1 MONTH OF FREE READING

at
www.ForgottenBooks.com

By purchasing this book you are eligible for one month membership to ForgottenBooks.com, giving you unlimited access to our entire collection of over 700,000 titles via our web site and mobile apps.

To claim your free month visit: www.forgottenbooks.com/free794733

* Offer is valid for 45 days from date of purchase. Terms and conditions apply.

ISBN 978-0-483-77616-6
PIBN 10794733

This book is a reproduction of an important historical work. Forgotten Books uses state-of-the-art technology to digitally reconstruct the work, preserving the original format whilst repairing imperfections present in the aged copy. In rare cases, an imperfection in the original, such as a blemish or missing page, may be replicated in our edition. We do, however, repair the vast majority of imperfections successfully; any imperfections that remain are intentionally left to preserve the state of such historical works.

Forgotten Books is a registered trademark of FB &c Ltd.
Copyright © 2017 FB &c Ltd.
FB &c Ltd, Dalton House, 60 Windsor Avenue, London, SW19 2RR.
Company number 08720141. Registered in England and Wales.

For support please visit www.forgottenbooks.com

THE
PLAYS
OF
WILLIAM SHAKESPEARE.

Vol. IV.

THE
PLAYS
OF
WILLIAM SHAKESPEARE.

VOLUME the FOURTH,

CONTAINING,

The LIFE and DEATH of RICHARD the SECOND.
The FIRST PART of KING HENRY the FOURTH.
The SECOND PART of KING HENRY the FOURTH.
The LIFE of KING HENRY the FIFTH.
The FIRST PART of KING HENRY the SIXTH.

LONDON:

Printed for J. and R. TONSON, C. CORBET, H. WOODFALL,
J. RIVINGTON, R. BALDWIN, L. HAWES, CLARK and
COLLINS, W. JOHNSTON, T. CASLON, T. LOWNDS,
and the Executors of B. DODD.
M,DCC,LXV.

THE
LIFE and DEATH
OF
RICHARD
THE
SECOND.

Vol. IV.   B

Dramatis Personæ.

KING Richard *the Second.*
Duke *of* York, } Uncles *to the King.*
John *of* Gaunt, *Duke of* Lancaster,
Bolingbroke, *Son to* John *of* Gaunt, *afterwards King* Henry *the Fourth.*
Aumerle, *Son to the Duke of* York.
Mowbray, *Duke of* Norfolk.
Earl of Salisbury.
Lord Berkley.
Bushy,
Bagot, } *Servants to King* Richard.
Green,
Earl of Northumberland.
Percy, *Son to* Northumberland.
Ross.
Willoughby.
Bishop of Carlisle.
Sir Stephen Scroop.
Fitzwater.
Surry.
Abbot of Westminster.
Sir Pierce *of* Exton.

Queen to King Richard.
Dutchess of Gloucester.
Dutchess of York.
Ladies, attending on the Queen.

Heralds, two Gardiners, Keeper, Messenger, Groom, and other Attendants.

SCENE, *dispersedly, in several Parts of* England.

Of this the Editions, earlier than the first Folio, are,
I. 4to, by *Valentine Simmes,* for *Andrew Wise,* 1598, of which I have a collation by Mr. Theobald.
II. 4to, for *Mathew Law,* 1615, from which the first Folio was printed.

[1]The LIFE and DEATH of

KING *RICHARD* II.

ACT I. SCENE I.

The COURT.

Enter King Richard, John of Gaunt, with other Nobles and Attendants.

King RICHARD.

OLD *John* of *Gaunt*, time-honour'd *Lancaster*,
Haſt thou, according to thy oath and bond,
Brought hither *Henry Hereford* thy bold ſon,
Here to make good the boiſt'rous late Appeal,
Which then our leiſure would not let us hear,
Againſt the Duke of *Norfolk*, *Thomas Mowbray?*
Gaunt. I have, my liege.
K. Rich. Tell me moreover, haſt thou ſounded him,

---

[1] *The* Life *and* Death *of King* Richard II.] But this Hiſtory comprizes little more than the Two laſt Years of this Prince. The Action of the Drama begins with *Bolingbroke's* appealing the Duke of *Norfolk*, on an Accuſation of high Treaſon, which fell out in the Year 1398; and it cloſes with the Murder of King *Richard* at *Pomfret*-Caſtle towards the End of the Year 1400, or the Beginning of the enſuing Year. THEOBALD.

If he appeal the Duke on ancient malice,
Or worthily, as a good Subject should,
On some known ground of treachery in him?

   Gaunt. As near as I could sift him on that argument,
On some apparent Danger seen in him
Aim'd at your Highness; no invet'rate malice.

   K. Rich. Then call them to our presence; face to face,
And frowning brow to brow. Ourselves will hear
Th' accuser, and th' accused freely speak.—
High-stomach'd are they Both, and full of ire;
In rage, deaf as the sea; hasty as fire.

SCENE II.

Enter Bolingbroke *and* Mowbray.

   Boling. May many years of happy days befal
My gracious Sovereign, my most loving Liege!

   Mowb. Each day still better other's happiness;
Until the heavens, envying earth's good hap,
Add an immortal title to your Crown!

   K. Rich. We thank you both, yet one but flatters us,
As well appeareth by the cause you come;
Namely, t'appeal each other of high Treason.
Cousin of *Hereford,* what dost thou object
Against the Duke of *Norfolk, Thomas Mowbray?*

   Boling. First (Heaven be the record to my speech!)
In the devotion of a Subject's love,
Tend'ring the precious safety of my Prince,
And free from other mis-begotten hate,
Come I Appellant to this princely presence.
—Now, *Thomas Mowbray,* do I turn to thee,
And mark my Greeting well; for what I speak,
My body shall make good upon this earth,
Or my divine soul answer it in heav'n:
Thou art a traitor and a miscreant;

Too good to be so, and too bad to live;
Since, the more fair and cryſtal is the ſky,
The uglier ſeem the clouds, that in it fly.
Once more, the more to aggravate the Note,
With a foul Traytor's Name ſtuff I thy throat;
And wiſh, ſo pleaſe my Sov'reign, ere I move,
What my Tongue ſpeaks, my [2] Right-drawn Sword
    may prove.

    Mowb. Let not my cold words here accuſe my zeal;
'Tis not the tryal of a woman's war,
The bitter clamour of two eager tongues,
Can arbitrate this cauſe betwixt us twain;
The blood is hot, that muſt be cool'd for this.
Yet can I not of ſuch tame patience boaſt,
As to be huſht, and nought at all to ſay.
Firſt, the fair Rev'rence of your Highneſs curbs me,
From giving reins and ſpurs to my free ſpeech;
Which elſe would poſt, until it had return'd
Theſe terms of Treaſon doubled down his throat.
Setting aſide his high blood's Royalty,
And let him be no kinſman to my Liege,
I do defie him, and I ſpit at him;
Call him a ſland'rous coward, and a villain;
Which to maintain, I would allow him odds,
And meet him, were I ty'd to run a-foot
Even to the frozen ridges of the *Alps*,
Or any other ground [*] inhabitable,
Where never *Engliſhman* durſt ſet his foot.
Mean time, let this defend my Loyalty;
By all my hopes, moſt falſly doth he lie.

    Boling. Pale trembling Coward, there I throw my
    Gage.
Diſclaiming here the kindred of a King,
And lay aſide my high blood's Royalty,
Which fear, not rev'rence, makes thee to except.
If guilty Dread hath left thee ſo much ſtrength,

---

  [2] *Right-drawn.*] Drawn in   [*] *Inhabitable.*] That is, *not*
a right or juſt Cauſe.   *habitable, uninhabitable.*

As to take up mine Honour's pawn, then stoop;
By that, and all the rights of Knighthood else,
Will I make good against thee, arm to arm,
What I have spoken, or thou canst devise.

Mowb. I take it up, and by that Sword I swear,
Which gently laid my Knighthood on my shoulder,
I'll answer thee in any fair degree,
Or chivalrous design of knightly tryal;
And when I mount, alive may I not light,
If I be traitor, or unjustly fight!

K. Rich. What doth our Cousin say to *Mowbray's* charge?
It must be great, that can inherit us
So much as of a thought of Ill in him.

Boling. Look, what I said, my life shall prove it true;
That *Mowbray* hath receiv'd eight thousand nobles,
In name of lendings for your Highness' soldiers,
The which he hath detain'd for lewd imployments;
Like a false traitor and injurious villain.
Besides, I say, and will in battle prove,
Or here, or elsewhere, to the furthest verge,
That ever was survey'd by *English* eye,
That all the treasons for these eighteen years,
Complotted and contrived in this Land,
Fetch from false *Mowbray* their first head and spring.
Further, I say, and further will maintain
Upon his bad Life to make all This good,
That he did plot the Duke of *Gloucester's* death;
Suggest his soon-believing adversaries;
And consequently, like a traitor coward,
Sluic'd out his inn'cent soul through streams of blood;
Which blood, like sacrificing *Abel's*, cries
Even from the tongueless caverns of the earth,
To me, for justice, and rough chastisement.
And by the glorious Worth of my Descent,
This arm shall do it, or this life be spent.

K. Rich. How high a pitch his resolution soars!

Thomas

Thomas of *Norfolk*, what fay'ſt thou to this?

Mowb. O, let my Sovereign turn away his face,
And bid his ears a little while be deaf,
Till I have told this Slander of his blood,
How God and good men hate ſo foul a liar.

K. Rich. Mowbray, impartial are our eyes and ears.
Were he our brother, nay, our Kingdom's heir,
As he is but our father's brother's ſon;
Now by ' my Scepter's awe, I make a vow,
Such neighbour-nearneſs to our ſacred blood
Should nothing priv'lege him, nor partialize
Th' unſtooping firmneſs of my upright ſoul.
He is our ſubject, *Mowbray*, ſo art thou;
Free ſpeech, and fearleſs, I to thee allow.

Mowb. Then, *Bolingbroke*, as low as to thy heart,
Through the falſe paſſage of thy throat, thou lieſt!
Three parts of that Receipt I had for *Calais*,
Disburſt I to his Highneſs' ſoldiers;
The other part reſerv'd I by conſent,
For that my ſovereign Leige was in my debt;
Upon remainder of a dear account,
Since laſt I went to *France* to fetch his Queen.
Now, ſwallow down that Lie.—For *Glouceſter's* death,
I ſlew him not; but, to mine own diſgrace,
Neglected my ſworn duty in that caſe.
For you, my noble lord of *Lancaſter*,
The honourable father to my foe,
Once did I lay an ambuſh for your life,
A treſpaſs that doth vex my grieved ſoul;
But ere I laſt receiv'd the Sacrament,
I did confeſs it, and exactly begg'd
Your Grace's pardon; and, I hope, I had it.
This is my fault; as for the reſt appeal'd,
It iſſues from the rancor of a villain,
A recreant and moſt degen'rate traitor;
Which in myſelf I boldly will defend,

---

³ *My Scepter's awe.*] The reverence due to my Scepter.

8 KING RICHARD II.

And interchangeably hurl down my gage
Upon this overweening traitor's foot;
To prove myself a loyal gentleman,
Even in the best blood chamber'd in his bosom.
In haste whereof, most heartily I pray
Your Highness to assign our tryal day.

   K. Rich. Wrath-kindled Gentlemen, be rul'd by me;
Let's purge this Choler without letting blood:
⁴ This we prescribe, though no physician;
Deep malice makes too deep incision:
Forget, forgive, conclude and be agreed;
Our Doctors say, this is no time to bleed.
Good Uncle, let this end where it begun;
We'll calm the Duke of *Norfolk*, you your Son.

   Gaunt. To be a make-peace shall become my age;
Throw down, my Son, the Duke of *Norfolk's* gage.

   K. Rich. And, *Norfolk*, throw down his.

   Gaunt. When, *Harry*? when
Obedience bids, I should not bid again.

   K. Rich. Norfolk, throw down, we bid; there is no boot *.

   Mowb. Myself I throw, dread Sovereign, at thy foot.
My life thou shalt command, but not my Shame;
The one my duty owes; but ⁵ my fair Name,
Despight of death, That lives upon my Grave,
To dark dishonour's use thou shalt not have.
I am disgrac'd, impeach'd, and baffled here,

---

⁴ *This we prescribe, though no physician,* &c.] I must make one Remark, in general, on the *Rhymes* throughout this whole play; they are so much inferior to the rest of the writing, that they appear to me of a different hand. What confirms this, is, that the context does every where exactly (and frequently much better) connect without the inserted rhymes, except in a very few places; and just there too, the rhyming verses are of a much better taste than all the others, which rather strengthens my conjecture.   POPE.

* *No boot.*] That is, no advantage, no use, in delay or refusal.

⁵ *My fair Name,* &c.] That is, *My name that lives on my grave in despight of death.* This easy passage most of the Editors seem to have mistaken.

Pierc'd

KING RICHARD II.

Pierc'd to the foul with flander's venom'd fpear:
The which no balm can cure, but his heart-blood
Which breath'd this poifon.

   K. Rich. Rage muft be withftood.
Give me his gage. Lions make Leopards tame.

   Mowb. Yea, but not change their fpots. Take but
      my fhame,
And I refign my gage. My dear, dear Lord,
The pureft treafure mortal times afford,
Is fpotlefs Reputation; That away,
Men are but guilded loam, or painted clay.
A jewel in a ten-times-barr'd-up cheft,
Is a bold fpirit in a loyal breaft.
Mine Honour is my life, both grow in one;
Take honour from me, and my life is done.
Then, dear my Liege, mine honour let me try;
In That I live, and for That will I die.

   K. Rich. Coufin, throw down your gage; do you
      begin.

   Boling. Oh, heav'n defend my foul from fuch foul fin!
Shall I feem creft-fall'n in my father's fight,
⁶ Or with pale beggar face impeach my height,
Before this out-dar'd Daftard? Ere my tongue
Shall wound my Honour with fuch feeble wrong,
Or found fo bafe a parle, my teeth fhall tear
⁷ The flavifh motive of recanting fear,
And fpit it bleeding, in his high difgrace,
Where fhame doth harbour, ev'n in *Mowbray's* face.
                            [*Exit* Gaunt.

   K. Rich. We were not born to fue, but to command,
Which fince we cannot do to make you friends,
Be ready, as your lives fhall anfwer it,
At *Coventry* upon Saint *Lambert's* day.

---

⁶ *Or with pale* beggar face—] i. e. with a face of fupplication. But this will not fatisfy the Oxford Editor, he turns it to *buggard fear.* WARBURTON.

⁷ *The flavifh* motive—] Motive, for inftrument. WARB. Rather that which fear puts in motion.

There

There shall your Swords and Lances arbitrate
The swelling diff'rence of your settled hate.
Since we cannot atone you, you shall see
Justice decide the Victor's Chivalry.
Lord Marshal, bid our officers at Arms
Be ready to direct these home-alarms. *[Exeunt.*

SCENE III.

Changes to the Duke of Lancaster's *Palace.*

Enter Gaunt *and Dutchess of* Gloucester.

Gaunt. ALas! * the part I had in *Glo'ster's* blood
Doth more sollicit me, than your Ex-
claims,
To stir against the butchers of his life.
But since correction lyeth in those hands,
Which made the fault that we cannot correct,
Put we our Quarrel to the Will of heav'n;
Who when it sees the hours ripe on earth,
Will rain hot vengeance on offenders' heads.

Dutch. Finds brotherhood in thee no sharper spur?
Hath love in thy old blood no living fire?
Edward's sev'n sons, whereof thy self art one,
Were as sev'n vials of his sacred blood;
Or sev'n fair branches, springing from one root:
Some of those sev'n are dry'd by Nature's Course;
Some of those branches by the Dest'nies cut:
But *Thomas*, my dear lord, my life, my *Glo'ster*,
One vial, full of *Edward's* sacred blood,
One flourishing branch of his most royal root,
Is crack'd, and all the precious liquor spilt;
Is hackt down, and his summer leaves all faded,
By Envy's hand and Murder's bloody axe.
Ah, *Gaunt!* his blood was thine; that bed, that womb,
That metal, that self-mould that fashion'd thee;

* *The part I had.*] That is, my relation of consanguinity to
Gloucester.   HANMER.

Made

KING RICHARD II.

Made him a man; and though thou liv'st and breath'st,
Yet art thou slain in him; thou dost consent
In some large measure to thy father's death;
In that thou seest thy wretched brother die,
Who was the model of thy father's life;
Call it not patience, *Gaunt*, it is despair.
In suff'ring thus thy brother to be slaughter'd,
Thou shew'st the naked pathway to thy life,
Teaching stern murther how to butcher thee.
That which in mean men we entitle Patience,
Is pale cold Cowardise in noble breasts,
What shall I say? to safeguard thine own life,
The best way is to 'venge my *Glo'ster's* death.

Gaunt. God's is the Quarrel; for God's Substitute,
His Deputy anointed in his sight,
Hath caus'd his death; the which if wrongfully,
Let God revenge, for I may never lift
An angry arm against his Minister.

Dutch. Where then, alas, may I complain myself?

Gaunt. To heav'n, the widow's Champion and Defence.

Dutch. Why then, I will: farewel, old *Gaunt*, farewel.
Thou go'st to *Coventry*, there to behold
Our Cousin *Hereford* and fell *Mowbray* fight.
O, sit my husband's wrongs on *Hereford's* spear,
That it may enter butcher *Mowbray's* breast!
Or, if misfortune miss the first career,
Be *Mowbray's* sins so heavy in his bosom,
That they may break his foaming Courser's back,
And throw the rider headlong in the lists,
⁸ A caitiff recreant to my cousin *Hereford!*
Farewel, old *Gaunt*; thy sometime brother's wife
With her companion Grief must end her life.

---

⁸ *A caitiff recreant—*] Caitiff originally signified a *prisoner*; next *a slave*, from the condition of prisoners; then a *scoundrel*, from the qualities of a slave.

Ἡμισυ τῆς ἀρετῆς ἀποαίνυται δούλιον ἦμαρ.

In this passage it partakes of all these significations.

Gaunt.

Gaunt. Sifter, farewel; I muft to *Coventry.*
As much Good ftay with thee, as go with me;
　Dutch. Yet one word more — grief boundeth where
　　it falls,
Not with the empty hollownefs, but weight:
I take my leave, before I have begun;
For Sorrow ends not, when it feemeth done.
Commend me to my brother, *Edmund York*:
Lo, this is all —— nay, yet depart not fo;
Though this be all, do not fo quickly go:
I fhall remember more. Bid him —— oh, what?
With all good fpeed at *Plafhie* vifit me.
Alack, and what fhall good old *York* fee there
But empty lodgings, and unfurnifh'd walls,
Unpeopled offices, untrodden ftones?
And what hear there for welcome, but my groans?
Therefore commend me, — let him not come there
To feek out forrow that dwells every where;
All defolate, will I from hence, and die;
The laft Leave of thee takes my weeping eye. [*Exeunt.*

SCENE IV.

The Lifts, at Coventry.

Enter the Lord-Marfhal, and Aumerle.

Mar. MY lord *Aumerle*, is *Harry Hereford* arm'd?
　　Aum. Yea; at all points, and longs to
　　　enter in.
　Mar. The Duke of *Norfolk*, fprightfully and bold,
Stays but the Summons of th' Appellant's trumpet.
　Aum. Why, then the Champions are prepar'd, and
　　ftay
For nothing but his Majefty's approach. [*Flourifh.*

The trumpets sound, and the King enters with Gaunt, Bushy, Bagot, *and others: when they are set, Enter the Duke of* Norfolk *in armour.*

K. Rich. Marshal, demand of yonder Champion
The cause of his arrival here in arms;
Ask him his name, and orderly proceed
To swear him in the justice of his Cause.
    Mar. In God's name and the King's, say who thou
        art?   [*To* Mowbray.
And why thou com'st, thus knightly clad in arms?
Against what man thou com'st, and what thy quarrel?
Speak truly on thy Knighthood, and thine Oath,
And so defend thee heaven, and thy valour!
    Mowb. My name is *Thomas Mowbray*, Duke of
        Norfolk,
Who hither come engag'd by my oath,
(Which, heav'n defend, a Knight should violate!)
Both to defend my Loyalty and Truth,
To God, my King, and his succeeding Issue [9],
Against the Duke of *Hereford*, that appeals me;
And by the grace of God, and this mine arm,
To prove him, in defending of myself,
A traitor to my God, my King, and me;
And, as I truly fight, defend me heav'n!

The trumpets sound. Enter Bolingbroke, *Appellant, in armour.*

K. Rich. Marshal, ask yonder Knight in arms,
Both who he is, and why he cometh hither,
Thus plated in habiliments of war;
And formally, according to our Law,

---

[9] ——— *his succeeding Issue.*] Such is the reading of the first folio; the later editions read *my* Issue. *Mowbray's Issue* was, by this accusation, in danger of an attainder, and therefore he might come among other reasons for their sake, but the old reading is more just and grammatical.

Depose

K. Rich. Farewel, my lord; securely I espy
Virtue with valour couched in thine eye.
Order the tryal, Marshal, and begin.

Mar. *Harry* of *Hereford, Lancaster* and *Derby,*
Receive thy Lance; and heav'n defend thy Right!

Boling. Strong as a tower in hope, I cry *Amen.*

Mar. Go bear this Lance to *Thomas* Duke of *Norfolk.*

1 *Her.* *Harry* of *Hereford, Lancaster* and *Derby.*
Stands here for God, his Sovereign, and Himself,
On pain to be found false and recreant,
To prove the Duke of *Norfolk, Thomas Mowbray,*
A traitor to his God, his King, and him;
And dares him to set forward to the fight.

2 *Her.* Here standeth *Thomas Mowbray,* Duke of
    Norfolk,
On pain to be found false and recreant,
Both to defend himself, and to approve
Henry of *Hereford, Lancaster* and *Derby,*
To God, his Sovereign, and to him, disloyal:
Courageously, and with a free desire,
Attending but the Signal to begin. [*A Charge sounded.*

Mar. Sound, Trumpets; and set forward, Com-
    batants.
—But stay, the King hath thrown his warder down.

K. Rich. Let them lay by their helmets and their
    spears,
And Both return back to their chairs again.
Withdraw with us, and let the trumpets sound,
While we return these Dukes what we decree.
    [*A long Flourish; after which, the King
    speaks to the Combatants.*

Draw near;———
And list, what with our Council we have done.
For that our Kingdom's earth should not be foil'd
With that dear blood, which it hath fostered;

---

substitutes, but the rhyme, to   obliged *Shakespeare* to write *jest,*
which sense is too often enslaved,   and obliges us to read it.

And,

KING RICHARD II. 17

And, for our eyes do hate the dire aspect
Of civil wounds plough'd up with neighbour swords;
[² And for we think, the eagle-winged pride
Of sky-aspiring and ambitious thoughts
With rival-hating Envy set you on,
To wake our Peace ³, which in our country's cradle
Draws the sweet infant breath of gentle sleep;]
Which thus rouz'd up with boist'rous untun'd drums,
And harsh resounding trumpets' dreadful Bray,
And grating shock of wrathful iron arms,

² *And for we think, the eagle-winged pride*, &c.] These five verses are omitted in the other editions, and restored from the first of 1598. POPE.

³ *To wake our Peace,———which thus rouz'd up———Might fright fair Peace,*] Thus the sentence stands in the common reading, absurdly enough: which made the Oxford Editor, instead of, *fright fair Peace*, read, *be affrighted*; as if these latter words could ever, possibly, have been blundered into the former by transcribers. But his business is to alter as his fancy leads him, not to reform errors, as the text and rules of criticism direct. In a word, then, the true original of the blunder was this: The Editors, before Mr. *Pope*, had taken their Editions from the Folios, in which the text stood thus,
——— *the dire aspect*
Of civil wounds plough'd up with neighbour swords;
Which thus rouz'd up,———
———*fright fair Peace,*
This is sense. But Mr. *Pope*, who carefully examined the first printed plays in Quarto (very much to the advantage of his Edition) coming to this place, found five lines, in the first Edition of this play printed in 1598, omitted in the first general collection of the poet's works; and not enough attending to their agreement with the common text, put them into their place. Whereas, in truth, the five lines were omitted by *Shakespeare* himself, as not agreeing to the rest of the context; which, on revise, he thought fit to alter. On this account I have put them into hooks, not as spurious, but as rejected on the author's revise; and, indeed, with great judgment; for,
To wake our Peace, which in our country's cradle
Draws the sweet infant breath of gentle sleep,
as pretty as it is in the image, is absurd in the sense; For Peace awake is still Peace, as well as when asleep. The difference is, that Peace asleep gives one the notion of a happy people sunk in sloth and luxury, which is not the idea the speaker would raise, and from which state, the sooner it was awaked the better.
WARBURTON.

VOL. IV. C Might

KING RICHARD II.

Might from our quiet Confines fright fair Peace,
And make us wade even in our kindred's blood:
Therefore, we banish you our Territories.
You, cousin *Hereford*, on pain of death,
Till twice five Summers have enrich'd our fields,
Shall not regreet our fair Dominions,
But tread the stranger paths of Banishment.

  Boling. Your will be done. This must my comfort be,
That Sun, that warms you here, shall shine on me:
And those his golden beams, to you here lent,
Shall point on me, and gild my Banishment.

  K. *Rich.* *Norfolk*, for thee remains a heavier Doom,
Which I with some unwillingness pronounce.
The fly-slow hours shall not determinate
The dateless limit of thy dear exile:
The hopeless word, of *never to return*,
Breathe I against thee, upon pain of life.

  Mowb. A heavy Sentence, my most sovereign Liege,
And all unlook'd for from your Highness' mouth.
A dearer merit, not so deep a maim [4],
As to be cast forth in the common air,
Have I deserved at your Highness' hands.
The language I have learn'd these forty years,
My native *English*, now I must forego;
And now my tongue's use is to me no more,
Than an unstringed viol, or a harp;
Or, like a cunning Instrument cas'd up,
Or being open, put into his hands
That knows no touch to tune the harmony.
Within my mouth you have engoal'd my tongue,
Doubly portcullis'd with my Teeth and Lips;
And dull, unfeeling, barren Ignorance
Is made my Goaler to attend on me.

---

[4] *A dearer merit, not so deep a maim, Have I deserved,* &c.———] To *deserve* a *merit* is a phrase of which I know not any example. I wish some copy would exhibit, *A dearer* mede, *and not so deep a maim.* To *deserve a mede* or *reward*, is regular and easy.

I am too old to fawn upon a nurse,
Too far in years to be a Pupil now;
What is thy Sentence then, but speechless death,
Which robs my tongue from breathing native breath?

    K. Richard. ³ It boots thee not to be compassionate;
After our Sentence, Plaining comes too late.

    Mowb. Then thus I turn me from my Country's light,
To dwell in solemn shades of endless night.

    K. Rich. Return again, and take an oath with ye.
Lay on our royal Sword your banish'd hands;
Swear by the duty that you owe to heav'n
⁶ (Our part therein we banish with yourselves)
To keep the oath that we administer.
You never shall, so help you truth, and heav'n!
Embrace each other's love in Banishment;
Nor ever look upon each other's face,
Nor ever write, regreet, or reconcile
This low'ring tempest of your home-bred hate;
Nor ever by advised purpose meet,
To plot, contrive, or complot any Ill,
'Gainst us, our State, our Subjects, or our Land.

    Boling. I swear.

    Mowb. And I, to keep all this.

    Boling. * *Norfolk,*—so far, as to mine enemy——
By this time, had the King permitted us,
One of our souls had wandred in the air,
Banish'd this frail sepulchre of our flesh,

---

³ *Compassionate,* for plaintive. WARBURTON.

⁶ *(Our part,* &c.] It is a question much debated amongst the writers of the Law of Nations, whether a banish'd man be still tied in allegiance to the state which sent him into exile. *Tully* and Lord Chancellor *Clarendon* declare for the affirmative: *Hobbs* and *Puffendorf* hold the negative. Our author, by this line, seems to be of the same opinion. WARB.

* Norfolk,—*so far,* &c.] I do not clearly see what is the sense of this abrupt line, but suppose the meaning to be this. *Hereford,* immediately after his oath of perpetual enmity addresses *Norfolk,* and, fearing some misconstruction, turns to the king and says—*so far as to mine enemy*—that is, *I should say nothing to him but what enemies may say to each other.*

As now our flesh is banish'd from this Land,
Confess thy treasons, ere thou fly this Realm;
Since thou haft far to go, bear not along
The clogging burthen of a guilty foul.
 Mowb. No, *Bolingbroke*; if ever I were traitor,
My Name be blotted from the Book of life,
And I from heaven banish'd as from hence!
But what thou art, heav'n, thou, and I do know,
And all too foon, I fear, the King shall rue.
Farewel, my Liege. Now no way can I stray,
Save back to *England*; all the world's my way [7]. [*Exit.*

SCENE V.

 K. Rich. Uncle, even in the glasses of thine eyes
I fee thy grieved heart, thy fad aspect
Hath from the number of his banish'd years
Pluck'd four away.—Six frozen winters spent, [*To* Bol.
Return with Welcome home from Banishment.
 Bolingb. How long a time lies in one little word!
Four lagging Winters, and four wanton Springs,
End in a word; such is the Breath of Kings.
 Gaunt. I thank my Liege, that in regard of me
He shortens four years of my son's exile:
But little vantage shall I reap thereby;
For ere the six years, that he hath to spend,
Can change their moons and bring their times about,
My oyl-dry'd lamp, and time-bewasted light,
Shall be extinct with age, and endless night:
My inch of taper will be burnt and done:
And blindfold death not let me fee my son.
 K. Rich. Why, uncle? thou hast many years to live.
 Gaunt. But not a minute, King, that thou canst give;
Shorten my days thou canst with sullen sorrow,

---

[7] ——— *all the world's my way.*] Perhaps *Milton* had this in his mind when he wrote these lines.

The world was all before them,
where to chuse
Their place of rest, and Providence
their guide.

And

KING RICHARD II.

And pluck nights from me, but not lend a morrow *;
Thou canst help time to furrow me with age,
But stop no wrinkle in his pilgrimage;
Thy word is current with him, for my death;
But dead, thy Kingdom cannot buy my breath.

K. Rich. Thy son is banish'd upon good advice,
Whereto thy tongue a party-verdict gave;
Why at our justice seem'st thou then to low'r?

Gaunt. Things, sweet to taste, prove indigestion sow'r.
You urg'd me as a judge; but I had rather,
You would have bid me argue like a father.
O, had it been a stranger, not my child,
To smooth his Fault, I would have been more mild:
Alas, I look'd, when some of you should f
I was too strict to make mine own away:
But you gave leave to my unwilling tongue,
Against my will, to do myself this wrong.
A partial slander † sought I to avoid,
And in the Sentence my own life destroy'd.

K. Rich. Cousin, farewel; and, uncle, bid him so:
Six years we banish him, and he shall go. [*Flourish.*
[*Exit.*

SCENE VI.

Aum. Cousin, farewel; what presence must not know,
From where you do remain, let paper show.

Mar. My lord, no leave take I; for I will ride
As far as land will let me, by your side.

Gaunt. Oh, to what purpose dost thou hoard thy words,
That thou return'st no Greeting to thy friends?

Boling. I have too few to take my leave of you,
When the tongue's office should be prodigal,
To breathe th' abundant dolour of the heart.

Gaunt. Thy grief is but thy absence for a time.

---

* *And pluck nights from me, but not lend a morrow;*] It is matter of very melancholy consideration, that all human advantages confer more power of doing evil than good

† *A partial slander—*] That is, the *reproach of partiality.* This is a just picture of the struggle between principle and affection.

Boling.

Boling. Joy abfent, grief is prefent for that time.
Gaunt. What is fix winters? they are quickly gone.
Boling. To men in joy; but grief makes one hour ten.
Gaunt. Call it a Travel, that thou tak'ft for pleafure.
Boling. My heart will figh, when I mifcall it fo,
Which finds it an inforced pilgrimage.
  Gaunt. The fullen paffage of thy weary fteps
Efteem a foil, wherein thou art to fet
The precious jewel of thy home-return.
  Boling. Nay, rather, ev'ry tedious ftride I make [8]
Will but remember me, what a deal of World
I wander from the Jewels that I love.
Muft I not ferve a long Apprentice-hood,
To foreign paffages, and in the End
Having my Freedom, boaft of Nothing elfe
But that I was a Journeyman to Grief? [*]
  Gaunt. [9] All Places that the Eye of Heaven vifits,
Are to a wife man ports and happy havens.
Teach thy neceffity to reafon thus:
There is no virtue like neceffity.
Think not, the King did banifh Thee;
But Thou the King. Woe doth the heavier fit,
Where it perceives it is but faintly borne.
Go fay, I fent thee forth to purchafe honour,

[8] *Boling. Nay, rather, ev'ry tedious Stride I make*] This, and the fix Verfes which follow, I have ventur'd to fupply from the old *Quarto*. The Allufion, 'tis true, to an *Apprenticeship*, and becoming a *Journeyman*, is not in the fublime Tafte, nor, as *Horace* has exprefs'd it, *fpirat Tragicum fatis*: however as there is no Doubt of the Paffage being genuine, the Lines are not fo defpicable as to deferve being quite loft. THEOBALD.

[*] —— *Journeyman to Grief?*] I am afraid our author in this place defigned a uery poor quibble, as *journey* fignifies both *travel* and a *day's work*. However, he is not to be cenfured for what he himfelf rejected.

[9] *All Places that the Eye of Heav'n vifits*, &c.] The fourteen verfes that follow, are found in the firft Edition. POPE.

I am inclined to believe that what Mr. *Theobald* and Mr *Pope* have reftored were expunged in the revifion by the authour: if the lines inclofed in crotchets are omitted, the fenfe is more coherent. Nothing is more frequent among dramatick writers, than to fhorten their dialogues for the ftage.

And

KING RICHARD II.   23

And not, the King exil'd thee. Or suppose,
Devouring Pestilence hangs in our air,
And thou art flying to a fresher clime.
Look, what thy soul holds dear, imagine it
To lye that way thou go'st, not whence thou com'st.
Suppose the singing birds, musicians;
The grass whereon thou tread'st, the presence-floor;
The flow'rs, fair ladies; and thy steps, no more
Than a delightful measure, or a dance.
For gnarling Sorrow hath less Pow'r to bite
The Man, that mocks at it, and sets it light.]
 Boling. Oh, who can hold a fire in his hand,
By thinking on the frosty *Caucasus?*
Or cloy the hungry edge of appetite,
By bare imagination of a feast?
Or wallow naked in *December* snow,
By thinking on fantastick Summer's heat?
Oh, no! the apprehension of the good
Gives but the greater feeling to the worse;
Fell sorrow's tooth doth never rankle more
Than when it bites, but lanceth not the sore.
 Gaunt. Come, come, my son, I'll bring thee on thy
   way;
Had I thy Youth, and Cause, I would not stay.
 Boling. Then, *England's* Ground, farewel; sweet
   soil, adieu,
My mother and my nurse, which bears me yet,
Where-e'er I wander, boast of this I can,
Though banish'd; yet a true-born *Englishman*[1].
            [*Exeunt.*

---

[1] —— *yet a true-born* Englishman.] Here the first act ought to end, that between the first and second acts there may be time for *John* of *Gaunt* to accompany his son, return and fall sick. Then the first scene of the second act begins with a natural conversation, interrupted by a message from *John* of *Gaunt,* by which the king is called to visit him, which visit is paid in the following scene. As the play is now divided, more time passes between the two last scenes of the first act, than between the first act and the second.

SCENE

SCENE VII.

Changes to the Court.

Enter King Richard, *and* Bagot, *&c. at one door;
and the Lord* Aumerle, *at the other.*

K. Rich. WE did, indeed, obferve———Coufin
Aumerle,
How far brought you high *Hereford* on his way?
Aum. I brought high *Hereford*, if you call him fo,
But to the next High-way, and there I left him.
  K. Rich. And fay, what ftore of parting tears were
    fhed?
  Aum. 'Faith, none by me; except the north-eaft
    wind,
(Which then blew bitterly againft our faces)
Awak'd the fleepy rheume; and fo by chance
Did grace our hollow Parting with a tear.
  K. Rich. What faid your coufin, when you parted
    with him?
  Aum. Farewel.
And, for my heart difdained that my tongue
Should fo prophane the word. That taught me craft
To counterfeit oppreffion of fuch grief,
That words feem'd buried in my forrow's Grave.
Marry, would the word *farewel* have lengthen'd hours,
And added years to his fhort Banifhment,
He fhould have had a volume of farewels;
But, fince it would not, he had none of me.
  K. Rich. He is our kinfman, Coufin; but 'tis doubt,
When time fhall call him home from Banifhment,
Whether our kinfman come to fee his friends.
Our-felf, and *Bufby, Bagot* here, and *Green,*
Obferv'd his Courtfhip to the common people:
How he did feem to dive into their hearts,
With humble and familiar courtefie?
                                What

What reverence he did throw away on slaves,
Wooing poor crafts-men with the craft of smiles,
And patient under-bearing of his fortune,
As 'twere to banish their Affects with him.
Off goes his bonnet to an oyster-wench;
A brace of dray-men bid, God speed him well!
And had the tribute of his supple knee;
With—Thanks, my countrymen, my loving friends—
As were our *England* in reversion his,
And he our Subjects' next degree in hope.

   Green. Well, he is gone, and with him go these
      thoughts.———
Now for the Rebels, which stand out in *Ireland*,
Expedient Manage must be made, my Liege;
Ere further leisure yield them further means
For their advantage, and your Highness' loss.

  K. Rich. We will our self in person to this war;
And, for our coffers with too great a Court,
And liberal largess, are grown somewhat light,
We are inforc'd to farm our royal Realm,
The Revenue whereof shall furnish us
For our affairs in hand; if they come short,
Our Substitutes at home shall have blank charters,
Whereto, when they shall know what men are rich,
They shall subscribe them for large sums of gold,
And send them after to supply our wants;
For we will make for *Ireland* presently.

          Enter Bushy.

  K. Rich. Bushy, what news?
  Bushy. Old *John* of *Gaunt* is sick, my lord,
Suddenly taken, and hath sent post-haste
T' intreat your Majesty to visit him.
  K. Rich. Where lyes he?
  Bushy. At *Ely-house.*
  K. Rich. Now put it, heav'n, in his physician's
     mind,

To help him to his Grave immediately.
The lining of his coffers shall make coats
To deck our soldiers for these *Irish* wars.
Come, gentlemen, let's all go visit him:
Pray heav'n, we may make haste, and come too late!
[*Exeunt.*

ACT II. SCENE I.

ELY-HOUSE.

Gaunt *brought in, sick; with the Duke of* York.

GAUNT.

WILL the King come, that I may breathe my last
In wholesome counsel to his unstay'd youth?
  York. Vex not your self, nor strive not with your breath;
For all in vain comes counsel to his ear.
  Gaunt. Oh, but, they say, the tongues of dying men
Inforce attention, like deep harmony:
Where words are scarce, they're seldom spent in vain;
For they breathe truth, that breathe their words in pain.
He, that no more must say, is listen'd more
Than they, whom youth and ease have taught to glose,
More are men's ends mark'd, than their lives before;
The setting Sun, and musick in the close,
As the last taste of sweets, is sweetest last;
Writ in remembrance, more than things long past.
Though *Richard* my life's counsel would not hear,
My death's sad Tale may yet undeaf his ear.
  York. His ear is stopt with other flatt'ring charms,
As praises of his State; there are, beside,
Lascivious meeters, to whose venom'd sound
The open ear of youth doth always listen:
Report

KING RICHARD II.

Report of Fashions in proud *Italy*²,
Whose manner still our tardy, apish, Nation
Limps after, in base aukward imitation.
Where doth the world thrust forth a vanity
(So it be new, there's no respect how vile)
That is not quickly buzz'd into his ears?
Then all too late comes counsel to be heard,
Where Will doth mutiny with wit's regard ³.
Direct not him, whose way himself will chuse *;
'Tis breath thou lack'st, and that breath wilt thou lose.

Gaunt. Methinks, I am a prophet new-inspir'd,
And, thus expiring, do foretel of him,
His rash, fierce blaze of riot cannot last;
For violent fires soon burn out themselves.
Small show'rs last long, but sudden storms are short;
He tires betimes, that spurs too fast betimes;
With eager feeding, food doth choak the feeder.
Light Vanity, insatiate Cormorant,
Consuming means, soon preys upon itself.
This royal Throne of Kings, this scepter'd Isle,
This Earth of Majesty, this Seat of *Mars*,
This other *Eden*, demy *Paradise*,
This fortress, built by Nature for her self,
Against infection⁴, and the hand of war;
This happy Breed of men, this little world,
This precious stone set in the silver sea,

² *Report of fashions in proud Italy,*] Our authour, who gives to all nations the customs of *England*, and to all ages the manners of his own; has charged the times of *Richard* with a folly not perhaps known then, but very frequent in *Shakespeare's* time, and much lamented by the wisest and best of our ancestors.
³ *Where Will doth mutiny with wit's regard.*] Where the will rebels against the notices of the understanding.

* —— *whose way himself will chuse*;] Do not attempt to *guide him who*, whatever thou shalt say, *will take his own course.*
† *Rash.* That is, *hasty, violent.*
⁴ *Against infection,* ——] I once suspected that for *infection* we might read *invasion*; but the copies all agree, and I suppose *Shakespeare* meant to say, that islanders are secured by their situation both *from* war and *pestilence.*

Which

Which serves it in the office of a wall,
Or as a moat defensive to a house,
Against the envy of less happier Lands [5];
This nurse, this teeming womb of royal Kings,
[6] Fear'd for their breed, and famous by their birth,
Renowned for their deeds, as far from home
For christian service and true chivalry,
As is the Sepulchre in stubborn *Jury*
Of the world's Ransom, blessed *Mary's* Son;
This land of such dear souls, this dear, dear Land,
Dear for her reputation through the world,
Is now leas'd out (I dye, pronouncing it)
Like to a Tenement, or pelting Farm.
England, bound in with the triumphant Sea,
Whose rocky shore beats back the envious siege
Of watry *Neptune*, is bound in with shame,
With inky blots, and rotten parchment-bonds.
That *England*, that was wont to conquer others,
Hath made a shameful Conquest of itself.
Ah! would the scandal vanish with my life,
How happy then were my ensuing death!

[5] *Less happier lands.*] So read all the editions, except *Hanmer's*, which has *less happy*. I believe *Shakespeare*, from the habit of saying *more happier* according to the custom of his time, inadvertently writ *less happier*.

[6] *Fear'd for their breed, and famous by their birth.*] The first edition in 4to, 1598, reads,
Fear'd by their breed, and famous for their birth.
The second 4to in 1615,
Fear'd by their breed, and famous by their birth.

The first folio, though printed from the second quarto, reads as the first. The particles in this authour seem often to have been printed by chance. Perhaps the passage, which appears a little disordered, may be regulated thus:

——————— *royal kings,*
Fear'd for their breed, and famous for their birth,
For Christian service, and true chivalry;
Renowned for their deeds as far from home
As is the Sepulchre.

SCENE II.

Enter King Richard, *Queen,* Aumerle, Bushy, Green, Bagot, Ross, *and* Willoughby.

York. The King is come, deal mildly with his youth:
For young hot colts, being rag'd, do rage the more.
  Queen. How fares our noble uncle, *Lancaster?*
  K. Rich. What comfort, man? How is't with aged *Gaunt?*
  Gaunt. Oh, how that Name befits my composition!
Old *Gaunt,* indeed, and gaunt in being old;
Within me grief hath kept a tedious fast,
And who abstains from meat, that is not gaunt?
For sleeping *England* long time have I watch'd,
Watching breeds leanness, leanness is all gaunt;
The pleasure, that some fathers feed upon,
Is my strict fast; I mean, my children's looks;
And, therein fasting, thou hast made me gaunt;
Gaunt am I for the Grave, gaunt as a Grave,
Whose hollow womb inherits nought but bones.
  K. Rich. Can sick men play so nicely with their names?
  Gaunt. No, misery makes sport to mock itself:
Since thou dost seek to kill my name in me,
I mock my name, great King, to flatter thee.
  K. Rich. Should dying men flatter those that live?
  Gaunt. No, no, men living flatter those that die.
  K. Rich. Thou, now a dying, say'st, thou flatter'st me.
  Gaunt. Oh! no, thou dyest, though I sicker be.
  K. Rich. I am in health, I breathe, I see thee ill.
  Gaunt. Now he, that made me, knows, I see thee ill.
Ill in myself, but seeing thee too, ill.
Thy death-bed is no lesser than the Land,

Wherein

KING RICHARD II.

Wherein thou lieſt in Reputation ſick;
And thou, too careleſs Patient as thou art,
Giv'ſt thy anointed body to the cure
Of thoſe phyſicians, that firſt wounded thee.
A thouſand flatt'rers ſit within thy Crown,
Whoſe compaſs is no bigger than thy head,
And yet incaged in ſo ſmall a verge,
Thy waſte is no whit leſſer than thy Land.
Oh, had thy Grandſire, with a prophet's eye,
Seen how his ſon's ſon ſhould deſtroy his ſons;
From forth thy reach he would have laid thy ſhame,
Depoſing thee before thou wert poſſeſt;
Who art poſſeſs'd now, to depoſe thyſelf.
Why, couſin, wert thou Regent of the world,
It were a ſhame to let this Land by leaſe;
But for thy world enjoying but this Land,
Is it not more than ſhame to ſhame it ſo?
Landlord of *England* art thou now, not King:
[7] Thy ſtate of law is bondſlave to the law;
And Thou———

K. Rich. And thou, a lunatick lean-witted fool,
Preſuming on an ague's privilege,

---

[7] *Thy* ſtate of law *is* bondſlave to the law :] *State of law,* i. e. *legal ſov'rainty.* But the Oxford Editor alters it to the *ſtate o'er law,* i. e. *abſolute ſov'rainty.* A doctrine, which, if our poet ever learnt at all, he learnt not in the reign when this play was written, Queen *Elizabeth's,* but in the reign after it, King *James's.* By *bondſlave to the law,* the poet means his being inſlaved to his favourite ſubjects. WARBURTON.

This ſentiment, whatever it be, is obſcurely expreſſed. I underſtand it differently from the learned commentator, being perhaps not quite ſo zealous for *Shakeſpeare's* political reputation. The reaſoning of *Gaunt,* I think, is this : *By ſetting thy royalties to farm, thou haſt reduced thyſelf to a ſtate below ſovereignty, thou art* now no longer king but landlord *of England, ſubject to the ſame reſtraint and limitations as other landlords; by making thy condition* a ſtate of law, *a condition upon which the common rules of law can operate,* thou art become a bondſlave to the law; *thou haſt made thyſelf amenable to laws from which thou wert originally exempt.*

Whether this interpretation be true, or no, it is plain that Dr. *Warburton's* explanation of *bondſlave to the law,* is not true.

Dar'ſt

KING RICHARD II.   31

Dar'st with thy frozen admonition
Make pale our cheek; chasing the royal blood
With fury from his native residence.
Now by my Seat's right-royal Majesty,
Wert thou not Brother to Great *Edward's* son,
This tongue that runs so roundly in thy head,
Should run thy head from thy unreverend shoulders.

  Gaunt. Oh, spare me not, my brother *Edward's* son,
For that I was his father *Edward's* son.
That blood already, like the Pelican,
Hast thou tapt out, and drunkenly carows'd.
My brother *Glo'ster*, plain well-meaning soul
(Whom fair befal in heav'n 'mong'st happy souls!)
May be a precedent and witness good,
That thou respect'st not spilling *Edward's* blood.
Join with the present Sickness that I have,
  And thy unkindness be like crooked age,
To crop at once a too-long-wither'd flower.
Live in thy shame, but die not shame with thee!
These words hereafter thy tormentors be!
Convey me to my Bed, then to my Grave:
 Love they to live, that love and honour have.
                              [*Exit, borne out.*

  K. *Rich.* And let them die, that Age and Sullens
       have;
For both hast thou, and both become the Grave.

  York. I do beseech your Majesty, impute

---

⁸ *And thy unkindness be like crooked age.*
To crop at once a too-long wither'd flow'r.] Thus stand these lines in all the copies, but I think there is an errour. Why should *Gaunt*, already *old*, call on any thing *like age* to end him? How can age be said to *crop at once?* How is the idea of *crookedness* connected with that of *cropping?* I suppose the poet dictated thus:
And thy unkindness be time's *crooked* edge
To crop at once ———
That is, *let thy unkindness be* time's scythe *to crop.*
Edge was easily confounded by the ear with *age*, and one mistake once admitted made way for another.

⁹ *Love they.*] That is, *let them love.*

His

His words to wayward ficklinefs, and age.
He loves you, on my life; and holds you dear
As *Harry* Duke of *Hereford*, were he here.

   K. Rich. Right, you fay true; as *Hereford's* love,
      fo his;
As theirs, fo mine; and all be, as it is.

SCENE III.

Enter Northumberland.

   North. My Liege, old *Gaunt* commends him to
      your Majefty.
   K. Rich. What fays old *Gaunt?*
   North. Nay, nothing; all is faid.
His tongue is now a ftringlefs inftrument,
Words, life, and all, old *Lancafter* hath fpent.

   York. Be *York* the next, that muft be bankrupt fo!
Though death be poor, it ends a mortal woe.

   K. Rich. The ripeft fruit firft falls, and fo doth he;
His time is fpent, our pilgrimage muft be.
So much for that.——Now for our *Irifh* wars;
We muft fupplant thofe rough rug-headed Kerns,
Which live like venom, where no venom elfe,
But only they, have privilege to live.
And, for thefe great affairs do afk fome charge,
To'rds our affiftance we do feize to us.
The plate, coin, revenues, and moveables,
Whereof our uncle *Gaunt* did ftand poffeft.

   York. How long fhall I be patient? Oh, how long
Shall tender Duty make me fuffer wrong?
Not *Glo'fter's* death, not *Hereford's* Banifhment,
Not *Gaunt's* rebukes, nor *England's* private wrongs,
Nor the prevention of poor *Bolingbroke*
About his marriage, nor my own difgrace,
Have ever made me fow'r my patient cheek;
Or bend one wrinkle on my Sovereign's face.
I am the laft of noble *Edward's* fons,

Of whom thy father, Prince of *Wales*, was first;
In war, was never Lion rag'd more fierce,
In peace, was never gentle Lamb more mild,
Than was that young and princely Gentleman:
His face thou haft, for even so look'd he,
Accomplish'd with the number of thy hours.
But when he frown'd, it was against the *French*,
And not against his friends; his noble hand
Did win what he did spend; and spent not That,
Which his triumphant father's hand had won.
His hands were guilty of no kindred's blood,
But bloody with the enemies of his kin.
Oh, *Richard!* *York* is too far gone with grief,
Or else he never would compare between.

 K. *Rich.* Why, uncle, what's the matter?
 York. O my Liege,
Pardon me, if you please; if not, I, pleas'd
Not to be pardon'd, am content withal.
Seek you to seize, and gripe into your hands,
The Royalties and Rights of banish'd *Hereford?*
Is not *Gaunt* dead, and doth not *Hereford* live?
Was not *Gaunt* just, and is not *Harry* true?
Did not the one deserve to have an heir?
Is not his heir a well-deserving son?
Take *Hereford's* Rights away, and take from time
His Charters, and his customary Rights;
Let not to-morrow then ensue to day;
Be not thyself; for how art thou a King,
But by fair sequence and succession?
If you do wrongfully seize *Hereford's* Right,
Call in his letters patents that he hath,
By his attorneys-general to sue
His livery, and * deny his offer'd homage;
You pluck a thousand dangers on your head;
You lose a thousand well-disposed hearts;
And prick my tender patience to those thoughts,

* *Deny his offer'd homage.*]   mage, by which he is to hold his
That is, *refuse* to admit the ho-   lands.

Which honour and allegiance cannot think.

K. Rich. Think what you will, we seize into our hands
His plate, his goods, his money, and his lands.

York. I'll not be by, the while; my Liege, farewel:
What will ensue hereof, there's none can tell.
But by bad courses may be understood,
That their events can never fall out good. [*Exit.*

K. Rich. Go, *Bushy*, to the Earl of *Wiltshire* straight,
Bid him repair to us to *Ely-house*,
To see this business done. To-morrow next
We will for *Ireland*; and 'tis time, I trow.
And we create, in absence of ourself,
Our uncle *York* Lord-governor of *England*,
For he is just, and always lov'd us well.
Come on, our Queen; to-morrow must we part;
Be merry, for our time of Stay is short. [*Flourish.*
[*Exeunt King, Queen,* &c.

SCENE IV.

Manent Northumberland, Willoughby, *and* Ross.

North. Well, Lords, the Duke of *Lancaster* is dead.
Ross. And living too, for now his son is Duke.
Willo. Barely in title, not in revenue.
North. Richly in both, if justice had her right.
Ross. My heart is great; but it must break with silence,
Ere't be disburden'd with a lib'ral tongue.

North. Nay, speak thy mind; and let him ne'er speak more,
That speaks thy words again to do thee harm.

Willo. Tends, what you'd speak, to the Duke of *Hereford*?
If it be so, out with it boldly, man:
Quick is mine ear to hear of good tow'rds him.

Ross. No good at all that I can do for him,
Unless you call it good to pity him,

Bereft

KING RICHARD II.

Bereft and gelded of his patrimony.

North. Now, afore heav'n, it's shame, such wrongs are borne
In him a royal Prince, and many more
Of noble blood in this declining Land;
The King is not himself, but basely led
By flatterers; and what they will inform
Merely in hate 'gainst any of us all,
That will the King severely prosecute
'Gainst us, our lives, our children, and our heirs.

Ross. The Commons hath he pill'd with grievous Taxes,
And lost their hearts; the Nobles he hath fin'd
For ancient quarrels, and quite lost their hearts.

Willo. And daily new exactions are devis'd;
As Blanks, Benevolences, I wot not what?
But what o' God's name doth become of this?

North. Wars have not wasted it, for warr'd he hath not,
But basely yielded upon compromise
That, which his Ancestors atchiev'd with blows;
More hath he spent in peace, than they in wars.

Ross. The Earl of *Wiltshire* hath the Realm in farm.

Willo. The King's grown bankrupt, like a broken man.

North. Reproach, and dissolution, hangeth over him.

Ross. He hath not money for these *Irish* wars,
His burthenous taxations notwithstanding,
But by the robbing of the banish'd Duke.

North. His noble Kinsman. Most degenerate King!
But, lords, we hear this fearful tempest sing,
Yet seek no shelter to avoid the storm:
We see the wind sit sore upon our sails,
[1] And yet we strike not, but securely perish.

Ross. We see the very wreck, that we must suffer;

---

[1] To *strike* the *sails*, is, to *contract* them when there is too much wind.

And unavoided is the danger now,
For suff'ring so the causes of our wreck.
 North. Not so; ev'n through the hollow eyes of Death
I spy life peering; but I dare not say,
How near the tidings of our comfort is.
 Willo. Nay, let us share thy thoughts, as thou dost ours.
 Ross. Be confident to speak, *Northumberland*;
We three are but thyself, and speaking so,
Thy words are but as thoughts, therefore be bold.
 North. Then thus, my friends. I have from *Port le Blanc*,
A bay in *Bretagne*, had intelligence,
That *Harry Hereford*, *Rainald* lord *Cobham*,
That late broke from the Duke of *Exeter*,
His brother, Archbishop late of *Canterbury*,
Sir *Thomas Erpingham*, Sir *John Rainston*,
Sir *John Norberie*, Sir *Robert Waterton*, and *Francis Coines*,
All these, well furnish'd by the Duke of *Bretagne*,
With eight tall ships, three thousand men of war,
Are making hither with all due expedience,
And shortly mean to touch our northern shore;
Perhaps, they had ere this; but that they stay
The first departing of the King for *Ireland*.
If then we shall shake off our slavish yoak,
Imp out our drooping Country's broken wing,
Redeem from broking Pawn the blemish'd Crown,
Wipe off the dust that hides our Scepter's gilt,
And make high Majesty look like itself.
Away with me in post to *Ravenspurg*;
But if you faint, as fearing to do so,
Stay, and be secret, and myself will go.
 Ross. To horse, to horse; urge Doubts to them that fear.
 Willo. Hold out my horse, and I will first be there.
           [*Exeunt.*
SCENE

SCENE V.

The COURT.

Enter Queen, Bushy, *and* Bagot.

Bushy. MAdam, your Majesty is much too sad:
You promis'd, when you parted with the King,
To lay aside self-harming heaviness,
And entertain a chearful disposition.
Queen. To please the King, I did; to please myself,
I cannot do it; yet I know no cause,
Why I should welcome such a guest as grief;
Save bidding farewel to so sweet a Guest
As my sweet *Richard.* Yet again, methinks,
Some unborn sorrow, ripe in fortune's womb,
Is coming tow'rd me; and my inward soul
² With nothing trembles, at something it grieves,
More than with parting from my lord the King.
Bushy. Each substance of a grief hath twenty shadows,
Which shew like grief itself, but are not so:
For sorrow's eye, glazed with blinding tears,
Divides one thing entire to many objects;
³ Like Perspectives, which, rightly gaz'd upon,

Shew

---

² *With* nothing *trembles, yet at* something *grieves.*] The following line requires that this should be read just the contrary way,
With something *trembles, yet at* nothing *grieves.*
WARBURTON.
All the old editions read,
———*my inward soul*
With nothing *trembles; at* something *it grieves.*

The reading, which Dr. *Warburton* corrects, is itself an innovation. His conjecture gives indeed a better sense than that of any copy, but copies must not be needlesly forsaken.
³ *Like* Perspectives, which, rightly *gaz'd upon,*
Shew nothing *but* confusion;
ey'd awry,
Distinguish form.] This is a fine similitude, and the thing

meant

Shew nothing but confusion; ey'd awry
Distinguish form.——So your sweet Majesty,
Looking awry upon your lord's departure,
Finds shapes of grief, more than himself, to wail;
Which look'd on, as it is, is nought but shadows
Of what it is not; gracious Queen, then weep not
More than your lord's departure; more's not seen:
Or if it be, 'tis with false sorrow's eye,
Which, for things true, weeps things imaginary.

Queen. It may be so; but yet my inward soul
Persuades me otherwise. Howe'er it be,
I cannot but be sad; so heavy-sad,
[4] As, though, on thinking, on no thought I think,
Makes me with heavy nothing faint and shrink.

Bushy. 'Tis nothing but Conceit, my gracious lady.

Queen. 'Tis nothing less; Conceit is still deriv'd
From some fore-father grief; mine is not so;
[5] For nothing hath begot my something grief;

Or

---

meant is this. Amongst *mathematical* recreations, there is one in *Optics*, in which a figure is drawn, wherein all the rules of *Perspective* are inverted: so that, if held in the same position with those pictures which are drawn according to the rules of *Perspective*, it can present nothing but confusion: and to be seen in form, and under a regular Appearance, it must be look'd upon from a contrary station: or, as *Shakspeare* says, *ey'd awry*.
WARBURTON.

[4] *As, though, on thinking, on no thought I think.*] We should read, *as though in thinking*: That is, *though musing, I have no distinct idea of calamity.* The involuntary and unaccountable depression of the mind, which every one has sometime felt, is here very forcibly described.

[5] *For nothing hath begot my something grief;*
Or something hath, the nothing that I grieve.]
With these lines I know not well what can be done. The Queen's reasoning, as it now stands, is this. My *trouble* is not *conceit*, for *conceit is still derived from some antecedent cause, some fore-father grief*; but with me the case is, that *either my real grief hath no real cause, or some real cause has produced a fany'd grief.* That is, *my grief is not conceit, because it either has not a cause like conceit, or it has a cause like conceit.* This can hardly stand. Let us try again, and read thus:
For nothing hath begot my something grief;

Not

KING RICHARD II. 39

Or something hath, the nothing that I grieve;
* 'Tis in reversion That I do possess;
But what it is, that is not yet known, what
I cannot name, 'tis nameless woe, I wot.

SCENE VI.

Enter Green.

Green. Heav'n save your Majesty! and well met,
 gentlemen:
I hope, the King is not yet shipt for *Ireland*.
 Queen. Why hop'st thou so? 'tis better hope, he is:
For his designs crave haste, his haste good hope:
Then wherefore dost thou hope, he is not shipt?
 Green. That he, our hope, ⁷ might have retir'd his
 Power?
And driv'n into despair an enemy's Hope,
Who strongly hath set footing in this Land.
The banish'd *Bolingbroke* repeals himself;

Not *something hath the nothing which I grieve.*
That is, **My grief is not conceit** ; *conceit is an imaginary uneasiness from some past occurrence.* But, on the contrary, here is *real grief without a real cause*; not a *real cause with a fanciful sorrow.* This, I think, must be the meaning; harsh at the best, yet better than contradiction or absurdity.
 ⁶ *'Tis in reversion that I do possess,*
 But *what it is, that is not yet known,* &c.] I am about to propose an interpretation which many will think harsh, and which I do not offer for certain. To *possess* a man, is, in *Shakespeare*, to *inform him fully*, to *make him comprehend.* To be *possessed*, is, *to be fully informed.* Of this sense the examples are

numerous.
 I have poss'st him my most stay Can be but short. Meas. for Meas.
 Is he possest what sum you need.
  Merch. of Venice.
I therefore imagine the Queen says thus:
 'Tis in reversion —— that I do possess. ——
 The event is yet in futurity—that I know with full conviction —*but what it is, that is not yet known.* In any other interpretation she must say that *she possess* what is not yet come, which, though it may be allowed to be poetical and figurative language, is yet, I think, less natural than my explanation.
 ⁷ *Might have retired his power.*] Might have drawn it back. A *French* sense.

D 4   And

And with uplifted arms is safe arriv'd
At *Ravenspurg.*
  Queen. Now God in heav'n forbid!
  Green. O, Madam, 'tis too true; and what is worse,
The lord *Northumberland*, his young son *Percy*,
The lords of *Ross*, *Beaumond*, and *Willoughby*,
With all their pow'rful friends, are fled to him.
  Bushy. Why have you not proclaim'd *Northumberland*,
And all of that revolted faction, traitors?
  Green. We have; whereon the Earl of *Worcester*
Hath broke his staff, resign'd his Stewardship;
And all the houshold servants fled with him
To *Bolingbroke.*
  Queen. So, *Green*, thou art the midwife of my woe,
And *Bolingbroke* * my sorrow's dismal heir.
Now hath my soul brought forth her prodigy,
And I, a gasping new-deliver'd mother,
Have woe to woe, sorrow to sorrow, join'd.
  Bushy. Despair not, Madam.
  Queen. Who shall hinder me?
I will despair, and be at enmity
With cozening hope; he is a flatterer,
A parasite, a keeper back of death;
Who gently would dissolve the bands of life,
Which false hopes linger, in extremity.

SCENE VII.

Enter York.

  Green. Here comes the Duke of *York.*
  Queen. With signs of war about his aged neck;
Oh, full of careful business are his looks!
Uncle, for heav'n's sake, comfortable words.
  York. Should I do so, I should bely my thoughts;

---

* *My sorrow's dismal heir.*] The authour seems to have used *heir* in an improper sense; an *heir* being one that *inherits by succession*, is here put for one that *succeeds*, though he *succeeds* but in order of time, not in order of descent.

Comfort's

Comfort's in heav'n, and we are on the earth,
Where nothing lives but Crosses, Care, and Grief,
Your husband he is gone to save far off,
Whilst others come to make him lose at home.
Here am I left to underprop this Land;
Who, weak with age, cannot support my self.
Now comes the sick hour, that his surfeit made;
Now shall he try his friends, that flatter'd him.

Enter a Servant.

Serv. My lord, your son was gone before I came.
York. He was—why, so—go all, which way it will—,
The Nobles they are fled, the Commons cold,
And will, I fear, revolt on *Hereford's* side.
Get thee to *Plashie*[s], to my sister *Glo'ster*;
Bid her send presently a thousand pound:
Hold, take my ring.
Serv. My lord, I had forgot
To tell, to-day I came by, and call'd there;
But I shall grieve you to report the rest.
York. What is't?
Serv. An hour before I came, the Dutchess dy'd.
York. Heav'n for his mercy, what a tide of woes
Come rushing on this woful land at once!
I know not what to do. I would to heav'n,
So my * untruth had not provok'd him to it,
The King had cut off my head with my brother's.
What, are there posts dispatch'd for *Ireland*?
How shall we do for mony for these wars?
Come, sister; cousin, I would say; pray, pardon me.—
Go, fellow, get thee home, provide some carts,
[*To the Servant.*
And bring away the armour that is there.
—Gentlemen, will you go and muster men?

[s] *Get thee to* Plashie, ———] The Lordship of *Plashie* was a Town of the Dutchess of *Gloucester's* in *Essex.* See *Hale's* Chronicle, p. 13.   THEOBALD.
* *Untruth.*] That is, *Dishonesty, treachery.*

If I know how to order thefe affairs,
Diforderly thus thruft into my hands,
Never believe me. They are both my kinfmen;
The one my Sovereign, whom both my oath
And duty bids defend; th' other again
My kinfman is, One whom the King hath wrong'd;
Whom confcience and my kindred bids to right.
Well, fomewhat we muft do.—Come, coufin, I'll
Difpofe of you.—Go mufter up your men,
And meet me prefently at *Berkley* caftle—
I fhould to *Plafhie* too; ———
But time will not permit. All is uneven,
And every thing is left at fix and feven.
[*Exeunt* York *and* Queen.

SCENE VIII.

Bufhy. The wind fits fair for news to go to *Ireland,*
But none returns; for us to levy Power,
Proportionable to the enemy,
Is all impoffible.

Green. Befides, our Nearnefs to the King in Love
Is near the Hate of thofe, love not the King.

Bagot. And that's the wav'ring Commons, for their love
Lies in their purfes; and who empties them,
By fo much fills their hearts with deadly hate.

Bufhy. Wherein the King ftands generally condemn'd.

Bagot. If judgment lye in them, then fo do we;
Becaufe we have been ever near the King.

Green. Well; I'll for Refuge ftraight to *Briftol* Caftle;
The Earl of *Wiltfhire* is already there.

Bufhy. Thither will I with you; for little office
The hateful Commons will perform for us;
Except, like curs, to tear us all in pieces:
Will you go with us?

Bagot. No, I'll to *Ireland* to his Majefty.
Farewel.

KING RICHARD II.

Farewel. If heart's Presages be not vain,
We three here part, that ne'er shall meet again.
  Bushy. That's as *York* thrives, to beat back *Bolingbroke.*
  Green. Alas, poor Duke! the task he undertakes
Is numb'ring sands, and drinking oceans dry;
Where one on his side fights, thousands will fly.
  Bushy. Farewel at once, for once, for all and ever.
  Green. Well, we may meet again.
  Bagot. I fear me, never.   [*Exeunt.*

SCENE IX.

Changes to a wild Prospect in Glocestershire.

Enter Bolingbroke *and* Northumberland.

Boling. HOW far is it, my lord, to *Berkley* now?
  North. I am a stranger here in *Glo'stershire,*
These high wild hills, and rough uneven ways,
Draw out our miles, and make them wearisome,
And yet your fair discourse has been as sugar,
Making the hard way sweet and delectable.
But, I bethink me, what a weary way,
From *Ravenspurg* to *Cotshold,* will be found
In *Ross* and *Willoughby,* wanting your Company;
Which, I protest, hath very much beguil'd
The tediousness and process of my travel;
But theirs is sweetned with the hope to have
The present benefit that I possess;
And hope to joy, is little less in joy,
Than hope enjoy'd. By this, the weary lords
Shall make their way seem short, as mine hath done,
By sight of what I have, your noble company,
  Boling. Of much less value is my company,
Than your good words. But who comes here?

Enter

Enter Percy.

North. It is my son, young *Harry Percy*,
Sent from my brother *Worcester*, whencesoever.
—*Harry*, how fares your uncle?
  Percy. I thought, my lord, t'have learn'd his health
    of you.
  North. Why, is he not with the Queen?
  Percy. No, my good lord, he hath forsook the Court,
Broken his staff of office, and dispers'd
The Houshold of the King.
  North. What was his reason?
He was not so resolv'd, when last we spake together.
  Percy. Because your lordship was proclaimed Traitor.
But he, my lord, is gone to *Ravenspurg*,
To offer service to the Duke of *Hereford*;
And sent me o'er by *Berkley*, to discover
What Pow'r the Duke of *York* had levy'd there;
Then with directions to repair to *Ravenspurg*.
  North. Have you forgot the Duke of *Hereford*, boy?
  Percy. No, my good lord; for that is not forgot,
Which ne'er I did remember; to my knowledge,
I never in my life did look on him.
  North. Then learn to known him now; this is the
    Duke.
  Percy. My gracious lord, I tender you my service,
Such as it is, being tender, raw, and young,
Which elder days shall ripen and confirm
To more approved service and desert.
  Boling. I thank thee, gentle *Percy*; and be sure,
I count my self in nothing else so happy,
As in a soul remembring my good friends:
And as my Fortune ripens with thy love,
It shall be still thy true love's recompence.
My heart this cov'nant makes, my hand thus seals it.
  North. How far is it to *Berkley*? and what stir
Keeps good old *York* there with his men of war?
                                        Percy.

KING RICHARD II.

Percy. There stands the Castle by yond tuft of trees,
Mann'd with three hundred men, as I have heard;
And in it are the lords, *York, Berkley, Seymour*;
None else of name, and noble estimate.

Enter Ross *and* Willoughby.

North. Here comes the lords of *Ross* and *Willoughby*,
Bloody with spurring, fiery-red with haste.
Boling. Welcome, my lords; I wot, your love pursues
A banish'd traitor; all my Treasury
Is yet but unfelt thanks, which, more enrich'd,
Shall be your love and labour's recompence.
Ross. Your presence makes us rich, most noble lord.
Willo. And far surmounts our labour to attain it.
Boling. Evermore, thanks, th' exchequer of the poor,
Which, 'till my infant-fortune comes to years,
Stands for my bounty. But who now comes here?

Enter Berkley.

North. It is my lord of *Berkley*, as I guess.
Berk. My lord of *Hereford*, my message is to you.
Boling. My lord, my answer is to *Lancaster*;
And I am come to seek that Name in *England*,
And I must find that Title in your tongue,
Before I make reply to aught you say.
Berk. Mistake me not, my lord; 'tis not my meaning
To raze one Title of your honour out.
To you, my lord, I come (what lord you will)
From the most glorious of this Land,
The Duke of *York*, to know what pricks you on
To take advantage of the absent time [9].
And fright our native peace with self-born arms.

[9] —— *the* absent *time,*] For unprepared. Not an inelegant synecdoche. WARBURTON. He means nothing more than, *time of the king's absence.*

SCENE

SCENE X.

Enter York.

Boling. I shall not need transport my words by you.
Here comes his Grace in person. Noble Uncle!
[*Kneels.*

York. Shew me thy humble heart, and not thy knee,
Whose duty is deceivable and false.
Boling. My gracious uncle!
York. Tut, tut!
Grace me no Grace, nor Uncle me no Uncle:——
I am no traitor's uncle; and that word Grace,
In an ungracious mouth, is but prophane.
Why have those banish'd and forbidden legs
Dar'd once to touch a dust of *England's* ground?
But more than why; why, have they dar'd to march
So many miles upon her peaceful bosom,
Frighting her pale-fac'd villages with war,
[1] And ostentation of despised arms?
Com'st thou because th' anointed King is hence?
Why, foolish boy, the King is left behind;
And in my loyal bosom lies his Power.
Were I but now the lord of such hot youth,
As when brave *Gaunt*, thy father, and myself
Rescu'd the *Black Prince*, that young *Mars* of men,
From forth the ranks of many thousand *French*;
Oh! then, how quickly should this arm of mine,

---

[1] *And ostentation of* DESPISED *arms?*] But sure the ostentation of despised arms would not *fright* any one. We should read
—— DISPOSED *arms.*
i. e. forces in battle-array. WAR. This alteration is harsh. Sir *T. Hanmer* reads *despightful.* Mr. *Upton* gives this passage as a proof that our authour uses the passive participle in an active sense. The copies all agree. Perhaps the old Duke means to treat him with contempt as well as with severity, and to insinuate that he despises his power, as being able to master it. In this sense, all is right.

Now

KING RICHARD II.

Now prisoner to the palsie, chastise thee,
And minister correction to thy fault.

Boling. My gracious uncle, let me know my fault;
* On what condition stands it, and wherein?

York. Ev'n in condition of the worst degree;
In gross Rebellion, and detested Treason.
Thou art a banish'd man, and here art come,
Before the expiration of thy time,
In braving arms against thy Sovereign.

Boling. As I was banish'd, I was banish'd *Hereford*;
But as I come, I come for *Lancaster*.
And, noble uncle, I beseech your Grace,
Look on my wrongs with an indifferent eye.
You are my father; for, methinks, in you
I see old *Gaunt* alive: O then, my father!
Will you permit, that I shall stand condemn'd
A wand'ring vagabond; my Rights and Royalties
Pluckt from my arms perforce, and giv'n away
To upstart unthrifts? † Wherefore was I born?
If that my cousin King be King of *England*,
It must be granted, I am Duke of *Lancaster*.
You have a son, *Aumerle*, my noble Kinsman:
Had you first dy'd, and he been thus trod down,
He should have found his uncle *Gaunt* a father,
To rowze his wrongs, and chase them to the bay.
I am deny'd to sue my livery here,
And yet my letters patents give me leave:
My father's Goods are all distrain'd and sold,
And these, and all, are all amiss imploy'd.
What would you have me do? I am a Subject,
And challenge law; attorneys are deny'd me;
And therefore personally I lay my Claim

* *On what condition.*] It should be, *in what condition.* That is, *in what degree of guilt.* The particles in the old editions are of little credit.

† *Wherefore was I born?*] To what purpose serves birth and lineal succession? I am Duke of *Lancaster* by the same right of birth as the King is king of *England*.

To

To mine Inheritance of free Defcent.
North. The noble Duke hath been too much abus'd.
Rofs. It ftands your Grace upon, to do him Right.
Willo. Bafe men by his endowments are made great.
York. My lords of *England*, let me tell you this,
I have had Feeling of my Coufin's wrongs,
And labour'd all I could to do him Right.
But, in this kind, to come in braving arms,
Be his own carver, and cut out his way,
To find out Right with wrongs, it may not be;
And you that do abet him in this kind,
Cherifh Rebellion, and are Rebels all.
North. The noble Duke hath fworn, his Coming is
But for his own; and, for the Right of That,
We all have ftrongly fworn to give him aid;
And let him ne'er fee joy, that breaks that oath.
York. Well, well, I fee the iffue of thefe arms;
I cannot mend it, I muft needs confefs,
Becaufe my Pow'r is weak, and all ill left;
But if I could, by him that gave me life,
I would attach you all, and make you ftoop
Unto the fovereign mercy of the King.
But fince I cannot, be it known to you,
I do remain as neuter. So, farewel.
Unlefs you pleafe to enter in the Caftle,
And there repofe you for this night.
Boling. An offer, Uncle, that we will accept.
But we muft win your Grace to go with us
To *Briftol-Caftle*, which, they fay, is held
By *Bufhy*, *Bagot*, and their complices;
The caterpillars of the Common-wealth,
Which I have fworn to weed, and pluck away.
York. It may be, I will go. But yet I'll paufe,
For I am loath to break our Country's Laws.
Nor friends nor foes, to me welcome you are;
Things paft Redrefs are now with me paft Care.
[*Exeunt.*

SCENE

KING RICHARD II.

[2] SCENE XI.

In WALES.

Enter Salisbury, *and a Captain.*

Cap. MY lord of *Salisbury*, we have ſtaid ten days,
And hardly kept our Countrymen together,
And yet we hear no tidings from the King;
Therefore we will diſperſe ourſelves.   Farewel.

Saliſ. Stay yet another day, thou truſty *Welſhman:*
The King repoſeth all his truſt in thee.

Cap: 'Tis thought, the King is dead: we will not
ſtay.
The Bay-trees in our Country all are wither'd,
And meteors fright the fixed ſtars of heav'n;
The pale-fac'd moon looks bloody on the earth;
And lean-look'd Prophets whiſper fearful Change.
Rich men look ſad, and ruffians dance and leap;
The one; in fear to loſe what they enjoy;
Th' other, in hope t'enjoy by rage and war.
Theſe ſigns forerun the death of Kings——
Farewel; our countrymen are gone and fled,
As well aſſur'd, *Richard* their King is dead. [*Exit.*

Saliſ. Ah, *Richard*, ah! with eyes of heavy mind,
I ſee thy Glory, like a ſhooting Star,

---

[2] Here is a ſcene ſo unartfully and irregularly thruſt into an improper place, that I cannot but ſuſpect it accidentally tranſpoſed; which, when the ſcenes were written on ſingle pages, might eaſily happen, in the wildneſs of *Shakeſpeare's* drama. This dialogue was; in the Author's draught, probably the ſecond ſcene of the enſuing act, and there I would adviſe the reader to inſert it, though I have not ventured on ſo bold a change. My conjecture is not ſo preſumptuous as may be thought. The play was not, in *Shakeſpeare's* time, broken into acts; the two editions publiſhed before his death exhibit only a ſequence of ſcenes from the beginning to the end, without any hint of a pauſe of action. In a drama ſo deſultory and erratick, left in ſuch a ſtate, tranſpoſitions might eaſily be made.

[3] *The bay-trees,* &c.] This enumeration of prodigies is in the higheſt degree poetical and ſtriking.

VOL. IV.   E   Fall

Fall to the base earth from the firmament.
Thy Sun sets weeping in the lowly West,
Witnessing Storms to come, woe, and unrest.
Thy friends are fled to wait upon thy foes;
And crossly to thy Good all fortune goes. [*Exit.*

ACT III. SCENE I.

Bolingbroke's *Camp at* Bristol.

Enter Bolingbroke, York, Northumberland, Ross, Percy, Willoughby, *with* Bushy *and* Green, *Prisoners.*

BOLINGBROKE.

BRING forth these men.———
Bushy and *Green*, I will not vex your souls
(Since presently your souls must part your bodies)
With too much urging your pernicious lives;
For 'twere no charity: yet to wash your blood
From off my hands, here, in the view of men,
I will unfold some causes of your deaths.
You have misled a Prince, a royal King,
A happy gentleman in blood and lineaments,
By you unhappy'd, and disfigur'd clean.
You have, in manner, with your sinful hours
Made a divorce betwixt his Queen and him;
Broke the Possession of a royal Bed,
And stain'd the Beauty of a fair Queen's cheeks
With tears drawn from her eyes, with your foul wrongs.
Myself, a Prince, by fortune of my birth,
Near to the King in blood, and near in love,
Till you did make him mis-interpret me,
Have stoopt my neck under your injuries;
And sigh'd my *English* breath in foreign clouds,

Eat-

KING RICHARD II.   51

Eating the bitter bread of Banishment,
While you have fed upon my Signiories,
Dis-park'd my Parks, and fell'd my forest-woods,
³ From mine own windows torn my houshold coat,
Raz'd out my Impress, leaving me no sign,
Save mens' opinions, and my living blood,
To shew the world I am a gentleman.
This, and much more, much more than twice all this,
Condemns you to the death. See them deliver'd
T'execution, and the hand of death.

Busby. More welcome is the stroke of death to me,
Than *Bolingbroke* to *England*.——Lords, farewel.

Green. My comfort is, that heav'n will take our
    souls,
And plague injustice with the pains of hell.

Boling. My lord *Northumberland,* see them dispatch'd.
—Uncle, you say the Queen is at your house;
For heav'n's sake, fairly let her be intreated;
Tell her, I send to her my kind Commends;
Take special care, my Greetings be deliver'd.

York. A gentleman of mine I have dispatch'd
With letters of your love to her at large.

Boling. ⁴ Thanks, gentle Uncle.—Come, my lords,
    away,

[To

---

³ *From mine own windows torn my houshold coat.*] It was the practice, when coloured glass was in use, of which there are still some remains in old seats and churches, to anneal the arms of the family in the windows of the house.

⁴ *Thanks, gentle Uncle; Come, my Lords, away,*
    To fight with *Glendower* and
    his Complices,
*A while to Work, and after
    Holyday.*] Tho' the intermediate Line has taken Posses-

sion of all the old Copies, I have great Suspicion of its being an Interpolation; and have therefore ventur'd to throw it out. The first and third Line rhime to each other; nor, do I imagine, this was casual, but intended by the Poet. Were we to acknowledge the Line genuine, it must argue the Poet of Forgetfulness and Inattention to History. *Bolingbroke* is, as it were, yet but just arrived; he is now at *Bristol*; weak in his Numbers; has had no Meeting with a Parliament;

E 2   nor

52　KING RICHARD II.

[To fight with *Glendower* and his Complices;]
A while to Work; and, after, Holy-day. [*Exeunt.*

SCENE II.

* *Changes to the coaſt of* Wales.

Flouriſh: Drums and Trumpets.

Enter King Richard, Aumerle, *Biſhop of* Carliſle, *and Soldiers.*

K. *Rich.* **B**Arkloughly-caſtle call you this at hand?
　　　Aum. Yea, my good lord; how brooks
　　　your Grace the air,
After your toſſing on the breaking Seas?
　K. *Rich.* Needs muſt I like it well. I weep for joy
To ſtand upon my Kingdom once again.
Dear Earth, I do ſalute thee with my hand,
Though Rebels wound thee with their horſes' hoofs:
As a long-parted mother with her child
Plays fondly with her tears, and ſmiles in meeting;
So weeping, ſmiling, greet I thee my Earth,
And do thee favour with my royal hands.
Feed not thy Sovereign's foe, my gentle Earth,
Nor with thy ſweets comfort his rav'nous ſenſe;
But let thy ſpiders that ſuck up thy venom,
And heavy-gaited toads, lye in their way;
Doing annoyance to the treacherous feet,
Which with uſurping ſteps do trample thee.

---

nor is ſo far aſſur'd of the Succeſſion, as to think of going to ſuppreſs Inſurrections before he is planted in the Throne. Beſides, we find, the Oppoſition of *Glendower* begins the *Firſt* Part of K. *Henry* IV; and *Mortimer's* Defeat by that hardy *Welſhman* is the Tidings of the firſt Scene of that Play. Again, tho' *Glendower*, in the very firſt Year of K. *Henry* IV. began to be troubleſome, put in for the Supremacy of *Wales*, and impriſon'd *Mortimer*; yet it was not 'till the ſucceeding Year, that the King employed any Force againſt him.
　　　　　　　　THEOBALD.
　This emendation, which I think is juſt, has been followed by Sir *T. Hanmer*, but is neglected by Dr. *Warburton*.

　* Here may be properly inſerted the laſt ſcene of the ſecond act.

Yield

KING RICHARD II.   53

ſtinging nettles to mine enemies;
when they from thy boſom pluck a flower,
 it, I pr'ythee, with a lurking adder;
e double tongue may with a mortal touch
v death upon thy Sovereign's enemies.
 not my ſenſeleſs conjuration, lords;
arth ſhall have a Feeling, and theſe ſtones
 armed ſoldiers, ere her native King
faulter under foul rebellious arms.
bop. 'Fear not, my Lord; that Pow'r, that made
    you King,
pow'r to keep you King, in ſpight of all.
eans, that heaven yields, muſt be embrac'd
ot neglected; elſe, if heaven would,
we would not heav'n's offer, we refuſe
roffer'd means of ſuccour and redreſs.
n. He means, my lord; that we are too remiſs;
ft *Bolingbroke*, through our ſecurity,
s ſtrong and great, in ſubſtance and in power.
Rich. Diſcomfortable Couſin, know'ſt thou not,
 when the ſearching eye of heav'n is hid
ind the globe, that lights the lower world;
 thieves and robbers range abroad unſeen,
rders, and in outrage bloody, here,
hen from under this terreſtrial ball
es the proud tops of the eaſtern pines,
larts his light through ev'ry guilty hole,
 murders, treaſons, and deteſted ſins,
loak of night being pluck'd from off their backs,
 bare and naked, trembling at themſelves.
hen this thief, this traitor *Bolingbroke*,

ar *not, my Lord.*] Of   ſuitable to the perſonage.
ech the four laſt lines were   * *Behind the globe,* &c.] I
 from the firſt edition by   ſhould read,
ope. They were, I ſup-   ——*the ſearching eye of heav'n
mitted by the players on-   is hid
orten the ſcenes, for they   Behind the globe,* and *lights the
rthy of the authour and   lower world.*

E 3   Who

Who all this while hath revell'd in the night,
Whilſt we were wand'ring with the Antipodes,
Shall ſee us riſing in our Throne, the eaſt;
His treaſons will ſit bluſhing in his face,
Not able to endure the ſight of day;
But, ſelf-affrighted, tremble at his ſin.
Not all the water in the rough rude ſea
Can waſh the balm from an anointed King;
⁶ The breath of worldly men cannot depoſe
The Deputy elected by the Lord.
For every man that *Bolingbroke* hath preſt,
To lift ſharp ſteel againſt our golden Crown,
Heav'n for his *Richard* hath in heav'nly Pay
A glorious Angel; then if angels fight,
Weak men muſt fall, for heav'n ſtill guards the **Right.**

SCENE III.

Enter Salisbury.

Welcome, my lord, how far off lies your Power?
   Saliſ. Nor near, nor further off, my gracious lord,
Than this weak arm: Diſcomfort guides my tongue,
And bids me ſpeak of nothing but Deſpair:
One day too late, I fear, my noble lord,
Hath clouded all thy happy days on earth.
Oh, call back yeſterday, bid time return,
And thou ſhalt have twelve thouſand fighting men.
To day, to day,———unhappy day, too late
O'erthrows thy joys, friends, fortune, and thy ſtate.
For all the *Welſhmen*, hearing thou wert dead,
Are gone to *Bolingbroke*, diſperſt and fled.

---

⁶ *The breath of worldly men.*] Here is the doctrine of indefeaſible right expreſſed in the ſtrongeſt terms; but our poet did not learn it in the reign of King *James,* to which it is now the practice of all writers, whoſe opinions are regulated by faſhion or intereſt, to impute the original of every tenet which they have been taught to think falſe or fooliſh.
                            Aum.

KING RICHARD II. 55

Aum. Comfort, my Liege, why looks your Grace
 so pale?
K. Rich. But now the blood of twenty thousand men
Did triumph in my face, and they are fled.
And till so much blood thither come again,
 Have I not reason to look pale, and dead?
All souls, that will be safe, fly from my side;
For time hath set a blot upon my pride.
 Aum. Comfort, my Liege; remember, who you are.
 K. Rich. I had forgot myself. Am I not King?
Awake, thou coward Majesty, thou sleepest;
Is not the King's name forty thousand names?
Arm, arm, my Name; a puny Subject strikes
 At thy great glory. Look not to the ground,
 fav'rites of a King, are we not high?
 High be our thoughts. I know, my uncle *York*
 hath pow'r to serve our turn. But who comes here?

SCENE IV.

Enter Scroop.

Scroop. More health and happiness betide my Liege,
Than can my care-tun'd tongue deliver him!
 K. Rich. [7] Mine ear is open, and my heart prepar'd.
The worst is worldly loss thou canst unfold.
Say, is my Kingdom lost? why, 'twas my care,
 And what loss is it, to be rid of care?
Strives *Bolingbroke* to be as great as we?
Greater he shall not be; if he serve God,
We'll serve him too, and be his fellow so.
Revolt our Subjects? that we cannot mend;

---

[7] *Mine ear is open,*] It seems to be the design of the poet to raise *Richard* to esteem in his fall, and consequently to interest the reader in his favour. He gives him only passive fortitude, the virtue of a confessor rather than of a king. In his prosperity we saw him imperious and oppressive, but in his distress he is wise, patient, and pious.

E 4 They

They break their faith to God, as well as us.
Cry, Woe, Destruction, Ruin, Loss, Decay;
The worst is death, and death will have his day.

Scroop. Glad am I, that your Highness is so arm'd
To bear the tidings of calamity.
Like an unseasonable stormy day,
Which makes the silver rivers drown their shores,
As if the world were all dissolv'd to tears;
So high above his limits swells the rage
Of *Bolingbroke*, cov'ring your fearful Land
With hard bright steel, and hearts more hard than st[eel]
White beards have arm'd their thin and hairless sca[lps]
Against thy Majesty; boys with women's voices
Strive to speak big, and clasp their female joints
In stiff unwieldy arms, against thy Crown.
⁸ Thy very Beadsmen learn to bend their bows
⁹ Of double-fatal Ewe, against thy State.
Yea, distaff-women manage rusty bills.
Against thy Seat both young and old rebel,
And all goes worse than I have pow'r to tell.

K. Rich. Too well, too well, thou tell'st a Tale ill.
¹ Where is the Earl of *Wiltshire?* where is *Bagot*

⁸ *The very Beadsmen learn to bend their bows.*] Such is the reading of all the copies, yet I doubt whether *beadsmen* be right, for the *bow* seems to be mentioned here as the proper weapon of a *beadsman*. The king's *beadsmen* were his chaplains. *Trenfa* calls himself the *beadsman* of his patron. *Beadsman* might likewise be any men maintained by charity to pray for their benefactor. *Hanmer* reads *the* very *beadsmen*, but *thy* is better.

⁹ *Of double fatal Ewe,——*] Called so, because the leaves the Ewe are poison, and the w[ood] is employed for instrument death; therefore *double* [fatal] should be with an hyphen.

WARBURT[ON]

¹ *Where is the Earl of* W[ilt]shire? *where is* Bagot? *What is become of* Bu[shy] *where is* Green?] [There] are *four* of them named; a[nd] within a very few Lines, [the] King, hearing they had m[ade] their Peace with *Bolingb*[roke] calls them THREE *Judas's*. [But] how was their Peace ma[de]

KING RICHARD II.

What is become of *Bufby?* where is *Green?*
That they have let the dang'rous enemy
Measure our confines with such peaceful steps?
If we prevail, their heads shall pay for it.
I warrant, they've made peace with *Bolingbroke.*
  Scroop. Peace they have made with him, indeed, my
    Lord.
  K. Rich. O villains, vipers, damn'd without re-
    demption!
Dogs, easily won to fawn on any man!
Snakes in my heart-blood warm'd, that sting my heart!
Three *Judaffes*, each one thrice worse than *Judas!*
Would they make peace? terrible hell make war
Upon their spotted souls for this offence!
  Scroop. Sweet love, I see, changing his property,
Turns to the sow'rest and most deadly hate.
Again uncurse their souls; their peace is made
With heads, and not with hands; those, whom you
    curse,
Have felt the worst of death's destroying hand,
And lie full low, grav'd in the hollow'd ground.
  Aum. Is *Bufby, Green,* and th' Earl of *Wiltfhire* dead?
  Scroop. Yea, all of them at *Briftol* lost their heads.
  Aum. Where is the Duke my Father, with his Power?

Why, with the Loss of their Heads. This being explained, *Aumerle* says, Is Bushy, Green, and th' Earl of Wiltshire *dead?* So that *Bagot* ought to be left out of the Question: and, indeed, he had made the best of his way for *Chefter*, and from thence had escap'd into *Ireland.* And so we find him, in the 2d Act, determining to do. *Bagot. No: I'll to* Ireland, *to his Majefty.* The Poet could not be guilty of so much Forgetfulness and Absurdity. The Transcribers must have blunder'd. It seems probable to me that he wrote, as I have conjecturally alter'd the Text,
  Where is the Earl of Wiltshire? *where is he got?*
i. e. into what Corner of my Dominions is he *flunk,* and *absconded?*   THEOBALD.
  This emendation Dr. *Warburton* adopts. *Hanmer* leaves a blank after *Wiltshire*. I believe the author, rather than transcriber, made a mistake. *Where is he got* does not found in my ear like an expression of *Shakespeare.*

          K. *Rich.*

KING RICHARD II.

K. Rich. No matter where; of comfort no man speak;
Let's talk of Graves, of Worms, and Epitaphs,
Make duſt our paper, and with rainy eyes
Write ſorrow on the boſom of the earth!
Let's chuſe executors, and talk of wills;
And yet not ſo—for what can we bequeath,
Save our depoſed bodies to the ground?
Our lands, our lives, and all are *Bolingbroke's*,
And nothing can we call our own, but death;
² And that ſmall model of the barren earth,
³ Which ſerves as paſte and cover to our bones.
For heav'n's ſake, let us ſit upon the ground,
And tell ſad ſtories of the death of Kings;
How ſome have been depos'd, ſome ſlain in war;
Some haunted by the Ghoſts they diſpoſſeſs'd;
Some poiſon'd by their wives, ſome ſleeping kill'd;
All murther'd.—For within the hollow Crown,
That rounds the mortal temples of a King,
Keeps Death his Court; and ⁴ there the Antick ſits,
Scoffing his State, and grinning at his Pomp;
Allowing him a breath, a little ſcene
To monarchize, be fear'd, and kill with looks;
Infuſing him with ſelf and vain conceit,
As if this fleſh, which walls about our life,
Were braſs impregnable; and, humour'd thus,
Comes at the laſt, and with a little pin
Bores through his caſtle-walls, and farewel King!
Cover your heads, and mock not fleſh and blood

---

² *And that ſmall* model *of the barren earth.*] He uſes *model* here, as he frequently does elſewhere, for *part, portion.*
　　　　　　　WARBURTON.
He uſes it rather for *mould.* That earth, which cloſing upon the body, takes its form. This interpretation the next line ſeems to authoriſe.

³ A metaphor, not of the moſt ſublime kind, taken from a pie.

⁴ *There the Antick ſits.*] Here is an alluſion to the *antick* or *fool* of old farces, whoſe chief part is to deride and diſturb the graver and more ſplendid perſonages.

With

With solemn Rev'rence; throw away respect,
² Tradition, form, and ceremonious duty,
For you have but mistook me all this while;
I live on bread like you, feel want like you,
Taste grief, need friends, like you; subjected thus,
How can you say to me, I am a King?

 Carl. My lord, wise men ne'er wail their present woes,
But presently prevent the ways to wail:
To fear the foe, since fear oppresseth strength,
Gives, in your weakness, strength unto your foe;
And so your follies fight against yourself:
Fear, and be slain; no worse can come from fight;
And fight and die, is ⁶ death destroying death:
Where fearing dying, pays death servile breath.

 Aum. My father hath a power, enquire of him,
And learn to make a body of a limb.

 K. Rich. Thou chid'st me well; proud *Bolingbroke,*
  I come
To change blows with thee, for our day of doom.
This ague-fit of fear is over-blown;
An easy task it is to win our own.
Say, *Scroop,* where lies our uncle with his Power?
Speak sweetly, man, although thy looks be sower.

 Scroop. Men judge by the complexion of the sky
  The state and inclination of the day;
So may you, by my dull and heavy eye,
 My tongue hath but a heavier tale to say.
I play the torturer, by small and small
To lengthen out the worst, that must be spoken.
Your uncle *York* is join'd with *Bolingbroke,*
And all your northern castles yielded up,
And all your southern gentlemen in arms
Upon his faction.

---

 ² *Tradition.*] This word seems here used in an improper sense, for *traditional practices:* That is, *established or customary homage.*

 ⁶ *Death destroying death*] That is, to *dye fighting,* is to return the evil that we suffer, to destroy the destroyers. I once read *death* defying *death,* but *destroying* is as well.

       K. *Rich.*

60   KING RICHARD II.
 K. *Rich.* Thou haſt ſaid enough.
Beſhrew thee, Couſin, which didſt lead me forth
          [*To* Aumerle.
Of that ſweet way I was in to Deſpair.
What ſay you now? what comfort have we now?
By heav'n, [7] I'll hate him everlaſtingly,
That bids me be of comfort any more.
Go to *Flint-caſtle*, there I'll pine away,
A King, woe's ſlave, ſhall kingly woe obey:
That Pow'r I have, diſcharge; and let 'em go
To ear the land, that hath ſome hope to grow,
For I have none. Let no man ſpeak again
To alter this, for counſel is but vain.
 Aum. My Liege, one word.
 K. *Rich.* He does me double wrong,
That wounds me with the flatt'ries of his tongue.
Diſcharge my Foll'wers; let them hence, away,
From *Richard's* night to *Bolingbroke's* fair day.
           [*Exeunt.*

SCENE V.

Bolingbroke's *Camp near* Flint.

Enter with drum and colours, Bolingbroke, York, Northumberland, *and Attendants.*

Boling. SO that by this intelligence we learn,
   The *Welſhmen* are diſpers'd; and *Saliſbury*
Is gone to meet the King, who lately landed
With ſome few private friends upon this Coaſt.
 North. The news is very fair and good, my lord,
Richard, not far from hence, hath hid his head.
 York. It would beſeem the lord *Northumberland*,

---

[7] *I'll hate him everlaſtingly, That bids me be of comfort.*] This ſentiment is drawn from nature. Nothing is more offenſive to a mind convinced that his diſtreſs is without a remedy, and preparing to ſubmit quietly to irreſiſtible calamity, than theſe petty and conjectured comforts which unſkilful officiouſneſs thinks it virtue to adminiſter.

To fay, King *Richard*. Ah, the heavy day,
When such a sacred King should hide his head!

North. Your Grace mistakes me; only to be brief,
Left I his Title out.

York. The time hath been,
Would you have been so brief with him, he would
Have been so brief with You, to shorten you,
* For taking so the Head, the whole Head's Length.

Boling. Mistake not, uncle, farther than you should.

York. Take not, good cousin, farther than you should,
Lest you mistake. The heav'ns are o'er your head.

Boling. I know it, uncle, nor oppose myself
Against their will. But who comes here?

Enter Percy.

Welcome, *Harry*; what, will not this castle yield?

Percy. The castle royally is mann'd, my lord,
Against your entrance.

Boling. Royally? why, it contains no King?

Percy. Yes, my good lord,
It doth contain a King. King *Richard* lies
Within the limits of yond lime and stone;
And with him lord *Aumerle*, lord *Salisbury*,
Sir *Stephen Scroop*, besides a clergy-man
Of holy reverence; who, I cannot learn.

North. Belike, it is the bishop of *Carlisle*.

Boling. Noble lord, [*To* North.
Go to the rude ribs of that ancient castle,
Through brazen trumpet send the breath of Parle
Into his ruin'd ears, and thus deliver.
Henry of *Bolingbroke* upon his knees
Doth kiss King *Richard's* hand, and sends allegiance
And faith of heart unto his royal person.
Ev'n at his feet I lay my arms and pow'r.
Provided, that my banishment repeal'd,

* *For taking so the head,—*] out restraint; to take undue li-
To *take the head is, to act with-* berties.

And

62   KING RICHARD II.
And lands restor'd again, be freely granted:
If not, I'll use th' advantage of my pow'r,
And lay the summer's dust with show'rs of blood,
Rain'd from the wounds of slaughter'd *Englishmen.*
The which, how far off from the mind of *Bolingbroke*
It is, such crimson tempest should bedrench
The fresh green lap of fair King *Richard's* Land,
My stooping duty tenderly shall shew.
Go signify as much, while here we march
Upon the grassy carpet of this Plain.
Let's march without the noise of threat'ning drum,
That from this Castle's tatter'd battlements
Our fair appointments may be well perus'd.
Methinks, King *Richard* and myself should meet
With no less terror than the elements
Of fire and water, when their thund'ring Shock,
At meeting, tears the cloudy cheeks of heav'n;
Be he the fire, I'll be the yielding water;
The rage be his, while on the earth I rain
My waters! on the earth, and not on him.
March on, and mark King *Richard* how he looks.

SCENE VI.

Parle without, and answer within; then a flourish.
  Enter, on the walls, King Richard, *the Bishop of*
  Carlisle, Aumerle, Scroop, *and* Salisbury.

  York. ⁸ See! see! King *Richard* doth himself appear,
As doth the blushing discontented Sun,
From out the fiery portal of the East,
When he perceives, the envious clouds are bent
To dim his Glory; and to stain the tract
Of his bright Passage to the Occident.

---

⁸ *See! see! King* Richard *doth himself appear,*] The following six lines are absurdly given to *Bolingbroke,* who is made to condemn his own conduct and disculp the King's. It is plain these six and the four following all belong to *York.*   WARB.

Yet

KING RICHARD II.

Yet looks he like a King; behold his eye,
As bright as is the Eagle's, lightens forth
Controlling Majesty; alack, for woe,
That any harm should stain so fair a show!

K. *Rich.* We are amaz'd, and thus long have we
    stood
To watch the fearful bending of thy knee, [*To* North.
Because we thought ourself thy lawful King;
And, if we be, how dare thy joints forget
To pay their awful duty to our presence?
If we be not, shew us the hand of God,
That hath dismiss'd us from our Stewardship.
For well we know, no hand of blood and bone
Can gripe the sacred handle of our Scepter,
Unless he do prophane, steal, or usurp.
And though you think, that all, as you have done,
Have torn their souls, by turning them from us,
And we are barren, and bereft of friends,
Yet know,—— My Master, God omnipotent,
Is must'ring in his clouds on our behalf
Armies of Pestilence; and they shall strike
Your children yet unborn, and unbegot,
That lift your vassal hands against my head,
And threat the Glory of my precious Crown.
Tell *Bolingbroke*, (for yond, methinks, he is)
That every stride he makes upon my Land
Is dangerous treason. He is come to ope
The purple Testament of bleeding War;
But ere the Crown, he looks for, live in peace [*],

Ten

---

[*] *But e'er the Crown, he looks for,* live in Peace, *Ten thousand bloody Crowns of Mothers' Sons Shall ill become the* Flow'r *of* England's *face;*] Tho' I have not disturb'd the Text here, I cannot but think it liable to Suspicion. A Crown living in Peace, as Mr. *Warburton* justly observ'd to me, is a very odd Phrase. He supposes; *But e'er the Crown, he looks for,* light *in Peace,* i. e. descend and settle upon *Bolingbroke's* Head in Peace.—— Again, I have a small Quarrel to the third line quoted. Would
the

64 KING RICHARD II.

Ten thousand bloody crowns of mothers' sons
Shall ill become the flow'r of *England's* face:
Change the complexion of her maid-pale peace
To scarlet indignation; and bedew
Her Pasture's grass with faithful *English* blood.

    North. The King of heav'n forbid, our lord the King
Should so with civil and uncivil arms
Be rush'd upon! no, thy thrice-noble cousin,
Harry of *Bolingbroke*, doth kiss thy hand,
And by the honourable tomb he swears,
That stands upon your royal grandsire's bones,
And by the Royalties of both your bloods,
Currents, that spring from one most gracious head
And by the bury'd hand of warlike *Gaunt* [1],
And by the worth and honour of himself,
Comprising all that may be sworn, or said,
His Coming hither hath no farther scope;

the Poet say, That bloody Crowns should disfigure the *Flow'rs* that spring on the Ground, and bedew the *Grass* with blood? Surely the two Images are too similar. I have suspected,
  Shall ill become the Floor *of* England's *Face*;
i. e. Shall make a dismal Spectacle on the Surface of the Kingdom's Earth. THEOBALD.
  Shall ill become the flow'r *of England's* face;] By *the flow'r of* England's *face*, is meant the choicest youths of *England*, who shall be slaughter'd in this quarrel, or have *bloody crowns. The flower of* England's *face*, to design her choicest Youth, is a fine and noble expression. *Pericles*, by a similar thought, said that the destruction of the *Athenian* youth was a fatality like cutting off the Spring from the Year. Yet the *Oxford Editor*,

who did not apprehend the figure, alters the line thus,
  "*Shall* misbecome *the flow'ry* England's *face.*"
Which means —— I know not what.   WARBURTON.
  Dr. *Warburton* has inserted *light in peace* in the text of his own edition, but *live in peace* is more suitable to *Richard's* intention, which is to tell him that though he should get the *crown* by rebellion, it will be long before it will *live* in peace, be so *settled as* to be firm, *The flow'r of* England's *face*, is very happily explained, and any alteration is therefore needless.

  [1] *And by the* bury'd *hand of warlike* Gaunt.] It should be read just the other way,
  And by the warlike *hand of* bury'd *Gaunt.*   WARBURT.
I see no great difference.

Then

KING RICHARD II. 65

ın for his lineal Royalties, and to beg
anchifement immediate on his knees;
ich on thy royal party granted once,
glitt'ring arms he will commend to ruft;
barbed fteeds to ftables; and his heart
aithful fervice of your Majefty.
fwears he, as he is a Prince, is juft;
as I am a Gentleman, I credit him.
Rich. Northumberland, fay—Thus the King re-
noble Coufin is right-welcome hither, [turns:
all the number of his fair demands
l be accomplifh'd without contradiction.
h all the gracious utterance thou haft,
k to his gentle Hearing kind Commends.
                      Exit North.
do debafe ourfelf, Coufin, do we not, [*To Aum.*
ook fo poorly, and to fpeak fo fair?
l we call back *Northumberland*, and fend
unce to the traitor, and fo die?
m. No, good my lord, let's fight with gentle words,
ime lend friends, and friends their helpful fwords.
Rich. Oh God, oh God! that e'er this tongue of
   mine,
laid the Sentence of dread Banifhment
ond proud man, fhould take it off again
words of Sooth [2]; oh, that I were as great
my grief, or leffer than my name!
at I could forget what I have been,
t remember what I muft be now!
'ft thou, proud heart? I'll give thee fcope to beat,
foes have fcope to beat both thee and me.
n. Northumberland comes back from *Bolingbroke*.
Rich. What muft the King do now? muft he
   fubmit?
King fhall do it. Muft he be depos'd?

ith *words of footh;*——] or foftnefs, a fignification yet re-
fweet as well as *true*. In tained in the verb to *footh*.
ce *footh* means *fweetnefs*

L. IV.   F   The

66 KING RICHARD II.

The King shall be contented: must he lose
The name of King? o' God's name, let it go.
I'll give my jewels for a set of beads;
My gorgeous palace for a hermitage;
My gay apparel, for an alms-man's gown;
My figur'd goblets, for a dish of wood;
My scepter, for a palmer's walking staff;
My subjects, for a pair of carved saints;
And my large Kingdom, for a little Grave;
A little, little Grave;—an obscure Grave;
Or I'll be bury'd in the King's high way [3],
Some way of common Trade, where Subjects' feet
May hourly trample on their Sovereign's head [4];
For on my heart they tread now, whilst I live;
And, bury'd once, why not upon my head?——
Aumerle, thou weep'st; my tender hearted cousin!
We'll make foul weather with despised tears;
Our sighs, and they, shall lodge the summer corn,
And make a dearth in this revolting Land.
Or shall we play the Wantons with our woes,
And make some pretty match, with shedding tears?
As thus, to drop them still upon one place,
Till they have fretted us a pair of Graves

[3] *Or I'll be buried in the King's high-way;*
Some Way of common Trade,—] As specious as this Reading appears, Mr. *Warburton*. Mr. *Bishop*, and I, all concurr'd in suspecting it, and in the Amendment which now possesses the Text;
Some way of common Tread,— *i.e.* a high Road. He subjoins immediately;
For on my heart they tread *now, while I live*;
And we know how much it is *Shakespeare's* way to diversify the Image with the same Word.
THEOBALD.
Dr. *Warburton* has put *tread* in his own text, but *trade* will serve very well in the sense either of *commerce* or *custom*.

[4] —— *on their sovereign's head:*] *Shakespeare* is very apt to deviate from the *pathetick* to the *ridiculous*. Had the speech of *Richard* ended at this line it had exhibited the natural language of submissive misery, conforming its intention to the present fortune, and calmly ending its purpose in death.

Within

Within the earth; and therein laid, there lies
Two kinsmen, digg'd their Graves with weeping eyes.
Would not this ill do well?——Well, well, I see
I talk but idly, and you mock at me.
                                    [*North. advances.*
Most mighty Prince, my lord *Northumberland*,
What says King *Bolingbroke?* will his Majesty
Give *Richard* leave to live, till *Richard* die?
You make a leg, and *Bolingbroke* says, ay.

  North. My lord, in the base court he doth attend
To speak with you, may't please you to come down.

  K. Rich. Down, down I come; like glist'ring *Phaëton*,
Wanting the manage of unruly jades.
                                    [*North. retires to Bol.*
In the base court? base court, where Kings grow base,
To come at traitors' Calls, and do them grace.
In the base court come down? down, court; down, King;
For Night-owls shriek, where mounting Larks should
  sing.

  Boling. What says his Majesty?
  North. Sorrow, and grief of Heart,
Makes him speak fondly, like a frantick Man;
                                    [*Richard comes to them.*
Yet is he come.
  Boling. Stand all apart,
And shew fair duty to his Majesty.
My gracious lord———   [*Kneels.*
  K. Rich. Fair cousin, you debase your princely knee,
To make the base earth proud with kissing it.
Me rather had, my heart might feel your love,
Than my unpleas'd eye see your courtesie.
Up, cousin, up; your heart is up, I know,
Thus high at least, although your knee be low.
                                    [*Touching his own head.*
  Boling. My gracious lord, I come but for mine own.
  K. Rich. Your own is yours, and I am yours, and all.
  Boling. So far be mine, my most redoubted lord,
As my true service shall deserve your love.
              F 2   K. *Rich.*

K. Rich. Well you deserve.—They well deserve to have,
That know the strong'st and surest way to get.
Uncle, give me your hand; nay, dry your eyes;
Tears shew their love, but want their remedies.
Cousin, I am too young to be your father,
Though you are old enough to be my heir.
What you will have, I'll give, and willing too;
For do we must, what force will have us do.
Set on towards *London*. Cousin, is it so?
Boling. Yea, my good lord.
K. Rich. Then I must not say, *no.* [*Flourish. Exeunt.*

SCENE VII.

A Garden, in the Queen's Court.

Enter Queen and two Ladies.

Queen. WHAT sport shall we devise here in this garden,
To drive away the heavy thought of care?
Lady. Madam, we'll play at bowls.
Queen. 'Twill make me think, the world is full of rubs,
And that my fortune runs against the bias.
Lady. Madam, we'll dance.
Queen. My legs can keep no measure in delight,
When my poor heart no measure keeps in grief.
Therefore no dancing, girl; some other sport.
Lady. Madam, we'll tell tales.
Queen. Of sorrow, or of joy?
Lady. Of either, Madam.
Queen. Of neither, girl.
For if of joy, being altogether wanting,
It doth remember me the more of sorrow;
Or if of grief, being altogether had,
It adds more sorrow to my want of joy.

KING RICHARD II. 69

hat I have, I need not to repeat,
vhat I want, it boots not to complain.
l. Madam, I'll ſing.
en. 'Tis well, that thou haſt cauſe,
ou ſhould'ſt pleaſe me better, would'ſt thou weep.
ly. I could weep, Madam, would it do you good.
en. And I could weep, would weeping do me
  good,
ever borrow any tear of thee.
iy, here comes the Gardiners.
tep into the ſhadow of theſe trees;⸺
retchedneſs unto a row of pins,

Enter a Gardiner, and two Servants.

l talk of State; for every one doth ſo,
nſt a Change; woe is fore-run with woe.
                   [*Queen and Ladies retire.*
d. Go, bind thou up yond dangling Apricots,
, like unruly children, make their Sire
with oppreſſion of their prodigal weight.

tinſt a Change; woe is
-run with woe.] But
s there, in the Gardiners'
of State, for matter of
woe? Beſides, this is in-
r a Sentence, but proves
imple one. I ſuppoſe
re wrote,
e is fore-run with mocks,
as ſome meaning in it;
iſies, that, when great
: on the decline, their
take advantage of their
, and treat them with-
iony. And this we find
e caſe in the following
it the Editors were ſeek-
. rhime. Tho' had they
ſo impatient they would
nd it gingled to what

followed, tho' it did not to what
went before. Warburton.

There is no need of any emendation. The poet, according to
the common doctrine of progno-
ſtication, ſuppoſes dejection to
forerun calamity, and a kingdom
to be filled with rumours of ſorrow when any great diſaſter is
impending. The ſenſe is that,
publick evils are always preſig-
nified by publick penſiveneſs, and
plaintive converſation. The conceit of rhyming *mocks* with *apri-*
cocks, which I hope *Shakeſpeare*
knew better how to ſpell, ſhows
that the commentator was re-
ſolved not to let his conjecture
fall for want of any ſupport that
he could give it.

F 3   Give

Give some supportance to the bending twigs.
Go thou, and, like an executioner,
Cut off the heads of too-fast-growing sprays,
That look too lofty in our Common-wealth;
All must be even in our Government.
You thus imploy'd, I will go root away
The noisom weeds, that without profit suck
The soil's fertility from wholsom flowers.

Serv. Why should we, in the compass of a pale,
Keep law, and form, and due proportion,
Shewing, as in a model, a firm state'?
When our Sea-walled garden, the whole Land,
Is full of weeds, her fairest flowers choak'd up,
Her fruit-trees all unprun'd, her hedges ruin'd,
Her knots disorder'd, and her wholsom herbs
Swarming with Caterpillars?

Gard. Hold thy peace.
He, that hath suffer'd this disorder'd Spring,
Hath now himself met with the Fall of leaf;
The weeds, that his broad spreading leaves did shelter,
That seem'd, in eating him, to hold him up;
Are pull'd up, root and all, by *Bolingbroke*;
I mean, the Earl of *Wiltshire*, *Busby*, *Green*.

Serv. What, are they dead?

Gard. They are,
And *Bolingbroke* hath seiz'd the wasteful King.
What pity is't, that he had not so trimm'd
And drest his Land, as we this Garden dress,
And wound the bark, the skin, of our fruit-trees;
Lest, being over proud with sap and blood,
With too much riches it confound itself;
Had he done so to great and growing men,
They might have liv'd to bear, and he to taste,
Their fruits of duty. All superfluous branches

⁵ —— *our firm state?*] How could he say *ours* when he immediately subjoins, that it was in- firm? We should read,
—— *A firm state.*
WARBURTON.

We

We lop away, that bearing boughs may live;
Had he done so, himself had borne the Crown,
Which waste and idle hours have quite thrown down.
　Serv. What, think you then, the King shall be depos'd?
　Gard. Deprest he is already; and depos'd,
'Tis doubted, he will be.　Letters last night
Came to a dear friend of the Duke of *York*,
That tell black tidings.
　Queen. Oh, I am prest to death, through want of speaking.
Thou *Adam's* likeness, set to dress this garden,
How dares thy tongue sound this unpleasing news?
What *Eve*, what Serpent hath suggested thee,
To make a second Fall of cursed man?
Why dost thou say, King *Richard* is depos'd?
Dar'st thou, thou little better Thing than earth,
Divine his downfal? say, where, when, and how
Cam'st thou by these ill tidings? Speak, thou wretch.
　Gard. Pardon me, Madam.　Little joy have I
To breathe these news; yet, what I say, is true.
King *Richard*, he is in the mighty hold
Of *Bolingbroke*; their fortunes both are weigh'd;
In your Lord's Scale is nothing but himself,
And some few Vanities that make him light;
But in the Balance of great *Bolingbroke*,
Besides himself, are all the *English* Peers,
And with that odds he weighs King *Richard* down.
Post you to *London*, and you'll find it so;
I speak no more, than every one doth know.
　Queen. Nimble Mischance, that art so light of foot,
Doth not thy Embassage belong to me?
And am I last, that know it? oh, thou think'st
To serve me last, that I may longest keep
Thy sorrow in my breast.　Come, ladies, go;
To meet, at *London*, *London's* King in woe.
What, was I born to this? that my sad Look
Should grace the triumph of great *Bolingbroke*?

Gard'ner,

KING RICHARD II.

Gard'ner, for telling me these news of woe,
I would, the plants, thou graft'st, may never grow.
　　　　　　　　　　[*Exeunt Queen and Ladies.*

Gard. Poor Queen, so that thy state might be no
　　　worse,
I would my skill were subject to thy Curse.
Here did she drop a tear; here, in this place,
I'll set a bank of Rue, sour *herb of grace*;
Rue, ev'n for ruth, here shortly shall be seen,
In the remembrance of a weeping Queen.
　　　　　　　　　　[*Exeunt Gard. and Serv.*

ACT IV. SCENE I.

In LONDON.

Enter, as, to the Parliament, Bolingbroke, Aumerle, Northumberland, Percy, Fitzwater, Surry, *Bishop of* Carlisle, *Abbot of* Westminster, *Herald, Officers, and* Bagot.

BOLINGBROKE.

CALL *Bagot* forth: now freely speak thy mind;
　What thou dost know of noble *Glo'ster's* death;
Who wrought it with the King, and who perform'd
The bloody office of his timeless end.

Bagot. Then set before my face the lord *Aumerle.*
Boling. Cousin, stand forth, and look upon that man.
Bagot. My Lord *Aumerle*, I know your daring tongue
Scorns to unsay, what it hath once deliver'd.
In that dead time when *Glo'ster's* death was plotted,

---

⁷ *I would, the plants, &c.*—] This execration of the queen is somewhat ludicrous, and unsuitable to her condition; the gardener's reflexion is better adapted to the state both of his mind and his fortune. Mr. *Pope*, who has been throughout this play very diligent to reject what he did not like, has yet, I know not why, spared the last lines of this act.

⁸ ———— *his timeless end.*] *Timeless* for *untimely.*　　WARB.

I heard

KING RICHARD II. 73

I heard you say, "Is not my arm of length,
" That reacheth from the reftful *Englifh* Court
" As far as *Calais* to my uncle's head?"
Amongst much other talk that very time,
I heard you say, "You rather had refufe
" The offer of an hundred thoufand crowns,
" Than *Bolingbroke* return to *England*; adding,
" How bleft this Land would be in this your Coufin's
  " death."

Aum. Princes, and noble Lords,
What anfwer fhall I make to this bafe man?
Shall I fo much difhonour my fair ftars [5],
On equal terms to give him chaftifement?
Either I muft, or have mine honour foil'd
With the attainder of his fland'rous lips.
There is my Gage, the manual feal of death,
That marks thee out for hell. Thou lieft,
And I'll maintain what thou haft faid, is falfe,
In thy heart-blood, though being all too bafe
To ftain the temper of my knightly fword.

Boling. Bagot, forbear; thou fhalt not take it up.

Aum. Excepting one, I would he were the beft
In all this prefence that hath mov'd me fo.

Fitzw. If that thy valour ftand on fympathies [9],

[5] ——*my fair* STARS,] I rather think it fhould be STEM, he being of the royal blood.
WARBURTON.
I think the prefent reading unexceptionable. The *birth* is fuppofed to be influenced by the *ftars*, therefore our authour with his ufual licence takes *ftars* for *birth*.

[9] *If that thy valour ftand on fympathies,*] Here is a tranflated fenfe much harfher than that of ftars explained in the foregoing note. *Aumerle* has challenged *Bagot* with fome hefitation, as not being his equal, and therefore one whom, according to the rules of chivalry, he was not obliged to fight, as a nobler life was not to be ftaked in duel againft a bafer. *Fitzwater* then throws down his *gage* a *pledge* of battle, and tells him that if he ftands upon *fympathies*, that is, upon *equality of blood*, the combat is now offered him by a man of rank not inferiour to his own. *Sympathy* is an *affection* incident at once to two fubjects. This *community of affection* implies a *likenefs or equality of nature*, and thence our poet tranfferred the term *to equality of blood*.

There

There is my Gage, *Aumerle*, in gage to thine.
By that fair Sun, that shews me where thou stand'st,
I heard thee say, and vauntingly thou spak'st it,
That thou wert cause of noble *Glo'ster's* death.
If thou deny'st it, twenty times thou liest;
And I will turn thy falshood to thy heart,
Where it was forged, with my rapier's point [1].

Aum. Thou dar'st not, coward, live to see the day.
Fitzw. Now, by my soul, I would it were this hour.
Aum. Fitzwater, thou art damn'd to hell for this.
Percy. Aumerle, thou liest; his honour is as true,
In this appeal, as thou art all unjust;
And that thou art so, there I throw my Gage
To prove it on thee, to th' extreamest point
Of mortal breathing. Seize it, if thou dar'st.

Aum. And if I do not, may my hands rot off,
And never brandish more revengeful steel
Over the glittering helmet of my foe.

[*] *Another Lord.* I take the earth to the like, forsworn
   Aumerle,
And spur thee on with full as many lies
As may be hollow'd in thy treach'rous ear
From sin to sin. Here is my honour's pawn,
Engage it to the tryal, if thou dar'st.

Aum. Who sets me else? by heav'n, I'll throw at all,
I have a thousand spirits in my breast,
To answer twenty thousand such as you.

Surry. My Lord *Fitzwater*, I remember well
The very time *Aumerle* and you did talk.

Fitzw. My Lord, 'tis true; you were in presence then;

---

[1] ——— *my rapier's point.*] *Shakespeare* deserts the manners of the age in which his drama is placed very often, without necessity or advantage. The edge of a sword had served his purpose as well as the *point of a rapier*, and he had then escaped the impropriety of giving the *English* nobles a weapon which was not seen in *England* till two centuries afterwards.

[*] This speech I have restored from the first edition in humble imitation of former editors, though, I believe, against the mind of the authour. For *the earth* I suppose we should read, *thy oath.*

And

And you can witness with me, this is true.
	Surry. As false, by heav'n, as heav'n itself is true.
	Fitzw. Surry, thou liest.
	Surry. Dishonourable boy,
That Lie shall lye so heavy on my sword,
That it shall render vengeance and revenge,
Till thou the lie-giver, and that Lie, rest
In earth as quiet, as thy father's scull.
In proof whereof, there is mine honour's pawn;
Engage it to the tryal, if thou dar'st.
	Fitz. How fondly dost thou spur a forward horse?
If I dare eat, or drink, or breathe, or live,
[2] I dare meet *Surry* in a wilderness,
And spit upon him, whilst I say, he lies,
And lies, and lies. There is my bond of faith,
To tie thee to my strong correction.
As I intend to thrive [3] in this new world,
Aumerle is guilty of my true appeal.
Besides I heard the banish'd *Norfolk* say,
That thou, *Aumerle,* didst send two of thy men
To execute the noble Duke at *Calais.*
	Aum. Some honest christian trust me with a gage,
That *Norfolk* lies. Here do I throw down this,
If he may be repeal'd, to try his honour.
	Boling. These Diff'rences shall all rest under gage,
Till *Norfolk* be repeal'd; repeal'd he shall be,
And, though mine enemy, restor'd again
To all his Signiories; when he's return'd,
Against *Aumerle* we will enforce his tryal.
	Carl. That honourable day shall ne'er be seen.
Many a time hath banish'd *Norfolk* fought
For Jesu Christ, in glorious christian field

[2] *I dare meet* Surry *in a wilderness.*] I dare meet him where no Help can be had by me against him. So in *Macbeth,*
—— *O be alive again,*
And dare me to the desert with thy sword.

[3] *In this new world,*] In this world where I have just begun to be an actor. *Surry* has, a few Lines above, called him boy.

Stream-

Streaming the Enſign of the chriſtian Croſs,
Againſt black Pagans, Turks, and Saracens:
Then, toil'd with works of war, retir'd himſelf
To *Italy*, and there at *Venice* gave
His body to that pleaſant Country's earth,
And his pure ſoul unto his captain Chriſt,
Under whoſe Colours he had fought ſo long.
   Boling. Why, Biſhop, is *Norfolk* dead?
   Carl. Sure as I live, my lord.
   Boling. Sweet peace conduct his ſoul
To th' boſom of good *Abraham!*—Lords appealants,
Your diff'rences ſhall all reſt under gage,
Till we aſſign you to your days of tryal.

SCENE II.

Enter York.

   York. Great Duke of *Lancaſter*, I come to thee
From plume-pluckt *Richard*, who with willing ſoul
Adopts thee Heir, and his high Scepter yields
To the Poſſeſſion of thy royal hand.
Aſcend his Throne, deſcending now from him,
And long live *Henry*, of that name the Fourth!
   Boling. In God's name, I'll aſcend the regal throne.
   Carl. Marry, heav'n forbid!
Worſt in this royal preſence may I ſpeak,
* Yet beſt beſeeming me to ſpeak the truth.
Would God, that any in this noble preſence
Were enough noble to be upright judge
Of noble *Richard*; then true Nobleneſs would
Learn him forbearance from ſo foul a wrong.
What Subject can give Sentence on his King?
And who ſits here, that is not *Richard's* Subject?
Thieves are not judg'd, but they are by to hear,
Although apparent Guilt be ſeen in them.

---

* *Yet beſt beſeeming me to ſpeak the truth.*] It might be read more grammatically, *Yet beſt beſeems it me to ſpeak the truth.* But I do not think it is printed otherwiſe than as *Shakeſpeare* wrote it.

And

⁵ And shall the Figure of God's Majesty,
His Captain, Steward, Deputy elect,
Anointed, crown'd, and planted many years,
Be judg'd by subject and inferior breath,
And he himself not present? oh, forbid it!
That, in a christian climate, souls refin'd
Should shew so heinous, black, obscene a deed.
I speak to Subjects, and a Subject speaks,
Stirr'd up by heav'n, thus boldly for his King.
My lord of *Hereford* here, whom you call King,
Is a foul traitor to proud *Hereford*'s King.
And if you crown him, let me prophesie,
The blood of *English* shall manure the ground,
And future ages groan for this foul act.
Peace shall go sleep with Turks and Infidels,
And in this seat of peace, tumultuous wars
Shall kin with kin, and kind with kind, confound.
Disorder, horror, fear and mutiny
Shall here inhabit, and this Land be call'd
The field of *Golgotha*, and dead men's sculls.
Oh, if you rear this house against this house,
It will the wofullest division prove,
That ever fell upon this cursed earth.
Prevent, resist it, let it not be so,
Lest children's children cry against you, woe.

  North. Well have you argu'd, Sir; and for your pains,
Of capital treason we arrest you here.
My lord of *Westminster*, be it your charge,
To keep him safely till his day of trial ⁶.

May't

---

⁵ *And shall the figure, &c.*] Here is another proof that our authour did not learn in King *James's* court his elevated notions of the right of kings. I know not any flatterer of the *Stuarts* who has expressed this doctrine in much stronger terms. It must be observed that the Poet intends from the beginning to the end to exhibit this bishop as brave, pious, and venerable.

⁶ *His day of trial.*] After this line, whatever follows, almost to the end of the act, containing the whole process

May't please you, lords, to grant the Common's suit?

Boling. Fetch hither *Richard*, that in common view
He may surrender. So we shall proceed
Without suspicion.

York. I will be his conduct. [*Exit.*

Boling. Lords, you that here are under our Arrest,
Procure your sureties for your days of answer.
Little are we beholden to your love,
And little look'd for at your helping hands.

SCENE III.

Enter King Richard, *and* York.

K. Rich. Alack, why am I sent for to a King,
Before I have shook off the regal thoughts
Wherewith I reign'd? I hardly yet have learn'd
T' insinuate, flatter, bow, and bend my knee.
Give sorrow leave a-while, to tutor me
To this submission. Yet I well remember
[7] The favours of these men: were they not mine?
Did they not sometime cry, all hail! to me?
So *Judas* did to *Christ*; but he, in twelve,
Found truth in all, but one; I, in twelve thousand,
none.
God save the King!——will no man say, *Amen?*
Am I both priest and clerk? well then, *Amen.*
God save the King, although I be not he;
And yet, *Amen*, if heav'n do think him me.
To do what service, am I sent for hither?

York. To do that office of thine own good will,
Which tired Majesty did make thee offer,
The Resignation of thy State and Crown.

cess of dethroning and debasing King *Richard*, was added after the first edition of 1598, and before the second of 1615. Part of the addition is proper, and part might have been forborn without much loss. The authour, I suppose, intended to make a very moving scene.

[7] *The favours.*] The countenances; the *features.*

K. *Rich.*

KING RICHARD II.

Rich. Give me the Crown.——Here, cousin,
  seize the Crown,
e, on this side, my hand; on that side, thine.
 is this golden Crown like a deep well,
t owes two buckets, filling one another;
ie emptier ever dancing in the air,
 other down, unseen and full of water;
t bucket down, and full of tears, am I;
iking my griefs, whilst you mount up on high.
oling. I thought you had been willing to resign.
Rich. My Crown, I am; but still my griefs are
  mine;
may my Glories and my State depose,
not my griefs; still am I King of those.
oling. Part of your Cares you give me with your
  Crown.
Rich. Your cares set up, do not pluck my cares
  down.
care, is loss of care, by old care done [o];
r care, is gain of care, by new care won.
 cares I give, I have, though given away;
y tend the Crown, yet still with me they stay.
oling. Are you contented to resign the Crown?
Rich. Ay, no;—no, ay;—for I must nothing be;
refore no no; for I resign to thee.
, mark me how I will undo myself;
e this heavy weight from off my head;
this unwieldy Scepter from my hand;
pride of kingly sway from out my heart;

---

he emptier ever dancing.] is a comparison not easily modated to the subject, very naturally introduced. best part is this line, in he makes the usurper the bucket.
My care, is loss of care, by ld care done;] Shakespeare obscures his meaning by playing with sounds. *Richard* seems to say here, that *his cares are not made less by the increase of* Bolingbroke's *cares,* for this reason, that *his care is the loss of care,* his grief is, that his regal cares are at an end, *by the cessation of the care to which he had been accustomed.*

With

KING RICHARD II.

With mine own tears I wash away [1] my Balm;
With mine own hands I give away my Crown;
With mine own tongue deny my sacred State;
With mine own breath release all duteous oaths;
All pomp and Majesty I do forswear;
My manors, rents, revenues, I forego;
My acts, decrees, and statutes I deny;
God pardon all oaths, that are broke to me!
God keep all vows unbroke, are made to thee!
Make me, that nothing have, with nothing griev'd,
And thou with all pleas'd, that hast all atchiev'd!
Long may'st thou live in *Richard's* Seat to sit,
And soon lye *Richard* in an earthy pit!
God save King *Henry*, unking'd *Richard* says,
And send him many years of sun-shine days!
What more remains?

North. No more; but that you read
These accusations, and these grievous crimes
Committed by your person, and your followers,
Against the State and Profit of this Land:
That, by confessing them, the souls of men
May deem that you are worthily depos'd.

K. Rich. Must I do so? and must I ravel out
My weav'd-up follies? Gentle *Northumberland*,
If thy offences were upon record,
Would it not shame thee, in so fair a troop,
To read a lecture of them? [2] if thou would'st,
There should'st thou find one heinous article,
Containing the deposing of a King;
And cracking the strong warrant of an oath,
Mark'd with a blot, damn'd in the book of heav'n.
Nay, all of you, that stand and look upon me,
Whilst that my wretchedness doth bait myself,
Though some of you with *Pilate* wash your hands,
Shewing an outward pity; yet you *Pilates*

---

[1] *My Balm.*] The oil of consecration. He has mentioned it before.

[2] *If thou would'st.* That is, if thou would'st read over a list of thy own deeds.

Have

KING RICHARD II.

here deliver'd me to my sow'r Cross,
vater cannot wash away your sin.
th. My lord, dispatch; read o'er these articles.
Rich. Mine eyes are full of tears, I cannot see;
et salt-water blinds them not so much,
iey can see a Sort of traitors here.
if I turn mine eyes upon myself,
myself a traitor with the rest;
have given here my soul's consent,
deck the pompous body of a King;
Glory base, a Sovereign a slave;
Majesty, a subject; State, a peasant.
th. My lord———
Rich. No lord of thine, thou haught-insulting
    man;
10 man's lord, I have no Name, no Title;
iot that Name was giv'n me at the Font,
is usurp'd. Alack, the heavy day,
I have worn so many winters out,
<now not now, what name to call myself!
hat I were a mockery-King of snow,
ing before the Sun of *Bolingbroke,*
elt myself away in water-drops!
King,—great King,—and yet not greatly good,
 my word be sterling yet in *England,* [*To Boling.*
 command a mirror hither straight,
it may shew me what a face I have,
it is bankrupt of his Majesty.
ling. Go some of you, and fetch a looking-glass.
rth. Read o'er this paper, while the glass doth
    come.
Rich. Fiend, thou torment'st me, ere I come to
    hell.
ling. Urge it no more, my lord *Northumberland.*

Sort] *A pack, a company.* fort in this sense was, perhaps,
                    WARBURTON. *Waller.*
 last who used the word   *A sort of lusty shepherds strive.*
L. IV.   G   *North.*

North. The Commons will not then be satisfy'd.
K. Rich. They shall be satisfy'd; I'll read enough,
When I do see the very Book, indeed,
Where all my sins are writ, and that's myself.

Enter One, with a Glass.

Give me that Glass, and therein will I read.
—No deeper wrinkles yet? hath Sorrow struck
So many blows upon this face of mine,
And made no deeper wounds? oh, flatt'ring Glass,
Like to my Followers in prosperity,
Thou dost beguile me.   Was this face, the face
That every day under his houshold roof
Did keep ten thousand men? was this the face,
That, like the Sun, did make beholders wink?
Is this the face, which fac'd so many follies,
That was at last out-fac'd by *Bolingbroke?*
A brittle Glory shineth in this face;
            [*Dashes the Glass against the Ground.*
As brittle, as the glory, is the face;
For there it is, crackt in an hundred shivers.
Mark, silent King, the Moral of this sport;
How soon my sorrow hath destroy'd my face.
  Boling. The shadow of your sorrow hath destroy'd
The shadow of your face.
  K. Rich. Say that again.
The shadow of my sorrow! ha, let's see;
'Tis very true, my grief lies all within;
And these external manners of laments
Are merely shadows to the unseen grief,
That swells with silence in the tortur'd soul;
There lies the substance.   And I thank thee, King,
For thy great bounty, that not only giv'st
Me cause to wail, but teachest me the way
How to lament the cause.   I'll beg one boon;
And then be gone, and trouble you no more.
Shall I obtain it?
                                            Boling.

ING RICHARD II. 83

Name it, fair Cousin.
. Fair Cousin! I am greater than a King:
I was a King, my flatterers
but Subjects; being now a Subject,
ing here to my flatterer:
eat, I have no need to beg.
Yet ask.
. And shall I have?
You shall.
. Then give me leave to go.
Whither?
. Whither you will, so I were from your sight.
Go some of you, convey him to the *Tower*.
. Oh, good! convey:———'Conveyers are
u all.
hus nimbly by a true King's fall. [*Exit.*
On *Wednesday* next we solemnly set down
nation: lords, prepare yourselves.
o, and lo be ready all.
ll but Abbot, Bishop of Carlisle *and* Aumerle.

SCENE IV.

A woeful pageant have we here beheld.
he woe's to come; the children yet unborn
this day as sharp to them as thorn [5].
ou holy Clergy-men, is there no Plot,
Realm of this pernicious blot.
Before I freely speak my mind herein,
not only take the Sacrament,

are ye all.] To says the deposed Prince, *jugglers*
rm often used in an who rise with this *nimble* dexte-
l so *Richard* under- rity *by the fall of a good king.*
ere. *Pistol* says of [5] *As sharp as thorn.*] This
ey *the wife it call;* pathetick denunciation shews
y is the word for that *Shakespeare* intended to im-
d, which seems to press his auditors with dislike of
o here. *Ye are all,* the deposal of *Richard.*

84 KING RICHARD II.
* To bury mine intents, but to effect
Whatever I shall happen to devise.
I see, your brows are full of discontent,
Your hearts of sorrow, and your eyes of tears.
Come home with me to supper, and I'll lay
A Plot, shall shew us all a merry day [6]. [*Exeunt.*

ACT V. SCENE I.

A Street in LONDON.

Enter Queen, and Ladies.

QUEEN.

THIS way the King will come: this is the way
[7] To *Julius Cæsar's* ill-erected Tower;
To whose flint-bosom my condemned lord
Is doom'd a prisoner, by proud *Bolingbroke*.
[8] Here let us rest, if this rebellious earth
Have any Resting for her true King's Queen.
   Enter King Richard, *and Guards.*
But soft, but see, or rather do not see,
My fair rose wither; yet look up; behold,
That you in pity may dissolve to dew,
And wash him fresh again with true-love tears.
[9] O thou, the model where old *Troy* did stand,
       [*To K. Richard.*
        Thou,

---

[6] *To bury, to conceal; to keep secret.*

9 In the first edition there is no personal appearance of King *Richard*, so that all to the line at which he leaves the stage was inserted afterwards.

[7] *To* Julius Cæsar's, &c.] The Tower of *London* is traditionally said to have been the work of *Julius Cæsar*.

[8] *Here let us rest, if, &c.*]
Here rest, if any rest can harbour here. MILTON.

[9] —*O thou, the model where old* Troy *did stand.*] The Queen uses comparative terms absolutely. Instead of saying,
       Thou

KING RICHARD II.

Thou map of honour, thou King *Richard's* tomb,
And not King *Richard*; thou moſt beauteous Inn,
Why ſhould hard-favour'd grief be lodg'd in thee,
When Triumph is become an ale-houſe Gueſt?

K. *Rich.* * Join not with grief, fair Woman, do not ſo,
To make my End too ſudden. Learn, good ſoul,
To think our former ſtate a happy dream,
From which awak'd, the truth of what we are
Shews us but this. ¹ I am ſworn brother, Sweet,
To grim Neceſſity; and he and I
Will keep a league till death. Hye thee to *France*,
And cloiſter thee in ſome Religious Houſe;
Our holy lives muſt win a new world's Crown,
Which our profane hours here have ſtricken down.

Queen. What, is my *Richard* both in ſhape and mind
Transform'd and weak? hath *Bolingbroke* depos'd
Thine intellect? hath he been in thy heart?
The Lion, dying, thruſteth forth his paw,
And wounds the earth, if nothing elſe, with rage
To be o'erpower'd; and wilt thou, pupil-like,
Take thy correction mildly, kiſs the rod,
And fawn on rage with baſe humility,
Which art a Lion and a King of beaſts?

K. *Rich.* A King of beaſts, indeed—if aught but beaſts,
I had been ſtill a happy King of men.
Good ſometime Queen, prepare thee hence for *France*;
Think, I am dead; and that ev'n here thou tak'ſt,

Thou who appeareſt as the ground on which the magnificence of *Troy* was once erected, ſhe ſays, O *thou, the model,* &c.
Thou map of honour. Thou figure of greatneſs.

* *Join not with grief,*] Do not thou unite with grief againſt me; do not, by thy additional ſorrows, enable grief to ſtrike me down at once. My own part of ſorrow I can bear, but thy affliction will immediately deſtroy me.

¹ —— *I am ſworn brother,* *To grim neceſſity;* ——] I have reconciled myſelf to neceſſity, I am in a ſtate of amity with the conſtraint which I have ſuſtained.

86   KING RICHARD II.

As from my death-bed, my laſt living Leave.
In winter's tedious nights ſit by the fire
With good old folks, and let them tell thee Tales
Of woeful ages, long ago betid;
And ere thou bid good Night, to quit their grief²,
Tell thou the lamentable Fall of me,
And ſend the hearers weeping to their beds.
For why?³ the ſenſeleſs brands will ſympathize
The heavy accent of thy moving tongue,
And in compaſſion weep the fire out;
And ſome will mourn in aſhes, ſome coal-black,
For the depoſing of a rightful King.

SCENE II.

Enter Northumberland *attended.*

North. My lord, the mind of *Bolingbroke* is chang'd
You muſt to *Pomfret*, not unto the *Tower.*
And, Madam, there is order ta'en for you,
With all ſwift-ſpeed, you muſt away to *France.*

K. Rich. Northumberland, thou ladder wherewith
The mounting *Bolingbroke* aſcends my Throne,
The time ſhall not be many hours of age
More than it is, ere foul ſin, gath'ring head,
Shall break into corruption; thou ſhalt think,
Though he divide the Realm, and give thee half,
It is too little, helping him to all;
And he ſhall think, that thou, which know'ſt the way
To plant unrightful Kings, wilt know again,
Being ne'er ſo little urg'd, another way
To pluck him headlong from th' uſurped Throne.
The love of wicked friends converts to fear;
That fear to hate; and hate turns one, or both,

---

² ——— *to quit their grief*] To retaliate their mournful ſtories.

³ *For why?* ———] The poet ſhould have ended this ſpeech with the foregoing line and have ſpared his childiſh prattle about the fire.

worthy danger, and deserved death.
North. My guilt be on my head, and there's an end.
Take leave and part, for you must part forthwith.
K. Rich. Doubly divorc'd? Bad men, ye violate
two-fold marriage; 'twixt my crown and me;
and then betwixt me and my married wife.
Let me unkiss the oath 'twixt thee and me.
                              [*To the Queen.*
And yet not so, for with a kiss 'twas made.
Part us, Northumberland. I, towards the North,
Where shiv'ring cold and sickness pines the clime;
My Queen to *France*, from whence, set forth in pomp,
She came adorned hither like sweet *May*;
Sent back like *Hollowmas*, or shortest day.
Queen. And must we be divided? must we part?
K. Rich. Ay, hand from hand, my Love, and heart from heart.
Queen. Banish us both, and send the King with me.
North. That were some Love, but little Policy.
Queen. Then whither he goes, thither let me go.
K. Rich. So two together weeping, make one woe.
Weep thou for me in *France*; I for thee here:
Better far off; than near, be ne'er the near [*].
Go, count thy way with sighs, I mine with groans:
Queen. So longest way shall have the longest moans.
K. Rich. Twice for one step I'll groan, the way being short,
And piece the way out with a heavy heart.
Come, come, in wooing sorrow let's be brief;
Since, wedding it, there is such length in grief.
One kiss shall stop our mouths, and dumbly part;
Thus give I mine, and thus take I thy heart. [*They kiss.*

---

[*] *Better far off, than near, be ne'er the near,*] To be nearer the nigher, or as it is commonly spoken in the mid land counties, *ne'er the ne'er*, is, to make no advance towards the good desired.

KING RICHARD II.

Queen. Give me mine own again; 'twere ne good part,
To take on me to keep, and kill thy heart. [*Kiss again.*
So, now I have mine own again, be gone,
That I may strive to kill it with a groan.

K. Rich. We make woe wanton with this fond delay:
Once more, adieu; the rest let sorrow say. [*Exeunt.*

SCENE III.

The Duke of YORK's Palace.

Enter York, and his Dutchess.

Dutch. MY lord, you told me, you would tell the rest,
When Weeping made you break the story off,
Of our two Cousins coming into *London.*

York. Where did I leave?

Dutch. At that sad stop, my lord,
Where rude mis-govern'd hands, from window-tops,
Threw dust and rubbish on King *Richard's* head.

York. Then, as I said, the Duke, great *Bolingbroke*
Mounted upon a hot and fiery steed,
Which his aspiring Rider seem'd to know,
With slow, but stately pace, kept on his course;
While all tongues cry'd, God save thee, *Bolingbroke!*
You wou'd have thought, the very windows spake,
So many greedy looks of young and old
Through casements darted their desiring eyes
Upon his visage; and that all the walls
With painted imag'ry had said at once,
Jesu, preserve thee! welcome, *Bolingbroke!*
Whilst he, from one side to the other turning,
Bare-headed, lower than his proud steed's neck,
Bespoke them thus; I thank you, Countrymen;
And thus still doing, thus he past along.

Dutch.

KING RICHARD II.

Dutch. Alas! poor *Richard*, where rides he the while?
York. As in a Theatre, the eyes of men,
After a well-grac'd Actor leaves the Stage,
Are idly bent [5] on him that enters next,
Thinking his prattle to be tedious:
Even so, or with much more contempt, men's eyes
Did scowl on *Richard*; no man cry'd, God save him;
No joyful tongue gave him his welcome home;
But dust was thrown upon his sacred head;
Which with such gentle sorrow he shook off,
His face still combating with tears and smiles,
The badges of his grief and patience;
That had not God, for some strong purpose, steel'd
The hearts of men, they must perforce have melted;
And barbarism itself have pitied him.
But heav'n hath a hand in these events,
To whose high will we bound our calm contents.
To *Bolingbroke* are we sworn Subjects now,
Whose State, and Honour, I for aye allow.

SCENE IV.

Enter Aumerle.

Dutch. Here comes my son *Aumerle*.
York. *Aumerle* that was,
But that is lost, for being *Richard's* Friend.
And, madam, you must call him *Rutland* now.
I am in parliament pledge for his truth,
And lasting fealty to the new-made King.
Dutch. Welcome, my son; who are the Violets now,
That strew the green lap of the new-come spring?
Aum. Madam, I know not, nor I greatly care:
God knows, I had as lief be none, as one.
York. Well, * bear you well in this new Spring of time,
Lest you be cropt before you come to Prime.

[5] *Are idly bent* ———] That is carelessly turned, thrown without attention. This the poet learned by his attendance and practice on the stage.
* — *bear you well*] That is, conduct yourself with prudence.

What

90 KING RICHARD II.

What news from *Oxford?* hold these Justs and Triumphs?

Aum. For aught I know, they do.

York. You will be there?

Aum. If God prevent me not, I purpose so.

York. What Seal is that, which hangs without thy bosom?
Yea, look'st thou pale? let me see the Writing †.

Aum. My lord, 'tis nothing.

York. No matter then who sees it.
I will be satisfied, let me see the Writing.

Aum. I do beseech your Grace to pardon me,
It is a matter of small consequence,
Which for some reasons I would not have seen.

York. Which, for some reasons, Sir, I mean to see.
I fear, I fear———

Dutch. What should you fear, my lord?
'Tis nothing but some bond he's enter'd into,
For gay apparel, against the triumph.

York. Bound to himself? what doth he with a bond,
That he is bound to? wife, thou art a fool.
Boy, let me see the Writing.

Aum. I do beseech you, pardon me; I may not shew it.

York. I will be satisfied, let me see it, I say.

[*Snatches it and reads.*

Treason! foul treason! villain, traitor, slave!

Dutch. What's the matter, my lord?

York. Hoa, who's within there? saddle my horse.
Heav'n, for his mercy! what treachery is here?

Dutch. Why, what is't, my lord?

York. Give me my boots, I say. Saddle my horse.
Now by my honour, by my life, my troth,
I will appeach the villain.

---

† *Yea, look'st thou pale? let me see the Writing.*] Such harsh and defective lines as this, are probably corrupt, and might be easily supplied, but that it would be dangerous to let conjecture loose on such slight occasions.

Dutch.

Dutch. What is the matter?
York. Peace, foolish woman.
Dutch. I will not Peace: what is the matter, son?
Aum. Good mother, be content; it is no more
Than my poor life must answer.
Dutch. Thy life answer!

SCENE V.

Enter Servant with boots.

York. Bring me my boots. I will unto the King.
Dutch. Strike him, *Aumerle.*—Poor boy, thou art amaz'd.—
Hence, villain, never more come in my sight.—
[*Speaking to the Servants.*
York. Give me my boots.
Dutch. Why, *York,* what wilt thou do?
Wilt not not hide the trespass of thine own?
Have we more sons? or are we like to have?
Is not my teeming date drunk up with time?
And wilt thou pluck my fair son from mine age,
And rob me of a happy mother's name?
Is he not like thee? is he not thine own?
York. Thou fond mad-woman,
Wilt thou conceal this dark Conspiracy?
A dozen of them here have ta'en the Sacrament,
And interchangeably have set their hands,
To kill the King at *Oxford.*
Dutch. He shall be none:
We'll keep him here; then what is that to him?
York. Away, fond woman: were he twenty times
My son, I would appeach him.
Dutch. Hadst thou groan'd for him,
As I have done, thou'dst be more pitiful.
But now I know thy mind; thou dost suspect,
That I have been disloyal to thy bed,

And

And that he is a baftard, not thy fon;
Sweet *York*, fweet hufband, be not of that mind;
He is as like thee as a man may be,
Nor like to me, nor any of my kin,
And yét I love him.

   York. Make way, unruly woman.   [*Exit.*
   Dutch. After, *Aumerle*, mount thee upon his horfe;
Spur poft, and get before him to the King,
And beg thy pardon, ere he do accufe thee.
I'll not be long behind; though I be old,
I doubt not but to ride as faft as *York:*
And never will I rife up from the ground,
'Till *Bolingbroke* have pardon'd thee, Away. [*Exeunt.*

SCENE VI.

Changes to the Court at Windfor *Caftle.*

Enter Bolingbroke, Percy, and other Lords.

Boling. CAN no man tell of my unthrifty fon?
        'Tis full three months, fince I did fee him
        laft.
If any plague hang over us, 'tis he:
I would to heav'n, my lords, he might be found.
* Enquire at *London*, 'mong the taverns there:
For there, they fay, he daily doth frequent,
With unreftrained loofe Companions,
Even fuch, they fay, as ftand in narrow lanes,
And beat our watch, and rob our paffengers,
While he, young, wanton, and effeminate boy,
Takes on the point of honour, to fupport
So diffolute a Crew.

   Percy. My lord, fome two days fince I faw the
       Prince,

---

* This is a very proper intro-   baucheries in his youth, and his
duction to the future character greatnefs in his manhood.
of *Henry* the fifth, to his de-

And

KING RICHARD II.

And told him of these Triumphs held at *Oxford*.

Boling. And what said the Gallant?

Percy. His answer was, he would unto the Stews,
And from the common'st Creature pluck a glove,
And wear it as a favour, and with that
He would unhorse the lustiest Challenger.

Boling. As dissolute, as desp'rate; yet through both
I see some sparks of hope; which elder days
May happily bring forth. But who comes here?

Enter Aumerle.

Aum. Where is the King?

Boling. What means our Cousin, that he stares,
And looks so wildly?

Aum. God save your Grace. I do beseech your Majesty,
To have some conf'rence with your Grace alone.

Boling. Withdraw yourselves, and leave us here alone.
What is the matter with our Cousin now?

Aum. For ever may my knees grow to the earth,
[*Kneels.*
My tongue cleave to my roof within my mouth,
Unless a pardon, ere I rise or speak!

Boling. Intended, or committed, was this fault?
If but the first, how heinous ere it be,
To win thy after-love, I pardon thee.

Aum. Then give me leave that I may turn the key,
That no man enter till the Tale be done.

Boling. Have thy desire. [*York within.*

York. My Liege, beware, look to thyself,
Thou hast a traitor in thy presence there.

Boling. Villain, I'll make thee safe. [*Drawing.*

Aum. Stay thy revengeful hand, thou hast no cause to fear.

York. Open the door, secure, fool-hardy King.
Shall I for love speak treason to thy face?
Open the door, or I will break it open.

SCENE

94 KING RICHARD II.

SCENE VII.

The King opens the door, enter York.

Boling. What is the matter, uncle? speak, take breath:
Tell us how near is danger,
That we may arm us to encounter it.
  York. Peruse this writing here, and thou shalt know
The Treason that my haste forbids me show.
  Aum. Remember, as thou read'st, thy promise past.
I do repent me, read not my name there;
My heart is not confed'rate with my hand.
  York. Villain, it was, ere thy hand set it down,
I tore it from the traytor's bosom, King,
Fear, and not love, begets his penitence;
Forget to pity him, lest thy pity prove
A serpent that will sting thee to the heart.
  Boling. O heinous, strong, and bold conspiracy!
O loyal father of a treach'rous son!
Thou clear, immaculate, and silver fountain,
From whence this stream, through muddy passages,
Hath had his current, and defil'd himself,
Thy overflow of good converts the bad [6];
And thine abundant goodness shall excuse
This deadly blot, in thy digressing son.
  York. So shall my virtue be his vice's bawd,
And he shall spend mine honour with his shame;
As thriftless sons their scraping fathers' gold.

In former copies,
[6] *Thy Overflow of Good converts to Bad*;] This is the Reading of all the printed Copies in general; and I never 'till lately suspected its being faulty. The Reading is disjointed, and inconclusive: My Emendation makes it clear and of a Piece. " Thy Overflow of Good changes " the Complexion of thy Son's " Guilt; and thy Goodness, be- " ing so abundant, shall excuse " his Trespass." THEOBALD.

Mine

mine honour lives, when his dishonour dies,
Or my sham'd life in his dishonour lies,
Thou kill'st me in his life; giving him breath,
The traytor lives, the true man's put to death.
[*Dutchess within.*
Dutch. What ho, my Liege! for heav'n's sake let me in.
Boling. What shrill-voic'd Suppliant makes this eager cry?
Dutch. A woman, and thine aunt, great King, 'tis I.
Speak with me, pity me, open the door;
A beggar begs that never begg'd before.
Boling. Our Scene is alter'd from a serious thing,
And now chang'd to *the Beggar, and the King*[7].
—My dang'rous Cousin, let your mother in;
I know, she's come to pray for your foul sin.
York. If thou do pardon, whosoever pray,
More sins for his forgiveness prosper may;
This fester'd joint cut off, the rest is sound;
This, let alone, will all the rest confound.

SCENE VIII.

Enter Dutchess.

Dutch. O King, believe not this hard-hearted man;
Love, loving not itself, none other can.
York. Thou frantick woman, what dost thou do here?
Shall thy old dugs once more a traytor rear?
Dutch. Sweet *York*, be patient; hear me, gentle Liege. [*Kneels.*
Boling. Rise up, good aunt.
Dutch. Not yet, I thee beseech;

---

[7] The *King and Beggar* seems to have been an interlude well known in the time of our au-thour, who has alluded to it more than once. I cannot now find that any copy of it is left.
For

For ever will I kneel upon my knees,
And never see day that the happy sees,
'Till thou give joy; until thou bid me joy,
By pard'ning *Rutland*, my transgressing boy.

   Aum. Unto my mother's pray'rs I bend my knee.
                                                                 [*Kneels.*

   York. Against them Both, my true joints bended be.
                                                                [*Kneels.*
Ill may'st thou thrive, if thou grant any grace!

   Dutch. Pleads he in earnest? look upon his face;
His eyes do drop no tears, his pray'r's in jest;
His words come from his mouth, ours from our breast;
He prays but faintly, and would be deny'd;
We pray with heart and soul, and all beside.
His weary joints would gladly rise, I know;
Our knees shall kneel, till to the ground they grow.
His pray'rs are full of false hypocrisy,
Ours of true zeal, and deep integrity;
Our prayers do out-pray his; then let them crave
That mercy, which true prayers ought to have.

   Boling. Good aunt, stand up.

   Dutch. Nay, do not say, stand up,
But pardon first; say afterwards, stand up.
An if I were thy nurse, thy tongue to teach,
Pardon should be the first word of thy speech.
I never long'd to hear a word till now,
Say, Pardon, King; let pity teach thee how.

   Boling. Good aunt, stand up.

   Dutch. I do not sue to stand,
Pardon is all the suit I have in hand.

   Boling. I pardon him, as heav'n shall pardon me.

   Dutch. O happy vantage of a kneeling knee!
Yet am I sick for fear; speak it again,
'Twice saying pardon, doth not pardon twain,
But makes one pardon strong.
The word is short, but not so short as sweet;
No word like pardon, for Kings mouths so meet.

   York.

KING RICHARD II. 97

York. Speak it in *French,* King; fay, *Pardonnez moy*[1].
Dutch. Doſt thou teach pardon, pardon to deſtroy?
Ah, my ſow'r husband, my hard-hearted lord,
That ſet'ſt the word itſelf, againſt the word;
Speak pardon, as 'tis current in our land,
The chopping *French* we do not underſtand.
Thine eye begins to ſpeak, ſet thy tongue there,
Or, in thy piteous heart, plant thou thine ear;
That, hearing how our plaints and prayers do pierce,
Pity may move thee pardon to rehearſe.
Boling. With all my heart
I pardon him.
Dutch. A God on earth thou art.
Boling. But for our truſty Brother-in-law, the
 Abbot[2],
With all the reſt of that conſorted crew,
Deſtruction ſtraight ſhall dog them at the heels.
Good Uncle, help to order ſeveral Powers
To *Oxford,* or where-e'er theſe traytors are.
They ſhall not live within this world, I ſwear;
But I will have them, if I once know where.
Uncle, farewel; and couſin too, adieu;
Your mother well hath pray'd, and prove you true.
Dutch. Come, my old ſon; I pray heav'n make
 thee new. [*Exeunt.*

[1] —— *Pardonnez moy.*] That is, *excuſe me,* a phraſe uſed when any thing is civilly denied. This whole paſſage is ſuch as I could well wiſh away.

[2] *But for our truſty Brother-in-law—the* Abbot —] The Abbot of *Weſtminſter* was an Eccleſiaſtic; but the Brother-in-law, meant, was *John* Duke of *Exeter* and Earl of *Huntingdon,* (own Brother to King *Richard* II.) and who had married with the Lady *Elizabeth* Siſter to *Henry* of *Bolingbroke.*   THEOBALD.

VOL. IV. H SCENE

SCENE IX.

Enter Exton *and a Servant.*

Exton. Didſt thou not mark the King, what wo
  he ſpake?
Have I no friend will rid me of this living fear?
Was it not ſo?
  Serv. Thoſe were his very words.
  Exton. Have I no friend?—quoth he; he ſpake
    twice,
And urg'd it twice together; did he not?
  S rv. He did.
  Exton. And ſpeaking it, he wiſtly look'd on me,
As who ſhall ſay,—I would, thou wert the man,
That would divorce this terror from my heart;
Meaning the King at *Pomfret*. Come, let's go:
I am the King's friend, and will rid his foe. [*Exeun*

SCENE X.

Changes to the Priſon at Pomfret-Caſtle.

Enter King Richard.

I Have been ſtudying, how to compare
  This priſon, where I live, unto the world;
And, for becauſe the world is populous,
And here is not a creature but myſelf,
I cannot do it; yet I'll hammer on't.
My brain I'll prove the female to my ſoul,
My ſoul, the father; and theſe two beget
A generation of ſtill-breeding thoughts;
And theſe ſame thoughts people this little world;
In humour, like the people of this world,
For no thought is contented. The better ſort,
As thoughts, of things divine, are intermixt

Wit

li scruples, and do set the word itself
inst the word; as thus; *Come, little ones*; and then
  again,
as hard to come, as for a Camel
read the postern of a needle's eye.
ights, tending to ambition, they do plot
kely wonders; how these vain weak nails
 tear a passage through the flinty ribs
his hard world, my ragged prison-walls,
 for they cannot, die in their own pride.
ghts tending to Content, flatter themselves,
 they are not the first of fortune's slaves,
hall not be the last; like silly beggars,
 sitting in the Stocks, refuge their shame
 many have, and others must sit there;
in this thought, they find a kind of ease,
ig their own misfortune on the back
ch as have before endur'd the like.
play I, in one prison, many people,
ione contented. Sometimes am I King,
treason makes me wish myself a beggar,
o I am. Then crushing penury
ides me, I was better when a King;
am I king'd again; and by and by,
, that I am unking'd by *Bolingbroke*,
raight am nothing. But what-e'er I am,
  nor any man, that but man is,
nothing shall be pleas'd, till he be eas'd
being nothing.—Musick do I hear?   [*Musick.*
1; keep time: how sow'r sweet musick is,
 time is broke, and no proportion kept?
in the musick of mens' lives;
ere have I the daintiness of ear,
ick time broke in a disorder'd string,
r the concord of my state and time,
ot an ear to hear my true time broke.
d time, and now doth time waste me,
w hath time made me his numbring clock,

My thoughts are minutes; and [1] with fighs they jar
Their watches to mine eyes the outward watch;
Whereto my finger, like a dial's point,
Is pointing still, in cleanfing them from tears.
Now, Sir, the founds, that tell what hour it is,
Are clamorous groans, that strike upon my heart,
Which is the bell; so fighs, and tears, and groans,
Shew minutes, hours, and times. O, but my time
Runs posting on, in *Bolingbroke's* proud joy,
While I stand fooling here, his jack o'th'clock.
This musick mads me, let it found no more;
For though it have help'd mad men to their wits,
In me, it seems, it will make wife men mad.
Yet blessing on his heart, that gives it me!
For 'tis a sign of love; and love to *Richard*
Is a strange brooch, in this all-hating world.

[1] —— *with fighs they jar, Their watches,* &c. ——] I think this expression must be corrupt, but I know not well how to make it better. The first quarto reads,
  My thoughts are minutes; and with fighs they jar,
  There watches to mine eyes the outward watch.
The second quarto:
  My thoughts are minutes, and with fighs they jar,
  There watches on unto mine eyes the outward watch.
The first folio agrees with the second quarto.
  Perhaps out of these two readings the right may be made. *Watch* seems to be used in a double sense, for a *quantity* time, and for the *instrument* t*o* measures time. I read, but w*ith* no great confidence, thus:
  My thoughts are minutes,
    with fighs they jar,
  Their watches on; mine eyes
    outward watch,
  Whereto, &c.

[2] —— *in this* ALL-HATI*NG world.*] We should r*ead* FALL-HATING, *i. e.* Love *to* *Richard* is a very rare jewel, *in* a world that shuns and av*oids* those who are fallen, or in a*dverse* fortunes. WARBURT*ON.*
  I believe the meaning is, *a* *world in which I am univer*sally *hated.*

SCE*NE*

SCENE XI.

Enter Groom.

Groom. Hail, royal Prince.
K. Rich. Thanks, noble Peer.
The cheapest of us is ten groats too dear.
What art? how com'st thou hither?
Where no man ever comes, but that sad dog,
That brings me food, to make misfortune live?
Groom. I was a poor groom of thy stable, King,
When thou wert King; who travelling tow'rds *York*,
With much ado, at length have gotten leave
To look upon my sometime Master's Face.
O, how it yearn'd my heart, when I beheld,
In *London* streets, that Coronation day,
When *Bolingbroke* rode on Roan Barbary,
That horse, that thou so often hast bestrid;
That horse, that I so carefully have dress'd.
K. Rich. Rode he on Barbary? tell me, gentle friend,
How went he under him?
Groom. So proudly, as he had disdain'd the ground.
K. Rich. So proud, that *Bolingbroke* was on his back!
That jade had eat bread from my royal hand,
This hand hath made him proud with clapping him;
Would he not stumble? would he not fall down,
Since pride must have a fall, and break the neck
Of that proud man, that did usurp his back?
Forgiveness, horse; why do I rail on thee,

---

[1] *Where no Man ever comes, but that sad Dog.*] I have ventur'd at a Change here, against the Authority of the Copies, by the Direction of Dr. *Warburton.* Indeed, *sad Dog* savours too much of the Comedian, the Oratory of the late facetious Mr. *Penkethman.* And *Drudge* is the word of Contempt, which our Author chuses to use on other like Occasions. THEOBALD.
Dr. *Warburton* says peremptorily, read *Drudge*—but I still persist in the old reading.

Since thou, created to be aw'd by man,
Waſt born to bear? I was not made a horſe,
And yet I bear a burthen like an aſs,
Spur-gall'd, and tir'd, by jaunting *Bolingbroke.*

SCENE XII.

Enter Keeper, with a diſh.

Keep. Fellow, give place; here is no longer
                                                    [*To the G*
K. *Rich.* If thou love me, 'tis time thou wert a
Groom. What my tongue dares not, that my
    ſhall ſay.   [
Keep. My lord, will't pleaſe you to fall to?
K. *Rich.* Taſte of it firſt, as thou wert wont
Keep. My lord, I dare not; for Sir *Pierce* of
Who late came from the King, commands th
    trary.
K. *Rich.* The Dev'l take *Henry* of *Lancaſt*
    thee!
Patience is ſtale, and I am weary of it.
                                          [*Beats the*
Keep. Help, help, help!

Enter Exton, *and Servants.*

K. *Rich.* How now, what means death in th
    aſſault?
Wretch, thine own hand yields thy death's inſtr
                    [*Snatching a Sword, and kill*
Go thou, and fill another room in hell. [*Kills*
                                [*Exton ſtrikes him*
That hand ſhall burn in never-quenching fire,
That ſtaggers thus my perſon; thy fierce hand
Hath with the King's blood ſtain'd the King
    Land.

Mount, mount, my soul! thy seat is up on high;
Whilst my gross flesh sinks downward, here to die.
[Dies.

Exton. As full of valour as of royal blood;
Both have I spilt: Oh, would the deed were good!
For now the devil, that told me, I did well,
Says, that this deed is chronicled in hell.
This dead King to the living King I'll bear;
Take hence the rest, and give them burial here.
[Exeunt.

SCENE XIII.

Changes to the Court at Windsor.

Flourish: Enter Bolingbroke, York, *with other Lords and attendants.*

Boling. KIND Uncle *York*, the latest news we hear,
Is, that the Rebels have consum'd with fire
Our town of *Cicester* in *Gloucestershire*;
But whether they be ta'en or slain, we hear not.

Enter Northumberland.

Welcome, my lord: what is the news?
North. First to thy sacred State wish I all happiness;
The next news is, I have to *London* sent
The heads of *Sal'sbury*, *Spencer*, *Blunt*, and *Kent*:
The manner of their Taking may appear
At large discoursed in this paper here.
[Presenting a Paper.
Boling. We thank thee, gentle *Percy*, for thy pains,
And to thy worth will add right-worthy gains.

Enter Fitz-water.

Fitz-w. My Lord, I have from *Oxford* sent to *London*

The heads of *Broccas*, and Sir *Bennet Seely*;
Two of the dangerous conforted traytors,
That fought at *Oxford* thy dire overthrow.

Boling. Thy pains, *Fitz water*, shall not be forgot,
Right noble is thy merit, well I wot.

Enter Percy, *and the Bishop of* Carlisle.

Percy. The grand Conspirator, *Abbot of Westminster*,
With clog of conscience, and four melancholy,
Hath yielded up his body to the Grave:
But here is *Carlisle*, living to abide
Thy kingly doom, and sentence of his pride.

Boling. Carlisle, this is your doom:
Chuse out some secret place, some reverend room
More than thou hast, and with it joy thy life;
So, as thou liv'st in peace, die free from strife.
For though mine enemy thou hast ever been,
High sparks of honour in thee I have seen.

Enter Exton, *with a coffin.*

Exton. Great King, within this Coffin I present
Thy bury'd fear; herein all breathless lies
The mightiest of thy greatest enemies,
Richard of *Bourdeaux*, by me hither brought.

Boling. Exton, I thank thee not; for thou hast
    wrought
A deed of slander with thy fatal hand,
Upon my head, and all this famous Land.

Exton. From your own mouth, my Lord, did I
    this deed.

Boling. They love not poison, that do poison need;
Nor do I thee; though I did wish him dead,
I hate the murth'rer, love him murthered.
The Guilt of Conscience take thou for thy labour,
But neither my good word, nor princely favour;
With *Cain* go wander through the shade of night,
And never shew thy head by day, or light.

                                        Lords

KING RICHARD II. 105

Lords, I proteſt, my ſoul is full of woe,
That blood ſhould ſprinkle me, to make me grow.
Come, mourn with me for what I do lament,
And put on ſullen Black, incontinnet:
I'll make a voyage to the Holy-land,
To waſh this blood off from my guilty hand.
March ſadly after, grace my Mourning here,
In weeping over this untimely Bier. [*Exeunt omnes.* ✲

✲ This play is extracted from the Chronicle of *Hollingſhead*, in which many paſſages may be found which *Shakeſpeare* has, with very little alteration, tranſplanted into his ſcenes; particularly a ſpeech of the biſhop of *Carliſle* in defence of King *Richard*'s unalienable right, and immunity from human juriſdiction.

Johnſon, who, in his *Catiline* and *Sejanus*, has inſerted many ſpeeches from the *Roman* hiſtorians, was, perhaps, induced to that practice by the example of *Shakeſpeare*, who had condeſkended ſometimes to copy more ignoble writers. But *Shakeſpeare* had more of his own than *Johnſon*, and, if he ſometimes was willing to ſpare his labour, ſhewed by what he performed at other times, that his extracts were made by choice or idleneſs rather than neceſſity.

This play is one of thoſe which *Shakeſpeare* has apparently reviſed; but as ſucceſs in works of invention is not always proportionate to labour, it is not finiſhed at laſt with the happy force of ſome other of his tragedies, nor can be ſaid much to affect the paſſions, or enlarge the underſtanding.

The First Part of
HENRY IV.
WITH THE
LIFE and DEATH
OF
HENRY, *Surnam'd* HOT-SPUR.

Dramatis Personæ.

KING Henry *the Fourth.*
Henry, *Prince of* Wales, } *Sons to the King.*
John, *Duke of* Lancaster,
Worcester.
Northumberland.
Hot-spur.
Mortimer.
Archbishop of York.
Dowglass.
Owen Glendower.
Sir Richard Vernon.
Sir Michell.
Westmorland.
Sir Walter Blunt.
Sir John Falstaff.
Poins.
Gads-hill.
Peto.
Bardolph.

Lady Percy, *Wife to* Hot-spur.
Lady Mortimer, *Daughter to* Glendower, *and Wife to* Mortimer.
Hostess Quickly.

Sheriff, Vintner, Chamberlain, Drawers, two Carriers, Travellers, and Attendants.

The persons of the drama were first collected by *Rowe.*

SCENE, *ENGLAND.*

Of this play the Editions are,
I. 1599, *S. S.* for *And. Wise.*
II. 1604.
III. 1608, for *Matthew Law.*
IV. 1613, *W. W.* for *Matt. Law.*
V. 1622, *T. P.* sold by *Mat-thew Law.* All in quarto.
VI. Folio 1623.
VII. 4to 1639, *John Norton,* sold by *Hugh Perry.*
VIII. Folio 1632, &c.
Of these Editions I have the I. V. VI. VII. VIII.

'The FIRST PART of

HENRY IV.

ACT I. SCENE I.

The Court *in* London.

Enter King Henry, *Lord* John *of* Lancaster, *Earl of* Westmorland, *and others.*

King HENRY.

SO shaken as we are, so wan with Care,
   Find we a time for frighted peace to pant [2],
   And breathe short-winded accents of new Broils
To be commenc'd in stronds a-far remote.

No

---

[1] *The 1st Part of Henry* IV.] The Transactions, contained in this historical Drama, are comprized within the Period of about 10 Months: For the Action commences with the News brought of *Hotspur* having defeated the *Scots* under *Archibald* Earl *Douglas* at *Holmedon*, (or *Halidown-hill*) which Battle was fought on *Holyrood*-day, (the 14th of *September*) 1402: and it closes with the Defeat and Death of *Hotspur* at *Shrewsbury*; which Engagement happened on *Saturday* the 21st of *July* (the Eve of St. *Mary Magdalen*) in the Year 1403. THEOBALD.

Shakespeare has apparently designed a regular connection of these dramatic histories from *Richard the second* to *Henry the fifth*. King *Henry*, at the end of *Richard* the second, declares his purpose to visit the Holy Land, which he resumes in this speech. Tho complaint made by king *Henry* in the last act of *Richard* the second, of the wildness of his son, prepares the reader for the frolicks which are here to be recounted, and the characters which are now to be exhibited.

[2] *Find out a time for frighted peace to pant,*

And

110   THE FIRST PART OF

No more the thirsty entrance of this Soil [3]
Shall damp her lips with her own children's blood;
No more shall trenching war channel her fields,
Nor bruise her flowrets with the armed hoofs
Of hostile paces.   [4] Those opposed eyes,

Which;

And breathe short-winded accents—] That is, *Let us soften peace to rest a while without disturbance, that she may recover breath to propose new wars.*

[3] *No more the thirsty entrance of this Soil*
Shall damp her lips with her own children's blood:] This nonsense should be read, *Shall* TREMPE, *i. e.* moisten, and refers to thirsty, in the preceding line: *Trempe*, from the *French, tremper*, properly signifies the moistness made by rain. WARB.

That these lines are absurd is soon discovered, but how this nonsense will be made sense is not so easily told; surely not by reading *trempe*, for what means he, that says, *the thirsty entrance of this* Soil *shall no more* trempe *her lips with her children's blood,* more than he that says *it shall not* damp *her lips?* To suppose the *entrance of the soil* to mean the *entrance* of a King upon *Dominion*, and King *Henry* to predict that *Kings shall enter hereafter without bloodshed,* is to give words such a latitude of meaning, that no nonsense can want a congruous interpretation.

The antient copies neither have *trempe* nor *damp*; the first 4to of 1599, that of 1622, the Folio of 1623, and the 4to of 1639, all read,

No more the thirsty entrance of this soil
Shall daube her lips with her own children's blood.

The Folios of 1632 and 1664 read, by an apparent errour of the press, *Shall* damb *her lips*, from which the later editors have idly adopted *damp*. The old reading helps the editor no better than the new, nor can I satisfactorily reform the passage. I think that *thirsty entrance* must be wrong, yet know not what to offer. We may read, but not very elegantly,

No more the thirsty entrails *of this soil*
Shall daubed *be with her own children's blood.*

The relative *her*, is inaccurately used in both readings; but to regard sense more than grammar is familiar to our authour.

We may suppose a verse or two lost between these two lines. This is a cheap way of palliating an editor's inability; but I believe such omissions are more frequent in *Shakespeare* than is commonly imagined.

[4] ———— *Those opposed eyes,*] The similitude is beautiful: But, what are *eyes meeting in intestine shocks, and marching all one way?* The true reading is, FILES; which appears not only from the integrity of the metaphor, *well beseeming*

Which, like the meteors of a troubled heav'n,
All of one nature, of one substance bred,
Did lately meet in the intestine shock
And furious close of civil butchery,
Shall now, in mutual, well-beseeming, ranks
March all one way; and be no more oppos'd
Against acquaintance, kindred, and allies;
The edge of war, like an ill-sheathed knife,
No more shall cut his master. Therefore, friends,
As far as to the sepulchre [5] of Christ,
Whose soldier now, under whose blessed Cross
We are impressed, and engag'd to fight,
Forthwith a Power of *English* shall we levy;
Whose arms were moulded in their mothers' womb
To chase these Pagans, in those holy fields
Over whose acres walk'd those blessed feet,
Which, fourteen hundred years ago, were nail'd
For our advantage on the bitter Cross.
But this our purpose is a twelvemonth old,
And bootless 'tis to tell you we will go;
Therefore, we meet not now. Then let me hear,
Of you my gentle Cousin *Westmorland*,

---

beseeming ranks march all one way; but from the nature of those *meteors* to which they are compared; namely long streaks of red, which represent the lines of armies; the appearance of which, and their likeness to such lines, gave occasion to all the superstition of the common people concerning armies in the air, &c. Out of mere contradiction, the *Oxford Editor* would improve my alteration of *files* to *arms*, and so loses both the integrity of the metaphor and the likeness of the comparison.   WARBURT.

This passage is not very accurate in the expression, but I think nothing can be changed.

[5] *As far as to the sepulchre*, &c.] The lawfulness and justice of the *holy wars* have been much disputed; but perhaps there is a principle on which the question may be easily determined. If it be part of the religion of the Mahometans, to extirpate by the sword all other religions, it is, by the law of self-defence, lawful for men of every other religion, and for Christians among others, to make war upon Mahometans, simply as Mahometans, as men obliged by their own principles to make war upon Christians, and only lying in wait till opportunity shall promise them success.

Which

What yesternight our Council did decree,
In forwarding this dear expedience [6].
　West. My Liege, this haste was hot in question,
[7] And many limits of the Charge set down
But yesternight: when, all athwart, there came
A Post from *Wales*, loaden with heavy news;
Whose worst was, that the noble *Mortimer*,
Leading the men of *Herefordshire* to fight
Against th' irregular and wild *Glendower*,
Was by the rude hands of that *Welshman* taken;
A thousand of his people butchered,
Upon whose dead corps there was such misuse,
Such beastly, shameless transformation,
By those *Welshwomen* done, as may not be,
Without much shame, re-told or spoken of.
　K. Henry. It seems then, that the tidings of th[is]
　　broil
Brake off our business for the holy Land.
　West. This, matcht with other, did, my gracio[us]
　　lord;
For more uneven and unwelcome news
Came from the North, and thus it did import.
On holy-rood day, the gallant *Hot-spur* there,
Young *Harry Percy*, and brave *Archibald*,
That ever-valiant and approved *Scot*,
At *Holmedon* spent a sad and bloody hour,
As by discharge of their artillery,
And shape of likelihood, the news was told;
For he, that brought it, in the very heat
And pride of their contention, did take horse,
Uncertain of the issue any way.
　K. Henry. Here is a dear and true-industrious frie[nd]
Sir *Walter Blunt*, new lighted from his horse,
Stain'd with the variation of each soil
Betwixt that *Holmedon*, and this Seat of ours:

[6] —— *this dear expedience.*]　[7] *And many* limits ——]
For *expedition.* WARBURTON.　*mits* for *estimates.* WARBU[RTON.]

KING HENRY IV.

And he hath brought us smooth and welcome news.
The Earl of *Dowglas* is discomfited;
Ten thousand bold *Scots*, three and twenty Knights,
Balk'd in their own blood did Sir *Walter* see
On *Holmedon's* plains. Of prisoners, *Hot-spur* took
Mordake the Earl of *Fife*, and eldest son
To beaten *Dowglas*, and the Earls of *Athol*,
Of *Murry*, *Angus*, and *Menteith*.
And is not this an honourable spoil?
A gallant prize? ha, cousin, is it not?

West. In faith, a conquest for a Prince to boast of.

K. Henry. Yea, there thou mak'st me sad, and
   mak'st me sin
In Envy, that my lord *Northumberland*
Should be the father of so blest a son,
A son, who is the theam of Honour's tongue,
Amongst a grove, the very streightest plant,
Who is sweet Fortune's Minion, and her Pride,
Whilst I, by looking on the praise of him,
See riot and dishonour stain the brow
Of my young *Harry*. O could it be prov'd,
That some night-tripping Fairy had exchang'd,
In cradle-cloaths, our children where they lay,
And call mine *Percy*, his *Plantagenet*;
Then would I have his *Harry*, and he mine.
But let him from my thoughts.——What think you,
  Cousin,
Of this young *Percy's* pride? the prisoners,
Which he in this adventure hath surpriz'd,
To his own use he keeps, and sends me word,
I shall have none but *Mordake* Earl of *Fife*.

West. This is his uncle's teaching, this is *Worcester*,
Malevolent to you in all aspects,
Which makes him plume himself [1], and bristle up
           The

---

[1] *Which makes him* PRUNE *himself.*—] Doubtless *Shakespeare* wrote PLUME. And to this the *Oxford Editor* gives his fiat.   WARBURTON.
I am not so confident as those two

VOL. IV.   I

THE FIRST PART OF

The Crest of youth against your Dignity.

K. Henry. But I have sent for him to answer this;
And for this cause a while we must neglect
Our holy purpose to *Jerusalem.*
Cousin, on *Wednesday* next our Council we
Will hold at *Windsor*, so inform the lords:
But come yourself with speed to us again;
For more is to be said, and to be done,
[9] Than out of anger can be utter'd.

West. I will, my Liege. [*Exeunt.*

SCENE II.

An Apartment of the Prince's.

Enter Henry *Prince of* Wales, *and Sir* John Falstaff.

Fal. NOW, Hal, what time of day is it, lad?

P. Henry. Thou art so fat-witted with drinking old sack, and unbuttoning thee after supper, and sleeping upon benches in the afternoon, that thou hast forgotten [1] to demand that truly, which thou would'st truly know. What a devil hast thou to do with the time of the day? Unless hours were cups of sack, and minutes capons, and clocks the tongues of bawds, and dials the signs of leaping-houses, and the blessed Sun himself a fair hot wench in flame-colour'd taffata. I see no reason why thou should'st be so superfluous, to demand the time of the day.

---

two editors. The metaphor is taken from a cock who in his pride *prunes himself*; that is picks off the loose feathers to smooth the rest. To *prune* and to *plume*, spoken of a bird, is the same.

[9] *Than out of anger can be uttered.*] That is, More is to be said than anger will suffer me to say: More than can issue from a mind distracted like mine.

[1] *To demand that truly, which thou wouldst truly know.*] The Prince's objection to the question seems to be, that *Falstaff* had asked in the *night* what was the time of day.

Fal.

Fal. Indeed, you come near me now, *Hal.* For we, that take purses, go by the moon and seven stars, and not by *Phœbus,* he, that wandring knight so fair. And I pray thee, sweet wag, when thou art King —— as God save thy Grace (Majesty, I should say; for grace thou wilt have none.) ——

P. Henry. What! none?

Fal. No, by my troth, not so much as will serve to be prologue to an egg and butter.

P. Henry. Well, how then? —— come —— roundly, roundly ——

Fal. Marry, then, sweet wag, when thou art King, let not us that are squires of the night's body, be call'd thieves of the day's booty. Let us be *Diana's* forester's, gentlemen of the shade, minions of the Moon; and let men say, we be men of good government, being governed as the Sea is, by our noble and chaste mistress the Moon, under whose countenance we—steal.

P. Henry. Thou say'st well, and it holds well too; for the fortune of us, that are the Moon's men, doth ebb and flow like the Sea; being govern'd as the Sea is, by the Moon. As for proof, now: a purse of gold most resolutely snatch'd on *Monday* night, and most dissolutely spent on *Tuesday* morning; [3] got with swearing, *lay by*; and spent with crying, *bring*

In former editions,
[2] *Let not Us, that are Squires of the Night's body, be call'd Thieves of the Day's* Beauty.] This conveys no manner of Idea to me. How could they be called Thieves of the Day's Beauty? They robbed by Moonshine; they could not steal the fair Day-light. I have ventured to substitute, *Booty:* and this I take to be the Meaning. Let us not be called *Thieves,* the Purloiners of that *Booty,* which, to be Proprietors, was the Purchase of honest Labour and Industry by Day. THEOBALD.

[3] *got with swearing,* lay by;] i. e. swearing at the passengers they robbed, *lay by your arms;* or rather, *lay by* was a phrase that then signified *stand still,* addressed to those who were preparing to rush forward. But the *Oxford Editor* kindly accommodates these old thieves with a new cant phrase, taken from *Bagshot-Heath* or *Finchly-Common,* of LUG-OUT. WARBURTON.

116   THE FIRST PART OF

in: now in as low an ebb as the foot of the l[
and by and by in as high a flow as the ridge [
gallows.

Fal. By the lord, thou fay'ſt true, lad: and
mine Hoſteſs of the tavern a moſt ſweet wench [
P. *Henry.* ⁴ As the honey of *Hybla,* my old

⁴ *As the Honey of* Hybla, *my Old* Lad *of the* Caſtle.] Mr. *Rowe* took notice of a Tradition, that this Part of *Falſtaff* was written originally under the Name of *Oldcaſtle.* An ingenious Correſpondent hints to me, that the Paſſage above quoted from our Author proves, what Mr. *Rowe* tells us was a Tradition. *Old* Lad of the *Caſtle* ſeems to have a Reference to *Oldcaſtle.* Beſides, if this had not been the Fact, why, in the Epilogue to the Second Part of *Henry* IV. where our Author promiſes to continue his Story with Sir *John* in it, ſhould he ſay, *Where, for any Thing I know,* Falſtaff *ſhall die of a Sweat, unleſs already he be killed with your hard Opinions: for* Oldcaſtle *dy'd a Martyr, and this is not the Man.* This looks like declining a Point, that had been made an Objection to him. I'll give a farther Matter in Proof, which ſeems almoſt to fix the Charge. I have read an old Play, called, *The famous Victories of* Henry *the* Vth, *containing the Honourable Battle of* Agincourt.——The Action of this Piece commences about the 14th Year of K. *Henry* IVth's Reign, and ends with *Henry* the Vth marrying Princeſs *Catharine* of *France.* The Scene opens with Prince *Henry's* Robberies. Sir *John Oldcaſtle* is one of h[and called *Jockie:* and Gads *hill* are two othe[rades.——From this ol[fect Sketch, I have a S[*Shakeſpeare* might form Parts of *Henry* the IVth, Hiſtory of *Henry* V: an[quently, 'tis not improba[he might continue the [of Sir *John Oldcaſtle,* [Deſcendants of that [moved Queen *Elizabeth* [mand him to change the [Th[*my old lad of the caſtle* alludes to the name S[firſt gave to this buffoo[ter, which was Sir J[*caſtle:* And when he [the name, he forgot to [this expreſſion that allu[The reaſon of the cha[this, one Sir *John Oldc[* ing ſuffered in the time [V. for the opinions of [it gave offence; and [the Poet altered it to *Fa[* endeavours to remove [dal, in the *Epilogue* to t[part of *Henry* IV. *Fa[* notice of this matte[*Church Hiſtory,*——S[have themſelves been [with, and others very [the memory of Sir John [whom they have fancie[companion, a jovial royſ[

KING HENRY IV.

the caftle; [5] and is not a buff-jerkin a moft fweet robe of durance.

Fal. How now, how now, mad wag; what, in thy quips and thy quiddities? what a plague have I to do with a buff-jerkin?

P. Henry. Why, what a pox have I to do with my Hoftefs of the tavern?

Fal. Well, thou haft called her to a reckoning many a time and oft.

P. Henry. Did I ever call thee to pay thy part?

Fal. No, I'll give thee thy due, thou haft paid all there.

P. Henry. Yea and elfewhere, fo far as my coin would ftretch; and where it would not, I have us'd my credit.

Fal. Yea, and fo us'd it, that were it not here apparent, that thou art heir apparent———But, I pr'ythee, fweet wag, fhall there be Gallows ftanding in *England*, when thou art King? and refolution thus fobb'd as it is, with the rufty curb of old father antick, the law? Do not thou, when thou art a King, hang a thief.

P. Henry. No: thou fhalt.

Fal. Shall I? O rare! By the Lord, I'll be a brave judge.

---

coward to boot. *The beft is, Sir John Falftaff hath relieved the memory of* fir John Oldcaftle, *and of late is fubftituted buffoon in his place.* Book 4. p. 16\. But, to be candid, I believe there was no malice in the matter. *Shakefpear* wanted a droll name to his character, and never confidered whom it belonged to: we have a like inftance in the *Merry Wives of Windfor*, where he calls his *French* Quack, *Caius*, a name, at that time very refpectable, as belonging to an eminent and learned phyfician, one of the founders of *Caius* College in *Cambridge*. WARBURTON.

[5] *And is not a buff jerkin a moft fweet robe of durance?*] To underftand the propriety of the Prince's anfwer, it muft be remarked that the fheriff's officers were formerly clad in buff. So that when *Falftaff* afks whether *his hoftefs is not a fweet wench*, the Prince afks in return, whether *it will not be a fweet thing to go to prifon by running in debt to this fweet wench*.

THE FIRST PART OF

sin for a man to labour in his vocation. *Poins!* ——
Now shall we know, if *Gads-hill* have set a match. O,
if men were to be sav'd by merit, what hole in hell
were hot enough for him!

SCENE III.

Enter Poins.

This is the most omnipotent Villain, that ever cry'd,
Stand, to a true Man.——

P. Henry. Good morrow, *Ned*.

Poins. Good morrow, sweet *Hal.* What says Monsieur Remorse? what says Sir *John* Sack and Sugar? *Jack!* how agree the devil and thou about thy soul, that thou soldest him on *Good-Friday* last, for a cup of *Madera*, and a cold capon's leg?

P. Henry. Sir *John* stands to his word; the devil shall have his bargain, for he was never yet a breaker of proverbs; *He will give the devil his due.*

Poins. Then thou art damn'd for keeping thy word with the devil.

P. Henry. Else he had been damn'd for cozening the devil.

Poins. But, my lads, my lads, to-morrow morning, by four o'clock, early at *Gads-hill*; there are pilgrims going to *Canterbury* with rich offerings, and traders riding to *London* with fat purses. I have visors for you all; you have horses for yourselves: *Gadshill* lies to night in *Rochester*, I have bespoke supper to-morrow night in *East cheap*; we may do it, as secure as sleep: if you will go, I will stuff your purses

---

observation made by *Pope*, hyperbolical enough, but not contradicted by the erroneous reading in this place, the speech not being so characteristick as to be infallibly applied to the speaker.

Theobald's triumph over the other Editors might have been abated by a confession, that the first edition gave him at least a glimpse of the emendation.

full of crowns; if you will not, tarry at home, and be hang'd.

Fal. Hear ye, *Yedward*; if I tarry at home, and go not, I'll hang you for going.

Poins. You will, chops?

Fal. Hal, wilt thou make one?

P. *Henry.* Who, I rob? I a thief? not I, by my faith.

Fal. There is neither honesty, manhood, nor good fellowship in thee, nor thou cam'st not of the blood royal, if thou dar'st not cry, *stand*, for ten shillings [3].

P. *Henry.* Well then, once in my days I'll be a madcap.

Fal. Why, that's well said.

P. *Henry.* Well, come what will, I'll tarry at home.

Fal. By the lord, I'll be a traitor then when thou art King.

P. *Henry.* I care not.

Poins. Sir *John*, I pr'ythee, leave the Prince and me alone; I will lay him down such reasons for this adventure, that he shall go.

Fal. Well, may'st thou have the spirit of persuasion, and he the ears of profiting, that what thou speak'st may move, and what he hears may be believ'd; that the true Prince may (for recreation-sake) prove a false thief; for the poor abuses of the time want countenance. Farewel, you shall find me in *East-cheap.*

P. *Henry.* Farewel, thou latter spring! Farewel, all-hallown summer! [*Exit* Falstaff.

Poins. Now, my good sweet hony lord, ride with us to-morrow. I have a jest to execute, that I cannot manage alone. [4] *Falstaff, Bardolph, Peto,* and *Gadshill,*

---

[3] The present reading may perhaps be right, but I think it necessary to remark, that all the old Editions read, *if thou darest not stand for ten shillings.*

[4] In former editions: Falstaff, HARVEY, ROSSIL, and Gads-hill *shall rob those men that*

bill, shall rob those men that we have already waylaid; yourself and I will not be there; and when they have the booty, if you and I do not rob them, cut this head from off my shoulders.

P. Henry. But how shall we part with them in setting forth?

Poins. Why, we will set forth before or after them; and appoint them a place of meeting, wherein it is at our pleasure to fail; and then will they adventure upon the exploit themselves, which they shall have no sooner atchiev'd, but we'll set upon them.

P. Henry. Ay, but, 'tis like, they will know us by our horses, by our habits, and by every other appointment, to be ourselves.

Poins. Tut, our horses they shall not see, I'll tye them in the wood; our visors we will change after we leave them; and, sirrah, I have cases of buckram for the nonce, to immask our noted outward garments.

P. Henry. But, I doubt, they will be too hard for us.

Poins. Well, for two of them, I know them to be as true-bred cowards as ever turn'd Back; and for the third, if he fights longer than he sees reason, I'll forswear arms. The virtue of this jest will be, the incom-

---

that we have already way-laid.] Thus We have two Persons named, as Characters in this Play, that never were among the *Dramatis Personæ*. But let us see who they were, that committed this Robbery. In the second Act, we come to a Scene of the *High-way*. *Falstaff*, wanting his Horse, calls out on *Hal*, *Poins*, *Bardolph*, and *Peto*. Presently, *Gadshill* joins 'em, with Intelligence of Travellers being at hand; upon which the Prince says,——You *four shall front 'em in the narrow Lane*, Ned Poins *and I will walk lower*. So that the *Four* to be concerned are *Falstaff*, *Bardolph*, *Peto*, and *Gadshill*. 'Accordingly, the Robbery is committed: and the Prince and *Poins* afterwards rob the *se* Four. In the *Boar's-Head* Tavern, the Prince rallies *Peto* and *Bardolph* for their running away; who confess the Charge. Is it not plain, that *Bardolph* and *Peto* were *two* of the *four* Robbers? And who then can doubt, but *Harvey* and *Rossil* were the Names of the Actors.

THEOBALD.

prehensible lies that this same fat rogue will tell us when we meet at supper; how thirty at least he fought with, what wards, what blows, what extremities he endured; and, in the [5] reproof of this, lies the jest.

P. Henry. Well, I'll go with thee; provide us all things necessary, and meet me to-morrow night in *East-cheap*, there I'll sup. Farewel.

Poins. Farewel, my lord. [*Exit* Poins.

P. Henry. I know you all, and will a while uphold
The unyok'd humour of your idleness;
Yet herein will I imitate the Sun,
Who doth permit the base contagious clouds
To smother up his beauty from the world;
That when he please again to be himself,
Being wanted, he may be more wondred at,
By breaking through the foul and ugly mists
Of vapours, that did seem to strangle him.
If all the year were playing holidays,
To sport would be as tedious as to work;
But when they seldom come, they wisht-for come,
And nothing pleaseth but rare Accidents.
So, when this loose behaviour I throw off,
And pay the debt I never promised;
By how much better than my word I am,
By so much [6] shall I falsifie men's hopes;
And, like bright metal on a sullen ground,
My Reformation glittering o'er my fault,
Shall shew more goodly, and attract more eyes,
Than that which hath no foil to set it off.

---

[5] *Reproof* is *confutation.*
[6] ——— *shall I falsifie men's* HOPES;] Just the contrary. We should read FEARS.
                                WARBURTON.

To *falsify hope* is to *exceed hope,* to give much where men *hoped* for little.

This speech is very artfully introduced to keep the Prince from appearing vile in the opinion of the audience; it prepares them for his future reformation, and, what is yet more valuable, exhibits a natural picture of a great mind offering excuses to itself, and palliating those follies which it can neither justify nor forsake.

THE FIRST PART OF

I'll so offend, to make offence a skill;
Redeeming time, when men think least I will. [*Exit.*

SCENE IV.

Changes to an Apartment in the Palace.

Enter King Henry, Northumberland, Worcester, Hot-spur, *Sir* Walter Blunt, *and others.*

K. *Henry.* MY blood hath been too cold and temperate,
Unapt to stir at these indignities;
And you have found me; for accordingly
You tread upon my patience: but be sure,
⁷ I will from henceforth rather be myself,
Mighty and to be fear'd, than my Condition;
Which hath been smooth as oyl, soft as young down,
And therefore lost that title of Respect,
Which the proud soul ne'er pays, but to the proud.

Wor. Our House, my sovereign Liege, little deserves

---

⁷ *I will from henceforth rather be myself,*
Mighty and to be fear'd, than my Condition;] *i. e.* I will from henceforth rather put on the character that becomes me, and exert the resentment of an injured King, than still continue in the inactivity and mildness of my natural disposition. And this sentiment he has well expressed, save that by his usual licence, he puts the word *condition* for *disposition*: which use of terms depraving our *Oxford Editor*, as it frequently does, he in a loss for the meaning, substitutes *in* for *than*,

Mighty and to be fear'd in ———
condition. So that by *condition*, in this reading, must be meant station, office. But it cannot be predicated of station and office, *that it is smooth as oyl, soft as young down,* which shews that *condition* must needs be licentiously used for *disposition*, as we said before. WAR.

The commentator has well explained the sense which was not very difficult, but is mistaken in supposing the use of *condition* licentious. *Shakespeare* uses it very frequently for *temper of mind*; and in this sense the vulgar still say a *good* or *ill-conditioned man.*

The

KING HENRY IV.

The scourge of Greatness to be used on it;
And that same Greatness too, which our own hands
Have help'd to make so portly.

North. My good lord,————

K. Henry. *Worcester*, get thee gone; for I do see
Danger and disobedience in thine eye.
O Sir, your presence is too bold and peremptory;
And Majesty might never yet endure
¹ The moody frontier of a servant brow.
You have good leave to leave us. When we need
Your use and counsel, we shall send for you.
[*Exit* Worcester.
You were about to speak. [*To* Northumberland.

North. Yes, my good lord.
Those Prisoners, in your Highness' name demanded,
Which *Harry Percy* here at *Holmedon* took,
Were, as he says, not with such strength deny'd
As was deliver'd to your Majesty.
Or Envy therefore, or Misprision,
Is guilty of this fault, and not my son.

Hot. My Liege, I did deny no prisoners;
But I remember, when the fight was done,
When I was dry with rage, and extream toil,
Breathless, and faint, leaning upon my sword;
Came there a certain lord, neat, trimly dress'd;
Fresh as a bridegroom, and his chin, new-reap'd,
Shew'd like a stubble land ² at harvest-home.
He was perfumed like a milliner;
And 'twixt his finger and his thumb, he held

---

¹ *The moody* FRONTIER————]
This is nonsense. We should
read FRONTLET, *i. e.* forehead.
WARBURTON.
So in *Lear*, when one of the
King's daughters frowns, he tells
her of her *frontlet*. All the editions read *frontier* in this place.

May it not mean, *Majesty will not
endure the moody brow of a servant
to border upon it, to be near it?
Shakespeare* has licences equal to
this.

² *At harvest-home.*] That is,
at a time of festivity.

A pouncet-

THE FIRST PART OF

[1] A pouncet-box, which ever and anon
He gave his nose: and took't away again;
Who, therewith angry, when it next came there,
Took it in snuff.——And still he smil'd, and talk't;
And as the soldiers bare dead bodies by,
He call'd them untaught knaves, unmannerly,
To bring a slovenly, unhandsome coarse
Betwixt the wind, and his Nobility.
With many holiday and lady terms
He question'd me: amongst the rest, demanded
My prisoners, in your Majesty's behalf.
[2] I, then all smarting with my wounds being cold,
To be so pester'd with a popinjay,
Out of my Grief, and my impatience,
Answer'd, neglectingly, I know not what;
He should, or should not; for he made me mad,
To see him shine so brisk, and smell so sweet,
And talk so like a waiting-gentlewoman,
Of guns, and drums, and wounds; (God save the mark!)

---

[1] *A pouncet-box,——*] A small box for musk or other perfumes then in fashion: The lid of which being cut with open work gave it its name; from *poinsoner*, to prick, pierce, or engrave.
WARBURTON.

[2] *I, then all smarting with my wounds being* COLD,
(To be so pester'd with a popinjay)] But in the beginning of the Speech he represents himself at this time not as *cold* but hot, and inflamed with rage and labour.
" *When I was dry with rage and extreme toil,* &c.
I am persuaded therefore that *Shakespeare* wrote and pointed it thus,
" *I then all smarting with my wounds; being* GAL'D
" *To be so pester'd with a popinjay,* &c.
WARBURTON.
Whatever *Percy* might say of his *rage* and *toil*, which is merely declamatory and apological, his wounds would at this time be certainly *cold*, and when they were *cold* would *smart*, and not before. If any alteration were necessary I should transpose the lines.
I then all smarting with my wounds being cold,
Out of my grief, and my impatience,
To be so pester'd with a popinjay,
Answer'd neglectingly.
A *popinjay* is a *parrot*.

And

And telling me, the sovereign'st thing on earth
Was Parmacity, for an inward bruise;
And that it was great pity, so it was,
This villainous salt petre should be digg'd
Out of the bowels of the harmless earth,
Which many a good tall fellow had destroy'd
So cowardly: And but for these vile guns,
He would himself have been a soldier.———
This bald, unjointed chat of his, my lord,
I answer'd indirectly, as I said;
And I beseech you, let not this report
Come current for an accusation,
Betwixt my love and your high Majesty.

Blunt. The circumstance consider'd, good my lord,
Whatever *Harry Percy* then had said,
To such a person, and, in such a place,
At such a time, with all the rest retold,
May reasonably die; and never rise
[3] To do him wrong, or any way impeach
What then he said, so he unsay it now.

K. Henry. Why, yet he doth deny his prisoners,

---

[3] *To do him wrong, or any way impeach What then he said, so he unsay it now.*] Let us consider the whole passage, which, according to the present reading, bears this literal sense. "Whatever *Percy* then said may reasonably die and never rise to impeach what he then said, so he unsay it now." This is the exact sense, or rather nonsense, which the passage makes in the present reading. It should therefore, without question, be thus printed and emended,

To do him wrong, or any way impeach.
What then he said, SES, *he* UNSAYS *it now.*

i. e. "Whatever *Percy* then said "may reasonably die, and ne- "ver rise to do him wrong or "any ways impeach him. For "see, my Liege, what he then "said, he now unsays." And the King's answer is pertinent to the words, as so emended — *why, yet he doth deny his prisoners, but with proviso,* &c. implying, "you are mistaken in saying, "*see he now unsays it.*" But the answer is utterly impertinent to what precedes in the common reading. WARBURTON.

The learned commentator has perplexed the passage. The construction is, *Let* what he then said *never rise to impeach* him, so he unsay it now.

Rut

THE FIRST PART OF

But with proviso and exception,
That we at our own charge shall ransom straight
His brother-in-law, the foolish *Mortimer*;
Who, on my soul, hath wilfully betray'd
The lives of those, that he did lead to fight
Against the great magician, damn'd *Glendower*;
Whose daughter, as we hear, the Earl of *March*
Hath lately marry'd. Shall our coffers then
Be empty'd, to redeem a traitor home?
Shall we buy treason? ⁴ and indent with fears,
When they have lost and forfeited themselves?
No; on the barren mountains let him starve;
For I shall never hold that man my friend,
Whose tongue shall ask me for one penny cost
To ransom home revolted *Mortimer*.

 Hot. Revolted *Mortimer*?
⁵ He never did fall off, my sovereign Liege,

---

4 —— *and indent with* fears.] The reason why he says, bargain and article with *fears*, meaning with *Mortimer*, is, because he supposed *Mortimer* had wilfully betrayed his own forces to *Glendower* out of fear, as appears from his next Speech. No need therefore to change *fears* to *foes*, as the *Oxford Editor* has done.
     WARBURTON.

The difficulty seems to me to arise from this, that the King is not desired to *article* or *contract with* Mortimer, but with another *for* Mortimer. Perhaps we may read,
 Shall we buy treason? and indent with peers,
 When they have lost and forfeited themselves?
Shall we purchase back a traytor? Shall we descend to a composition with *Worcester, Northumber-*

land, *and young Percy, who by* disobedience *have lost and forfeited* their honours and *themselves?*

5 *He never did fall off, my sovereign Liege,*
 But BY *the chance of war;*—]
A poor apology for a soldier, and a man of honour, that he fell off, and revolted by the chance of war. The Poet certainly wrote,
 But 'BIDES *the chance of war.*
i. e. he never did revolt, but abides the chance of war, as a prisoner. And if he still endured the rigour of imprisonment, that was a plain proof he was not revolted to the enemy. Hot-*spur* says the same thing afterwards,
 —— *suffer'd his kinsman* March
 —— *to be encag'd in* Wales.
Here again the *Oxford Editor*

KING HENRY IV. 129

ut by the chance of war; 'to prove That true,
eeds no more but one tongue; for all thoſe wounds,—
hoſe mouthed wounds, which valiantly he took,
When on the gentle *Severn's* ſedgy bank,
i ſingle oppoſition, hand to hand,
e did confound the beſt part of an hour
i changing hardiment with great *Glendower*;
hree times they breath'd, and three times did they
    drink,
'pon agreement, of ſwift *Severn's* flood;
Who then affrighted with their bloody looks,
an fearfully among the trembling reeds,
nd hid his criſpe head in the hollow bank,
lood-ſtained with theſe valiant Combatants.
Never did bare and rotten Policy

ikes this correction his own, at the ſmall expence of changing *des* to *bore*. WARBURTON. The plain meaning is, *he came into the enemy's power but by chance of war*. To 'bide the *uſe of war* may well enough niſy to *ſtand the hazard of a 'tle*, but can ſcarcely mean to *lure the ſeverities of a priſon*. e King charged *Mortimer* that *wilfully betrayed* his army, and, he was then with the enemy, ls him *revolted Mortimer*. Hot- r replies, that he never *fell off* it is, fell into *Glendower's* ds, *but by the chance of war*. hould not have explained thus iouſly a paſſage ſo hard to be ſtaken, but that two Editors re already miſtaken it.

6 —————— *to prove that true; Needs no more but one tongue, For all thoſe wounds*, &c.] is paſſage is of obſcure con- ction. The later editors int it, as they underſtood, that

for the wounds a tongue *was need- ful*, and only *one tongue*. This is harſh. I rather think it is a broken ſentence. *To prove the loyalty of* Mortimer, ſays Hot- ſpur, one *ſpeaking witneſs is ſuffi- cient, for his wounds* proclaim his loyalty, *thoſe mouthed wounds*, &c.

7 *Who then affrighted*, &c.] This paſſage has been cenſured as ſounding nonſenſe, which re- preſents a ſtream of water as ca- pable of fear. It is miſunder- ſtood. *Severn* is here not the *flood*, but the tutelary power of the flood, who was frighted, and hid his head in *the hollow bank*.

8 *Never did bare and rotten policy*.] All the quarto's which I have ſeen read *bare* in this place. The firſt folio, and all the ſubſequent editions, have *baſe*. I believe *bare* is right: *never did policy lying open to de- tection ſo colour its workings*.

VOL. IV.   K   Colour

130 THE FIRST PART OF

Colour her working with such deadly wounds;
Nor never could the noble *Mortimer*
Receive so many, and all willingly;
Then let him not be slander'd with Revolt.

  K. Henry. Thou dost belie him, *Percy*, thou beliest
    him;
He never did encounter with *Glendower*;
He durst as well have met the Devil alone,
As *Owen Glendower* for an enemy.
Art not asham'd? [9] but, sirrah, from this hour
Let me not hear you speak of *Mortimer*.
Send me your prisoners with the speediest means,
Or you shall hear in such a kind from me
As will displease you.—My Lord *Northumberland*,
We licence your departure with your son.
—Send us your prisoners, or you'll hear of it.
                     [*Exit K. Henry.*

  Hot. And if the devil come and roar for them,
I will not send them. I'll after strait,
And tell him so; for I will ease my heart,
[1] Although it be with hazard of my head.

  North. What, drunk with choler? stay, and pause
    a while;
Here comes your uncle.

Enter Worcester.

  Hot. Speak of *Mortimer?*
Yes, I will speak of him; and let my son
Want mercy, if I do not join with him.
In his behalf, I'll empty all these veins,

---

[9] — *but*, sirrah, *from this hour.*] The *Oxford Editor* is a deal more courtly than his old plain *Elizabeth* author. He changes *sirrah* therefore to *Sir*: And punctilios of this kind he very carefully discharges throughout his edition: which it may be enough once for all just to have taken notice of.   WARBURTON.

[1] *Although it be with hazard,* &c.] So the first folio, and all the following editions. The quarto's read,

Although I make a hazard of my head.

                     And

And shed my dear blood drop by drop in dust,
But I will lift the down-trod *Mortimer*
As high i'th' Air as this unthankful King,
As this ingrate and cankred *Bolingbroke*.

North. Brother, the King hath made your Nephew
   mad.   [*To* Worcester.

Wor. Who strook this heat up, after I was gone?

Hot. He will, forsooth, have all my prisoners;
And when I urg'd the ransom once again
Of my wife's brother, then his cheek look'd pale,
And on my face he turn'd an [3] eye of death,
Trembling ev'n at the name of *Mortimer*.

Wor. I cannot blame him; was he not proclaim'd,
By *Richard* that dead is, the next of blood?

North. He was; I heard the Proclamation;
And then it was, when the unhappy King
(Whose wrongs in us, God pardon!) did set forth
Upon his *Irish* expedition,
From whence he, intercepted, did return
To be depos'd, and shortly murthered.

Wor. And for whose death, we in the world's wide
   mouth
Live scandaliz'd, and foully spoken of.

Hot. But soft, I pray you. Did King *Richard* then
Proclaim my brother *Mortimer*
Heir to the Crown?

North. He did: myself did hear it.

Hot. Nay, then I cannot blame his cousin King,
That wish'd him on the barren mountains starv'd.
But shall it be, that you, that set the Crown
Upon the head of this forgetful man,
And for his sake wear the detested blot

---

[2] *But I will lift the* downfall'n *Mortimer*] The quarto of 1599 reads *down-trod Mortimer*: which is better. WARB. All the quartos that I have seen read *down-trod*, the three folios read *downfall*.

[3] *An eye of death.*] That is, an eye menacing death. *Hotspur* seems to describe the King as trembling with rage rather than fear.

Of murd'rous Subornation? shall it be,
That you a world of curses undergo,
Being the agents or base second means,
The cords, the ladder, or the hangman rather?
(O pardon me, that I descend so low,
To shew the line and the predicament
Wherein you range under this subtle King)
Shall it for shame be spoken in these days,
Or fill up Chronicles in time to come,
That men of your Nobility and Power
Did gage them Both in an unjust behalf,
As Both of you, God pardon it! have done,
To put down *Richard*, that sweet lovely Rose,
And plant this Thorn, this Canker *Bolingbroke?*
And shall it in more shame be further spoken,
That you are fool'd, discarded, and shook off
By him, for whom these shames ye underwent?
No; yet times serves, wherein you may redeem
Your banish'd honours, and restore yourselves
Into the good thoughts of the world again.
Revenge the jeering, and * disdain'd contempt
Of this proud King, who studies day and night
To answer all the debt he owes unto you,
Ev'n with the bloody payments of your deaths:
Therefore, I say ——

Wor. Peace, Cousin, say no more.
And now I will unclasp a secret book,
And to your quick-conceiving discontents
I'll read you matter deep and dangerous;
As full of peril and advent'rous spirit,
As to o'er-walk a current, roaring loud,
⁂ On the unsteadfast footing of a spear.

Hot. If he fall in, good night, or sink or swim—
Send Danger from the east unto the west,
So Honour cross it from the north to south,

---

* *Disdain'd* for *disdainful*.   ⁂ *On the unsteadfast footin*
of a spear.] i. e. of a spear laid across.   WARBURTON

KING HENRY IV. 133

them grapple.——— O! the blood more stirs
: a Lion, than to start a Hare.
. Imagination of some great exploit
im beyond the bounds of patience.
By heav'n, methinks, it were an easy leap,
To

av'n, methinks, &c]
critic of the size of
:. calls this speech,
y ceremony, *a ridicu-
and absolute madness.*
ald talks in the same
ie *French* critics had
e people just enough
nd where *Shakespeare*
essed the rules of the
ic writers; and, on
ions, they are full of
rigid cant, of *fable,
diction, unities,* &c.
iother thing to get to
'*s* sense: to do this re-
tle of their own. For
hich, they could not
: poet here uses an al-
covering to express a
very natural thought.
, all on fire, exclaims
kstering and *bartering*
, and dividing it into
! says he, could I be
hen I had purchased
iould wear her digni-
t a Rival—what then?

*n, methinks, it were an
ap.
bright honour from the
ic'd Moon:*
ome great and shin-
er in the most elevated
lready in possession of
would, methinks, be
eater acts, to eclipse
and pluck all his ho-
him;

Or *dive into the bottom of the
deep,
And pluck up drowned honour by
the locks:*
i. e. or what is still more difficult, tho' there were in the world
no great examples to incite and
fire my emulation, but that honour was quite sunk and buried
in oblivion, yet would I bring it
back into vogue, and render it
more illustrious than ever. So
that we see, tho' the expression
be sublime and daring, yet the
thought is the natural movement
of an heroic mind. *Euripides* at
least thought so, when he put
the very same sentiment, in the
same words, into the mouth of
*Etrocles—I will not, madam, dis-
guise my thoughts; I could scale
heaven, I could descend to the very
entrails of the earth, if so be that
by that price I could obtain a kingdom.* WARBURTON.
Though I am very far from
condemning this speech with *Gil-
don* and *Theobald* as *absolute madness*, yet I cannot find in it that
profundity of reflection and beauty of allegory which the learned
commentator has endeavoured to
display. This sally of *Hot-spur*
may be, I think, soberly and ra-
tionally vindicated as the violent
eruption of a mind inflated with
ambition and fired with resentment; as the boastful clamour
of a man able to do much, and
eager to do more; as the hasty

K 3   motion

134 THE FIRST PART OF

To pluck bright honour from the pale-fac'd Moon;
Or dive into the bottom of the Deep,
Where fathom-line could never touch the ground,
And pluck up drowned Honour by the locks;
So he, that doth redeem her thence, might wear
Without Corrival all her Dignities.
' But out upon this half-fac'd fellowship!

Wor. He apprehends * a world of figures here,
But not the form of what he should attend.
—Good Cousin, give me audience for a while.

Hot. I cry you mercy.

Wor. Those same noble *Scots*,
That are your prisoners——

Hot. I'll keep them all;
By heav'n, he shall not have a *Scot* of them;
No, if a *Scot* would save his soul, he shall not;
I'll keep them, by this hand.

Wor. You start away,
And lend no ear unto my purposes;
Those prisoners you shall keep.

Hot. I will; that's flat.——
He said, he would not ransom *Mortimer*,
Forbad my tongue to speak of *Mortimer*;
But I will find him when he lies asleep,
And in his ear I'll holla, *Mortimer!*

---

motion of turbulent desire; as the dark expression of indetermined thoughts. The passage from *Euripides* is surely not allegorical, yet it is produced, and properly, as parallel.

' *Put out upon this half-fac'd fellowship!*] I think this finely expressed. The image is taken from one who turns from another, so as to stand before him with a side face; which implied neither a full consorting, nor a separation. WARB.

I cannot think this word rightly explained. It alludes rather to dress. A coat is said to be *faced*, when part of it, as the sleeves or bosom, is covered with something finer and more splendid than the main substance. The mantua-makers still use the word. *Half-fac'd fellowship* is then partnership but half adorned, partnership which yet wants half the show of dignities and honours.

* —*a world of figures here*, &c] *Figure* is used here equivocally. As it is applied to *Hot-spur's* speech, it is a *rhetorical mode*; as opposed to *form*, it means *appearance* or *shape*.

Nay,

Nay, I will have a Starling taught to speak
Nothing but *Mortimer*, and give it him,
To keep his anger still in motion.

Wor. Hear you, cousin, a word.

Hot. All Studies here I solemnly defy,
Save how to gall and pinch this *Bolingbroke*.
And that same sword-and-buckler Prince of *Wales*,
But that, I think, his father loves him not,
And would be glad he met with some mischance,
'd have him poison'd with a pot of ale.

Wor. Farewel, my kinsman! I will talk to you,
When you are better temper'd to attend.

North. Why, what a wasp-tongu'd and impatient fool,
Art thou, to break into this woman's mood,
Tying thine ear to no tongue but thine own?

Hot. Why, look you, I am whipt and scourg'd with rods,
Nettled, and stung with pismires, when I hear
Of this vile politician *Bolingbroke*.
In *Richard*'s time—what do ye call the place?——
A plague upon't!—it is in *Glo'stershire*————
'Twas where the mad-cap Duke his uncle kept——
His uncle *York*—where I first bow'd my knee
Unto this King of Smiles, this *Bolingbroke*,
When you and he came back from *Ravenspurg*.

North. At *Berkley* castle.

Hot. You say true:
Why, what a deal of candy'd Courtesy
This fawning greyhound then did proffer me!
Look, when his * *infant fortune came to age*,—
And *gentle Harry Percy*—and *kind cousin*—
The Devil take such cozeners—God forgive me—
Good uncle, tell your tale, for I have done.

---

[7] *And that same sword-and-buckler Prince of* Wales.] A Royster, or turbulent fellow, that fought in the taverns, or raised disorders in the streets, was called a *swash-buckler*. In this sense *sword and-buckler* is used here.

* Alluding to what passed in King *Richard*, Act II. Sc.

K 4

136   THE FIRST PART OF

Wor. Nay, if you have not, to't again;
We'll stay your leisure.
Hot. I have done, i'faith.
Wor. Then once more to your *Scottish* prisoners.
[*To* Hot-spur.
Deliver them without their ransom straight,
And make the *Dowglas*' Son your only mean
For Pow'rs in *Scotland*; which, for divers reasons
Which I shall send you written, be assur'd,
Will easily be granted.—You, my lord, [*To* North.
Your Son in *Scotland* being thus employ'd,
Shall secretly into the bosom creep
Of that same noble Prelate, well belov'd,
Th' Archbishop.
Hot. York, is't not?
Wor. True, who bears hard
His brother's death at *Bristol*, the lord *Scroop*.
ᵃ I speak not this in estimation,
As what, I think, might be; but what, I know,
Is ruminated, plotted and set down;
And only stays but to behold the face
Of that occasion, that shall bring it on.
Hot. I smell it. On my life, it will do well.
North. Before the game's a-foot, thou still lett'st * slip.

ᵃ *I speak not this in* estimation,] *Estimation* for *conjecture*. But between this and the foregoing verse it appears there were some lines which are now lost. For, consider the sense. What was it that was *ruminated, plotted, and set down?* Why, as the text stands at present, that the Archbishop *bore his brother's death hard*. It is plain then that they were some *consequences* of that resentment which the speaker informed *Hot-spur* of, and to which his conclusion of, *I speak not this by conjecture, but on good proof*, must be referred. But some player, I suppose, thinking the speech too long, struck them out.
WARBURTON.

If the Editor had, before he wrote his note, read ten lines forward, he would have seen that nothing is omitted. *Worcester* gives a dark hint of a conspiracy. *Hot-spur smells it*, that is, *guesses it*. *Northumberland* reproves him for not suffering *Worcester* to tell his design. *Hot-spur*, according to the vehemence of his temper, still follows his own conjecture.

* *To let slip* is, to loose the greyhound.

Hot.

KING HENRY IV.

It cannot chuse but be a noble Plot;
˼en the Power of *Scotland* and of *York*
˼ with *Mortimer*---ha!
. So they shall.
In faith, it is exceedingly well aim'd.
. And 'tis no little reason bids us speed
e our heads, by raising of a head *;
:ar ourselves as even as we can,
˹ing will always think him in our debt;
˼nk, we deem ourselves unsatisfy'd,
: hath found a time to pay us home.
e already, how he doth begin
ke us strangers to his looks of love.
He does, he does; we'll be reveng'd on him.
. Cousin, farewel. No further go in this,
˼ by letters shall direct your course.
time is ripe, which will be suddenly,
˼l to *Glendower*, and lord *Mortimer*,
: you and *Dowglas*, and our Pow'rs at once,
vill fashion it) shall happily meet,
r our fortunes in our own strong arms,
˼ now we hold at much uncertainty,
'h. Farewel, good brother; we shall thrive, I trust.
Uncle, adieu. O let the hours be short,
elds, and blows, and groans applaud our sport!
[*Exeunt.*

ead is a *body of forces*.
˼ is a natural description
state of mind between
at have conferred, and
˼t have received, obliga-
tions too great to be satisfied.
That this would be the event
of *Northumberland*'s disloyalty,
was predicted by King *Richard*
in the former play.

ACT

138 THE FIRST PART OF

ACT II. SCENE I.

An Inn at Rocheſter.

Enter a Carrier with a Lanthorn in his Hand.

1 CARRIER.

HEIGH ho! an't be not four by the day, I'll be hang'd. *Charles' wain* is over the new chimne[y], and yet our horſe not packt. What, oſtler?

Oſt. [*within.*] Anon, anon.

1 *Car.* I pr'ythee, *Tom*, beat *Cutt's* ſaddle, put [a] few flocks in the point; the poor jade is wrung in th[e] withers, ¹ out of all ceſs.

Enter another Carrier.

2 *Car.* Peaſe and beans are ² as dank here as a do[g], and that is the next way to give poor jades the ³ bot[ts]: this houſe is turn'd upſide down, ſince *Robin* Oſtle[r] dy'd.

1 *Car.* Poor fellow never joy'd ſince the price o[f] oats roſe; it was the death of him.

2 *Car.* I think, this be the moſt villianous houſe i[n] all *London* road for fleas: I am ſtung like a Tench.

1 *Car.* Like a Tench? by th' Maſs, there's ne'e[r]

---

¹ *out of all* ceſs] The Oxford Editor, not underſtanding this phraſe, has alter'd it to—*out of all* caſe. As if it were likely that a blundering tranſcriber ſhould change ſo common a word as *caſe* for *ceſs*? which, it is probable, he underſtood no more than this critic; but it means *out of all meaſure*: the phraſe being taken from a *ceſs*, tax [or] ſubſidy; which being by regul[ar] and moderate rates, when a[ny] thing was exorbitant, or out [of] meaſure, it was ſaid to be, *o[ut] of all ceſs.* WARBURTO[N]

² *as* dank.] *i. e.* wet, rotte[n] POP[E]

³ *Botts* are worms in the ſ[to]mach of a horſe.

a Ki[ng]

KING HENRY IV.

a King in Christendom could be better bit than I have been since the first cock.

2 Car. Why, they will allow us ne'er a jourden, and then we leak in your chimney: and your chamber-lie breeds fleas [4] like a Loach.

1 Car. What, ostler!—Come away, and be hang'd, come away.

2 Car. I have a gammon of bacon, and two [5] razes of ginger to be deliver'd as far as *Charing-cross:*

1 Car. 'Odsbody, the Turkies in my panniers are quite starv'd. What, ostler! a plague on thee! hast thou never an eye in thy head? canst not hear? an 'twere not as good a deed as drink, to break the pate of thee, I am a very villain.—Come and be hang'd— hast no faith in thee?

Enter Gads-hill.

Gads. Good-morrow, carriers. What's o'clock?

Car. I think, it be two o'clock.

Gads. I pr'ythee, lend me thy lanthorn, to see my gelding in the stable.

1 Car. Nay, soft, I pray ye; I know a trick worth two of that, i'faith.

Gads. I pr'ythee, lend me thine.

2 Car. Ay, when? canst tell?—lend me thy lanthorn, quoth a!——marry, I'll see thee hang'd first.

Gads. Sirrah, carrier, what time do you mean to come to *London?*

2 Car. Time enough to go to bed with a Candle, I warrant thee.—Come, neighbour *Mugges,* we'll call

---

[4] *like a* Loach.] *Scotch,* a lake. WARBURTON.

[5] *And two* Razes *of Ginger.*] As our Author in several Passages mentions a *Race* of Ginger, I thought proper to distinguish it from the *Raze* mentioned here. The former signifies no more than a single Root of it; but a *Raze* is the *Indian* Term for a *Bale* of it. THEOBALD.

up

up the gentlemen; they will along with Company, for they have great Charge. [*Exeunt Carriers.*

SCENE II.

Enter Chamberlain.

Gads. What, ho, chamberlain!—

Cham. At hand, quoth pick-purse.

Gads. That's ev'n as fair, as at hand, quoth the chamberlain; for thou varieſt no more from picking of purſes, than giving direction doth from labouring. Thou lay'ſt the plot how.

Cham. Good-morrow, maſter *Gads-hill*. It holds current, that I told you yeſternight. There's a ⁶ Franklin, in the wild of *Kent*, hath brought three hundred marks with him in gold; I heard him tell it to one of his company laſt night at ſupper, a kind of auditor, one that hath abundance of charge too, God knows what. They are up already, and call for eggs and butter. They will away preſently.

Gads. Sirrah, if they meet not with ⁷ St. *Nicholas'* clarks, I'll give thee this neck.

Cham. No, I'll none of it; I pr'ythee, keep that for the hangman; for I know thou worſhipp'ſt St. *Nicholas* as truly as a man of falſhood may.

Gads. What talk'ſt thou to me of the hangman? if I hang, I'll make a fat pair of gallows. For if I hang, old Sir *John* hangs with me, and thou know'ſt, he's no ſtarveling. Tut, there are other *Trojans* that thou dream'ſt not of, the which, for ſport-ſake, are content to do the profeſſion ſome grace; that would, if mat-

---

⁶ *Franklin* is a little gentleman.

⁷ *St.* Nicholas' *clarks.*] St. *Nicholas* was the Patron Saint of ſcholars: And *Nicholas*, or Old *Nick*, is a cant name for the Devil. Hence he equivocally calls robbers, St. *Nicholas's clarks.*
　　　　　　　WARBURTON.

KING HENRY IV.

ters should be look'd into for their own credit sake, make all whole. I am join'd with no foot-land-rakers, no long-staff-sixpenny-strikers, none of those mad Mustachio-purple-hu'd-malt-worms; but with nobility and tranquillity; burgo-masters, and great Oneyers; such as can hold in, such as will strike sooner

---

—— I am joined with no foot land rakers,——] That is, with no padders, no wanderers on foot. No *long staff sixpenny strikers*, no fellows that infest the road with long staffs and knock men down for sixpence. *None of those mad mustachio purple hued maltworms, none of those whose faces are red with drinking ale.*

—— burgo masters, and great one eyers.] Perhaps oneraires, *Trustees*, or *Commissioners*; says Mr. *Pope*. But how this Word comes to admit of any such Construction, I am at a loss to know. To Mr. *Pope*'s second Conjecture, of *cunning Men that look sharp and aim well*, I have nothing to reply seriously: but chuse to drop it. The reading which I have substituted, I owe to the Friendship of the ingenious *Nicholas Hardinge*, Esq. A *Moneyer* is an Officer of the Mint, which makes Coin and delivers out the King's Money. *Moneyers* are also taken for Bankers, or those that make it their trade to turn and return Money. Either of these Acceptations will admirably square with our author's Context.

THEOBALD.

This is a very acute and judicious attempt at emendation, and it is not undeservedly adopted by Dr. *Warburton*. Sir *T. Hanmer* reads great *owners*, not without equal or greater likelihood of truth. I know not however whether any change is necessary; *Gads-hill* tells the *Chamberlain* that he is joined with no mean wretches but *with burgomasters and great ones*, or as he terms them in merriment by a cant termination, *great-oneyers*, or *greatone eers*, as we say *privateer, auctioneer, circuiteer*. This is I fancy the whole of the matter.

—— such as will strike sooner than speak; and speak sooner than DRINK; *and* DRINK *sooner than pray;*——] According to the specimen given us in this play, of this dissolute gang, we have no reason to think they *were less ready to drink than speak*. Besides, it is plain, a natural gradation was here intended to be given of their actions, relative to one another. But what has *speaking, drinking* and *praying* to do with one another? We should certainly read THINK in both places instead of *drink*; and then we have a very regular and humourous climax. *They will strike sooner than speak; and speak sooner than* THINK; *and* THINK *sooner than pray*. By which last words is meant, that *Tho' perhaps they may now and then reflect on their crimes, they will never repent of them*. The *Oxford Editor* has dignified this correction by his adoption of it. WARBURTON.

than

142   THE FIRST PART OF

than speak: and speak sooner than think; and th[en]
sooner than pray; and yet I lye, for they pray [con]
tinually unto their saint the Common-wealth; or [ra]
ther, not pray to her, but prey on her; for they [ride]
up and down on her, and make her their boots.

Cham. What, the common-wealth their boots? [Will]
she hold out water in foul way?

Gads. ² She will, she will; justice hath liquor'd [her.]
We steal as in a castle, cock-sure; we have the rec[eipt]
of Fern-seed ³, we walk invisible.

Cham. Nay, I think rather you are more beho[lding]
to the night, than the Fern-seed, for your walking [in]
visible.

Gads. Give me thy hand: thou shalt have a [share]
in our purchase, as I am a true man.

Cham. Nay, rather let me have it, as you ar[e a]
false thief.

Gads. Go to, * *Homo* is a common name to all [men.]
—Bid the ostler bring my gelding out of the sta[ble.]
Farewell, ye muddy knave.   [Ex[eunt.]

---

² *She will, she will; justice hath liquor'd her.*] A Satire on chicane, in courts of justice; which supports ill men in their violations of the law, under the very cover of it. WARBURTON.

³ ———— *we have the receipt of Fern-seed,* ————] Fern is one of those plants, which have their seed on the back of the leaf so small as to escape the sight. Those who perceived that *fern* was propagated by semination, and yet could never see the seed, were much at a loss for a solution of the difficulty; and as

wonder always endeavou[rs to] augment itself, they asc[ribed] to *Fern-seed* many strange [pro]perties, some of which the r[omantic] virgins have not yet forgot[ten or] exploded.

* —— Homo *is a name* [common to all men.] Gads-hill had promised as h[e was] a *true man*, the chamberlain [advises] him to promise rather as [a] *false thief*; to which Gads[hill an]swers, that though he might [have] reason to change the word [yet] he might have spared ma[n, for] *homo* is a name common [to all] men, and among others to th[ieves.]

SCE[NE

KING HENRY IV. 143

SCENE III.

Changes to the Highway.

Enter Prince Henry, Poins, *and* Peto.

Poins. COME, shelter, shelter, I have removed *Falstaff's* horse, and he frets like a gumm'd velvet.

P. Henry. Stand close.

Enter Falstaff.

Fal. Poins, *Poins*, and be hang'd, *Poins!*

P. Henry. Peace, ye fat-kidney'd rascal, what a brawling dost thou keep?

Fal. What, *Poins, Hal!* ——

P. Henry. He is walk'd up to the top of the hill, I'll go seek him.

Fal. I am accurst to rob in that thief's company: the rascal hath remov'd my horse, and ty'd him, I know not where. If I travel but [4] four foot by the square farther afoot, I shall break my wind. Well, I doubt not but to die a fair death for all this, if I 'scape hanging for killing that rogue. I have forsworn his company hourly any time this two and twenty year, and yet I am bewitch'd with the rogue's company. If the rascal have not given me [5] medicines to make me love him, I'll be hang'd; it could not be else; I have drunk medicines. *Poins! Hal!* a Plague upon you

---

[4] —— *four foot by the square.*] The thought is humourous, and alludes to his bulk: Insinuating, that his legs being four foot asunder, when he advanced four foot, this put together made *four foot square.* WARBURTON.
I am in doubt whether there is so much humour here as is suspected: *four foot by the square* is probably no more than *four foot by a rule.*

[5] —— *medicines to make me love him,*] Alluding to the vulgar notion of *love-powder.*

I both.

144 THE FIRST PART OF

both. *Bardolph! Peto!* I'll ftarve, ere I'll [6] rob a foot further. An 'twere not as good a deed as to drink, to turn true man, and to leave thefe rogues, I am the verieft varlet that ever chew'd with a tooth. Eight yards of uneven ground, is threefcore and ten miles afoot with me; and the ftony hearted villains know it well enough. A plague upon't, when thieves cannot be true one to another. [*They whiftle.*] Whew!— a plague upon you all. Give me my horfe; you rogues, give me my horfe, and be hang'd.

P. Henry. Peace, ye fat guts! lye down, lay thine ear clofe to the ground, and lift if thou canft hear the tread of travellers.

Fal. Have you any levers to lift me up again, being down? 'Sblood, I'll not bear mine own flefh fo far afoot again, for all the coin in thy father's exchequer. What a plague mean ye, [7] to colt me thus?

P. Henry. Thou lieft, thou art not colted, thou art uncolted.

Fal. I pr'ythee, good Prince *Hal*, help me to my horfe, good King's fon.

P. Henry. Out, you rogue! fhall I be your oftler?

Fal. Go hang thyfelf in thy own heir-apparent garters[8]; if I be ta'en, I'll peach for this. An I have not ballads made on you all, and fung to filthy tunes, let a cup of fack be my poifon. When a jeft is fo forward, and afoot too!—I hate it.

Enter Gads-hill.

Gads. Stand,——
Fal. So I do againft my will.

---

[6] —— *rob a foot further.*] This is only a flight errour which yet has run through all the copies. We fhould read *rub* a foot. So we now fay *rub* on.

[7] *To colt* is, to fool, to trick, but the prince taking it in another fenfe oppófes it by *uncolt,* that is, *unhorfe.*

[8] —— *heir-apparent garters;*] Alluding to the order of the garter, in which he was enrolled as heir apparent.

Poins.

KING HENRY IV.

Poins. O, 'tis our Setter, I know his voice. [9] *Bardolph.*—What news?

Gads. Cafe ye, cafe ye; on with your vifors; there's ony of the King's coming down the hill, 'tis going to the King's Exchequer.

Fal. You lie, you rogue, 'tis going to the King's tavern.

Gads. There's enough to make us all.

Fal. To be hang'd.

P. Henry. Sirs, you four fhall front them in the narrow lane; *Ned Poins* and I will walk lower; if they 'cape from your encounter, then they light on us.

Peto. But how many be of them?

Gads. Some eight or ten.

Fal. Zounds! will they not rob us?

P. Henry. What, a coward, Sir *John Paunch*.

Fal. Indeed, I am not *John* of *Gaunt*, your grandfather; but yet no coward, *Hal*.

P. Henry. Well, we'll leave that to the proof.

Poins. Sirrah, *Jack*, thy horfe ftands behind the hedge; when thou need'ft him, there fhalt thou find him. Farewel, and ftand faft.

Fal. Now cannot I ftrike him, if I fhould be hang'd.

P. Henry. Ned, where are our difguifes?

Poins. Here, hard by. Stand clofe.

Fal. Now, my mafters, happy man be his dole, fay I; every man to his bufinefs.

---

[9] Bardolph—*What news.*] In all the copies that I have feen *Poins* is made to fpeak upon the entrance of *Gadshill* thus, O, 'tis our Setter, I know his voice.—Bardolph, *What news?* This is abfurd; he knows *Gadshill* to be the *fetter*, and afks *Bardolph what news.* To countenance this impropriety, the later editions have made *Gadshill* and *Bardolph* enter together, but the old copies bring in *Gadshill* alone, and we find that Falftaff, who knew their ftations, calls to *Bardolph* among others for his horfe, but not to *Gadshill* who was pofted at a diftance. We fhould therefore read,
 Poins. *O 'tis our fetter,* &c.
 Bard. *What news?*
 Gadfh. *Cafe ye,* &c.

VOL. IV. L SCENE

SCENE IV.

Enter Travellers.

Trav. Come, neighbour; the boy shall lead our horses down the hill: we'll walk a foot a while, and ease our legs.

Thieves. Stand, ⸺

Trav. Jesu bless us!

Fal. Strike; down with them, cut the villains' throats; ah! whorson caterpillars; bacon-fed knaves; they hate us youth; down with them, fleece them.

Trav. O, we are undone, both we and ours for ever.

Fal. Hang ye, gorbellied knaves, are you undone? no, ye fat chuffs, I would your store were here. On, bacons, on! what, ye knaves? young men must live; you are grand jurors, are ye? we'll jure ye, i'faith.

[*Here they rob and bind them: Exeunt.*

Enter Prince Henry *and* Poins.

P. Henry. The thieves have bound the true men. Now could thou and I rob the thieves and go merrily to *London*, it would be argument for a week, laughter for a month, and a good jest for ever.

Poins. Stand close, I hear them coming.

Enter Thieves again at the other part of the stage.

Fal. Come, my masters, let us share, and then to horse before day; an the Prince and *Poins* be not two arrant Cowards, there's no equity stirring. There's no more valour in that *Poins*, than in a wild Duck.

P. Henry. Your mony.

Poins. Villains!

[*As they are sharing, the Prince and* Poins *set upon them. They all run away, and Falstaff after a blow*

KING HENRY IV. 147

blow or two runs away too, leaving the booty behind them.]

Henry. Got with much eafe. Now merrily to horfe:
thieves are fcatter'd, and poffeft with fear
rongly, that they dare not meet each other;
takes his fellow for an officer.
y, good *Ned.* Now *Falſtaff* fweats to death,
lards the lean earth as he walks along:
e't not for laughing, I fhould pity him.
ins. How the rogue roar'd! [*Exeunt.*

SCENE V.

Lord Percy's *Houſe.*

Enter Hot-fpur *folus, reading a letter.*

T for mine own part, my lord, I could be well contented to be there, in reſpect of the love I bear ouſe. He could be contented to be there; why is t then? *in reſpect of the love he bears our Houſe!* ws in this, he loves his own barn better than he our Houſe. Let me fee fome more. *The purpoſe dertake is dangerous.* Why, that's certain: 'tis rous to take a cold, to fleep, to drink: but I tell ny lord fool, out of this nettle, danger, we pluck ower, fafety. *The purpoſe you undertake is danger- he friends you have named uncertain, the time it nſorted, and your whole plot too light, for the rpoize of ſo great an oppoſition.* Say you fo, fay ? I fay unto you again, you are a fhallow cow- hind, and you lie. What a lack-brain is this? lord, our plot is a good plot as ever was laid; riends true and conftant; a good plot, good s, and full of expectation; an excellent plot, very friends. What a frofty-fpirited rogue is this? my lord of *York* commends the plot, and the

L 2 general

general courſe of the action. By this hand, I were now by this raſcal, I could brain him with his lady's fan. Is there not my father, my uncle, and myſelf, Lord *Edmund Mortimer*, my lord of *York*, and *Owen Glendower*? Is there not beſides, the *Dowglas*? have I not all their letters, to meet me in arms by the ninth of the next month? and are there not ſome of them ſet forward already? What a Pagan raſcal is this? an infidel. Ha! you ſhall ſee now, in very ſincerity of fear and cold heart, will he to the King, and lay open all our proceedings. O, I could divide myſelf, and go to buffets, for moving ſuch a diſh of ſkimm'd milk with ſo honourable an action. Hang him, let him tell the King. We are prepared; I will ſet forward to night.

SCENE VI.

Enter Lady Percy.

How now, *Kate!* I muſt leave you within theſe two hours.
    Lady. O my good lord, why are you thus alone?
For what offence have I this fortnight been
A baniſh'd woman from my *Harry's* bed?
Tell me, ſweet lord, what is't that takes from thee
Thy ſtomach, pleaſure, and thy golden ſleep?
Why doſt thou bend thy eyes upon the earth,
And ſtart ſo often, when thou ſitt'ſt alone?
Why haſt thou loſt the freſh blood in thy cheeks,
And given my treaſures and my rights of thee,
To thick-ey'd muſing, and curs'd melancholy?
In thy faint ſlumbers I by thee have watcht,
And heard thee murmur tales of iron wars,
Speak terms of manage to thy bounding ſteed;
Cry, *courage! to the field!* and thou haſt talk'd
Of ſallies, and retires; of trenches, tents,

KING HENRY IV.

Of palisadoes, frontiers [1], parapets;
Of basilisks, of cannon, culverin,
Of prisoner's ransom, and of soldiers slain,
And all the current of a heady fight.
Thy spirit within thee hath been so at war,
And thus hath so bestir'd [2] thee in thy sleep,
That beads of sweat have stood upon thy brow,
Like bubbles in a late disturbed stream;
And in thy face strange motions have appear'd,
Such as we see when men restrain their breath
On some great sudden haste. O, what portents are
   these?
Some heavy business hath my lord in hand,
And I must know it; else he loves me not.
  Hot. What, ho! is *Gilliams* with the packet gone?

Enter Servant.

Serv. He is, my lord, an hour agone.
Hot. Hath *Butler* brought those horses from the
   Sheriff?
Serv. One horse, my lord, he brought ev'n now.
Hot. What horse? a roan, a crop-ear, is it not?
Serv. It is, my lord.
Hot. That roan shall be my Throne.
Well, I will back him strait. O *Esperance!*
Bid *Butler* lead him forth into the Park.
Lady. But hear you, my Lord.
Hot. What say'st thou, my Lady?
Lady. What is it carries you away?
Hot. Why, my horse, my love, my horse.
Lady. [3] Out, you mad-headed ape!

A weazle

---

[1] For *frontier* Sir *Thomas Hanmer*, and after him Dr. *Warburton*, read very plausibly *fortins*.

[2] *And thus hath so bestir'd—*] Perhaps, *And thought hath so disturb'd.*

[3] *Out, you mad-headed ape!*] This and the following speech of the lady are in the early editions printed as prose; those editions are indeed in such cases of no great authority, but per-

A weazle hath not such a deal of spleen
As you are tost with.
In faith, I'll know your business, that I will.
I fear, my brother *Mortimer* doth stir
About his Title, and hath sent for you
To line his enterprize: but if you go——

    Hot. So far afoot, I shall be weary, love.

    Lady. Come, come, you Paraquito, answer me
Directly to this question, I shall ask.
I'll break thy little Finger, *Harry.*
An if thou wilt not tell me all things true.

    Hot. Away, away, you trifler:—love! I love th
        not [4],
I care not for thee, *Kate*; this is no world
To play with [5] mammets, and to tilt with lips.
We must have bloody noses, and crack'd crowns,
And pass them current too — gods me! my horse.
What say'st thou, *Kate?* what wouldst thou have w
    me?

    Lady. Do ye not love me? do you not, indeed?
Well, do not then. For, since you love me not,
I will not love myself. Do you not love me?
Nay, tell me, if you speak in jest, or no?

    Hot. Come, wilt thou see me ride?
And when I am o'horse-back, I will swear,
I love thee infinitely. But hark you, *Kate,*
I must not have you henceforth question me,
Whither I go; nor reason, where about;
Whither I must, I must; and, to conclude,
This evening must I leave thee, gentle *Kate.*
I know you wise; but yet no further wise
Than *Harry Percy's* wife. Constant you are,

---

haps they were right in this place, for some words have been left out to make the metre.

  [4] *Hot. Away, away, you trifler:
——love! I love thee not,*]
This I think would be better thus,
  Hot. Away, you trifler.
  Lady. Love!
  Hot I love thee not.
This is no time, go.

  [5] —— *mammets.*] Puppe

But yet a woman; and for secresie,
No lady closer, for I well believe,
Thou wilt not utter what thou dost not know;
And so far will I trust thee, gentle *Kate*.

Lady. How! so far?

Hot. Not an inch further. But hark you, *Kate*,
Whither I go, thither shall you go too;
To-day will I set forth, to-morrow you.
Will this content you, *Kate?*

Lady. It must of force. [*Exeunt.*

SCENE VII.

Changes to the Boar's-Head Tavern *in* East-cheap.

Enter Prince Henry *and* Poins.

P. Henry. NED, pr'ythee come out of that fat room and lend me thy hand to laugh a little.

Poins. Where hast been, *Hal?*

P. Henry. With three or four loggerheads, amongst three or fourscore hogsheads. I have sounded the very base string of humility. Sirrah, I am sworn brother to a leash of drawers, and can call them all by their Christian names, as *Tom, Dick*, and *Francis*. They take it already upon their conscience, that though I be but Prince of *Wales*, yet I am the King of courtesie; telling me flatly, I am no proud *Jack*, like *Falstaff*, but a *Corinthian*[6], a lad of mettle, a good boy (by the Lord, so they call me); and when I am King of *England*, I shall command all the good lads in *East-cheap*. They call drinking deep, dying scarlet; and when you breathe in your watering, they cry, hem! and bid you play it off.——To conclude, I am so good a proficient in one quarter of an hour, that I can drink with any tinker in his own language during my life. I tell

[6] —*Corinthian,*] A wencher.

thee, *Ned*, thou haſt loſt much honour, that thou wert not with me in this action; but, ſweet *Ned*,—to ſweeten which name of *Ned*, I give thee this penny-worth of ſugar, clapt even now into my hand by an under-ſkinker [7], one that never ſpake other *Engliſh* in his life, than *Eight Shillings and Six Pence*, and *You are welcome, Sir :* with this ſhrill addition, *Anon, anon, Sir; Score a pint of baſtard in the half moon,* or ſo. But, *Ned*, to drive away the time till *Falſtaff* come, I pr'y-thee, do thou ſtand in ſome bye-room, while I queſtion my puny drawer, to what end he gave me the ſugar; and do thou never leave calling *Francis*, that his tale to me may be nothing but, *anon*. Step aſide, and I'll ſhew thee a precedent.   [*Poins retires*.

Poins. Francis ———
P. *Henry.* Thou art perfect.
Poins. Francis ———

SCENE VIII.

Enter Francis *the Drawer* [8].

Fran. Anon, anon, Sir.—Look down into the pom-granet, *Ralph.*
P. *Henry.* Come hither, *Francis.*
Fran. My lord.
P. *Henry.* How long haſt thou to ſerve, *Francis?*
Fran. Forſooth, five years, and as much as to—
Poins. Francis, ———
Fran. Anon, anon, Sir.
P. *Henry.* Five years; by'rlady, a long leaſe for the clinking of pewter. But, *Francis*, dareſt thou be ſo

---

[7] *under-ſkinker,*] A tapſter; an under-drawer. *Skink* is *drink*, and a *ſkinker* is *one that ſerves drink at* table.

[8] *Enter* Francis *the drawer.*] This ſcene, helped by the dif- traction of the drawer, and gri-maces of the prince, may enter-tain upon the ſtage, but afford not much delight to the reader. The authour has judiciouſly made it ſhort.

KING HENRY IV. 153

valiant, as to play the coward with thy indenture, and shew it a fair pair of heels, and run from it?

Fran. O lord, Sir, I'll be sworn upon all the books in *England*, I could find in my heart——

Poins. Francis,——

Fran. Anon, anon, Sir.

P. Henry. How old art thou, *Francis*?

Fran. Let me see, about *Michaelmas* next I shall be——.

Poins. Francis,——

Fran. Anon, Sir.—Pray you stay a little, my lord.

P. Henry. Nay, but hark you, *Francis*, for the sugar thou gavest me, 'twas a pennyworth, was't not?

Fran. O lord, I would it had been two.

P. Henry. I will give thee for it a thousand pound: ask me when thou wilt, and thou shalt have it.

Poins. Francis.

Fran. Anon, anon.

P. Henry. Anon, *Francis*? no, *Francis*; but to-morrow, *Francis*; or, *Francis*, on *Thursday*; or, indeed, *Francis*, when thou wilt. But, *Francis*,——

Fran. My lord?

P. Henry. Wilt thou rob this leathern-jerkin, crystal-button, knot-pated, agat ring, puke-stocking [9], caddice-garter, smooth tongue, *Spanish*-pouch.

Fran. O lord, Sir, who do you mean?

P. Henry. Why then your brown [1] bastard is your only drink; for look you, *Francis*, your white canvas

---

[9] The prince intends to ask the drawer whether he will rob his master whom he denotes by many contemptuous distinctions, of which all are easily intelligible but *puke-stocking*, which may have indeed a dirty meaning, but it is not the meaning here intended, for the prince designs to mention the materials of the stocking. There is something wrong which I cannot rectify.

[1] —— *brown bastard*—] *Bastard* was a kind of sweet wine. The prince finding the drawer not able, or not willing, to understand his instigation, puzzles him with unconnected prattle, and drives him away.

doublet

doublet will fully. In *Barbary*, Sir, it cannot come to so much.

Fran. What, Sir?

Poins. Francis,——

P. Henry. Away, you rogue, dost thou not hear them call?

Here they both call; the drawer stands amazed, not knowing which way to go.

Enter Vintner.

Vint. What, stand'st thou still, and hear'st such a Calling? Look to the guests within. [*Exit drawer.*] My lord, old Sir *John* with half a dozen more are at the door; shall I let them in?

P. Henry. Let them alone a while, and then open the door. [*Exit Vintner.*] *Poins,*——

Enter Poins.

Poins. Anon, anon, Sir.

P. Henry. Sirrah, *Falstaff* and the rest of the thieves are at the door; shall we be merry?

Poins. As merry as Crickets, my lad. But hark ye, what cunning match have you made with this jest of the drawer? come, what's the issue?

P. Henry. I am now of all humours, that have shew'd themselves humours, since the old days of goodman *Adam*, to the pupil age of this present twelve o'clock at midnight. What's o'clock, *Francis*?

Fran. Anon, anon, Sir.

P. Henry. That ever this fellow should have fewer words than a Parrot, and yet the son of a Woman!—— His industry is up stairs and down stairs; his eloquence the parcel of a reckoning.—²I am not yet of *Percy*'s mind,

---

² —— *I am not yet of* Percy's *mind,*] The drawer's answer had interrupted the prince's train of discourse. He was proceeding thus, *I am now of all humours that have shew'd themselves humours*

KING HENRY IV. 155

mind, the hot-spur of the north; he that kills me some six or seven dozen of *Scots* at breakfast, washes his hands and says to his wife, *Fy upon this quiet life! I want work.* O my sweet Harry, says she, *how many hast thou kill'd to-day?* Give my roan horse a drench, says he, and answers, *some fourteen,* an hour after; *a trifle, a trifle.* I pr'ythee, call in *Falstaff*; I'll play *Percy,* and that damn'd Brawn shall play dame *Mortimer* his wife. *Ribi* [3], says the drunkard. Call in ribs, call in tallow.

SCENE IX.

Enter Falstaff, Gads-hill, Bardolph, *and* Peto.

Poins. Welcome, *Jack*; where hast thou been?

Fal. A plague on all cowards, I say, and a vengeance too, marry and *Amen!*—Give me a cup of sack, boy—Ere I lead this life long, I'll sow nether socks, and mend them, and foot them too. A plague on all cowards!—Give me a cup of sack, rogue.—Is there no virtue extant? [*He drinks.*

P. Henry. Didst thou never see *Titan* kiss a dish of butter? (* pitiful-hearted *Titan!*) that melted at the
sweet

——I am not yet of Percy's *mind.* That is, *I am willing to indulge myself in gaiety and frolick, and try all the varieties of human life. I am not yet of* Percy's *mind,* who thinks all the time lost that is not spent in bloodshed, forgets decency and civility, and has nothing but the barren talk of a brutal soldier.

[3] *Ribi,* that is, *drink.* Hanmer. All the former editions have *rivo,* which certainly had no meaning, but yet was perhaps the cant of *English* taverns.

[4] —*pitiful-hearted* Titan, *that melted at the sweet Tale of the Sun?*] This absurd Reading possesses all the Copies in general; and tho' it has pass'd thro' such a Number of Impressions, is Nonsense, which we may pronounce to have arisen at first from the Inadvertence, either of Transcribers, or the Compositors at Press 'Tis well known, *Titan* is one of the poetical Names of the *Sun*; but we have no authority from Fable for *Titan's* melting away at his own sweet Tale, as *Narcissus* did at the Reflection of his own Form. The Poet's

sweet tale of the Sun? if thou didst, then behold that compound.

Fal. You rogue, [5] here's lime in this sack too; there is nothing but roguery to be found in villainous man;

Poet's Meaning was certainly this: *Falstaff* enters in a great Heat, after having been robb'd by the *Prince* and *Poins* in Disguise: and the Prince seeing him in such a Sweat, makes the following *Simile* upon him: " Do but look upon that Compound of Grease; ——his Fat drips away with the Violence of his Motion, just as *Butter* does with the Heat of the *Sun-Beams* darting full upon it." THEOBALD.

Didst thou never see Titan *kiss a dish of butter? pitiful-hearted* Titan! *that melted at the sweet tale of the Sun?*] This perplexes Mr. *Theobald*; he calls it nonsense, and indeed, having made nonsense of it, changes it to *pitiful hearted Butter*. But the common reading is right: And all that wants *restoring* is a parenthesis into which (*pitiful-hearted* Titan!) should be put. *Pitiful-hearted* means only *amorous*, which was *Titan's* character: the pronoun *that* refers to *butter*. But the *Oxford Editor* goes still further, and not only takes without ceremony Mr. *Theobald's* bread and *butter*, but turns *tale* into *face*; not perceiving that the heat of the Sun is figuratively represented as a *love tale*, the poet having before called him *pitiful-hearted*, or amorous.
WARBURTON.

[5] —— *here's lime in this sack too; there is nothing but roguery to be found in villainous man*;] Sir *Richard Hawkins*, one of Queen *Elizabeth's* sea captains, in his voyages, p. 379. says, *Since the* Spanish *sacks have been common in our taverns, which for conservation are mingled with* lime *in the making, our nation complains of calentures, of the stone, the dropsy, and infinite other distempers not heard of before this wine came into frequent use. Besides, there is no year that it wasteth not two millions of crowns of our substance by conveyance into foreign countries.* This latter, indeed, was a substantial evil. But as to *lime's* giving the *stone*, this sure must be only the good old man's prejudice; since in a wiser age by far, an old woman made her fortune, by shewing us that *lime* was a *cure* for the *stone*. Sir *John Falstaff*, were he alive again, would say she deserved it, for satisfying us that we might drink sack in safety: But that liquor has been long since out of date. I think Lord *Clarendon*, in his Apology, tells us, *That sweet wines, before the Restoration, were so much to the* English *taste, that we engrossed the whole product of the* Canaries; *and that not a pipe of it was expended in any other country in* Europe. But the banished Cavaliers brought home with them the goust for *French* wines, which has continued ever since; and from whence, perhaps, we may more truly date the greater frequency of the *stone*. WARB.

KING HENRY IV. 157

yet a coward is worfe than a cup of fack with lime in it; a villainous coward—Go thy ways, old *Jack*, die when thou wilt, if manhood, good manhood, be not forgot upon the face of the earth, then am I a fhotten herring. There live not three good men unhang'd in *England*, and one of them is fat, and grows old, God help, the while! a bad world; I fay.—⁶ I would, I were a weaver; I could fing all manner of fongs.—A plague on all cowards, I fay ftill!

P. Henry. How now, *Woolfack*, what mutter you?

Fal. A King's fon! If I do not beat thee out of thy Kingdom with a dagger of lath, and drive all thy Subjects afore thee like a flock of wild geefe, I'll never wear hair on my face more. You Prince of *Wales!*

P. Henry. Why, you whorfon round man! what's the matter?

Fal. Are you not a coward? anfwer me to that, and *Poins* there?

P. Henry. Ye fat paunch, an ye call me coward, I'll ftab thee.

Fal. I call thee coward! I'll fee thee damn'd ere I call thee coward; but I would give a thoufand pound I could run as faft as thou can'ft. You are ftrait

---

⁶ —— *I would, I were a weaver; I could fing pfalms, &c.*] In the perfecutions of the proteftants in *Flanders* under *Philip* II. thofe who came over into *England* on that occafion, brought with them the woolen manufactory. Thefe were Calvinifts, who were always diftinguifhed for their love of pfalmody.
WARBURTON.

In the firft editions the paffage is read thus, *I could fing pfalms or any thing.* In the firft folio thus, *I could fing all manner of fongs.* Many expreffions bordering on indecency are found in the firft editions, which are afterwards corrected. The reading of the three laft editions, *I could fing pfalms and all manner of fongs,* is made without authority out of different copies.

I believe nothing more is here meant than to allude to the practice of weavers, who having their hands more employed than their minds, amufe themfelves frequently with fongs at the loom. The knight, being full of vexation, wifhes he could fing to divert his thoughts.

Weavers are mentioned as lovers of mufick in the *Merchant of* Venice. Perhaps *to fing like a Weaver* might be proverbial.

enough

enough in the shoulders, you care not who sees your back. Call you that backing of your friends? a plague upon such backing! give me them that will face me—Give me a cup of sack; I am a rogue if I drunk to day.

P. Henry. O villain, thy lips are scarce wip'd since thou drunk'st last.

Fal. All's one for that.   [*He drinks.*
A plague on all cowards, still, say I!

P. Henry. What's the matter?

Fal. What's the matter! here be four of us, have ta'en a thousand pound this morning.

P. Henry. Where is it, *Jack?* where is it?

Fal. Where is it? taken from us, it is. A hundred upon poor four of us.

P. Henry. What a hundred, man?

Fal. I am a rogue, if I were not at half-sword with a dozen of them two hours together. I have escaped by miracle. I am eight times thurst through the doublet, four through the hose, my buckler cut through and through, my sword hack'd like a hand-saw, *ecce signum.* [*Shews his sword.*] I never dealt better since I was a man.—All would not do. A plague on all cowards!—Let them speak; if they speak more or less than truth, they are villains, and the sons of darkness.

P. Henry. Speak, Sirs, how was it?

Gads. We four set upon some dozen.

Fal. Sixteen, at least, my lord.

Gads. And bound them.

Peto. No, no, they were not bound.

Fal. You rogue, they were bound, every man of them, or I am a *Jew* else, an *Ebrew Jew.*

Gads. As we were sharing, some six or seven fresh men set upon us.

Fal. And unbound the rest, and then came in the other.

P. Henry. What, fought ye with them all?

Fal.

Fal. All? I know not what ye call all; but if I fought not with fifty of them, I am a bunch of radish: if there were not two or three and fifty upon poor old *Jack*, then am I no two-legg'd creature.

Poins. Pray heav'n you have not murthered some of them.

Fal. Nay, that's paſt praying for. I have pepper'd two of them; two, I am ſure, I have pay'd, two rogues in buckram ſuits. I tell thee what, *Hal*; If I tell thee a lie, ſpit in my face, call me horſe. Thou know'ſt my old ward; here I lay, and thus I bore my point; four rogues in buckram let drive at me.

P. Henry. What four? thou ſaidſt but two, even now.

Fal. Four, *Hal*, I told thee four.

Poins. Ay, ay, he ſaid four.

Fal. Theſe four came all a front, and mainly thruſt at me; I made no more ado, but took all their ſeven points in my target, thus.

P. Henry. Seven, why, there were but four, even now.

Fal. In buckram.

Poins. Ay, four, in buckram ſuits.

Fal. Seven, by theſe hilts, or I am a villain elſe.

P. Henry. Pr'ythee let him alone, we ſhall have more anon.

Fal. Doſt thou hear me, *Hal?*

P. Henry. Ay, and mark thee too, *Jack.*

Fal. Do ſo, for it is worth the liſtening to. Theſe nine in buckram, that I told thee of——

P. Henry. So, two more already.

Fal. ⁷ Their points being broken———

Poins. Down fell his hoſe.

---

⁷ *Their points being broken—down fell his hoſe.*] To underſtand *Poins's* joke, the double meaning of *point* muſt be remembered, which ſignifies *the ſharp end of a weapon, and the lace of a garment.*

Fal.

P. Henry. Content:---and the argument shall be thy running away.

Fal. Ah!---no more of that, *Hal*, if thou lovest me.

SCENE X.

Enter Hostess.

Host. O Jesu! my lord the Prince!

P. Henry. How now, my lady the hostess, what say'st thou to me?

Host. Marry, my lord, there is a Nobleman of the Court at door would speak with you; he says, he comes from your father.

P. Henry. [1] Give him as much as will make him a royal man, and send him back again to my mother.

Fal. What manner of man is he?

Host. An old man.

Fal. What doth gravity out of his bed at midnight? Shall I give him his answer?

P. Henry. Pr'ythee, do, *Jack*.

Fal. Faith, and I'll send him packing. [*Exit.*

P. Henry. Now, Sirs, by'r lady, you fought fair; so did you, *Peto*; so did you, *Bardolph*; you are Lions too, you ran away upon instinct; you will not touch the true Prince; no. Fie!

Bard. 'Faith, I ran when I saw others run.

P. Henry. Tell me now in earnest; how came *Falstaff*'s sword so hackt?

Peto. Why, he hackt it with his dagger, and said, he would swear truth out of *England*, but he would

---

[1] *There is a Nobleman ---- give him as much as will make him a royal man.*] I believe here is a kind of jest intended. He that had received a *noble* was, in cant language, called a *nobleman*: in this sense the Prince catches the word, and bids the landlady give him as much as will make him a royal man, that is, a real or royal, and send him away.

make

KING HENRY IV.

you believe it was done in fight, and perfuaded
to the like.

d. Yea, and to tickle our nofes with fpear-grafs,
e them bleed; and then beflubber our garments
and fwear it was ² the blood of true men. I did
lid not thefe feven years before, I blufh'd to
is monftrous devices.

'enry. O villain, thou ftolleft a cup of fack eigh-
ars ago, and wert ³ taken with the manner, and
ce thou haft blufh'd *extempore*. Thou hadft ⁴ fire
ord on thy fide, and yet thou ranneft away;
ftinct hadft thou for it?

l. My lord, do you fee thefe meteors? do you
thefe exhalations?

enry. I do.

!. What think you they portend?

nry. ⁵ Hot livers, and cold purfes.

'. Choler, my lord, if rightly taken.

nry. No, if rightly taken, halter.

SCENE XI.

Re-enter Falftaff.

mes lean *Jack*, here comes bare-bone. How
r fweet creature of ⁶ bombaft? How long is't
ck, fince thou faw'ft thy own knee?

ood of true men.] That
men with whom they
 boneft men, oppofed

in *the manner.*] The
d Folio read *with the*
hich is right. Taken
manner is a law phrafe,
n common ufe, to fig-
in the fact. But the
'itor alters it, for bet-
of the fenfe, to
in the MANOUR.

i. e. I fuppofe, by the lord of it,
as a ftrey.   WARBURTON.
⁴ The *fire* was in his face. A
red face is termed a *firy face*.
While I affirm a firy face
Is to the owner no difgrace.
    Legend *of Capt.* Jones.
⁵ *Hot livers, and cold purfes.*]
That is, *drunkennefs* and *poverty*.
To *drink* was, in the language
of thofe times, to *heat* the *liver*.
⁶ *Bombaft* is the ftuffing of
cloaths.

M 2   Fal.

Fal. My own knee? When I was about thy years Hal, I was an Eagle's talon in the wafte; I could have crept into any alderman's thumb-ring. A plague on fighing and grief, it blows up a man like a bladder. There's villainous news abroad; here was Sir *John Braby* from your Father; you muft go to the Court in the morning. That fame mad fellow of the north, *Percy*, and he of *Wales*, that gave *Amamon* the baftinado, and made *Lucifer* cuckold, and fwore the devil his true Liegeman upon the crofs of a *Welfh*-hook: what a plague call you him———

Poins. O, *Glendower.*

Fal. Owen, Owen; the fame; and his fon in law *Mortimer*, and old *Northumberland*, and that fprightly *Scot* of *Scots*, *Dowglas*, that runs a horfeback up a hill perpendicular.

P. Henry. He that rides at high fpeed, and with a [7] piftol kills a fparrow flying.

Fal. You have hit it.

P. Henry. So did he never the Sparrow.

Fal. Well; that rafcal has good mettle in him, he will not run.

P. Henry. Why, what a rafcal art thou then, to praife him fo for running?

Fal. A horfeback, ye cuckow! but afoot, he will not budge a foot.

P. Henry. Yes, *Jack*, upon inftinct.

Fal. I grant ye, upon inftinct: well, he is there too, and one *Mordake*, and a thoufand [8] blue caps more. *Worcefter* is ftoln away by night. Thy father's beard is

---

[7] *Shakefpeare* never has any care to preferve the manners of the time. *Piftols* were not known in the age of *Henry*. Piftols were, I believe, about our author's time, eminently ufed by the *Scots*. Sir *Henry Wotton* fomewhere makes mention of a *Scotifh piftol*.

[8] *Blue-caps.*] A name of ridicule given to the *Scots* from their blue *bonnets*.

turn'd

KING HENRY IV. 165

rn'd white with the news.[9] You may buy land now cheap as stinking mackerel.

P. Henry. Then 'tis like, if there come a hot *June*, d this civil buffetting hold, we shall buy maidenheads, as they buy hob-nails, by the hundred.

Fal. By the mass, lad, thou say'st true; it is like e shall have good trading that way.—But tell me, al, art not thou horribly afeard, thou being heir pparent? Could the world pick thee out three such emies again as that fiend *Dowglas*, that spirit *Percy*, d that devil *Glendower?* art thou not horribly afraid? th not thy blood thrill at it?

P. Henry. Not a whit, i'faith; I lack some of thy stinct.

Fal. Well, thou wilt be horribly chid to-morrow, hen thou com'st to thy father; if thou do love me, ractise an answer.

P. Henry. Do thou stand for my father, and examine e upon the particulars of my life.

Fal. Shall I? content. This Chair shall be my State, his Dagger my Scepter, and this Cushion my Crown.

P. Henry.[1] Thy state is taken for a joint-stool, thy golden scepter for a leaden dagger, and thy precious ich Crown for a pitiful bald crown.

Fal. Well, an the fire of grace be not quite out of thee, now shalt thou be moved—Give me a cup of Sack to make mine eyes look red, that it may be

---

[9] *You may buy land*, &c.] In former times the prosperity of the nation was known by the value of land as now by the price f stocks. Before *Henry* the seventh made it safe to serve the ing regnant, it was the practice f every revolution for the conueror to confiscate the estates of hose that opposed, and perhaps f those who did not assist him. Those, therefore, that foresaw a change of government, and thought their estates in danger, were desirous to sell them in haste for something that might be carried away.

[1] This answer might, I think, have better been omitted. It contains only a repetition of *Falstaff's* mock-royalty.

M 3 thought

166 THE FIRST PART OF

thought I have wept; for I muſt ſpeak in paſſion, and I will do it in ² King *Cambyſes'* vein.

P. Henry. Well, here is ³ my leg.

Fal. And here is my ſpeech—Stand aſide, Nobility——

Hoſt. This is excellent ſport, i'faith.

Fal. Weep not, ſweet Queen, for trickling tears are vain.

Hoſt. O the father! how he holds his countenance?

Fal. For God's ſake, lords, convey my triſtful Queen, For tears do ſtop the flood-gates of her eyes.

Hoſt. O rare, he doth it as like one of thoſe harlotry Players, as I ever ſee.

Fal. Peace, good pint-pot; peace, good tickle-brain— ⁴ Harry, I do not only marvel, where thou ſpendeſt thy time, but alſo, how thou art accompany'd; for ⁵ though the camomile, the more it is trodden on, the faſter it grows, yet youth, the more it is waſted, the ſooner it wears. Thou art my ſon; I have partly thy mother's word, partly my own opinion; but chiefly, a villainous trick of thine eye, and a fooliſh hanging of thy nether lip, that doth warrant me. If then thou be ſon to me, here lyeth the point; why, being ſon to me, art thou 'ſo pointed at? Shall the

---

² A lamentable tragedy, mixed full of pleaſant mirth, containing the life of *Cambyſes* King of *Perſia*. By *Thomas Preſton*.
THEOBALD.
I queſtion if *Shakeſpeare* had ever ſeen this tragedy; for there is a remarkable peculiarity of meaſure, which, when he profeſſed to ſpeak in *King* Cambyſes' *vein*, he would hardly have miſſed, if he had known it.

³ *My leg.*] That is, My obeiſance to my father.

⁴ Harry, *I do not only marvel,* &c.] A ridicule on the public oratory of that time.   WARB.

⁵ *Though camomile,* &c.] This whole ſpeech is ſupremely comick. The ſimile of camomile uſed to illuſtrate a contrary effect, brings to my remembrance an obſervation of a later writer of ſome merit, whom the deſire of being witty has betrayed into a like thought. Meaning to enforce with great vehemence the mad temerity of young ſoldiers, he remarks, that *though* Bedlam *be in the road to* Hogſden, *it is out of the way to promotion.*

bleſſed

KING HENRY IV.

1 of heav'n prove ⁶ a micher, and eat black-
queſtion not to be aſk'd. Shall the ſon of
)rove a thief and take purſes? a queſtion
. There is a thing, *Harry*, which thou
heard of, and it is known to many in our
the name of pitch; this pitch, as ancient
report, doth defile; ſo doth the company
'ſt; for, *Harry*, now do I not ſpeak to thee
ut in tears; not in pleaſure, but in paſſion;
ls only, but in woes alſo.——And yet there is
man, whom I have often noted in thy com-
I know not his name.

'. What manner of man, an it like your

goodly portly man, i'faith, and a corpu-
chearful look, a pleaſing eye, and a moſt
age; and, as I think, his age ſome fifty,
idy, inclining to threeſcore: and now, I
me, his name is *Falſtaff*. If that man
ewdly given, he deceives me; for, *Harry*,
 in his looks. If then the ⁷ fruit may be
the tree, as the tree by the fruit, then pe-
I ſpeak it, there is virtue in that *Falſtaff*;
vith, the reſt baniſh. And tell me now,
ity varlet, tell me, where haſt thou been
?

'. Doſt thou ſpeak like a King? Do thou
le, and I'll play my father.
poſe me.——If thou doſt it half ſo gravely,
illy, both in word and matter, hang me up
s for a ⁸ rabbet-ſucker, or a poulterer's hare.

,] *i. e.* Truant; to
rk out of ſight, a
. WARBURTON.
i is to a truant-boy,
g to go to ſchool,
;o home, lurks in
 picks wild fruits.
fage is happily re-

ſtored by Sir *Thomas Hanmer*.

⁸ *Rabbet-ſucker* is, I ſuppoſe,
a *fucking rabbet*. The jeſt is in
comparing himſelf to ſomething
thin and little. So a *poulterer's
hare*, a hare hung up by the
hind legs without a ſkin, is long
and ſlender.

M 4   P. *Henry.*

P. Henry. Well, here I am set.

Fal. And here I stand; judge, my masters.

P. Henry. Now, *Harry,* whence come you?

Fal. My noble lord, from *East-cheap.*

P. Henry. The Complaints I hear of thee are grievous.

Fal. 'Sblood, my lord, they are false.—— Nay, I'll tickle ye for a young Prince.

P. Henry. 'Sweareft thou, ungracious boy? henceforth ne'er look on me. Thou art violently carried away from grace; there's a devil haunts thee, in the likeness of a fat old man! a tun of man is thy companion. Why dost thou converse with that trunk of humours, that [9] boulting hutch of beastliness, that swoln parcel of dropsies, that huge bombard of sack, that stufft cloak-bag of guts, that roasted [1] *Manning-tree* Ox with the pudding in his belly, that reverend vice, that grey iniquity, that father ruffian, that vanity in years? Wherein is he good, but to taste sack and drink it? wherein neat and cleanly, but to carve a capon and eat it? wherein [*] cunning, but in craft? wherein crafty, but in villany? wherein villainous, but in all things? wherein worthy, but in nothing?

Fal. I would, your Grace would [2] take me with you. Whom means your Grace?

P. Henry. That villainous abominable mis-leader of youth, *Falstaff,* that old white-bearded Satan.

Fal. My lord, the man I know.

P. Henry. I know thou dost.

Fal. But to say, I know more harm in him than in my self, were to say more than I know. That

---

[9] *Boulting-hutch.*] *Boulting-hutch* is, I think, a *meal-bag.*

[1] Of the *Manning-tree* Ox I can give no account, but the meaning is clear.

[*] *Cunning* was not yet debased to a bad meaning. It signified *knowing* or *skilful.*

[2] *Take me with you.*] That is, go no *faster than I can follow* you. Let me know your meaning.

KING HENRY IV. 169

he is old, the more is the pity, his white hairs do witness it; but that he is, saving your reverence, a whoremaster, that I utterly deny. If sack and sugar be a fault, God help the wicked. If to be old and merry, be a sin, then many an old Host, that I know, is damn'd. If to be fat, be to be hated, then *Pharoah's* lean kine are to be lov'd. No, my good lord, banish *Peto*, banish *Bardolph*, banish *Poins*; but for sweet *Jack Falstaff*, kind *Jack Falstaff*, true *Jack Falstaff*, valiant *Jack Falstaff*, and therefore more valiant, being as he is, old *Jack Falstaff*, banish not him thy *Harry's* company; banish plump *Jack*, and banish all the world.

P. *Henry*. I do, I will.

[*Knocking; and* Hostess *goes out.*

Enter Bardolph *running*.

Bard. O, my lord, my lord, the Sheriff with a most monstrous Watch is at the door.

Fal. Out, you rogue!—Play out the Play; I have much to say in behalf of that *Falstaff*.

Re-enter the Hostess.

Host. O, my lord, my lord!

Fal. Heigh, heigh, the devil rides upon a fiddle-stick: what's the matter?

Host. The Sheriff and all the watch are at the door: they are come to search the house. Shall I let them in?

Fal. Dost thou hear, *Hal?* never call a true piece of gold a counterfeit; thou art essentially mad, without seeming so.

P. *Henry*. And thou a natural coward, without instinct.

Fal. I deny your *major*. If you will deny the Sheriff, so, if not, let him enter. If I become not a cart as well as another man, a plague on my bringing up; I

hope

THE FIRST PART OF

hope I shall as soon be strangled with a halter, as another.

P. Henry. Go, * hide thee behind the arras, the rest walk up above. Now, my masters, for a true face and good conscience.

Fal. Both which I have had; but their date is out, and therefore I'll hide me.

[*Exeunt* Falstaff, Bardolph, &c.

P. Henry. Call in the Sheriff.———

SCENE XII.

Enter Sheriff and Carrier.

Now, master Sheriff, what is your will with me?

Sher. First, pardon me, my lord.—A hue and cry Hath follow'd certain men unto this house.

P. Henry. What men?

Sher. One of them is well known, my gracious lord, A gross fat man.

Car. As fat as butter.

P. Henry. The man, I do assure you, is not here, For I myself at this time have imploy'd him; And, Sheriff, I engage my word to thee, That I will, by to-morrow dinner-time, Send him to answer thee, or any man, For any thing he shall be charg'd withal; And so let me intreat you leave the house.

Sher. I will, my lord. There are two gentlemen Have in this robbery lost three hundred marks.

P. Henry. It may be so; if he have robb'd these men, He shall be answerable; and so farewel.

Sher. Good night, my noble lord.

---

* —*hide thee behind the arras,*] The bulk of *Falstaff* made him not the fittest to be concealed behind the hangings, but every poet sacrifices something to the scenery; if *Falstaff* had not been hidden, he could not have been found asleep, nor had his pockets searched.

P. Henry.

KING HENRY IV.

P. Henry. I think, it is good-morrow, is it not?
Sher. Indeed, my lord, I think it be two o'clock.
[*Exit.*
P. Henry. This oily rascal is known as well as *Paul's*; go call him forth [3].
Peto. Falstaff—— fast asleep, behind the arras, and snorting like a horse.
P. Henry. Hark, how hard he fetches breath. Search his Pockets.
[*He searches his pockets, and finds certain papers.*
P. Henry. What hast thou found?
Peto. Nothing but papers, my lord.
P. Henry. Let's see, what be they? read them.
Peto. Item, a capon, 2 *s.* 2 *d.*
Item, Sawce, 4 *d.*
Item, Sack, two gallons, 5 *s.* 8 *d.*
Item, Anchoves and sack after supper, 2 *s.* 6 *d.*
Item, Bread, a halfpenny.
P. Henry. O monstrous! but one halfpenny-worth of bread, to this intolerable deal of sack? What there is else, keep close, we'll read it at more advantage; there let him sleep till day. I'll to the Court in the morning: we must all to the wars, and thy place shall

---

[3] *go call him forth*,] The scenery here is somewhat perplexed. When the sheriff came, the whole gang retired, and *Falstaff* was hidden. As soon as the sheriff is sent away, the Prince orders *Falstaff* to be called: by whom? by *Peto*. But why had not *Peto* gone up stairs with the rest, and if he had, why did not the rest come down with him? The conversation that follows between the prince and *Peto*, seems to be apart from the others.
I cannot but suspect that for *Peto* we should read *Poins*: what had *Peto* done that *his place should be* honourable, or that he should be trusted with the plot against *Falstaff? Poins* has the prince's confidence, and is a man of courage.
This alteration clears the whole difficulty; they all retired but *Poins*, who, with the prince, having only robbed the robbers, had no need to conceal himself from the travellers. We may therefore boldly change the scenical direction thus, *Exeunt* Falstaff, Bardolph, Gad-hill, *and* Peto; *manent the* Prince *and* Poins.

be

be honourable. I'll procure this fat rogue a charge of foot, and, [4] I know, his death will be a march of twelvescore. The mony shall be paid back again with advantage. Be with me betimes in the morning; and so good-morrow, *Peto*.

Peto. Good-morrow, good my lord. [*Exeunt.*

ACT III. SCENE I.

The Archdeacon of Bangor's *House in* Wales.

Enter Hot-spur, Worcester, *Lord* Mortimer, *and* Owen Glendower.

Mortimer.

THESE promises are fair, the parties sure,
And our [5] Induction full of prosp'rous hope.
Hot. Lord *Mortimer*, and cousin *Glendower*,
Will you sit down?
And, uncle *Worcester*———a plague upon it!
I have forgot the map.
Glend. No, here it is.
Sit, cousin *Percy;* sit, good cousin *Hot-spur;*
For, by that name, as oft as *Lancaster*
Doth speak of you, his cheek looks pale; and with
A rising sigh, he wisheth you in heav'n.
Hot. And you in hell, as often as he hears
Owen Glendower spoke of.
Glend. I blame him not; at my Nativity,
The front of heav'n was full of fiery shapes,
Of burning Cressets; know, that, at my birth,

---

[4] ——— *I know, his death will be a march of twelvescore.*] i. e. It will kill him to march so far twelvescore yards.
[5] ——— *induction*] That is, entrance; beginning.

Th

The frame and the foundation of the earth
Shook like a coward.
 Hot. So it wou'd have done
At the same season, if your mother's cat
Had kitten'd, though yourself had ne'er been born.
 Glend. I say, the earth did shake when I was born.
 Hot. I say, the earth then was not of my mind,
If you suppose, as fearing you, it shook.
 Glend. The heav'ns were all on fire, the earth did
  tremble.
 Hot. O, then the earth shook to see the heav'ns on
  fire,
And not in fear of your nativity.
 Diseased Nature oftentimes breaks forth
In strange eruptions; and the teeming earth
Is with a kind of colick pinch'd and vext,
By the imprisoning of unruly wind
Within her womb; which, for enlargement striving,
Shakes the old beldame earth, and topples down
High tow'rs and moss-grown steeples. At your birth,
Our grandam earth, with this distemperature,
In passion shook.
 Glend. Cousin, of many men
I do not bear these crossings. Give me leave
To tell you once again, that at my birth
The front of heav'n was full of fiery shapes;
The goats ran from the mountains, and the herds
Were strangely clamrous in the frighted fields.
These signs have mark'd me extraordinary,
And all the courses of my life do shew,
I am not in the roll of common men.
Where is he living, clipt in with the sea
That chides the banks of *England, Wales,* or *Scotland,*
Who calls me pupil, or hath read to me?

---

* *Diseased Nature*——] The Poet has here taken, from the Perverseness and contrariousness of *Hotspur's* temper, an opportunity of raising his character, by a very rational and philosophical confutation of superstitious errour.

And bring him out, that is but woman's son,
Can trace me in the tedious ways of art,
Or hold me pace in deep experiments.
   Hot. I think, there is no man speaks better Weſ
—I'll to dinner.
   Mort. Peace, cousin *Percy*; you will make him ma
   Glend. I can call spirits from the wasty deep.
   Hot. Why, so can I, or so can any man:
But, will they come when you do call for them?
   Glend. Why, I can teach thee to command the dev
   Hot. And I can teach thee, coz, to shame the dev
By telling truth; *Tell truth, and shame the devil.*—
If thou hast pow'r to raise him, bring him hither,
And I'll be sworn, I've pow'r to shame him hence.
Oh, while you live, tell truth, and shame the devil.
   Mort. Come, come!
No more of this unprofitable chat.
   Glend. Three times hath *Henry Bolingbroke* mac
     head
Against my pow'r; thrice from the banks of *Wye*,
And sandy-bottom'd *Severn*, have I sent
Him bootless home, and weather-beaten back.
   Hot. Home, without boots, and in foul weather to
How 'scapes he agues, in the devil's name?
   Glend. Come, here's the Map: Shall we divide o
     Right,
According to our threefold order ta'en?
   Mort. Th' Archdeacon hath divided it
Into three limits, very equally:
England, from *Trent*, and *Severn* hitherto,
By south and east, is to my part assign'd;
All westward, *Wales*, beyond the *Severn* shore,
And all the fertile land within that bound,
To *Owen Glendower*; and, dear Coz, to you
The remnant northward, lying off from *Trent*.
And our Indentures tripartite are drawn,
Which being sealed interchangeably
(A business, that this night may execute),

To-morrow, cousin *Percy*, you and I,
And my good lord of *Wor'ster*, will set forth,
To meet your father, and the *Scottish* Power,
As is appointed us, at *Shrewsbury*.
My father *Glendower* is not ready yet,
Nor shall we need his help these fourteen days.
—Within that space, you may have drawn together
Your tenants, friends, and neighbouring gentlemen.
[*To* Glendower.

Glend. A shorter time shall send me to you, lords,
And in my conduct shall your ladies come,
From whom you now must steal, and take no leave,
For there will be a world of water shed,
Upon the parting of your wives and you.

Hot. [7] Methinks, my moiety, north from *Burton* here,
In quantity equals not one of yours.
See, how this river comes me crankling in,
And cuts me, from the best of all my land,
A huge half-moon, a monstrous cantle out.
I'll have the Current in this place damm'd up:
And here the smug and silver *Trent* shall run
In a new channel, fair and evenly;
It shall not wind with such a deep indent,
To rob me of so rich a bottom here.

Glend. Not wind? it shall, it must; you see, it doth.

Mort. But mark, he bears his course, and runs me up
With like advantage on the other side,
Gelding th' opposed continent as much,
As on the other side it takes from you.

Wor. Yes, but a little charge will trench him here,
And on this north side win this cape of land,
And then he runs straight and even.

---

[7] *Methinks, my moiety,*—] *Hot-spur* is here just such a divider as the *Irishman* who made *three halves*: Therefore, for the honour of *Shakespeare*, I will suppose, with the *Oxford Editor*, that he wrote *portion*. WARB.
I will not suppose it.
Hot.

176 THE FIRST PART OF

Hot. I'll have it so, a little charge will do it.
Glend. I will not have it alter'd.
Hot. Will not you?
Glend. No, nor you shall not.
Hot. Who shall say me *nay?*
Glend. Why, that will I.
Hot. Let me not understand you then,
Speak it in *Welsh.*
Glend. I can speak *English*, lord, as well as you,
For I was train'd up in the *English* Court,
Where, being young, I framed to the harp
Many an *English* Ditty, lovely well,
And gave the * tongue a helpful ornament;
A virtue, that was never seen in you.
Hot. Marry, and I'm glad of it with all my heart,
I had rather be a kitten, and cry, *mew!*
Than one of these same meeter-ballad-mongers;
I'd rather hear a brazen candlestick turn'd,
Or a dry wheel grate on the axle-tree,
And that would nothing set my teeth on edge,
Nothing so much as mincing Poetry;
'Tis like the forc'd gate of a shuffling nag.
Glend. Come, you shall have *Trent* turn'd.
Hot. I do not care; I'll give thrice so much land
To any well-deserving friend;
But in the way of bargain, mark ye me,
I'll cavil on the ninth part of a hair.
Are the indentures drawn? shall we be gone?
Glend. The moon shines fair, you may away by night;
* (I'll haste the writer) and withal,
Break with your Wives of your departure hence.
I am afraid my daughter will run mad;
So much she doteth on her *Mortimer.* [*Exit.*

* *The tongue.*] The *English* language.

* (*I'll haste the writer*) He means the writer of the articles. **Pope.**

SCENE

SCENE II.

Fie, coufin *Percy*, how you crofs my father?
cannot chufe.   Sometime he angers me,
     lling of the Moldwarp and the Ant [a],
  mer *Merlin*, and his prophecies;
  a dragon, and a finlefs fifh,
 wing Griffin, and a moulting Raven,
 ing Lion, and a ramping Cat,
  h a deal of fkimble-fkamble ftuff,
  me from my faith.   I tell you what,
  l me the laft night at leaft nine hours,
 ning up the feveral devils names,
 ere his lackeys: I cry'd, *hum,*—and *well,*—
 k'd him not a word,   O, he's as tedious
  'd horfe, or as a railing wife;
 han a fmoaky houfe.   I'd rather live
 eefe and garlick, in a windmil, far,
  ed on cates, and have him talk to me,
 ummer-houfe in chriftendom.
  In faith, he is a worthy gentleman;
 ngly well read, and profited [1]
 ge concealments; valiant as a Lion;
 nd'rous affable; as bountiful
 es of *India*.   Shall I tell you, coufin?
ls your temper in a high refpect,
 rbs himfelf, even of his natural fcope,
 rou do crofs his humour; 'faith, he does;
 nt you, that man is not alive
  o have tempted him as you have done,
 it the tafte of danger and reproof.
 not ufe it oft, let me intreat you.

---

of the Moldwarp and   See *Hall's* Chronicle, folio 20.
Ant,] This alludes to   Pope.
   phecy which is faid to   [1] ——————— *profited*
uced *Owen Glendower*   *In ftrange concealments;*———]
ms againft King *Henry.*   Skilled in wonderful *fecrets.*

Wor. In faith, my lord, you are too * wilful blame,
And, since your coming here, have done enough
To put him quite besides his patience.
You must needs learn, lord, to amend this fault;
Though sometimes it shews greatness, courage, blood,
(And that's the dearest grace it renders you)
Yet oftentimes it doth present harsh rage,
Defect of manners, want of government,
Pride, haughtiness, opinion, and disdain;
The least of which, haunting a Nobleman,
Loseth men's hearts, and leaves behind a stain
Upon the beauty of all parts besides,
Beguiling them of commendation.

   Hot. Well, I am school'd: good manners be your
      speed!
Here come our wives, and let us take our leave.

SCENE III.

Enter Glendower, *with the ladies.*

   Mort. This is the deadly spight that angers me,
My wife can speak no *English*, I no *Welsh*.

   Glend. My daughter weeps, she will not part with you,
She'll be a soldier too, she'll to the wars.

   Mort. Good father, tell her, she and my aunt *Percy*
Shall follow in your conduct speedily.

[Glendower *speaks to her in* Welsh, *and she an-
    swers him in the same.*

   Glend. She's desp'rate here, a peevish self-will'd
      harlotry,
That no persuasion can do good upon.

                    [*Lady speaks in* Welsh.

   Mort. I understand thy looks; that pretty *Welsh*,
Which thou pour'st down from those two swelling
      heavens,

---

* — *too wilful-blame,*] This is a mode of speech with which I am not acquainted. Perhaps it might be read *too wilful-blunt,* or *too wilful-bent,* or thus, Indeed, *my lord, you are to* blame, too wilful.

I am

too perfect in, and, but for shame,
ch a parly should I answer thee.
            [*The Lady again in* Welsh.
erstand thy kisses, and thou mine;
hat's a feeling disputation;
will never be a truant, love,
I have learn'd thy language; for thy tongue
's *Welsh* as sweet as ditties highly penn'd,
by a fair Queen in a summer's bower,
 ravishing division to her lute.
nd. Nay, if thou melt, then will she run mad.
            [*The Lady speaks again in* Welsh.
rt. O, I am Ignorance itself in this.
nd. She bids you,
n the wanton rushes lay you down²,
rest your gentle head upon her lap,
he will sing the song that pleaseth you;
 on your eye-lids crown the God of Sleep,
ming your blood with pleasing heaviness;
ng such diff'rence betwixt wake and sleep⁴,
the diff'rence betwixt day and night,
hour before the heav'nly-harness'd team
is his golden progress in the east.
rt. With all my heart I'll sit, and hear her sing:
at time will ⁵ our book, I think, be drawn.
nd. Do so;

*l on the wanton rushes lay
u down.*] It was the cus-
this country, for many
to strew the floors with
as we now cover them
arpets.
*d on your eye-lids crown
'e God of Sleep,*] The ex-
n is fine; intimating, that
od of Sleep should not only
his eye lids, but that he
fit crown'd, that is, pleased
lighted. WARBURTON.

4 *Making such diff'rence betwixt wake and sleep,*] She
will lull you by her song into
soft tranquillity, in which you
shall be so near to sleep as to be
free from perturbation, and so
much awake as to be sensible of
pleasure; a state partaking of
sleep and wakefulness, as the
twilight of night and day.
⁵ —— *our book,*—] Our paper of conditions.

180 THE FIRST PART OF
" And those musicians, that shall play to you
Hang in the air a thousand leagues from hence;
Yet strait they shall be here. Sit, and attend.

Hot. Come, *Kate*, thou art perfect in lying down: come, quick, quick, that I may lay my head in thy lap.

Lady. Go, ye giddy goose.　　　[*The musick plays.*

Hot. Now I perceive the devil understands *Welsh*: and 'tis no marvel, he is so humorous, by'r lady, he's a good musician.

Lady. Then would you be nothing but musical, for you are altogether govern'd by humours. Lie still, ye thief, and hear the lady sing in *Welsh*.

Hot. I had rather hear *Lady*, my brach, howl in *Irish*.

Lady. Would'st have thy head broken?

Hot. No.

Lady. Then be still.

Hot. [7] Neither. 'Tis a woman's fault.

Lady. Now God help thee!

Hot. To the *Welsh* lady's bed.

Lady. What's that?

Hot. Peace, she sings.

　　　　　　　[*Here the Lady sings a* Welsh *song.*
Come, I'll have your song too.

Lady. Not mine in good sooth.

Hot. Not yours, in good sooth! you swear like a comfit-maker's wife; not you, *in good sooth*; and, *as true as I live*; and, *as God shall mend me*; and, *as sure as day:* and givest such sarcenet surety for thy oaths, as if thou never walk'd'st further than *Finsbury*. Swear me, *Kate*, like a lady, as thou art,

---

[6] *And* THOSE *musicians, that shall play to you*
Hang in the air————*Yet*]
The particle *yet* being used here adversatively, must have a particle of concession preceding it.

I read therefore
And THO' TH' *musicians*————
　　　　　WARBURTON.

[7] *Neither. 'Tis a woman's fault.*] I do not plainly see what is a woman's fault.

A good

KING HENRY IV.

A good mouth-filling oath, and leave *infooth*,
And such protest of pepper-ginger-bread,
To [1] velvet-guards, and *Sunday*-citizens.
Come, sing.
  Lady. I will not sing.
  Hot. [2] 'Tis the next way to turn tailor, or be *Robin-red-breast* teacher. If the indentures be drawn, I'll away within these two-hours; and so come in when ye will. [*Exit.*
  Glen. Come, come, lord *Mortimer*, you are as slow, As hot lord *Percy* is on fire to go.
By this our book is drawn: we will but seal,
And then to horse immediately.
  Mort. With all my heart. [*Exeunt.*

SCENE IV.

Changes to the Presence-chamber in Windsor.

Enter King Henry, *Prince of* Wales, *Lords and others.*

  K. Henry. LORDS, give us leave, the Prince of Wales and I
Must have some private conference; but be near,
For we shall presently have need of you.———
 [*Exeunt Lords.*
I know not, whether God will have it so,
For some displeasing service I have done,
That, in his secret doom, out of my blood
He'll breed revengement, and a scourge for me,
But thou dost in thy passages of life
Make me believe that thou art only mark'd

---

[1] *Velvet guards.*] To such as wove their cloaths adorned with reds of velvet, which was, I suppose, the finery of Cockneys.
[2] *'Tis the next way to turn taylor, &c.*] I suppose *Percy* means, that *singing* is a mean quality, and therefore he excuses his lady.
[9] *For some displeasing service*—] *service* for *action*, simply.
 WARBURTON.

THE FIRST PART OF

For the hot vengeance and the rod of heav'n,
To punish my mis-treadings. Tell me else,
Could such inordinate and low desires,
Such poor, such base, such lewd, [1] such mean attempts,
Such barren pleasures, rude society,
As thou art match'd withal and grafted to,
Accompany the greatness of thy blood
And hold their level with thy princely heart?

   P. Henry. So please your Majesty, I would I could
Quit all offences with as clear excuse,
As well, as, I am doubtless, I can purge
My self of many I am charg'd withal.
[2] Yet such extenuation let me beg,
As, in reproof of many tales devis'd,
Which oft the ear of greatness needs must hear,
By smiling pick-thanks and base news-mongers,
I may for some things true wherein my youth
Hath faulty wander'd and irregular,
Find pardon on my true submission.

   K. Henry. Heav'n pardon thee. Yet let me wonder, Harry,
At thy affections, which do hold a wing
Quite from the flight of all thy ancestors.
Thy place in council thou hast rudely lost,
Which by thy younger brother is supply'd;
And art almost an alien to the hearts
Of all the court and princes of my blood.
The hope and expectation of thy time
Is ruin'd, and the soul of ev'ry man
Prophetically does fore-think thy Fall.
Had I so lavish of my presence been,

---

[1] —*such lewd, such mean* AT-TEMPTS,] *Shakespear* certainly wrote ATTAINTS, *i. e.* unlawful actions. WARB.

[2] *Yet such extenuation let me beg,* &c.] The construction is somewhat obscure. Let me beg so much extenuation, that, *upon confutation of many false charges, I may be pardon'd* some that are true. I should read *on reproof* instead of *in reproof,* but concerning *Shakespeare's* particles there is no certainty.

So

KING HENRY IV.

n-hackney'd in the eyes of men,
d cheap to vulgar company,
that did help me to the crown,
kept ³ loyal to poſſeſſion,
ne in reputeleſs baniſhment,
of no mark, nor likelihood.
ſeldom ſeen, I could not ſtir,
a comet, I was wonder'd at,
would tell their children, *this is he*;
ould ſay, *where? which is* Bolingbroke?
n I ſtole all courteſie from heav'n,
myſelf in much humility,
pluck allegiance from men's hearts,
ts and ſalutations from their mouths,
e preſence of the crowned King.
keep my perſon freſh and new,
nce, like a robe pontifical,
, but wonder'd at; and ſo my State,
ut ſumptuous, ſhewed like a feaſt,
by rareneſs, ſuch ſolemnity.
ing King, he ambled up and down
low jeſters, and ⁵ raſh bavin wits,
led, and ſoon burnt; ² 'ſcarded his State;

poſſeſſion.] *True* to thence, by which power is beſt
then *poſſeſſion* of the procured, is called a theft. The
thought is exquiſitely great and
n I ſtole all courteſie beautiful. WARBURTON.
av'n,] This is an al- 5 *Raſh bavin wits.*] *Raſh* is
he ſtory of *Prome-* *heady, thoughtleſs. Bavin* is
who ſtole *fire* from *Bruſhwood*, which, fired, burns
as with *this* he made fiercely, but is ſoon out.
with *that*, Boling- 6 In former copies,
a King. As the ——— CARDED *his State*]
ſuppoſed jealous in *Richard* is here repreſented as
g *reaſon* to them- laying aſide his royalty, and mix-
getting *fire* from ing himſelf with common jeſters.
ch lighted it up in This will lead us to the true read-
was called a theft; ing, which I ſuppoſe is,
er is their preroga- 'SCARDED *his State;*
getting *courteſie* from *i. e.* diſcarded, threw off. WARB.

N 4 Mingled

184 THE FIRST PART OF

Mingled his Royalty with carping fools;
Had his great name profaned with their scorns;
[7] And gave his countenance, against his name,
To laugh at gybing boys, and stand the push
[8] Of every beardless, vain comparative;
Grew a companion to the common streets,
Enfeoff'd himself to popularity.
That, being daily swallow'd by men's eyes,
They surfeited with honey, and began
To loath a taste of sweetness; whereof a little
More than a little is by much too much.
So when he had occasion to be seen,
He was but, as the Cuckow is in *June*,
Heard, not regarded; seen, but with such eyes,
As, sick and blunted with community,
Afford no extraordinary gaze;
Such as is bent on sun-like Majesty,
When it shines seldom in admiring eyes;
But rather drowz'd, and hung their eye-lids down,
Slept in his face, and rendred such aspect
As cloudy men use to their adversaries,
Being with his presence glutted, gorg'd and full.
And in that very line, *Harry*, stand'st thou;
For thou hast lost thy Princely privilege
With vile participation; not an eye,
But is a-weary of thy common sight,
Save mine, which hath desir'd to see thee more;
Which now doth, what I would not have it do,
Make blind itself with foolish tenderness. [*Weeping.*

---

[7] *And gave his countenance, against his name.*] Made his presence injurious to his reputation.

[8] *Of every beardless, vain comparative.*] Of every boy whose vanity incited him to try his wit against the King's.

When *Lewis* XIV. was asked, why, with so much wit, he never attempted raillery, he answered, that he who practised raillery ought to bear it in his turn, and that to stand the butt of raillery was not suitable to the dignity of a King. *Scudery's Conversation.*

P. Henry.

P. Henry. I shall hereafter, my thrice gracious lord,
Be more myself.

K. Henry. For all the world,
As thou art at this hour was *Richard* then,
When I from *France* set foot at *Ravenspurg*;
And ev'n as I was then, is *Percy* now.
Now by my scepter, and my soul to boot,
' He hath more worthy interest to the State,
Than thou, the shadow of succession!
For, of no Right, nor colour like to Right,
He doth fill fields with harness; in the Realm
Turns head against the Lion's armed jaws;
And, being no more in debt to years than thou,
Leads ancient lords and rev'rend bishops on,
To bloody battles, and to bruising arms.
What never dying honour hath he got
Against renowned *Dowglas,* whose high deeds,
Whose hot incursions, and great name in arms,
Holds from all soldiers chief majority,
And military Title capital,
Through all the Kingdoms that acknowledge Christ?
Thrice hath this *Hot-spur, Mars* in swathing cloaths,
This infant warrior, in his enterprises,
Discomfited great *Dowglas,* ta'en him once,
Enlarged him, and made a friend of him,
To fill the mouth of deep defiance up,
And shake the peace and safety of our Throne.
And what say you to this? *Percy, Northumberland,*
Th' Archbishop's Grace of *York, Dowglas,* and *Mortimer,*
Capitulate against us, and are up.
But wherefore do I tell this news to thee?
Why, *Harry,* do I tell thee of my foes,

' *He hath more worthy interest to the state, Than thou, the shadow of succession!*] This is obscure. I believe the meaning is,—*Hot-spur* hath a right to the kingdom more worthy than thou, who hast only the *shadowy right of lineal succession,* while he has real and solid power.

Which

186 THE FIRST PART OF

Which art my near'ſt and * deareſt enemy?
Thou that art like enough through vaſſal fear,
Baſe inclination, and the ſtart of ſpleen,
To fight againſt me under *Percy's* pay,
To dog his heels, and curt'ſie at his frowns,
To ſhow how much thou art degenerate.

P. Henry. Do not think ſo, you ſhall not find it ſo:
And heav'n forgive them, that ſo much have ſway'd
Your Majeſty's good thoughts away from me!
I will redeem all this on *Percy's* head.
And in the cloſing of ſome glorious day,
Be bold to tell you, that I am your ſon.
When I will wear a garment all of blood,
' And ſtain my favours in a bloody maſk,
Which, waſh'd away, ſhall ſcower my ſhame with it.
And that ſhall be the day, when e'er it lights,
That this ſame child of honour and renown,
This gallant *Hot-ſpur*, this all-praiſed Knight,
And your unthought of *Harry*, chance to meet.
For every honour ſitting on his helm,
'Would they were multitudes, and on my head
My ſhames redoubled! for the time will come,
That I ſhall make this northern youth exchange
His glorious deeds for my indignities.
Percy is but my factor, good my lord,
T' engroſs up glorious deeds on my behalf;
And I will call him to ſo ſtrict account,
That he ſhall render every glory up,
Yea, even the ſlighteſt worſhip of his time,
Or I will tear the reck'ning from his heart.
This in the name of heav'n I promiſe here;
The which, if I perform, and do ſurvive,
I do beſeech your Majeſty, may ſalve
The long-grown wounds of my intemperance.

* *Deareſt* is *moſt fatal, moſt* read *favour*, i. e. countenance.
mischievous. WARBURTON
' *And ſtain my* favours *in a*
bloody maſk,] We ſhould

Favours are *features.*

KING HENRY IV. 187

not, the end of life cancels all bonds;
nd I will die an hundred thousand deaths,
e break the smallest parcel of this vow.
K. *Henry.* A hundred thousand Rebels die in this!
ou shalt have Charge, and sovereign Trust herein.

Enter Blunt.

w now, good *Blunt?* thy looks are full of speed.
Blunt. So is the business that I come to speak of.
d *Mortimer* of *Scotland* hath sent word,
at *Dowglas* and the *English* rebels met
' eleventh of this month, at *Shrewsbury:*
mighty and a fearful head they are,
promises be kept on every hand,
ever offer'd foul play in a State.
K. *Henry.* The Earl of *Westmorland* set forth to day,
th him my son, lord *John* of *Lancaster;*
this advertisement is five days old.
Wednesday next, *Harry,* thou shalt set forward:
Thursday, we ourselves will march: our meeting
t *Bridgnorth;* and, *Harry,* you shall march
rough *Glo'stershire:* by which some twelve days
 hence
r general forces at *Bridgnorth* shall meet,
r hands are full of business: let's away,
vantage feeds him fat, while men delay. [*Exeunt.*

SCENE V.

hanges to the Boar's-head Tavern in East-cheap.

Enter Falstaff *and* Bardolph.

l. BARDOLPH, am not I fall'n away vilely, since
this last action? Do I not bate? do I not
indle? Why, my skin hangs about me like an old
y's loose gown; I am wither'd, like an old apple
John.

John. Well, I'll repent, and that suddenly, while I am in some liking; I shall be out of heart shortly, and then I shall have no strength to repent. An I have not forgotten what the inside of a church is made of, I am a pepper-corn, [2] a brewer's horse. The inside of a church!—Company, villainous company hath been the spoil of me.

Bard. Sir *John*, you are so fretful, you cannot live long.

Fal. Why, there is it; come, sing me a bawdy song, to make me merry. I was as virtuously given, as a gentleman need to be; virtuous enough; swore little; diced not above seven times a week; went to a bawdy-house not above once in a quarter of an hour; paid mony that I borrow'd, three or four times; liv'd well, and in good compass; and now I live out of all order, out of all compass.

Bard. Why, you are so fat, Sir *John*, that you must needs be out of all compass, out of all reasonable compass, Sir *John*.

Fal. Do thou amend thy face, and I'll amend my life. Thou art our Admiral thou bearest the lanthorn in the poop, but 'tis in the nose of thee; thou art the knight of the burning lamp [3].

Bard. Why, Sir *John*, my face does you no harm.

Fal. No, I'll be sworn; I make as good use of it, as many a man doth of a death's head, or a *memento mori*. I never see thy face, but I think upon hell-fire, and *Dives* that liv'd in purple; for there he is in his robes, burning, burning.—— If thou wert any way given to virtue, I would swear by thy face; my oath

---

[2] *A* brewer's horse.] I suppose a *brewer's* horse was apt to be lean with hard work.

[3] *The knight of the burning lamp.*] This is a natural picture. Every man who feels in himself the pain of deformity, however, like this merry knight, he may affect to make sport with it among those whom it is his interest to please, is ready to revenge any hint of contempt upon one whom he can use with freedom.

should

KING HENRY IV.

should be, *by this fire*; but thou art altogether given over; and wert indeed, but for the light in thy face, the son of utter darkness. When thou rann'st up *Gadshill* in the night to catch my horse, if I did not think, thou had'st been an *ignis fatuus*, or a ball of wild fire, there's no purchase in mony. O, thou art a perpetual triumph, an everlasting bonfire light; thou hast saved me a thousand marks in links and torches, walking with thee in the night betwixt tavern and tavern; but the sack, that thou hast drunk me, would have bought me lights as * good cheap, as the dearest chandler's in *Europe*. I have maintained that *Salamander* of yours with fire, any time this two and thirty years, heav'n reward me for it!

Bard. 'Sblood, I would, my face were in your belly.

Fal. God-a-mercy! so should I be sure to be heart-burn'd.

Enter Hostess.

How now, dame *Partlet* the hen, have you enquir'd yet who pick'd my pocket?

Host. Why, Sir *John!* what do you think, Sir *John?* do you think, I keep thieves in my house? I have search'd, I have enquired, so has my husband, man by man, boy by boy, servant by servant. The tithe of a hair was never lost in my house before.

Fal. Ye lie, hostess; *Bardolph* was shav'd, and lost many a hair; and I'll be sworn, my pocket was pick'd; go to, you are a woman, go.

Host. Who I? I defie thee; I was never call'd so in mine own house before.

Fal. Go to, I know you well enough.

Host. No, Sir *John :* you do not know me, Sir *John :* I know you, Sir *John*; you owe me mony, Sir *John*,

* *Good cheap.*] Cheap is *market*, and *good cheap* therefore is *a len marché*.

and

setting thy knighthood aside, thou art a knave to call me so.

Fal. Setting thy womanhood aside, thou art a beast to say otherwise.

Host. Say, what beast, thou knave, thou?

Fal. What beast? why, an Otter.

P. Henry. An Otter, Sir *John*, why an Otter?

Fal. Why? she's neither fish nor flesh; a man knows not where to have her.

Host. Thou art an unjust man in saying so: thou, or any man knows where to have me; thou knave, thou!

P. Henry. Thou say'st true, hostess, and he slanders thee most grossly.

Host. So he doth you, my lord, and said this other day, you ow'd him a thousand pound.

P. Henry. Sirrah, do I owe you a thousand pound?

Fal. A thousand pound, *Hal*? a million; thy love is worth a million, thou ow'st me thy love.

Host. Nay, my lord, he call'd you *Jack*, and said, he would cudgel you.

Fal. Did I, *Bardolph*?

Bard. Indeed, Sir *John*, you said so.

Fal. Yea, if he said, my ring was copper.

P. Henry. I say, 'tis copper. Dar'st thou be as good as thy word now?

Fal. Why, *Hal*, thou know'st, as thou art but a man, I dare; but as thou art a Prince, I fear thee, as I fear the roaring of the Lion's whelp.

P. Henry. And why not as the Lion?

Fal. The King himself is to be fear'd as the Lion; dost thou think, I'll fear thee, as I fear thy father? nay, if I do, let my Girdle break!

P. Henry. O, if it should, how would thy guts fall about thy knees! But, Sirrah, there's no room for faith, truth, nor honesty, in this bosom of thine; it is all fill'd up with guts and midriff. Charge an honest woman with picking thy pocket! why, thou whorson, impudent,

KING HENRY IV.

impudent, [9] imboss'd rascal, if there were any thing in thy pocket but tavern-reckonings, *Memorandums* of bawdy-houses, and one poor penny-worth of sugar-candy to make thee long-winded; if thy pocket were enrich'd with any other injuries but these, I am a villain. And yet [1] you will stand to it, you will not pocket up wrongs. Art thou not asham'd?

Fal. Dost thou hear, *Hal?* thou know'st in the state of innocency, *Adam* fell: and what should poor *Jack Falstaff* do, in the days of villainy? Thou seest, I have more flesh than another man, and therefore more frailty.—You confess then, you pickt my pocket?

P. Henry. It appears so by the story.

Fal. Hostess, I forgive thee; go make ready Breakfast. Love thy husband, look to thy servants, and cherish thy guests; thou shalt find me tractable to any honest reason. Thou seest, I am pacify'd still.—Nay, pr'ythee, be gone. [*Exit Hostess.*

Now, *Hal*, to the news at Court? For the robbery, lad, how is that answer'd?

P. Henry. O my sweet beef, I must still be good angel to thee. The mony is paid back again.

Fal. O, I do not like that paying back; 'tis a double labour.

P. Henry. I am good friends with my father, and may do any thing.

Fal. Rob me the exchequer the first thing thou do'st, and do it with unwash'd hands too.

Bard. Do, my Lord.

P. Henry. I have procur'd thee, *Jack*, a Charge of foot.

Fal. I would, it had been of horse. Where shall I

---

[9] *impudent, imboss'd rascal,—*] *imbossed* is *swoln, puffy.*

[1] *—and yet you will stand to it, you will not pocket up wrongs:*] Some part of this merry dialogue seems to have been lost. I suppose *Falstaff*, in pressing the robbery upon his hostess, had declared his resolution *not to pocket up wrongs* or *injuries*, to which the prince alludes.

Vol. IV. O find

194 THE FIRST PART OF

find one, that can steal well? O, for a fine thief, of two and twenty, or thereabout; I am heinously unprovided. Well, God be thank'd for these rebels, they offend none but the virtuous; I laud them, I praise them.

P. Henry. Bardolph,————

Bard. My Lord?

P. Henry. Go bear this letter to lord *John* of *Lancaster*, to my brother *John*. This to my Lord of *Westmorland;* go.—² *Peto,* to horse; for thou and I have thirty miles to ride yet ere dinner-time. *Jack,* meet me to-morrow in the *Temple-Hall* at two o'clock in the afternoon, there shalt thou know thy charge, and there receive mony and order for their furniture.
The Land is burning, *Percy* stands on high;
And either they, or we, must lower lie.

Fal. Rare words! brave world!—Hostess, my breakfast, come.
Oh, I could wish, this tavern were my drum! [*Exeunt*

ACT IV. SCENE I.

Changes to SHREWSBURY.

Enter Hot-spur, Worcester, *and* Dowglas.

HOT-SPUR.

WELL said, my noble *Scot.* If speaking truth,
In this fine age, were not thought flattery,
Such attribution should the *Dowglas* have,
As not a soldier of this season's stamp
Should go so gen'ral current through the World.

---

² *Peto, to horse;* ————] I cannot but think that *Peto* is again put for *Poins*. I suppose the copy had only a P——. We have *Peto* afterwards, not riding with the Prince, but lieutenant to *Falstaff.*

By

KING HENRY IV.

By heav'n, I cannot flatter, I defy
The tongues of foothers, but a braver place
In my heart's love hath no man than yourfelf:
Nay, tafk me to my word; approve me, Lord.

Dowg. Thou art the King of honour;
No man fo potent breathes upon the ground,
But I will beard him———

Hot. Do fo, and 'tis well ———

Enter a Meffenger.

What letters haft thou there?———
I can but thank you.

Meff. Thefe letters come from your father.

Hot. Letters from him? why comes he not himfelf?

Meff. He cannot come, my lord, he's grievous fick.

Hot. Heav'ns! how has he the leifure to be fick
In fuch a juftling time? who leads his Pow'rs?
Under whofe government come they along?

Meff. [3] His letters bear his mind, not I.

Hot. His mind!

Wor. I pr'ythee, tell me, doth he keep his bed?

Meff. He did, my lord, four days ere I fet forth;
And at the time of my departure thence,
He was much fear'd by his phyficians.

Wor. I would, the ftate of time had firft been whole,
Ere he by ficknefs had been vifited;
His health was never better worth than now.

Hot. Sick now? droop now? this ficknefs doth infect
The very life-blood of our enterprife;
'Tis catching hither, even to our Camp.

---

[3] *Meff. His letters bear his mind, not I his mind,*] The line fhould be read and divided thus, *Meff. His letters bear his mind, not I. Hot. His mind!* *Hotfpur* had afked *who leads his powers?* The *Meffenger* anfwers, *His letters bear his mind.* The other replies, *His mind!* As much as to fay, I inquire not about his mind, I want to know where his powers are. This is natural, and perfectly in character. WARBURTON.

O 2 He

He writes me here, that inward ſickneſs——
And that his friends by deputation
Could not ſo ſoon be drawn; nor thought he meet
To lay ſo dangerous and dear a Truſt
⁴ On any ſoul remov'd, but on his own.
Yet doth he give us bold advertiſement,
That with our ſmall conjunction we ſhould on,
To ſee how fortune is diſpos'd to us;
For, as he writes, there is no quailing now,
Becauſe the King is certainly poſſeſt
Of all our purpoſes. What ſay you to it?

Wor. Your father's ſickneſs is a maim to us.

Hot. A perilous gaſh, a very limb lopt off.
And yet, in faith, 'tis not—His preſent want
Seems more than we ſhall find it. Were it good,
To ſet the exact wealth of all our ſtates
All at one Caſt; to ſet ſo rich a Main
On the nice hazard of one doubtful hour?
It were not good; for ⁵ therein ſhould we read
The very bottom, and the ſoul of hope,
The very liſt, the very utmoſt Bound
Of all our fortunes.

Dowg. Faith, and ſo we ſhould;
Where now remains a ſweet reverſion.
We now may boldly ſpend upon the hope
Of what is to come in:
⁶ A comfort of retirement lives in this.

Hot. A rendezvous, a home to fly unto,
If that the Devil and and Miſchance look big

---

⁴ *On any ſoul removed.*] On any *leſs near* to himſelf; on any whoſe intereſt is *remote*.

⁵ —— *therein ſhould we read The very bottom, and the ſoul of hope,*] To read *the bottom and ſoul of hope, and the bound of fortune,* though all the copies and all the editors have received it, ſurely cannot be right. I can think on no other word than *riſque*.
Therein ſhould we riſque The very bottom, &c.
The *liſt* is the *ſelvage*; figuratively, the utmoſt line of circumference, the utmoſt extent.

⁶ *A comfort of retirement.*] A ſupport to which we may have recourſe.

Upon the Maidenhead of our affairs.

Wor. But yet I would your father had been here;
⁷ The quality and hair of our attempt
Brooks no division; it will be thought
By some, that know not why he is away,
That wisdom, loyalty, and meer dislike
Of our proceedings, kept the Earl from hence;
And think, how such an apprehension
May turn the tide of fearful faction,
And breed a kind of question in our cause;
For well you know, ⁸ we of th' offending side
Must keep aloof from strict arbitrement;
And stop all sight-holes, every loop, from whence
The eye of reason may pry in upon us.
This absence of your father draws a curtain,
That shews the ignorant a kind of fear
Before not dreamt upon.

Hot. You strain too far;
I rather of his absence make this use,

---

⁷ *The quality and hair of our attempt.*] The *hair* seems to be *the complexion, the character.* The metaphor appears harsh to us, but, perhaps, was familiar in our authour's time.

⁸ *We of th' offending side.*] All the later editions have this reading; but all the older copies which I have seen, from the first quarto to the edition of *Rowe,* read, *we of the* off'ring *side.* Of this reading the sense is obscure, and therefore the change has been made; but since neither *offering* nor *offending* are words likely to be mistaken, I cannot but suspect that *offering* is right, especially as it is read in the first copy of 1599, which is more correctly printed than any single edition, that I have yet seen, of a play written by *Shakespeare.*

The *offering* side may signify that party, which, acting in opposition to the law, strengthens itself only by *offers*; encreases its numbers only by *promises.* The King can raise an army, and continue it by threats of punishment; but those, whom no man is under any obligation to obey, can gather forces only by *offers* of advantage: and it is truly remarked, that they, whose influence arises from *offers,* must keep danger out of sight.

The *offering side* may mean simply the *assailant,* in opposition to the *defendant,* and it is likewise true of him that *offers* war, or makes an invasion, that his cause ought to be kept clear from all objections.

O 3 'It

THE FIRST PART OF

nds a luſtre, and more great opinion,
arger Dare to our great enterpriſe,
an if the Earl were here; for men muſt think,
we without his help can make a head,
) puſh againſt the Kingdom; with his help,
'e ſhall o'erturn it topſie turvy down.
-Yet all goes well, yet all our joints are whole.

Doug. As heart can think; there is not ſuch a w[or]t
poke of in *Scotland*, as this term of fear.

SCENE II.

Enter Sir Richard Vernon.

Hot. My couſin *Vernon*, welcome, by my ſoul!
Ver. Pray God, my news be worth a welcome, lord
The Earl of *Weſtmorland*, ſev'n thouſand ſtrong,
Is marching hither, with Prince *John* of *Lancaſter.*
Hot. No harm; what more?
Ver. And further, I have learn'd,
The King himſelf in perſon hath ſet forth,
Or hitherwards intended ſpeedily
With ſtrong and mighty preparation.
Hot. He ſhall be welcome too: where is his ſon?
The nimble-footed mad-cap Prince of *Wales*,
And his comrades, that daft the world aſide
And bid it paſs?
Ver. [9] All furniſht, all in arms,

---

[9] *All furniſht, all in arms,*
All plumb'd like Eſtridges, that
with the wind
Baited like Eagles.] To bait
with the wind appears to me an
improper expreſſion. To bait
is in the ſtyle of falconry, to
beat the wing, from the *French*
battre, that is, to flutter in preparation for flight

Beſides, what is the r
of *Eſtridges,* that baited
wind like Eagles; for the
that, in the uſual conſ
muſt relate to *Eſtridges.*
Sir *Thomas Hanmer* r
All plumb'd like Eſtr
with the wind
Baiting *like Eagles.*
By which he has eſcaj

KING HENRY IV. 199

All plum'd like Estridges, that with the wind
Baited like Eagles, having lately bath'd:
Glittering in golden coats like images,
As full of spirit as the month of *May*,
And gorgeous as the Sun at *Midsummer;*
Wanton as youthful goats, wild as young bulls.
¹ I saw young *Harry*, with his beaver on,
² His cuisses on his thighs, gallantly arm'd,
Rise from the ground like feather'd *Mercury;*
And vaulted with such ease into his seat,
As if an Angel dropt down from the clouds,
To turn and wind a fiery *Pegasus*,
³ And witch the world with noble horsemanship.

    Hot. No more, no more; worse than the Sun in
      March,
This praise doth nourish agues; let them come.

---

the difficulty, but has yet left impropriety sufficient to make his reading questionable.
   I read,
    All furnish'd, all in arms,
    All plum'd like Estridges that
      wing the wind
    Baited like Eagles.
This gives a strong image. They were not only plum'd like Estridges, but their plumes fluttered like those of an Estridge on the wing mounting against the wind. A more lively representation of young men ardent for enterprize perhaps no writer has ever given.

   ¹ *I saw young* Harry, *with his beaver* on.] We should read, *beaver* up. It is an impropriety to say *on:* For the beaver is only the visiere of the Helmet, which, let down, covers the face. When the soldier was not upon action he wore it *up*, so that his face might be seen (hence

Vernon says he *saw* young *Harry.)* But when upon action, it was let down to cover and secure the face. Hence in the second part of *Henry* IV it is said,
   Their armed staves in charge,
    their beavers down.
          WARBURTON.
   There is no need of all this note, for *beaver* may be a *helmet;* or the prince, trying his armour, might wear his beaver down.
   ² *His* cuisses *on his thighs,*—] *Cuisses, French,* armour for the thighs.   POPE.
   The reason why his *cuisses* are so particularly mentioned, I conceive to be, that his horsemanship is here praised, and the *cuisses* are that part of armour which most hinders a horseman's activity.
   ³ *And* witch *the world*—] For bewitch, charm.   POPE.

O 4   They

THE FIRST PART OF

They come like Sacrifices in their trim,
And to the fire-ey'd maid of smoaky war,
All hot, and bleeding, will we offer them.
The mailed *Mars* shall on his altar sit
Up to the ears in blood. I am on fire,
To hear this rich reprisal is so nigh,
And yet not ours. Come, let me take my horse,
Who is to bear me, like a thunder bolt,
Against the bosom of the Prince of *Wales*.
Harry to *Harry* shall, hot horse to horse———
Meet, and ne'er part, 'till One drop down a coarse.
Oh, that *Glendower* were come!

Ver. There is more news:
I learn'd in *Worcester*, as I rode along,
He cannot draw his Pow'r this fourteen days.

Doug. That's the worst tidings that I hear of yet.

Wor. Ay, by my faith, that bears a frosty sound.

Hot. What may the King's whole Battle reach unto?

Ver. To thirty thousand.

Hot. Forty let it be;
My father and *Glendower* being both away,
The Pow'r of us may serve so great a day.
Come, let us take a muster speedily;
Dooms-day is near; die all, die merrily.

Doug. Talk not of dying, I am out of fear
Of death, or death's hand, for this one half year.

[*Exeunt.*

---

⁴ *Harry to Harry shall, hot horse to horse,*
Meet, and ne'er part.] This reading I have restored from the first edition. The second edition in 1622, reads,
Harry to Harry shall, not horse to horse,
Meet, and ne'er part.
which has been followed by all the criticks except Sir *Tho.* Hanmer, who, justly remarking the impertinence of the negative, reads,
Harry to Harry shall,
horse to horse
Meet, and ne'er part.
But the unexampled expression of *meeting to*, for *meeting with* or simply *meeting*, is yet left. The ancient reading is surely right.

SCENE

KING HENRY IV.

SCENE III.

Changes to a publick Road, near Coventry.

Enter Falstaff *and* Bardolph.

Fal. Bardolph, get thee before to *Coventry*; fill me a bottle of sack. Our soldiers shall march through; we'll to *Sutton-cold-field* to-night.

Bard. Will you give me mony, captain?

Fal. Lay out, lay out.

Bard. This bottle makes an angel.

Fal. And if it do, take it for thy labour; and if it make twenty, take them all, I'll answer the coynage. Bid my lieutenant * *Peto* meet me at the town's end.

Bard. I will, captain; farewel. [*Exit.*

Fal. If I be not asham'd of my soldiers, I am a [5] souc'd gurnet. I have mis-us'd the King's Press damnably; I have got, in exchange of an hundred and fifty soldiers, three hundred and odd pounds. I press me none but good housholders, yeomens sons; enquire me out contracted batchelors, such as had been ask'd twice on the banes; such a commodity of warm slaves, as had as lieve hear the devil, as a drum; such as fear the report of a culverin, [6] worse than a struck fowl, or a hurt wild duck. I press me none but such

---

* *Lieutenant* Peto.] This passage proves that *Peto* did not go with the prince.

[5] *Souc'd gurnet.*] I believe a *souced gurnet* is a *pickled anchovy.* Much of *Falstaff's* humour consists in comparing himself to somewhat little.

[6] *Worse than a struck fowl, or a hurt wild duck.*] The repetition of the same image disposed Sir *Tho. Hanmer,* and after him Dr. *Warburton,* to read, in opposition to all the copies, a struck *Deer,* which is indeed a proper expression, but not likely to have been corrupted. *Shakespeare,* perhaps, wrote a struck *sorel,* which, being negligently read by a man not skilled in hunter's language, was easily changed to struck *fowl. Sorel* is used in *Love's labour lost* for a young *deer,* and the terms of the chase were, in our authour's time, familiar to the ears of every gentleman.

toasts

THE FIRST PART OF

toasts and butter, with hearts in their bellies no bigger than pins' heads, and they have bought out their services. And now my whole Charge consists of ancients, corporals, lieutenants, gentlemen of companies, slaves as ragged as *Lazarus* in the painted cloth, where the Glutton's dogs licked his sores; and such as indeed were never soldiers, but discarded unjust servingmen, ⁷ younger sons to younger brothers; revolted tapsters, and ostlers-trade-fall'n, the cankers of a calm world and a long peace; ⁸ ten times more dishonourably

---

⁷ *Younger sons to younger brothers;*] *Raleigh*, in his discourse on *war*, uses this very expression for men of desperate fortune and wild adventure. Which borrowed it from the other I know not, but I think the play was printed before the discourse.

⁸ —— *ten times more dishonourably ragged than an old-*fac'd *Antient.*] *Shakespeare* uses this Word so promiscuously, to signify an Ensign or Standard bearer, and also the Colours or Standard borne, that I cannot be at a Certainty for his Allusion here. If the Text be genuine, I think, the Meaning must be; as dishonourably ragged as one that has been an Ensign all his days; that has let Age creep upon him, and never had Merit enough to gain Preferment. Mr. *Warburton*, who understands it in the Second Construction, has suspected the Text, and given the following ingenious Emendation.—— "How " is an old-fac'd *Ancient*, or *En-* " *sign*, dishonourably ragged? " On the contrary, Nothing is " esteemed more honourable " than a ragged Pair of *Colours*. " A very little Alteration will

" restore it to its original Sense, " which contains a Touch of " the strongest and most fine- " turned Satire in the World;
Ten times more dishonourably ragged, than an old Feast Ancient
" *i. e.* the *Colours* used by the " City-Companies in their Feasts " and Processions. For each " Company had one with its pe- " culiar Device, which was u- " sually display'd and borne a- " bout on such Occasions. No- " thing could be more witty " or satirical than this Compa- " rison. For as *Falstaff's* Rag- " gamuffians were reduced to " their tatter'd Condition thro' " their riotous Excesses; so this " old Feast Ancient became torn " and shatter'd, not in any man- " ly Exercise of Arms, but a- " midst the Revels of drunken " Bacchanals." THEOBALD.
Dr. *Warburton's* emendation is very acute and judicious; but I know not whether the licentiousness of our authour's diction may not allow us to suppose that he meant to represent his soldiers, as *more ragged, though less honourably ragged, than an old ancient.*

ragged,

KING HENRY IV.   203

...gged, than an old-feast ancient; and such have I to
...l up the rooms of them that have bought out their
...rvices; that you would think, I had a hundred and
...ty tatter'd Prodigals, lately come from swine-keep-
...g, from eating draff and husks. A mad fellow met
...e on the way, and told me, I had unloaded all the
...bbets, and prest the dead bodies. No eye hath
...en such skare-crows: I'll not march through *Coven-*
...y with them, that's flat. Nay, and the villains
...arch wide betwixt the legs, as if they had * gyves on;
...r, indeed, I had the most of them out of prison.
...here's but a shirt and half in all my company; and
...e half-shirt is two napkins tack'd together, and
...rown over the shoulders like a herald's coat without
...eeves; and the shirt, to say the truth, stoll'n from
...y Host of St. *Albans*; or the red-nos'd Inn keeper
...f *Daintry*. But that's all one, they'll find linen
...nough on every hedge.

Enter Prince Henry, *and* Westmorland.

P. Henry. How now, blown *Jack?* how now, quilt?
Fal. What, *Hal?*—How now, mad wag, what a
...evil dost thou in *Warwickshire?*—My good lord of
...*estmorland*, I cry you mercy; I thought, your Ho-
...our had already been at *Shrewsbury.*
West. 'Faith, Sir *John*, 'tis more than time that I
...ere there, and you too; but my Powers are there
...lready. The King, I can tell you, looks for us all;
...e must away all to night.
Fal. Tut, never fear me, I am as vigilant, as a Cat
...o steal cream.
P. Henry. I think, to steal cream, indeed; for thy
...heft hath already made thee butter. But tell me, *Jack*,
...hose fellows are these that come after?
...*al.* Mine, *Hal*, mine.
...*. Henry.* I did never see such pitiful rascals.

* **gyves on;**] *i. e.* shackles.   POPE.

Fa.

Fal. Tut, tut, ¹ good enough to tofs: food for powder, food for powder; they'll fill a pit, as well as better; tufh, man, mortal men, mortal men.

Weſt. Ay, but, Sir *John*, methinks, they are exceeding poor and bare, too beggarly.

Fal. Faith, for their poverty, I know not where they had that; and for their bareneſs, I am ſure, they never learn'd that of me.

P. Henry. No, I'll be ſworn, unleſs you call three fingers on the ribs, bare. But, firrah, make haſte. *Percy* is already in the field.

Fal. What, is the King encamp'd?

Weſt. He is, Sir *John*; I fear, we ſhall ſtay too long.

Fal. Well,
The latter end of a fray, and beginning of a feaſt,
Fits a dull Fighter, and a keen Gueſt.   [*Exeunt.*

SCENE IV.

Changes to SHREWSBURY.

Enter Hot-ſpur, Worceſter, Dowglas, *and* Vernon.

Hot. WE'll fight him to-night.
Wor. It may not be.
Dowg. You give him then advantage.
Ver. Not a whit.
Hot. Why ſay you ſo? looks he not for ſupply?
Ver. So do we.
Hot. He is certain; ours is doubtful.
Wor. Good couſin, be advis'd; ſtir not to night.
Ver. Do not, my lord.
Dowg. You do not counſel well;
You ſpeak it out of fear, and from cold heart.
Ver. Do me no ſlander, *Dowglas*; by my life,

---

¹ *Good enough to toſs.*] That is, to toſs upon a pike.

And

And I dare well maintain it with my life,
If well-respected honour bid me on,
I hold as little counsel with weak fear,
As you, my lord, or any *Scot* that lives.
Let it be seen to-morrow in the battle,
Which of us fears.

Dowg. Yea, or to-night.

Ver. Content.

Hot. To-night, say I.

Ver. Come, come, it may not be: I wonder much,
Being men of [a] such great Leading as you are,
That you foresee not what impediments
Drag back our expedition; certain horse
Of my cousin *Vernon's* are not yet come up;
Your uncle *Worcester's* horse came but to-day,
And now their pride and mettle is asleep,
Their courage with hard labour tame and dull,
That not a horse is half half of himself.

Hot. So are the horses of the enemy,
In gen'ral, journey-bated, and brought low;
The better part of ours are full of Rest.

Wor. The number of the King's exceedeth ours:
For God's sake, cousin, stay till all come in.

[*The trumpets sound a parley.*

SCENE V.

Enter Sir Walter Blunt.

Blunt. I come with gracious offers from the King,
If you vouchsafe me hearing, and respect.

Hot. Welcome, Sir *Walter Blunt:* and would to God,
You were of our determination;
Some of us love you well; and ev'n those some
Envy your great deservings, and good name,

[a] *Such great leading*] Such *Conduct*, such experience in martial business.

Be-

Becaufe you are not of our quality;
But ftand againft us like an enemy.

Blunt. And heav'n defend, but ftill I fhould ftand fo,
So long as out of limit, and true rule,
You ftand againft anointed Majefty!
But, to my Charge—The King hath fent to know
The nature of your griefs, and whereupon
You conjure from the breaft of civil peace
Such bold hoftility, teaching his duteous Land
Audacious cruelty. If that the King
Have any way your good deferts forgot,
Which he confeffeth to be manifold,
He bids you name your griefs, and with all fpeed
You fhall have your defires, with intereft,
And pardon abfolute for yourfelf, and thefe,
Herein mif-led by your fuggeftion.

Hot. The King is kind, and well we know, the King
Knows at what time to promife, when to pay.
My father and my uncle, and myfelf,
Did give him that fame Royalty he wears;
And when he was not fix and twenty ftrong,
Sick in the world's regard, wretched and low,
A poor unminded Out-law, fneaking home,
My father gave him welcome to the fhore;
And when he heard him fwear, and vow to God,
He came to be but Duke of *Lancafter*,
To fue his livery and beg his peace,
With tears of innocence and terms of zeal,
My father, in kind heart and pity mov'd,
Swore him affiftance, and perform'd it too.
Now, when the Lords and Barons of the Realm
Perceiv'd, *Northumberland* did lean to him,
They, more and lefs, came in with cap and knee,
Met him in boroughs, cities, villages,
Attended him on bridges ftood in lanes,
Laid gifts before him, proffer'd him their oaths,
Gave him their heirs, as pages following him,

Even

KING HENRY IV.

at the heels, in golden multitudes.
esently, as Greatness knows itself,
me a little higher than his vow
to my father, while his blood was poor,
n the naked shore at *Ravenspurg*.
ow, forsooth, takes on him to reform
certain Edicts, and some strait Decrees,
lay too heavy on the Common-wealth;
out upon abuses, seems to weep
his Country's wrongs; and by this face,
eeming brow of justice, did he win
earts of all that he did angle for;
eded further, cut me off the heads
l the Fav'rites that the absent King
putation left behind him here,
he was personal in the *Irish* war.
nt. I came not to hear this.
. Then, to the point ———
rt time after, he depos'd the King,
after That depriv'd him of his life,
in the neck of that, * task'd the whole State.
ake that worse, suffer'd his kinsman *March*,
is, if every Owner were right plac'd,
l his King, to be incag'd in *Wales*,
without ransom to lie forfeited;
ac'd me in my happy Victories,
it to entrap me by intelligence,
my uncle from the Council-board,
ge dismiss'd my father from the Court,
oath on oath, committed wrong on wrong,
n conclusion drove us to seek out
head of safety; and withal to pry
is Title too, the which we find
direct for long continuance.

this whole speech he al- | suppose it should be, *task'd the*
gain to some passages in | *whole state*.
the second. | + *This head of safety*.] This *army*
sk'd *the whole State*.] I | from which I hope for protection.
 | *Blunt*.

Blunt. Shall I return this anſwer to the King?

Hot. Not ſo, Sir *Walter*; we'll withdraw awhile.
—Go to the King, and let there be impawn'd
Some ſurety for a ſafe return again;
And in the morning early ſhall my uncle
Bring him our purpoſes. And ſo farewel.

Blunt. I would, you would accept of grace and love!

Hot. It may be, ſo we ſhall.

Blunt. Pray heav'n, you do! [*Exeunt.*

SCENE VI.

Changes to the Archbiſhop of York's *Palace.*

Enter the Archbiſhop of York, *and Sir* Michaell.

York. HIE, good Sir *Michaell*, bear this [5] ſealed brief
With winged haſte to the Lord Mareſhal;
This to my couſin *Scroop*, and all the reſt
To whom they are directed. If you knew
How much they do import, you wou'd make haſte.

Sir *Mich.* My lord, I gueſs their tenour.

York. Like enough.
To-morrow, good Sir *Michaell*, is a day,
Wherein the fortune of ten thouſand men
Muſt bide the touch; for, Sir, at *Shrewſbury*,
As I am truly giv'n to underſtand,
The King, with mighty and quick-raiſed power,
Meets with lord *Harry;* and, I fear, Sir *Michaell,*
What with the ſickneſs of *Northumberland,*
Whoſe pow'r was * in the firſt proportion,
And what with *Owen Glendower's* abſence thence,
Who with them was [6] a rated ſinew too,

---

[5] *Sealed brief.*] A brief is ſimply a *letter.*

* *In the firſt proportion*] Whoſe quota was larger than that of any other man in the confederacy.

[6] — *a rated ſinew too,*] So the firſt edition, *i. e.* accounted a ſtrong aid.   POPE.

A *ſtrength* on which we reckoned; a *help* of which we made account.

And

KING HENRY IV.

comes not in, o'er-rul'd by prophecies.
, the pow'r of *Percy* is too weak,
age an inftant tryal with the King.
Mich. Why, my good lord, there's *Dowglas*, and
lord *Mortimer.*
rk. No, *Mortimer* is not there.
Mich. But there is *Mordake*, *Vernon*, *Harry Percy*,
there's my lord of *Worcefter*, and a head
allant warriors, noble gentlemen.
rk. And fo there is; but yet the King hath drawn
fpecial head of all the Land together,
Prince of *Wales*, lord *John* of *Lancafter*,
noble *Weftmorland*, and warlike *Blunt*;
many more corrivals, and dear men
ftimation and command in arms.
Mich. Doubt not, my lord, they fhall be well
oppos'd.
rk. I hope no lefs; yet, needful 'tis to fear.
to prevent the worft, Sir *Michaell*, fpeed;
f lord *Percy* thrive not, ere the King
ifs his Power, he means to vifit us;
he hath heard of our Confederacy,
'tis but wifdom to make ftrong againft him;
efore make hafte, I muft go write again
ther friends; and fo farewel, Sir *Michaell*. [*Exeunt.*

THE FIRST PART OF

⁷ACT V. SCENE I.

The Camp of SHREWSBURY.

Enter King Henry, *Prince of* Wales, *Lord* John *of* Lancaster, *Earl of* Westmorland, *Sir* Walter Blunt, *and* Falstaff.

K. HENRY.

HOW bloodily the Sun begins to peer
  Above yon busky hill! the day looks pale
At his distemperature.
 P. Henry. The southern wind
Doth play the trumpet ⁸ to his purposes,
And, by his hollow whistling in the leaves,
Foretels a tempest, and a blust'ring day.
 K. Henry. Then with the losers let it sympathize,
For nothing can seem foul to those that win.
      [*The Trumpet sounds.*

Enter Worcester, *and Sir* Richard Vernon.

 K. Henry. How now, my lord of *Wor'ster?* 'tis not well
That you and I should meet upon such terms
As now we meet. You have deceiv'd our Trust,
And made us doff our easie robes of peace,
To crush our old limbs in ungentle steel;

---

⁷ *Act* V.] It seems proper to be remarked, that in the editions printed while the authour lived, this play is not broken into acts. The division which was made by the players in the first folio seems commodious enough; but, being without authority, may be changed by any editor who thinks himself able to make a better.

⁸ *To his purposes.*] That is, to *the sun's,* to that which the sun portends by his unusual appearance.

This

KING HENRY IV.

...is is not well, my lord, this is not well.
...hat say you to't? will you again unknit
...is churlish knot of all-abhorred war,
...d move in that obedient Orb again,
...here you did give a fair and natural light,
...d be no more an exhal'd meteor,
...prodigy of fear, and a portent
...broached mischief, to the unborn times?
Wor. Hear me, my Liege.
...mine own part, I could be well content
...entertain the lag end of my life
...th quiet hours, for I do protest,
...ave not sought the day of this dislike.
K. Henry. You have not fought it, Sir? how comes it then?
Fal. Rebellion lay in his way, and he found it.
P. Henry. Peace, Chewet, peace.
Wor. It pleas'd your Majesty, to turn your looks
...favour from myself, and all our House,
...d yet I must remember you, my lord,
...e were the first and dearest of your friends;

Fal. Rebellion lay in his way, be found it.
Prince. Peace, Chevet, peace.] ...is, I take to be an arbitrary ...inement of Mr. *Pope's*: nor ...l easily agree, that *Chevet* it ...*kspeare's* Word here. Why ...uld Prince *Henry* call *Falstaff* ...fter, for interposing in the ...coarse betwixt the King and ...*rcester?* With Submission, he ...not take him up here for his ...easonable Size, but for his ill- ...'d and unseasonable Chatter-
  I therefore have preserv'd ...Reading of the old Books. *Chewet*, or *Chuet*, is a noisy ...tering Bird, a *Pie*. This ...es a proper Reproach to *Fal-* *staff* for his medling and impertinent Jest. And besides, if the Poet had intended that the Prince should sleer at *Falstaff*, on Account of his Corpulency, I doubt not, but he would have called him *Bolster* in plain *English*, and not have wrapp'd up the Abuse in the *French* Word *Chevet*. In another Passage of this Play, the Prince honestly calls him *Quilt?* As to Prince *Henry*, his Stock in this Language was so small, that when he comes to be King, he hammers out one small Sentence of it to Princess *Catharine*, and tells her, *It is as easy for him to conquer the Kingdom as to speak so much more* French. THEOBALD.

P 2 For

THE FIRST PART OF

For you, [1] my staff of office I did break
In *Richard's* time, and posted day and night
To meet you on the way, and kiss your hand;
When yet you were in place and in account
Nothing so strong and fortunate, as I:
It was myself, my brother, and his son,
That brought you home, and boldly did out-dare
The dangers of the time. You swore to us,
And you did swear that Oath at *Doncaster*,
That you did nothing purpose 'gainst the State,
Nor claim no further than your new-fall'n Right;
The Seat of *Gaunt*, Dukedom of *Lancaster*.
To this, we sware our aid; but in short space
It rain'd down fortune show'ring on your head,
And such a flood of greatness fell on you,
What with our help, what with the absent King,
What with the injuries of a wanton time,
The seeming suff'rances that you had borne,
And the contrarious winds that held the King
So long in the unlucky *Irish* wars,
That all in *England* did repute him dead;
And from this swarm of fair advantages
You took occasion to be quickly woo'd,
To gripe the gen'ral Sway into your hand;
Forgot your oath to us at *Doncaster*,
And being fed by us, you us'd us so,
As that ungentle gull, the Cuckow's bird, [2]
Useth the Sparrow, did oppress our nest,
Grew by our feeding to so great a bulk,
That ev'n our love durst not come near your sight
For fear of swallowing; but with nimble wing
We were inforc'd for safety's sake to fly
Out of your sight, and raise this present head,

---

[1] *My staff of office.*] See *Richard the second.*

[2] *As that ungentle gull, the cuckow's bird.*] The cuckow's chicken, who, being hatched and fed by the sparrow, in whose nest the cuckow's egg was laid, grows in time able to devour her nurse.

Whereby

hereby [3] we stand oppofed by fuch means
you yourfelf have forg'd againft yourfelf,
unkind ufage, dangerous countenance,
 d violation of all faith and troth,
 orn to us in your younger enterprize.
K. *Henry.* Thefe things, indeed, you have articulated,
 oclaim'd at market-croffes, read in churches.
  face the garment of Rebellion
ith fome fine colour, that may pleafe the eye
f fickle Changelings and poor Difcontents;
 hich gape, and rub the elbow at the news
f hurly-burly innovation.
nd never yet did Infurrection want
 ich water-colours, to impaint his caufe,
or moody beggars, ftarving for a time
f pell-mell havock and confufion.

P. *Henry.* In both our armies there is many a foul
 iall pay full dearly for this bold encounter,
  once they join in tryal. Tell your Nephew,
he Prince of *Wales* doth join with all the world
 praife of *Henry Percy.* By my hopes,
his prefent enterprize fet'off his head,
do not think a braver gentleman,
More active-valiant, or more valiant-young,
 lore daring, or more bold, is now alive,
 o grace this latter age with noble deed.
or my part, I may fpeak it to my fhame,
 have a truant been to Chivalry,
 ind fo, I hear, he doth account me too.
 et this before my father's Majefty——
 am content that he fhall take the odds
)f his great Name and Eftimation,
 ind will, to fave the blood on either fide,
 ry fortune with him, in a fingle fight.

[3] *We ſtand oppoſed,* &c.] We mer reads, more *valued* young.
 nd in oppofition to you.   I think the prefent gingle has
4 *More active-valiant, or more* more of *Shakeſpeare.*
 valiant-young.] Sir *T. Han-*

K. *Henry.*

K. *Henry.* And, Prince of *Wales*, so dare we venture thee,
Albeit, Considerations infinite
Do make against it. No, good *Wor'ster*, no,
We love our People well; even those we love,
That are misled upon your Cousin's part;
And, will they take the offer of our Grace,
Both he, and they, and you, yea, every man
Shall be my friend again, and I'll be his.
So tell your Cousin, and return me word
What he will do. But if he will not yield,
Rebuke and dread Correction wait on us,
And they shall do their office. So, be gone;
We will not now be troubled with Reply;
We offer fair, take it advisedly.
[*Exit* Worcester, *with* Vernon.

P. *Henry.* It will not be accepted, on my life.
The *Dowglas* and the *Hotspur* both together
Are confident against the world in arms.

K. *Henry.* Hence, therefore, every Leader to his Charge.
For on their answer we will set on them.
And God befriend us, as our cause is just! [*Exeunt.*

SCENE II.

Manent Prince Henry *and* Falstaff.

Fal. Hal, if thou see me down in the battle, and bestride me, so; 'tis a point of friendship.

P. *Henry.* Nothing but a Colossus can do thee that friendship. Say thy prayers, and farewel.

Fal. I would it were bed-time, *Hal*, and all well.

P. *Henry.* Why, thou owest heav'n a death.
[*Exit P.* Henry [*].

Fal. 'Tis not due yet: I would be loth to pay him before his day. What need I be so forward with him that calls not on me? Well, 'tis no matter, honour

[*] This *exit* is remarked by Mr. *Upton.*

pricks

KING HENRY IV. 215

ie on; but how if honour prick me off, when
on? how then? Can honour set to a leg? no:
'm? no: or take away the grief of a wound?
our hath no skill in surgery then? no. What
r? a word. What is that word honour? Air;
Reckoning.—Who hath it? he that dy'd a
ay. Doth he feel it? no. Doth he hear it? no.
nsible then? yea, to the dead; but will it not
1 the living? no; why? Detraction will not
. Therefore, I'll none of it; ' honour is a
itcheon, and so ends my catechism. [*Exit.*

SCENE III.

Changes to Percy's *Camp.*

ter Worcester, *and Sir* Richard Vernon.

), No, my nephew must not know, Sir
  Richard,
eral kind offer of the King.
Twere best, he did.
Then we are all undone.
: possible, it cannot be,
ng should keep his word in loving us;
  suspect us still, and find a time
ish this offence in other faults.
ion, all our lives, shall be stuck full of eyes;
son is but trusted like a Fox,
:'er so tame, so cherish'd, and lock'd up,

r *is a* meer scutcheon,] processions. And by *meer scutcheon*
:ry fine. The reward is insinuated, that, whether alive
actions formerly was or dead, honour was but a name.
honourable bearing in   WARBURTON.
1 of arms bestow'd upon   ' *Suspicion, all our lives, shall*
   But *Falstaff* having   *be stuck full of eyes.*] The
honour often came not same image of *suspicion* is exhi-
death, he calls it very bited in a *Latin* tragedy, called
scutcheon, which is the *Roxana*, written about the same
:raldry borne in funeral time by Dr. *William Alabaster*.

P 4   Will

Will have a wild trick of his anceſtors.
Look how we can, or ſad, or merrily,
Interpretation will miſquote our looks;
And we ſhall feed like Oxen at a ſtall,
The better cheriſh'd, ſtill the nearer death.
My nephew's treſpaſs may be well forgot,
It hath th' excuſe of youth and heat of blood;
And [7] an adopted name of privilege,
A hair-brain'd *Hot-ſpur*, govern'd by a Spleen:
All his Offences live upon my head,
And on his father's; we did train him on;
And his corruption, being ta'en from us,
We as the ſpring of all, ſhall pay for all.
Therefore, good couſin, let not *Harry* know,
In any caſe the offer of the King.

Ver. Deliver what you will, I'll ſay, 'tis ſo.
Here comes your couſin.

SCENE IV.

Enter Hot-ſpur *and* Dowglas.

Hot. My uncle is return'd.
—Deliver up my lord of *Weſtmorland*.
—Uncle, what news?
Wor. The King will bid you battle preſently.
Dowg. Defy him by the lord of *Weſtmorland*.
Hot. Lord *Dowglas*, go you then and tell him ſo.
Dowg. Marry, I ſhall; and very willingly.
[*Exit* Dowgl:
Wor. There is no ſeeming mercy in the King.
Hot. Did you beg any? God forbid!
Wor. I told him gently of our grievances,
Of his oath-breaking; which he mended thus,
By now forſwearing that he is forſworn.

---

[7] *An adopted name of privilege,*   name of *Hot-ſpur* will privile
A hair brain'd Hot-ſpur.] The   him from cenſure.

He calls us rebels, traitors, and will scourge
With haughty arms this hateful name in us.

Enter Dowglas.

Dowg. Arm, gentlemen, to arms; for I have thrown
A brave defiance in King *Henry's* teeth,
⁸ And *Westmorland*, that was ingag'd, did bear it;
Which cannot chuse but bring him quickly on.

Wor. The Prince of *Wales* stept forth before the King,
And, Nephew, challeng'd you to single fight.

Hot. O, would the quarrel lay upon our heads,
And that no man might draw short breath to day,
But I and *Harry Monmouth!* Tell me, tell me,
How shew'd his talking? seem'd it in contempt?

Ver. No, by my soul; I never in my life
Did hear a challenge urg'd more modestly,
Unless a brother should a brother dare,
To gentle exercise and proof of arms.
He gave you all the duties of a man,
Trim'd up your praises with a princely tongue,
Spoke your deservings like a chronicle,
Making you ever better than his Praise:
⁹ By still dispraising Praise, valu'd with You.
And, which became him like a Prince indeed,

---

⁸ *And* Westmorland, *that was ingag'd.*] *Engag'd* is, delivered as an hostage. A few lines before, upon the return of *Worcester*, he orders *Westmorland* to be dismissed.

⁹ *By still dispraising Praise, valued with You*] This foolish line is indeed in the Folio of 1623, but it is evidently the players' nonsense. WARB.
This line is not only in the first folio, but in all the editions before it that I have seen. Why it should be censured as nonsense I know not. To vilify praise, compared or *valued* with merit superiour to praise, is no harsh expression. There is another objection to be made. Prince *Henry*, in his challenge of *Percy*, had indeed commended him, but with no such hyperboles as might represent him above praise, and there seems to be no reason why *Vernon* should magnify the Prince's candour beyond the truth. Did then *Shakespeare* forget the foregoing scene? or are some lines lost from the prince's speech?

He

THE FIRST PART OF

[1] He made a blushing cital of himself,
And chid his truant youth with such a grace,
As if he master'd there a double spirit,
Of teaching, and of learning, instantly.
There did he pause; but let me tell the world,
If he out-live the envy of this day,
England did never owe so sweet a hope,
So much misconstrued in his wantonness.

Hot. Cousin, I think, thou art enamoured
Upon his follies; never did I hear
[2] Of any Prince, so wild, at liberty.
But be he as he will, yet once ere night,
I will embrace him with a soldier's arm,
That he shall shrink under my courtesie.
Arm, arm with speed. And fellows, soldiers, friends,
Better consider what you have to do,
Than I, that have not well the gift of tongue,
Can lift your blood up with persuasion.

SCENE V.

Enter a Messenger.

Mess. My lord, here are letters for you.
Hot. I cannot read them now.
O Gentlemen, the time of life is short,
To spend that shortness basely were too long,
Tho' life did ride upon a dial's point,
Still ending at th' arrival of an hour.
And if we live, we live to tread on Kings;
If die; brave death, when Princes die with us!
Now, for our consciences, the arms are fair,
When the intent for bearing them is just.

---

[1] *He made a blushing cital of himself,*] *Cital* for taxation. POPE.

[2] *Of any Prince, so wild, at liberty.*] Of any prince that played such pranks, and was not confined as a madman.

KING HENRY IV.

Enter another Messenger.

Mess. My lord, prepare, the King comes on apace.
Hot. I thank him, that he cuts me from my tale,
 I profess not talking; only this,
 each man do his best. And here draw I
 sword, whose temper I intend to stain
 th the best blood that I can meet withal,
 the adventure of this perilous day.
 ow, *Esperanza! Percy!* and set on;
 nd all the lofty Instruments of war,
 d by that musick let us all embrace,
 r, heav'n to earth, some of us never shall
 cond time do such a courtesie.
[*They embrace, then exeunt. The Trumpets sound.*

SCENE VI.

King entereth with his power: Alarm to the Battle. Then enter Dowglas, *and Sir* Walter Blunt.

unt. What is thy name, that thus in battle cros-
 sest me?
 t honour dost thou seek upon my head?
wg. Know then, my name is *Dowglas,*
 I do haunt thee in the battle thus,
 use some tell me that thou art a King.
unt. They tell me true.
wg. The lord of *Stafford* dear to day hath bought
 likeness; for instead of thee, King *Harry,*
 sword hath ended him; so shall it thee,
 fs thou yield thee as my prisoner.
unt. I was not born to yield, thou haughty *Scot,*

---

low, Esperanza!—] This
e word of battle on *Percy's*
See *Hall's* Chronicle, fo-
Pope.

⁴ *For (heav'n to earth)*—]
i. e. one might wager heaven to
earth.   Warburton.

And

And thou shalt find a King that will revenge
Lord *Stafford's* death.

Fight, Blunt *is slain, then enter* Hot-spur.

Hot. O *Dowglas,* hadst thou fought at *Holmedon* thus,
I never had triumphed o'er a *Scot.*
Dowg. All's done, all's won, here breathless lies the
    King.
Hot. Where?
Dowg. Here.
Hot. This, *Dowglas?* no. I know his face full well;
A gallant Knight he was, his name was *Blunt,*
Semblably furnish'd like the King himself.
Dowg. Ah! fool go with thy soul, whither it goes!
A borrow'd title hast thou bought too dear.
Why didst thou tell me that thou wert a King?
Hot. The King hath many marching in his coats.
Dowg. Now by my sword, I will kill all his coats;
I'll murther all his wardrobe piece by piece,
Until I meet the King.
Hot. Up and away,
Our soldier stand full fairly for the day.   [*Exeunt.*

SCENE VII.

Alarm, enter Falstaff *solus.*

Fal. Though I could 'scape [5] shot free at *London,* I
fear the shot here, here's no scoring, but upon the pate.
Soft, who art thou? Sir *Walter Blunt?* there's honour
for you; [6] here's no vanity!—I am as hot as moulten
    lead,

---

[5] *Shot free at* London.] A play upon *shot,* as it means the part of a reckoning, and a missive weapon discharged from artillery.

[6] *here's no vanity*] In our author's time the *negative,* in common speech, was used to design, ironically, the excess of a thing. Thus *Ben Johnson,* in *Every Man in his Humour,* says, O HERE'S NO FOPPERY! 'Death, *I can endure the stocks better.*
    Mem-

KING HENRY IV.

d, and as heavy too; heav'n keep lead out of me, I
ed no more weight than mine own bowels!—I have
my rag-o-muffians where they are pepper'd, there's
t three of my hundred and fifty left alive; and they
: for the town's end, to beg during life. But who
nes here?

Enter Prince Henry.

P. Henry. What, stand'st thou idle here? lend me
thy sword;
any a noble man lies stark and stiff
nder the hoofs of vaunting enemies;
hose deaths are unreveng'd. Lend me thy sword.
Fal. O *Hal,* I pr'ythee, give me leave to breathe a
nile. ' Turk *Gregory* never did such deeds in arms,
I have done this day. ⁸ I have paid *Percy,* I have
ade him sure.

P. Henry. He is, indeed, and living to kill thee:
pr'ythee, lend me thy sword.

eaning, as the passage shews, at the *foppery* was excessive. nd so in many other places. it the *Oxford Editor,* not appre-nding this, has alter'd it to, *ere's vanity!* WARBURTON.
I am in doubt whether this terpretation, though ingenious id well supported, is true. 'he words may mean, here is :al honour, *no vanity,* or *no pty appearance.*
⁷ Turk Gregory *never did ich deeds in arms,*] Meaning *Iregory* the seventh, called *Hil-ebrand.* This furious frier sur-nounted almost invincible obsta-les to deprive the emperor of iis right of investiture of bishops, vhich his predecessors had long ittempted in vain. *Fox,* in his history, had made this *Gregory* so odious, that I don't doubt but the good protestants of that time were well pleased to hear him thus characterised, as uniting the attributes of their two great ene-mies, the *Turk* and *Pope,* in one.
WARBURTON.
⁸ *I have paid* Percy, *I have made him sure.*
P. Henry. *He is, indeed, and,* &c.] The Prince's Answer, which is apparently connected with *Fal-staff's* last words, does not co-here so well as if the knight had said,
I have made him sure; Percy's safe enough.
Perhaps a word or two like these may be lost.

Fal.

THE FIRST PART OF

Fal. Nay, *Hal*, if *Percy* be alive, thou get'ſt not my ſword, but take my piſtol, if thou wilt.

P. Henry. Give it me. What, is it in the caſe?

Fal. Ay, *Hal*, 'tis hot. There's that will ſack a city.

[*The Prince draws it out, and finds it a bottle of ſack.*

P. Henry. What, is it a time to jeſt and dally now?

[*Throws it at him, and Exit.*

Fal. ⁹ If *Percy* be alive, I'll pierce him. If he do come in my way, ſo; if he do not, if I come in his, willingly, let him make a * carbonado of me. I like not ſuch grinning honour as Sir *Walter* hath; give me life, which if I can ſave, ſo; if not, honour comes unlook'd for, and there's an end. [*Exit.*

SCENE VIII.

Alarm, Excurſions. Enter the King, the Prince, Lord John of Lancaſter, and the Earl of Weſtmoreland.

K. Henry. I pr'ythee, *Harry*, withdraw thyſelf, thou bleedeſt too much. Lord *John* of *Lancaſter*, go go you with him.

Lan. Not I, my lord, unleſs I did bleed too.

P. Henry. I do beſeech your Majeſty make up, Leſt your retirement do amaze your friends.

K. Henry. I will do ſo.
My lord of *Weſtmorland*, lead him to his Tent.

Weſt. Come, my lord, I'll lead you to your Tent.

⁹ *If* Percy *be alive*, I'll *pierce him*;] Certainly, he'll *pierce him*, i. e. Prince *Henry* will, who is juſt gone out to ſeek him. Beſides, *I'll pierce* him, contradicts the whole turn and humour of the ſpeech. WARBURTON.

I rather take the conceit to be this. To *pierce a veſſel* is to *tap* it. *Falſtaff* takes up his bottle which the Prince had toſſed at his head, and being about to animate himſelf with a draught, cries, if *Percy be alive I'll pierce him*, and ſo draws the cork. I do not propoſe this with much confidence.

* A *carbonado* is a piece of meat cut croſwiſe for the gridiron.

P. Henry.

P. Henry. Lead me, my lord? I do not need your help;
And heav'n forbid, a shallow scratch should drive
The Prince of *Wales* from such a field as this,
Where stain'd Nobility lies trodden on,
And Rebels arms triumph in massacres!

Lan. We breathe too long; come, cousin *Westmorland,*
Our duty this way lies; for heav'ns sake, come.

P. Henry. By heav'n, thou hast deceiv'd me, *Lancaster,*
I did not think thee lord of such a spirit;
Before, I lov'd thee as a brother, *John*;
But now, I do respect thee as my soul.

K. Henry. I saw him hold Lord *Percy* at the point,
With lustier maintenance than I did look for
Of such an ungrown warrior.

P. Henry. Oh, this boy
Lends mettle to us all. [*Exeunt.*

Manet King Henry. *Enter* Dowglas.

Dowg. Another King? they grow, like *Hydra's* heads.
I am the *Dowglas,* fatal to all those
That wear those colours on them. What art thou,
That conterfeit'st the person of a King?

K. Henry. The King himself, who, *Dowglas,* grieves at heart,
So many of his shadows thou hast met,
And not the very King. I have two boys
Seek *Percy* and thyself about the field;
But seeing thou fall'st on me so luckily,
I will assay thee; so defend thyself.

Dowg. I fear, thou art another counterfeit,
And yet, in faith, thou bear'st thee like a king;
But mine, I'm sure, thou art, whoe'er thou be,
And thus I win thee.
[*They fight, the King being in danger.*
Enter

THE FIRST PART OF

Enter Prince Henry.

P. Henry. Hold up thy head, vile *Scot*, or thou art like
Never to hold it up again; the Spirits
Of *Sherley, Stafford, Blunt*, are in my arms.
It is the Prince of *Wales* that threatens thee,
Who never promiseth, but means to pay.
[*They fight*, Dowglas *flyeth.*
Chearly, my lord; how fares your Grace?
Sir *Nicholas Gawsey* hath for succour sent,
And so hath *Clifton*; I'll to *Clifton* strait.

K. Henry. Stay, and breathe awhile;
Thou hast redeem'd my lost opinion,
And shew'd, thou mak'st some tender of my life,
In this fair rescue thou hast brought to me.

P. Henry. O heav'n, they did me too much injury,
That ever said, I hearken'd for your death.
If it were so, I might have let alone
Th' insulting hand of *Dowglas* over you;
Which would have been as speedy in your end,
As all the pois'nous potions in the world,
And sav'd the treach'rous labour of your son.

K. Henry. Make up to *Clifton*, I'll to Sir *Nicholas Gawsey*. [*Exit.*

SCENE IX.

Enter Hotspur.

Hot. If I mistake not, thou art *Harry Monmouth.*
P. Henry. Thou speak'st as if I would deny my name.
Hot. My name is *Harry Percy.*
P. Henry. Then I see
A very valiant Rebel of that name.
I am the Prince of *Wales*: and think not, *Percy*,

re with me in Glory any more.
tars keep not their motion in one sphere;
n one *England* brook a double Reign,
rry *Percy* and the Prince of *Wales*.
 Nor shall it, *Harry*, for the hour is come
l the one of us; and would to heav'n,
ime in arms were now as great as mine!
'enry. I'll make it greater, ere I part from thee;
l the budding honours on thy crest
p, to make a garland for my head.
 I can no longer brook thy vanities. [*Fight.*

Enter Falstaff.

 Well said, *Hal*; to it, *Hal.*—Nay, you shall
boy's play here, I can tell you.

)owglas, *he fights with* Falstaff, *who falls down
if he were dead. The Prince kills* Percy.

 O, *Harry*, thou hast robb'd me of my youth.
r brook the loss of brittle life,
 those proud titles thou hast won of me,
vound my thoughts, worse than thy sword my
 flesh;
)ught's the slave of life, and life time's fool,
ne, that takes survey of all the world,
ave a stop. O, I could prophesie,
it the earthy and cold hand of death,
n my tongue. No, *Percy*, thou art dust,
od for ——— [*Dies.*

---

e *proud Titles thou hast* | *wounds his thoughts*; but *thought*,
t *of me*; | being *dependent on life*, must cease
wound my thoughts ——— | with it, and will soon be at an
bought's the flave of life, | end. *Life*, on which *thought*
life time's fool; | depends, is itself of no great va-
'ime ——— *must have a* | lue, being the *fool* and sport of
.] *Hotspur* in his last | *time*; of *time* which, with all its
endeavours to console | dominion over sublunary things,
The glory of the Prince | must itself at last *be stopped*
. IV. Q P. *Henry.*

THE FIRST PART OF

P. Henry. For worms, brave *Percy.* Fare thee well,
    great heart!
* Ill-weav'd ambition, how much art thou shrunk!
When that this body did contain a spirit,
² A Kingdom for it was too small a bound:
But now two paces of the vilest earth
Is room enough. This earth, that bears thee dead,
Bears not alive so stout a gentleman.
If thou wert sensible of courtesy,
I should not make so great a show of zeal;
³ But let my favours hide thy mangled face,
And, ev'n in thy behalf, I thank myself
For doing these fair Rites of tenderness.
Adieu, and take thy praise with thee to heav'n;
Thy ignominy sleep with thee in the Grave,
But not remember'd in thy epitaph.
            [*He sees* Falstaff *on the ground.*
—What! old acquaintance! could not all this flesh
Keep in a little life? poor *Jack!* farewel!
I could have better spar'd a better man.
Oh, I should have a heavy miss of thee,
If I were much in love with Vanity.
Death hath not struck ⁴ so fair a Deer to day,
Though many a † dearer in this bloody fray:
Imbowell'd will I see thee by and by,
Till then, in blood by noble *Percy* lye.   [*Exit.*

---

* *Ill-weav'd ambition, &c.*—] A metaphor taken from cloath, which *shrinks* when it is *ill-weav'd*, when its texture is loose.

² *Carminibus confide bonis—jacet ecce Tibullus*
Vix manet e toto parva quod urna capit.   OVID.

³ *But let my favours hide thy mangled face,*] We should read *favour*, face or countenance. He stooping down here to kiss *Hot-spur*.   WARBURTON.
He rather covers his face with a scarf to hide the ghastliness of death.

⁴ *So fair a deer.*] This is the reading of the first edition, and of the other quartos. The first folio has *fat*, which was followed by all the editors.

There is in these lines a very natural mixture of the serious and ludicrous produced by the view of *Percy* and *Falstaff.* I wish all play on words had been forborn.

† *a dearer*] Many *of greater value.*

I   SCENE

KING HENRY IV.

SCENE X.

Falſtaff *riſes.*

Fal. Imbowell'd!—if thou imbowel me to day, I'll give you leave to * powder me, and eat me to-morrow! 'Sblood, 'twas time to counterfeit, or that hot termagant *Scot* had paid me ſcot and lot too. Counterfeit? I lie, I am no counterfeit; to die, is to be a counterfeit; for he is but the counterfeit of a man, who hath not the life of a man; but to counterfeit dying, when a man thereby liveth, is to be no counterfeit, but the true and perfect image of life, indeed. The better part of valour is diſcretion; in the which better part I have ſaved my life. I am afraid of this gun-powder *Percy*, though he be dead. How if he ſhould counterfeit too, and riſe? I am afraid, he would prove the better counterfeit; therefore I'll make him ſure; yea, and I'll ſwear, I kill'd him. Why may not he riſe as well as I? Nothing confutes me but eyes, and no body ſees me. Therefore, ſirrah, with a new wound in your thigh, come you along with me. [*Takes* Hot-ſpur *on his back.*

SCENE XI.

Enter Prince Henry, *and* John *of* Lancaſter.

P. Henry. Come, brother *John*, full bravely haſt
    thou fleſht
Thy maiden ſword.
  Lan. But ſoft! whom have we here?
Did you not tell me, this fat man was dead?
  P. Henry. I did, I ſaw him dead,
And breathleſs on the ground.—Art thou alive,
Or is it fancy plays upon our eye-ſight?
I pr'ythee, ſpeak; we will not truſt our eyes
Without our ears. Thou art not what thou ſeem'ſt.

* *To powder is to ſalt.*

Fal.

Fal. No, that's certain; I am not a * double man; but if I am not *Jack Falstaff*, then am I a *Jack*. There is *Percy*, if your father will do me any honour, so; if not, let him kill the next *Percy* himself. I look either to be Earl or Duke, I can assure you.

P. Henry. Why, *Percy* I kill'd myself, and saw thee dead.

Fal. Did'st thou? Lord, Lord, how the world is giv'n to lying! I grant you, I was down, and out of breath, and so was he; but we rose both at an instant, and fought a long hour by *Shrewsbury* clock. If I may be believed, so; if not, let them, that should reward valour, bear the sin upon their own heads. I'll take't on my death, I gave him this wound in the thigh; if the man were alive, and would deny it, I would make him eat a piece of my sword.

Lan. This is the strangest Tale that e'er I heard.

P. Henry. This is the strangest fellow, brother *John*.
Come, bring your luggage nobly on your back;
For my part, if a Lie may do thee grace,
I'll gild it with the happiest terms I have.
[*A retreat is sounded*.
The trumpets sound retreat, the day is ours.
Come, brother, let's to th' highest of the field,
To see what friends are living, who are dead. [*Exeunt.*

Fal. I'll follow, as they say, for reward. He that rewards me, heav'n reward him! If I do grow great, I'll grow less; for I'll purge, and leave sack, and live cleanly, as a noble man should do. [*Exit.*

SCENE XII.

The Trumpets sound. Enter King Henry, **Prince of** Wales, *Lord* John *of* Lancaster, *Earl of* Westmorland, *with* Worcester *and* Vernon *Prisoners.*

K. Henry. Thus ever did Rebellion find rebuke.

* —'*a double man;*] That is, I am not *Falstaff*, and *Percy* together, though having *Percy* on my back, I seem double.

Ill-spirited *Wor'ster*, did we not send grace,
Pardon, and terms of love to all of you?
And would'st thou turn our offers contrary?
Misuse the tenor of thy kinsman's trust?
Three Knights upon our party slain to-day,
A noble Earl, and many a creature else,
Had been alive this hour,
If like a christian thou had'st truly borne
Betwixt our armies true intelligence.

Wor. What I have done, my safety urg'd me to;
And I embrace this fortune patiently,
Since not to be avoided it falls on me.

K. Henry. Bear *Worcester* to death, and *Vernon* too.
Other Offenders we will pause upon.

[*Exeunt* Worcester *and* Vernon, *guarded.*

How goes the field?

P. Hen. The gallant *Scot*, lord *Douglas*, when he saw
The fortune of the day quite turned from him,
The noble *Percy* slain, and all his men
Upon the foot of fear, fled with the rest,
And, falling from a hill, he was so bruis'd,
That the pursuers took him. At my Tent
The *Dowglas* is, and I beseech your Grace,
I may dispose of him.

K. Henry. With all my heart.

P. Henry. Then, brother *John* of *Lancaster*, to you
This honourable bounty shall belong.
Go to the *Dowglas*, and deliver him
Up to his pleasure, ransomless and free.
His valour, shown upon our crests to-day,
Hath taught us how to cherish such high deeds,
Ev'n in the bosom of our adversaries.

Lan.[+] I thank your Grace for this high courtesie,
Which I shall give away immediately.

K. Henry. Then this remains, that we divide our
Power.

[+] These two lines are added from the quarto. POPE. I suspect that they were rejected by *Shakespeare* himself.

You son *John*, and my cousin *Westmorland*,
Tow'rds *York* shall bend you, with your dearest speed,
To meet *Northumberland* and Prelate *Scroop*,
Who, as we hear, are busily in arms.
Myself and You, son *Harry*, will tow'rds *Wales*,
To fight with *Glendower* and the Earl of *March*.
Rebellion in this land shall lose his sway,
Meeting the check of such another day;
And since this business so far fair is done,
Let us not leave, till all our own be won.   [*Exeunt*.

The Second Part of HENRY IV.

Containing his DEATH:

AND THE

CORONATION

OF

King HENRY V.

Dramatis Personæ.

KING Henry *the Fourth.*
Prince Henry.
Prince John *of* Lancaster.
Humphry *of* Gloucester.
Thomas *of* Clarence.
Northumberland ⎫
The Archbishop of York, ⎪
Mowbray, ⎪
Hastings, ⎪
Lord Bardolph, ⎬ *against the King.*
Travers, ⎪
Morton, ⎪
Coleville, ⎭
Warwick, ⎫
Westmorland, ⎪
Surrey, ⎪
Gower, ⎬ *of the King's Party.*
Harcourt, ⎪
Lord Chief Justice, ⎭
Falstaff, Poins, Bardolph, Pistol, Peto, *and* Page.
Shallow *and* Silence, *Country Justices.*
Davy, *Servant to* Shallow.
Phang *and* Snare, *two Serjeants.*
Mouldy, ⎫
Shadow, ⎪
Wart, ⎬ *Country Soldiers.*
Feeble, ⎪
Bulcalf, ⎭

Lady Northumberland.
Lady Percy.
Hostess Quickly.
Doll Tear-sheet.

Drawers, Beadles, Grooms, &c.

I. Quarto, printed by *V. S.* for *Andrew Wise* and *William A[?]*
1600.
II. Folio, 1623.

INDUCTION.

Enter RUMOUR, *painted full of Tongues.*

OPEN your ears; for which of you will stop
 The Vent of Hearing, when loud *Rumour* speaks?
From the Orient to the drooping West,
Making the wind my post-horse, still unfold
The Acts commenced on this Ball of Earth.
Upon my tongues continual slanders ride,
The which in every language I pronounce;
Stuffing the ears of men with false reports.
I speak of Peace, while covert enmity,
Under the smile of safety, wounds the world;
And who but *Rumour*, who but only I,
Make fearful musters and prepar'd defence,
Whilst the big year, swoll'n with some other griefs,
Is thought with child by the stern tyrant War,
And no such matter? *Rumour* is a pipe
Blown by surmises, jealousies, conjectures;
And, of so easy and so plain a stop,
That the blunt monster with uncounted heads,
The still discordant wavering multitude,
Can play upon it. But what need I thus

---

¹ *Enter* RUMOUR,—] This speech of *Rumour* is not inelegant nor unpoetical, but is wholly useless, since we are told nothing which the first scene does not clearly and naturally discover. The only end of such prologues is to inform the audience of some facts previous to the action, of which they can have no knowledge from the persons of the drama.

² —*painted full of tongues.*] This direction, which is only to be found in the first Edition in Quarto of 1600, explains a passage in what follows, otherwise obscure.   POPE.

³ ——— *Rumour is a pipe*] Here the poet imagines himself describing *Rumour*, and forgets that *Rumour* is the speaker.

My

234   INDUCTION.
My well-known body to anatomize.
Among my houſhold? Why is *Rumour* here?
I run before King *Harry's* victory;
Who in a bloody field by *Shrewſbury*
Hath beaten down young *Hot-ſpur* and his troops;
Quenching the flame of bold rebellion
Ev'n with the Rebels' blood.   But what mean I
To ſpeak ſo true at firſt? my office is
To noiſe abroad, that *Harry Monmouth* fell
Under the Wrath of noble *Hot-ſpur's* ſword;
And that the King before the *Dowglas'* rage
Stoop'd his anointed head as low as death.
This have I rumour'd through the peaſant towns,
Between that royal field of *Shrewſbury,*
And this worm-eaten Hold of ragged ſtone⁴;
Where *Hot-ſpur's* father, old *Northumberland,*
Lies crafty ſick.   The Poſts come tiring on;
And not a man of them brings other news
Than they have learn'd of me. From *Rumour's* tongues,
They bring ſmooth comforts falſe, worſe than true
          wrongs.   [*Exit.*

⁴ *And this worm-eaten* Hole *of ragged Stone;*] Nor-tʰumberland had retir'd and for-tified himſelf in his Caſtle, a Place of Strength in thoſe Times, though the Building might be impaired by its Antiquity; and therefore, I believe, our Poet wrote.
     And this worm-eaten Hold *of ragged Stone.*   THEOBALD.

[5] The Second Part of
HENRY IV.[6]

ACT I. SCENE I.

Northumberland's Castle.

Enter Lord Bardolph; *the Porter at the door.*

BARDOLPH.

WHO keeps the gate here, hoa? where is the Earl?

Port. What shall I say you are?

Bard. Tell thou the Earl,

---

[5] *The second Part of* Henry IV. The Transactions comprized in [th]is History take up about nine [ye]ars. The Action commences [wi]th the Account of *Hot-spur's* [be]ing defeated and killed; and [clo]ses with the Death of K. Hen[ry] IV, and the Coronation of *Henry* V. THEOBALD.

[6] Mr. *Upton* thinks these two [pla]ys improperly called the *first* [and] *second parts* of Henry the [four]th. The first play ends, he [says,] with the peaceful settle[men]t of *Henry* in the kingdom [by] the defeat of the rebels. [Th]is is hardly true, for the re-

bels are not yet finally suppressed. The second, he tells us, shews *Henry* the *fifth* in the various lights of a good-natured rake, till, on his father's death, he assumes a more manly character. This is true; but this representation gives us no idea of a dramatick action. These two plays will appear to every reader, who shall peruse them without ambition of critical discoveries, to be so connected that the second is merely a sequel to the first; to be two only because they are too long to be one,

That

That the lord *Bardolph* doth attend him here.

  Port. His lordship is walk'd forth into the Orchard;
Please it your Honour, knock but at the gate,
And he himself will answer.

Enter Northumberland.

  Bard. Here's the Earl.
  North. What news, lord *Bardolph?* ev'ry minute now
Should be the [7] father of some stratagem.
The times are wild: Contention, like a horse
Full of high feeding, madly hath broke loose,
And bears down all before him.
  Bard. Noble Earl,
I bring you certain news from *Shrewsbury.*
  North. Good, if heav'n will!
  Bard. As good as heart can wish.
The King is almost wounded to the death:
And in the fortune of my lord your Son,
Prince *Harry* slain outright; and both the *Blunts*
Kill'd by the hand of *Dowglas*; young Prince *John,*
And *Westmorland,* and *Stafford,* fled the field;
And *Harry Monmouth's* brawn, the hulk Sir *John,*
Is prisoner to your son. O, such a day,
So fought, so follow'd, and so fairly won,
Came not till now, to dignify the times,
Since *Cæsar's* fortunes!
  North. How is this deriv'd?
Saw you the field? came you from *Shrewsbury?*
  Bard. I spake with one, my lord, that came from thence,
A gentleman well bred, and of good name;
That freely render'd me these news for true.
  North. Here comes my servant *Travers,* whom I sent

---

[7] *father of some* stratagem.] *Stratagem,* for vigorous action.
                                    WARBURTON.

KING HENRY IV. 237

day laſt to liſten after news.
. My lord, I over-rode him on the way,
is furniſh'd with no certainties,
ian he, haply, may retain from me.

SCENE II.

Enter Travers.

). Now, *Travers*, what good tidings come
with you?
My lord, Sir *John Umfrevil* turn'd me back
)yful tidings; and, being better hors'd,
e me. After him came ſpurring hard
eman, almoſt fore-ſpent with ſpeed,
pp'd by me to breathe his bloodied horſe;
l the way to *Cheſter*; and of him
nand what news from *Shrewſbury*.
me, that Rebellion had ill luck;
.t young *Harry Percy's* ſpur was cold.
at he gave his able horſe the head,
nding forward, ſtruck his agile heels
the panting ſides of his poor jade
he ⁸ rowel-head; and, ſtarting ſo,
t'd in running to devour the way,
no longer queſtion.
. Ha? —— again ——
young *Harry Percy's* ſpur was cold?
n had ill luck?
  My lord, I'll tell you;
)ung lord your ſon have not the day,
inc Honour, for a ⁹ ſilken point
my Barony. Ne'er talk of it.

---

⁸-head] I think that only a ſingle ſpike.
rved in old prints the *⁹ Silken point.*] A *point* is a
oſe times to have been *ſtring tagged,* or *lace.*
                                    North.

238 THE SECOND PART OF

North. Why should the gentleman, that rode by *Travers*,
Give then such instances of loss?
Bard. Who he?
He was [1] some hilding fellow, that had stoll'n
The horse he rode on; and, upon my life,
Spake at adventure. Look, here comes more news.

SCENE III.

Enter Morton.

North. Yea, this man's brow, like to a title-leaf,
Foretels the nature of a tragick volume.
So looks the strond, whereon th' imperious flood
Hath left a witness'd usurpation.
Say, *Morton*, didst thou come from *Shrewsbury?*
Mort. I ran from *Shrewsbury*, my noble Lord,
Where hateful Death put on his ugliest Mask
To fright our Party.
North. How doth my son, and Brother?
Thou tremblest; and the whiteness in thy cheek
Is apter than thy tongue to tell thy errand.
Even such a man, so faint, so spiritless,
So dull, so dead in look, [2] so woe-be-gone,
Drew *Priam's* curtain in the dead of night,
And would have told him half his *Troy* was burn'd,
But *Priam* found the fire, ere he his tongue,
And I my *Percy's* death, ere thou report'st it.
This thou would'st say: your son did thus, and thus;
Your brother, thus; so fought the noble *Douglas:*
Stopping my greedy ear with their bold deeds;

---

[1] — *some hilding fellow,* —] For *hinderling,* i. e. base, degenerate. POPE.

[2] *So woe-be-gone.*] The word was common enough amongst the old *Scottish* and *English* poets, as G. *Douglas, Chaucer,* lord *Buckhurst, Fairfax*; and signifies, *far gone in woe.* WARBURTON.

But

the end, to stop mine ear indeed,
haſt a ſigh to blow away this praſe,
g with brother, ſon, and all are dead!
t. Dowglas is living, and your brother, yet;
r my lord your ſon ——
th. Why, he is dead.
hat a ready tongue ſuſpicion hath.
at but but fears the thing he would not know,
by inſtinct, knowledge from other's eyes,
vhat he fear'd is chanc'd. Yet, *Morton*, ſpeak,
ou thy Earl, his Divination lies;
will take it as a ſweet Diſgrace,
ake thee rich for doing me ſuch wrong.
t. You are too Great, to be by me gainſaid:
ſpirit is too true, your fears too certain.
h. * Yet for all this, ſay not, that *Percy's* dead.
ſtrange confeſſion in thine eye,

ſpirit.] The impreſ-
n your mind, by which
eive the death of your

for all this, ſay not, &c.]
radiction in the firſt part
eech might be imputed
traction of *Northumber-*
nd, but the calmneſs
lection, contained in the
ſeems not much to
ce ſuch a ſuppoſition.
nture to diſtribute this
a manner which will,
eem more commodious,
t wiſh the reader to for-
the moſt commodious
ays the true reading.

Yet for all this, ſay not
'ercy's dead.
I ſee a ſtrange confeſ-
n thine eye,

Thou ſhak'ſt thy head, and holdſt it
fear, or ſin,
To ſpeak a truth. If he be ſlain,
ſay ſo.
The tongue offends not, that reports
his death;
And he doth ſin, that doth belie the
dead.
Not he that ſaith the dead is not
alive.
Morton. *Yet the firſt bringer of*
unwelcome news
Hath but a loſing office, and his
tongue
Sounds ever after as a ſullen bell.
Remember'd, tolling a departing
friend.
Here is a natural interpoſition
of *Bardolph* at the beginning, who
is not pleaſed to hear his news
confuted, and a proper preparation of *Morton* for the tale which
he is unwilling to tell.

Thou

Thou shak'st thy head, and ⁵ hold'st it fear, or sin,
To speak a truth. ⁶ If he be slain, say so.
The tongue offends not, that reports his death;
And he doth sin, that doth belie the dead,
Not he, which says the dead is not alive.
Yet the first bringer of unwelcome news
Hath but a losing office, and his tongue
Sounds ever after as a sullen bell,
Remember'd, tolling a departing friend.

Bard. I cannot think, my lord, your son is dead.

Mort. I'm sorry, I should force you to believe
That, which, I would to heav'n, I had not seen;
But these mine eyes saw him in bloody state,
Rend'ring faint quittance, wearied and out-breath'd,
To *Henry Monmouth*; whose swift wrath beat down
The never-daunted *Percy* to the earth,
From whence, with life, he never more sprung up,
In few, his death, whose spirit lent a fire
Even to the dullest peasant in his Camp,
Being bruited once, took fire and heat away
From the best-temper'd courage in his troops;
⁷ For from his metal was his party steel'd;

Which

⁵ ——— *hold'st it* fear, *or sin.*] *Fear,* for danger. WARBURTON.

⁶ *If he be slain, say so.*] The words *say so* are in the first folio, but not in the quarto: they are necessary to the verse, but the sense proceeds as well without them.

⁷ *For from his* metal *was his party steel'd*; *Which once in him* ABATED,———] The word *metal* is one of those hacknied metaphorical terms, which resumes so much of a literal sense as not to need the idea (from whence the figure is taken) to be kept up. So that it may with elegance enough be said,

his metal *was abated,* as well as *his courage was abated.* See what is said on this subject on *Love's Labour's Lost,* Act V. But when the writer shews, as here, both before and after, [———*his party steel'd*——— *turn'd on themselves like dull and heavy lead*] that his intention was not to drop the idea from whence he took his metaphor, that he cannot say with propriety and elegance, his *metal was elated*; because what he predicates of *metal,* must be then convey'd in a term conformable to the metaphor. Hence I conclude that *Shakespeare* wrote,

Which

ı once in him abated, all the rest
l on themselves, like dull and heavy lead.
 the thing, that's heavy in its self,
 enforcement, flies with greatest speed;
 our men, heavy in *Hot-spur's* loss,
 ɔ this weight such lightness with their fear,
 rrows fled not swifter toward their aim,
 lid our soldiers, aiming at their safety,
 ɔm the field. Then was that noble *Wor'ster*
 on ta'en prisoner: and that furious *Scot*,
 loody *Dowglas*, whose well-labouring sword
 ιree times slain th' appearance of the King,
 vail his stomach, and did grace the shame
 ɔse that turn'd their backs; and in his flight,
 ling in fear, was took. The sum of all
 t the King hath won; and hath sent out
 ·dy Pow'r to encounter you, my lord,
 the conduct of young *Lancaster*
 ⁷estmorland. This is the news at full.
 th. For this, I shall have time enough to mourn;
 on there is physick, and this news,
 ɔould, had I been well, have made me sick,
 sick, hath in some measure made me well.
 ɔ the wretch, whose fever-weaken'd joints,
 rengthless hinges, buckle ⁹ under life,
 ent of his fit, breaks like a fire
 ˙ his keeper's arms; ev'n so my limbs,
 ∶n'd with grief, being now inrag'd with grief,
 ιrice themselves. Hence, therefore, thou nice
    crutch;

---

nce in him REDATED,—
ited. WARBURTON.
is a great effort to pro-
le effect. The commen-
es not seem fully to un-
 the word *abated*, which
 ɛre put for the general
 diminished, nor for the
 f *blunted* as applied to a
.. IV.

single edge, but for *reduced to a lower temper*, or, as the work-men now call it, *let down*. It is very proper.
⁸ *'Gan vail his stomach.*—]
Began to fall his courage, to let his spirits sink under his fortune.
⁹ — *buckle*] Bend; yield to pressure.

R   A scaly

242 THE SECOND PART OF

A scaly gauntlet now with joints of steel
Must glove this hand. And hence, thou sickly quoif,
Thou art a guard too wanton for the head,
Which Princes, flesh'd with conquest, aim to hit.
Now bind my brows with iron, and approach
[1] The rugged'st hour that time and spight dare bring
To frown upon th' enrag'd *Northumberland!*
Let heav'n kiss earth! now let not nature's hand
Keep the wild flood confin'd; let order die,
And let this world no longer be a stage
To feed contention in a lingring act:
But let one spirit of the first-born *Cain*
Reign in all bosoms, that each heart being set
On bloody courses, the rude scene may end,
And darkness be the burier of the dead![2]

   Bard. [3] This strained passion doth you wrong, my lord!
Sweet Earl, divorce not wisdom from your honour.

   Mort. The lives of all your loving complices
Lean on your health; the which, if you give o'er
To stormy passion, must perforce decay.
[4] You cast th'event of war, my noble lord,

And

---

[1] The old Edition,
The ragged'st *Hour that Time and* Spight *dare bring To frown,* &c.——] There is no Consonance of Metaphors betwixt *ragged* and *frown*; nor, indeed, any Dignity in the Image. On both Accounts, therefore, I suspect, our Author wrote, as I have reformed the Text, *The* rugged'st *Hour,* &c. THEOB.

[2] The conclusion of this noble speech is extremely striking. There is no need to suppose it exactly philosophical; *darkness* in poetry may be absence of eyes as well as privation of light. Yet we may remark, that by an ancient opinion it has been held, that if the human race, for whom the world was made, were extirpated, the whole system of sublunary nature would cease.

[3] *This strained passion,* &c.—] This line is only in the first edition, where it is spoken by *Umfreville,* who speaks no where else. It seems necessary to the connection. POPE.

[4] *You cast th' event of war,* &c.] The fourteen lines from hence to *Bardolph's* next speech are not to be found in the first editions till that in the Folio of 1623. A very great number of other lines in this play

KING HENRY IV.

And summ'd th'account of chance, before you said,
Let us make head. It was your presurmise,
That, in the dole of blows, your son might drop;
You knew, he walk'd o'er perils, on an edge
More likely to fall in, than to get o'er;
You were advis'd, his flesh was capable
Of wounds and scars; and that his forward spirit
Would lift him where most trade of danger rang'd;
Yet did you say, *Go forth.* And none of this,
Though strongly apprehended, could restrain
The stiff-borne action. What hath then befall'n,
Or what hath this bold enterprize brought forth,
More than That being, which was like to be?

Bard. We all, that are engaged to this loss,
Knew, that we ventur'd on such dang'rous seas,
That, if we wrought out life, 'twas ten to one;
And yet we ventur'd for the gain propos'd,
Choak'd the respect of likely peril fear'd;
And since we are o'er-set, venture again.
Come, we will all put forth, body and goods.

Mort. 'Tis more than time; and my most noble
    lord,
I hear for certain, and do speak the truth:
[5] The gentle Arch-bishop of *York* is up
With well-appointed Powers. He is a man,
Who with a double surety binds his followers.
My lord, your son had only but the corps,
But shadows, and the shews of men to fight;
For that same word, Rebellion, did divide
The action of their bodies from their souls,

---

play are inserted after the first edition in like manner, but of such spirit and mastery generally, that the insertions are plainly by *Shakespeare* himself. POPE.
 To this note I have nothing to add, but that the editor speaks of more editions than I believe him to have seen, there having been but one edition yet discovered by me that precedes the first folio.
  [5] *The gentle,* &c.—] These one-and-twenty lines were added since the first edition.

And they did fight with queafinefs, conftrain'd,
As men drink potions, that their weapons only
Seem'd on our fide, but for their fpirits and fouls,
This word, Rebellion, it had froze them up,
As fifh are in a pond. But now, the Bifhop
Turns Infurrection to Religion;
Suppos'd fincere and holy in his thoughts,
He's follow'd both with body and with mind,
And doth enlarge his Rifing with the blood
Of fair King *Richard*, fcrap'd from *Pomfret* ftones;
Derives from heav'n his quarrel and his caufe;
Tells them, he doth ⁶ beftride a bleeding land
Gafping for life under great *Bolingbroke*,
And more, and lefs, do flock to follow him.

North. I knew of this before, but to fpeak truth,
This prefent grief had wip'd it from my mind.
Go in with me, and counfel every man
The apteft way for fafety and revenge.
Get pofts, and letters, and make friends with fpeed;
Never fo few, nor never yet more need.   [*Exeunt.*

SCENE IV.

Changes to a Street in London.

Enter Sir John Falftaff, *with his Page bearing his fword and buckler.*

Fal. SIrrah, you, giant! what fays the doctor to my water?

Page. He faid, Sir, the water it felf was a good healthy water. But for the party that own'd it, he might have more difeafes than he knew for.

Fal. Men of all forts take a pride to gird at me.

---

⁶ *Tells them, he doth beftride a bleeding land.*] That is, ftands over his country to defend her as fhe lies bleeding on the ground. So *Falftaff* before fays to the *Prince*, *If thou fee me down*, Hal, *and beftride me, fo; it is an office of friendfhip.*

The

KING HENRY IV.

The brain of this foolish-compounded-clay, Man, is not able to invent any thing that tends to laughter, more than I invent, or is invented on me. I am not only witty in myself, but the cause that wit is in other men. I do here walk before thee, like a sow, that hath overwhelmed all her litter but one. If the Prince put thee into my service for any other reason than to set me off, why, then I have no judgment. Thou whorson mandrake [7], thou art fitter to be worn in my cap, than to wait at my heels. [8] I was never mann'd with an agate till now: but I will neither set you in gold nor silver, but in vile apparel, and send you back again to your master, for a jewel: The *Juvenal*, the Prince your master! whose chin is not yet fledg'd; I will sooner have a beard grow in the palm of my hand, than he shall get one on his cheek; yet he will not stick to say, his face is a face-royal. Heav'n may finish it when it will, it is not a hair amiss yet; he may keep it still as a face-royal [9], for a barber shall never earn sixpence out of it; and yet he will be crowing, as if he had writ man ever since his father was a batchelor. He may keep his own grace, but he is almost out of mine, I can assure him.—What said Mr. *Dombledon*, about the satten of my short cloak and slops?

---

[7] *Mandrake* is a root supposed to have the shape of a man; it is now counterfeited with the root of briony.

[8] *I was never mann'd*] That is, I never before had an agate for my man.

I was never mann'd with an agate till now:] Alluding to the little figures cut in *agates*, and other hard stones, for seals: and therefore he says, *I will set you either in gold nor silver.* The Oxford Editor alters this to *ag-let*, a tag to the points then in use (a word indeed which our authour uses to express the same thought). But *aglets*, tho' they were sometimes of gold or silver, were never *set* in those metals.
WARBURTON.

[9] — *he may keep it still as a face royal,*] That is, a face exempt from the touch of vulgar hands. So a *stag royal* is not to be hunted, a *mine royal* is not to be dug.

R 3

Page. He said, Sir, you should procure him better assurance than *Bardolph*; he would not take his bond and yours, he lik'd not the security.

Fal. Let him be damn'd like the Glutton, may his tongue be hotter. A whorson *Achitophel*, a rascally yea-forsooth knave, to bear a gentleman in [1] hand, and then stand upon *security*.—The whorson-smooth-pates do now wear nothing but high-shoes, and bunches of keys at their girdles; and if a man is thorough with them in honest taking up [2], then they must stand upon *security*. I had as lief they would put rats-bane in my mouth, as offer to stop it with security. I looked he should have sent me two and twenty yards of satten, as I am a true Knight, and he sends me *Security*. Well, he may sleep in security, for he hath the horn of abundance. And [3] the lightness of his wife shines through it, and yet cannot he see, though he have his own lanthorn to light him. Where's *Bardolph?*

Page. He's gone into *Smithfield* to buy your Worship a horse.

Fal. [4] I bought him in *Paul's*, and he'll buy me a horse in *Smithfield*. If I could get me but a wife in the Stews, I were mann'd, hors'd, and wiv'd.

---

[1] *To bear in hand*, is *to keep in expectation*.

[2] — *if a man is thorough with them in honest taking up*,] That is, *If a man by taking up goods is in their debt*. *To be thorough* seems to be the same with the present phrase, *to be in with a tradesman*.

[3] *the lightness of his wife shines through it, and yet cannot he see, though he have his own lanthorn to light him.*] This joke seems evidently to have been taken from that of *Plautus: Quò ambulas tu, qui Vulcanum in cornu conclusum geris. Amph.* Act 1. Scene 1. and much improved. We need not doubt that a joke was here intended by *Plautus*, for the proverbial term of *horns*, for *cuckoldom* is very ancient, as appears by *Artemidorus*, who says, Προλέγει αὐτῷ ὅτι ἡ γυνή σου πορνεύσει, καὶ τὸ λεγόμενον κέρατα αὐτῷ ποιήσει, καὶ οὕτως ἀπέβη. Ὀνείροι, lib. 2. cap. 12. And he copied from those before him. WARBURT.

[4] *I bought him in* Paul's,] At that time the resort of idle people, cheats, and knights of the post.
WARBURTON.

SCENE V.

Enter Chief Juſtice, and Servants.

ge. Sir, here comes the Nobleman that committed
rince for ſtriking him, about *Bardolph*.
l. Wait clóſe, I will not ſee him.
Juſt. What's he that goes there?
rv. Falſtaff, an't pleaſe your lordſhip.
Juſt. He that was in queſtion for the robbery?
rv. He, my lord. But he hath ſince done good
:e at *Shrewsbury*; and, as I hear, is now going
ſome charge to the lord *John* of *Lancaſter*.
Juſt. What to *York?* call him back again.
rv. Sir *John Falſtaff,*———
l. Boy, tell him I am deaf.
ge. You muſt ſpeak louder, my maſter is deaf.
Juſt. I am ſure, he is, to the hearing of any
good. Go pluck him by the elbow. I muſt
with him.
rv. Sir *John*———
l. What! a young knave and beg! are there not
? is there not employment? doth not the King
Subjects? do not the Rebels need ſoldiers? though
a ſhame to be on any ſide but one, it is worſe
e to beg, than to be on the worſt ſide, were it
e than the name of Rebellion can tell how to
: it.
rv. You miſtake me, Sir.
l. Why, Sir, did I ſay you were an honeſt man?
ig my knight-hood and my ſoldierſhip aſide, I
lied in my throat, if I had ſaid ſo.
rv. I pray you, Sir, then ſet your knight-hood
your ſoldierſhip aſide, and give me leave to tell
you lie in your throat, if you ſay I am any other
an honeſt man.
al. I give thee leave to tell me ſo? I lay aſide
, which grows to me? if thou gett'ſt any leave

248 THE SECOND PART OF

of me, hang me; if thou tak'ſt leave, thou wert better be hang'd. You * hunt-counter, hence; avaunt.

Serv. Sir, my lord would ſpeak with you.

Ch. Juſt. Sir *John Falſtaff*, a word with you.

Fal. My good lord! God give your lordſhip good time of day. I am glad to ſee your lordſhip abroad; I heard ſay, your lordſhip was ſick. I hope, your lordſhip goes abroad by advice. Your lordſhip, though not clean paſt your youth, hath yet ſome ſmack of age in you; ſome reliſh of the ſaltneſs of time; and I moſt humbly beſeech your lordſhip, to have a reverend care of your health.

Ch. Juſt. Sir *John*, I ſent for you before your expedition to *Shrewsbury*.——

Fal. If it pleaſe your lordſhip, I hear, his Majeſty is return'd with ſome diſcomfort from *Wales*.

Ch. Juſt. I talk not of his Majeſty. You would not come when I ſent for you.——

Fal. And I hear moreover, his Highneſs is fallen into this ſame whorſon apoplexy.

Ch. Juſt. Well, heav'n mend him! I pray, let me ſpeak with you.

Fal. This apoplexy is, as I take it, a kind of lethargy, an't pleaſe your lordſhip, a kind of ſleeping in the blood, a whorſon tingling.

Ch. Juſt. What tell you me of it? be it, as it is.

Fal. It hath its original from much grief; from ſtudy and perturbation of the brain. I have read the cauſe of it in *Galen*. It is a kind of deafneſs.

Ch. Juſt. I think, you are fallen into that diſeaſe: for you hear not what I ſay to you.

Fal. ⁵ Very well, my lord, very well; rather, an't
pleaſe

---

* *Hunt-counter.*] That is, *blunderer*. He does not, I think, allude to any relation between the judge's ſervant and the counter-priſon.

⁵ Fal. *Very well, my Lord, very well:*] In the *Quarto* Edition, printed in 1600, this Speech ſtands thus;

Old. *Very well, my Lord, very well:* I had not obſerv'd this, when I wrote my Note, to the firſt part
of

KING HENRY IV.

please you, it is the disease of not list'ning, the malady of not marking, that I am troubled withal.

Ch. Just. To punish you by the heels, would amend the attention of your ears; and I care not if I do become your physician.

Fal. I am as poor as *Job*, my lord, but not so patient. Your lordship may minister the potion of imprisonment to me, in respect of poverty; but how I should be your Patient to follow your prescriptions, the wise may make some dram of a scruple, or, indeed, a scruple itself.

Ch. Just. I sent for you, when there were matters against you for your life, to come speak with me.

Fal. As I was then advis'd by my Counsel learned in the laws of this land-service, I did not come.

Ch. Just. Well, the truth is, Sir *John*, you live in great infamy.

Fal. He that buckles him in my belt, cannot live in less.

Ch. Just. Your means are very slender, and your waste is great.

Fal. I would it were otherwise; I would, my means were greater, and my waste slenderer.

Ch. Just. You have mis-led the youthful Prince.

Fal. The young Prince hath mis-led me. I am the fellow with the great belly, and he my dog [6].

Ch. Just. Well, I'm loth to gall a new-heal'd wound; your day's service at *Shrewsbury* hath a little gilded over your night's exploit on *Gads-hill*. You may thank the unquiet time, for your quiet o'er-posting that action.

of *Henry* IV. concerning the Tradition of *Falstaff*'s Character having been first called *Oldcastle*. This almost amounts to a self-evident Proof, of the Thing being so: and that the Play being printed from the State-Manuscript, *Oldcastle* had been all along altered into *Falstaff*, except in this single Place by an Oversight: of which the Printers, not being aware, continued these initial Traces of the Original Name. THEOBALD.

[6] I do not understand this joke. Dogs lead the blind, but why does a dog lead the fat?

Fal.

250 THE SECOND PART OF

Fal. My lord ———

Ch. Juſt. But ſince all is well, keep it ſo: wake not a ſleeping Wolf.

Fal. To wake a Wolf, is as bad as to ſmell a Fox.

Ch. Juſt. What? you are as a candle, the better part burnt out.

Fal. [7] A waſſel candle, my lord; all tallow; but if I did ſay of wax, my growth would approve the truth.

Ch. Juſt. There is not a white hair on your face, but ſhould have his effect of gravity.

Fal. His effect of gravy, gravy, gravy.———

Ch. Juſt. You follow the young Prince up and down, like his [8] ill angel.

Fal. Not ſo, my lord, your angel is light: but I hope, he that looks upon me, will take me without weighing; and yet, in ſome reſpects, I grant, I cannot go; I cannot * tell. Virtue is of ſo little regard in theſe [9] coſter-mongers' days, that true valour is turned bear-herd; pregnancy is made a tapſter, and hath his quick wit waſted in giving reckonings; all the other

---

[7] *A waſſel candle, &c.*] A *waſſel candle* is a large candle lighted up at a feaſt. There is a poor quibble upon the word *wax*, which ſignifies *encreaſe* as well as the *matter of the honey-comb*.

[8] *You follow the young Prince up and down like his* evil *Angel.*] What a precious Collator has Mr. *Pope* approved himſelf in this Paſſage! Beſides, if this were the true Reading, *Falſtaff* could not have made the witty and humorous Evaſion he has done in his Reply. I have reſtor'd the Reading of the oldeſt *Quarto*. The Lord Chief Juſtice calls *Falſtaff* the Prince's *ill Angel* or Genius: which *Falſtaff* turns off by ſaying, an *ill Angel* (meaning the Coin call'd an *Angel*) is *light*; but, ſurely, it can't be ſaid that he wants *Weight*: ergo,——the Inference is obvious. Now Money may be call'd *ill*, or *bad*; but it is never call'd *evil*, with Regard to its being under Weight. This Mr. *Pope* will facetiouſly call reſtoring *loſt Puns:* But if the Author wrote a *Pun*, and it happens to be *loſt* in an Editor's Indolence, I ſhall, in ſpite of his Grimace, venture at bringing it back to Light. THEOBALD.

* *I cannot tell*] I cannot be taken in a reckoning: I cannot paſs current.

[9] *In theſe coſter-mongers' days.*] In theſe times when the prevalence of trade has produced that meanneſs that rates the merit of every thing by money.

gifts

gifts appertinent to man, as the malice of this age shapes them, are not worth a goose-berry. You, that are old, consider not the capacities of us that are young; you measure the heat of our Livers, with the bitterness of your Galls; and we that are in the vaward of our youth, I must confess, are wags too.

Ch. Just. Do you set down your name in the scrowl of youth, that are written down old, with all the chatacters of age? Have you not a moist eye? a dry hand? a yellow cheek? a white beard? a decreasing leg? an ncreasing belly? Is not your voice broken? your wind hort? your chin double? 'your wit single? and every part about you blasted with antiquity? and will you yet call yourself young? fie, fie, fie, Sir *John*.

Fal. My lord, I was born about three of the clock n the afternoon, with a white head, and something a ound belly. For my voice, I have lost it with halowing and singing of Anthems. To approve my outh further, I will not. The truth is, I am only ld in judgment and understanding, and he, that will aper with me for a thousand marks, let him lend me he money, and have at him. For the box o'th' ear hat the Prince gave you, he gave it like a rude Prince, nd you took it like a sensible lord. I have checkt him for it; and the young Lion repents: marry, not n ashes and sack-cloth, but in new silk and old sack.

Ch. Just. Well, heav'n send the Prince a better Companion.

Fal. Heav'n send the companion a better Prince. I cannot rid my hands of him.

Ch. Just. Well, the King hath sever'd you and Prince

---

[1] *——your wit single?*] We call a man *single-witted* who attains but one species of knowkdge. This sense I know not how to apply to *Falstaff*, and rather think that the *Chief Justice* hints at a calamity always incident to a gray-haired wit, whose misfortune is, that his merriment is unfashionable. His allusions are to forgotten facts; his illustrations are drawn from notions obscured by time; his *wit* is therefore *single*, such as none has any part in but himself.

Harry.

Harry. I hear, you are going with lord *John* of *Lancaster*, againſt the Archbiſhop and the Earl of *Northumberland.*

Fal. Yes, I thank your pretty ſweet wit for it; but look you, pray, all you that kiſs my lady Peace at home, that our armies join not in a hot day; for, by the Lord, I take but two ſhirts out with me, and I mean not to ſweat extraordinarily; if it be a hot day, if I brandiſh any thing but a bottle, would I might never ſpit white again. There is not a dangerous action can peep out his head, but I am thruſt upon it. Well, I cannot laſt ever. —— But it was always yet the trick of our *Engliſh* Nation, if they have a good thing, to make it too common. If ye will needs ſay, I am an old man, you ſhould give me Reſt: I would to God, my name were not ſo terrible to the enemy as it is! I were better to be eaten to death with a ruſt, than to be ſcour'd to nothing with perpetual motion.

Ch. Juſt. Well, be honeſt, be honeſt, and heav'n bleſs your expedition!

Fal. Will your lordſhip lend me a thouſand pound, to furniſh me forth?

Ch. Juſt. Not a penny, not a penny; you are too impatient to bear croſſes. Fare you well. Commend me to my couſin *Weſtmoreland.* [*Exit.*

Fal. If I do, fillip me with ⁸ a three man beetle —— A man can no more ſeparate age and covetouſneſs, than he can part young limbs and letchery; but the gout galls the one, and the pox pinches the other, and ſo both the degrees prevent my curſes. Boy, ——

Page. Sir?

Fal. What money is in my purſe?

Page. Seven groats and two pence.

Fal. I can get no remedy againſt this conſumption of the purſe. Borrowing only lingers and lingers it out, but the diſeaſe is incurable. Go bear this letter to my lord of *Lancaſter*, this to the Prince, this to

---

⁸ *... a three-man beetle* --A bcetle wielded by three men. POPE.

the

the Earl of *Weſtmorland,* and this to old Mrs. *Urſula,* whom I have weekly ſworn to marry ſince I perceived the firſt white hair on my chin. About it; you know where to find me. A pox of this gout! or, a gout of this pox! for the one, or t'other, plays the rogue with my great toe; it is no matter, if I do halt, I have the wars for my colour, and my penſion ſhall ſeem the more reaſonable. A good wit will make uſe of any thing; I will turn diſeaſes to commodity. [*Exeunt.*

SCENE VI.

Changes to the Archbiſhop of York's *Palace.*

Enter Archbiſhop of York, Haſtings, Thomas Mowbray *(Earl Marſhal) and Lord* Bardolph.

York. THUS have you heard our cauſe, and know
 our means;
Now, my moſt noble friends, I pray you all,
Speak plainly your opinion of our hopes.
And firſt, Lord Marſhal, what ſay you to it?

 Mowb. I well allow th' occaſion of our arms,
But gladly would be better ſatisfied
How in our means we ſhould advance our ſelves
To look with forehead bold and big enough
Upon the pow'r and puiſſance of the King?

 Haſt. Our preſent muſters grow upon the file
To five and twenty thouſand men of choice;
And our Supplies live largely in the hope
Of great *Northumberland,* whoſe boſom burns
With an incenſed fire of injuries.

 Bard. The queſtion then, lord *Haſtings,* ſtandeth
 thus;
Whether our preſent five and twenty thouſand
May hold up head without *Northumberland?*

 Haſt. With him we may.

 Bard. Ay, marry, there's the point:
But if without him we be thought too feeble,

254 THE SECOND PART OF

My judgment is, we should not step too far
Till we had his assistance by the hand.
For in a theme so bloody-fac'd as this,
Conjecture, expectation, and surmise,
Of aids uncertain should not be admitted.

York. 'Tis very true, lord *Bardolph*; for, indeed,
It was young *Hot-spur's* case at *Shrewsbury*.

Bard. It was, my lord, who lin'd himself with hope,
Eating the air, on promise of Supply;
Flatt'ring himself with project of a Power
Much smaller than the smallest of his thoughts;
And so, with great imagination,
Proper to madmen, led his Pow'rs to death,
And, winking, leap'd into destruction.

Hast. But, by your leave, it never yet did hurt
To lay down likelihoods and forms of hope.

Bard. Yes, if this present quality of war,
Indeed the instant action; a cause on foot
Lives so in hope, as in an early Spring
We see th' appearing buds; which, to prove fruit,
Hope gives not so much warrant, as Despair,

---

[3] ——*step too far*] The four following lines were added in the second edition.

[4] *Yes, if this present quality of war,*] These first twenty lines were first inserted in the folio of 1623.
The first clause of this passage is evidently corrupted. All the folio editions and Mr. *Rowe's* concur in the same reading, which Mr. *Pope* altered thus,

Yes, if this present quality of war
Impede *the instant act.*

This has been silently followed by Mr. *Theobald,* Sir *Tho. Hanmer,* and Dr. *Warburton;* but the corruption is certainly deeper, for in the present reading *Bardolph* makes the inconvenience of *hope* to be that it may cause delay, when indeed the whole tenour of his argument is to recommend delay to the rest that are too forward. I know not what to propose, and am afraid that something is omitted, and that the injury is irremediable. Yet perhaps, the alteration requisite is no more than this,

*Yes, in this present quality of war,
Indeed of instant action.*

It never, says *Hastings, did harm to lay down likelihoods of hope. Yes,* says *Bardolph,* it has done harm *in this present quality of war,* in a state of things, such as is now before us, *of war, indeed of instant action.* This is obscure, but Mr. *Pope's* reading is still less reasonable.

That

ts will bite them. When we mean to build,
survey the plot, then draw the model;
n we see the figure of the house,
st we rate the cost of the erection;
 we find out-weighs ability,
we then but draw a-new the model
offices? at least, desist
at all? much more, in this great Work,
 almost to pluck a Kingdom down,
nother up, should we survey
of situation, and the model;
ipon a sure foundation,
surveyors, know our own estate,
: such a work to undergo,
. against his opposite; or else,
'y in paper and in figures,
· names of men instead of men,
that draws the model of a house
is pow'r to build it, who, half through,
r, and leaves his part-created cost
subject to the weeping clouds,
e for churlish winter's tyranny.
Grant, that our hopes, yet likely of fair birth,
: still born, and that we now possest
)st man of expectation,
'e are a body strong enough,
'e are, to equal with the King.   [sand?
What, is the King but five and twenty thou-
To us, no more; nay, not so much, lord
ardolph.
visions, as the times do brawl,
:ee heads; one Pow'r against the *French*,
against *Glendower;* perforce, a third
: up us; so is the unfirm King
livided; and his coffers sound
low poverty and emptiness.   [gether,
That he should draw his sev'ral strengths to-
: against us in full puissance,
                              Need

Need not be dreaded.

Haft. If he should do so[5],
He leaves his back unarm'd, the *French* and *Welsh*
Baying him at the heels; never fear That.

Bard. Who, is it like, should lead his forces hither?

Haft. The Duke of *Lancaster,* and *Westmorland*:
Against the *Welsh,* himself and *Harry Monmouth*:
But who is substituted 'gainst the *French,*
I have no certain notice.

York. [6] Let us on;
And publish the occasion of our arms.
The Commonwealth is sick of their own choice;
Their over-greedy love hath surfeited.
An habitation giddy and unsure
Hath he, that buildeth on the vulgar heart.
O thou fond Many! with what loud applause
Did'st thou beat heav'n with blessing *Bolingbroke,*
Before he was, what thou would'st have him be?
And now, being trim'd up in thine own desires,
Thou, beastly feeder, art so full of him,
That thou provok'st thyself to cast him up.
So, so, thou common dog, didst thou disgorge
Thy glutton bosom of the royal *Richard,*
And now thou would'st eat thy dead vomit up,
And howl'st to find it. What Trust is in these times?
They, that when *Richard* liv'd, would have him die,
Are now become enamour'd on his Grave;
Thou, that threw'st dust upon his goodly head,
When through proud *London* he came sighing on
After th' admired heels of *Bolingbroke,*
Cry'st now, O Earth, yield us that King again,

---

[5] *If he should do so,*] This passage is read in the first editions thus: *If he should do so, French and* Welsh *he leaves his back unarm'd, they baying him at the heels, never fear that.* These lines, which were evidently printed from an interlined copy not understood, are properly regulated in the next edition, and are here only mentioned to show what errors may be suspected to remain.

[6] *Let us on, &c.*] This excellent speech of *York* was one of the passages added by *Shakespeare* after his first Edition. POPE

         ıd take thou this. O thoughts of men accurſt!
ſt and to come, ſeem beſt; things preſent, worſt.
Mowb. Shall we go draw our numbers and ſet on?
Haſt. We are time's ſubjects, and time bids, be gone.
                                                   [*Exeunt.*

ACT II. SCENE I.

A Street in LONDON.

Enter Hoſteſs, with two Officers, Phang *and* Snare.

HOSTESS.

MR. *Phang*, have you enter'd the action?
    Phang. It is enter'd.
Hoſt. Where's your yeoman? is he a luſty yeoman?
ll he ſtand to it?
Phang. Sirrah, where's *Snare?*
Hoſt. O Lord, ay, good Mr. *Snare.*
Snare. Here, here,
Phang. Snare, we muſt arreſt Sir *John Falſtaff.*
Hoſt. Ay, good Mr. *Snare*, I have enter'd him and
    all.
Snare. It may chance coſt ſome of us our lives, for
    he will ſtab.
Hoſt. Alas-the-day! take heed of him; he ſtab'd
: in mine own houſe, and that moſt beaſtly; he
res not what miſchief he doth, if his weapon be out.
e will foin like any devil; he will ſpare neither man,
ɔman, nor child.
Phang. If I can cloſe with him, I care not for his
    thruſt.
Hoſt. No, nor I neither.——I'll be at your elbow.

258 THE SECOND PART OF

Phang. If I but fift him once; ⁷ if he come but within my vice.

Hoſt. I am undone by his going; I warrant you, he is an infinitive thing upon my ſcore. Good Mr. *Phang*, hold him ſure; good Mr. *Snare*, let him not 'ſcape. He comes continually to *Pie corner*, ſaving your manhoods, to buy a ſaddle: and he is indited to dinner to the ⁸ *Lubbars-head* in *Lombard-ſtreet*, to Mr. *Smooth's* the *Silkman*. I pray ye, ſince my exion is enter'd, and my caſe ſo openly known to the world, let him be brought in to his anſwer. ⁹ A hundred mark is a long Lone, for a poor lone woman to bear; and I have borne, and borne, and borne, and have been fub'd off, and fub'd off, from this day to that day, that it is a ſhame to be thought on. There is no honeſty in ſuch dealing, unleſs a woman ſhould be made an Aſs and a beaſt, to bear every knave's wrong.

Enter Falſtaff, Bardolph, *and the boy.*

Yonder he comes, and that arrant ¹ malmſey-noſe knave *Bardolph* with him. Do your offices, do your offices, Mr. *Phang* and Mr. *Snare*, do me, do me, do me your offices.

Fal. How now? whoſe mare's dead? what's the matter?

---

⁷ *If he comes but within my vice.*] *Vice* or *graſp*. A metaphor taken from a ſmith's vice: There is another reading in the old Edition, *view*, which I think not ſo good.   POPE.

⁸ —— *Lubbar's-head*] This is, I ſuppoſe, a colloquial corruption of the *Libbard's* head.

⁹ *A hundred mark is a long* one,] A long *one?* A long What? It is almoſt needleſs to obſerve, how familiar it is with our Poet to play the Chimes upon Words ſimilar in Sound, and *differing* in Signification: and therefore I make no Queſtion but he wrote,

A hundred Marks is a long Lone for a poor lone Woman to bear: i. e. 100 Marks is a good round Sum for a poor Widow to venture on Truſt.   THEOBALD.

¹ *Malmſey-noſe.*] That is, red noſe, from the colour of malmſey wine.

Phang.

KING HENRY IV.

Phang. Sir *John,* I arreſt you at the ſuit of Mrs. Quickly.

Fal. Away, varlets. Draw, *Bardolph,* cut me off the villain's head; throw the quean in the kennel.

Hoſt. Throw me in the kennel? I'll throw thee in the kennel. Wilt thou? wilt thou? thou baſtardly rogue. Murder, murder! O thou [2] hony-ſuckle villain, wilt thou kill God's officers and the King's? O thou hony-feed rogue! thou art a hony-feed, a man queller, and a woman-queller.

Fal. Keep them off, *Bardolph.*

Phang. A reſcue, a reſcue!

Hoſt. Good people, bring a reſcue or two; [3] thou wo't, wo't thou? thou wo't, wo't thou? do, do, thou rogue, do, thou hemp-feed!

Fal. [4] Away, you ſcullion, you rampallian, you fuſtarian: I'll tickle your cataſtrophe.

SCENE II.

Enter Chief Juſtice attended.

Ch. Juſ. What's the matter? keep the peace here, ha!

Hoſt. Good my lord, be good to me. I beſeech you, ſtand to me.

Ch. Juſ. How now, Sir *John?* what, are you brawling here?
Doth this become your place, your time, and buſineſs?
You ſhould have been well on your way to *York.*

---

[2] *Hony-ſuckle villain — hony-[feed] rogue.*] The landlady's corruption of *homicidal* and *homicide*. THEOBALD.

Thou wo't, wo't thou? &c] The firſt folio reads, I think, leſs properly, *thou wilt not? thou wilt not?*

[4] *Fal. Away, you ſcullion.*] This ſpeech is given to the *page* in all the editions to the folio of 1664. It is more proper for *Falſtaff,* but that the boy muſt not ſtand quite ſilent and uſeleſs on the ſtage.

S 2 —Stand

—Stand from him, fellow; wherefore hang'ſt thou on him?

Hoſt. O my moſt worſhipful lord, an't pleaſe your Grace, I am a poor widow of *Eaſt-cheap*, and he is arreſted at my ſuit.

Ch. Juſ. For what ſum?

Hoſt. It is more than for ſome, my lord, it is for all; all I have; he hath eaten me out of houſe and home; he hath put all my ſubſtance into that fat belly of his. —But I will have ſome of it out again, or I'll ride thee o'nights, like the mare.

Fal. I think, I am as like to ride the mare, if I have any 'vantage of ground to get up.

Ch. Juſ. How comes this, Sir *John?* fie; what man of good temper would endure this tempeſt of exclamation? are you not aſham'd to inforce a poor widow to ſo rough a courſe to come by her own?

Fal. What is the groſs ſum that I owe thee?

Hoſt. Marry, if thou wert an honeſt man, thyſelf, and the mony too. Thou didſt ſwear to me on a par- cel-gilt goblet, ſitting in my *Dolphin*-chamber, at the round table, by a ſea-coal fire, on *Wedneſday* in *Whitſun- week*, when the Prince broke thy head [5] for likening his father to a ſinging-man of *Windſor*; thou didſt ſwear to me then, as I was waſhing thy wound, to marry me, and make me my lady thy wife. Canſt thou deny it? did not good-wife *Keech*, the butcher's wife, come in then, and call me goſſip *Quickly?* coming in to bor- row a meſs of vinegar; telling us, ſhe had a good diſh of prawns; whereby thou didſt deſire to eat ſome; whereby I told thee, they were ill for a green wound; and didſt not thou, when ſhe was gone down ſtairs,

---

[5] *For likening his father to a ſinging man.*] Such is the read- ing of the firſt edition, all the reſt have *for likening him to a ſinging man.* The original edi- tion is right; the prince might allow familiarities with himſelf, and yet very properly break the knight's head when he ridiculed his father.

deſire

KING HENRY IV.

e me to be no more fo familiarity with fuch poor
)le, faying, that ere long they fhould call me Ma-
? and didft thou not kifs me, and bid me fetch
 thirty fhillings? I put thee now to thy book-oath;
 it, if thou canft.
al. My lord, this is a poor mad foul; and fhe
 up and down the town, that her eldeft fon is like
    She hath been in good cafe, and the truth is,
 :rty hath diftracted her. But for thefe foolifh
 cers, I befeech you, I may have redrefs againft
 a.
b. Juft. Sir *John*, Sir *John*, I am well acquainted
 your manner of wrenching the true caufe the falfe
 . It is not a confident brow, nor the throng of
 ds that come with fuch more than impudent faw-
 fs from you, can thruft me from a level confide-
 m. ' ⁶ I know, you have practifed upon the eafy-
 ling fpirit of this woman.
ʼʃt. Yes, in troth, my lord.
b. Juft. Pry'thee, peace.—Pay her the debt you
 her, and unpay the villainy you have done her;
)ne you may do with fterling mony, and the other
    current repentance.
il. My lord, I will not undergo ⁷ this fneap with-
 ·eply. You call honourable boldnefs impudent
 inefs; if a man will court'fie and fay nothing, he
 rtuous. No, my lord, my humble duty remem-
 l, I will not be your fuitor; I fay to you, I defire
 erance from thefe officers, being upon hafty em-
    ment in the King's affairs.
b. Juft. You fpeak, as having power to do wrong;

---

⁶ *know you have practifed*] *and perfon.* Without this the fol-
firft quarto it is read thus. lowing exhortation of the Chief
have, *as it appears to me,* Juftice is lefs proper.
ed upon the eafy yielding   ⁷ *This fneap*] A *Yorkfhire* word
of this woman, *and made* for *rebuke.*   POPE.
·ve your ufes both in purfe

S 3   but

but [1] anſwer in the effect of your reputation, and ſa-
tisfy the poor woman.

Fal. Come hither, hoſteſs. [*Aſide.*

SCENE III.

Enter a Meſſenger.

Ch. Juſt. Maſter *Gower*, what news?
Gower. The King, my lord, and *Henry* Prince of
Wales
Are near at hand: the reſt the paper tells.

Fal. As I am a gentleman———
Hoſt. Nay, you ſaid ſo before.
Fal. As I am a gentleman;——— come, no more
words of it.

Hoſt. By this heav'nly ground I tread on, I muſt
be fain to pawn both my plate, and the tapeſtry of my
dining chambers.

Fal. Glaſſes, glaſſes, is the only drinking; and for
thy walls, a pretty ſlight drollery, or the ſtory of the
Prodigal, or the [9] *German* Hunting in water-work, is
worth a thouſand of [1] theſe bed-hangings, and theſe
fly-bitten tapeſtries. Let it be ten pound, if thou canſt.
Come, if it were not for thy humours, there is not a
better wench in *England.* Go, waſh thy face, and
draw thy action. Come, thou muſt not be in this humour with me; do'ſt not know me? Come, come, I
know, thou waſt ſet on to this.

Hoſt. Pr'ythee, Sir *John*, let it be but twenty nobles; I am loth to pawn my plate, in good earneſt, la.

---

[1] *Anſwer in the effect of your reputation.*] That is, *anſwer in a manner ſuitable to your character.*

[9] German *Hunting in water-work,*] *i. e.* in water-colours.
WARBURTON.

[1] *Theſe* BED-*hangings,*] We ſhould read DEAD-*hangings, i. e.* faded. WARBURTON.
I think the preſent reading may well ſtand. He recommends painted paper inſtead of tapeſtry; which he calls *bed-hangings,* in contempt, as fitter to make curtains than to hang walls.

Fal. Let it alone, I'll make other shift; you'll be a fool still———

Host. Well, you shall have it, though I pawn my gown. I hope, you'll come to supper. You'll pay me all together?

Fal. Will I live?—Go with her, with her: hook on, hook on. [*To the officers.*

Host. Will you have *Doll Tear-sheet* meet you at supper?

Fal. No more words. Let's have her.
[*Exeunt Hostess and Serjeant.*

Ch. Just. I have heard better news.

Fal. What's the news, my good lord?

Ch. Just. Where lay the King last night?

Gower. At *Basingstoke*, my lord.

Fal. I hope, my lord, all's well. What is the news, my lord?

Ch. Just. Come all his forces back?

Gower. No; fifteen hundred foot, five hundred horse Are march'd up to my lord of *Lancaster*, Against *Northumberland* and the Arch-bishop.

Fal. Comes the King back from *Wales*, my noble lord?

Ch. Just. You shall have letters of me presently. Come, go along with me, good Mr. *Gower*.

Fal. My lord,———

Ch. Just. What's the matter?

Fal. Master *Gower*, shall I intreat you with me to dinner?

Gower. I must wait upon my good lord here, I thank you, good Sir *John*.

Ch. Just. Sir *John*, you loiter here too long, being you are to take soldiers up in the countries as you go.

Fal. Will you sup with me, master *Gower*?

Ch. Just. What foolish master taught you these manners, Sir *John*?

Fal. Master *Gower*, if they become me not, he was a fool

a fool that taught them me. This is the right fencing grace, my lord, tap for tap, and so part fair.

Ch. Just. Now the Lord lighten thee, thou art a great fool! [*Exeunt.*

SCENE IV.

Continues in LONDON.

Enter Prince Henry *and* Poins.

P. Henry. TRUST me, I am exceeding weary.

Poins. Is it come to that? I had thought, weariness durst not have attach'd one of so high blood.

P. Henry. It doth me, though it discolours the complexion of my Greatness to acknowledge it. Doth it not shew vilely in me to desire small beer?

Poins. Why, a Prince should not be so loosely studied, as to remember so weak a composition.

P. Henry. Belike then, my appetite was not princely got; for, in troth, I do now remember the poor creature, small beer. But, indeed, these humble considerations make me out of love with my Greatness. What a disgrace is it to me to remember thy name? or to know thy face to-morrow? or to take note how many pair of silk stockings thou hast? (*viz.* these, and those that were the peach-colour'd ones;) or to bear the inventory of thy shirts, as one for superfluity, and one other for use; but that the tennis-court-keeper knows better than I, for it is a low ebb of linnen with thee, when thou keepest not racket there; as thou hast not done a great while, because the rest of thy low Countries have made a shift to eat up thy holland [a]. *Poins.*

---

[a] The quarto of 1600 adds, *And God knows, whether those, that bawl out of the ruins of thy linen, shall inherit his Kingdom: but the midwives say, the children are not in the fault; whereupon the world increases, and kindred are mightily strengthened.*] Th passag

KING HENRY IV. 265

ns. How ill it follows, after you have labour'd
d, you should talk so idly? tell me, how many
young Princes would do so, their fathers lying
as yours at this time is.

Henry. Shall I tell thee one thing, *Poins?*

ns. Yes, and let it be an excellent good thing.

Henry. It shall serve among wits of no higher
ng than thine.

ns. Go to; I stand the push of your one thing,
ou'll tell.

Henry. Why, I tell thee, it is not meet that I
be sad now my father is sick; albeit, I could
thee, as to one it pleases me, for fault of a
, to call my friend, I could be sad, and sad in-
oo.

ns. Very hardly, upon such a subject.

Henry. By this hand, thou think'st me as far in
evil's book, as thou and *Falstaff*, for obduracy
rsistency. Let the end try the man. But, I tell
ny heart bleeds inwardly that my father is so
nd keeping such vile company, as thou art,
1 reason taken from me ³ all ostentation of sor-

ns. The reason?

Henry. What would'st thou think of me, if I
weep.

ns. I would think thee a most princely hypocrite.

Henry. It would be every man's thought; and
rt a blessed fellow, to think as every man thinks.
a man's thought in the world keeps the road-way

Mr *Pope* restored from
edition. I think it may
e omitted, and therefore
raded it to the margin.
tted in the first folio, and
sequent editions before
's, and was perhaps ex-
oy the authour. The edi-
viling to lose any thing

of *Shakespeare's*, not only insert
what he has added, but recal
what he has rejected.

³ *All ostentation of sorrow.*]
Ostentation is here not *boastful
shew,* but simply *shew. Mer-
chant of* Venice.
—*One well studied in a sad* ostent
To please his Grandame.

better

266   THE SECOND PART OF

better than thine. Every man would think me an hypocrite, indeed. And what excites your moſt worſhipful thought to think ſo?

Poins. Why, becauſe you have ſeemed ſo lewd, and ſo much ingraffed to *Falſtaff*.

P. Henry. And to thee.

Poins. Nay, by this light, I am well ſpoken of, I can hear it with mine own ears; the worſt they can ſay of me is, that I am a ſecond brother, and that I am a * proper fellow of my hands; and thoſe two things, I confeſs, I cannot help. Look, look, here comes *Bardolph*.

P. Henry. And the Boy that I gave *Falſtaff*; he had him from me chriſtian, and, ſee, if the fat villain have not transform'd him ape.

SCENE V.

Enter Bardolph *and* Page.

Bard. Save your Grace.

P. Henry. And yours, moſt noble *Bardolph*.

Bard. [*to the Boy*] ⁵ Come, you virtuous aſs, and baſhful fool, muſt you be bluſhing? wherefore bluſh you now; what a maidenly man at arms are you become? Is it ſuch a matter to get a pottle-pot's maiden-head?

Page. He call'd me even now, my lord, through a red lattice, and I could diſcern no part of his face from the window; at laſt, I ſpy'd his eyes, and, methought,

---

* *Proper fellow of my hands.*] A *tall* or *proper* man of his hands was a *ſtout fighting man*.

⁵ Poins. *Come, you virtuous aſs*, &c.] Tho' all the Editions give this Speech to *Poins*, it ſeems evident by the Page's immediate Reply, that it muſt be placed to *Bardolph*. For *Bardolph* had call'd to the Boy from an Alehouſe, and, 'tis likely, made him half-drunk: and, the Boy being aſham'd of it, 'tis natural for *Bardolph*, a bold unbred Fellow, to banter him on his aukward Baſhfulneſs.

THEOBALD.

he

he had made two holes in the ale-wive's new petticoat, and peep'd through.

P. Henry. Hath not the boy profited?

Bard. Away, you whorfon upright rabbet, away!

Page. Away, you rafcally *Althea's* dream, away!

P. Henry. Inftruct us, boy. What dream, boy?

Page. Marry, my lord, *Althea* dream'd, fhe was deliver'd of a firebrand; and therefore I call him her dream [6].

P. Henry. A crowns-worth of good interpretation. —There it is, boy. [*Gives him money.*

Poins. O that this good bloffom could be kept from cankers! Well, there is fix pence to preferve thee.

Bard. If you do not make him be hang'd among you, the Gallows fhall be wrong'd.

P. Henry. And how doth thy mafter, *Bardolph?*

Bard. Well, my good lord; he heard of your Grace's coming to town. There's a letter for you.

P. Henry. Deliver'd with good refpect;—and how doth the [7] *Martlemas,* your Mafter?

Bard. In bodily health, Sir.

Poins. Marry, the immortal part needs a phyfician; but that moves not him; though that be fick, it dies not.

P. Henry. I do allow [8] this wen to be as familiar with me as my dog; and he holds his place; for, look you, how he writes.

Poins reads. John Falftaff, knight,——Every man muft know that, as often as he hath occafion to name himfelf: even like thofe that are kin to the King, for

---

[6] *Shakespeare* is here miftaken in his Mythology, and has confounded *Althea's* firebrand with *Hecuba's*. The firebrand of *Althea* was real: but *Hecuba*, when fhe was big with *Paris*, dreamed that fhe was delivered of a firebrand that confumed the kingdom.

[7] *The* Martlemas, *your Mafter,*] That is, the *autumn,* or rather the *latter spring.* The old fellow with juvenile paffions.

[8] *This wen.*] The fwoln excrefcence of a man.

they

268   THE SECOND PART OF

they never prick their finger but they say, *there is some of the King's blood spilt. How comes that?* says he that takes upon him not to conceive⁹: the answer is as ready as a borrower's cap; *I am the King's poor cousin, Sir.*

P. *Henry.* Nay, they will be akin to us, or they will fetch it from *Japhet.* But, to the letter.

Poins. *Sir* John Falstaff, *knight, to the son of the King, nearest his father,* Harry *Prince of* Wales, *Greeting.* Why, this is a certificate.

¹ P. *Henry.* Peace.

Poins. *I will imitate the honourable* Romans *in brevity.* Sure, he means brevity in breath; short-winded. *I commend me to thee, I commend thee, and I leave thee. Be not too familiar with* Poins, *for he misuses thy favours so much, that he swears, thou art to marry his Sister* Nell. *Repent at idle times as thou may'st, and so farewel. Thine, by yea and no; which is as much as to say, as thou usest him.* Jack Falstaff *with my familiars:* John *with my brothers and sisters:* and Sir John *with all* Europe.

Poins. My Lord, I will steep this letter in sack, and make him eat it.

P. *Henry.* ² That's to make him eat twenty of his words. But do you use me thus, *Ned?* must I marry your Sister?

Poins. May the wench have no worse fortune! But I never said so.

P. *Henry.* Well, thus we play the fools with the

⁹ *The Answer is as ready as a* borrow'd *Cap.*] But how is a *borrow'd* Cap so ready? Read, a *Borrower's* Cap: and then there is some Humour in it For a Man, that goes to borrow Mony, is of all Others the most complaisant: His Cap is always at hand. WARBURTON.

¹ *Prince* Henry.] All the editors, except Sir *Thomas Hanmer,*

have left this letter in confusion making the *Prince* read part, and *Poins* part. I have followed his correction.

² *That's to make him eat* TWENTY *of his words.*] What just twenty, when the letter contain'd above eight times twenty we should read PLENTY; and in this word the joke, as slender as it is, consists. WARBURTON.

time,

time, and the spirits of the wise sit in the clouds and mock us. Is your master here in *London*?

Bard. Yes, my lord.

P. Henry. Where sups he? doth the old Boar feed in the old frank *?

Bard. At the old place, my lord, in *East-cheap*.

P. Henry. What company?

Page. ³ *Ephesians*, my lord, of the old church.

P. Henry. Sup any women with him?

Page. None, my lord, but old Mrs. *Quickly*, and Mrs. *Doll Tear-sheet*.

P. Henry. What Pagan may that be?

Page. A proper gentlewoman, Sir, and a kinswoman of my master's.

P. Henry. Even such kin, as the parish heifers are to the town Bull. Shall we steal upon them, *Ned*, at supper?

Poins. I am your shadow, my lord, I'll follow you.

P. Henry. Sirrah, you boy, and *Bardolph*, no word to your master that I am yet come to town. There's for your silence.

Bard. I have no tongue, Sir.

Page. And for mine, Sir, I will govern it.

P. Henry. Fare ye well: go. This *Dol Tear-sheet* should be some road.

Poins. I warrant you, as common as the way between St. *Albans* and *London*.

P. Henry. How might we see *Falstaff* bestow himself to-night in his true colours, and not ourselves be seen?

Poins. ⁴ Put on two leather jerkins and aprons, and wait upon him at his table, as drawers.

---

* *Frank* is *sty*.   Pope.

³ *Ephesians*, &c.] *Ephesian* was a term in the cant of these times of which I know not the precise notion: it was, perhaps, a *toper*. So the *Host* in *the Merry Wives of* Windsor:

It is thine Host, thine Ephesian *calls*.

⁴ *Put on two leather jerkins.*] This was a plot very unlikely to succeed where the *Prince* and the drawers were all known; but it produces merriment, which our author found more useful than probability.

P. Henry.

P. Henry. From a God to a Bull? ⁵ a heavy defcenfion. It was *Jove's* cafe. From a Prince to a prentice? a low transformation; that fhall be mine. For in every thing, the purpofe muft weigh with the folly. Follow me, *Ned.* [*Exeunt.*

SCENE VI.

Changes to Northumberland's *Caftle.*

Enter Northumberland, *Lady* Northumberland, *and Lady* Percy.

North. I Pr'ythee, loving wife, and gentle daughter,
Give even way unto my rough affairs.
Put not you on the vifage of the times,
And be like them to *Percy*, troublefome.
 L. North. I have given over, I will fpeak no more;
Do what you will; your wifdom be your guide.
 North. Alas, fweet wife, my Honour is at pawn,
And, but my Going, nothing can redeem it.
 L. Percy. Oh, yet, for heav'ns fake, go not to thefe wars.
The time was, father, that you broke your word,
When you were more endear'd to it than now;
When your own *Percy*, when my heart-dear *Harry*,
Threw many a northward look, to fee his father

---

⁵ *a heavy* defcenfion.] Other readings have it *declenfion*. Mr. *Pope* chofe the firft. On which Mr *Theobald* fays, *But why not declenfion? are not the terms properly fynonymous?* If fo, might not Mr. *Pope* fay in his turn, then why not *defcenfion?* But it is not fo. And *defcenfion* was preferred with judgment. For *defcenfion* fignifies a *voluntary* going down; *declenfion,* a *natural* and neceffary. Thus when we fpeak of the Sun, poetically, as a charioteer, we fhould fay his *defcenfion*: if phyfically, as a mere globe of light, his *declenfion.*   WARBURTON.

Defcenfion is the reading of the firft edition.

Mr. *Upton* propofes that we fhould read thus by tranfpofition. *From a God to a Bull, a low transformation;—from a Prince to a Prentice, a heavy declenfion.* This reading is elegant, and perhaps right.

Bring

Bring up his Pow'rs; but he did long in vain!
Who then perfuaded you to ftay at home?
There were two Honours loft; yours and your fon's.
For yours, may heav'nly glory brighten it!
For his, it ftuck upon him as the Sun
In the grey vault of heav'n; and by his light
Did all the chivalry of *England* move
To do brave acts. He was indeed the glafs,
Wherein the noble Youth did drefs themfelves.
'He had no legs, that practis'd not his gait;
And fpeaking thick, which Nature made his blemifh,
Became the accents of the valiant;
For thofe, that could fpeak low and tardily,
Would turn their own perfection to abufe,
To feem like him: So that in fpeech, in gait,
In diet, in affections of delight,
In military rules, humours of blood,
He was the mark and glafs, copy and book,
That fafhion'd others. And him, wondrous him!
O miracle of men! him did you leave
Second to None, unfeconded by You,
To look upon the hideous God of War
In difadvantage; to abide a field,
Where nothing but the found of *Hot-fpur's* Name
Did feem defenfible. So you left Him.
Never, O, never do his Ghoft the wrong,
To hold your honour more precife and nice
With others, than with him. Let them alone:
The Marfhal and the Archbifhop are ftrong.
Had my fweet *Harry* had but half their numbers,
To day might I, (hanging on *Hot-fpur's* neck)
Have talk'd of *Monmouth's* Grave.

North. Befhrew your heart,
Fair daughter, you do draw my fpirits from me,
With new-lamenting ancient over-fights.

' *He had no legs,* &c.] The of thofe added by *Shakefpeare*
twenty-two following lines are after his firft edition. POPE.

But

But I muſt go and meet with danger there,
Or it will ſeek me in another place,
And find me worſe provided.

 L. North. Fly to *Scotland*,
'Till that the Nobles and the armed Commons
Have of their puiſſance made a little taſte.

 L. Percy. If they get ground and 'vantage of the King,
Then join you with them, like a rib of ſteel,
To make ſtrength ſtronger. But, for all our loves,
Firſt let them try themſelves. So did your ſon:
He was ſo ſuffer'd; ſo came I a widow;
And never ſhall have length of Life enough,
[7] To rain upon remembrance with mine eyes,
That it may grow and ſprout as high as heav'n,
For recordation to my noble husband.

 North. Come, come, go in with me. 'Tis with my mind
As with the tide ſwell'd up unto his height,
That makes a ſtill-ſtand, running neither way.
Fain would I go to meet the Archbiſhop,
But many thouſand reaſons hold me back:
I will reſolve for *Scotland;* there am I,
'Till time and 'vantage crave my company. [*Exeunt.*

---

[7] *To rain upon remembrance—*]
Alluding to the plant, roſemary, ſo called, and uſed in funerals.---
Thus in *The Winter's Tale,*
 For you there's roſemary *and* rue, *theſe keep*
 Seeming and favour all the winter long,
Grace *and* remembrance *be unto you both,* &c.
For as rue was called *herb of grace,* from its being uſed in exorciſms: ſo roſemary was called *remembrance,* from its being a cephalic. W<small>ARBURTON</small>.

SCENE

SCENE VII.

...nges to the Boar's-head Tavern in East-cheap.

Enter two Drawers.

1 Draw. WHAT the devil hast thou brought there? Apple-*Johns*? thou know'st, Sir *John* ...t endure an apple-*John*.

Draw. Mass! thou sayest true. The prince once ...dish of Apple-*Johns* before him, and told him ... were five more Sir *Johns*, and, putting off his ...said, I will now take my leave of these six dry, ...l, old, wither'd knights. It anger'd him to the ...; but he hath forgot That.

Draw. Why then, cover, and set them down; and ... thou can'st find out [1] *Sneak's* Noise; Mrs. *Tear-*...would fain hear some musick. [2] Dispatch!—The ... where they sup is too hot, they'll come in ...ht.

Draw. Sirrah, here will be the Prince, and Master ... anon; and they will put on two of our jerkins ...prons, and Sir *John* must not know of it. Bar- ...hath brought word.

Draw. Then [3] here will be old *Utis:* it will be an ...ent stratagem.

Draw. I'll see, if I can find out *Sneak.* [*Exeunt.*

---

[1] — Sneak's *Noise;*] Sneak ... street minstrel, and there- ...e drawer goes out to listen ...an hear him in the neigh- ...od.

[2] *Dispatch,* &c.] This period ... the first edition. POPE.

[3] — *here will be old* Utis;] *Utis,* an old word yet in use in some countries, signifying a *merry festival,* from the *French, Huit, octo,* ab *A. S.* Eahta. *Octava Festi alicujus.* SKINNER. POPE.

SCENE VIII.

Enter Hoſteſs and Dol.

Hoſt. I'faith, ſweet-heart, methinks now you are in an excellent good temperality, your pulſidge beats as extraordinarily as heart would deſire, and your colour, I warrant you, is as red as any roſe; but, i'faith, you have drank too much canaries, and that's a marvellous ſearching wine; and it perfumes the blood, ere we can ſay *what's this.* How do you now?

Dol. Better than I was. Hem.——

Hoſt. Why, that was well ſaid. A good heart's worth gold. Look, here comes Sir *John*.

Enter Falſtaff.

Fal. When Arthur *firſt in Court*—empty the jourden —*and was a worthy King:* how now, Mrs. *Dol.*

Hoſt. Sick of a calm; yea, good ſooth.

Fal. So is all her feĉt [2]; if they be once in a calm, they are ſick.

Dol. You muddy raſcal, is that all the comfort you give me?

Fal. [3] You make fat raſcals, Mrs. *Dol.*

Dol. I make them! gluttony and diſeaſes make them, I make them not.

Fal. If the cook make the gluttony, you help to make the Diſeaſes, *Dol*; we catch of you, *Dol*, we catch of you; grant That, my poor Vertue, grant That.

Dol. Ay, marry, our chains and our jewels.

---

[2] *So is all her feĉt;*——] I khow not why *feĉt* is printed in all the copies, I believe *ſex* is meant.

[3] *You make fat raſcals.*] Fal-ſtaff alludes to a phraſe of the foreſt; *lean* deer are called *raſcal* deer. He tells her ſhe calls him wrong, being *fat* he cannot be a *raſcal.*

Fal.

KING HENRY IV.

Fal. [4] Your brooches, pearls and owches.—For to serve bravely, is to come halting off, you know; to come off the breach with his pike bent bravely, and to surgery bravely; to venture upon the charg'd chambers bravely——

Dol. Hang yourself, you muddy Conger, hang yourself!

Host. By my troth, this is the old fashion; you two never meet, but you fall to some discord; you are both, in good troth, as [5] rheumatick as two dry toasts, you cannot one bear with another's confirmities. What the good-jer? one must bear, and that must be you; you are the weaker vessel, as they say, the emptier vessel.

[*To* Dol.

Dol. Can a weak empty vessel bear such a huge full hogshead? there's a whole merchant's venture of *Bourdeaux* stuff in him; you have not seen a hulk better stuft in the Hold. Come, I'll be friends with thee, *Jack*.—Thou art going to the wars, and whether I shall ever see thee again or no, there is no body cares.

SCENE IX.

Enter Drawer.

Draw. Sir, [6] ancient *Pistol* is below and would speak with you.

Dol. Hang him, swaggering rascal, let him not come

---

[4] *Your* brooches, *pearls and* owches:] *Brooches* were chains of gold that women wore formerly about their necks. *Owches* were bosses of gold set with diamonds. POPE.

I believe *Falstaff* gives these splendid names as we give that of *carbuncle* to something very different from gems and ornaments, but the passage deserves not a laborious research.

[5] *Rheumatick.*] She would say *splenetick.* HANMER.

As two dry toasts, which cannot meet but they grate one another.

[6] *Ancient* Pistol is the same as *ensign* Pistol. *Falstaff* was captain, *Peto* lieutenant, and *Pistol* ensign, or *ancient*.

hither;

276 THE SECOND PART OF

hither; it is the foul-mouth'dst rogue in *England.*

Host. If he swagger, let him not come here. No; by my faith, I must live amongst my neighbours, I'll no swaggerers. I am in good name and fame with the very best. Shut the door, there comes no swaggerers here, I have not liv'd all this while to have swaggering now. Shut the door, I pray you.

Fal. Dost thou hear, Hostess? ———

Host. Pray you pacify yourself, Sir *John?* there comes no swaggerers here.

Fal. Do'st thou hear—it is mine Ancient.

Host. Tilly-fally, Sir *John,* never tell me; your Ancient swaggerer comes not in my doors. I was before master *Tisick* the deputy the other day; and, as he said to me—it was no longer ago than *Wednesday* last—neighbour *Quickly,* says he;—master *Domb* our minister was by then—neighbour *Quickly,* says he, receive those that are civil; for, faith he, you are in an ill name (now he said so, I can tell whereupon); for, says he, you are an honest woman, and well thought on; therefore take heed, what guests you receive. Receive, says he, no swaggering companions.—There come none here. You would bless you to hear what he said. No, I'll no swaggerers.

Fal. He's no swaggerer, Hostess; a tame cheater, i'faith; you may stroak him as gently as a puppey-greyhound; he will not swagger with a *Barbary* hen, if her feathers turn back in any shew of resistance. Call him up, drawer.

Host. Cheater, call you him? [7] I will bar no honest man my house, nor no cheater; but I do not love

---

[7] *I will bar no honest man my house, nor no* cheater;] The humour of this consists in the woman's mistaking the title of *Cheater* (which our ancestors gave to him whom we now, with better manners, call a *Gamester*) for that officer of the exchequer called an *Escheater,* well known to the common people of that time; and named, either corruptly or satirically, a *Cheater.*
WARBURTON.

swagger-

swaggering, by my troth; I am the worse, when one says swagger. Feel, masters, how I shake, look you, I warrant you.

Dol. So you do, hostess.

Host. Do I? yea, in very truth, do I, as if it were an aspen leaf. I cannot abide swaggerers.

SCENE X.

Enter Pistol, Bardolph *and* Page.

Pist. Save you, Sir *John*.

Fal. Welcome, ancient *Pistol*. Here, *Pistol*, I charge you with a cup of sack, do you discharge upon mine hostess.

Pist. I will discharge upon her, Sir *John*, with two bullets.

Fal. She is Pistol-proof, Sir, you shall hardly offend her.

Host. Come, I'll drink no proofs, nor no bullets; I will drink no more than will do me good, for no man's pleasure. I———

Pist. Then to you, Mrs. *Dorothy*, I will charge you.

Dol. Charge me! I scorn you, scurvy companion! what you poor, base, rascally, cheating, lack-linnen mate. Away, you mouldy rogue, away, I'm meat for your master.

Pist. I know you, Mistress *Dorothy*.

Dol. Away, you cut-purse rascal, you filthy bung, away. By this wine, I'll thrust my knife in your mouldy chaps, if you play the sawcy cuttle with me. Away, you bottle-ale rascal, you basket-hilt stale jugler. You.— Since when, I pray you, Sir?—what, with two [*] points on your shoulder? much [¹]!

Pist,

---

[*] As a mark of his commission.
[¹] *what, with two points on your shoulder? much!*] Much was a common expression of disdain at that time, of the same sense with that more modern one, *Marry*

Pist. I will murther your ruff for this.

Fal. ⁹ No more, *Piſtol*; I wou'd not have you go off here. Diſcharge yourſelf of our company, *Piſtol.*

Hoſt. No, good captain *Piſtol*; not here, ſweet captain.

Dol. Captain! thou abominable damn'd cheater, art thou not aſham'd to be call'd captain? if Captains were of my mind, they would truncheon you out of taking their names upon you, before you have earn'd them. You a captain! you ſlave! for what? for tearing a poor whore's ruff in a bawdy-houſe?—he a captain! hang him, rogue, ¹ he lives upon mouldy ſtew'd prunes and dry'd cakes. A captain! theſe villains will make the word *captain* as odious as the word *occupy*; which was an excellent good word, before it was ill ſorted; therefore captains had need look to it.

Bard. Pray thee, go down, good Antient.

Fal. Hark thee hither, miſtreſs *Dol.*

Pist. Not I. I tell thee what, Corporal *Bardolph*,—I could tear her. I'll be reveng'd on her.

Page. Pray thee, go down.

Pist. I'll ſee her damn'd firſt: to *Pluto*'s damned lake, to the infernal deep, where *Erebus* and tortures vile alſo. Hold hook and line, ſay I; down! down, dogs; down, fates; have we not *Hiren* here?"

Hoſt. Good captain *Peeſel*, be quiet, it is very late; I beſeech you now, aggravate your choler.

Pist. Theſe be good humours, indeed. Shall pack-horſes

Marry come up. The *Oxford Editor* not apprehending this, alters it to *march.* WARBURT.

I cannot but think the emendation right. This uſe of *much* I do not remember, nor is it here proved by any example.

⁹ *No more,* Piſtol, &c.] This is from the old edition of 1600. POPE.

¹ — *he lives upon mouldy ſtew'd prunes and dry'd cakes.*] That is, he lives at other mens coſt, but is not admitted to their tables, and gets only what is too ſtale to be eaten in the houſe.

And

llow-pamper'd jades of *Asia*,
nnot go but thirty miles a day,
with *Cæsars*, and with * *Cannibals*,
an Greeks? nay, rather damn them with
berus, and let the welkin roar.
fall foul for toys?
By my troth, captain, these are very bitter

Begone, good Ancient. This will grow to a
on.
Die men, like dogs; give crowns like pins;
: not *Hiren* here?
)' my word, captain, there's none such here.
e good-jer? do you think, I would deny her?
e quiet.
Then feed, and be fat, my fair *Calipolis*; come,
some sack. + *Si fortuna me tormenta, spero
ta.*

ow pamper'd jades of &c.] These lines are a quotation out of an old an play intitled, *Tamnquests, or the Scyrd.* THEOBALD.
l is used by a blunder al. This was afterd by *Congreve's Bluff Bluff* is a character taken from this of ol.
e not Hiren *here? ' my Word, Captain, such here.*] i. e. Shall have this trusty and Sword by my Side? ng *Arthur's* Swords Caliburne and Ron; the Confessor's, Curharlemagne's, Joyeuse; Durindana; Rinaldo's, and Rogero's, Balisarjtol, in Imitation of

these Heroes, calls his Sword *Hiren*. I have been told, *Amadis de Gaul* had a Sword of this Name. *Hirir* is to strike: From hence it seems probable that *Hiren* may be deriv'd; and so signify a *swashing, cutting* Sword ——— But what wonderful Humour is there in the good Hostess so innocently mistaking *Pistol's* Drift, fancying that he meant to fight for a Whore in the House, and therefore telling him, *On my Word, Captain, there's none such here; what the good-jer! do you think, I would deny her?* THEOBALD.

+ Sir *Tho.* Hanmer reads, *Si fortuna me tormenta, il sperare me contenta*, which is undoubtedly the true reading, but perhaps it was intended that *Pistol* should corrupt it.

280 THE SECOND PART OF

Fear we broad sides? no, let the fiend give fire:
Give me some sack; and, sweet-heart, lye thou there.
[Laying down his sword.
⁵ Come we to full points here; and are *& cætera*'s nothing?

Fal. *Pistol*, I would be quiet.

Pist. ⁶ Sweet knight, I kiss thy neif. What! we have seen the seven stars.

Dol. Thrust him down stairs, I cannot endure such a fustian rascal.

Pist. Thrust him down stairs? know we not ⁷ galloway nags?

Fal. Quoit him down, *Bardolph*, like a shove-groat shilling. Nay, if he do nothing but speak nothing, he shall be nothing here.

Bard. Come, get you down stairs.

Pist. What, shall we have incision! shall we imbrew? then Death
Rock me asleep, abridge my doleful days:
Why, then let grievous, ghastly, gaping wounds
Untwine the sisters three. Come, *Atropos*, I say.
[Snatching up his sword.

Host. Hoere's goodly stuff toward.

Fal. Give me my rapier, boy.

Dol. I pr'ythee, *Jack*, I pr'ythee, do not draw.

Fal. Get you down stairs.
[Drawing, and driving Pistol out.

Host. Here's a goodly tumult; I'll forswear keeping house, before I'll be in these tirrits and frights. So; murther, I warrant now. Alas, alas, put up your naked weapons, put up your naked weapons.

---

⁵ *Come we to full points,* &c.] That is, shall we stop here, shall we have no further entertainment.

⁶ *Sweet Knight, I kiss thy Neif.*] i. e. I kiss thy Fist. Mr. Pope will have it, that *neif* here is from *nativa*; i. e. a Woman-Slave that is born in one's house; and that *Pistol* would kiss *Falstaff*'s domestic Mistress *Dol Tearsheet*. THEOBALD.

⁷ *Galloway nags.*] That is, common backneys.

4
Dol.

KING HENRY IV.

I pr'ythee, *Jack*, be quiet, the rascal is gone.
ou whorson, little valiant villain, you!
. Are you not hurt i'th' groin? methought,
de a shrewd thrust at your belly.
Have you turn'd him out of doors?
d. Yes, Sir, the rascal's drunk. You have hurt
ir, in the shoulder.
A rascal, to brave me!——
Ah, you sweet little rogue, you. Alas, poor
ow thou sweat'st? Come, let me wipe thy face——
n, you whorson chops—ah, rogue! I love thee,
art as valourous as *Hector* of *Troy*, worth five
amemnon; and ten times better than the nine
ies. A villain!
A rascally slave; I will toss the rogue in a
t.
Do, if thou dar'st for thy heart: if thou do'st,
vass thee between a pair of sheets.

Enter Musick.

e. The musick is come, Sir.
Let them play; play, Sirs. Sit on my knee,
A rascal, bragging slave! the rogue fled from
quick-silver.
I'faith, and thou follow'd'st him like a church,
vhorson little *tydie Bartholomew* Boar-pig, when
ou leave fighting on days, and foining on nights,
gin to patch up thine old body for heaven?

e tydy Bartholomew *Boar-* | *Bartholomew Boar-pig* is a little
tidy Sir *T. Hanmer* reads | pig made of paste, sold at *Bar-*
: they are both words of | *tholomew* fair, and given to chil-
ent, and equally proper. | dren for a fairing.

SCENE

THE FIRST PART OF

SCENE XI.

Enter Prince Henry *and* Poins.

Fal. Peace, good *Dol*, do not speak like a death's head, do not bid me remember mine end.

Dol. Sirrah, what humour is the Prince of?

Fal. A good shallow young fellow; he would have made a good Pantler, he would have chipp'd bread well.

Dol. They say, *Poins* has a good wit.

Fal. He a good wit? hang him, baboon!—his wit is as thick as *Tewksbury* mustard, there is no more conceit in him, than is in a mallet.

Dol. Why doth the Prince love him so then?

Fal. Because their legs are both of a bigness, and he plays at quoits well, and ⁹ eats conger and fennel, and drinks off candles' ends for flap dragons, and rides the wild mare with the boys, and jumps upon joint-stools, and swears with a good grace, and wears his boot very smooth like unto the sign of the leg, and breeds no bate with telling of ¹ discreet stories; and such other gambol faculties he hath, that shew a weak mind and an able body, for the which the Prince admits him, for the Prince himself is such another, the weight of an hair will turn the scales between their *Averdupais*.

P. Henry. Would not this * Nave of a wheel have his ears cut off?

Poins. Let us beat him before his whore.

P. Henry. Look, if the wither'd Elder hath not his poll claw'd like a Parrot.

Poins. Is it not strange, that desire should so many years out-live performance?

---

⁹ *Eats conger and fennel, and drinks off candles' ends.* These qualifications I do not understand.

¹ *discreet stories;*] We should read *indiscreet.* WARB.

* *Nave of a wheel.*] Nave and *knave* are easily reconciled, but why *nave of a wheel?* I suppose for his roundness. He was called *round man* in contempt before.

Fal.

Fal. Kiss me, *Dol.*
P. Henry. *Saturn* and *Venus* this year in conjunction! what says the almanack to that?
Poins. And, look, whether the fiery *Trigon*, his man, be not lisping to his master's old Tables, his note-book, his counsel-keeper?
Fal. Thou dost give me flattering busses.
Dol. By my troth, I kiss thee with a most constant art.
Fal. I am old, I am old.
Dol. I love thee better than I love e'er a scurvy young boy of them all.
Fal. What stuff wilt thou have a kirtle of? I shall receive money on *Thursday*. Thou shalt have a cap tomorrow. A merry song, come — it grows late, we'll to bed. Thou wilt forget me when I am gone.
Dol. By my troth, thou wilt set me a weeping if thou say'st so. Prove, that ever I dress myself handsome till thy return ——— Well, hearken the end.
Fal. Some sack, *Francis*.
P. Henry. Poins. Anon, anon, Sir.
Fal. Ha! a bastard son of the King's! and art not thou *Poins* his brother?
P. Henry. Why, thou globe of sinful continents, what a life dost thou lead?
Fal. A better than thou: I am a gentleman, thou art a drawer.
P. Henry. Very true, Sir; and I come to draw you out by the ears,

---

[2] *Saturn and* Venus *this year* conjunction.] This was indeed a prodigy. The Astrologers, says Ficinus, remark, that *Saturn* and *Venus* are never conjoined.

[3] LISPING TO *his master's old* Tables, &c.] We should read ASPIRING TOO *his master's old* Tables, &c.] i. e. embracing his master's cast-off whore, and now his bawd [*his note book, his counsel-keeper.*] We have the same phrase again in *Cymbaline*,
You clasp young Cupid's Tables.
WARBURTON.
This emendation is very specious. I think it right.

[4] *Ha! a Bastard*, &c.] The improbability of this scene is scarcely balanced by the humour,
Host.

284 THE SECOND PART OF

Host. Oh, the Lord preserve thy good Grace! Welcome to *London.*—Now heav'n bless that sweet face of thine. What, are you come from *Wales?*

Fal. Thou whorson-mad compound of majesty, by this light flesh and corrupt blood, thou art welcome.
[*Leaning his hand upon Dol.*

Dol. How! you fat fool, I scorn you.

Poins. My lord, he will drive you out of your revenge, and turn all to a merriment, if you take not the heat.

P. Henry. You whorson [5] candle-mine, you, how vilely did you speak of me even now, before this honest, virtuous, civil gentlewoman?

Host. 'Blessing on your good heart, and so she is, by my troth.

Fal. Didst thou hear me?

P. Henry. Yes; and you knew me, as you did when you ran away by *Gads-hill*; you knew, I was at your back, and spoke it on purpose to try my patience.

Fal. No, no, no; not so; I did not think, thou wast within hearing.

P. Henry. I shall drive you then to confess the wilful abuse, and then I know how to handle you.

Fal. No abuse, *Hal*, on my honour, no abuse.

P. Henry. Not to dispraise me, and call me pantler; and bread-chipper, and I know not what!

Fal. No abuse, *Hal.*

Poins. No abuse!

Fal. No abuse, *Ned*, in the world; honest *Ned*, none. I disprais'd him before the wicked, that the wicked might not fall in love with him; in which doing, I have done part of a careful friend, and a true subject.—And thy father is to give me thanks for it. No abuse, *Hal*, none, *Ned*, none; no, boys, none.

P. Henry. See now, whether pure fear and entire cowardise doth not make thee wrong this virtuous

---
[5] *Candle-mine.*] Thou inexhaustible magazine of tallow.

gentle-

KING HENRY IV. 285

entlewoman, to close with us? Is she of the wicked? thine Hostess here of the wicked? or is the boy of he wicked? or honest *Bardolph*, whose zeal burns in is nose, of the wicked?

Poins. Answer, thou dead Elm, answer.

Fal. The fiend hath prickt down *Bardolph* irrecoveible, and his face is *Lucifer's* privy-kitchen, where he oth nothing but roast malt-worms. For the boy, iere is a good angel about him, but the devil out bids im too.

P. Henry. For the women,——

Fal. For one of them, she is in hell already, ⁶ and irns, poor soul! for the other, I owe her money; d whether she be damn'd for that, I know not.

Host. No, I warrant you.

Fal. No, I think, thou art not; I think thou art iit for that. Marry, there is another indictment upi thee, for suffering flesh to be eaten in thy house, ntrary to the law, for the which, I think, thou wilt owl.

Host. All victuallers do so. What is a joint of mutin or two in a whole *Lent*?

P. Henry. You, gentlewoman.

Dol. What says your Grace?

Fal. His Grace says that, which his flesh rebels gainst.

Host. Who knocks so loud at door? Look to the oor there, *Francis*.

⁶ *And burns, poor soul.*] This *Sir T. Hanmer's* reading. Undoubtedly right. The other editions had, *she is in hell already,* and burns poor souls. The venereal disease was called in these times the *brennynge* or *burning.*

SCENE

SCENE VI.

Enter Peto.

P. Henry. Peto, how now? what news?

Peto. The King your father is at *Westminster*,
And there are twenty weak and wearied posts
Come from the North; and, as I came along,
I met and overtook a dozen captains,
Bare-headed, sweating, knocking at the taverns,
And asking every one for Sir *John Falstaff*.

P. Henry. By heavens, *Poins*, I feel me much to blame,
So idly to profane the precious time;
When tempest of commotion, like the South
Borne with black vapour, doth begin to melt
And drop upon our bare unarmed heads.
Give me my sword, and cloak. *Falstaff*, good night.
[*Exeunt Prince and* Poins.

Fal. Now comes in the sweetest morsel of the night, and we must hence, and leave it unpick'd. More knocking at the door?—how now? what's the matter?

Bard. You must away to Court, Sir, presently; a dozen captains stay at door for you.

Fal. Pay the musicians, Sirrah. Farewel, Hostess; farewel, *Dol*. You see, my good wenches, how men of merit are sought after; the undeserver may sleep, when the man of action is call'd on. Farewel, good wenches; if I be not sent away post, I will see you again, ere I go.

Dol. I cannot speak; if my heart be not ready to burst——well, sweet *Jack*, have a care of thyself.

Fal. Farewel, farewel. [*Exit.*

Host. Well, fare thee well. I have known thee these twenty-nine years, come pescod-time; but an honester and truer hearted man—well, fare thee well.

Bard. Mrs. *Tear-sheet*.

Host.

Host. What's the matter?
Bard. Bid Mistress *Tear-Sheet* come to my master.
Host. O run, *Dol,* run; run, good *Dol.* [*Exeunt.*

ACT III. SCENE I.

The Palace in LONDON.

Enter King Henry *in his Night-Gown, with a Page.*

K. HENRY.

GO, call the Earls of *Surrey* and of *Warwick;*
But, ere they come, bid them o'er-read these letters,
And well consider of them. Make good speed.
[*Exit Page.*
How many thousands of my poorest Subjects
Are at this hour asleep! O gentle sleep,
Nature's soft Nurse, how have I frighted thee,
That thou no more wilt weigh my eye-lids down,
And steep my senses in forgetfulness?
Why rather, Sleep, ly'st thou in smoaky cribs,
Upon uneasy pallets stretching thee,
And husht with buzzing night-flies to thy slumber;
Than in the perfum'd chambers of the Great,
Under the Canopies of costly State,
And lull'd with sounds of sweetest melody?
O thou dull God, why ly'st thou with the vile
In loathsome beds, and leav'st the kingly couch
' A watch-case, or a common larum bell?
Wilt

. ⁷ The first scene is not in my copy of the first edition.
⁸ *A watch-case,* &c.] This alludes to the watchmen set in garrison towns upon some eminence attending upon an alarum-bell, which he was to ring out in case of fire, or any approaching danger. He had a case or box to shelter him from the weather, but

THE SECOND PART OF

Wilt thou, upon the high and giddy maſt,
Seal up the ſhip-boy's eyes, and rock his brains,
In cradle of the rude imperious Surge;
And in the Viſitation of the winds,
Who take the ruffian billows by the top,
Curling their monſtrous heads, and hanging them
With deaf'ning clamours in the ſlip'ry ſhrouds,
That, with the hurley, death itſelf awakes?
Can'ſt thou, O partial Sleep, give thy repoſe
To the wet ſea-boy in an hour ſo rude?
And, in the calmeſt and the ſtilleſt night,
With all appliances and means to boot,
Deny it to a King? ' then, happy lowly clown,
Uneaſy lyes the head, that wears a Crown.

SCENE II.

Enter Warwick *and* Surrey.

War. Many good morrows to your Majeſty!
K. Henry. Is it good morrow, lords?
War. 'Tis one o'clock, and paſt.
K. Henry. ' Why, then, good morrow to you. Well,
    my lords,

Have

---

but at his utmoſt peril he was not to ſleep whilſt he was upon duty. Theſe alarum bells are mentioned in ſeveral other places of *Shakeſpeare.*   HANMER.

⁹ —— *then, happy* LOW! LYE DOWN;] Evidently corrupted from *happy* LOWLY CLOWN. Theſe two lines making the juſt concluſion from what preceded. *If ſleep will fly a king and conſort itſelf with beggars, then happy the* lowly clown, *and uneaſy the* crown'd head.
    WARBURTON.

Dr. *Warburton* has not admitted this emendation into his text: I am glad to do it the juſtice which its authour has neglected.

¹ In the old Edition:
Why then good morrow to you all, my Lords:

Have you read o'er, &c.] The King ſends Letters to *Surrey* and *Warwick,* with Charge that they ſhould read them and attend him. Accordingly here *Surrey* and *Warwick* come, and no body elſe. The King would hardly have ſaid *Good morrow* to You All,

KING HENRY IV.

read o'er the letters I sent you?
We have, my Liege.
Then you perceive the body of our Kingdom,
it is; what rank diseases grow,
what danger, near the heart of it.
It is but as a body yet distemper'd,
its former strength may be restor'd,
 advice and little medicine;
Northumberland will soon be cool'd.
Oh heav'n, that one might read the book
fate,
e revolution of the times
ntains level, and the Continent,
solid firmness, melt itself
a; and, other times, to see
y girdle of the Ocean
or *Neptune's* hips; how Chances mock,
ges fill the cup of alteration
's liquors! O, if this were seen,
est youth viewing his progress through,
ls past, what crosses to ensue,

ers. THEOBALD.
mer and Dr. *War-*
eceived this emen-
d *well* for *all*. The
way is of no im-

as a body YET *dif-*
] What would he
We should read,
a body SLIGHT *dis-*
 WARBURTON.
t reading is right.
t is, according to
ck, a disproportio-
f humours, or in-
nate heat and radi-
', is less than actu-
ng only the state
s or produces dif-
difference between
sase, seems to be

much the same as between *dis-*
position and *habit*.
³ *My lord* Northumberland
will soon be COOL'D.] I believe
Shakespeare wrote SCHOOL'D;
tutor'd, and brought to submission. WARBURTON.
Cool'd is certainly right.
⁴ —— *O, if this were seen,* &c.]
These four lines are supplied from
the Edition of 1600. WARB.
My copy wants the whole
scene, and therefore these lines.
There is some difficulty in the
line,
What perils past, what crosses to
ensue,
because it seems to make *past pe-*
rils equally terrible with *ensuing*
crosses.

U Wou'd

Wou'd shut the book, and sit him down and die.
'Tis not ten Years gone,
Since *Richard* and *Northumberland*, great Friends,
Did feast together; and in two years after
Were they at wars. It is but eight years since,
This *Percy* was the man nearest my soul;
Who, like a brother, toil'd in my affairs,
And laid his love and life under my foot;
Yea, for my sake, ev'n to the eyes of *Richard*
Gave him defiance. But which of you was by?
(You, cousin *Nevil*, as I may remember) [*To War.*
When *Richard*, with his eye brim-full of tears [5],
Then check'd and rated by *Northumberland*,
Did speak these words, now prov'd a prophecy.
' *Northumberland, thou ladder by the which*
' *My cousin* Bolingbroke *ascends my Throne:*'
Though then, Heav'n knows, I had no such intent;
But that Necessity so bow'd the State,
That I and Greatness were compell'd to kiss:
' *The time will come,* thus did he follow it,
' *The time will come, that foul sin, gathering head,*
' *Shall break into corruption:*' so went on,
Foretelling this same time's condition,
And the division of our amity.
War. There is a history in all
Figuring the Nature of the times deceas'd;
The which observ'd, a man may prophesy,
With a near aim, of the main chance of things
As yet not come to life, which in their seeds
And weak beginnings lie intreasured.
Such things become the hatch and brood of time;
And by the necessary form of this [6],
King *Richard* might create a perfect guess,

[5] He refers to King *Richard*, act 5. scene 2. But whether the King's or the authour's memory fails him, so it was, that *Warwick* was not present at that conversation.

[6] *And by the necessary form of this,*] I think we might better read, *The necessary form of things.* The word *this* has no very evident antecedent.

KING HENRY IV. 291.

Northumberland, then falſe to him,
hat feed grow to a greater falſeneſs,
uld not find a ground to root upon,
You.
. Are theſe things then neceſſities *?
; meet them like neceſſities;
ıme word even now cries out on us.
ıe Biſhop and *Northumberland*
ouſand ſtrong.
:annot be:
h double, like the voice and echo,
rs of the fear'd. Pleaſe it your Grace
:d. Upon my life, my lord,
, that you already have ſent forth,
this prize in very eaſily.
you the more, I have receiv'd
ıſtance that *Glendower* is dead.
ty hath been this fortnight ill,
nſeaſon'd hours perforce muſt add
ickneſs.
I will take your counſel;
ıeſe inward wars once out of hand,
ear lords, unto the Holy Land'. [*Exeunt.*

bings then neceſ-   through the firſt edition, and
               there is therefore no evidence
et them like neceſ- that the diviſion of the acts was
   am inclined to   made by the authour. Since then
               every editor has the ſame right
et them like neceſ- to mark the intervals of action
               as the players, who made the pre-
he reſiſtleſs vio-   ſent diſtribution, I ſhould propoſe
ty; then comes   that this ſcene may be added to
ollowing line: the foregoing act, and the re-
e word even now move from *London* to *Glouceſter-*
us.   *ſhire* be made in the intermediate
d neceſſity.   time, but that it would ſhorten
the Holy Land.] the next act too much, which has
the former, pro- not even now its due proportion
nbroken tenour   to the reſt.

U 2   SCENE

SCENE III.

Changes to Justice Shallow's *Seat in* Gloucestershire.

Enter Shallow *and* Silence, *Justices; with* Mouldy, Shadow, Wart, Feeble, *and* Bull-calf.

Shal. COME on, come on, come on; give me your hand, Sir; an early stirrer, [a] by the rood. And how doth my good cousin *Silence?*

Sil. Good morrow, good cousin *Shallow.*

Shal. And how doth my cousin, your bed-fellow? and your fairest daughter, and mine, my god-daughter *Ellen?*

Sil. Alas, a black ouzel, cousin *Shallow.*

Shal. By yea, and nay, Sir, I dare say, my cousin *William* is become a good scholar. He is at *Oxford* still, is he not?

Sil. Indeed, Sir, to my cost.

Shal. He must then to the Inns of Court shortly. I was once of *Clement's* Inn; where, I think, they will talk of mad *Shallow* yet.

Sil. You were call'd lusty *Shallow* then, cousin.

Shal. I was call'd any thing, and I would have done any thing, indeed, too, and roundly too. There was I, and little *John Doit of Staffordshire,* and black *George Bare,* and *Francis Pickbone,* and *Will Squele* a *Cotswold* man, you had not four such swinge-bucklers in all the Inns of Court again; and I may say to you, we knew where the *Bona-Roba's* were, and had the best of them all at commandment. Then was *Jack Falstaff,* now Sir *John,* a boy, and page to *Thomas Mowbray,* Duke of *Norfolk.*

[a] —— *by the rood.*] *i. e.* the cross. POPE.

Sil.

Sil. This Sir *John*, coufin, that comes hither anon about Soldiers?

Shal. The fame Sir *John*, the very fame. I faw him break *Schoggan's* head at the Court-gate, when he was a crack, not thus high; and the very fame day I did fight with one *Sampfon Stockfifh*, a fruiterer, behind *Gray's-Inn*. O the mad days that I have fpent! and to fee how many of mine old acquaintance are dead?

Sil. We fhall all follow, coufin.

Shal. Certain, 'tis certain, very fure, very fure. Death (as the Pfalmift faith) is certain to all, all fhall die. How a good yoke of Bullocks at *Stamford* Fair?

Sil. Truly, coufin, I was not there.

Shal. Death is certain. Is old *Double* of your town living yet?

Sil. Dead, Sir.

Shal. Dead!—fee, fee—he drew a good bow. And dead?—he fhot a fine fhoot. *John* of *Gaunt* loved him well, and betted much money on his head. Dead!—he would have [9] clapt in the clowt at twelve fcore, and carried you a fore hand fhaft a [1] fourteen and fourteen and a half, that it would have done a man's heart good to fee.———How a fcore of ewes now?

Sil. Thereafter as they be. A fcore of good ewes may be worth ten pounds.

Shal. And is old *Double* dead?

SCENE IV.

Enter Bardolph, *and* Page.

Sil. Here come two of Sir *John Falftaff's* men, as I think.

Shal. Good-morrow, honeft gentlemen.

Bard. I befeech you, which is Juftice *Shallow*?

---

[9] —— *clapt in the clowt*] i. e. hit the white mark. WARBURT.

[1] —*fourteen and fourteen and a half*,] That is, fourteen fcore of yards.

THE SECOND PART OF

Shal. I am *Robert Shallow*, Sir, a poor Esquire of this Country, one of the King's Justices of the peace. What is your good pleasure with me?

Bard. My captain, Sir, commends him to you, my captain Sir *John Falstaff*; a tall gentleman, by heav'n! and a most gallant leader.

Shal. He greets me well, Sir, I knew him a good back-sword man. How doth the good Knight? may I ask, how my lady his wife doth?

Bard. Sir, pardon, a soldier is better accommodated than with a wife.

Shal. It is well said, Sir; and it is well said indeed too, *better accommodated*——it is good, yea, indeed, is it; good phrases, surely, are, and ever were, very commendable. *Accommodated*——it comes of *accommodo;* [2] very good, a good phrase.

Bard. Pardon me, Sir, I have heard the word. Phrase, call you it? By this day, I know not the phrase, but I will maintain the word with my sword, to be a soldier-like word, and a word of exceeding good command. *Accommodated*, that is, when a man is, as they say, accommodated; or, when a man is, being whereby he may be thought to be accommodated, which is an excellent thing.

---

[2] —*very good, a good phrase*] *Accommodate* was a modish term of that time, as *Ben Johnson* informs us: *You are not to cast or wring for the perfuming terms of the time, as* accommodation, complement, spirit, *&c. but use them properly in their places as others.* Discoveries. Hence *Bardolph* calls it a word of *exceeding good command.* His definition of it is admirable, and highly satirical: nothing being more common than for inaccurate speakers or writers, when they should define, to put their hearers off with a synonymous term; or, for want of that, even with the same term differently *accommodated*; as in the instance before us. WARBURT.

SCENE

SCENE V.

Enter Falstaff.

al. It is very juſt.—Look, here comes good Sir
Giye me your good hand: give me your Wor-
good hand. Truſt me, you look well, and bear
years very well. Welcome, good Sir *John*.
l. I am glad to ſee you well, good maſter *Robert*
ow.—Maſter *Sure-card*, as I think,———
al. No, Sir *John*, it is my couſin *Silence*; in Com-
n with me.
l. Good maſter *Silence*, it well befits, you ſhould
the peace.
Your good Worſhip is welcome. [*Embraces him.*
l. Fie, this is hot weather—Gentlemen; have you
ded me here half a dozen of ſufficient men?
al. Marry, have we, Sir. Will you ſit?
l. Let me ſee them, I beſeech you.
ıl. Where's the roll? where's the roll? where's
oll? Let me ſee, let me ſee, let me ſee. So, ſo,
Yea, marry, Sir. *Ralph Mouldy:*—let them
r as I call. Let them do ſo, let them do ſo. Let
e, where is *Mouldy?*
ul. Here, if it pleaſe you.
ıl. What think you, Sir *John?* a good-limb'd
: young, ſtrong, and of good friends.
. Is thy name *Mouldy?*
ul. Yea, if it pleaſe you.
. 'Tis the more time thou wert us'd.
l. Ha, ha, ha, moſt excellent, i'faith. Things,
re mouldy, lack uſe. Very ſingular good. Well
ir *John*, very well ſaid.
. Prick him.
ıl. I was prickt well enough before, if you could
et me alone. My old dame will be undone now
e to do her huſbandry, and her drudgery; you
need

need not to have prickt me, there are other men fitter to go out than I.

Fal. Go to: peace, *Mouldy*, you shall go. *Mouldy*, it is time you were spent.

Moul. Spent?

Shal. Peace, fellow, peace. Stand aside. Know you where you are? For the other, Sir *John*.—Let me see—*Simon Shadow*.

Fal. Ay, marry, let me have him to fit under: he's like to be a cold soldier.

Shal. Where's *Shadow*?

Shad. Here, Sir.

Fal. Shadow, whose son art thou?

Shad. My mother's son, Sir.

Fal. Thy mother's son! like enough; and thy father's shadow; so the son of the female is the shadow of the male; it is often so, indeed, but not of the father's substance.

Shal. Do you like him, Sir *John*?

Fal. Shadow will serve for summer; prick him; for we have a number of shadows do fill up the muster-book [3].

Shal. Thomas Wart.

Fal. Where's he?

Wart. Here, Sir.

Fal. Is thy name *Wart*?

Wart. Yea, Sir.

Fal. Thou art a very ragged wart.

Shal. Shall I prick him down, Sir *John*?

Fal. It were superfluous; for his apparel is built upon his back, and the whole frame stands upon pins; prick him no more.

Shal. Ha, ha, ha.—You can do it, Sir; you can do it: I commend you well. *Francis Feeble*.

---

[3] *we have a number of shadows do fill up the muster-book.*] That is, we have in the muster-book many names for which we receive pay, though we have not the men.

Feeble. Here, Sir.

Fal. What trade art thou, *Feeble?*

Feeble. A woman's tailor, Sir.

Shal. Shall I prick him, Sir?

Fal. You may: but if he had been a man's tailor, he would have prick'd you. Wilt thou make as many holes in an enemy's battel, as thou haſt done in a woman's petticoat?

Feeble. I will do my good will, Sir; you can have no more.

Fal. Well ſaid, good woman's tailor; well ſaid, courageous *Feeble.* Thou wilt be as valiant as the wrathful Dove, or moſt magnanimous mouſe. Prick the woman's tailor well, maſter *Shallow,* deep, maſter *Shallow.*

Feeble. I would, *Wart* might have gone, Sir.

Fal. I would, thou wert a man's tailor, that thou might'ſt mend him, and make him fit to go. I cannot put him to be a private ſoldier, that is the leader of ſo many thouſands. Let that ſuffice, moſt forcible *Feeble.*

Feeble. It ſhall ſuffice.

Fal. I am bound to thee, reverend *Feeble.* Who is the next?

Shal. Peter *Bull-calf* of the Green.

Fal. Yea, marry, let us ſee *Bull-calf.*

Bul. Here, Sir.

Fal. Truſt me, a likely fellow. Come, prick me *Bull-calf,* till he roar again.

Bul. Oh, good my lord captain,———

Fal. What, doſt thou roar before th'art prickt?

Bul. Oh, Sir, I am a diſeaſed man.

Fal. What diſeaſe haſt thou?

Bul. A whorſon Cold, Sir; a cough, Sir, which I caught with ringing in the King's affairs, upon his Coronation-day, Sir.

Fal. Come, thou ſhalt go to the wars in a gown:

we will have away thy Cold, and I will take such order that thy friends shall ring for thee. Is here all?

Shal. There is two more called than your number, you must have but four here, Sir; and so, I pray you, go in with me to dinner.

Fal. Come, I will go drink with you, but I cannot tarry dinner. I am glad to see you, in good troth, master *Shallow*.

Shal. O, Sir *John*, do you remember since we lay all night in the wind-mill in Saint *George's* fields?

Fal. No more of that, good master *Shallow*, no more of that.

Shal. Ha! it was a merry night. And is *Jane Night-work* alive?

Fal. She lives, master *Shallow*.

Shal. She never could away with me.

Fal. Never, never. She would always say, she could not abide master *Shallow*.

Shal. By the mass, I could anger her to the heart. She was then a * *Bona-roba*. Doth she hold her own well?

Fal. Old, old, master *Shallow*.

Shal. Nay, she must be old, she cannot chuse but be old; certain, she's old, and had *Robin Night-work* by old *Night-work*, before I came to *Clement's* Inn.

Sil. That's fifty-five years ago.

Shal. Ha, cousin *Silence*, that thou hadst seen That, that this knight and I have seen!—— hah, Sir *John*, said I well?

Fal. We have heard the chimes at midnight, Master *Shallow*.

Shal. That we have, that we have, in faith, Sir *John*, we have. Our watch-word was, hem, boys.—Come, let's to dinner.—Oh, the days that we have seen! come, come.

* *Bona-Roba.*] A fine showy wanton.

Bul.

Bul. [*aside to* Bardolph] Good master corporate *Bardolph*, stand my friend, and here is four *Harry* ten shillings in *French* Crowns for you; in very truth, Sir, I had as lief be hang'd, Sir, as go; and yet for my own part, Sir, I do not care, but rather because I am unwilling, and for my own part, have a desire to stay with my friends; else, Sir, I did not care for mine own part so much.

Bard. Go to; stand aside.

Moul. And good master corporal captain, for my old Dame's sake stand my friend; she hath no body to do any thing about her when I am gone, and she's old and cannot help her self; you shall have forty, Sir.

Bard. Go to; stand aside.

Feeble, I care not, a man can die but once; we owe God a death, I will never bear a base mind; if it be my destiny, so; if it be not, so. No man is too good to serve his Prince; and let it go which way it will, he that dies this year is quit for the next.

Bard. Well said, thou art a good fellow.

Feeble. 'Faith, I will bear no base mind.

Fal. Come, Sir, which men shall I have?

Shal. Four of which you please.

Bard. Sir, a word with you :—[5] I have three pound to free *Mouldy* and *Bull-calf.*

Fal. Go to: well.

Shal. Come, Sir *John,* which four will you have?

Fal. Do you chuse for me.

Shal. Marry then, *Mouldy, Bull-calf, Feeble,* and *Shallow.*

Fal. Mouldy, and *Bull-calf*——For you, *Mouldy,* stay at home till you are past service; and for your part, *Bull-calf,* grow till you come unto it. I will none of you.

---

[5] —— *I have three pound.*] Here seems to be a wrong computation. He had forty shillings for each. Perhaps he meant to conceal part of the profit.

Shal.

Shal. Sir *John,* Sir *John,* do not yourself wrong; they are your likeliest men, and I would have you serv'd with the best.

Fal. Will you tell me, master *Shallow,* how to chuse a man? care I for the limb, the thewes, the stature, bulk and big semblance of a man? give me the spirit, master *Shallow.* Here's *Wart*; you see what a ragged appearance it is, he shall charge you and discharge you with the motion of a pewterer's hammer; come off and on, [6] swifter than he that gibbets on the brewer's bucket. And this same half-fac'd fellow *Shadow,* give me this man, he presents no mark to the enemy; the fo-man may with as great aim level at the edge of a pen-knife. And, for a retreat, how swiftly will this *Feeble,* the woman's tailor, run off? O give me the spare men, and spare me the great ones. Put me a caliver [7] into *Wart's* hand, *Bardolph.*

Bard. Hold, *Wart,* traverse; thus, thus, thus.

Fal. Come, manage me your caliver. So, very well, go to, very good, exceeding good. O, give me always a little, lean, old, chopt, bald shot [8]. Well said, *Wart,* thou art a good scab. Hold, there is a tester for thee.

Shal. He is not his craft-master, he doth not do it right. I remember at *Mile-End Green,* when I lay at *Clement's* Inn, [9] I was then Sir *Dagonet* in *Arthur's* Show,

---

[6] ———— *swifter than he that gibbets on the brewer's bucket.*] Swifter than he that carries beer from the vat to the barrel, in buckets hung upon a gibbet or beam crossing his shoulders.

[7] *Caliver,* a hand gun.

[8] ——— *bald shot.*] Shot is us'd for *shooter,* one who is to fight by shooting.

[9] ——— *I was then Sir Dagonet in Arthur's Show;*] The only Intelligence I have gleaned of this worthy Wight, Sir *Dagonet,* is from *Beaumont* and *Fletcher* in their *Knight* of the *burning Pestle.*

Boy. *Besides, it will shew favouredly to have a Grocer Prentice to court a King's Daughter.*

Cit. *Will it so, Sir? You are well read in Histories! I pray you what was Sir* Dagonet? *Was not he Prentice to a Grocer in London? Read the Play of The Four Prentices of London, where they toss their Pikes so:* &c.

THEOBALD.

The story of Sir *Dagonet* is to be

KING HENRY IV.

Show, there was a little quiver fellow, and he would manage you his piece thus; and he would about, and about, and come you in, and come you in; rah, tah, tah, would he say; bounce, would he say, and away again would he go, and again would he come. I shall never see such a fellow.

Fal. These fellows will do well. Master *Shallow*, God keep you; farewel, master *Silence*. I will not use many words with you, fare you well, gentlemen both. I thank you, I must a dozen mile to night. *Bardolph*, give the soldiers coats.

Shal. Sir *John*, heaven bless you, and prosper your affairs, and send us peace. As you return, visit my house. Let our old acquaintance be renewed: peradventure, I will with you to the Court.

Fal. I would you would, master *Shallow*.

Shal. Go to; I have spoke at a word. Fare you well. [*Exeunt* Shal. *and* Sil.

Fal. Fare you well, gentle gentlemen. On, *Bardolph*, lead the men away. As I return, I will fetch off these Justices. I do see the bottom of Justice *Shallow*. How subject we old men are to this Vice of lying! this same starv'd Justice hath done nothing but prate to me of the wildness of his youth, and the feats he hath done about *Turnball-street*; and every third word a lie, more duly paid to the hearer than the *Turk's* tribute. I do remember him at *Clement's* Inn, like a man made after supper of a cheese-paring. When he was naked, he was for all the world like a forked radish, with a head fantastically carv'd upon

---

be found in *La Mort d'Arthure*, an old romance much celebrated in our authour's time, or a little before it. *When papistry*, says *Ascham* in his *Schoolmaster*, *as a standing pool overflowed all* England, *few books were read in our tongue, saving certain books of chivalry, as they said, for pastime and pleasure; which books, as some say, were made in monasteries by idle monks. As one, for example, La Mort d'Arthure. In this romance Sir Dagonet is King Arthur's fool.* Shakespeare would not have shown his *justice* capable of representing any higher character.

it

302 THE SECOND PART OF

it with a knife. He was so forlorn, that his dimensions to any thick sight were invincible. He was the very *Genius* of famine, yet leacherous as a Monkey, and the whores call'd him Mandrake. He came ever in the rere-ward of the fashion; and sung those tunes to the [1] over-scutcht huswives that he heard the carmen whistle, and sware they were his *Fancies*, or his *Goodnights*. [2] And now is this Vice's dagger become a Squire, and talks as familiarly of *John* of *Gaunt* as if he had been sworn brother to him, and I'll be sworn, he never saw him but once in the Tilt-yard, and then he broke his head for crouding among the Marshal's men. I saw it, and told *John* of *Gaunt* he [3] beat his own name; for you might have truss'd him and all his apparel into an Eel-skin; the case of a treble hoboy was a Mansion for him — a Court — and now hath he land and beeves. Well, I will be acquainted with him, if I return; and it shall go hard but I will make him a [4] philosopher's two stones to me. [5] If the young Dace be a bait for the old Pike; I
see

[1] *Over scutcht*] i. e. whipt, carted. POPE.
I rather think that the word means *dirty*, or *grimed*, the word *huswives* agrees better with this sense. *Shallow* crept into mean houses, and boasted his accomplishments to the *dirty* women.

[2] *And now is this* Vice's *Dagger.*] By *Vice* here the Poet means that *droll* Character in the old Plays (which I have several times mentioned in the course of these Notes) equipped with Asses Ears and a Wooden Dagger. It is very satirical in *Falstaff* to compare *Shallow's* Activity and Impertinence to such a Machine as a *wooden Dagger* in the Hands and Management of a *Buffoon.*
THEOBALD.

[3] —— *beat his own name*;] That is, beat *gaunt*, a fellow so slender that his name might have been *gaunt*.

[4] —— *philosopher's two stones*] One of which was an universal medicine, and the other a transmuter of baser metals into gold.
WARBURTON.
I believe the commentator has refined this passage too much. *A philosopher's two stones*, is only more than the *philosopher's stone*. The *universal medicine* was never, so far as I know, conceived to be a stone, before the time of *Butler's stone*.

[5] *If the young Dace*] That is,
If

see no reason in the law of nature but I may snap at him. Let time shape, and there's an end. [*Exeunt.*

ACT IV. SCENE I.

Changes to a Forest in Yorkshire.

Enter the Archbishop of York, Mowbray, Hastings, *and* Colevile.

York.

WHAT is this forest call'd?
  Hast. 'Tis *Gaultree* forest.
York. Here stand, my lords, and send discoverers forth,
To know the numbers of our enemies.
  Hast. We have sent forth already.
  York. 'Tis well done.
My friends and brethren in these great affairs,
I must acquaint you, that I have receiv'd
New-dated letters from *Northumberland*,
Their cold intent, tenour and substance thus.—
Here doth he wish his person, with such Powers
As might hold sortance with his quality,
The which he could not levy; whereupon
He is retir'd, to ripe his growing fortunes,
To *Scotland*; and concludes in hearty prayers
That your attempts may over-live the hazard
And fearful meeting of their opposite.
  Mowb. Thus do the hopes we have in him touch ground,
And dash themselves to pieces.

If the pike may prey upon the dace, weaker, Falstaff *may with great if it be the law of nature that propriety devour* Shallow.
the stronger may seize upon the
                                            Enter

Enter a Messenger.

Haſt. Now, what news?

Meſſ. Weſt of this foreſt, ſcarcely off a mile,
In goodly form comes on the enemy,
And by the ground they hide, I judge their number
Upon, or near, the rate of thirty thouſand.

Mowb. The juſt proportion that we gave them out.
Let us ſway on [6], and face them in the field.

SCENE II.

Enter Weſtmorland.

York. What well-appointed leader fronts us here?

Mowb. I think, it is my lord of *Weſtmorland*.

Weſt. Health and fair Greeting from our General,
The Prince, Lord *John*, and Duke of *Lancaſter*.

York. Say on, my lord of *Weſtmorland*, in peace:
What doth concern your coming?

Weſt. Then, my lord,
Unto your Grace do I in chief addreſs
The ſubſtance of my ſpeech. If that Rebellion
Came like itſelf, in baſe and abject routs,
[7] Led on by bloody youth, goaded with rage,
And countenanc'd by boys and beggary;
I ſay, if damn'd Commotion ſo appear'd
In his true, native, and moſt proper ſhape,
You, reverend Father, and theſe noble lords,
Had not been here to dreſs the ugly form

---

[6] *Let us ſway on,——*] We ſhould read *way on, i. e.* march on. WARBURTON.

I know not that I have ever ſeen *ſway* in this ſenſe, but I believe it is the true word, and was intended to expreſs the uniform and forcible motion of a compact body. There is a ſenſe of the noun in *Milton* kindred to this, where ſpeaking of a weighty ſword, he ſays, *It deſcends with huge two-handed ſway.*

[7] *Led on by bloody youth,—*] I believe *Shakeſpeare* wrote, *heady youth*. WARBURTON.

I think *bloody* can hardly be right, perhaps it was *moody*, that is, *furious*. So in Scene 8 of this Act.

Being moody *give him line and ſcope
Till that his paſſions, like a whale on ground,
Confound themſelves with working.*

KING HENRY IV.

base and bloody insurrection
th your fair honours. You, my lord Arch-bishop,
ose see is by a civil peace maintain'd,
ose beard the silver hand of peace hath touch'd,
ose learning and good letters peace hath tutor'd,
ose white investments figure innocence,
e dove and very blessed Spirit of Peace;
erefore do you so ill translate your self,
t of the speech of peace, that bears such grace,
) the harsh and boist'rous tongue of war?
rning your books to * graves, your ink to blood,
ur pens to launces, and your tongue divine
a loud trumpet and a point of war?
ork. Wherefore do I this? so the question stands [b].
fly, to this end. We are all diseas'd,
d with our surfeiting and wanton hours,
ve brought ourselves into a burning fever,
d we must bleed for it; of which disease
late King *Richard* being infected, dy'd.
, my most noble lord of *Westmorland*,
ke it not on me here as a physician;
do I, as an enemy to peace,
op in the throngs of military men;
rather shew a while like fearful war,
diet rank minds, sick of happiness,
I purge th' obstructions, which begin to stop
very veins of life. Hear me more plainly.
ve in equal balance justly weigh'd
at wrongs our arms may do, what wrongs we suffer,
d find our griefs heavier than our offences.
see, which way the stream of time doth run,

For *graves* Dr. *Warburton* plausibly reads *glaves*, and lowed by Sir *Thomas Han*-

In this speech, after the first lines, the next twenty-five either omitted in the first on, or added in the second.

The answer, in which both the editions agree, apparently refers to some of these lines, which therefore may be probably supposed rather to have been dropped by a player desirous to shorten his speech, than added by the second labour of the authour.

Vol. IV.   X   And

And are inforc'd from our moſt Quiet ſphere [a],
By the rough torrent of occaſion;
And have the ſummary of all our griefs,
When time ſhall ſerve, to ſhew in articles;
Which long ere this we offer'd to the King,
And might by no ſuit gain our audience.
When we are wrong'd and would unfold our griefs,
We are deny'd acceſs unto his perſon,
Ev'n by thoſe men that moſt have done us wrong.
The danger of the days but newly gone,
Whoſe memory is written on the earth
With yet-appearing blood, and the Examples
Of every minute's inſtance, preſent now,
Have put us in theſe ill beſeeming arms,
Not to break peace, or any branch of it,
But to eſtabliſh here a peace, indeed,
Concurring both in name and quality.

Weſt. When ever yet was your appeal deny'd?
Wherein have you been galled by the King?
What Peer hath been ſuborn'd to grate on you,
That you ſhould ſeal this lawleſs bloody book
Of forg'd Rebellion with a Seal divine,
* And conſecrate Commotion's Civil edge [b]?

---

[a] In former Editions:
And are inforc'd from our moſt quiet THERE,] This is ſaid in anſwer to *Weſtmorland's* upbraiding the Archbiſhop for engaging in a courſe which ſo ill became his profeſſion,
——*You my lord Archbiſhop,*
Whoſe See is by a civil peace maintain'd, &c.
So that the reply muſt be this,
And are inforc'd from our moſt quiet SPHERE. WARB.

* *And conſecrate,* &c.] In one of my old *Quarto's* of 1600 (for I have Two of the ſelf-ſame Edition; one of which, 'tis evident, was corrected in ſome Paſſages during the working off the whole Impreſſion) I found this Ve— I have ventur'd to ſubſtitute for *Edge,* with regard to the formity of Metaphor. the Sword of Rebellion, dr by a Biſhop, may in ſome be ſaid to be conſecrated his Reverence. THEOB

' *And conſecrate Commo Civil* Edge'] So the books read. But Mr. *Th* changes *edge* to *page,* out o gard to the *uniformity* (as he it) *of the metaphor.* But h not underſtand what was by edge. It was an old cu continued from the time c firſt croiſades, for the po

KING HENRY IV.

York. ⁱ My brother General, the Common-wealth,
To Brother born an houshold Cruelty,
make my quarrel in particular.

West. There is no need of any such redress;
Or if there were, it not belongs to you.

Mowb. Why not to him in part, and to us all
That feel the bruises of the days before;
And suffer the condition of these times
To lay an heavy and unequal hand
Upon our honours?

West. O my good Lord *Mowbray*,

consecrate the general's sword, which was employ'd in the service of the church. To this I from the line in question alludes. As to the cant of *uniformity of metaphor* in writing, this is to be observed, that changing the allusion in the same sentence is indeed vicious, and what *Quintilian* condemns, *Multi quum inimicum à tempestate sumpserint, inundo aut ruinâ finiunt.* But when the comparison or allusion is fairly separated from another, by distinct sentences, the case is different. So it is here; in one sentence we see *the book of religion stamp'd with a seal divine*; in the other, *the sword of civil war consecrated*. But this change of the metaphor is not only allowable, but fit. For the dwelling overlong upon *one* occasions a discourse to degenerate into a dull kind of allegorism.

WARBURTON.

What Mr. *Theobald* says of the editions seems to be true, my copy reads, *commotion's ere edge*, but *civil* is undoubtedly right, and one would wonder how *bitter* could intrude if *civil* had been written first; perhaps the authour himself made the change.

ⁱ *My brother general, &c.* — *I make my quarrel in particular.*] The sense is this, *My brother general, the Common-wealth, which ought to distribute its benefits equally, is become an enemy to those of his own house, to brothers-born, by giving some all, and others none; and this* (says he) *I make my quarrel or grievance, that honours are unequally distributed*; the constant birth of male-contents, and source of civil commotions.

WARBURTON.

In the first folio the second line is omitted; yet that reading, unintelligible as it is, has been followed by Sir *T. Hanmer*. How difficultly sense can be drawn from the best reading the explication of Dr. *Warburton* may show. I believe there is an errour in the first line, which perhaps may be rectified thus,

My quarrel *general, the commonwealth,*
To Brother born an houshold cruelty,
I make my quarrel in particular.

That is, my *general* cause of discontent is publick mismanagement, my *particular* cause a domestick injury done to my *natural brother*, who had been beheaded by the King's order.

* Conſtrue the times to their neceſſities,
And you ſhall ſay, indeed, it is the time,
And not the King, that doth you injuries.
Yet, for your part, it not appears to me,
† Or from the King, or in the preſent time,
That you ſhould have an inch of any ground
To build a grief on. Were you not reſtor'd
To all the Duke of *Norfolk's* Seigniories,
Your noble and right-well remember'd father's?

Mowb. What thing, in honour, had my father loſt,
That need to be reviv'd and breath'd in me?
The King, that lov'd him, as the State ſtood then,
Was, force per force, compell'd to baniſh him.
And then, when *Harry Bolingbroke* and he
Being mounted and both rowſed in their ſeats,
Their neighing Courſers daring of the ſpur.
‡ Their armed ſtaves in charge, their beavers down,
Their eyes of fire ſparkling through ſights of ſteel,
And the loud trumpet blowing them together;
Then, then, when there was nothing could have ſta
My father from the breaſt of *Bolingbroke*,
O, when the King did throw his warder down,
His own life hung upon the ſtaff he threw;
Then threw he down himſelf, and all their lives,
That by indictment, or by dint of ſword,
Have ſince miſcarried under *Bolingbroke*. [not wh

Weſt. You ſpeak, Lord *Mowbray*, now, you kn
The Earl of *Hereford* was reputed then
In *England* the moſt valiant gentleman.
Who knows, on whom fortune would then have ſmil'
But if your father had been victor there,

---

* *Conſtrue the times to their neceſſities*] That is, judge of what is done in theſe times according to the exigencies that over-rule us.

† *Or from the King, &c.*] Whether the faults of government be imputed to the *time* or the *king*, it appears not that have, for your part, been inj either by the *king* or the *tim*

‡ *Their armed ſtaves in cha* An armed ſtaff is a lance. T in charge, is to be fixed for th counter.

He ne'er had borne it out of *Coventry*;
For all the country in a general voice
Cry'd hate upon him; all their prayers and love
Were set on *Hereford*, whom they doated on,
And bless'd, and grac'd, indeed, more than the King.
But this is mere digression from my purpose. ——
Here come I from our princely General,
To know your griefs, to tell you from his Grace,
That he will give you audience, and wherein
It shall appear that your demands are just,
You shall enjoy them; every thing set off,
That might so much as think you enemies.

Mowb. But he hath forc'd us to compel this offer,
And it proceeds from policy, not love.

West. *Mowbray*, you over-ween to take it so;
This offer comes from mercy, not from fear.
For lo! within a ken, our army lies,
Upon mine honour, all too confident
To give admittance to a thought of fear.
Our battle is more full of names than yours,
Our men more perfect in the use of arms,
Our armour all as strong, our cause the best;
Then reason wills, our hearts should be as good.
Say you not then, our offer is compell'd.

Mowb. Well; by my will, we shall admit no parley.

West. That argues but the shame of your offence,
A rotten case abides no handling.

Hast. Hath the Prince *John* a full commission,
In very ample virtue of his father,
To hear and absolutely to determine
Of what conditions we shall stand upon?

West. That is intended in the General's name [4]:

---

[3] *And bless'd and grac'd more than the King himself.*] The Two oldest Folio's (which first gave us this Speech of *Westmorland*) read this Line thus;
And bless'd and grac'd and did more than the King.
Dr. *Thirlby* reform'd the Text very near to the Traces of the corrupted Reading. THEOBALD.

[4] *This is intended in the General's name:*] That is, this power is included in the name or office of a general. We wonder that you can ask a question so trifling.

I muse,

310 THE SECOND PART OF

I muse, you make so slight a question.

 York. Then take, my lord of *Westmorland*, this
For this contains our general grievances, [schedule,
Each several article herein redress'd;
All members of our cause, both here and hence,
That are insinewed to this action,
Acquitted by a true * substantial form;
And present executions of our wills
⁵ To us, and to our purposes, confin'd;
⁶ We come within our awful banks again,
And knit our powers to the arm of peace. [lords,

 West. This will I shew the General. Please you,
⁷ In sight of both our battles, we may meet;
And either end in peace, which heav'n so frame!
Or to the place of difference call the swords,
Which must decide it.

 York. My lord, we will do so.   [*Exit* West.

* *Substantial form*] That is, by a pardon of due form and legal validity.

⁵ *To us, and to our* PURPOSES, *confin'd;*] This schedule we see consists of three parts, 1. A redress of general grievances. 2. A pardon for those in arms. 3. Some demands of advantage for them. But this third part is very strangely expressed.

*And present execution of our wills
To us and to our* PURPOSES *confin'd.*

The first line shews they had something to demand, and the second expresses the modesty of that demand. The demand, says the speaker, *is confined to us and to our purposes.* A very modest kind of restriction truly! only as extensive as their appetites and passions. Without question *Shakespeare* wrote,

To us and to our PROPERTIES *confin'd;*

i. e. we desire no more than security for our *liberties* and *properties:* and this was no unreasonable demand. WARBURTON.

This passage is so obscure that I know not what to make of it. Nothing better occurs to me, than to read *consign'd*, for *confin'd.* That is, let the execution of our demands be put into our hands according to our declared purposes.

⁶ *We come within our* AWFUL *banks again,*]
We should read LAWFUL. WARB.

Awful banks are the proper limits of reverence.

⁷ The old copies: *We may meet At either end in peace; which Heav'n so frame!*] That easy, but certain, Change in the Text, I owe to Dr. *Thirlby.* THEOBALD.

SCENE

KING HENRY IV. 311
SCENE III.

owb. There is a thing within my bosom tells me,
no conditions of our peace can stand.
st. Fear you not that; if we can make our peace
 such large terms and so absolute,
r conditions shall insist upon,
peace shall stand as firm as rocky mountains.
owb. Ay, but our valuation shall be such,
 ev'ry slight and false-derived cause,
 ev'ry idle, nice and wanton reason,
 to the King taste of this action.
t, were our loyal faiths martyrs in love,
hall be winnow'd with so rough a wind,
 ev'n our corn shall seem as light as chaff,
good from bad find no partition.
rk. No, no, my lord, note this; the King is weary
 dainty and such picking grievances:
e hath found, to end one doubt by death,
ves two greater in the heirs of life.
therefore will he [9] wipe his tables clean,
keep no tell-tale to his memory,
 may repeat and history his loss
ew remembrance. For full well he knows,
annot so precisely weed this land,
is misdoubts present occasion;
foes are so enrooted with his friends,
, plucking to unfix an enemy,
loth unfasten so and shake a friend.
at this Land, like an offensive wife,

---

 former Editions:
t, were our royal *faiths
martyrs in love.*] If *royal*
can mean *faith to a king*,
 cannot mean it without
violence done to the lan-
. I therefore read, with
Hanmer, loyal faiths, which
per, natural, and suitable
intention of the speaker.

* *Of dainty and such picking
grievancies.*] I cannot but
think that this line is corrupted,
and that we should read,
*Of picking out such dainty griev-
ances.*
[9] —— *wipe his tables clean.*]
Alluding to a table-book of slate,
ivory, &c. WARBURTON.

X 4 That

That hath enrag'd him on to offer strokes,
As he is striking, holds his infant up,
And hangs resolv'd correction in the arm
That was uprear'd to execution.

Haſt. Besides, the King hath wasted all his rods
On late offenders, that he now doth lack
The very instruments of chastisement;
So that his pow'r, like to a fangless Lion,
May offer, but not hold.

York. 'Tis very true:
And therefore be assur'd, my good lord Marshal,
If we do make our atonement well,
Our peace will, like a broken limb united,
Grow stronger for the breaking.

Mowb. Be it so.
Here is return'd my lord of *Westmorland.*

Enter Westmorland.

Weſt. The Prince is here at hand, pleaseth your lordship
To meet his Grace, just distance 'tween our armies?

Mowb. Your Grace of *York* in God's name then
set forward.

York. Before, and greet his Grace.—My lord, we
come.

SCENE IV.

Enter Prince John *of* Lancaſter.

Lan. You're well encounter'd here, my cousin *Mowbray;*
Good day to you, my gentle lord Arch-bishop;
And so to you, lord *Haſtings,* and to all.
My lord of *York,* it better shew'd with you,
When that your flock, assembled by the bell,
Encircled you, to hear with reverence
Your exposition on the holy text,
Than now to see you here an iron man,
Cheering a rout of Rebels with your drum,
Turning the word to sword, and life to death.
That man, that sits within a monarch's heart,

And ripens in the sun-shine of his favour,
Would he abuse the count'nance of the King,
Alack, what mischiefs might he set abroach,
In shadow of such Greatness? With you, lord Bishop,
It is ev'n so. Who hath not heard it spoken,
How deep you were within the books of heav'n?
To us, the Speaker in his Parliament,
To us, th' imagin'd voice of heav'n it self,
The very opener and intelligencer
Between the grace, ¹ the sanctities of heav'n,
And our dull workings. O, who shall believe
But you misuse the rev'rence of your place,
Employ the countenance and grace of heav'n,
As a false favourite doth his Prince's name
In deeds dishon'rable? you've * taken up,
Under the counterfeited zeal of God,
The Subjects of his Substitute, my father;
And both against the peace of heav'n and him
Have here up-swarm'd them.

York. Good my lord of *Lancaster*,
I am not here against your father's peace,
But, as I told my lord of *Westmorland*,
The time mis-order'd doth ² in common sense
Crowd us and crush us to this monstrous form,
To hold our safety up. I sent your Grace
The parcels and particulars of our grief,
The which hath been with scorn shov'd from the Court;
Whereon this *Hydra*-son of war is born,
Whose dangerous eyes may well be charm'd asleep
With Grant of our most just and right desire,
And true Obedience, of this madness cur'd,

---

¹ *The sanctities of Heav'n.*] This expression *Milton* has copied.
Around him all the Sanctities of heav'n
Stood thick as stars.

* *To take up,* is to *levy*, to *raise in arms.*
² *In common* SENSE] I believe, *Shakespeare* wrote *common* FENCE, *i.e.* drove by self-defence. WARB.
C:mmon *sense* is the *general sense* of general danger.

Stoop

THE SECOND PART OF

Stoop tamely to the foot of Majesty.

Mowb. If not, we ready are to try our fortunes
To the last man.

Hast. And though we here fall down,
We have Supplies to second our attempt;
If they miscarry, theirs shall second them.
³ And so Success of mischief shall be born,
And heir from heir shall hold his quarrel up,
While *England* shall have generation.

Lan. You are too shallow, *Hastings*, much too shallow,
To sound the bottom of the after-times.

West. Pleaseth your Grace, to answer them directly,
How far-forth you do like their articles?

Lan. I like them all, and do allow them well,
And swear here, by the honour of my blood,
My father's purposes have been mistook;
And Some about him have too lavishly
Wrested his meaning and authority.
My lord, these griefs shall be with speed redrest;
Upon my life, they shall. If this may please you,
Discharge your Pow'rs unto their several Counties,
As we will ours; and here, between the armies,
Let's drink together friendly, and embrace;
That all their eyes may bear those tokens home,
Of our restored love and amity.

York. I take your princely word for these Redresses.

Lan. I give it you; and will maintain my word;
And thereupon I drink unto your Grace.

Hast. Go, captain, and deliver to the army
This news of peace; let them have pay, and part.
I know, it will well please them. Hie thee, captain.
 [*Exit* Colevile.

York. To you, my noble lord of *Westmorland*.

West. I pledge your Grace; and if you knew what
 pains
I have bestow'd, to breed this present peace,
You would drink freely; but my love to ye

---

³ *And so Success of mischief—*] *Success*, for succession. WAR
Sha

KING HENRY IV.

Shall shew itself more openly hereafter.
  York. I do not doubt you.
  West. I am glad of it.
Health to my lord, and gentle cousin *Mowbray.*
  Mowb. You wish me health in very happy season,
For I am on the sudden something ill.
  York. Against ill chances men are ever merry,
But heaviness fore-runs the good event.
  West. [4] Therefore be merry, Coz, since sudden sorrow
Serves to say thus; some good thing comes to-morrow.
  York. Believe me, I am passing light in spirit.
  Mowb. So much the worse, if your own rule be true. [*Shouts.*
  Lan. The word of peace is render'd; hark! they shout.
  Mowb. This had been chearful after victory.
  York. A peace is of the nature of a conquest;
For then both parties nobly are subdu'd,
And neither party loser.
  Lan. Go, my lord.
And let our army be discharged too, [*Exit* West.
—And, good my lord, so please you, [5] let our trains
March by us, that we may peruse the men
We should have cop'd withal.
  York. Go, good lord *Hastings:*
And, ere they be dismiss'd, let them march by.
            [*Exit* Hastings.
  Lan. I trust, lords, we shall lie to-night together.

---

[4] *Therefore, be merry, Coz.*] That is: *therefore*, notwithstanding this sudden impulse to heaviness, *be merry, for such sudden dejections forebode good.*

[5] *Let our trains,* &c.] That is, our army on each part, that we may both see those that were to have opposed us.

SCENE

SCENE V.

Re-enter Westmorland.

Now, cousin, wherefore stands our army still?
  West. The Leaders, having charge from you to stand,
Will not go off untill they hear you speak.
  Lan. They know their duties.

Re-enter Hastings.

  Hast. My lord, our army is dispers'd already;
Like youthful Steers unyoak'd, they took their course
East, west, north, south; or like a school broke up,
Each hurries towards his home and sporting-place.
  West. Good tidings, my lord *Hastings*; for the which
I do arrest thee, traitor, of high treason;
And you, lord Arch-bishop; and you, lord *Mowbray*;
Of capital treason I attach you both.
  Mowb. Is this proceeding just and honourable?
  West. Is your assembly so?
  York. Will you thus break your faith?
  Lan. I pawn'd you none;
I promis'd you Redress of these same grievances,
Whereof you did complain; which, by mine honour,
I will perform with a most christian care.
But for you, Rebels, look to taste the due
Meet for rebellion and such acts as yours.
Most shallowly did you these arms commence,
Fondly brought here, and foolishly sent hence.
Strike up our drums, pursue the scatter'd stray,
Heav'n, and not we, have safely fought to-day.

Some

KING HENRY IV.   317

guard these traitors to the block of death,
on's true bed and yielder up of breath ⁶. [*Exeunt.*
[*Alarm. Excursions.*

SCENE VI.

Enter Falstaff *and* Colevile.

l. What's your name, Sir? of what condition are
and of what place, I pray?
le. I am a Knight, Sir; and my name is *Colevile*
e dale.
l. Well then, *Colevile* is your name, a Knight is
degree, and your place, the dale. *Colevile* shall
)e your name, a traitor your degree, and the dun-
your place, a place deep enough. So shall you
be *Colevile* of the dale.
le. Are not you Sir *John Falstaff?*
l. As good a man as he, Sir, who e'er I am. Do
eld, Sir, or shall I sweat for you? if I do sweat,
are the drops of thy lovers, and they weep for thy
1; therefore rowze up fear and trembling, and do
vance to my mercy.
le. I think, you are Sir *John Falstaff,* and in that
ght yield me.
al. I have a whole school of tongues in this belly
nine, and not a tongue of them all speaks any
r word but my name. An I had but a belly of any
fferency, I were simply the most active fellow in
)pe; my womb, my womb, my womb, undoes
Here comes our General.

⁶ It cannot but raise some in- thus slightly by the poet, with-
ation to find this horrible out any note of censure or detes-
tion of faith passed over tation.

Enter

Enter Prince John *of* Lancaster, *and* Westmorland.

Lan. [7] The heat is past, follow no farther now,
Call in the Pow'rs, good cousin *Westmorland*.
                                    [*Exit* West.
Now, *Falstaff*, where have you been all this while?
When every thing is ended, then you come.
These tardy tricks of yours will, on my life,
One time or other break some Gallows' back.

Fal. I would be sorry, my lord, but it should be thus. I never knew yet, but rebuke and check was the reward of valour. Do you think me a swallow, an arrow, or a bullet? Have I, in my poor and old motion, the expedition of thought? I speeded hither with the very extreamest inch of possibility; I have founder'd ninescore and odd posts; and here, travel-tainted as I am, have in my pure and immaculate valour taken Sir *John Colevile* of the dale, a most furious Knight and valorous enemy. But what of that? he saw me and yielded; that I may justly say with the hook-nos'd fellow of *Rome* there, *Cæsar*, —— I came, saw, and overcame.

Lan. It was more of his courtesy than your deserving.

Fal. I know not; here he is, and here I yield him; and I beseech your Grace, let it be book'd with the rest of this day's deeds; or, by the lord, I will have it in a particular ballad else, with mine own picture on the top of it, *Colevile* kissing my foot; to the which course if I be enforc'd, if you do not all shew like gilt two-pences to me; and I, in the clear sky of fame, o'ershine you as much as the full Moon doth the cinders of the element, which shew like pin's heads to her; believe not the word of the noble. Therefore let me have Right, and let desert mount.

Lan. Thine's too heavy to mount.

[7] *The heat is past.*] That is, the violence of resentment, the eagerness of revenge.

Fal.

Fal. Let it shine then.

Lan. Thine's too thick to shine.

Fal. Let it do something, my good lord, that may do me good, and call it what you will.

Lan. Is thy name *Colevile*?

Cole. It is, my lord.

Lan. A famous Rebel art thou, *Colevile.*

Fal. And a famous true Subject took him.

Cole. I am, my lord, but as my betters are,
That led me hither; had they been rul'd by me,
You should have won them dearer than you have.

Fal. I know not how they sold themselves; but thou, like a kind fellow, gav'st thy self away *gratis*; and I thank thee for thee.

SCENE VII.

Enter Westmorland.

Lan. Now, have you left pursuit?

West. Retreat is made, and execution stay'd.

Lan. Send *Colevile* then with his Confederates
To *York*, to present execution.
Blunt, lead him hence; and see you guard him sure.
[*Ex. with* Colevile.
And now dispatch we tow'rd the Court, my lords;
I hear, the King, my father, is sore sick;
Our news shall go before us to his Majesty,
Which, cousin, you shall bear to comfort him,
And we with sober speed will follow you.

Fal. My lord, I beseech you, give me leave to go through *Glo'stershire*; and when you come to Court, *pray, * stand my good Lord in your good report.

---

* *Stand my good Lord in your good report.*] We must either read, *pray let me stand*, or by a construction somewhat harsh, understand it thus. *Give me leave to go—and—stand. To stand in a report*, referred to the reporter, is *to persist*, and *Falstaff* did not ask the prince to persist in his present opinion.

Lan.

Lan. Fare you well, *Falstaff*; ⁸ I, in my condition, shall better speak of you than you deserve. [*Exit.*

Fal. I would, you had but the wit; 'twere better than your dukedom. Good faith, ⁹ this same young sober-blooded Boy doth not love me; nor a man cannot make him laugh; but that's no marvel, he drinks no wine. There's never any of these demure boys come to any proof; for thin drink doth so over-cool their blood, and making many fish-meals, that they fall into a kind of male green-sickness; and then, when they marry, they get wenches. They are generally fools and cowards; which some of us should be too, but for inflammation. A good Sherris-Sack hath a two-fold operation in it; it ascends me into the brain, dries me there all the foolish, dull and crudy vapours which environ it; makes it apprehensive, quick, ¹ forgetive, full of nimble, fiery, and delectable shapes; which deliver'd o'er to the voice, the tongue, which is the birth, becomes excellent wit. The second property of your excellent Sherris, is, the warming of the blood; which before cold and settled, left the liver white and pale; which is the badge of pusillanimity and cowardise; but the Sherris warms it, and makes it course from the inwards, to the parts extreme; it illuminateth the face, which, as a beacon, gives warning to all the rest of this little Kingdom, Man, to arm; and then the vital commmoners and inland petty spirits muster me all to their captain, the heart; who, great, and puft up with this retinue, doth any deed of

---

⁸ —— *I, in my condition, Shall better speak of you than you deserve,*] I know not well the meaning of the word *condition* in this place; I believe it is the same with *temper of mind:* I shall, *in my good nature*, speak better of you than you merit.

⁹ *This same sober-blooded boy doth not love me, nor a man cannot make him laugh.*] *Falstaff* speaks here like a veteran in life. The young prince did not love him, and he despaired to gain his affection, for he could not make him laugh. Men only become friends by community of pleasures. He who cannot be softened into gayety cannot easily be melted into kindness.

¹ *Forgetive* from *forge*; inventive, imaginative.

courage

KING HENRY IV.

courage; and this valour comes of Sherris. So that skill in the weapon is nothing without sack, for that sets it a-work; and learning a meer hoard of gold kept by a devil, 'till Sack commences it, and sets it in act and use. Hereof comes it, that Prince *Harry* is valiant; for the cold blood he did naturally inherit of his father, he hath, like lean, steril, and bare land, manured, husbanded, and till'd, with excellent endeavour of drinking good, and good store of fertil Sherris, that he is become very hot and valiant. If I had a thousand sons, the first human principle I would teach them should be to forswear thin potations, and to addict themselves to Sack.

Enter Bardolph.

How now, *Bardolph.*

Bard. The army is discharged all, and gone.

Fal. Let them go; I'll through *Gloucestershire*, and there will I visit master *Robert Shallow*, Esquire; [2] I have him already tempering between my finger and my thumb, and shortly will I seal with him. Come away.
[*Exeunt.*

SCENE VIII.

Changes to the Palace at Westminster.

Enter King Henry, Warwick, Clarence, *and* Gloucester.

K. Henry. NOW, lords, if heav'n doth give successful end
To this debate that bleedeth at our doors,
We will our youth lead on to higher fields,
And draw no swords but what are sanctify'd.
Our Navy is address'd, our Pow'r collected,
Our Substitutes in absence well invested,
And every thing lyes level to our wish;

[2] *I have him already tempering* &c.] A very pleasant allusion to the old use of sealing with soft wax. WARBURTON.

THE SECOND PART OF

Only we want a little perfonal ftrength,
And paufe us, till thefe Rebels, now a foot,
Come underneath the yoke of Government.

War. Both which, we doubt not, but your Majefty
Shall foon enjoy.

K. Henry. Humphrey, my fon of *Gloucefter,*
Where is the Prince your brother?

Glou. I think he's gone to hunt, my lord, at
Windfor.

K. Henry. And how accompanied?

Glou. I do not know, my lord.

K. Henry. Is not his brother, *Thomas* of *Clarence,*
with him?

Glou. No, my good lord, he is in prefence here.

Cla. What would my lord and father?

K. Henry. Nothing but well to thee, *Thomas* of
Clarence,
How chance thou art not with the Prince thy brother?
He loves thee, and thou doft neglect him, *Thomas*;
Thou haft a better place in his affection,
Than all thy brothers; cherifh it, my boy;
And noble offices thou may'ft effect
Of mediation, after I am dead,
Between his greatnefs and thy other brethren.
Therefore omit him not; blunt not his love;
Nor lofe the good advantage of his grace,
By feeming cold, or carelefs of his will.
For he is gracious, if he be obferv'd,
He hath a tear for pity, and a hand
Open as Day, for melting charity,
Yet notwithftanding, being incens'd, he's flint;
As [3] humourous as winter, and as fudden
As flaws [4] congealed in the fpring of day.

His

---

[3] *Humourous as winter,*] That is, changeable as the weather of a winter's day. *Dryden* fays of *Almanzor,* that he is *humerous as wind.*

[4] ——*congealed in the fpring of day*] Alluding to the opinion of fome philofophers, that the vapours being congealed in the air by cold, (which is moft
intenfe

KING HENRY IV.

His temper therefore must be well observ'd;
Chide him for faults, and do it reverently,
When you perceive his blood inclin'd to mirth,
But being moody, give him line and scope,
'Till that his passions, like a Whale on ground,
Confound themselves with working. Learn this,
  Thomas,
And thou shalt prove a shelter to thy friends,
A hoop of gold to bind thy brothers in,
That the united vessel of their blood,
Mingled with venom of suggestion,
As, force-per force, the age will pour it in,
Shall never leak, though it doth work as strong
As *Aconitum,* or 5 rash gun-powder.
 Cla. I shall observe him with all care and love.
 K. Henry. Why art thou not at *Windsor* with him,
  Thomas?
 Cla. He is not there to-day; he dines in *London.*
 K. Henry. And how accompanied? canst thou tell
  that?
 Cla. With *Poins,* and other his continual followers.
 K. Henry. Most subject is the fattest soil to weeds;
And he, the noble image of my youth,
Is over spread with them; therefore my grief
Stretches it self beyond the hour of death.
The blood weeps from my heart, when I do shape,
In forms imaginary, th' unguided days
And rotten times that you shall look upon,
When I am sleeping with my ancestors.
For when his headstrong riot hath no curb,
When rage and hot blood are his councellors,
When means and lavish manners meet together,

---

intense towards the morning) and being afterwards ratified and let loose by the warmth of the sun, occasion those sudden and impetuous gusts of wind which are called *Flaws*.   HANMER.

5 *Rash gun powder*] *Rash* is quick, violent, sudden. This representation of the prince, is a natural picture of a young man whose passions are yet too strong for his virtues.

Oh,

324   THE SECOND PART OF

Oh, with what wings shall his * affection fly
To'ward fronting peril and oppos'd decay?

War. My gracious lord, you look beyond him quite;
The prince but studies his companions,
Like a strange tongue, wherein to gain the language,
'Tis needful, that the most immodest word
Be look'd upon and learn'd; which once attain'd,
Your highness knows, comes to no farther use,
But to be known and hated. So, like gross terms,
The Prince will in the perfectness of time
Cast off his followers; and their memory
Shall as a pattern or a measure live,
By which his grace must mete the lives of others;
Turning past evils to advantages.

K. Henry. 6 'Tis seldom, when the Bee doth leave her comb
In the dead carrion.—Who's here? *Westmorland!*

SCENE IX.

Enter Westmorland.

West. Health to my Sovereign, and new happiness
Added to that, which I am to deliver!
Prince *John*, your son, doth kiss your Grace's hand:
Mowbray, the Bishop *Scroop*, *Hastings*, and all,
Are brought to the correction of your Law;
There is not now a rebel's sword unsheath'd,
But Peace puts forth her Olive ev'ry where.
The manner how this action hath been borne,
Here at more leisure, may your Highness read,
With every course, 7 in his particular.

K. Henry.

---

* —*his affection*] His passions; his inordinate desires.

6 *'Tis seldom when the bee,* &c.] As the bee, having once placed her comb in a carcase, stays by her honey, so he that has once taken pleasure in bad company, will continue to associate with those that have the art of pleasing him.

7 *In his particular.*] We should read, I think, in *this* particular: that

K. Henry. O *Westmorland,* thou art a summer bird,
Which ever in the haunch of winter sings
The lifting up of day.

Enter Harcourt.

Look, here's more news.
  Har. From enemies heav'n keep your Majesty:
And, when they stand against you, may they fall
As those that I am come to tell you of!
The Earl *Northumberland,* and the lord *Bardolph,*
With a great Pow'r of *English* and of *Scots,*
Are by the Sh'riff of *Yorkshire* overthrown.
The manner and true order of the fight,
This packet, please it you, contains at large.
  K. Henry. And wherefore should these good news
    make me sick?
Will fortune never come with both hands full,
But write her fair words still in foulest letters?
She either gives a stomach, and no food;
Such are the poor, in health; or else a feast,
And takes away the stomach; such the rich,
That have abundance and enjoy it not.
I should rejoice now at these happy news,
And now my sight fails, and my brain is giddy.
O me, come near me, now I am much ill!
  Glou. Comfort your Majesty!
  Cla. Oh, my royal father!
  West. My sovereign lord, chear up your self, look up.
  War. Be patient, Princes; you do know, these fits
Are with his Highness very ordinary.
Stand from him, give him air; he'll straight be well.
  Cla. No, no, he cannot long hold out these pangs;
Th' incessant care and labour of his mind
Hath wrought the mure, that should confine it in,

---

it is, in this *detail,* in this ac-   8 *Hath wrought the* mure,—]
count which is minute and distinct.   *i. e.* the wall.   Pope.

326 THE SECOND PART OF

So thin, that life looks through, and will break out.

Glou. 9 The people fear me; for they do observe
1 Unfather'd heirs and loathly births of Nature.
2 The Seasons change their manners, as the year
Had found some months asleep, and leap'd them over.

Cla. The river hath thrice flow'd, no ebb between;
And the old folk, time's doting chronicles,
Say, it did so a little time before
That our great Gransire *Edward* sick'd and dy'd.

War. Speak lower, Princes, for the King recovers.

Glou. This apoplex will, certain, be his end.

K. Henry. I pray you, take me up, and bear me hence
Into some other chamber. Softly, 'pray.
Let there be no noise made, my gentle friends,
3 Unless some dull and favourable hand
Will whisper musick to my weary spirit.

War. Call for the musick in the other room.

K. Henry. Set me the crown upon the pillow here.

Cla. His eye is hollow, and he changes much.

War. Less noise, less noise.

---

9 *The people fear me;* ———] i. e. make me afraid; which sense the *Oxford Editor* not taking, alters it to *fear it.* WARB.

1 *Unfather'd heirs.*] That is, equivocal births; animals that had no animal progenitors; productions not brought forth according to the stated laws of generation.

2 *The seasons change their manners,* ———] This is finely expressed; alluding to the terms of *rough* and *harsh,* and *mild* and *soft,* applied to weather. WARB.

3 *Unless some* DULL AND *favourable hand.*] Thus the old editions read it Evidently corrupt. *Shakespear* seems to have wrote, *Unless some* DOLEING *favourable hand.*
Doleing, i. e. a hand using soft melancholy airs. WARBURTON.

I rather think that *dull* signifies, *melancholy, gentle, soothing. Doleing* cannot be received without some example of its use, which the commentator has not given, and my memory will not supply.

SCENE

KING HENRY IV.

SCENE X.

Enter Prince Henry.

P. Henry. Who saw the Duke of *Clarence?*
Cla. I am here, brother, full of heaviness.
P. Henry. How now! rain within doors, and none abroad?
How doth the King?
Glou. Exceeding ill.
P. Henry. Heard he the good news yet?
Tell it him.
Glou. He alter'd much upon the hearing it.
P. Henry. If he be sick with joy,
He'll recover without physick.
War. Not so much noise, my lords. Sweet Prince, speak low;
The King, your father, is dispos'd to sleep.
Cla. Let us withdraw into the other room.
War. Will't please your grace to go along with us?
P. Henry. No; I will sit, and watch here by the King. [*Exeunt all but P.* Henry.
Why doth the Crown lye there upon his pillow,
Being so troublesome a bed fellow?
O polish'd perturbation! golden care!
That keep'st the ports of slumber open wide
To many a watchful night. Sleep with it now.—
Yet not so sound, and half so deeply sweet,
As he, whose brow, with homely biggen bound,
Snores out the watch of night. O majesty!
When thou dost pinch thy bearer, thou dost sit
Like a rich armor worn in heat of day,
That scalds with safety. By his gates of breath
There lies a downy feather, which stirs not;
Did he suspire, that light and weightless Down
Perforce must move.—My gracious lord! my father!
—This sleep is sound, indeed; this is a sleep,

Y 4 That

That from this golden Rigol hath divorc'd
So many *English* Kings. Thy Due from me
Is tears, and heavy sorrows of the blood;
Which nature, love, and filial tenderness
Shall, O my dear father, pay thee plenteously.
My due from thee is this imperial Crown,
Which, as immediate from thy place and blood,
Derives it self to me. Lo, here it sits,
[*Putting it on his head.*
Which heav'n shall guard; and put the world's whole
 strength
Into one giant arm, it shall not force
This lineal Honour from me. This from thee
Will I to mine leave, as 'tis left to me. [*Exit.*

SCENE XI.

Enter Warwick, Gloucester, *and* Clarence.

K. Henry. *Warwick! Gloucester! Clarence!*
Cla. Doth the King call?
War. What would your Majesty? how fares your
 Grace?
K. Henry. Why did you leave me here alone, my
 lords?
Cla. We left the Prince my brother here, my Liege,
Who undertook to sit and watch by you.
K. Henry. The Prince of *Wales*? where is he? let
 me see him.
War. This door is open, he is gone this way.
Glou. He came not through the chamber where we
 stay'd.
K. Henry. Where is the Crown? who took it from
 my pillow?
War. When we withdrew, my Liege, we left it
 here.
K. Henry. The Prince hath ta'en it hence; go seek
 him out.

Is

KING HENRY IV.

e so hasty, that he doth suppose
sleep my death? find him, my lord of *Warwick*,
d chide him hither straight; this part of his
joins with my disease, and helps to end me.
, sons, what things you are! how quickly nature
s to revolt, when gold becomes her object?
this, the foolish over-careful fathers
ve broke their sleeps with thought, their brains with
  care,
ir bones with industry; for this, engrossed
: canker'd heaps of strange-atchieved gold;
this, they have been thoughtful to invest
ir sons with arts and martial exercises,
en, like the Bee, culling from ev'ry flow'r,
 thighs are packt with wax, our mouths with
  honey,
bring it to the hive; and, like the Bees,
murder'd for our pains! this bitter taste
eld his engrossments to the dying father.

Enter Warwick.

r, where is he, that will not stay so long,
l his friend, Sickness, hath determin'd me?
ar. My lord, I found the Prince in the next room,
hing with kindly tears his gentle cheeks;
h such a deep demeanour in great sorrow,
t Tyranny, which never quaft but blood,
uld by beholding him have wash'd his knife
h gentle eye-drops.   He is coming hither.
. *Henry*. But wherefore did he take away the
  Crown?

Enter Prince Henry.

where he comes.   Come hither to me *Harry*—
epart the chamber, leave us here alone.
                                  [*Exeunt Lords*.

4 *Yield his engrossments*.] His accumulations.

P. *Henry*.

THE SECOND PART OF

  P. Henry. I never thought to hear you speak again.
  K. Henry. Thy wish was father, *Harry*, to that
    thought;
I stay too long by thee, I weary thee.
Dost thou so hunger for my empty Chair,
That thou wilt needs invest thee with my Honours,
Before thy hour be ripe? O foolish youth!
Thou seek'st the Greatness, that will overwhelm thee.
Stay but a little; for my cloud of Dignity
Is held from falling with so weak a wind,
That it will quickly drop; my day is dim.
Thou hast stoln that, which, after some few hours,
Were thine without offence; and at my death
Thou hast seal'd up my expectation; *.
Thy life did manifest, thou lov'dst me not;
And thou wilt have me die assur'd of it.
Thou hid'st a thousand daggers in thy thoughts,
Which thou hast whetted on thy stony heart,
To stab at half an hour of my frail life.
What! canst thou not forbear me half an hour?
Then get thee gone, and dig my Grave thyself,
And bid the merry bells ring to thy ear
That thou art crowned, not that I am dead.
—Let all the tears, that should bedew my herse,
Be drops of balm to sanctify thy head;
Only compound me with forgotten dust,
Give that, which gave thee life, unto the worms.—
Pluck down my officers, break my decrees;
For now a time is come to mock at form;
Henry the Fifth is crown'd. Up, Vanity!
Down, royal State! All you sage Counsellors, hence;
And to the *English* Court assemble now,
From ev'ry region, apes of Idleness;
Now, neighbour confines, purge you of your scum;
Have you a ruffian that will swear, drink, dance,
Revel the night, rob, murder, and commit
The oldest sins the newest kind of ways?

  * —*seal'd up my expectation;*] Thou hast *confirmed* my opinion.

KING HENRY IV.

)y, he will trouble you no more;
id shall double gild his treble Guilt,
l shall give him office, honour, might;
: Fifth *Harry* from curb'd licence plucks
uzzle of restraint, and the wild dog
esh his tooth on every innocent.
poor kingdom, sick with civil blows,
:hat my care could not withold thy riots,
vilt thou do when riot is thy care?
a wilt be a wilderness again,
l with Wolves, thy old inhabitants.
nry. O pardon me, my Liege! but for my
    tears,   [*Kneeling.*
oift impediments unto my speech,
ore-stall'd this dear and deep rebuke,
i with grief had spoke, and I had heard
urse of it so far. There is your Crown;
 that wears the crown immortally,
uard it yours! If I affect it more,
s your Honour, and as your Renown,
ie no more from this obedience rise,

and *shall double gild his ult;*] Evidently the of some foolish Playe: : nust make a difference what *Shakespear* might 'd to have written off . what he had corrected. enes are of the latter :refore such lines by no be esteemed his. But r. *Pope*, (who judicious- out this line) not one *ear*'s Editors seem ever id so reasonable and ne- rule in their heads, :y set upon correcting r. WARBURTON. not why this commen- ild speak with so much : what he cannot know, .ine so positively what

so capricious a writer as our poet might either deliberately or wan- tonly produce. This line is in- deed such as disgraces a few that precede and follow it, but it suits well enough with the *daggers hid in thought, and whet- ted on the flinty hearts;* and the answer which the prince makes, and which is applauded for wis- dom, is not of a strain much higher than this ejected line.

* This is obscure in the con- struction, though the general meaning is clear enough. The order is, *this obedience which is taught this exterior bending by my duteous spirit;* or, *this obedience which teaches this exterior bend- ing to my inwardly duteous spirit.* I know not which is right.

Which

Which my moſt * true and inward-duteous ſpirit
Teacheth this proſtrate and exterior bending.
Heav'n witneſs with me, when I here came in,
And found no courſe of breath within your Majeſty,
How cold it ſtruck my heart! If I do feign,
O let me in my preſent wildneſs die,
And never live to ſhew th' incredulous world
The noble change that I have purpoſed.
Coming to look on you, thinking you dead,
(And dead almoſt, my Liege, to think you were)
I ſpake unto the Crown, as having ſenſe,
And thus upbraided it. The care on thee depending
Hath fed upon the body of my father;
Therefore thou beſt of gold art worſt of gold;
Other, leſs fine in carrat, is more precious,
Preſerving life 6 in med'cine potable,
But thou, moſt fine, moſt honour'd, moſt renowned,
Haſt eat thy bearer up. Thus, Royal Liege,
Accuſing it, I put it on my head,
To try with it, as with an enemy,
That had before my face murder'd my father,
The quarrel of a true inheritor.
But if it did infect my blood with joy,
Or ſwell my thoughts to any ſtrain of pride,
If any rebel or vain ſpirit of mine
Did with the leaſt affection of a welcome
Give entertainment to the Might of it;
Let heav'n for ever keep it from my head,
And make me as the pooreſt vaſſal is,
That doth with awe and terror kneel to it!

 K. *Henry.* O my ſon!
Heav'n put it in thy mind to take it hence,

---

* *True* is *loyal.*

6 *In med'cine potable*] There has long prevailed an opinion that a ſolution of gold has great medicinal virtues, and that incorruptibility of gold might be communicated to the body impregnated with it. Some have pretended to make *potable* gold among other frauds practiſed on credulity.

That

KING HENRY IV. 333

ou might'st win the more thy father's love,
; so wisely in excuse of it.
ither, *Harry*, sit thou by my bed;
ır, I think, the very latest counsel,
er I shall breathe. Heav'n knows, my son,
by-paths and indirect crook'd ways
ıis crown; and I myself know well,
ɔublesome it sate upon my head.
it shall descend with better quiet,
pinion, better confirmation;
he 7 soil of the atchievement goes
e into the earth. It seem'd in me
ın honour snatch'd with boist'rous hand,
ad many living to upbraid
ı of it by their assistances;
laily grew to quarrel and to blood-shed,
ding supposed peace. 9 All these bold fears
:est, with peril I have answered,
my reign hath been but as a Scene,
that Argument; and now my death
es the mode; for what in me was purchas'd,
ɔon thee in a much fairer sort;
the garland wear'st ² successively.

is *spot*, *dirt*, *turpitude*,

ıding supposed *peace*.—]
or undermined.
  WARBURTON.
counterfeited, *imagined*,

'll THESE *bold* FEARS.]
I certainly read,
'll THEIR *bold* FEATS,
, commotions of con-
  WARBURTON.
is no need of alteration.
ere used in the active
that which causes *fear*.
ges *the* mode;] *Mode*,
:s not signify fashion,

but *time* and *measure* in singing,
or the *pitch* in speaking: *Modus*,
a word peculiar to the ancient
Drama: For the metaphor is
continued from the words immediately preceding,
——— *as a Scene*,
Acting that Argument———
  WARBURTON.
Mode is here in its usual
sense, the *form* or *state of things*.
Nothing is more easy than to
make obscurities and clear them.
 2 *Successively*.] To order of
succession Every usurper snatches
a claim of hereditary right as
soon as he can.

       Yet

THE SECOND PART OF

Yet though thou stand'st more sure than I could do,
Thou art not firm enough, since griefs are green,
And all thy friends, which thou must make thy friends,
Have but their stings and teeth newly ta'en out,
By whose fell-working I was first advanc'd,
And by whose pow'r I well might lodge a fear,
To be again displac'd; which to avoid
I cut them off, and had a purpose now
3 To lead out many to the Holy Land;
Lest Rest and lying still might make them look
Too near into my State. Therefore, my *Harry*,
Be it thy course to busy giddy minds
With foreign Quarrels; that action, hence, borne out,
May waste the memory of former days.
More would I, but my Lungs are wasted so,
That strength of speech is utterly deny'd me.
4 How I came by the Crown, O God, forgive!
And grant it may with thee in true peace live.

P. *Henry*. My gracious Liege,
You won it, wore it, kept it, gave it me;
Then plain and right must my Possession be;
Which I with more than with a common pain,
'Gainst all the world, will rightfully maintain.

---

3 *To lead* OUT *many to the Holy Land;*] As plausible as this reading is, it is corrupt. *Shakespear*, I think, wrote,
To lead OUR *many* —— *our many* or *meiny, i. e.* our people.
WARBURTON.

As plausible as this emendation is I think it wrong. The sense is: *Of those who assisted my usurpation, some I have cut off, and many I intended to lead abroad.* This journey to the Holy Land, of which the king very frequently revives the mention, had two motives, religion, and policy. He durst not wear the ill-gotten crown without expiation, but in the act of expiation he contrives to make his wickedness successful.

4 *How I came,* &c.] This is a true picture of a mind divided between heaven and earth. He prays for the prosperity of guilt while he deprecates its punishment.

Enter

Enter Lord John *of* Lancaster, *and* Warwick.

K. *Henry.* Look, look, here comes my *John* of Lancaster.
Lan. Health, peace and happiness to my royal father!
K. *Henry.* Thou bring'st me happiness and peace, son *John*;
But health, alack, with youthful wings is flown
From this bare, wither'd Trunk. Upon thy sight
My worldly business makes a period.
Where is my lord of *Warwick?*
P. *Henry.* My lord of *Warwick.*——
K. *Henry.* Doth any name particular belong
Unto the lodging where I first did swoon?
War. 'Tis call'd *Jerusalem*, my noble lord.
K. *Henry.* Laud be to God! even there my life must end.
It hath been prophesy'd to me many years,
I should not die but in *Jerusalem*,
Which vainly I suppos'd the Holy Land.
But bear me to that chamber, there I'll lye:
In that *Jerusalem* shall *Harry* die. [*Exeunt.*

THE SECOND PART OF

ACT V. SCENE I.

Shallow's *Seat in* Glo'ſterſhire.

Enter Shallow, Silence, Falſtaff, Bardolph, *and Page.*

SHALLOW.

BY cock and pye, Sir, you ſhall not away to night. What! *Davy,* I ſay——

Fal. You muſt excuſe me, maſter *Robert Shallow.*

Shal. 5 I will not excuſe you; you ſhall not be excuſed. Excuſes ſhall not be admitted: there is no excuſe ſhall ſerve: you ſhall not be excus'd. Why, *Davy!*——

Enter Davy.

Davy. Here, Sir.

Shal. Davy, Davy, Davy, let me ſee, *Davy,* let me ſee;—yea, marry, *William* Cook, bid him come hither.—Sir *John,* you ſhall not be excus'd.

Davy. Marry, Sir, thus. 6 Thoſe precepts cannot be ſerv'd; and, again, Sir, ſhall we ſow the headland with wheat?

Shal. With red wheat, *Davy.* But, for *William* Cook.——Are there no young Pidgeons?

Davy. Yea, Sir——Here is now the Smith's note for ſhoeing, and plow-irons.

---

5 *I will not excuſe you,* &c.] The ſterility of Juſtice *Shallow's* wit is admirably deſcribed, in thus making him, by one of the fineſt ſtrokes of nature, ſo often vary his phraſe, to expreſs one and the ſame thing, and that the commoneſt. WARBURTON.

6 *Thoſe precepts cannot be ſerv'd.*] *Precept* is a juſtice's warrant. To the offices which *Falſtaff* gives *Davy* in the following ſcene, may be added that of juſtice's clerk. *Davy* has almoſt as many employments as *Scrub* in the Stratagem.

Shal.

Shal. Let it be cast and paid—— Sir *John*, you shall not be excus'd. [*Goes to the other side of the stage.*

Davy. Now, Sir, a new link to the bucket must needs be had. And, Sir, do you mean to stop any of *William*'s wages about the sack he lost the other day at *Hinckly* Fair?

Shal. He shall answer it. Some Pigeons, *Davy*, a couple of short-legg'd Hens, a joint of mutton, and any pretty little tiny kickshaws. Tell *William* Cook.

Davy. Doth the man of war stay all night, Sir?

Shal. Yes, *Davy*. I will use him well. A friend i'th' Court is better than a penny in purse. Use his men well, *Davy*, for they are errant knaves, and will back-bite.

Davy. No worse than they are back-bitten, Sir; for they have marvellous foul linnen.

Shal. Well conceited, *Davy*. About thy business, *Davy*.

Davy. I beseech you, Sir, to countenance *William Visor* of *Wancot* against *Clement Perkes* of the hill.

Shal. There are many complaints, *Davy*, against that *Visor*; that *Visor* is an arrant knave, on my knowledge.

Davy. I grant your Worship, that he is a knave, Sir; but yet God forbid, Sir, but a knave should have some countenance at his friend's request. An honest man, Sir, is able to speak for himself, when a knave is not. I have serv'd your Worship truly, Sir, these eight years; and if I cannot once or twice in a quarter bear out a knave against an honest man, I have but very little credit with your Worship. The knave is mine honest friend, Sir, therefore, I beseech your Worship, let him be countenanced.

Shal. Go to, I say, he shall have no wrong. Look about, *Davy*. Where are you, Sir *John*? Come, off with your boots. Give me your hand, master *Bardolph*.

Bard. I am glad to see your Worship.

Vol. IV.   Z   *Shal.*

THE SECOND PART OF

Shal. I thank thee with all my heart, kind master *Bardolph*. And welcome my tall fellow. [*To the Page.*] Come, Sir *John*.

Fal. I'll follow you, good master *Robert Shallow*. [*Exeunt* Shallow, Silence, *&c.*] *Bardolph*, look to our horses.———If I were saw'd into quantities, I should make four dozen of such 7 bearded hermites-staves as master *Shallow*. It is a wonderful thing to see the semblable coherence of his mens' spirits and his; they, by observing of him, do bear themselves like foolish justices; he, by conversing with them, is turn'd into a justice-like servingman. Their spirits are so married in conjunction, with the participation of society, that they flock together in consent, like so many wild Geese. If I had a suit to master *Shallow*, I would humour his men with the imputation of being near their master; if to his men, I would curry with master *Shallow*, that no man could better command his servants. It is certain, that either wise Bearing or ignorant Carriage is caught, as men take diseases, one of another, therefore let men take heed of their company. I will devise matter enough out of this *Shallow* to keep Prince *Henry* in continual laughter the wearing out of six fashions, which is four terms or 8 two actions, and he shall laugh without *Intervallums*. O, it is much, that a lie with a slight oath, and a jest with a sad brow, will do with a 9 fellow that never had the ache in his shoulders. O, you shall see him laugh, till his face be like a wet cloak ill laid up.

Shal. [*within.*] Sir *John*———

---

7 *Bearded-hermites staves.*] He had before called him *the starved Justice*. His want of flesh is a standing jest.

8 *Two actions*] There is something humorous in making a spendthrift compute time by the operation of an action for debt.

9 *Fellow that never had the ache.*] That is, a young fellow one whose disposition to merriment, time and pain have not yet impaired.

Fal.

Fal. I come, master *Shallow*; I come, master *Shal-*
v. [*Exit* Falstaff.

SCENE II.

Changes to the Court, in LONDON.

ter the Earl of Warwick, *and the Lord Chief Justice.*

ar. HOW now, my lord Chief Justice, whither away?
Ch. Just. How doth the King?
War. Exceeding well; his cares are now all ended.
Ch. Just. I hope, not dead?
War. He's walk'd the way of Nature;
id to our purposes he lives no more.
Ch. Just. I would his Majesty had call'd me with him:
ie service, that I truly did his life,
ith left me open to all injuries.
War. Indeed I think the young King loves you not.
Ch. Just. I know, he doth not; and do arm myself
welcome the condition of the time,
hich cannot look more hideously on me,
an I have drawn it in my fantasy.

ter Lord John *of* Lancaster, Gloucester, *and* Clarence.

War. Here come the heavy issue of dead *Harry*.
that the living *Harry* had the temper
him, the worst of these three gentlemen,
w many Nobles then should hold their places,
at must strike sail to spirits of vile sort!
Ch. Just. Alas, I fear all will be overturn'd.
Lan. Good morrow, cousin *Warwick*.
Glou. Cla. Good morrow, cousin.
Lan. We meet, like men that had forgot to speak.
Z 2 *War.*

THE SECOND PART OF

War. We do remember; but our argument
Is all too heavy to admit much Talk.

Lan. Well, peace be with him that hath made us
heavy!

Ch. Juſt. Peace be with us, leſt we be heavier!

Glou. O, good my lord, you've loſt a friend, indeed;
And I dare ſwear, you borrow not that face
Of ſeeming ſorrow; it is, ſure, your own.

Lan. Tho' no man be aſſur'd what grace to find,
You ſtand in coldeſt expectation.
I am the ſorrier; 'would, 'twere otherwiſe.

Cla. Well, you muſt now ſpeak Sir *John Falſtaff*
fair,
Which ſwims againſt your ſtream of quality.

Ch. Juſt. Sweet Princes, what I did, I did in Honour,
Led by th' impartial conduct of my ſoul;
And never ſhall you ſee, that I will beg
[1] A ragged and foreſtall'd remiſſion.
If truth and upright innocency fail me,
I'll to the King my maſter that is dead,
And tell him who hath ſent me after him.

War. Here comes the Prince.

Enter Prince Henry.

Ch. Juſt. Heav'n ſave your Majeſty!

K. Henry. This new and gorgeous garment, Majeſty!

---

[1] *A* RAGGED *and foreſtall'd remiſſion.*] *Ragged* has no ſenſe here. We ſhould read, *A* rated *and* forſtail'd *remiſſion.* i.e. a remiſſion that muſt be ſought for, and bought with ſupplication. WARBURTON.

Different minds have different perplexities. I am more puzzled with *foreſtall'd* than with *ragged,* for *ragged,* in our authour's licentious diction, may eaſily ſignify *beggarly, mean, baſe, ignominious*; but *foreſtalled* I know not how to apply to *remiſſion* in any ſenſe primitive or figurative. I ſhould be glad of another word, but cannot find it. Perhaps by *foreſtall'd* remiſſion, he may mean a pardon begged by a voluntary confeſſion of offence, and *anticipation* of the charge.

Sits

KING HENRY IV.

ts not so easy on me, as you think.
rothers, you mix your sadness with some fear;
his is the *English*, not the *Turkish* Court;
ot *Amurath* an *Amurath* succeeds,
it *Harry*, *Harry*. Yet be sad, good brothers,
or, to speak truth, it very well becomes you:
rrow so royally in you appears,
hat I will deeply put the fashion on,
nd wear it in my heart. Why then, be sad;
it entertain no more of it, good brothers,
han a joint burthen laid upon us all.
or me, by heav'n, I bid you be assur'd,
l be your father and your brother too,
:t me but bear your love, I'll bear your cares.
:t weep that *Harry*'s dead? and so will I;
it *Harry* lives, that shall convert those tears
r number into hours of happiness.
Lan. &c. We hope no other from your Majesty.
K. Henry. You all look strangely on me; and you
most; [*To the Ch. Just.*
ou are, I think, assur'd, I love you not.
Ch. Just. I am assur'd, if I be measur'd rightly,
our Majesty hath no just cause to hate me.
K. Henry. No! might a Prince of my great hopes
forget
great indignities you laid upon me?
hat! rate, rebuke, and roughly send to prison
h' immediate heir of *England*? was this easy?—
lay this be wash'd in *Lethe*, and forgotten?
Ch. Just. I then did use the person of your father,
he image of his Power lay then in me;
nd in th' administration of his Law,

---

1 *Not the* Turkish *court.*] Not a court where the prince that ints the throne puts his brothers to death.

3 *Was this easy?*] That is, *was this not grievous?* Shakespeare has *easy* in this sense elsewhere.

Z 3 While

While I was busie for the Common-wealth,
Your Highness pleased to forget my Place,
The Majesty and Pow'r of Law and Justice,
The image of the King whom I presented,
And struck me in my very Seat of Judgment;
Whereon, as an offender to your father,
I gave bold way to my authority,
And did commit you. If the deed were ill,
Be you contented, wearing now the Garland,
To have a son set your decrees at naught,
To pluck down justice from your awful bench,
4 To trip the course of law, and blunt the sword
That guards the peace and safety of your person,
Nay more, to spurn at your most royal image,
5 And mock your working in a second body.
Question your royal thoughts, make the case your
Be now the father, and propose a son,
Hear your own dignity so much profan'd,
See your most dreadful laws so loosely flighted,
Behold your self so by a son disdain'd,
And then imagine me taking your part,
And in your pow'r so silencing your son.
After this cold conlid'rance, sentence me;
And, as you are a King, speak 6 in your State,
What I have done that misbecame my place,
My person, or my Liege's Sovereignty.

   K. *Henry.* You are right Justice, and you w
      this well,
Therefore still bear the balance and the sword;
And I do wish, your Honours may increase,
Till you do live to see a son of mine
Offend you, and obey you, as I did.

   4 *To trip the course of Law.*] To defeat the process of justice, a metaphor taken from the act of tripping a runner.

   5 *To mock your working in a second body.*] To treat with contempt your acts executed by a representative.

   6 *In your state.*] In yo[ur] gal character and office, no[t] the passion of a man inte[r] but with the impartiality [of a] Legislator.

shall I live to speak my father's words;
Happy am I, that have a man so bold,
That dares do justice on my proper son;
And no less happy, having such a son,
That would deliver up his Greatness so
Into the hand of justice.'—You committed me;
[F]or which I do commit into your hand
[Th'] unstain'd sword that you have us'd to bear;
[W]ith this * remembrance, that you use the same
[W]ith a like bold, just, and impartial spirit,
[As] you have done 'gainst me. There is my hand,
[You] shall be as a father to my youth,
[My] voice shall sound, as you do prompt mine ear,
[An]d I will stoop and humble my intents,
[To] your well-practis'd wise directions.
[An]d, Princes all, believe me, I beseech you;
[M]y father is gone wild into his Grave,
[Fo]r in his tomb lye my affections;
[An]d with his spirit ⁷ sadly I survive,
[To] mock the expectations of the world;
[To] frustrate prophecies, and to raze out
[ro]tten opinion, which hath writ me down
[af]ter my seeming. Tho' my tide of blood
[ha]th proudly flow'd in vanity 'till now;
[No]w doth it turn and ebb back to the sea,
[W]here it shall mingle with ⁹ the state of floods,
[An]d flow henceforth in formal Majesty.

⁷ *Remembrance.*] That is, *addition.*

⁷ *My father is gone wild.*] Mr. [Pop]e, by substituting *wail'd* for [wi]ld, without sufficient considera[tio]n, afforded Mr. *Theobald* much [mat]ter of ostentatious triumph.

⁸ *Sadly I survive.*] *Sadly* is [the] same as *soberly, seriously, [grav]ely. Sad* is opposed to *wild.*

⁹ ———— *the state of floods,*] [i.] e. the *assembly,* or general [me]eting of the floods. For all

rivers, running to the sea, are there represented as holding their *sessions.* This thought naturally introduced the following,
Now call we our high Court of Parliament.
But the *Oxford Editor*, much a stranger to the phraseology of that time in general, and to his author's in particular, out of mere loss for his meaning, reads it backwards, *the floods of state*.
WARBURTON.

Z 4 Now

Now call we our high Court of Parliament;
And let us chuse such limbs of noble counsel,
That the great body of our state may go
In equal rank with the best govern'd nation;
That War or Peace, or both at once, may be
As things acquainted and familiar to us;
In which you, father,. shall have foremost hand.
[*To the Lord Chief Justice.*
Our Coronation done, we will accite
As I before remember'd, all our State,
And (Heav'n consigning to my good intents)
No Prince, nor Peer, shall have just cause to say,
Heav'n shorten *Harry*'s happy life one day. [*Exeunt.*

SCENE IV.

Changes to Shallow's *Seat in* Gloucestershire.

Enter Falstaff, Shallow, Silence, Bardolph, *the Page,*
and Davy.

Shal. NAY, you shall see mine orchard, where in an arbour we will eat a last year's pippin of my own grafting, with * a dish of carraways, and so forth.—Come, cousin *Silence.*—And then to bed.

Fal. You have here a goodly dwelling, and a rich.

Shal. Barren, barren, barren. Beggars all, beggars all, Sir *John.* Marry, good air. Spread, *Davy,* spread, *Davy;* well said, Davy.

Fal. This *Davy* serves you for good uses; he is your servingman, and your husbandman.

Shal. A good varlet, a good varlet, a very good varlet, Sir *John.* — By th' Mass, I have drank too

---

* *a dish of carraways.*] A comfit or confection so called in our author's time. A passage in *Le Vigneul Marville*'s *Mesanges d'Historie et de Litt.* will explain this odd treat. *Dans le dernier siecle ou l'on avoit le goût delicat,* on ne croioit pas pouvoir vivre sans Dragées. Il n'etoit fils de bonne mere, qui n'eut sont Dragier; et il est raporté dans l'histoire du duc de Guise, que quand il fut tué à Blois il avoit son Dragier à la main. WARB.

much

much Sack at supper.———A good varlet. Now sit down, now sit down: come, cousin.

Sil. Ah, sirrah, quoth-a,
We shall do nothing but eat, and make good chear, [Singing.
And praise heav'n for the merry year;
When flesh is cheap and females dear,
And lusty lads roam here and there;
So merrily, and ever among, so merrily, &c.

Fal. There's a merry heart. Good master *Silence*, I'll give you a health for that anon.

Shal. Give Mr. *Bardolph* some wine, *Davy*.

Davy. Sweet Sir, sit; I'll be with you anon; most sweet Sir, sit. Master Page, sit; good master Page, sit; * proface. What you want in meat, we'll have in drink; but you must bear; [1] the heart's all. [*Exit.*

Shal. Be merry, master *Bardolph*; and, my little soldier there, be merry.

Sil. [Singing.] *Be merry, be merry, my wife has all;*
For women are Shrews, both short and tall;
'Tis merry in hall, when beards wag all,
And welcome merry Shrovetide.
Be merry, be merry.

Fal. I did not think, master *Silence* had been a man of this mettle.

Sil. Who I? I have been merry twice and once ere now.

Re-enter Davy.

Davy. There is a dish of leather-coats for you.

Shal. Davy,———

Davy. Your Worship—I'll be with you streight— A cup of wine, Sir?

---

* *Proface.*] *Italian* from *profaccia; that is, much good may it do you.* - HANMER.
I rather think *proface* is uttered by mistake for *perforce. Davy* impertinently asks *Bardolph* and the Page, who, according to their place, were standing, to sit down. *Bardolph* complies; the Page, knowing his duty, declines the seat, and *Davy* cries *proface,* and sets him down by force.

[1] *The heart's all.*] That is, the intention with which the entertainment is given. The humour consists in making *Davy* act as master of the house.

THE SECOND PART OF

Sil. [Singing] *A cup of wine,*
That's brisk and fine,
And drink unto the leman mine;
And a merry heart lives long-a.

Fal. Well said, master *Silence.*

Sil. If we shall be merry, now comes in the sweet of the night.

Fal. Health and long life to you, master *Silence.*

Sil. Fill the cup, and let it come. I'll pledge you, were't a mile to the bottom.

Shal. Honest *Bardolph*, welcome; if thou want'st any thing and wilt not call, beshrew thy heart. Welcome, my little tiny thief, and welcome, indeed, too. I'll drink to master *Bardolph*, and to all the [2] cavaleroes about *London*.

Davy. I hope to see *London*, ere I die.

Bard. If I might see you there, *Davy*,——

Shal. You'll crack a quart together? ha——will you not, master *Bardolph?*

Bard. Yes, Sir, in a pottle pot.

Shal. By God's liggens, I thank thee; the knave will stick by thee, I can assure thee that. He will not out, he is true-bred.

Bard. And I'll stick by him, Sir.

[*One knocks at the door.*

Shal. Why, there spoke a King. Lack nothing, be merry. Look, who's at the door there, ho.——Who knocks?

Fal. Why, now you have done me right.

Sil. [Singing.] *Do me right, and dub me Knight,*
[3] *Samingo.* Is't not so?

Fal. 'Tis so.

---

[2] *Cavaleroes.*] This was the term by which an airy splendid irregular fellow was distinguished. The soldiers of King *Charles* were called *Cavaliers* from the gayety which they affected in opposition to the sour faction of the parliament.

[3] Samingo] He means to say, *San Domingo.* HANMER.
Of *Samingo*, or *San Domingo*, I see not the use in this place.
Sil.

KING HENRY IV.   347

Is't so? why, then say, an old man can do what.

vy. If it please your Worship, there's one *Pistol* from the Court with news.

l. From the Court? let him come in.

SCENE V.

Enter Pistol.

now, *Pistol?*

l. Sir *John*, 'save you, Sir.

'. What wind blew you hither, *Pistol?*

t. Not the ill wind which blows no man good.
. Knight; thou art now one of the greatest men
 Realm.

Indeed, I think he be, but goodman *Puff* of
1.

l. Puff?

n thy teeth, most recreant coward base,
 John, I am thy *Pistol* and thy friend;
 1elter skelter have I rode to thee;
 .idings do I bring, and lucky joys,
 golden times, and happy news of price.
. I pr'ythee now, deliver them like a man of
 this world.

'. A foutra for the world and worldlings base!
 k of *Africa* and golden joys.
. O base *Assyrian* Knight, what is thy news?
 King *Cophetua* know the truth thereof.

old man can do somewhat.] goes a courting to a young girl. be observed that *Shake- Shallow* is an old man in both in the *Merry Wives of* plays. r, which he wrote after 5 *Let King* Cophetua, *&c*] y, for the greater com- Lines taken from an old bombast ness of his plot, changed play of *King Cophetua*: of whom, of *Silence.* He is here as we learn from *Shakespear*, advanced in years, with a there were ballads too. WARB. the university: he there See *Love's labour lost.*

Sil.

348   THE SECOND PART OF

Sil. *And* Robin-hood, Scarlet, *and* John.   [*Sings.*

Pist. Shall dunghill curs confront the *Helicons?*
And shall good news be baffled?
Then *Pistol* lay thy head in Fury's lap.

Shal. Honest gentleman, I know not your breeding.

Pist. Why then, lament therefore.

Shal. Give me pardon, Sir. If, Sir, you come with news from the Court, I take it, there is but two ways: either to utter them; or to conceal them. I am, Sir, under the King, in some authority.

Pist. Under which King? 6 *Bezonian*, speak or die.

Shal. Under King *Harry.*

Pist. Harry the Fourth? or Fifth?

Shal. Harry the Fourth.

Pist. A foutra for thine office!
Sir *John*, thy tender Lambkin now is King.
Harry the Fifth's the man.   I speak the truth.
When *Pistol* lies, do this, and * fig me like
The bragging *Spaniard.*

Fal. What, is the old King dead?

Pist. As nail in door.   The things I speak are just.

Fal. Away, *Bardolph*, saddle my horse. Master *Robert Shallow*, chuse what office thou wilt in the Land, 'tis thine. *Pistol*, I will double charge thee with Dignities.

Bard. O joyful day; I would not take a Knighthood for my fortune.

Pist. What? I do bring good news.

Fal. Carry master *Silence* to bed. Master *Shallow*, my Lord *Shallow*, be what thou wilt; I am fortune's

---

6 —— *Bezonian, speak or die.*] So again *Suffolk* says in 2d *Henry* VI.
   Great men oft die by vile Bezonians.
It is a term of Reproach, frequent in the Writers contemporary with our Poet. *Bisognoso*, a needy Person; thence metaphorically, a base Scoundrel.
                    THEOBALD.

* —— *Fig me like The bragging Spaniard.*] To fig, in *Spanish*, *Higas dar*, is to insult by putting the thumb between the fore and middle fingers. From this *Spanish* custom we yet say in contempt, *a fig for you.*
                    Steward.

KING HENRY IV. 349

Steward. Get on thy boots, we'll ride all night. Oh, sweet *Pistol!*—Away *Bardolph*—Come, *Pistol,* utter more to me; and withal devise something to do thyself good. Boot, boot, master *Shallow.* I know, the young King is sick for me. Let us take any man's horses; the Laws of *England* are at my commandment. Happy are they which have been my friends; and woe to my Lord Chief Justice!

Pist. Let vultures vile seize on his lungs also! Where is the life that late I led, say they? Why, here it is, welcome this pleasant day. [*Exeunt.*

SCENE VIII.

Changes to a Street in LONDON.

Enter Hostess Quickly, Doll Tear-sheet, *and Beadles.*

Host. NO, thou arrant knave, I would I might die, that I might have thee hang'd; thou hast drawn my shoulder out of joint.

Bead. The constables have deliver'd her over to me; and she shall have whipping cheer enough, I warrant her. There hath been a man or two kill'd about her.

Dol. [8] Nut-hook, nut-hook, you lye. Come on. I'll tell thee what, thou damn'd tripe-visag'd rascal, if the child, I go with, do miscarry, thou hadst better thou hadst struck thy mother, thou paper-fac'd villain.

Host. O the Lord, that Sir *John* were come, he would make this a bloody day to some body. But I pray God, the fruit of her womb miscarry.

Bead. If it do, you shall have a dozen of cushions again, you have but eleven now. Come, I charge you both go with me; for the man is dead, that you and *Pistol* beat among you.

---

[7] *Where is the life that late I led.*——] Words of an old ballad. WARBURTON.

[8] It hath been already observ'd on the *Merry Wives of* Windsor, that *Nut-hook* seems to have been in those times a name of reproach for a catch-poll.

Dol.

THE SECOND PART OF

Dol. I'll tell thee what, thou thin man in a Censer! I will have you as soundly swing'd for this, you blue-bottle rogue! ¹—You filthy famish'd correctioner! if you be not swing'd, I'll forswear half-kirtles. ²

Bead. Come, come, you she-Knight-arrant, come.

Host. O, that Right should thus o'ercome Might! Well, of sufferance comes ease.

Dol. Come, you rogue, come. Bring me to a Justice.

Host. Yes, come, you starv'd blood-hound.

Dol. Goodman death, goodman bones!——

Host. Thou Atomy, thou?

Dol. Come, you thin thing: come, you rascal!

Bead. Very well. [*Exeunt.*

SCENE VII.

A publick Place near Westminster-*Abbey*.

Enter two Grooms, strewing rushes.

1 *Groom.* MORE rushes, more rushes.

2 *Groom.* The trumpets have sounded twice.

1 *Groom.* It will be two of the clock ere they come from the Coronation: despatch, despatch.

[*Exeunt Grooms.*

Enter Falstaff, Shallow, Pistol, Bardolph, *and the boy*.

Fal. Stand here by me, master *Robert Shallow*, I

---

9 — thou *thin man in a Censer!*] These old Censers of thin metal had generally at the bottom the figure of some saint raised up with the hammer, in a barbarous kind of imbossed or chased work. The hunger-starved Beadle is compared, in substance, to one of these thin raised figures, by the same kind of humour that *Pistol*, in the *Merry Wives*. calls *Slender*, a *laten bilboe*. WARB.

1 *blue bottle rogue!*] A name I suppose given to the beadle from the colour of his livery.

2 *half-kirtles*.] Probably the dress of the prostitutes of that time.

* It has been already observed, that, at ceremonial entertainments, it was the custom to strew the floor with rushes. *Casus de Ephemera*.

I will

KING HENRY IV. 351

will make the King do you grace. I will leer upon him as he comes by, and do but mark the countenance that he will give me.

Pist. Bless thy lungs, good Knight.

Fal. Come here, *Pistol*; stand behind me. O, if I had had time to have made new liveries, I would have bestow'd the thousand pound I borrow'd of you. [*To Shallow.*] But it is no matter, this poor Show doth better; this doth infer the zeal I had to see him.

Shal. It doth so.

Fal. It shews my earnestness of affection.

Pist. It doth so.

Fal. My devotion.

Pist. It doth, it doth, it doth. 3

Fal. As it were, to ride day and night, and not to deliberate, not to remember, not to have patience to shift me.

Shal. It is most certain.

Fal. But to stand stained with travel, and sweating with desire to see him, thinking of nothing else, putting all affairs else in oblivion, as if there were nothing else to be done but to see him.

Pist. 'Tis *semper idem*; for *absque hoc nihil est*. 'Tis all in every part. 4

Shal. 'Tis so, indeed.

Pist. My Knight, I will enflame thy noble liver,
And make thee rage.
Thy *Dol* and *Helen* of thy noble thoughts
Is in base durance and contagious prison;

---

3 The two little answers here given to *Pistol*, are transferred by Sir T. Hanmer to *Shallow*, the repetition of *it doth* suits *Shallow* best.

4 'Tis all in every part,] The sentence alluded to is,
'Tis all in all, and all in every part.
And so doubtless it should be read. 'Tis a common way of expressing one's approbation of a right measure, to say, 'tis all in all. To which this phantastic character adds, with some humour, *and all in every part:* which, both together, make up the philosophic sentence, and compleat the absurdity of *Pistol's* phraseology. WARBURTON.

Haul'd

THE SECOND PART OF

Haul'd thither by mechanick dirty hands.
Rouze up revenge from Ebon den, with fell *Alecto's*
    snake,
For *Dol* is in.   *Pistol* speaks nought but truth.
  Fal. I will deliver her.
  Pist. There roar'd the sea; and trumpet-clangour sounds.

SCENE VIII.

The Trumpets sound.   Enter the King, and his train.

  Fal. God save thy Grace, King *Hal*, my royal *Hal!*
  Pist. The heav'ns thee guard and keep, most royal imp of fame!
  Fal. God save thee, my sweet boy!
  King. My Lord Chief Justice, speak to that vain
    man.
  Ch. Just. Have you your wits? know you, what 'tis
    you speak?
  Fal. My King, my *Jove*, I speak to thee, my heart!
  King. I know thee not, old man. Fall to thy prayers:
How ill white hairs become a fool and jester!
I have long dream'd of such a kind of man,
So surfeit-swell'd, so old, and so * profane;
But, being awake, I do despise my dream.
Make less thy body hence, and more thy grace;
Leave gormandizing. Know, the Grave doth gape 5
    For

---

  * *Profane*, in our authour, often signifies *love of talk* without the particular idea now given it. So in *Othello, Is he not a profane and very liberal counsellor.*
  5 —— *Know, the Grave doth gape*
    For thee, thrice wider than for other men.
  Reply not to me with a fool-born jest;] Nature is highly touched in this passage. The king having shaken off his vanities, schools his old companion for his follies with great severity: he assumes the air of a preacher; bids him fall to his *prayers, seek grace,* and leave *gormandizing.* But that word unluckily presenting him with a pleasant idea, he cannot forbear pursuing it. *Know, the Grave doth gape for thee thrice wider,* &c. and is just falling back into *Hal*, by an humourous allusion to *Falstaff*'s bulk; but he perceives it immediately, and
    fearing

KING HENRY IV.

, thrice wider than for other men.
)t to me with a fool-born jest,
not, that I am the thing I was,
'n doth know, so shall the world perceive,
ave turn'd away my former self,
those that kept me company.
ou dost hear I am as I have been,
h me, and thou shalt be as thou wast,
r and the feeder of my riots;
I banish thee, on pain of death,
e done the rest of my mis-leaders,
)me near our person by ten miles. [6]
)etence of life, I will allow you,
 of means enforce you not to Evil;
we hear you do reform yourselves,
according to your strengths and qualities
 advancement. Be't your charge, my Lord,
:rform'd the tenour of our word.
 [*Exit King*, &c.

John should take the
f it, checks both him-
knight, with
to me with a fool-born

ies the thread of his
nd goes moralizing
 end of the chapter.
et copies nature with
 and shews us how
e to fall back into
oms, when the change
le by degrees, and
) a habit, but deter-
once on the motives
nterest or reason.
 WARBURTON.
Rowe observes, that
rs lament to see *Fal-*
lly used by his old
. if it be considered
t knight has never
 sentiment of gene-
with all his power

of exciting mirth, has nothing
in him that can be esteemed,
no great pain will be suffered
from the reflection that he is
compelled to live honestly, and
maintained by the king, with a
promise of advancement when he
shall deserve it.

I think the poet more blame-
able for *Poins*, who is always
represented as joining some virtues with his vices, and is therefore treated by the prince with apparent distinction, yet he does nothing in the time of action, and
though after the bustle is over he
is again a favourite, at last va-
nishes without notice. *Shake-*
speare certainly lost him by heed-
lessness, in the multiplicity of his
characters, the variety of his action, and his eagerness to end the
play.

SCENE

SCENE IX.

Fal. Master *Shallow*, I owe you a thousand pound.

Shal. Ay, marry, Sir *John*, which I beseech you to let me have home with me.

Fal. That can hardly be, Mr. *Shallow*. Do not you grieve at this; I shall be sent for in private to him. Look you, he must seem thus to the world. Fear not your advancement, I will be the man yet that shall make you great.

Shal. I cannot perceive how, unless you give me your doublet, and stuff me out with straw. I beseech you, good Sir *John*, let me have five hundred of my thousand.

Fal. Sir, I will be as good as my word. This, that you heard, was but a colour.

Shal. A colour, I fear, that you will die in, Sir *John*.

Fal. Fear no colours. Go with me to dinner. Come, lieutenant *Pistol*; come, *Bardolph*. I shall be sent for soon at night.

Enter Chief Justice and Prince John.

Ch. Just. Go, carry Sir *John Falstaff* to the *Fleet*.*
Take all his company along with him.

Fal. My Lord, my Lord,———

Ch. Just. I cannot now speak. I will hear you soon. ——Take them away.

Pist. Si fortuna me tormento, spera me contento.

[*Exeunt.*

---

* I do not see why *Falstaff* is carried to the Fleet. We have never lost sight of him since his dismission from the king; he has committed no new fault, and therefore incurred no punishment; but the different agitations of fear, anger, and surprise in him and his company, made a good scene to the eye; and our author, who wanted them no longer on the stage, was glad to find this method of sweeping them away.

Manent

KING HENRY IV.

Manent Lancaster, *and Chief Justice.*

Lan. I like this fair proceeding of the King's.
He hath intent, his wonted followers
Shall all be very well provided for;
But they are banish'd, till their conversations
Appear more wise and modest to the world.
Ch. Just. And so they are.
Lan. The King hath call'd his Parliament, my Lord.
Ch. Just. He hath.
Lan. I will lay odds, that ere this year expire,
We bear our civil swords and native fire
As far as *France*. I heard a bird so sing,
Whose musick, to my thinking, pleas'd the King.
Come, will you hence? * [*Exeunt.*

---

* I fancy every reader, when he ends this play, cries out with *Desdemona*, O most lame and impotent conclusion! As this play was not, to our knowledge, divided into acts by the authour, I could be content to conclude it with the death of *Henry* the fourth.

In that Jerusalem shall Harry dye. These scenes which now make the fifth act of *Henry* the fourth, might then be the first of *Henry* the fifth; but the truth is, that they do unite very commodiously to either play. When these plays were represented, I believe they ended as they are now ended in the books; but *Shakespeare* seems to have designed that the whole series of action from the beginning of *Richard* the second, to the end of *Henry* the fifth, should be considered by the reader as one work, upon one plan, only broken into parts by the necessity of exhibition.

None of *Shakespeare's* plays are more read than the first and second parts of *Henry* the fourth. Perhaps no authour has ever in two plays afforded so much delight. The great events are interesting, for the fate of kingdoms depends upon them; the slighter occurrences are diverting, and, except one or two, sufficiently probable; the incidents are multiplied with wonderful fertility of invention, and the characters diversified with the utmost nicety of discernment, and the profoundest skill in the nature of man.

The prince, who is the hero both of the comick and tragick part, is a young man of great abilities and violent passions, whose sentiments are right, though his actions are wrong; whose virtues are obscured by negligence, and whose understanding is dissipated by levity. In his idle hours he is rather loose than wicked, and when the occasion forces out his latent qualities, he is great without effort, and brave without tumult. The trifler is roused into a hero, and the hero again reposes in the trifler. This character is great, original, and just.

Piercy is a rugged soldier, cholerick, and quarrelsome, and has only the soldier's virtues, generosity and courage.

But *Falstaff* unimitated, unimitable *Falstaff*, how shall I describe thee? Thou compound of sense and vice; of sense which may be admired but not esteemed, of vice which may be despised, but hardly detested. *Falstaff* is a character loaded with faults, and with those faults which naturally produce contempt. He is a thief, and a glutton, a coward, and a boaster, always ready to cheat the weak, and prey upon the poor; to terrify the timorous and insult the defenceless. At once obsequious and malignant, he satirises in their absence those whom he lives by flattering. He is familiar with the prince only as an agent of vice, but of this familiarity he is so proud as not only to be supercilious and haughty with common men, but to think his interest of importance to the duke of *Lancaster*. Yet the man thus corrupt, thus despicable, makes himself necessary to the prince that despises him, by the most pleasing of all qualities, perpetual gaiety, by an unfailing power of exciting laughter, which is the more freely indulged, as his wit is not of the splendid or ambitious kind, but consists in easy escapes and sallies of levity, which make sport but raise no envy. It must be observed that he is stained with no enormous or sanguinary crimes, so that his licentiousness is not so offensive but that it may be borne for his mirth.

The moral to be drawn from this representation is, that no man is more dangerous than he that with a will to corrupt, hath the power to please; and that neither wit nor honesty ought to think themselves safe with such a companion when they see *Henry* seduced by *Falstaff*.

PILOGUE.*

Spoken by a DANCER.

ST *my fear*; *then, my court'sy*; *last, my speech.*
y *fear is your displeasure*; *my court'sy*, *my duty*;
speech, to beg your pardons. If you look for a
eech now, you undo me; *for what I have to say*
ine own making, and what, indeed, I should say,
 doubt, prove mine own marring. But to the
, *and so to the venture. Be it known to you, (as*
ry well) I was lately here in the end of a dis-
Play, to pray your patience for it, and to promise
tter. I did mean, indeed, to pay you with this;
f, like an ill venture, it come unluckily home, I
 and you, my gentle creditors, lose. Here, I pro-
ou, I would be, and here I commit my body to your
: *bate me some, and I will pay you some, and,*
 debtors do, promise you infini.ely.

y *tongue cannot entreat you to acquit me, will you*
d *me to use my legs? and yet that were but light*
', *to dance out of your debt. But a good conscience*
ke any possible satisfaction, and so will I. + All
tlewomen here have forgiven me; *if the gentle-*
ill not, then the gentlemen do not agree with the
omen, which was never seen before in such an

word more, I beseech you; *if you be not too much*
with fat meat, our humble author will continue
y with Sir John *in it, and make you merry with*

s epilogue was merely one part of the audience by the
al, and alludes to some favour of the other, has been
l transaction. played already in the epilogue to
is trick of influencing *As you like it.*

EPILOGUE.

fair Catharine *of* France; *where, for any thing I k*
Falſtaff *ſhall die of a Sweat, unleſs already he be*
with your hard opinions; [1] *for* Oldcaſtle *died a m*
and this is not the man. My tongue is weary: wh
legs are too, I will bid you good night, and ſo kneel
before you: but, indeed, to pray for the Queen.

[1] *for* Oldcaſtle *died a martyr,*] Sir *John* Oldcaſtle was pu
This alludes to a play in which *Falſtaff.*

THE
LIFE
OF
HENRY V.

Dramatis Personæ.

KING Henry *the Fifth.*
Duke of Gloucester, \
Duke of Bedford,   } *Brothers to the King.*
Duke of Clarence, /
Duke of York,   } *Uncles to the King.*
Duke of Exeter,
Earl of Salisbury.
Earl of Westmorland.
Earl of Warwick.
Archbishop of Canterbury.
Bishop of Ely.
Earl of Cambridge, \
Lord Scroop,   } *Conspirators against the King.*
Sir Thomas Grey,   /
Sir Thomas Erpingham, Gower, Fluellen, Mackmorris, Jamy, *Officers in King* Henry's *Army.*
Nym, Bardolph, Pistol, *Boy, formerly Servants to* Falstaff, *now Soldiers in the King's Army.*
Bates, Court, Williams, *Soldiers.*
Charles, *King of* France.
The Dauphin.
Duke of Burgundy.
Constable, Orleans, Rambures, Bourbon, Grandpree, *French Lords.*
Governor of Harfleur.
Mountjoy, *a Herald.*
Ambassadors to the King of England.
Isabel, *Queen of* France.
Catharine, *Daughter to the King of* France.
Alice, *a Lady attending on the Princess* Catharine.
Quickly, Pistol's *Wife, an Hostess.*
C H O R U S.
Lords, Messengers, French *and* English *Soldiers, with other Attendants.*
The Scene, *at the beginning of the Play, lies in* England; *but afterwards, wholly in* France.

Of this play the editions are, I. 1600, *Tho. Crede* for *Tho. Millington,* 4to.
II. 1608, for *J. P.* 4to.
III. 1623, *&c.* Folio. I have the second quarto and folio. The folio edition is much enlarged.

ROLOGUE.

For a Muse of fire, that would ascend
The brightest heaven of invention!
ngdom for a stage, ² Princes to act,
Monarchs to behold the swelling scene!
should the warlike Harry, like himself,
ne the port of Mars; and, at his heels,
bt in, like hounds, should famine, sword and fire
ch for employment. But pardon, gentles all,
flat unraised spirit, that hath dar'd,
his unworthy scaffold, to bring forth
reat an object. Can this Cock-pit hold
asty field of France? or may we cram,
thin this wooden O, 4 the very caskes
did affright the air, at Agincourt?
ardon; since a crooked figure may
t in little place a million;
let us, cyphers to this great accompt,
your imaginary forces work.
se, within the girdle of these walls

) *for a Muse of fire, &c.*] goes upon the notion of the tetic System, which imaseveral Heavens one above er ; the last and highest of was one of fire.
    WARBURTON.
lludes likewise to the afnature of fire, which, by ity, at the separation of the took the highest seat of all ements.
———— *Princes to act,*
monarchs to behold.]
eare does not seem to set e enough between the pers and spectators.

3 *Within this wooden O.*] Nothing shews more evidently the power of custom over language, than that the frequent use of calling a circle an *O* could so much hide the meanness of the metaphor from *Shakespeare*, that he has used it many times where he makes his most eager attempts at dignity of stile.
4 *The very caskes.*] The helmets.
5 *Imaginary forces.*] *Imaginary* for *imaginative*, or your powers of fancy. Active and passive words are by this author frequently confounded.

Are

PROLOGUE.

Are now confin'd two mighty monarchies;
6 *Whose high-up-reared and abutting fronts*
The perillous narrow ocean parts asunder.
Piece out our imperfections with your thoughts,
Into a thousand parts divide one man,
7 *And make imaginary puissance.*
Think, when we talk of horses, that you see them
Printing their proud hoofs i' th' receiving earth.
8 *For 'tis your thoughts that now must deck our Kings,*
Carry them here and there, jumping o'er times,
Turning th' accomplishment of many years
Into an hour-glass; for the which supply,
Admit me Chorus *to this history;*
Who, prologue-like, your humble patience pray,
Gently to hear, kindly to judge, our Play.

6 *Whose high up-reared, and abutting fronts,*
THE PERILLOUS *narrow ocean parts asunder.*] Without doubt the author wrote,
Whose high-up-reared, and abutting fronts
PERILLOUS, THE *narrow ocean parts asunder;*]
for his purpose is to shew, that the highest danger arises from the shock of their meeting; and that it is but a little thing which keeps them asunder. This sense my emendation gives us, as the common reading gives us a contrary; for those whom a *perillous ocean parts asunder*, are in no danger of meeting. WARB.

7 *And make imaginary puissance.*]
This passage shews that *Shakespeare* was fully sensible of the absurdity of shewing battles on the theatre, which indeed is never done but tragedy becomes farce. Nothing can be represented to the eye but by something like it, and *within's*
O nothing very like a battle can be exhibited.

8 *For 'tis your thoughts that now must deck our Kings,*
Carry them here and there]
We should read *king* for *kings*. The prologue relates only to this single play. The mistake was made by referring *them* to *kings* which belongs to *thoughts*. The sense is, *your thoughts must give the king his proper greatness*, and therefore your thoughts *here and there.*

The

[1] The LIFE of King *HENRY* V.

ACT I. SCENE I.

An Antechamber *in the* English *Court, at* Kenilworth.

Enter the Archbishop of Canterbury, *and* Bishop *of* Ely.

[2] *Archbishop of* CANTERBURY.

MY lord, I'll tell you—That self bill is urg'd,
  Which, in th' eleventh year o' th' last King's reign,
Was like, and had, indeed against us past,
But that the scambling and unquiet time
Did push it out of further question.

---

[1] *The Life of* Henry V.] This play was writ (as appears from a passage in the chorus to the fifth act) at the time of the Earl of *Essex*'s commanding the forces in *Ireland* in the reign of Queen *Elizabeth*, and not till after *Henry* the VIth had been played, as may be seen by the conclusion of this play.   POPE.

The Life *of K.* Henry.] The Transactions compriz'd in this Historical Play, commence about the latter end of the first, and terminate in the 8th Year of this King's reign; when he married *Catharine* Princess of *France*, and closed up the Differences betwixt *England* and that Crown. THEO.

[2] *Archbishop of* Canterbury.] This first scene was added since the edition of 1608, which is much short of the present editions, wherein the speeches are generally enlarged and raised: Several whole scenes besides, and all the chorus's also, were since added by *Shakespeare*.   POPE.

Ely.

Ely. But how, my lord, shall we resist it now?

Cant. It must be thought on; if it pass against us,
We lose the better half of our possession;
For all the temporal lands, which men devout
By testament have given to the Church,
Would they strip from us; being valu'd thus,
As much as would maintain, to the King's honour,
Full fifteen Earls and fifteen hundred Knights,
Six thousand and two hundred good Esquires;
And to relief of lazars, and weak age
Of indigent faint souls, past corporal toil,
A hundred alm-houses, right well supply'd;
And to the coffers of the King, beside,
A thousand pounds by th' year. Thus runs the bill.

Ely. This would drink deep.

Cant. 'Twould drink the cup and all.

Ely. But what prevention?

Cant. The King is full of grace and fair regard.

Ely. And a true lover of the holy Church.

Cant. The courses of his youth promis'd it not.
The breath no sooner left his father's body,
But that his wildness mortify'd in him,
Seem'd to die too; yea, at that very moment,
* Consideration, like an angel, came,
And whipt th' offending *Adam* out of him;
Leaving his body as a Paradise,
T' invelope and contain celestial spirits.
Never was such a sudden scholar made,
Never came reformation in a flood ³
With such a heady current, scow'ring faults;
Nor ever *Hydra*-headed wilfulness

---

* *Consideration, like an angel,* &c.] As paradise when sin and *Adam* were driven out by the angel became the habitation of celestial spirits, so the king's heart, since *consideration* has driven out his follies, is now the receptacle of wisdom and of virtue.

³ *Never came reformation like a flood*] Alluding to the method by which *Hercules* cleansed the famous stables when he turned a river through them. *Hercules* still is in our author's head when he mentions the *Hydra*.

So soon did lose his seat, and all at once,
As in this King.
    Ely. We're blessed in the change.
    Cant. Hear him but reason in divinity, 4
And, all admiring with an inward wish
You would desire, the King were made a Prelate.
Hear him debate of common-wealth affairs,
You'd say it hath been all in all his study.
List his discourse of war, and you shall hear
A fearful battle render'd you in musick.
Turn him to any cause of policy,
The *Gordian* knot of it he will unloose,
Familiar as his garter. When he speaks,
The air, a charter'd libertine, is still; 5
And the mute wonder lurketh in men's ears,
To steal his sweet and hony'd sentences.

    4. *Hear him but reason in divinity,* &c.] This speech seems to have been copied from King *James*'s prelates, speaking of their *Solomon*; when Archbishop *Whitgift*, who, as an eminent writer says, *died soon afterwards, and probably doated then,* at the *Hampton-Court* conference, declared himself *verily persuaded, that his* sacred *Majesty spake by the Spirit of God.* And, in effect, this scene was added after King *James*'s accession to the crown: So that we have no way of avoiding its being esteemed a compliment to *him,* but by supposing it was a satire on *his bishops.*   WARBURTON.
    Why these lines should be divided from the rest of the speech and applied to king *James,* I am not able to conceive; nor why an opportunity should be so eagerly snatched to treat with contempt that part of his character which was least contemptible. King *James*'s theological knowledge was not inconsiderable. To preside at disputations is not very suitable to a king, but to understand the questions is surely laudable. The poet, if he had *James* in his thoughts, was no skilful encomiast; for the mention of *Harry*'s skill in war, forced upon the remembrance of his audience the great deficiency of their present king; who yet with all his faults, and many faults he had, was such that Sir *Robert Cotton* says, *he would be content that* England *should never have a better, provided that it should never have a worse.*

    5 *The air,* &c.] This line is exquisitely beautiful.

So that the Art, and practic part of life, [6]
Must be the mistress to this theorique.
Which is a wonder how his Grace should glean it,
Since his addiction was to courses vain;
His companies unletter'd, rude and shallow;
His hours filled up with riots, banquets, sports;
And never noted in him any study,
Any retirement, any sequestration
From open haunts and popularity.

Ely. The Strawberry grows underneath the nettle,
And wholesome berries thrive, and ripen best,
Neighbour'd by fruit of baser quality.
And so the Prince obscur'd his contemplation
Under the veil of wildness; which, no doubt,
Grew like the summer grass, fastest by night,
Unseen, yet crescive in his faculty. [7]

Cant. It must be so; for miracles are ceased:
And therefore we must needs admit the means,
How things are perfected.

---

[6] *So that the* Art *and* practic *part of Life,*] All the Editions, if I am not deceiv'd, are guilty of a slight Corruption in this Passage. The Archbishop has been shewing, what a Master the King was in the Theory of Divinity, War and Policy: so that it must be expected (as I conceive, he would infer;) that the King should now wed that Theory to Action, and the putting the several Parts of his Knowledge into Practice. If this be our author's Meaning, I think, we can hardly doubt but he wrote,

So that the Act, *and practic,* &c. Thus we have a Consonance in the Terms and Sense. For Theory is the Art, and Study of the Rules of any Science; and Action, the Exemplification of those Rules by Proof and Experiment. THEOBALD.

This emendation is received by Dr. *Warburton,* but it appears to me founded upon a misinterpretation. The true meaning seems to be this. He discourses with so much skill on all subjects, that *the art and practice of life must be the mistress or teacher of his theorique,* that is, *that his theory must have been taught by art and practice,* which, says he, is strange since he could see little of the true art or practice among his loose companions, nor ever retired to digest his practice into theory: *Art* is used by the authour for *practice,* as distinguished from *science* or *theory.*

[7] —— *crescive in his faculty.*] Encreasing in its proper power.

Ely.

Ely. But, my good Lord,
[ho]w now for mitigation of this bill,
[urg]'d by the Commons? doth his Majesty
[inc]line to it, or no?
Cant. He seems indifferent;
 rather swaying more upon our part,
[th]an cherishing th' exhibiters against us.
[Fo]r I have made an offer to his Majesty,
[Up]on our spiritual Convocation,
[An]d in regard of causes now in hand
[W]hich I have open'd to his Grace at large
[As] touching *France*, to give a greater Sum,
[th]an ever at one time the Clergy yet
[Di]d to his predecessors part withal.
Ely. How did this offer seem receiv'd, my Lord?
Cant. With good acceptance of his Majesty;
[Sa]ve that there was not time enough to hear
[As], I perceiv'd, his Grace would fain have done
[T]he severals, and unhidden passages [2]
[O]f his true titles to some certain Dukedoms,
[A]nd, generally, to the Crown and seat of *France*,
[D]eriv'd from *Edward* his great grandfather.
Ely. What was th' impediment, that broke this off?
Cant. The *French* Ambassador upon that instant
[C]rav'd audience; and the hour, I think, is come
[T]o give him hearing. Is it four o'clock?
Ely. It is.
Cant. Then go we in to know his embassy;
[W]hich I could with a ready guess declare,
[B]efore the *Frenchman* speaks a word of it.
Ely. I'll wait upon you, and I long to hear it.
[*Exeunt.*

---

2 *The severals, and unhidden passages*] This line I suspect of corruption, though it may be fairly enough explained: the *passages* of his *titles* are the *lines* of *succession*, by which his claims descend. *Unhidden* is *open, clear*.

SCENE

SCENE II.

Opens to the Presence.

Enter King Henry, Gloucester, Bedford, Clarence, Warwick, Westmorland, *and* Exeter.

K. *Henry.* WHERE is my gracious Lord of Canterbury?
Exe. Not here in presence.
K. *Henry.* Send for him, good uncle.
West. Shall we call in th' ambassador, my Liege?
K. *Henry.* Not yet, my cousin; we would be resolv'd,
Before we hear him, of some things of weight,
That * task our thoughts, concerning us and *France.*

Enter the Archbishop of Canterbury, *and Bishop of* Ely.

Cant. God and his angels guard your sacred throne,
And make you long become it!
K. *Henry.* Sure, we thank you.
My learned Lord, we pray you to proceed;
And justly and religiously unfold,
Why the law *Salike,* that they have in *France,*
Or should, or should not, bar us in our claim.
And, God forbid, my dear and faithful Lord,
That you should fashion, wrest, or bow your reading;
Or nicely charge your understanding soul
With opening titles † miscreate, whose right
Suites not in native colours with the truth.
For, God doth know, how many now in health
Shall drop their blood, in approbation
Of what your reverence shall incite us to.

9 *Shall we call in,* &c.] Here began the old play.   POPE.
* *task*] Keep busied with scruples and laborious disquisitions.
1 *Or nicely charge your understanding soul*] Take heed lest by nice and subtle sophistry you burthen your knowing soul, or knowingly burthen your soul, with the guilt of advancing a false title, or of maintaining, by specious fallacies, a claim which, if shewn in its native and true colours, would appear to be false.
† *miscreate*—] Ill begotten; illegitimate; spurious.

Therefore

KING HENRY V. 369

'ore take heed, how you impawn our perſon, [a]
ou awake our ſleeping ſword of war
arge you in the name of God, take heed.
ver two ſuch kingdoms did contend
ıt much fall of blood; whoſe guiltleſs drops
ery one a woe, a ſore complaint,
him, whoſe wrong gives edge unto the ſwords,
ɪake ſuch waſte in brief mortality.
this conjuration, ſpeak, my Lord;
will hear, note, and believe in heart,
vhat you ſpeak is in your conſcience waſht,
e as ſin with baptiſm.
. Then hear me, gracious Sovereign, and you
Peers,
we your lives, your faith, and ſervices,
imperial throne. There is no bar [3]
ke againſt your Highneſs' claim to *France*,
s which they produce from *Pharamond*;
:m Salicam *Mulieres nè ſuccedant*;
man ſhall ſucceed in Salike *land:*
Salike land the *French* unjuſtly gloſs
the realm of *France*, and *Pharamond*
under of this law and female bar.
ɛir own authors faithfully affirm,
he land *Salike* lies in *Germany*,
n the floods of *Sala* and of *Elve*,

ake heed how you im-
ɪn our perſon;] The
ıft of the king is to im-
ɔn the archbiſhop a due
the caution with which
ſpeak. He tells him
crime of unjuſt war, if
ɔe unjuſt, ſha.l reſt upon

re take heed how you im-
ɔn your perſon.
ink it ſhould be read.
ed how you pledge your-
r honour, your happi-
ſupport of bad advice.

Dr. *Warburton* explains *im-*
pawn by *engage*, and ſo eſcapes
the difficulty.

3 ——— *There is no bar*, &c.]
This whole ſpeech is copied (in
a manner *verbatim*) from *Hall's*
Chronicle, *Henry* V. year the ſecond, folio 4. xx, xxx, xl, &c.
In the firſt edition it is very imperfect, and the whole hiſtory
and names of the princes are
confounded; but this was afterwards ſet right, and corrected
from his original, Hall's *Chro-*
nicle. POPE.

. IV.　　　　　B b　　　　　Where

Where *Charles* the great, having subdu'd the *Saxons*,
There left behind and settled certain *French*,
Who, holding in disdain the *German* women,
For some dishonest manners of their life,
Establish'd then this law; to wit, no female
Should be inheritrix in *Salike* land,
Which *Salike*, as I said, 'twixt *Elve* and *Sala*,
Is at this day in *Germany* call'd *Meisen*.
Thus doth it well appear, the *Salike* law
Was not devised for the realm of *France*;
Nor did the *French* possess the *Salike* land,
Until four hundred one and twenty years
After defunction of King *Pharamond*,
Idly suppos'd the founder of this law;
Who died within the year of our redemption
Four hundred twenty-six; and *Charles* the great,
Subdu'd the *Saxons*, and did seat the *French*
Beyond the river *Sala* in the year
Eight hundred five. Besides, their writers say,
King *Pepin*, which deposed *Childerick*,
Did as heir general, being descended
Of *Blithild*, which was daughter to King *Clothair*,
Make claim and title to the Crown of *France*.
Hugh Capet also, who usurp'd the Crown
Of *Charles* the Duke of *Lorain*, sole heir male
Of the true line and stock of *Charles* the great,
To fine his title with some shews of truth, [4]
Though, in pure truth, it was corrupt and naught,
Convey'd himself as heir to th' Lady *Lingare*,
Daughter to *Charlemain*, who was the son
To *Lewis* th' Emperor, which was the son
Of *Charles* the great. Also King *Lewis* the ninth,

---

4. *To fine his title*, &c] This is the reading of the 4to of 1608, that of the folio is, *To find his title*. I would read,
  To line his title with shows of truth.
To line may signify at once to decorate and strengthen. In *Macbeth*:
  He did line the rebels with hidden help and vantage.
Dr. *Warburton* says, that *to fine his title*, is to refine or improve it. The reader is to judge.

Who was sole heir to the usurper *Capet*,
Could not keep quiet in his conscience,
Wearing the Crown of *France*, 'till satisfy'd
That fair Queen *Isabel*, his grandmother,
Was lineal of the lady *Ermengere*,
Daughter to *Charles* the foresaid Duke of *Lorain*:
By the which match the line of *Charles* the great
Was re-united to the Crown of *France*.
So that, as clear as is the summer's sun,
King *Pepin*'s title, and *Hugh Capet*'s claim,
King *Lewis*' Satisfaction, all appear
To hold in right and title of the female;
So do the Kings of *France* until this day,
Howbeit they would hold up this *Salike* law,
To bar your Highness claiming from the female;
And rather chuse to hide them in a net,
Than amply to imbare their crooked titles, *
Usurpt from you and your progenitors.

   K. *Henry.* May I with right and conscience make this claim?

   Cant. The sin upon my head, dread Sovereign!
For in the book of *Numbers* it is writ,
When the son dies, let the inheritance
Descend unto the daughter. Gracious Lord,
Stand for your own, unwind your bloody flag,
Look back into your mighty ancestors;
Go, my dread Lord, to your great grandsire's tomb,
From whom you claim; invoke his warlike spirit,

---

* Mr. *Pope* reads:
Than openly imbrace.] But where is the *Antithesis* betwixt *hide* in the preceding Line, and *imbrace* in this? The two old *Folio*'s read, *Than amply to imbarre*—We certainly must read, as Mr. *Warburton* advis'd me,—*Than amply to* imbare—lay open, display to View. I am surpriz'd Mr. *Pope* did not start this Conjecture, as Mr. *Rowe* has led the way to it in his Edition, who reads;
Than amply to make bare *their crook'd Titles.* THEOBALD.
Mr. *Theobald* might have found in the quarto of 1608, this reading,
Than amply to embrace *their crooked causes*,
out of which line Mr. *Pope* formed his reading, erroneous indeed, but not merely capricious.

B b 2   And

And your great uncle *Edward* the black Prince,
Who on the *French* ground play'd a Tragedy,
Making defeat on the full pow'r of *France*,
While his moſt mighty Father, on a hill,
Stood ſmiling, to behold his Lion's whelp
Forage in blood of *French* Nobility.
O noble *Engliſh*, that could entertain
With half their forces the full pow'r of *France*,
And let another half ſtand laughing by,
All out of work, and cold for action!

Ely. Awake remembrance of theſe valiant dead, [5]
And with your puiſſant arm renew their feats.
You are their heir, you ſit upon their throne;
The blood, and courage, that renowned them,
Runs in your veins; and my thrice puiſſant Liege
Is in the very *May*-morn of his youth,
Ripe for exploits and mighty enterpriſes.

Exe. Your brother Kings and Monarchs of the earth
Do all expect that you ſhould rouze yourſelf,
As did the former Lions of your blood.

Weſt. They know, your Grace hath cauſe; and means
 and might [6]
So hath your Highneſs; never King of *England*
Had Nobles richer, and more loyal Subjects;
Whoſe hearts have left their bodies here in *England*,
And lie pavilion'd in the field of *France*.

Cant. O, let their bodies follow, my dear Liege, [7]
With blood and ſword, and fire, to win your right.
In aid whereof, we of the Spiritualty

---

[5] Theſe four ſpeeches were added after the firſt edition.

[6] *They know your* Grace hath *cauſe, and means, and might,* So *hath your Highneſs* ———] We ſhould read,
——— *your* Race had *cauſe.* ——
which is carrying on the ſenſe of the concluding words of *Exeter.*
As did the former Lions of your blood.
meaning *Edward* III, and the Black Prince. Warburton.

I do not ſee but the preſent reading may ſtand as I have pointed it.

[7] Theſe two lines Dr. *Warburton* gives to *Weſtmorland*, but with ſo little reaſon that I have continued them to *Canterbury.* The credit of old copies, though not great, is yet more than nothing.

Will raise your Highness such a mighty sum,
As never did the Clergy at one time
Bring in to any of your ancestors.

K. Henry. We must not only arm t'invade the *French*,
But lay down our proportions to defend
Against the *Scot*, who will make road upon us
With all advantages.

Cant. They of those Marches, gracious Sovereign,
Shall be a wall sufficient to defend
Our Inland from the pilfering borderers.

K. Henry. We do not mean the coursing snatchers only,
But fear the main intendment of the *Scot*,
Who hath been still a [8] giddy neighbour to us;
For you shall read, that my great grandfather
Never went with his forces into *France*, [9]
But that the *Scot* on his unfurnisht kingdom
Came pouring, like a tide into a breach,
With ample and brim fulness of his force,
Galling the gleaned land with hot assays,
Girding with grievous siege castles and towns,
That *England*, being empty of defence,
Hath shook, and trembled, at th' ill neighbourhood.

Cant. She hath been then more fear'd than harm'd,
  my Liege;
For hear her but exampled by herself,
When all her chivalry hath been in *France*,
And she a mourning widow of her Nobles,
She hath herself not only well defended,
But taken and impounded as a stray
The King of *Scots*, whom she did send to *France*,
To fill King *Edward*'s fame with prisoner Kings;
And make your chronicle as rich with praise, [1]

As

---

[8] ——— *giddy neighbour* ———] That is, inconstant, changeable.

[9] Never went with his *forces into* France] *Shakespeare* wrote the line thus,
Ne'er went with his FULL *forces into* France.

The following expressions of *unfurnisht kingdom, gleaned land,* and *empty of defence,* shew this.
        WARBURTON.
There is no need of alteration.

[1] *And make his chronicle as rich with*

As is the ouzy bottom of the Sea
With funken wreck and fumlefs treafuries.
  Exet. But there's a faying very old and true.[2]
If that you will France *win, then with* Scotland *firſt begin.*[3]
For once the Eagle *England* being in prey,
To her unguarded neſt the Weazel, *Scot,*
Comes fneaking, and fo fucks her princely eggs;
Playing the Moufe in abfence of the Cat,
To taint, and havock, more than fhe can eat.[4]
  Ely. It follows then, the Cat muſt ſtay at home,
Yet that is but a cruſh'd neceſſity;[5]
Since we have locks to fafeguard neceſſaries,

And

with PRAISE,] He is ſpeaking of King *Edward*'s prifoners; fo that it appears *Shakeſpeare* wrote,

—— *as rich with* PRIZE,

i. e. captures, booty. Without this, there is neither beauty nor likenefs in the fimilitude. WARB.

The change of *praife* to *prize,* I believe no body will approve; the fimilitude between the chronicle and fea confiſts only in this, that they are both full, and filled with fomething valuable. Befides, Dr. *Warburton* prefuppofes a reading which exiſts in no ancient copy, for *bis chronicle* as the later editions give it, the quarto has *your,* the folio *their chronicle.*

Your and *their* written by contraction y^r are juſt alike, and *her* in the old hands is not much unlike y^r. I believe we ſhould read *her* chronicle.

2 Ely. *But there's a faying,* &c.] This fpeech, which is diſſuafive of the war with *France,* is abfurdly given to one of the churchmen in confederacy to puſh the King upon it, as appears by the firſt fcene of this act. Befides, the poet had here an eye to *Hall,* who gives this obfervation to the Duke of *Exeter.* But the editors have made *Ely* and *Exeter* change fides, and fpeak one another's fpeeches; for this, which is given to *Ely,* is *Exeter*'s; and the following given to *Exeter,* is *Ely*'s. WARBURTON.

3 *If that you will* France *win,* &c.] *Hall*'s Chronicle. *Hen.* V. year 2. fol. 7. p. 2. x. POPE.

4 *To tear and havock more than fhe can eat.*] 'Tis not much the Quality of the Moufe to tear the Food it comes at, but to run over and defile it. The old Quarto reads, *ſpoils;* and the two firſt folio's, *tame:* from which laſt corrupted Word, I think, I have retriev'd the Poet's genuine Reading, *taint.* THEOB.

5 *Yet that is but a* curs'd *Neceſſity;*] So the old Quarto. The *folio*'s read *cruſò'd:* Neither of the Words convey any tolerable Idea; but give us a counter reafoning, and not at all pertinent. We ſhould read, *'ſcus'd neceſſity.* 'Tis *Ely*'s bufinefs to

ſhew

KING HENRY V.

'etty traps to catch the petty thieves.
that the armed hand doth fight abroad,
vifed head defends itfelf at home;
vernment, though high, and low, and lower, *
:o parts, doth deep in one confent,
eing in a full and natural clofe,
nufick.

Therefore heav'n doth divide
te of man in divers functions,
endeavour in continual motion, 6
ich is fixed, as an aim or butt,
nce. For fo work the honey Bees;
'es, that by a rule in nature teach
t of order to a peopled kingdom.
ave a King, and officers of fort;
fome, like magiftrates, correct at home,
like merchants, venture trade abroad, 7

Others

re is no real Neceffity
g at home: he muft
mean, that tho' there
ning Neceffity, yet it is
may be well *excus'd* and
WARBURTON.
r the old readings nor
ndation feem very fa
. A curfed *neceffity* has
a 'fcus'd *neceffity* is fo
t one would not admit
thing elfe can be found.
l *neceffity* may mean, a
hich is *fubdu'd* and *over-*
by contrary reafons We
ad a *crude* neceffity, a
t *complete*, or not well
d and digefted, but it
fh.
Hanmer reads,
is not o'courfe a neceffity.
Government, *though*
, *and low, and* lower,]
ndation and expreffion
hought feems to be bor-

row'd from *Cicero* de *Republica*,
lib. 2. *Sic ex* fummis, *& me-*
diis, *&* infimis *interjectis* Ordinibus, *ut* fonis, *moderatam ratione Civitatem*, Confenfu *diffimiliorum* concinere; *& quæ* Harmonia *à* Muficis *dicitur in Cantu,*
eam effe in Civitate Concordiam.
THEOBALD.
6 *Setting endeavour in continual
motion,*
*To which is fixed, as an aim or
butt.*
Obedience.] Neither the fenfe
nor the conftruction of this paffage is very obvious. The conftruction is, *endeavour — as an
aim or butt to which endeavour,
obedience is fixed*. The fenfe is,
that all endeavour is to terminate in obedience, to be fubordinate to the publick good and
general defign of government.
7 *Others, like merchants,* VEN
TURE *trade abroad;* What

376   KING HENRY V.

Others, like soldiers, armed in their stings,
Make boot upon the summer's velvet buds,
Which pillage they with merry march bring home
To the tent-royal of their Emperor,
Who busy'd in his majesty, surveys
The singing mason building roofs of gold;
The civil citizens kneading up the honey; [8]
The poor mechanick porters crowding in
Their heavy burdens at his narrow gate,
The sad-ey'd Justice with his surly hum,
Delivering o'er to executors pale
The lazy yawning drone. I thus infer,
That many things, having full reference
To one consent, may work contrariously.
As many arrows, loosed several ways,
Come to one mark; as many ways meet in one town;
As many fresh streams meet in one salt sea;
As many lines close in the dial's center;
So may a thousand actions once a-foot, [9]

is the *venturing trade?* I am persuaded we should read and point it thus,
  Others, like merchant-venturers, trade abroad.
             WARBURTON.

If the whole difficulty of this passage consist in the obscurity of the phrase *to venture trade*, it may be easily cleared. To *venture trade* is a phrase of the same import and structure as to *hazard battle*. Nothing could have raised an objection but the desire of being busy.

8 *The civil Citizens* KNEADING *up the honey*;] This may possibly be right; but I rather think that *Shakespear* wrote HEADING *up the honey*; alluding to the putting up merchandise in casks. And this is in fact the case. The honey being headed up in separate and distinct cells by a thin membrane of wax drawn over the mouth of each of them, to hinder the liquid matter from running out.
             WARBURTON.

To head *the honey* can hardly be right; for though we *head* the cask, no man talks of *heading* the commodities. To *knead* gives an easy sense, though not physically true. The bees do in fact *knead* the wax more than the honey, but that *Shakespear* perhaps did not know.

9 *So may a thousand actions,* ONCE *a-foot.*] The speaker is endeavouring to shew, that the state is able to execute many projected actions at once, and conduct them all to their completion,

nd in one purpose, and be all well borne
Without defeat. Therefore to *France*, my Liege;
Divide your happy *England* into four,
Whereof take you one quarter into *France*,
And you withal shall make all *Gallia* shake,
If we, with thrice such powers left at home,
Cannot defend our own doors from the dog,
Let us be worried; and our Nation lose
The name of hardiness and policy.

   K. *Henry*. Call in the messengers, sent from the *Dauphin*.
Now are we well resolv'd; and by God's help
And yours, the noble sinews of our power,
France being ours, we'll bend it to our awe,
Or break it all to pieces. There we'll sit,
Ruling in large and ample empery,
O'er *France*, and all her almost kingly Dukedoms,
Or lay these bones in an unworthy urn,
Tombless, with no remembrance over them.
Either our History shall with full mouth
Speak freely of our acts; or else our grave,
Like *Turkish* mute, shall have a tongueless mouth;
Not worshipt with a waxen epitaph.

SCENE III.

Enter Ambassadors of France.

Now are we well prepar'd to know the pleasure
Of our fair cousin *Dauphin*; for we hear,
Your greeting is from him, not from the King.

   Amb. May't please your Majesty to give us leave
Freely to render what we have in charge,
Or shall we sparingly shew you far off

---

pletion, without impeding or jostling one another in their course. *Shakespeare*, therefore, must have wrote, *actions 't once a foot, i. e.* at once: or, on foot together. WARBURTON.

Sir *T. Hanmer* is more kind to this emendation by reading *acts at once*. The change is not necessary, the old text may stand.

The

The *Dauphin*'s meaning, and our embaſſy?

 K. Henry. We are no tyrant, but a Chriſtian King,
Unto whoſe grace our paſſion is as ſubject,
As are our wretches fetter'd in our priſons;
Therefore, with frank and with uncurbed plainneſs,
Tell us the *Dauphin*'s mind.

 Amb. Thus then, in few.
Your Highneſs, lately ſending into *France*,
Did claim ſome certain Dukedoms in the right
Of your great predeceſſor, *Edward* the third;
In anſwer of which claim, the Prince our maſter
Says, that you favour too much of your youth,
And bids you be advis'd. There's nought in *France*,
That can be with a nimble gilliard won;
You cannot revel into Dukedoms there.
He therefore ſends you, meeter for your ſpirit,
This tun of treaſure; and in lieu of this,
Deſires you, let the Dukedoms, that you claim,
Hear no more of you. This the *Dauphin* ſpeaks.

 K. Henry. What treaſure, uncle?

 Exe. Tennis-balls, my Liege.

 K. Henry. We're glad, the *Dauphin* is ſo pleaſant
   with us.
His preſent, and your pains, we thank you for.
When we have match'd our rackets to theſe balls,
We will in *France*, by God's grace, play a ſet,
Shall ſtrike his father's Crown into the hazard.
Tell him, h'ath made a match with ſuch a wrangler,
That all the Courts of *France* will be diſturb'd
With * chaces. And we underſtand him well,
How he comes o'er us with our wilder days;
Not meaſuring, what uſe we made of them.
We never valu'd this poor ſeat of *England*,
And therefore, living hence, [1] did give ourſelf

---

* *Chace* is a term at tennis.

[1] *And therefore, living* hence,
————] This expreſſion has ſtrength and energy: He never valued *England*, and therefore lived *hence*, i. e. as if abſent from it. But the *Oxford Editor* alters *hence* to *here*. WARBURTON.

barb'rous licence; as 'tis ever common,
at men are merriest, when they are from home.
tell the *Dauphin*, I will keep my State,
like a King, and shew my sail of Greatness
en I do rouze me in my throne of *France*.
or that I have laid by my Majesty,
d plodded like a man for working days;
I will rise there with so full a glory,
at I will dazzle all the eyes of *France*,
, strike the *Dauphin* blind to look on us.
d tell the pleasant Prince, this mock of his
th turn'd † his balls to gun-stones; and his soul
ll stand sore charged for the wasteful vengeance,
at shall fly with them. Many thousand widows
ll this his Mock mock out of their dear husbands,
ck mothers from their sons, mock castles down;
d some are yet ungotten and unborn,
at shall have cause to curse the *Dauphin*'s scorn.
this lies all within the will of God,
whom I do appeal; and in whose name,
l you the *Dauphin*, I am coming on
'venge me as I may; and to put forth
rightful hand in a well-hallow'd cause.
get you hence in peace; and tell the *Dauphin*,
jest will savour but of shallow wit,
en thousands weep, more than did laugh at it.
Convey them with safe conduct —Fare ye well.
[*Exeunt Ambassadors.*

xe. This was a merry message.
. Henry. We hope to make the sender blush at it.
erefore, my Lords, omit no happy hour,
at may give furth'rance to our expedition;
we have now no thoughts in us but *France*,
e those to God, that run before our business.

For that I have laid by, &c.]
ualify myself for this under-
g, I have descended from my
n, and studied the arts of
o a lower character.

† *His balls to gun-stones.*] When
ordnance was first used, they discharged balls not of iron but of
stone.

There-

Therefore, let our proportions for these wars
Be soon collected, and all things thought upon,
That may with reasonable swiftness add
More feathers to our wings; for, God before,
We'll chide this *Dauphin* at his father's door.
Therefore let every man now task his thought,
That this fair action may on foot be brought. [*Exeunt.*

ACT II. SCENE I.

Enter CHORUS.

Chorus. NOW all the youth of *England* are on fire,[2]

And

[2] In this place, in all the editions hitherto, is inserted the chorus which I have postponed. That chorus manifestly is intended to advertise the spectators of the change of the scene to *Southampton,* and therefore ought to be placed just before that change, and not here, where the scene is still continued in *London.*
POPE.

Now all the Youth of England] I have replaced this *Chorus* here, by the Authority of the Old *Folio's*; and ended the first *Act,* as the Poet certainly intended. Mr. *Pope* remov'd it, because (says he) *This Chorus manifestly is intended to advertise the Spectators of the Change of the Scene to* Southampton; *and therefore ought to be placed just before that Change, and not here.* 'Tis true, the Spectators are to be informed, that, when they next see the King, they are to suppose him at *Southampton.* But this does not imply any Necessity of this Cho-rus being contiguous to that Change. On the contrary, the very concluding Lines vouch absolutely against it.

*But, till the King come forth, and not till then,
Unto Southampton do we shift our Scene.*

For how absurd is such a Notice, if the Scene is to change, so soon as ever the *Chorus* quits the Stage? Besides, unless this *Chorus* be prefixed to the Scene betwixt *Nim, Bardolph,* &c. We shall draw the Poet into another Absurdity. *Pistol, Nim,* and *Bardolph* are in this Scene talking of going to the Wars in *France:* but the King had but just, at his quitting the Stage, declar'd his Resolutions of commencing this War: And without the Interval of an *Act,* betwixt that Scene and the Comic Characters entring, how could they with any Probability be informed of this intended Expedition?
THEOBALD.

I think

And silken dalliance in the wardrobe lies;
Now thrive the armourers, and honour's thought
Reigns solely in the breast of every man;
They sell the pasture now, to buy the horse;
Following the mirror of all Christian Kings,
With winged heels, as *English* Mercuries.
³ For now sits expectation in the air,
And hides a sword from hilts unto the point
With Crowns imperial, Crowns, and Coronets
Promis'd to *Harry* and his followers.
The *French*, advis'd by good intelligence
Of this most dreadful preparation,
Shake in their fear; and with pale policy
Seek to divert the *English* purposes.
O *England!* model to thy inward greatness,
Like little body with a mighty heart;
What might'st thou do, that honour would thee do,
Were all thy children kind and natural!
But see, thy fault *France* hath in thee found out;
A nest of hollow bosoms, which he fills
With treach'rous crowns; and three corrupted men,
One, *Richard* Earl of *Cambridge*, and the second,
Henry Lord *Scroop* of *Masham*, and the third,
Sir *Thomas Grey* Knight of *Northumberland*,
Have for the gilt of *France* (O guilt, indeed!)
Confirm'd conspiracy with fearful *France*.

I think Mr. *Pope* mistaken in transposing this Chorus, and Mr. *Theobald* in concluding the act with it. The chorus evidently introduces that which follows, not comments on that which precedes, and therefore rather begins than ends the Act, and so I have printed it. Dr. *Warburton* follows Mr. *Pope*.

3 *For now sits expectation in the air,*

And hides a sword from hilts unto the point
With Crowns imperial, &c.] The imagery is wonderfully fine, and the thought exquisite. *Expectation sitting in the air* designs the height of their ambition; and the *Sword hid from the hilt to the point with Crowns and Coronets*, that all sentiments of danger were lost in the thoughts of glory. WARBURTON.

And

4 And by their hands this 5 grace of Kings muſt die,
If hell and treaſon hold their promiſes,
Ere he take ſhip for *France*; and in *Southampton*.
Linger your patience on, and well digeſt
Th' abuſe of diſtance, while we force a play,
The ſum is paid, the traitors are agreed,
The King is ſet from *London*, and the ſcene
Is now tranſported, gentles, to *Southampton*:
There is the play-houſe now, there muſt you ſit;
And thence to *France* ſhall we convey you ſafe,
And bring you back, charming the narrow ſeas
To give you gentle paſs; for if we may,

4 *And by their hands this grace of Kings muſt die,*
If hell and treaſon hold their promiſes,
Ere he take ſhip for France; *and in* Southampton.
Linger your patience on, and well digeſt
Th' abuſe of diſtance, while we force a play.
The ſum is paid, the traitors are agreed,
The King is ſet from London, *and the ſcene*
Is now tranſported, gentles, to Southampton:
There is the play-houſe now.]
I ſuppoſe every one that reads theſe lines looks about for a meaning which he cannot find. There is no connection of ſenſe nor regularity of tranſition from one thought to the other. It may be ſuſpected that ſome lines are loſt, and in that caſe the ſenſe is irretrievable. I rather think the meaning is obſcured by an accidental tranſpoſition, which I would reform thus:

And by their hands this grace of Kings muſt die,
If hell and treaſon hold their promiſes.
The ſum is paid, the traitors are agreed,
The King is ſet from London, *and the ſcene*
Is now tranſported, gentles, to Southampton
Ere he take ſhip for France.
And in Southampton
Linger your patience on, and well digeſt
Th' abuſe of diſtance, which we force a play.
There is the play-houſe now.
This alteration reſtores ſenſe, and probably the true ſenſe. The lines might be otherwiſe ranged, but this order pleaſes me beſt.

5 —— *this grace of Kings*—] i. e. he who does greateſt honour to the title. By the ſame kind of phraſeology the uſurper in *Hamlet* is call'd the *Vice of Kings*, i. e. the opprobrium of them. WARBURTON.

We'll

KING HENRY V. 383

5 We'll not offend one stomach with our play.
7 But, till the King come forth, and not till then,
Unto *Southampton* do we shift our scene. [*Exit.*

SCENE II.

Before Quickly's *House in* Eastcheap.

Enter Corporal Nim, *and Lieutenant* Bardolph.

Bard. WELL met, Corporal *Nim.* [8]
Nim. Good morrow, Lieutenant *Bardolph.* [9]
Bard. What, are Ancient *Pistol* and you friends yet?
Nim. For my part, I care not. I say little; but when time shall serve, [1] there shall be—[*smiles.*] But that

---

6 *We'll not offend one stomach.*] That is, you shall pass the sea without the qualms of sea-sickness.

7 *But, 'till the King come forth.*] Here seems to be something omitted. Sir *T. Hanmer* reads,

But when the King comes forth,

which, as the passage now stands, is necessary. These lines, obscure as they are, refute Mr. *Pope's* conjectures on the true place of the chorus; for they shew that something is to intervene before the scene changes to *Southampton.*

8 Bard. *Well met, corporal Nim.*] I have chose to begin the 2d *Act* here, because each Act may close regularly with a *Chorus.* Not that I am persuaded, this was the poet's intention to mark the *Intervals* of his *Acts* as the *Chorus* did on the old *Grecian* Stage. He had no occasion of this sort: since, in his Time, the Pauses of Action were filled up, as now, with a Lesson of Musick: But the Reasons for this Distribution are explained before.
THEOBALD.

I have already shewn why in this edition the act begins with the chorus.

9 *Lieutenant* Bardolph.] At this scene begins the connection of this play with the latter part of King *Henry* IV. The characters would be indistinct, and the incidents unintelligible, without the knowledge of what passed in the two foregoing plays.

1 *there shall be* [smiles] I suspect *smiles* to be a marginal direction crept into the text. It is natural for a man, when he threatens, to break off abruptly, and conclude, *But that shall be as it may.* But this fantastical fellow is made to smile disdainfully while he threatens; which circumstance was marked for the player's direction in the margin.
WARBURTON.

shall

shall be as it may. I dare not fight, but I will wink and hold out mine iron; it is a simple one; but what tho? it will toast cheese, and it will endure cold as another man's sword will; and there's an end.

Bard. I will bestow a breakfast to make you friends, ² and we'll be all three sworn brothers to *France.* Let it be so, good corporal *Nim.*

Nim. Faith, I will live so long as I may, that's the certain of it; and when I cannot live any longer, I will do as I may; that is my rest, that is the rendezvous of it.

Bard. It is certain, corporal, that he is married to *Nel Quickly*; and certainly she did you wrong, for you were troth-plight to her.

Nim. I cannot tell, things must be as they may; men may sleep, and they may have their throats about them at that time; and some say, knives have edges. It must be as it may. Tho' ³ patience be a tir'd Mare, yet she will plod. There must be conclusions. Well, I cannot tell,——

Enter Pistol *and* Quickly.

Bard. Here comes ancient *Pistol* and his wife. Good corporal, be patient here. How now, mine host *Pistol?*

Pist. Base tyke, call'st thou me host?
Now by this hand, I swear, I scorn the term:
Nor shall my *Nell* keep lodgers.

Quick. No, by my troth, not long: for we cannot lodge and board a dozen or fourteen gentlewomen, that live honestly by the prick of their needles, but it will be thought we keep a bawdy-house straight. O welli-

---

² *And we'll all be sworn brothers to* France.] We should read, *we'll all go sworn brothers to* France, *or we'll all be sworn brothers in* France.

³ *Patience be a tir'd mare.*]

The folio reads by corruption, *tired* name, from which Sir T. Hanmer, sagaciously enough, derived *tired Dame.* Mr. *Theobald* retrieved from the quarto *tired Mare,* the true reading.

day

KING HENRY V.

y, if he be not drawn⁴! Now we shall see
lultery, and murder committed.
  Good lieutenant, good corporal, offer no-
re.
  Pish!——
ish, for thee ⁵, *Island* dog; thou prick-ear'd
land.
. Good corporal *Nim*, shew thy valour and put
word.
Will you shog off? I would have you *solus*.
Solus, egregious dog! O viper vile!
s in thy most marvellous face,
s in thy teeth, and in thy throat,
hy hateful lungs, yea, in thy maw, perdy,
hich is worse, within thy nasty mouth;
rt the *solus* in thy bowels;
an take, and *Pistol's* cock is up,
hing fire will follow.
I am not *Barbason*, you cannot conjure me: I
humour to knock you indifferently well; if
v foul with me, *Pistol*, I will scour you with
r as I may, in fair terms. If you would walk
ould prick your guts a little in good terms as I
d that's the humour of it.
) braggard vile, and damned furious wight!

*lliday Lady, if he be
w.*] I cannot under-
Drift of this Expres-
e be not *hewn*, must
he be not *cut down*;
t Case, the very Thing
d, which *Quickly* was
ve of. But I rather
r Fright arises upon
r Swords drawn: and
tured to make a flight
  accordingly. *If he
wn*, for, *if he has not
drawn*, is an Expres-

sion familiar with our Poet. THE-
  ⁵ *Island dog*] I believe we
should read *Iceland dog*. He
seems to allude to an account
credited in *Elizabeth's* time,
that in the North there was a nation with human bodies and dogs
heads.
  ⁶ *For I can take.*] I know
not well what he can *take*. The
quarto reads *talk*. In our authour *to take*, is sometimes to
blust, which sense may serve in
this place.

IV.   C c   The

The grave doth gape,[7] and doating death is near;
Therefore exhale.

Bard. Hear me, hear me, what I say. He that strikes the first stroke, I'll run him up to the hilts as I am a soldier.

Pist. An Oath of mickle might; and fury shall abate.
Give me thy fist, thy fore foot to me give;
Thy spirits are most tall.

Nim. I will cut thy throat one time or other in fair terms, that is the humour of it.

Pist. Coup à gorge, that is the word. I defy thee again.
O hound of *Crete*, think'st thou my spouse to get?
No, to the spittle go,
And from the powd'ring tub of infamy
Fetch forth the lazar Kite of *Cressia's* kind,
Dol Tear-sheet, she by name, and her espouse.
I have, and I will hold the *Quondam Quickly*
For th' only she. And *pauca*,—there's enough—Go to.

Enter the Boy.

Boy. Mine host *Pistol*, you must come to my master, and your hostess; he is very sick, and would to bed. Good *Bardolph*, put thy nose between his sheets, and do the office of a warming pan; faith, he's very ill.

Bard. Away, you rogue.

Quick. By my troth, he'll yield the crow a pudding one of these days; the King has kill'd his heart. Good husband, come home presently. [*Exit* Quickly.

Bard. Come, shall I make you two friends? We must to *France* together; why the devil should we keep knives to cut one another's throats?

Pist. Let floods o'erswell, and fiends for food howl on!——

[7] *Doating death is near.*] The quarto has *groaning* death.

Nim.

Nim. You'll pay me the eight shillings, I won of
 at betting?
Pist. Base is the slave, that pays.
Nim. That now I will have; that's the humour of

Pist. As manhood shall compound, push home.
                              [*Draw.*
Bard. By this sword, he that makes the first thrust,
kill him; by this sword, I will.
Pist. Sword is an oath, and oaths must have their
 rse.
Bard. Corporal *Nim*, an thou wilt be friends, be
 nds; an thou wilt not, why then be enemies with
 too. Pry'thee, put up.
Pist. A noble shalt thou have and present pay,
 d liquor likewise will I give to thee;
 d friendship shall combine and brotherhood.
 live by *Nim*, and *Nim* shall live by me,
 not this just? for I shall Suttler be
 to the camp, and profits will accrue.
 re me thy hand.
Nim. I shall have my noble?
Pist. In cash most justly paid.
Nim. Well then, that's the humour of't.

Re-enter Quickly.

Quick. As ever you came of women, come in quick-
 o Sir *John*: ah, poor heart, he is so shak'd of a
 ning quotidian tertian, that it is most lamentable
 behold. Sweet men, come to him.
Nim. The King hath run bad humours on the
 ight, that's the even of it.
Pist. *Nim*, thou hast spoken the right, his heart is
 ted and corroborate.
Nim. The King is a good King, but it must be as
 lay; he passes some humours and careers.

Pist. Let us condole the Knight; for, lambkins! we will live. [*Exeunt.*

SCENE III.

Changes to SOUTHAMPTON.

Enter Exeter, Bedford, *and* Westmorland.

Bed. 'FORE God, his Grace is bold to trust these traitors.
Exe. They shall be apprehended by and by.
West. How smooth and even they do bear themselves,
As if allegiance in their bosoms sate,
Crowned with faith and constant loyalty!
Bed. The King hath note of all that they intend,
By interception which they dream not of.
Exe. Nay, but the man that was his bedfellow,
Whom he hath lull'd and cloy'd with gracious favours,
That he should for a foreign purse so sell
[3] His Sovereign's life to death and treachery!
[*Trumpets sound.*

Enter the King, Scroop, Cambridge, Grey, *and Attendants.*

K. Henry. Now sits the wind fair, and we will aboard.
My Lord of *Cambridge,* and my Lord of *Masham,*
And you my gentle Knight, give me your thoughts:
Think you not, that the pow'rs, we bear with us,
Will cut their passage through the force of *France*;
Doing the execution and the act

---

[3] *To death and treachery.*] Here the quarto inserts a line omitted in all the following editions.
Exet. *O! the lord of Masham!*

For

KING HENRY V. 389

which we have in head assembled them?

oop. No doubt, my Liege, if each man do his best.

Henry. I doubt not that; since we are well persuaded
arry not a heart with us from hence
grows not in a fair consent with ours,
eave not one behind that doth not wish
fs and conquest to attend on us.

n. Never was monarch better fear'd, and lov'd,
is your Majesty; there's not, I think, a subject
fits in heart-grief and uneasiness
r the sweet shade of your government.

y. True; those that were your father's enemies
steept their gauls in honey, and do serve you
h hearts create of duty and of zeal.

Henry. We therefore have great cause of thank-
fulness,
shall forget the office of our hand
er than quittance of desert and merit
rding to the weight and worthiness.

oop. So service shall with steeled sinews toil,
labour shall refesh itself with hope
o your Grace incessant services.

Henry. We judge no less. Uncle of *Exeter,*
ʒe the man committed yesterday,
rail'd against our person. We consider,
s excess of wine that set him on,
on his ² more advice we pardon him.

oop. That's mercy, but too much security;
iim be punish'd, Sovereign, lest example

---

r which we have IN HEAD *ssembled them?*] This is not glish phraseology. I am ded *Shakespeare* wrote, *which we have* IN AID *assembled them?*
ag to the tenures of those
                    WARBURTON.
strange that the commen-
tator should forget a word so eminently observable in this writer, as *head* for *an army formed.*

¹ *Hearts create.*] Hearts compound.d or *made up* of duty and zeal

² *More advice.*] On his return to more *coolness of mind.*

Cc 3   Breed,

Breed, by his suff'rance, more of such a kind.

K. Henry. O, let us yet be merciful.

Cam. So may your Highness, and yet punish too.

Grey. You shew great mercy, if you give him life,
After the taste of much correction.

K. Henry. Alas, your too much love and care of me
Are heavy orisons 'gainst this poor wretch.
If little faults [3], proceeding on distemper,
Shall not be wink'd at [4], how shall we stretch our eye,
When capital crimes, chew'd, swallow'd and digested,
Appear before us? We'll yet enlarge that man,
Though *Cambridge, Scroop,* and *Grey,* in their dear care
And tender preservation of our person,
Would have him punish'd. Now to our *French* causes—
Who are the late Commissioners?

Cam. I one, my Lord.
Your Highness bad me ask for it to-day.

Scroop. So did you me, my Liege.

Grey. And I, my Sovereign.

K. Henry. Then *Richard,* Earl of *Cambridge,* there
is yours;
There yours, Lord *Scroop* of *Masham;* and Sir Knight,
Grey of *Northumberland,* this same is yours.
Read them, and know, I know your worthiness.
My Lord of *Westmorland* and uncle *Exeter,*
We will aboard to-night.—Why, how now, gentlemen?
What see you in those papers, that you lose
So much complexion?—look ye, how they change!
Their cheeks are paper.—Why, what read you there,
That hath so cowarded, and chas'd your blood

---

[3] ——*proceeding on distemper,*] i. e. sudden passions. WARBURTON.
Perturbation of mind. *Temper* is equality or calmness of mind, from an equipoise or due mixture of passions. *Distemper* of mind is the predominance of a passion, as *distemper* of body is the predominance of a *humour.*

[4] *How shall we stretch our eye.*] If we may not wink at small faults, how wide must we open our eyes at great.

KING HENRY V.

Out of appearance?

Cam. I confess my fault,
And do submit me to your Highness' mercy.

Grey. Scroop. To which we all appeal.

K. Henry. The mercy, that was [5] quick in us but late,
By your own counsel is suppress'd and kill'd.
You must not dare for shame to talk of mercy,
For your own reasons turn into your bosoms,
As dogs upon their masters, worrying you.
See you, my Princes and my noble Peers,
These *English* monsters! My Lord *Cambridge* here,
You know, how apt our love was to accord
To furnish him with all appertinents
Belonging to his Honour; and this man
Hath for a few light crowns lightly conspir'd,
And sworn unto the practices of *France*
To kill us here in *Hampton*. To the which,
This Knight, no less for bounty bound to us
Than *Cambridge* is, hath likewise sworn. But O!
What shall I say to thee, Lord *Scroop*, thou cruel,
Ingrateful, savage, and inhuman creature!
Thou that didst bear the key of all my counsels,
That knew'st the very bottom of my soul,
That almost might'st have coin'd me into gold,
Wouldst thou have practis'd on me for thy use;
May it be possible, that foreign hire
Could out of thee extract one spark of evil,
That might annoy my finger? 'Tis so strange
That [6] though the truth of it stand off as gross
As black and white, my eye will scarcely see it.

[5] *Quick*] That is, *living*.

[6] *Though the truth stand off as gross. As black and white.*] Though the truth be as apparent and visible as black and white contiguous to each other. To *stand off* is *être relevé*, to be prominent to the eye, as the strong parts of a picture.

[7] Treason and murder ever kept together,
As two yoak-devils sworn to either's purpose,
[8] Working so grosly in a natural cause,
That admiration did not whoop at them.
But thou, 'gainst all proportion, didst bring in
Wonder to wait on treason, and on murder;
And whatsoever cunning fiend it was,
That wrought upon thee so prepost'rously,
Hath got the voice in hell for excellence;
And other devils, that suggest by-treasons,
Do botch and bungle up damnation,
With patches, colours, and with forms being fetcht
From glist'ring semblances of piety,
But [9] he, that temper'd thee, bade thee stand up;
Gave thee no instance why thou shouldst do treason,
Unless to dub thee with the name of traitor.
If that same Dæmon, that hath gull'd thee thus,
Should with his Lion-gait walk the whole world,
He might return to vasty *Tartar* back,
And tell the legions, I can never win
A soul so easy as that *Englishman's*.
[1] Oh, how hast thou with jealousy infected
The sweetness of affiance! Shew men dutiful?
Why so didst thou. Or seem they grave and learn'd?
Why so didst thou. Come they of noble family?

---

[7] *Treason and murder* ——] What follows to the end of this speech is additional since the first edition. POPE.

[8] *Working so grosly*——] Grosly for commonly, which the Oxford Editor not understanding, alters it to closely. WARBURT.

Grosly is neither closely nor commonly, but palpably; with a plain and visible connexion of cause and effect.

[9] *He that temper'd thee*] Though *temper'd* may stand for form'd or moulded, yet I fancy *tempted* was the authour's word, for it answers better to *suggest* in the opposition.

[1] *Oh, how hast thou with jealousy infected The sweetness of affiance!*] Shakespeare urges this aggravation of the guilt of treachery with great judgment. One of the worst consequences of breach of trust is the diminution of that confidence which make the happiness of life, and the dissemination of suspicion, which is the poison of society.

Why

KING HENRY V.

idst thou.   Seem they religious?
idst thou.   Or are they spare in diet,
  gross passion or of mirth, or anger,
in spirit, not swerving with the blood,
'd and deck'd in modest compliment,
rking with the eye without the ear,
in purged judgment trusting neither?
d so finely boulted didst thou seem.
  thy fall hath left a kind of blot,
  the full-fraught man, the best endu'd,

'd and deck'd in modest
 ent.]
ompliment, that is,
   WARBURTON.
 will not much help
unless he knows to
is to be applied. I
 eaning to be this.
 having mentioned
 perance in diet, pas-
his decency in dress,
 at he was *decked in
 ment*; that is, he was
with ornaments, but
 ht be worn without
 tation. *Compliment*
 ething more than is
 so *compliment* in lan-
 at we say *ad concili-
 iam*, more than is
 iterally meant.
 orking with the eye
 e ear.] He is here
 character of a com-
 man, and says, he did
  eye without the confir-
 s ear. But when men
 ght proof, they think
 ufficient evidence, and
 or the confirmation of
 . Prudent men, on
 ry, won't trust the
 he ear, till it be con-
 the demonstration of

the eye. And this is that conduct for which the king would
here commend him. So that we
must read,
  Not working with the ear, but
  with the eye.
       WARBURTON.
  The author's meaning I
should have thought not so difficult to find, as that an emendation should have been proposed.
The king means to say of *Scroop*,
that he was a cautious man, who
knew that *fronti nulla fides*, that
a specious appearance was deceitful, and therefore did not
work with the eye without the ear.
did not trust the air or look of
any man till he had tried him by
enquiry and conversation. Surely
this is the character of a prudent
man.

  4 —— *and so finely* boulted *didst
      thou seem,* ——] i.e. refined
or purged from all faults. POPE.
  Boulted is the same with *sifted*,
and has consequently the meaning of *refined*.

  6 *To* MAKE *the full-fraught
      man,*—] We should read,
To MARK *the full-fraught man*.
i.e. *marked* by the *blot* he speaks
of in the preceding line.
           WARBURTON.
                    With

With some suspicion. I will weep for thee.
For this revolt of thine, methinks, is like
Another fall of man.————Their faults are open;
Arrest them to the answer of the law,
And God acquit them of their practices!

Exe. I arrest thee of high treason, by the name of *Richard* Earl of *Cambridge*.

I arrest thee of high treason, by the name of *Henry* Lord *Scroop* of *Masham*.

I arrest thee of high treason, by the name of *Thomas Grey*, Knight of *Northumberland*.

Scroop. Our purposes God justly hath discover'd,
And I repent my fault, more than my death,
Which I beseech your Highness to forgive,
Although my body pay the price of it.

Cam. For me, the gold of *France* did not seduce,
Although I did admit it as a motive
The sooner to effect what I intended;
But God be thanked for prevention,
Which I in suff'rance heartily rejoice for,
Beseeching God and you to pardon me.

Grey. Never did faithful subject more rejoice
At the discovery of most dangerous treason,
Than I do at this hour joy o'er myself,
Prevented from a damned enterprize.
⁶ My fault, but not my body, pardon, Sovereign.

K. Henry. God quit you in his mercy! Hear your sentence.

You have conspir'd against our royal person,
Join'd with an enemy proclaim'd, and from his coffers
Receiv'd the golden earnest of our death,

---

⁶ One of the conspirators against Queen *Elizabeth*, I think *Parry*, concludes his letter to her with these words, A culpa, but not a pœna; absolve me, most dear Lady. This letter was much read at that time, and the author doubtless copied it.

This whole scene was much enlarged and improved after the first edition; the particular insertions it would be tedious to mention, and tedious without much use.

Wherein

Wherein you would have sold your King to slaughter,
His Princes and his Peers to servitude,
His subjects to oppression and contempt,
And his whole kingdom into desolation.
'Touching our person, seek we no revenge;
But we our kingdom's safety must so tender,
Whose ruin you three sought, that to her laws
We do deliver you. Go therefore hence,
Poor miserable wretches, to your death;
The taste whereof God of his mercy give
You patience to endure, and true Repentance
Of all your dear offences!—Bear them hence. [*Exeunt*.
—Now, Lords, for *France*; the enterprize whereof
Shall be to you, as us, like glorious.
We doubt not of a fair and lucky war,
Since God so graciously hath brought to light
This dangerous treason lurking in our way,
To hinder our beginning. Now we doubt not,
But every rub is smoothed in our way.
Then forth, dear countrymen; let us deliver
Our puissance into the hand of God,
Putting it straight in expedition.
Chearly to sea. The signs of war advance;
No King of *England*, if not King of *France*. [*Exeunt*.

SCENE IV.

Changes to Quickly's *house in* Eastcheap.

Enter Pistol, Nim, Bardolph, *Boy and* Quickly.

Quick. PR'ythee, honey-sweet husband, let me bring thee to *Staines*.
Pist. No, for my manly heart doth yern.
Bardolph, be blith. *Nim*, rouze thy vaunting vein.
Boy, bristle thy courage up; for *Falstaff* he is dead,
And we must yern therefore.

Bard.

Bard. Would I were with him wheresome'er he is, either in heaven or in hell.

Quick. Nay, sure, he's not in hell; he's in *Arthur's* bosom, if ever man went to *Arthur's* bosom. He made a ⁷ finer end, and went away, an it had been any chrisom child. A' parted even just between twelve and one, even at the ⁸ turning o' th' tide. For after I saw him fumble with the sheets, and play with flowers, and smile upon his finger's end, I knew there was but one way; ⁹ for his nose was as sharp as a pen, and a' babled of green fields. How now, Sir *John?* quoth I; what, man? be of good cheer. So a' cried out, God, God, God, three or four times. Now I, to comfort him, bid him, a' should not think of God;

---

⁷ *Finer end*, for *final*.

⁸ *Turning o' th' Tide.*] It has been a very old opinion, which *Mead, de imperio Solis*, quotes, as if he believed it, that nobody dies but in the time of ebb; half the deaths in *London* confute the notion, but we find that it was common among the women of the poet's time.

⁹ *for his nose was as sharp as a pen*, and a table of green fields.] These words, *a table of greenfields*, are not to be found in the old editions of 1600 and 1608. This nonsense got into all the following editions by a pleasant mistake of the stage editors, who printed from the common piece-meal-written parts in the play-house. A table was here directed to be brought in (it being a scene in a tavern where they drink at parting) and this direction crept into the text from the margin. *Greenfield* was the name of the property-man in that time who furnish'd implements, &c. for the actors, *A table of Greenfield's*. POPE.

So reasonable an account of this blunder Mr. *Theobald* would not acquiesce in. He thought *a table of* Greenfield's part of the text, only corrupted, and that it should be read, *he babled of greenfield*, because men do so in the ravings of a calenture. But he did not consider how ill this agrees with the nature of the Knight's illness, who was now in no *babling* humour: and so far from wanting cooling in *greenfields*, that his feet were cold, and he just expiring.

WARBURTON.

Upon this passage Mr. *Theobald* has a note that fills a page, which I omit in pity to my readers, since he only endeavours to prove, what I think every reader perceives to be true, that at this time no *table* could be wanted. Mr. *Pope*, in an appendix to his own edition in *twelves*, seems to admit *Theobald's* emendation, which we would have allowed to be uncommonly happy, had we not been prejudiced against it by a conjecture with which, as it excited merriment, we are loath to part

I hop'd,

KING HENRY V.   397

I hop'd, there was no need to trouble himself with any such thoughts yet. So a' bade me lay more cloathes on his feet. I put my hand into the bed and felt them, and they were as cold as a stone; then I felt to his knees, and so upward, and upward, and all was as ¹ cold as any stone.

Nim. They say, he cried out of Sack.

Quick. Ay, and that a' did.

Bard. And of women.

Quick. Nay, that a' did not.

Boy. Yes; that he did; and said, they were devils incarnate.

Quick. A' could never abide carnation, 'twas a colour he never lik'd.

Boy. He said once, the deule would have him about women.

---

¹ *Cold as any stone.*] Such is the end of *Falstaff*, from whom *Shakespeare* had promised us in his epilogue to *Henry* IV. that we should receive more entertainment. It happened to *Shakespeare* as to other writers, to have his imagination crowded with a tumultuary confusion of images, which, while they were yet unsorted and unexamined, seemed sufficient to furnish a long train of incidents, and a new variety of merriment, but which, when he was to produce them to view, shrunk suddenly from him, or could not be accommodated to his general design. That he once designed to have brought *Falstaff* on the scene again, we know from himself; but whether he could contrive no train of adventures suitable to his character, or could match him with no companions likely to quicken his humour, or could open no new vein of pleasantry, and was afraid to continue the same strain lest it should not find the same reception, he has here for ever discarded him, and made haste to dispatch him, perhaps for the same reason for which *Addison* killed Sir *Roger*, that no other hand might attempt to exhibit him.

Let meaner authors learn from this example, that it is dangerous to sell the bear which is yet not hunted, to promise to the publick what they have not written.

This disappointment probably inclined Queen *Elizabeth* to command the poet to produce him once again, and to shew him in love or courtship. This was indeed a new source of humour, and produced a new play from the former characters.

I forgot to note in the proper place, and therefore note here, that *Falstaff's* courtship, or *The Merry Wives of* Windsor, should be read between *Henry* IV. and *Henry* V.

Quick.

398 KING HENRY V.

Quick. He did in some sort, indeed, handle women; but then he was rheumatick, and talk'd of the whore of *Babylon*.

Boy. Do you not remember, he saw a Flea stick upon *Bardolph's* nose, and said, it was a black foul burning in hell?

Bard. Well, the fuel is gone, that maintain'd that fire. That's all the riches I got in his service.

Nim. Shall we shog? the King will be gone from *Southampton*.

Pist. Come, let's away. My love, give me thy lips. Look to my chattles, and my moveables. —
* Let senses rule.—The word is, * *pitch and pay*;
Trust none, for oaths are straws; men's faiths are wafer-cakes,
And hold-fast is the only dog, my Duck;
Therefore *Caveto* be thy counsellor.
Go, clear thy † crystals.—Yoke-fellows in arms,
Let us to *France*, like Horse leeches, my boys,
To suck, to suck, the very blood to suck.

Boy. And that is but unwholsome food, they say.

Pist. Touch her soft mouth and march.

Bard. Farewel, hostess.

Nim. I cannot kiss, that is the humour of it; but adieu.

Pist. Let housewifery appear; keep close, I thee command.

Quick. Farewel; adieu. [*Exeunt.*

---

* *Let senses rule*] I think this is wrong, but how to reform it I do not well see. Perhaps we may read,
Let sense us *rule.*
Pistol is taking leave of his wife, and giving her advice as he kisses her; he sees her rather weeping than attending, and supposing that in her heart she is still longing to go with him part of the way, he cries, *Let sense us rule*, that is, *let us not give way to foolish fondness, but be ruled by our better understanding.* He then continues his directions for her conduct in his absence.

* — *pitch and pay*;] I know not the meaning of *pitch*. Perhaps it should be *pinch and pay*; that is, as the language is of the present alehouses, *touch pot, touch penny.*

† *clear thy crystals.*] Dry thine eyes.

SCENE

KING HENRY V. 399

SCENE V.

Changes to the French King's Palace.

French *King, the Dauphin, the Duke of* Burgundy, *and the Constable.*

ing. THUS come the *English* with full power upon us,
l more than carefully it us concerns
nswer royally in our defences.
efore the Dukes of *Berry,* and of *Britain,*
rabant, and of *Orleans,* shall make forth,
you, Prince *Dauphin,* with all swift dispatch,
ne, and new repair our towns of war,
men of courage, and with means defendant;
England his Approaches makes as fierce,
aters to the sucking of a gulph.
s us then to be as provident,
ar may teach us out of late examples,
by the fatal and neglected *English*
n our fields.
u. My most redoubted father,
most meet we arm us 'gainst the foe:
peace itself should not so dull a Kingdom,
ugh war nor no known quarrel were in question,
that defences, musters, preparations,
ild be maintain'd, assembled, and collected,
vere a war in expectation.

nd more than CAREFULLY *t us concerns*] This was a :fs indeed, that required than care to discharge it. perſuaded *Shakeſpear* wrote, *e than* CARELESLY.
King is ſuppoſed to hint at the Dauphin's wanton it in ſending over tennis- to *Henry:* which, ariſing

from over-great confidence of their own power, or contempt of their enemies, would naturally breed *careliſneſs.* WARBURTON.
I do not ſee any defect in the preſent reading; *more than carefully* is *with more than common care,* a phraſe of the ſame kind with *better than well.*

There-

Therefore, I say, 'tis meet we all go forth,
To view the sick and feeble parts of *France*;
And let us do it with no shew of fear,
No, with no more, than if we heard that *England*
Were busied with a *Whitson* morris-dance,
For, my good Liege, she is so idly king'd,
Her scepter so fantastically borne,
By a vain, giddy, shallow, humorous youth,
That fear attends her not.

   Con. O peace, Prince *Dauphin!*
⁴ You are too much mistaken in this King.
Question your Grace the late ambassadors,
With what great state he heard their embassy;
How well supply'd with noble counsellors,
* How modest in exception, and withal
How terrible in constant resolution,
And you shall find, his vanities fore-spent
⁵ Were but the out-side of the *Roman Brutus*,
Covering discretion with a coat of folly;
As gardeners do with ordure hide those roots,
That shall first spring and be most delicate.

   Dau. Well, 'tis not so, my Lord high **Constable**,
But tho' we think it so, is no matter.

---

⁴ *You are too much mistaken in this King:* &c.] This part is much enlarged since the first writing. POPE.

* *How modest in exception*—] How diffident and decent in making objections.

⁵ *Were but the out-side of the Roman Brutus.*] *Shakespeare* not having given us, in the first or second part of *Henry* IV, or in any other place but this, the remotest hint of the circumstance here alluded to, the comparison must needs be a little obscure to those who don't know or reflect that some historians have told us, that *Henry* IV. had entertain'd a deep jealousy of his son's aspiring superior genius. Therefore, to prevent all umbrage, the prince withdrew from publick affairs, and amused himself in consorting with a dissolute crew of robbers. It seems to me, that *Shakspeare* was ignorant of this circumstance when he wrote the two parts of *Henry* IV. for it might have been so managed as to have given new beauties to the character of *Hal*, and great improvements to the plot. And with regard to these matters, *Shakespeare* generally tells us all he knew, and as soon as he knew it. WARBURTON.

In

causes of defence, 'tis best to weigh
the enemy more mighty than he seems;
So the proportions of defence are fill'd,
Which of a weak, and niggardly projection
Doth like a miser spoil his coat with scanting
A little cloth.

Fr. King. Think we King *Harry* strong;
And, Princes, look you strongly arm to meet him.
The kindred of him hath been flesh'd upon us,
And he is bred out of that bloody strain,
That haunted us in our familiar paths.
Witness our too much memorable shame,
When *Cressy*-battle fatally was struck:
And all our Princes captiv'd by the hand
Of that black name, *Edward* black Prince of *Wales*;
While that his mounting fire, on mountain standing,
Up in the air, crown'd with the golden sun,
Saw his heroic seed, and smil'd to see him
Mangle the work of nature, and deface
The patterns, that by God and by *French* fathers
Had twenty years been made. This is a stem
Of that victorious stock; and let us fear
The native mightiness and [9] fate of him.

Enter a Messenger.

Mess. Ambassadors from *Harry*, King of *England*,
Do crave admittance to your Majesty.

[6] *That* HAUNTED *us—*] We should assuredly read HUNTED: the integrity of the metaphor requires it. So, soon after, the King says again,
You see this Chace *is hotly followed.* WARBURTON.
The emendation weakens the passage. To *haunt* is a word of the utmost horror, which shews that they dreaded the *English* as Goblins and spirits.

[7] *While that his* MOUNTAIN *fire, on mountain standing.*] We should read, MOUNTING, ambitious, aspiring. WARBURTON.

[8] *Up in the air, crown'd with the golden sun,*] A nonsensical line of some player. WARBURTON.
And why of a player? There is yet no proof that the players have interpolated a line.

[9] *The fate of him.*] His fate is what is allotted him by destiny, or what he is fated to perform.

Vol. IV. D d Fr.

Fr. King. We'll give them prefent audience. Go, and bring them.

—You fee, this chafe is hotly follow'd, friends.

Dau. Turn head, and ftop purfuit; for coward dogs
Moft * fpend their mouths, when, what they feem to
    threaten,
Runs far before them. Good, my Sovereign,
Take up the *Englifh* fhort; and let them know
Of what a monarchy you are the head.
Self-love, my Liege, is not fo vile a fin,
As felf-neglecting.

SCENE VI.

Enter Exeter.

Fr. King. From our brother *England?*
Exe. From him; and thus he greets your Majefty.
He wills you in the name of God Almighty,
That you diveft yourfelf, and lay apart
The borrow'd glories that, by gift of heaven,
By law of nature and of nations, 'long
To him and to his heirs; namely, the Crown,
And all the wide-ftretch'd honours, that pertain
By cuftom and the ordinance of times,
Unto the Crown of *France.* That you may know,
'Tis no finifter nor no aukward claim,
Pick'd from the worm-holes of long-vanifh'd days,
Nor from the duft of old oblivion rak'd,
He fends you this moft ¹ memorable Line,
In every branch truly demonftrative,
        [*Gives the* French *King a Paper.*
Willing you overlook this pedigree;
And when you find him evenly deriv'd
From his moft fam'd of famous anceftors,

---

* *Spend their mouths,*] That is *bark*; the fportfman's term.

¹ *Memorable Line.*] This genealogy; this deduction of his lineage.

Edward

KING HENRY V.

rd the Third; he bids you then refign
Crown and Kingdom, indirectly held
him the native and true challenger.
 King. Or elfe what follows?
. Bloody conftraint; for if you hide the Crown
in your hearts, there will he rake for it.
therefore in fierce tempeft is he coming,
inder, and in earthquake, like a *Jove,*
, if requiring fail, he may compel.
ds you, in the bowels of the Lord,
er up the Crown; and to take mercy
ie poor fouls for whom this hungry war
s his vafty jaws; upon your head
ing the widows' tears, the orphans' cries,
: dead mens' blood, the pining maidens' groans,
ufbands, fathers, and betrothed lovers,
fhall be fwallow'd in this controverfy.
is his claim, his threatning, and my meffage;
s the *Dauphin* be in prefence here,
hom exprefly I bring Greeting too.
 King. For us, we will confider of this further.
orrow fhall you bear our full intent
to our brother *England.*
u. For the *Dauphin,*
d here for him; what to him from *England?*
. Scorn and defiance, flight regard, contempt,
iny thing that may not mif-become
mighty fender, doth he prize you at.
fays my King; and if your father's Highnefs
>t, in grant of all demands at large,
en the bitter mock you fent his Majefty;
call you to fo hot an anfwer for it,
caves and womby vaultages of *France*

e dead mens' blood.] The
ion of the images were
:gular if we were to read

Turning the dead mens' blood,
 the widows' tears,
The orphans' cries, the pining
 maidens' groans, &c.

· upon your head

Shall

KING HENRY V.

[2] Shall hide your trespass, and return your mock
In second accent to his ordinance.

Dau. Say, if my father render fair reply
It is against my will, for I desire
Nothing but odds with *England*; to that end,
As matching to his youth and vanity,
I did present him with those *Paris* balls.

Exe. He'll make your *Paris Louvre* [3] shake for it,
Were it the mistress court of mighty *Europe*.
And, be assur'd, you'll find a difference,
As we his subjects have in wonder found,
Between the promise of his greener days,
And these he masters now; now he weighs time
Even to the utmost grain, which you shall read
In your own losses, if he stay in *France*.

Fr. King. To-morrow you shall know our mind at
  full.   [*Flourish.*

Exe. Dispatch us with all speed, lest that our King
Come here himself to question our delay;
For he is footed in this land already.

Fr. King. You shall be soon dispatch'd with fair
  conditions.
A night is but small breath, and little pause,
To answer matters of this consequence.   [*Exeunt.*

ACT III. SCENE I.

Enter CHORUS.

Chorus. THUS with imagin'd wing our swift scene
  flies,
In motion of no less celerity
Than that of thought. Suppose, that you have seen

[2] *Shall* HIDE *your trespass,*—] Mr. *Pope* rightly corrected it, *Shall* CHIDE ——— WARBURTON.
I doubt whether it be *rightly corrected.* The meaning is, that the authors of this insult shall fly to caves for refuge.

[3] — *Paris Louvre*] This palace was, I think, not built in those times.

The

KING HENRY V.

The well-appointed King at *Hampton* Peer [4]
Embark his royalty, and his brave fleet
With silken streamers the young *Phœbus* fanning.
Play with your fancies; and in them behold,
Upon the hempen tackle, ship-boys climbing;
Hear the shrill whistle, which doth order give
To sounds confus'd; behold the threaden sails,
Borne with th' invisible and creeping wind,
Draw the huge bottoms thro' the furrow'd sea,
Breasting the lofty surge. O, do but think,
You stand upon the rivage [5], and behold
A city on th' inconstant billows dancing;
For so appears this Fleet majestical,
Holding due course to *Harfleur*. Follow, follow,
Grapple your minds to sternage of this navy.
And leave your *England*, as dead midnight still,
Guarded with grandsires, babies and old women,
Or past, or not arriv'd, to pith and puissance;
For who is he, whose chin is but enrich'd
With one appearing hair, that will not follow
These cull'd and choice-drawn cavaliers to *France*?
Work, work your thoughts, and therein see a siege;
Behold the ordnance on their carriages
With fatal mouths gaping on girded *Harfleur*,
Suppose, th' ambassador from *France* comes back;
Tells *Harry*, that the King doth offer him
Catharine his daughter, and with her to dowry
Some petty and unprofitable Dukedoms:

---

[4] *The well-appointed King at Dover peer Embark his Royalty;*—] Thus all the Editions downwards, implicitly, after the first *Folio*. But could the Poet possibly be so discordant from himself (and the Chronicles, which he copied) to make the King here embark at *Dover*; when he has before told us so precisely, and that so often over, that he embark'd at *Southampton?* I dare acquit the Poet from so flagrant a Variation. The Indolence of a Transcriber, or a Compositor at Press, must give Rise to such an Error. They seeing *Peer* at the End of the Verse, unluckily thought of *Dover*-peer, as the best known to them: and so unawares corrupted the Text. THEOBALD.

[5] — *rivage*] The *bank* or shore.

The offer likes not; and the nimble gunner
With lynstock [6] now the devilish cannon touches,
And down goes all before him. Still be kind,
And eke out our performance with your mind. [*Exit.*

SCENE II.
Before HARFLEUR.
[*Alarm and Cannon go off.*]

Enter King Henry, Exeter, Bedford, *and* Gloucester, *Soldiers, with scaling ladders.*

K. Henry. ONCE more unto the breach, dear friends,
once more;
* Or close the wall up with the *English* dead.
In peace, there's nothing so becomes a man
As modest stillness and humility;
But when the blast of war blows in our ears,
Then imitate the action of the Tyger;
Stiffen the sinews, summon up the blood,
Disguise fair nature with hard-favour'd rage;
Then lend the eye a terrible aspect;
Let it pry thro' the † portage of the head,
Like the brass cannon; let the brow o'erwhelm it,
As fearfully, as doth a galled rock
O'er-hang and jutty ‡ his confounded base,
Swill'd with the wild and wasteful ocean.
Now set the teeth, and stretch the nostril wide;
Hold hard the breath, and bend up every spirit [7]
To his full height. Now on, you noblest *English,*

---

6 — *lynstock*] The staff to which the match is fixed when ordnance is fired.

* *Or close the wall, &c*] Here is apparently a chasm. One line at least is lost which contained the other part of a disjunctive proposition. The King's speech is, Dear friends, either win the town, or close up the wall with our dead. The old 4to gives no help.

† *Portage of the head.*] Portage, open space, from *port*, a gate. Let the eye appear in the head, as cannon through the batt'ements, or embrasures, of a fortification.

‡ *His confounded base.*] His worn or wasted base.

7 — *bend up every spirit*] A metaphor from the bow.

Whose

Whose blood is fetcht from fathers of war proof;
Fathers, that, like so many *Alexanders*,
Have in these parts from morn till even fought,
And sheath'd their swords for lack of argument [a].
Dishonour not your mothers; now attest,
That those, whom you call'd fathers, did beget you.
Be copy now to men of grosser blood,
And teach them how to war. And you, good yeomen,
Whose limbs were made in *England*, shew us here
The mettle of your pasture, let us swear
That you are worth your breeding, which I doubt not;
For there is none of you so mean and base,
That hath not noble lustre in your eyes.
See you stand like Greyhounds in the slips,
Straining upon the start; the game's a-foot,
Follow your spirit; and, upon this charge,
Cry, God for *Harry! England!* and St. *George!*

[*Exeunt* King, *and* Train.
[*Alarm, and Cannons go off.*

SCENE III.

Enter Nim, Bardolph, Pistol, *and Boy*.

Bard. On, on, on, on, on. To the breach, to the breach.

Nim. 'Pray thee, corporal, stay; the knocks are too hot, and for mine own part, I have not a [*] case of lives. The humour of it is too hot, that is the very plain song of it.

Pist. The plain song is most just, for humours do abound,
Knocks go and come; God's vassals drop and die;
    And sword and shield,
    In bloody field,
Doth win immortal fame.

---

[a] *Argument* is *matter, or sub-ject*.

[*] *A case of lives*] A set of lives, of which, when one is worn out, another may serve.

Boy. 'Wou'd I were in an ale-house in *London*, I would give all my fame for a pot of ale and safety.

Pist. And I;
If wishes would prevail with me [9],
My purpose should not fail with me,
But thither would I hye.

Enter Fluellen.

Flu. Up to the breach, you dogs; avaunt, you cullions.

Pist. Be merciful, great Duke, to men of mould [1],
Abate thy rage, abate thy manly rage;
Good bawcock, 'bate thy rage; use lenity, sweet chuck.

Nim. These be good humours; your honour wins bad humours. [*Exeunt.*

Boy. As young as I am, I have observed these three swashers. I am boy to them all three; but all they three, though they would serve me, could not be man to me; for, indeed, three such Anticks do not mount to a man. For *Bardolph*, he is white-liver'd and red-fac'd; by the means whereof he faces it out, but fights not. For *Pistol*, he hath a killing tongue and a quiet sword; by the means whereof he breaks words, and keeps whole weapons. For *Nim*, he hath heard, that men of few words are the [2] best men; and therefore he scorns to say his prayers, lest he should be thought a coward; but his few bad words are match'd with as few good deeds; for he never broke any man's head but his own, and that was against a post when he was drunk. They will steal any thing, and call it purchase. *Bardolph* stole a lute-case, bore it twelve leagues, and

---

[9] This passage I have replaced from the first folio, which is the only authentic copy of this play. These lines, which perhaps are part of a song, Mr. *Pope* did not like, and therefore changed them, in conformity to the imperfect play in 4to, and was followed by the succeeding editors. For *prevail* I should read *avail*.

[1] —— *to men of mould,*] To men of *earth*, to poor mortal men.

[2] —— *best men;*] That is, *bravest*; so in the next line, *good deeds* are *brave actions*.

sold

KING HENRY V. 409

sold it for three half-pence. *Nim* and *Bardolph* are sworn brothers in filching; and in *Calais* they stole a fire shovel; I knew, by that piece of service, the men would carry coals [3]. They would have me as familiar with mens pockets, as their gloves or their handkerchers, which makes much against my manhood; for if I would take from another's pocket to put into mine, it is plain pocketting up of wrongs. I must leave them, and seek some better service; their villainy goes against my weak stomach, and therefore I must cast it up. [*Exit Boy.*

Enter Gower, *and* Fluellen.

Gower. Captain *Fluellen*, you must come presently to the mines; the Duke of *Gloucester* would speak with you.

Flu. To the mines? tell you the Duke, it is not so good to come to the mines; for look you, the mines are not according to the disciplines of the war; the concavities of it is not sufficient; for, look you, th' athversary (you may discuss unto the Duke, look you) is digt [4] himself four yards under the countermines; by *Cheshu*, I think a' will [5] plow up all, if there is not petter directions.

Gower. The Duke of *Gloucester*, to whom the order of the siege is given, is altogether directed by an *Irish* man, a very valliant gentleman, i'faith.

Flu. It is captain *Macmorris*, is it not?

Gower. I think, it be.

Flu. By *Cheshu* he is an Ass, as is in the world; I will verify as much in his beard. He has no more

---

[3] —— *the men would carry coals.*] It appears that in *Shakespeare's* age, *to carry coals* was, I know not why, *to endure affronts.* So in *Romeo* and *Juliet,* one servingman asks another whether he will *carry coals.*

[4] —— *is digt himself four yards under the countermines :*] *Fluellen* means, that the enemy had digged himself *countermines* four yards under the *mines.*

[5] —— *will plow up all.*] That is, *he will* blow *up all.*

directions

directions in the true disciplines of the wars, look you, of the *Roman* disciplines, than is a Puppy-dog.

Enter Macmorris, *and Capt.* Jamy.

Gower. Here he comes, and the *Scots* Captain, Captain *Jamy* with him.

Flu. Captain *Jamy* is a marvellous valorous gentleman, that is certain; and of great expedition and knowledge in the antient wars, upon my particular knowledge of his directions; by *Cheshu*, he will maintain his argument as well as any military man in the world, in the disciplines of the pristine wars of the *Romans*.

Jamy. I say, gudday, Captain *Fluellen*.

Flu. Godden to your worship, good captain *James*.

Gower. How now, captain *Macmorris*, have you quitted the mines? have the pioneers given o'er?

Mac. By Chrish law, tish ill done; the work ish give over, the trumpet sound the retreat. By my hand, I swear, and by my father's soul, the work ish ill done; it ish give over; I would have blowed up the town, so Chrish save me law, in an hour. O tish ill done, tish ill done; by my hand, tish ill done.

Flu. Captain *Macmorris*, I beseech you now, will you vouchsafe me, look you, a few disputations with you, as partly touching or concerning the disciplines of the war, the *Roman* wars, in the way of argument, look you, and friendly communication; partly to satisfy my opinion; and partly for the satisfaction, look you, of my mind; as touching the direction of the military discipline, that is the point.

Jamy. It sall be very gud, gud feith, gud captains bath; and I sall quit you [6] with gud leve, as I may pick occasion; that sall I, marry.

[6] — *I sha'll quit you*] That is, I sha'l, with your permission, requite you, that is, answer you, or interpose with my arguments, as I shall find opportunity.

Mac.

Mac. It is no time to difcourfe, fo Chrifh fave me: the day is hot, and the weather and the wars, and the King and the Duke; it is not time to difcourfe, the town is befeech'd, and the trumpet calls us to the breach, and we talk, and by Chrifh do nothing, 'tis fhame for us all; fo God fa'me, 'tis fhame to ftand ftill; it is fhame, by my hand; and there is throats to be cut, and works to be done, and there is nothing done, fo Chrifh fa' me law.

Jamy. By the mefs, ere theife eyes of mine take themfelves to flomber, aile do gud fervice, or aile ligge i'th' ground for it; ay, or go to death; and aile pay it as valoroufly as I may, that fal I furely do, the breff and the long; marry, I wad full fain heard fome queftion 'tween you tway.

Flu. Captain *Macmorris*, I think, look you, under your correction, there is not many of your nation —

Mac. Of my nation? what ifh my nation? ifh a villain, and a baftard, and a knave, and a rafcal? what ifh my nation? who talks of my nation?

Flu. Look you, if you take the matter otherwife than is meant, captain *Macmorris*, peradventure, I fhall think you do not ufe me with that affability as in difcretion you ought to ufe me, look you; being as good a man as yourfelf, both in the difciplines of wars, and in the derivation of my birth, and in other particularities.

Mac. I do not know you fo good a man as myfelf; fo Chrifh fave me, I will cut off your head.

Gower. Gentlemen both, you will miftake each other.
Jamy. Au! that's a foul fault. [*A Parley founded.*
Gower. The town founds a parley.
Flu. Captain *Macmorris*, when there is more better opportunity to be requir'd, look you, I'll be fo bold as to tell you, I know the difciplines of war; and there's an end.* [*Exeunt.*

* It were to be wifhed that the poor merriment of this dialogue had not been purchafed with fo much profanenefs.

SCENE

SCENE IV.

Before the Gates of Harfleur.

Enter King Henry *and his Train.*

K. Henry. HOW yet resolves the Governor of
the town?
This is the latest parle we will admit;
Therefore to our best mercy give yourselves,
Or, like to men proud of destruction,
Defy us to our worst. As I'm a soldier,
A name, that, in my thoughts, becomes me best,
If I begin the batt'ry once again,
I will not leave the half-atchieved *Harfleur*
'Till in her ashes she lie buried.
The gates of mercy shall be all shut up;
And the flesh'd soldier, rough and hard of heart,
In liberty of bloody hand shall range
With conscience wide as hell, mowing like grass
Your fresh fair virgins, and your flow'ring infants.
What is it then to me, if impious war,
Array'd in flames like to the Prince of fiends,
Do with his smircht complexion all fell feats [7],
Enlinkt to waste and desolation?
What is't to me, when you yourselves are cause,
If your pure maidens fall into the hand
Of hot and forcing violation?
What rein can hold licentious wickedness,
When down the hill he holds his fierce career?
We may, as bootless, spend our vain command
Upon th' enraged soldiers in their spoil,
As send our precepts to th' *Leviathan*
To come a shoar. Therefore, you men of *Harfleur*,
Take pity of your town and of your people,

---

[7] ———— *fell feats,* All the savage practices naturally
Enlinkt to waste and desolation?] concomitant to the sack of cities.

While

KING HENRY V. 413

yet my soldiers are in my command;
le yet the cool and temp'rate wind of grace
lows the filthy and contagious clouds
dy murder, spoil and villainy.
; why, in a moment, look to see
lind and bloody soldier with foul hand
the locks of your shrill-shrieking daughters;
fathers taken by the silver beards,
heir most reverend heads dasht to the walls;
naked infants spitted upon pikes,
the mad mothers with their howls confus'd
eak the clouds; as did the wives of *Jewry*,
rod's bloody-hunting slaughter-men.
say you? will you yield, and this avoid?
ilty in defence, be thus destroy'd?

Enter Governor upon the Walls.

. Our expectation hath this day an end;
)auphin, whom of succours we entreated,
ns us, that his pow'rs are not yet ready
se so great a siege. Therefore, great King,
ield our town and lives to thy soft mercy,
our gates, dispose of us and ours,
e no longer are defensible.
Henry. Open your gates. Come, uncle *Exeter*,
u and enter *Harfleur*, there remain,
ortify it strongly 'gainst the *French*.
iercy to them all. For us, dear Uncle,
vinter coming on, and sickness growing
our soldiers, we'll retire to *Calais*.
ght in *Harfleur* we will be your guest,
orrow for the march we are addrest.
   [*Flourish, and enter the town.*

'bile yet the cool and | very harsh metaphor. To *over-*
np'rate wind of grace | *blow* is to *drive away*, or *to keep*
blows the filthy and conta- | *off.*
us clouds, &c.] This is a

SCENE

Alice. De nayles, madame.

Cath. De nayles, de arme, de ilbow.

Alice. Sauf voſtre bonneur, d'elbow.

Cath. Ainſi, dis je d' elbow, de neck, de ſin: comment appellez vous les pieds, & de robe.

Alice. Le foot, madame, & le coun.

Cath. Le foot, & le. coun! O Seigneur Dieu! ces ſont des mots mauvais, corruptibiles & impudiques, & non pour les dames d'honneur d'uſer: je ne voudrois prononcer ces mots devant les Seigneurs de France, pour tout le monde! il faut le foot, & le coun; neant-moins. Je reciteray une autrefois ma leçon enſemble; d' band, de fugre, de nayles, d'arme, d'elbow, de neck, de ſin, de foot, de coun.

Alice. Excellent, madame.

Cath. C'eſt aſſez pour une fois, allons nous en diſner.

[*Exeunt.*

SCENE VI.

Preſence-Chamber in the French Court.

Enter the King of France, the Dauphin, Duke of Bourbon, the Conſtable of France, and others.

Fr. King. 'TIS certain, he hath paſs'd the river
    Some.

Con. And if he be not fought withal, my Lord,
Let us not live in *France*; let us quit all,
And give our vineyards to a barb'rous people.

Dau. O *Dieu vivant!* ſhall a few ſprays of us,
The emptying of our fathers' luxury [1],
Our Syens, put in wild and ſavage [2] ſtock,
Sprout up ſo ſuddenly into the clouds,
And over-look their grafters?

---

[1] ——— *our fathers' luxury,*] In this place, as in others, *luxury* means *luſt*.

[2] *Savage* is here uſed in the *French* original ſenſe, for *ſilvan, uncultivated,* the ſame with *wild.*

Bour.

KING HENRY V.

Bour. Normans, but bastard *Normans;* Norman bastards.
Mort de ma vie! if thus they march along
Unfought withal, but I will sell my Dukedom,
To buy a foggy and a dirty farm
In that nook-shotten [3] Isle of *Albion.*

   Con. Dieu de Batailles! why, whence have they this mettle?
Is not their climate foggy, raw and dull?
On whom, as in despight, the Sun looks pale,
Killing their fruit with frowns? can sodden water [4],
A drench for sur-reyn'd jades, their barly-broth,
Decoct their cold blood to such valiant heat?
And shall our quick blood, spirited with wine,
Seem frosty? Oh! for honour of our land,
Let us not hang like frozen isicles
Upon our house-tops, while more frosty people
Sweat drops of gallant blood in our rich fields:
Poor, we may call them, in their native Lords.

   Dau. By faith and honour,
Our madams mock at us, and plainly say,
Our mettle is bred out; and they will give
Their bodies to the lust of *English* youth,
To new-store *France* with bastard warriors.

   Bour. They bid us to the *English* dancing-schools,
And teach *La volta's* high, and swift *Corantos;*
Saying, our grace is only in our heels;
And that we are most lofty run-aways.

   Fr. King. Where is *Mountjoy*, the herald? speed him hence;

---

[3] *In that nook-shotten Isle of Albion.*] *Shotten* signifies any thing *projected:* So *nook-shotten Isle*, is an Isle that shoots out into capes, promontories and necks of land, the very figure of *Great-Britain.* WARBURTON.

[4] —— *can sodden water,*
A drench for sur-reyn'd jades,—]
The exact meaning of *sur-reyn'd* I do not know. It is common to give horses over-ridden or feverish, ground malt and hot water mixed, which is called *a mash.* To this he alludes.

Let him greet *England* with our sharp defiance.
Up, Princes, and with spirit of honour edg'd,
Yet sharper than your swords, hie to the field.
Charles Delabreth, [5] high constable of *France;*
You dukes of *Orleans, Bourbon,* and of *Berry,*
Alanson, Brabant, Bar, and *Burgundy,*
Jaques Chatillion, Rambures, Vaudemont,
Beaumont, Grandpree, Rouffie, and *Faulconbridge,*
Loys, Leftraile, Bouciqualt, and *Charaloys,*
High Dukes, great Princes, Barons, Lords and Knights,
For your great seats now quit you of great shames,
Bar *Harry England,* that sweeps through our land
With penons painted in the blood of *Harfleur;*
Rush on his host, as doth the melted snow [6]
Upon the vallies; whose low vassal seat
The *Alps* doth spit and void his rheum upon.
Go down upon him, you have pow'r enough,
And in a captive chariot into *Roan*
Bring him our prisoner.

   Con. This becomes the great.
Sorry am I, his numbers are so few,
His soldiers sick, and famisht in their march;
For, I am sure, when he shall see our army,
He'll drop his heart into the sink of fear,
And for atchievement offer us his ransom.

   Fr. King. Therefore, Lord Constable, haste on
    Mountjoy,

---

[5] *Charles Delabreth,* &c.] Milton somewhere bids the *English* take notice how their names are misspelt by foreigners, and seems to think that we may lawfully treat foreign names in return with the same neglect. This privilege seems to be exercised in this catalogue of *French* names, which, since the sense of the authour is not afferted, I have left it as I found it.

[6] The poet has here defeated himself by passing too soon from one image to another. To be the *French* rush upon the *Engli[sh]* as the torrents formed from melted snow stream from the *Alp[s]* was at once vehement and proper, but its force is destroyed b[y] the grossness of the thought i[n] the next line.

And let him say to *England*, that we send
To know what willing ransom he will give.
Prince *Dauphin*, you shall stay with us in *Roan*.

Dau. Not so, I do beseech your Majesty.

Fr. King. Be patient, for you shall remain with us.
Now forth, Lord Constable, and Princes all;
And quickly bring us word of *England's* fall. [*Exeunt.*

SCENE VII.

The English *Camp.*

Enter Gower *and* Fluellen.

Gow. HOW now, captain *Fluellen*, come you from the bridge?

Flu. I assure you, there is very excellent services committed at the pridge.

Gow. Is the Duke of *Exeter* safe?

Flu. The Duke of *Exeter* is as magnanimous as *Agamemnon*, and a man that I love and honour with my soul, and my heart, and my duty, and my life, and my living, and my uttermost power. He is not, God be praised and plessed, any hurt in the world; he is maintain the pridge most valiantly, with excellent discipline. There is an Antient lieutenant there at the pridge, I think, in my very conscience, he is as valiant a man as *Mark Anthony*, and he is a man of no estimation in the world, but I did see him do gallant services.

Gow. What do you call him?

Flu. He is call'd Ancient *Pistol*.

Gow. I know him not.

Enter Pistol.

Flu. Here is the man.

Pist. Captain, I thee beseech to do me favours:

420 KING HENRY V.

The Duke of *Exeter* doth love thee well.

Flu. I, I praise God, and I have merited some love at his hands.

Pist. Bardolph, a soldier firm and sound of heart,
And buxom valour, hath by cruel fate,
And giddy fortune's furious fickle wheel,
That Goddess blind that stands upon the rolling restless stone——

Flu. By your patience, Ancient *Pistol:* Fortune is painted plind, with a muffler before her eyes, [7] to signify to you that fortune is plind; and she is painted also with a wheel, to signify to you, which is the moral of it, that she is turning and inconstant and mutabilities and variations; and her foot, look you, is fixed upon a spherical stone, which rowles, and rowles, and rowles; in good truth, the Poet makes a most excellent description of it. Fortune is an excellent moral.

Pist. Fortune is *Bardolph's* foe, and frowns on him,
For he hath stol'n a [8] *Pix*, and hanged must a' be,
Damned death!

Let

---

[7] *Fortune is painted* PLIND, *with a muffler before her eyes, to signify to you that fortune is plind;*] Here the fool of a player was for making a joke, as *Hamlet* says, *not set down for him, and shewing a most pitiful ambition* to be witty. For *Fluellen*, though he speaks with his country accent, yet is all the way represented as a man of good plain sense. Therefore, as it appears he knew the meaning of the term *plind*, by his use of it, he could never have said that *Fortune was painted plind, to signify she was plind.* He might as well have said afterwards, *that she was painted inconstant, to signify she was inconstant.* But there he speaks sense, and so unquestionably, he did here. We should therefore strike out the first *plind*, and read,

Fortune is painted with a muffler, &c. WARBURTON.

[8] The old editions, *For he hath stol'n a Pax,*] "And this is conformable to History, (says Mr. *Pope*) a Soldier (as *Hall* tell us) being hang'd at this Time for such a Fact."—Both *Hall* and *Holingshead* agree as to the point of the *Theft*; but as to the Thing *stolen*, there is not that Conformity betwixt them and Mr. *Pope*. It was an ancient custom, at the Celebration of Mass, that when the Priest pronounc'd these Words, *Pax Domini sit semper vobiscum !* both Clergy and People kiss'd one another.

KING HENRY V.

Let gallows gape for dog, let man go free,
And let not hemp his wind-pipe suffocate;
But *Exeter* hath given the doom of death,
For *Pix* of little Price. Therefore, go speak,
The Duke will hear thy voice;
And let not *Bardolph's* vital thread be cut
With edge of penny-cord, and vile reproach.
Speak, Captain, for his life, and I will thee requite.

Flu. Ancient *Pistol*, I do partly understand your meaning.

Pist. Why then rejoice therefore.

Flu. Certainly, Ancient, it is not a thing to rejoice at; for if, look you, he were my brother, I would desire the Duke to use his good pleasure, and put him to executions; for disciplines ought to be used.

Pist. Die and be damn'd, and *Figo* for thy friendship!

Flu. It is well.

Pist. The fig of *Spain*——— [*Exit* Pist.

Flu. Very good.

Gow. Why, this is an arrant counterfeit rascal, I remember him now; a bawd, a cut-purse.

Flu. I'll assure you, he utter'd as prave words at the pridge, as you shall in a summer's day: but it is very well; what he has spoke to me, that is well, I warrant you, when time is serve.

Gow. Why, 'tis a gull, a fool, a rogue, that now and then goes to the wars, to grace himself at his re-

another. And this was call'd *Osculum Pacis*, the Kiss of *Peace*. But that custom being abrogated, a certain Image is now presented to be kiss'd, which is call'd a *Pax*. But it was not this Image which *Bardolph* stole; it was a *Pix*; or little Chest (from the *Latin* Word, *Pixis*, a Box); in which the consecrated *Host* was used to be kept. "A foolish

" Soldier (says *Hall* expressly,
" and *Holingshead* after him;)
" stole a *Pix* out of a Church."
THEOBALD.

What *Theobald* says is true, but might have been told in fewer words: I have examined the passage in *Hall*. Yet Dr. *Warburton* rejected the emendation, and continued *Pope's* note without animadversion.

turn into *London*, under the form of a soldier. Such fellows are perfect in the great commanders' names, and they will learn you by rote where services were done; at such and such a sconce, at such a breach, at such a convoy; who came off bravely, who was shot, who disgrac'd, what terms the enemy stood on; and this they con perfectly in the phrase of war, which they trick up with new-turn'd oaths; and what a beard of the general's cut, and a horrid suite of the camp, will do among foaming bottles and ale-wash'd wits, is wonderful to be thought on! But you must learn to know ² such slanders of the age, or else you may be marvellously mistook.

Flu. I tell you what, captain *Gower*; I do perceive, he is not the man that he would gladly make shew to the world he is; if I find a hole in his coat, I will tell him my mind. Hear you, the King is coming, and I must speak with him from the pridge ¹.

---

² *Such slanders of the age*] This was a character very troublesome to wise men in our authour's time. It is the practice with him, says *Ascham*, to be near like though he never look'd on my in the face, yet some warlike sign must be us'd, as a slovenly buskin, or an over-staring frouncèd head, as though out of every hair's top should suddenly start a good big oath.

¹ *I must speak with him from the pridge.*] "*Speak with him* "*from the Bridge*, Mr. Pope tells "us, is added in the latter "Editions; but that it is plain "from the Sequel, that the "Scene here continues, and "the affair of the Bridge is "over." This is a most inaccurate Criticism. Tho' the Affair of the Bridge be over, is that a Reason, that the King must receive no Intelligence from thence? *Fluellen*, who comes from the Bridge, wants to acquaint the King with the Transactions that had happened there. This he calls *speaking to the King from the Bridge*. THEOBALD.

With this Dr. *Warburton* concurs.

SCENE

SCENE VIII.

Drum and Colours. Enter the King, and his poor soldiers.

Flu. God plefs your Majefty.

K. Henry. How now, *Fluellen*, cam'ft thou from the bridge?

Flu. I, fo pleafe your Majefty: the Duke of *Exeter* has very gallantly maintain'd the pridge; the *French* is gone off, look you, and there is gallant and moft prave paffages; marry, th' athverfary was have poffeffion of the pridge, but he is enforced to retire, and the Duke of *Exeter* is mafter of the pridge. I can tell your Majefty, the Duke is a prave man.

K. Henry. What men have you loft, *Fluellen?*

Flu. The perdition of th' athverfary hath been very great, very reafonably great; marry, for my part, I think, the Duke hath loft never a man but one that is like to be executed for robbing a church, one *Bardolph*, if your Majefty know the man; his face is all bubukles, and whelks, and knobs, and flames of fire; and his lips blows at his nofe, and it is like a coal of fire; fometimes plue, and fometimes red; but his nofe is executed, and his fire's * out.

K. Henry. We would have fuch offenders fo cut off;
And give exprefs charge, that in all our march
There fhall be nothing taken from the villages,
But fhall be paid for; and no *French* upbraided,
Or yet abufed in difdainful language;
When lenity and cruelty play for kingdoms,
The gentler gamefter is the foonest winner.

---

* *his fire's out.*] This is the laft time that any fport can be made with the red face of *Bardolph*, which, to confefs the truth, feems to have taken more hold on *Shakefpeare's* imagination than on any other. The conception is very cold to the folitary reader, though it may be fomewhat invigorated by the exhibition on the ftage. This poet is always more careful about the prefent than the future, about his audience than his readers

E e 4

Tucket sounds. Enter Mountjoy.

Mount. You know me [2] by my habit.
K. Henry. Well then, I know thee; what shall I know of thee?
Mount. My master's mind.
K. Henry. Unfold it.
Mount. Thus says my King. Say thou to *Harry England*,
Although we seemed dead, we did but sleep;
Advantage is a better soldier than rashness.
Tell him, we could at *Harfleur* have rebuk'd him,
But that we thought not good to bruise an injury,
'Till it were ripe. Now, speak we [3] on our cue,
With voice imperial. *England* shall repent
His folly, see his weakness, and admire
Our suff'rance. Bid him therefore to consider,
What must the ransom be, which must proportion
The losses we have borne, the subjects we
Have lost, and the disgrace we have digested,
To answer which, his pettiness would bow under.
First for our loss, too poor is his Exchequer;
For the effusion of our blood, his army
Too faint a number; and for our disgrace,
Ev'n his own person kneeling at our feet
A weak and worthless satisfaction.
To this, defiance add; and for conclusion,
Tell him he hath betrayed his followers,
Whose condemnation is pronounc'd. So far
My King and master; and so much my office.
K. Henry. What is thy name? I know thy quality.
Mount. Mountjoy.

---

[2] *By my habit.*] That is, by his herald's coat. The person of a herald being inviolable was distinguished in those times of formality by a peculiar dress, which is likewise yet worn on particular occasions.

[3] *On our cue.*] In our turn. This phrase the author learned among players, and has imparted it to kings.

K. Henry.

KING HENRY V. 425

K. Henry. Thou doſt thy office fairly. Turn thee back,
And tell thy King, I do not ſeek him now;
But could be willing to march on to *Calais*
Without impeachment; for to ſay the ſooth,
Though 'tis no wiſdom to confeſs ſo much
Unto an enemy of craft and vantage,
My people are with ſickneſs much enfeebled,
My numbers leſſen'd; and thoſe few I have,
Almoſt no better than ſo many *French*;
Who, when they were in health, I tell thee, herald,
I thought, upon one pair of *Engliſh* legs
Did march three *Frenchmen.* Yet, forgive me God,
That I do brag thus; this your air of *France*
Hath blown that vice in me; I muſt repent.
Go, therefore, tell thy maſter, here I am,
My ranſom is this frail and worthleſs trunk,
My army but a weak and ſickly guard,
Yet [4], God before, tell him we will come on,
Though *France* himſelf, and ſuch another neighbour,
Stand in our way. There's for thy labour, *Mountjoy,*
Go, bid thy maſter well adviſe himſelf:
If we may paſs, we will; if we be hinder'd,
We ſhall your tawny ground with your red blood
Diſcolour; and ſo, *Mountjoy,* fare you well.
The ſum of all our anſwer is but this;
We would not ſeek a battle as we are,
Yet, as we are, we ſay, we will not ſhun it:
So tell your maſter.

Mount. I ſhall deliver ſo. Thanks to your Highneſs. [*Exit.*

---

[4] *God before.*] This was an expreſſion in that age for *God being my guide,* or when uſed to another, *God be thy guide.* So in an old dialogue between a herdſman and a maiden going on pilgrimage to *Walſingham,* the herdſman takes his leave in theſe words,

Now go thy ways, and God *before.*

To *prevent* was uſed in the ſame ſenſe.

Glou.

KING HENRY V.

Glou. I hope, they will not come upon us now.

K. Henry. We are in God's hand, brother, not in theirs.
March to the bridge; it now draws towards night;
Beyond the River we'll encamp ourselves;
And on to-morrow bid them march away. [*Exeunt.*

⁵SCENE IX.

The French *Camp near* Agincourt.

Enter the Constable of France, *the Lord* Rambures, Orleans, Dauphin, *with others.*

Con. TUT, I have the best armour of the world. Would it were day!

Orl. You have an excellent armour, but let my horse have his due.

Con. It is the best horse of *Europe.*

Orl. Will it never be morning?

Dau. My Lord of *Orleans*, and my Lord high Constable, you talk of horse and armour,——

Orl. You are as well provided of both, as any Prince in the world.

Dau. What a long night is this! I will not change my horse with any that treads but on four pasterns; *ca, ha? le Cheval volant*, the *Pegasus, chez les Narines de feu* ⁶! he bounds from the earth, as if his entrails were hairs; when I bestride him, I soar, I am a Hawk; he trots the air, the earth sings when he touches it; the

---

⁵ SCENE IX] This scene is shorter, and I think better, in the first editions of 1600 and 1608. But as the enlargements appear to be the author's own, I would not omit them. POPE.

⁶ *he bounds from the earth, as if his entrails were hairs;*] Alluding to the bounding of tennis-balls, which were stuffed with hair, as appears from *Much ado about Nothing. And the old ornament of his cheek hath already stufft tennis-balls.* WARBURTON.

basest

afest horn of his hoof is more musical than the pipe of *Hermes*.

Orl. He's of the colour of the nutmeg.

Dau. And of the heat of the ginger. It is a beast for *Perseus*; he is pure air and fire; and the dull elements of earth and water never appear in him, but only in patient stillness while his rider mounts him; he is indeed a horse [7]; and all other jades you may call beasts.

Con. Indeed, my Lord, it is a most absolute and excellent horse.

Dau. It is the prince of palfreys; his neigh is like the bidding of a monarch, and his countenance enforces homage.

Orl. No more, cousin.

Dau. Nay, the man hath no wit, that cannot, from the rising of the lark to the lodging of the lamb, vary deserved praise on my palfry; it is a theme as fluent as the sea; turn the sands into eloquent tongues, and my horse is argument for them all; 'tis a subject for a Sovereign to reason on, and for a Sovereign's Sovereign to ride on; and for the world familiar to us and unknown to lay apart their particular functions and wonder at him. I once writ a sonnet in his praise, and began thus [8], *Wonder of nature.*———

Orl. I have heard a sonnet begin so to one's mistress.

Dau. Then did they imitate that, which I compos'd to my courser; for my horse is my mistress.

Orl. Your mistress bears well.

Dau. Me, well;——which is the prescript praise, and perfection, of a good and particular mistress.

---

[7] *And all other* jades *you may call* beasts.] It is plain that *jades* and *beasts* should change places, it being the first word and not the last, which is the term of reproach; as afterwards it is said, *I had as lieve have my mistress a jade.* WARBURTON.

[8] *Wonder of nature.*———] Here, I suppose, some foolish poem of our author's time is ridiculed; which indeed partly appears from the answer. WARB.

Con.

Con. Methought, yesterday your mistress shrewdly shook your back.

Dau. So, perhaps did yours.

Con. Mine was not bridled.

Dau. O, then, belike, she was old and gentle; and you rode, like a *Kerne* of *Ireland*, your *French* hose off, and in your strait Trossers [a].

Con. You have good judgment in horsemanship.

Dau. Be warn'd by me then; they that ride so and ride not warily, fall into foul bogs; I had rather have my horse to my mistress.

Con. I had as lieve have my mistress a jade.

Dau. I tell thee, Constable, my mistress wears her own hair.

Con. I could make as true a boast as that, if I had a Sow to my mistress.

Dau. Le chien est retourné à son proper vomissement, & la truie lavée au bourbier; thou mak'st use of any thing.

Con. Yet do I not use my horse for my mistress; or any such proverb, so little kin to the purpose.

Ram. My Lord Constable, the armour, that I saw in your tent to-night, are those stars, or suns upon it?

Con. Stars, my Lord.

Dau. Some of them will fall to-morrow, I hope.

Con. And yet my sky shall not want.

Dau. That may be, for you bear many superfluously; and 'twere more honour, some were away.

Con. Ev'n as your horse bears your praises, who would trot as well, were some of your brags dismounted.

Dau. Would I were able to load him with his desert. Will it never be day? I will trot to-morrow a mile, and my way shall be paved with *English* faces.

---

[a] *Like a Kerne of Ireland, your French hose off, and in your strait Strossers.*] Thus all the Editions have mistaken this Word, which should be *Trossers;* and signifies, a pair of Breeches. THEOBALD.

KING HENRY V.

n. I will not say so, for fear I should be fac'd out
y way; but I would it were morning, for I would
be about the ears of the *English.*

m. Who will go to hazard with me for twenty
/b prisoners?

n. You must first go yourself to hazard ere you
them.

u. 'Tis mid-night, I'll go arm myself.   [*Exit.*

l. The *Dauphin* longs for morning.

m. He longs to eat the *English.*

n. I think, he will eat all he kills.

l. By the white hand of my lady, he's a gallant
ce.

n. Swear by her foot, that she may tread out the

l. He is simply the most active gentleman of
ce.

m. Doing is activity, and he will still be doing.

rl. He never did harm, that I heard of.

m. Nor will do none to-morrow: he will keep
good name still.

rl. I know him to be valiant,

n. I was told that, by one that knows him better
you.

rl. What's he?

m. Marry, he told me so himself; and he said,
ar'd not who knew it.

rl. He needs not, it is no hidden virtue in him.

on. By my faith, Sir, but it is; never any body
it, but * his lacquey; ¹ 'tis a hooded valour, and
n it appears, it will bate.

rl. Ill-will never said well.

---

bis lacquey;] He has beaten   as soon as the hood is off *bait*
ody yet but his foot-boy.   or flap the wing. The meaning
   "*'Tis a hooded valour, and*   is, the dauphin's valour has ne-
it appears, it will bait.]   ver been let loose upon an ene-
is said with allusion to fal-   my, yet, when he makes his
which are kept *hooded* when   first essay, we shall see how he
are not to fly at game, and   will flutter.

Con.

From camp to camp, through the foul womb of night,
The hum of either army stilly sounds;
That the fixt Sentinels almost receive
The secret whispers of each other's watch.
Fire answers fire; and through their paly flames
Each battle sees *the other's umber'd face.
Steed threatens steed, in high and boastful neighs
Piercing the night's dull ear; and from the tents,
The armourers accomplishing the knights,
With busy hammers closing rivets up,
Give dreadful note of preparation.
The country cocks do crow, the clocks do toll;
And (the third hour of drousy morning nam'd)
Proud of their numbers and secure in soul,
The confident and over lusty *French*
⁵ Do the low-rated *English* play at dice;
And chide the cripple tardy-gated night,
Who, like a foul and ugly witch, does limp
So tediously away. The poor condemned *English*,
Like sacrifices, by their watchful fires
Sit patiently, and inly ruminate
The morning's danger: and their gesture sad,
⁶ Invest in lank-lean cheeks and war-worn coats,
Presented them unto the gazing moon
So many horrid ghosts. Who now beholds
The royal captain of this ruin'd band
Walking from watch to watch, from tent to tent,
Let him cry, *Praise and glory on his head!*

⁴ —— *the other's* umber'd *face.*] Umber'd or *umbrid,* is a term in blazonry, and signifies shadowed. WARBURTON.

⁵ *Do the low-rated* English *play at dice;*] i. e. do play them away at dice. WARBURTON.

⁶ INVESTING *lank lean cheeks,* &c.] *A gesture investing cheeks and coats* is nonsense. We should read,
INVEST IN *lank-lean cheeks,* which is sense, i. e. their sad gesture was cloath'd, or set off, in lean-cheeks and worn-coats. The image is strong and picturesque. WARBURTON.

For

KING HENRY V.

For forth he goes, and visits all his host,
Bids them good morrow with a modest smile,
And calls them brothers, friends, and countrymen.
Upon his royal face there is no note,
How dread an army hath enrounded him;
Nor doth he dedicate one jot of colour
Unto the weary and all-watched night,
But freshly looks and over-bears attaint,
With chearful semblance and sweet majesty;
That ev'ry wretch, pining and pale before,
Beholding him, plucks comfort from his looks.
A largess universal, like the sun,
His lib'ral eye doth give to ev'ry one,
Thawing cold 7 fear. Then, mean and gentle, all
Behold, as may unworthiness define,
A little touch of *Harry* in the night.
And so our scene must to the battle fly,
Where, O for pity! we shall much disgrace,
With four or five most vile and ragged foils,
Right ill dispos'd, in brawl ridiculous,
The name of *Agincourt*. Yet sit and see,
Minding true things by what their mock'ries be. [*Exit.*

SCENE II.

The English *Camp, at* Agincourt.

Enter King Henry *and* Gloucester.

Henry. GLo'ster, 'tis true, that we are in great danger;

——— *Fear; that mean and gentle all, Behold, as may,* &c.] As this stood, it was a most perplex'd and nonsensical Passage: and could not be intelligible, but I have corrected it. The Poet, in addressing himself to every degree of his Audience, tells them; he'll shew (as well as his unworthy Pen and Powers can describe it) a little Touch, or Sketch of this Hero in the Night.
THEOBALD.

7 *Minding true things.*] To *mind* is the same, as *to call to remembrance.*

The greater therefore should our courage be.

Enter Bedford.

—Good morrow, brother *Bedford*.—God Almighty!
There is some soul of goodness in things evil,
Would men observingly distil it out;
For our bad neighbour makes us early stirrers,
Which is both healthful, and good husbandry.
Besides, they are our outward consciences,
And preachers to us all; admonishing,
That we should dress us fairly for our end.
Thus may we gather honey from the weed,
And make a moral of the devil himself.

Enter Erpingham.

Good morrow, old Sir *Thomas Erpingham*,
A good soft pillow for that good white head
Were better than a churlish turf of *France*.

Erping. Not so, my Liege; this lodging likes me
    better :
Since I may say, now lie I like a King.

K. Henry. 'Tis good for men to love their present pain
Upon example; so the spirit is eased,
And when the mind is quicken'd, out of doubt,
The organs, though defunct and dead before,
Break up their drowsy grave, and newly move
With casted [1] slough and fresh legerity.
Lend me thy cloak, Sir *Thomas.* Brothers both,
Commend me to the Princes in our camp,
Do my good morrow to them, and anon
Desire them all to my pavillion.

Glou. We shall, my Liege.

Erping. Shall I attend your grace?

K. Henry. No, my good kight,
Go with my brothers to my lords of *England*.

---

[1] *Slough* is the skin which the serpent annually throws off, and by the change of which he is supposed to regain new vigour and fresh youth. *Legerity* is lightness, nimbleness.

I and

KING HENRY V. 435
I and my bosom must debate a while,
And then I would no other company.

Erping. The Lord in heaven bless thee, noble Harry!

K. *Henry.* God a-mercy, old heart, thou speak'st chearfully. [*Exeunt.*

SCENE III.

Enter Pistol.

Pistol. *Qui va là?*

K. *Henry.* A friend.

Pist. Discuss unto me, art thou officer?
Or art thou base, common and popular?

K. *Henry.* I am a gentleman of a company.

Pist. Trail'st thou the puissant pike?

K. *Henry.* Even so. What are you?

Pist. As good a gentleman as the Emperor.

K. *Henry.* Then you are a better than the King.

Pist. The King's a bawcock, and a heart of gold,
A lad of life, an imp of fame,
Of parents good, of fist most valiant;
I kiss his dirty shoe, and from my heart-string
I love the lovely bully. What's thy name?

K. *Henry.* Harry le Roy.

Pist. Le Roy! a *Cornish* name: art thou of *Cornish* crew?

K. *Henry.* No, I am a *Welshman.*

Pistol. Know'st thou *Fluellen?*

K. *Henry.* Yes.

Pist. Tell him, I'll knock his leek about his pate,
Upon St. *David's* day.

K. *Henry.* Do not you wear your dagger in your cap that day, lest he knock that about yours.

Pist. Art thou his friend?

K. *Henry.* And his kinsman too.

Pist. The *Figo* for thee then!

F f 2   K. *Henry.*

K. Henry. I thank you. God be with you.
Pist. My name is *Pistol* call'd. [*Exit.*
K. Henry. It sorts well with your fierceness.
[*Manet King* Henry.

Enter Fluellen, *and* Gower *severally.*

Gow. Captain *Fluellen.*———
Flu. So; in the name of *Jesu* Christ, speak fewer; it is the greatest admiration in the universal world, when the true and auncient prerogatifes and laws of the wars is not kept. If you would take the pains but to examine the wars of *Pompey* the great, you shall find, I warrant you, that there is no tittle tattle, nor pibble pabble, in *Pompey's* camp; I warrant you, you shall find the ceremonies of the wars, and the cares of it, and the forms of it, and the sobrieties of it, and the modesty of it to be otherwise.
Gow. Why, the enemy is loud, you hear him all nigh.
Flu. If the enemy is an ass and a fool, and a prating coxcomb, is it meet, think you, that we should also, look you, be an ass and a fool, and a prating coxcomb, in your own conscience now?
Gow. I will speak lower.
Flu. I pray you, and beseech you, that you will.
[*Exeunt.*
K. *Henry.* Though it appear a little out of fashion, There is much care and valour in this *Welshman.*

SCENE IV.

Enter three Soldiers, John Bates, Alexander Court, *and* Michael Williams.

Court. Brother *John Bates,* is not that the morning which breaks yonder?

Bates. I think it be, but we have no great cause to desire the approach of day.

Will. We see yonder the beginning of the day, but, I think, we shall never see the end of it. Who goes there?

K. Henry. A friend.

Will. Under what captain serve you?

K. Henry. Under Sir *Thomas Erpingham*.

Will. A good old commander, and a most kind gentleman. I pray you, what thinks he of our estate?

K. Henry. Even as men wreck'd upon a sand, that, look to be wash'd off the next tide.

Bates. He hath not told his thought to the King?

K. Henry. No; nor is it meet, he should; for tho' I speak it to you, I think, the King is but a man as I am: the Violet smells to him as it doth to me; the element shews to him as it doth to me; all his senses have but human [9] conditions. His ceremonies laid by, in his nakedness he appears but a man; and tho' his affections are higher mounted than ours, yet when they stoop, they stoop with the like wing; therefore when he sees reason of fears as we do, his fears, out of doubt, be of the same relish as ours are; yet in reason no man should possess him with any appearance of fear, lest he, by shewing it, should dishearten his army.

Bates. He may shew what outward courage he will; but, I believe, as cold a night as 'tis, he could wish himself in the *Thames* up to the neck; and so I would he were, and I by him at all adventures, so we were quit here.

K. Henry. By my troth, I will speak my conscience of the King; I think, he would not wish himself any where but where he is.

---

[9] *Conditions* are *qualities*. The meaning is, that objects are represented by his senses to him, as to other men by theirs. What is danger to another is danger likewise to him, and when he feels fear it is like the fear of meaner mortals.

Bates. Then 'would he were here alone; so should he be sure to be ransom'd, and many poor men's lives saved.

K. Henry. I dare say, you love him not so ill to wish him here alone; howsoever you speak this to feel other men's minds. Methinks, I could not die any where so contented as in the King's company; his cause being just, and his quarrel honourable.

Will. That's more than we know.

Bates. Ay, or more than we should seek after; for we know enough, if we know we are the King's subjects; if his cause be wrong, our obedience to the King wipes the crime of it out of us.

Will. But if the cause be not good, the King himself hath a heavy reckoning to make; when all those legs, and arms, and heads, chop'd off in a battle, shall join together at the latter day, and cry all, *We dy'd at such a place,* some, swearing; some, crying for a surgeon; some, upon their wives left poor behind them; some, upon the debts they owe; some, upon their children [1] rawly left. I am afear'd there are few die well, that die in battle; for how can they charitably dispose of any thing, when blood is their argument? now, if these men do not die well, it will be a black matter for the King that led them to it, whom to disobey were against all proportion of subjection.

K. Henry. So, if a son, that is sent by his father about merchandize, do fall into some lewd action and miscarry, the imputation of his wickedness, by your rule, should be imposed upon his father that sent him; or if a servant, under his master's command transporting a sum of mony, be assail'd by robbers, and die in many irreconcil'd iniquities; you may call the

---

[1] *Rawly.*] That is, *without preparation, hastily, suddenly.* What is not matured is raw.

So in *Macbeth.*
Why in this rawness left he wife and children.

business

business of the master the author of the servant's damnation. But this is not so: the King is not bound to answer the particular endings of his soldiers, the father of his son, nor the master of his servant; for they purpose not their death, when they purpose their services. Besides, there is no King, be his cause never so spotless, if it come to the arbitrement of swords, can try it out with all unspotted soldiers; some, peradventure, have on them the guilt of premeditated and contrived murder; some of beguiling virgins with the broken seals of perjury; some, making the wars their bulwark, that have before gored the gentle bosom of peace with pillage and robbery. Now if these men have defeated the law, and out-run native punishment; though they can out-strip men, they have no wings to fly from God. War is his beadle, war is his vengeance; so that here men are punished, for before-breach of the King's laws, in the King's quarrel now: where they feared the death, they have borne life away; and where they would be safe, they perish. Then if they die unprovided, no more is the King guilty of their damnation, than he was before guilty of those impieties for which they are now visited [2]. Every subject's duty is the King's, but every subject's soul is his own. Therefore should every soldier in the wars do as every sick man in his bed, wash every moth out of his conscience; and dying so, death is to him advantage; or not dying, the time was blessedly lost, wherein such preparation was gained: and, in him that escapes, it were not sin to think, that making God so free an offer, he let him outlive that day to see his greatness, and to teach others how they should prepare.

Will. 'Tis certain, that every man that dies ill, the

---

[2] This is a very just distinction, and the whole argument is well followed, and properly concluded.

ill is upon his own head, the King is not to anfwer for it.

Bates. I do not defire he fhould anfwer for me, and yet I determine to fight luftily for him.

K. Henry. I myfelf heard the King fay, he would not be ranfom'd.

Will. Ay, he faid fo, to make us fight chearfully; but, when our throats are cut, he may be ranfom'd, and we ne'er the wifer.

K. Henry. If I live to fee it, I will never truft his word after.

Will. You pay him then; that's a perilous fhot out of an Elder-gun [3], that a poor and private difpleafure can do againft a monarch! you may as well go about to turn the fun to ice, with fanning in his face with a Peacock's feather; you'll never truft his word after! come, 'tis a foolifh faying.

K. Henry. Your reproof is fomething too round: I fhould be angry with you, if the time were convenient.

Will. Let it be a quarrel between us, if you live.

K. Henry. I embrace it.

Will. How fhall I know thee again?

K. Henry. Give me any gage of thine, and I will wear it in my bonnet, then if ever thou dar'ft acknowledge it, I will make it my quarrel.

Will. Here's my glove; give me another of thine.

K. Henry. There.

Will. This will I alfo wear in my cap; if ever thou come to me and fay, after to-morrow, this is my glove; by this hand, I will give thee a box on the ear.

K. Henry. If ever I live to fee it, I will challenge it.

Will. Thou dar'ft as well be hang'd.

K. Henry. Well, I will do it, though I take thee in the King's company.

---

[3] *That's a perilous fhot out of an Elder-gun.*] In the old play the thought is more opened. It is a great difpleafure that an elder gun can do againft a cannon.

Will.

KING HENRY V. 441

Will. Keep thy word: fare thee well.

Bates. Be friends, you *English* fools, be friends; we have *French* quarrels enow, if you could tell how to reckon.

K. Henry. Indeed, the *French* may lay * twenty *French* crowns to one, they will beat us, for they bear them on their shoulders; but it is no *English* treason to cut *French* crowns, and to-morrow the King himself will be a clipper. [*Exeunt soldiers.*

SCENE V.

Manet King Henry.

⁴ Upon the King! let us our lives, our souls,
Our debts, our careful wives, our children and
Our sins, lay on the King; he must bear all.
O hard condition, and twin-born with greatness,
Subject to breath of ev'ry fool, whose sense
No more can feel but his own wringing.
What infinite heart-ease must Kings neglect,
That private men enjoy? and what have Kings,
That private have not too, save ceremony?
Save gen'ral ceremony?———
And what art thou, thou idol ceremony?
What kind of God art thou, that suffer'st more
Of mortal griefs, than do thy worshippers?
⁵ What are thy rents? what are thy comings in?

O

---

* *Twenty* French *crowns.*] This conceit, rather too low for the King, has been already explained, as alluding to the venereal disease.

⁴ *Upon the King!* &c.] This beautiful speech was added after the first edition.   POPE.

There is something very striking and solemn in this soliloquy, into which the king breaks immediately as soon as he is left alone. Something like this, on less occasions, every breast has felt. Reflection and seriousness rush upon the mind upon the separation of a gay company, and especially after forced and unwilling merriment.

⁵ *What are thy* rents? *What are thy* comings in?

O ceremony, shew me but thy worth:

What! is thy SOUL OF *adoration?*] Thus is the last line given us, and the nonsense of it made worse by the ridiculous pointing. We should read, *What*

KING HENRY V.

O ceremony, shew me but thy worth,
What is thy soul, O adoration?
Art thou aught else but place, degree, and form,
Creating awe and fear in other men?
Wherein thou art less happy, being fear'd,
Than they in fearing.
What drink'st thou oft, instead of homage sweet,
But poison'd flatt'ry? O be sick, great greatness,
And bid thy ceremony give thee cure.
Think'st thou, the fiery fever will go out
With titles blown from adulation?
Will it give place to flexure and low bending?
Can'st thou, when thou command'st the beggar's knee,
Command the health of it? no, thou proud dream,
That play'st so subtly with a King's repose;
I am a King, that find thee; and I know,
'Tis not the balm, the scepter and the ball,
The sword, the mace, the crown imperial,
The enter-tissued robe of gold and pearl,
The ⁶ farsed title running 'fore the King,
The throne he sits on, nor the tide of pomp

is thy TOLL, O *adoration!* Let us examine how the context stands with my emendation: *What are thy rents? What are thy comings-in? What is thy worth? What is thy toll?*—— (*i. e.* the *duties*, and *imposts*, thou receivest:) All here is consonant, and agreeable to a sensible exclamation. So King *John:* —— *No Italian priest shall tythe or* TOLL *in our dominions.* But the *Oxford Editor*, now he finds the way open for alteration, reads, *What is thy shew of adoration.* By which happy emendation, what is about to be enquired into, is first taken for granted: namely, that *ceremony* is but a shew. And to make room for this word here, which is found in the immediate preceding line, he degrades it there. but puts as good a word indeed in its stead, that is to say, *toll.* WARBURTON.

This emendation is not ill conceived, yet I believe it is erroneous. The first copy reads, *What? is the soul of Adoration* This is incorrect, but I think we may discover the true reading easily enough to be, *What is thy soul, O adoration?* That is, *O reverence paid to Kings, what art thou within? What are thy real qualities? What is thy intrinsick value?*

⁶ *Farsed title running, &c.*] *Farsed* is *stuffed* The tumid pufty titles with which a king's name is always introduced. This I think is the sense.

That

KING HENRY V.   443

That beats upon the high shore of this world;
No, not all these thrice-gorgeous ceremonies,
Not all these, laid in bed majestical,
' Can sleep so soundly as the wretched slave;
Who, with a body fill'd, and vacant mind,
Gets him to rest, cramm'd with distressful bread,
Never sees horrid night, the child of hell,
But, like a lacquey, from the rise to set,
Sweats in the eye of *Phœbus*; and all night
Sleeps in *Elysium*; next day, after dawn,
Doth rise, and help *Hyperion* to his horse;
And follows so the ever-running year
With profitable labour to his grave:
And, but for ceremony, such a wretch,
Winding up days with toil, and nights with sleep,
Hath the fore-hand and vantage of a King.
The slave, a member of the country's peace,
Enjoys it; but in gross brain little wots,
What watch the King keeps to maintain the peace;
Whose hours the peasant best advantages.

S C E N E VI.

Enter Erpingham.

Erp. My Lord, your Nobles, jealous of your ab-
    sence,
Seek through your camp to find you.
    K. Henry. Good old Knight,
Collect them all together at my tent:
I'll be before thee.
    Erp. I shall do't, my Lord.   [*Exit.*
    K. Henry. O God of battles! steel my soldiers
        hearts;

' *Can sleep so soundly,* &c.] bus, *and to sleep in* Elysium, are
These lines are exquisitely pleas- expressions very poetical.
ing. *To sweat in the eye of* Phœ-

444　KING HENRY V.

Poſſeſs them not with fear [8]; take from them now
The ſenſe of reck'ning; leſt th' oppoſed numbers
Pluck their hearts from them.—Not to-day, O Lord,
O not to day, think not upon the fault
My father made in compaſſing the crown.
I *Richard's* body have interred new,
And on it have beſtow'd more contrite tears,
Than from it iſſu'd forced drops of blood.
Five hundred Poor I have in yearly pay,
Who twice a-day their wither'd hands hold up
Tow'rd heav'n to pardon blood; and I have built
Two chauntries, where the ſad and ſolemn prieſts
Sing ſtill for *Richard's* ſoul.　More will I do;
Tho' all that I can do, is nothing worth,
[9] Since that my penitence comes after all,
Imploring pardon.

Enter

---

[8] In former editions:
———*take from them now*
The Senſe of reck'ning of th'
oppoſed Numbers:
Pluck their hearts from them]
Thus the firſt *folio.* The Poet might intend, " Take from them "the Senſe of reckoning thoſe "oppoſed Numbers; *which* "might pluck their Courage "from them." But the *relative* not being expreſs'd, the Senſe is very obſcure.　THEOB.

The change is admitted by Dr. *Warburton,* and rightly. Sir *T. Hanmer* reads,
———*th' oppreſſ'd numbers*
Which ſtand before them.
This reading he borrowed from the old quarto, which gives the paſſage thus,
Take from them now the ſenſe
of reckoning,
That the oppoſed multitudes that
ſtand before them
May not appall their courage.

[9] *Since that my penitence comes*
after ALL,
Imploring pardon] We muſt obſerve, that *Henry* IV. had committed an injuſtice, of which he, and his *ſon,* reap'd the fruits. But reaſon tells us, juſtice demands that they who ſhare the profits of iniquity, ſhall ſhare alſo in the puniſhment. Scripture again tells us, that when men have ſinned, the Grace of God gives frequent invitations to repentance; which, in the language of Divines, are ſtiled *Calls.* Theſe if neglected, or careleſly dallied with, are, at length, irrecoverably withdrawn, and then repentance comes to late. All this ſhews that the unintelligible reading of the text ſhould be corrected thus,
———*comes after* CALL.
WARBURTON.

I wiſh the commentator had explained his meaning a little
better;

Enter Gloucester.

Glou. My Liege.
K. *Henry.* My brother *Glo'ster's* voice?
I know thy errand, I will go with thee,
The day, my friends, and all things stay for me.
[*Exeunt.*

SCENE VII.

Changes to the French Camp.

Enter the Dauphin, Orleans, Rambures *and* Beaumont.

Orl. THE Sun does gild our armour; up, my Lords.
Dau. Montez Cheval: my horse, *valet, lacquay:* ha!
Orl. O brave spirit!
Dau. Via!——les eaux & la terre.——
Orl. Rien puis! 'le air & feu.——
Dau. Ciel! Cousin *Orleans.*

Enter Constable.

Now, my Lord Constable!
Con. Hark, how our Steeds for present service neigh.

better; for his comment is to me less intelligible than the text. I know not what he thinks of the king's penitence, whether coming *in consequence of call,* it is sufficient; or whether coming when *calls have ceased,* it is ineffectual. The first sense will suit but ill with the position, that *all which he can do is nothing worth,* and the latter as ill with the intention of *Shakespeare,* who certainly does not mean to represent the king as abandoned and reprobate.

The old reading is in my opinion easy and right. *I do all this,* says the King, *though all that I can do is nothing worth,* is so far from an adequate expiation of the crime, *that penitence comes after all, imploring pardon* both of the crime and the expiation.

Dau.

Dau. Mount them, and make incision in their hides,
That their hot blood may spin in *English* eyes,
And daunt them with superfluous courage: ha!

Ram. What, will you have them weep our Horses'
  blood?
How shall we then behold their natural tears?

Enter a Messenger.

Mess. The *English* are embattel'd, you *French* Peers.
Con. To horse! you gallant Princes, strait to horse!
Do but behold yon poor and starved band,
And your fair shew shall suck away their souls;
Leaving them but the shales and husks of men.
There is not work enough for all our hands,
Scarce blood enough in all their sickly veins
To give each naked curtle-ax a stain;
That our *French* gallants shall to-day draw out,
And sheath for lack of sport. Let's but blow on them,
The vapour of our valour will o'erturn them.
'Tis positive 'gainst all exception, Lords,
That our superfluous lacqueys and our peasants,
Who in unnecessary action swarm
About our squares of battle, were enow
To purge this field of such a hilding foe;
Tho' we, upon this mountain's basis by,
Took stand for idle speculation;
But that our honours must not. What's to say?
A very little, little, let us do;
And all is done. Then let the trumpets sound
¹ The tucket sonance, and the note to mount,
For our approach shall so much dare the field,
That *England* shall couch down in fear, and yield.

¹ *The tucket-sonance,* &c] He uses terms of the field as if they were going out only to the chase for sport. *To dare the field* is a phrase in falconry. Birds are dared when, by the falcon in the air, they are terrified from rising, so that they will be sometimes taken by the hand.
  Such an easy capture the lords expected to make of the *English*.

Enter

KING HENRY V.

Enter Grandpree.

Grand. Why do you stay so long, my Lords of France?
Yon Island carrions, desp'rate of their bones,
Ill-favour'dly become the morning field:
Their ragged curtains poorly are let loose,
And our air shakes them passing scornfully.
Big *Mars* seems bankrupt in their beggar'd host,
And faintly through a rusty bever peeps.
The horsemen sit like fixed candlesticks,
With torch-staves in their hand; and their poor jades
Lob down their heads, dropping the hide and hips:
The gum down-roping from their pale dead eyes;
And in their pale dull mouths the gimmal bitt [2]
Lies foul with chew'd grass, still and motionless:
And [3] their executors, the knavish Crows,
Fly o'er them, all impatient for their hour.
Description cannot suit itself in words,
To demonstrate the life of such a battle,
In life so liveless as it shews itself.

Con. They've said their prayers, and they stay for death.

Dau. Shall we go send them dinners and fresh suits,
And give their fasting Horses provender,
And, after, fight with them?

Con. [4] I stay but for my guard: on, to the field;
I will the banner from a trumpet take,
And use it for my haste. Come, come, away!
The sun is high, and we out-wear the day. [*Exeunt.*

---

[2] *Gimmal* is in the western countries a *ring*; a *gimmal bit* is therefore a *bit* of which the parts were one within another.

[3] *Their executors, the knavish crows*] The crows who are to have the disposal of what they shall leave, their hides and their flesh.

[4] *I stay but for my guard.*] It seems, by what follows, that *guard* in this place means rather something of ornament or of distinction than a body of attendants.

SCENE

448 KING HENRY V.

SCENE VIII.

The English *CAMP.*

Enter Gloucester, Bedford, Exeter, Erpingham, *with all the Host;* Salisbury *and* Westmorland.

Glou. WHERE is the King?
Bed. The King himself is rode to view their battle.
West. Of fighting men they have full threescore thousand.
Exe. There's five to one; besides, they all are fresh.
Sal. God's arm strike with us, 'tis a fearful odds!
God be wi' you, Princes all; I'll to my charge.
If we no more meet till we meet in heav'n,
Then joyfully, my noble Lord of *Bedford*,
My dear Lord *Glo'ster*, and my good Lord *Exeter*,
And my kind kinsman, warriors all, adieu!
Bed. Farewel, good *Salisbury*, and good luck go with thee! [5]
Exe. to Sal. Farewel, kind Lord; fight valiantly to-day:
And yet I do thee wrong to mind thee of it,
For thou art fram'd of the firm truth of valour.
[*Exit* Sal.
Bed. He is as full of valour, as of kindness;
Princely in both.

Enter King Henry.

West. O, that we now had here
But one ten thousand of those men in *England*,
That do no work to-day!

---

[5] In the old editions:
Bed. Farewel, good Salisbury,
and good Luck go with thee,
And yet I do thee wrong to mind
thee of it,
For thou art fram'd of the firm
Truth of Valour.
Exe. Farewel, kind Lord: fight
valiantly to-day.] What! does he do *Salisbury* Wrong to wish him good luck? The ingenious Dr. *Thirlby* prescrib'd to me the Transposition of the Verses, which I have made in the Text: and the old Quarto's plainly lead to such a Regulation. THEOBALD.

K. Henry.

K. Henry. What's he, that wishes so?
My cousin *Westmorland?* No, my fair cousin,
If we are mark'd to die, we are enow
To do our country loss; and if to live,
The fewer men, the greater share of honour.
God's will! I pray thee, wish not one man more.
* By *Jove*, I am not covetous of gold,
Nor care I, who doth feed upon my cost,
It yerns me not, if men my garments wear,
Such outward things dwell not in my desires;
But if it be a sin to covet honour,
I am the most offending soul alive.
No, faith, my Lord, wish not a man from *England*:
God's peace! I would not lose so great an honour,
As one man more, methinks, would share from me,
For the best hopes I have. Don't wish one more;
Rather proclaim it *(Westmorland)* through my host,
That he, which hath no stomach to this fight,
Let him depart: his pass-port shall be made,
And crowns for convoy put into his purse:
We would not die in that man's company,
That fears his fellowship to die with us.
This day is call'd the feast of *Crispian*.
He that out-lives this day, and comes safe home,
Will stand a tip-toe when this day is nam'd,
And rouze him at the name of *Crispian*;
He that shall live this day, and see old age,
Will yearly on the vigil feast his neighbours,
And say, to-morrow is Saint *Crispian*;
Then will he strip his sleeve, and shew his scars.
Old men forget; yet shall not all forget,
But they'll remember, † with advantages,
What feats they did that day. Then shall our names,

---

* *By* Jove] The king prays like a christian, and swears like a heathen.

† *With advantages.*] Old men, notwithstanding the natural forgetfulness of age, shall remember *their feats of this day*, and remember to tell them *with advantage*. Age is commonly boastful, and inclined to magnify past acts and past times.

KING HENRY V.

Familiar in their mouth as houshold words,
Harry the King, *Bedford*, and *Exeter*,
Warwick and *Talbot*, *Salisbury* and *Glo'ster*,
Be in their flowing cups freshly remember'd.
This story shall the good man teach his son,
And *Crispin Crispian* shall ne'er go by,
" From this day to the ending of the world,
But we in it shall be remembered,
We few, we happy few, we band of brothers;
For he, to-day that sheds his blood with me,
Shall be my brother; be he ne'er so vile,
This day shall * gentle his condition.
And gentlemen in *England*, now a-bed,
Shall think themselves accurs'd, they were not here;
And hold their manhoods cheap, while any speaks,
That fought with us upon St. *Crispian's* day †.

Enter Salisbury.

Sal. My sov'reign Lord, bestow yourself with speed:
The *French* are ⁷ bravely in their battles set,
And will with all expedience charge on us.

K. Henry. All things are ready, if our minds be so.

West. Perish the man, whose mind is backward
  now!

K. Henry. Thou dost not wish more help from *England*, cousin?

West. God's will, my Liege. 'Would you and I alone
Without more help could fight this royal battle!

---

⁶ *From this day to the ending.*]
It may be observed that we are apt to promise to ourselves a more lasting memory than the changing state of human things admits. This prediction is not verified; the feast of *Crispin* passes by without any mention of *Agincourt*. Late events obliterate the former: the civil wars have left in this nation scarcely any tradition of more ancient history.

* *Gentle his condition.*] This day shall advance him to the rank of a gentleman.

† *Upon St.* Crispian's *day.*] This speech, like many others of the declamatory kind, is too long. Had it been contracted to about half the number of lines, it might have gained force, and lost none of the sentiments.

⁷ *Bravely* is *splendidly, ostentatiously.*

K. *Henry.*

KING HENRY V.

K. Henry. Why, now thou haſt unwiſh'd five thou-
    ſand men [8],
Which likes me better than to wiſh us one.
—You know your places. God be with you all!

SCENE IX.

A Tucket ſounds. Enter Mountjoy.

Mount. Once more I come to know of thee, King
    Harry,
If for thy ranſom thou wilt now compound,
Before thy moſt aſſured over-throw;
For, certainly, thou art ſo near the gulf,
Thou needs muſt be englutted. Thus, in mercy,
The Conſtable deſires thee. Thou wilt mind
Thy followers of repentance, that their ſouls
May make a peaceful and a ſweet retire
From off theſe fields, where, wretches, their poor bodies
Muſt lie and feſter.

K. Henry. Who hath ſent thee now?

Mount. The Conſtable of *France.*

K. Henry. I pray thee, bear my former anſwer back.
Bid them atchieve me, and then ſell my bones.
Good God! why ſhould they mock poor fellows thus?
The man, that once did ſell the lion's ſkin
While the beaſt liv'd, was kill'd with hunting him.
And many of our bodies ſhall, no doubt,
Find native graves; upon the which, I truſt,
Shall witneſs live in braſs of this day's work.
And thoſe that leave their valiant bones in *France,*
Dying like men, tho' buried in your dunghills,
They ſhall be fam'd; for there the ſun ſhall greet them,
And draw their honours reeking up to heav'n,

[8] *Thou haſt unwiſh'd five thou-ſand men.*] By wiſhing only thyſelf and me, thou haſt wiſhed five thouſand men away. *Shakeſpeare* never thinks on ſuch trifles as numbers. In the laſt ſcene the *French* are ſaid to be *full threeſcore thouſand,* which *Exeter* declares to be *five to one*; but, by the King's account, they are twelve to one.

452   KING HENRY V.

Leaving their earthly parts to choak your clime,
The smell whereof shall breed a plague in *France.*
⁹ Mark then a bounding valour in our *English:*
That being dead, like to the bullet's grazing,
Breaks out into a second course of mischief,
¹ Killing in relapse of mortality.
Let me speak proudly; tell the Constable,
We are but ² warriors for the working day:
Our gayness, and our guilt, are all be-smirch'd
With rainy marching in the painful field.
There's not a piece of feather in our host,
Good argument, I hope, we will not fly,
And time hath worn us into slovenry.
But, by the mass, our hearts are in the trim:
And my poor soldiers tell me, yet ere night
They'll be in fresher robes; or they will pluck
The gay new coats o'er the *French* soldiers' heads,
And turn them out of service. If they do,
As, if God please, they shall, my ransom them
Will soon be levy'd. Herald, save thy labour,
Come thou no more, for ransom, gentle herald;
They shall have none, I swear, but these my joints:

⁶ *Mark then* abounding *Valour in our* English.] Thus the Old *Folio's.* The *Quarto's,* more erroneously still,

Mark then aboundant——
Mr. *Pope* degraded the Passage in both his Editions, because, I presume, he did not understand it. I have reformed the Text, and the Allusion is exceedingly beautiful; comparing the Revival of the *English* Valour to the *rebounding* of a Cannon-ball.
                        THEOBALD.

¹ *Killing in relapse of mortality.*] What it is *to kill in relapse of mortality,* I do not know. I suspect that it should be read,

Killing in reliques of mortality.

That is, continuing to *kill* when they are the *reliques* that *death* has left behind it.

That the allusion is, as Mr. *Theobald* thinks, *exceedingly beautiful,* I am afraid few readers will discover. The *valour* of a putrid body, that destroys by the stench, is one of the thoughts that do no great honour to the poet. Perhaps from this putrid valour *Dryden* might borrow the posthumous empire of Don *Sebastian,* who was to reign wheresoever his atoms should be scattered.

² *Warriors for the working day.*] We are soldiers but coarsely dressed, we have not on our holiday apparel.

Which

KING HENRY V.

Which if they have, as I will leave 'em them
Shall yield them little. Tell the Constable.
Mount. I shall King *Harry*, and so fare thee well.
Thou never shall hear herald any more. [*Exit.*
  K. *Henry.* I fear, thou'lt once more come again for
Ransom.

Enter York.

York. My Lord, most humbly on my knee I beg
The leading of the vaward.
  K. *Henry.* Take it brave *York*; now, soldiers, march
    away.
And how thou pleasest, God, dispose the day! [*Exeunt.*

SCENE X.

The Field of Battle.

Alarm, Excursions. Enter Pistol, *French soldier,
and Boy.*

Pist. YIELD, cur.
  Fr. Sol. *Je pense, que vous estes le gentil-
    homme de bonne qualité.*
  Pist. Quality, calmy, custure me, art thou a gen-
tleman? [3] what is thy name? discuss.
  Fr. Sol. *O Seigneur Dieu!*
  Pist. O, Signieur Dewe should be a gentleman.
Perpend my words, O Signieur Dewe, and mark;
O Signieur Dewe, [4] thou diest on point of fox,

---

[3] *Quality, CALMY, CUSTURE me, art thou a gntl man?*] We should read this nonsense thus,
  Quality, CALITY—CONSTRUE *me, are thou a gentl man?* *i. e.* tell me, let me understand whether thou be'st a gentleman.
  WARBURTON.

[4] *Thou diest on point of fox*] *Point of fox* is an expression which, if the editors understood it, they should have explained. I suppose we may better read,

  On point of faulchion.

G g 3   except

454 KING HENRY V.

Except, O Signieur, thou do give to me
Egregious ransom.

Fr. Sol. *O, prennez misericorde, ayez pitié de moy.*

Pist. Moy shall not serve, I will have forty moys;
[5] For I will fetch thy rym out at thy throat,
In drops of crimson blood.

Fr. Sol. *Est-il impossible d'eschapper la force de ton bras?*

Pist. Brass, cur.
Thou damned and luxurious mountain Goat,
Offer'st me brass?

Fr. Sol. *O pardonnez moy.*

Pist. Say'st thou me so? is that a ton of [6] moys?
Come hither, Boy, ask me this slave in *French*,
What is his name?

Boy. *Escoutez, comment estes vous appellé?*

Fr. Sol. *Monsieur le Fer.*

Boy. He says his name is Mr. *Fer.*

Pist. Mr. *Fer!* I'll fer him, and ferk him, and ferret him: discuss the same in *French* unto him.

Boy. I do not know the *French* for *fer*, and *ferret*, and *ferk*.

Pist. Bid him prepare, for I will cut his throat.

Fr. Sol. *Que dit-il, Monsieur?*

Boy. *Il me commande de vous dire que vous vous teniez prest; car ce soldat icy est disposé tout à cette heure de couper vostre gorge.*

Pist. Owy, cuppelle gorg, paramafoy, pesant,
Unless thou give me crowns, brave crowns,
Or mangled shalt thou be by this my sword.

Fr. Sol. *O, je vous supplie pour l'amour de Dieu, me pardonner; je suis gentilhomme de bonne maison, gardez ma vie, & je vous donneray deux cent escus.*

[5] For *I will fetch thy* RYM] we should read,
OR *I will fetch thy* RANSOM *out of thy throat.* WARB.
I know not what to do with *rym.* The measure gives reason to suppose that it stands for some monosyllable; and besides, *ransome* is a word not likely to have been corrupted,

[6] *Moy* is a piece of money, whence *Moi d'or,* or *moi* of gold.

Pist.

Pist. What are his words?

Boy. He prays you to save his life, he is a gentleman of a good house, and for his ransom he will give you two hundred crowns.

Pist. Tell him, my fury shall abate, and I
The Crowns will take.

Fr. Sol. Petit Monsieur, que dit-il?

Boy. Encore qu'il est contre son jurement, de pardonner aucun prisonnier, neantmoins pour les escus que vous l'avez promettes, il est content de vous donner la liberté, le franchisement.

Fr. Sol. Sur mes genoux je vous donne mille remerciemens, & je m' estime heureux que je suis tombé entre les mains d'un Chevalier, je pense, le plus brave, valiant, & tres estimé Signeur d'Angleterre.

Pist. Expound unto me, boy.

Boy. He gives you upon his knees a thousand thanks and esteems himself happy that he hath fall'n into the hands of one, as he thinks, the most brave, valorous, and thrice-worthy Signieur of *England*.

Pist. As I suck blood, I will some mercy shew. Follow me, cur.

Boy. Suivez le grand capitain.

[*Ex.* Pist. *and* Fr. Sol.

I did never know so full a voice issue from so empty a heart; but the saying is true, The empty vessel makes the greatest sound. *Bardolph* and *Nim* had ten times more valour than this roaring devil i' th' old play [7]; every one may pare his nails with a wooden dagger: yet they are both hang'd; and so would this be, if he durst steal any thing advent'rously. I must stay with the lacqueys, with the luggage of our camp; the *French* might have a good prey of us, if he knew of it: for there is none to guard it but boys. [*Exit.*

---

[7] In modern puppet-shows, which seem to be copied from the old farces, *Punch* sometimes fights the devil and always overcomes him. I suppose the *Vice* of the old farce, to whom *Punch* succeeds, used to fight the devil with a wooden dagger.

SCENE XI.

Another part of the Field of Battle.

Enter Constable, Orleans, Bourbon, Dauphin, *and* Rambures.

Con. O Diable!

Orl. O Signeur! le jour est perdu, tout est perdu.

Dau. Mort de ma vie! all is confounded, all!
Reproach and everlasting shame
Sits mocking in our plumes. [*A short alarm.*
O *meschante fortune!*——do not run away.

Con. Why, all our ranks are broke.

Dau. O perdurable shame! let's stab ourselves.
Be these the wretches, that we play'd at dice for?

Orl. Is this the King we sent to for his ransom?

Bour. Shame, and eternal shame, nothing but shame!
[a] Let us die, instant—Once more back again;
The man, that will not follow *Bourbon* now,
Let him go hence, and with his cap in hand
Like a base pander hold the chamber door,
Whilst by a slave, no gentler than a dog,
His fairest daughter is contaminated.

Con. Disorder, that hath spoil'd us, friend us now!
Let us on heaps go offer up our lives.

Orl. We are enow, yet living in the field,
To smother up the *English* in our throngs;
If any order might be thought upon.

Bour. The devil take order now! I'll to the throng;
Let life be short, else shame will be too long. [*Exeunt.*

---

[a] *Let us die, instant: Once more back again;*] This Verse, which is quite left out in Mr. *Pope*'s Editions, stands imperfect in the first *Folio.* By the addition of a Syllable, I think, I have retriev'd the Poet's Sense. It is thus in the Old Copy;
Let us die in once more back again. THEOBALD.

KING HENRY V.

SCENE XII.

Alarm. Enter the King and his train, with prisoners.

K. Henry. Well have we done, thrice valiant countrymen.
But all's not done; the *French* yet keep the field.
   Exe. The Duke of *York* commends him to your Majesty.
   K. Henry. Lives he, good uncle? thrice within this hour
I saw him down, thrice up again, and fighting,
From helmet to the spur all bleeding o'er.
   Exe. In which array, brave soldier, doth he lie,
Larding the plain; and by his bloody side,
Yoak-fellow to his honour-owing wounds,
The noble Earl of *Suffolk* also lies.
Suffolk first dy'd, and *York*, all haggled over,
Comes to him where in gore he lay insteep'd,
And takes him by the beard; kisses the gashes,
That bloodily did yawn upon his face,
And cries aloud, " tarry, my cousin *Suffolk*,
" My soul shall thine keep company to heav'n:
" Tarry, sweet soul, for mine, then fly a-breast:
" As in this glorious and well-foughten field
" We kept together in our chivalry."
Upon these words I came, and cheer'd him up;
He smil'd me in the face, gave me his hand,
And with a feeble gripe, says, " dear my Lord,
" Commend my service to my Sovereign."
So did he turn, and over *Suffolk's* neck
He threw his wounded arm, and kist his lips,
And so espous'd to death, with blood he seal'd
A testament of noble ending love.
The pretty and sweet manner of it forc'd
Those waters from me, which I would have stop'd;
But I had not so much of man in me,
But all my mother came into mine eyes,
And gave me up to tears.
                                 K. Henry.

458 KING HENRY V.

K. Henry. I blame you not;
⁹ For, hearing this, I must perforce compound
With mistful eyes, or they will issue too.   [*Alarm.*
But, hark, what new alarum is this same?
The *French* have re-inforc'd their scatter'd men:
Then every soldier kill his prisoners.
Give the word through.   [*Exeunt.*

¹SCENE XIII.

Alarms continued; after which, Enter Fluellen *and* Gower.

Flu. ² Kill the poys and the luggage! 'tis expresly against the law of arms; 'tis as arrant a piece of
Knavery,

---

⁹ *For, hearing this, I must perforce compound*
With mixtful *eyes,*——] The poet must have wrote, *mistful:* i. e. just ready to over-run with tears. The word he took from his observation of Nature: for just before the bursting out of tears the eyes grow dim as if in a mist.   WARBURTON.

¹ SCENE XIII.] Here, in the other editions, they begin the fourth act, very absurdly, since both the place and time evidently continue, and the words of *Fluellen* immediately follow those of the King just before.   POPE.

² *Kill the Poyes and the luggage! 'tis expresly against the Law of Arms;*] In the Old *Folio's,* the 4th Act is made to begin here. But as the Matter of the *Chorus,* which is to come betwixt the 4th and 5th Acts, will by no means fort with the *Scenery* that here follows; I have chose to fall in with the other Regulation. Mr. *Pope* gives a Reason, why this Scene should be connective to the preceding Scene; but his Reason, according to Custom, is a mistaken one. *The words of* Fluellen (he says,) *immediately follow those of the King just before.* The King's last Words, at his going off, were;
Then ev'ry Soldier kill his Prisoners:
Give the Word through.
Now Mr. *Pope* must very accurately suppose, that *Fluellen* overhears this: and that by replying: *Kill the Poyes, and the luggage; 'tis expresly against the Law of Arms;*—— he is condemning the King's Order, as against martial Discipline. But this is a most absurd Supposition. *Fluellen* neither overhears, nor replies to, what the King had said: nor has *kill the Poyes and the Luggage* any reference to the Soldiers' killing their Prisoners. Nay, on the contrary (as there is no *Interval* of an *Act* here) there must be some little Pause betwixt the King's going off, and *Fluellen's*
Entring

KING HENRY V.

Knavery, mark you now, as can be desir'd in your conscience now, is it not?

Gow. 'Tis certain, there's not a boy left alive; and the cowardly rascals, that ran away from the battle, have done this slaughter. Besides, they have burn'd or carried away all that was in the King's tent; wherefore the King most worthily has caus'd every soldier to cut his prisoner's throat. O 'tis a gallant King!

Flu. I, he was porn at *Monmouth*, captain *Gower*; what call you the town's name, where *Alexander* the pig, was born?

Gow. Alexander the great.

Flu. Why, I pray you, is not pig, great? the pig, or the great, or the mighty, or the huge, or the magnanimous, are all one reckonings, save the phrase is a little variations.

Gow. I think, *Alexander* the great was born in *Macedon*; his father was called *Philip* of *Macedon*, as I take it.

Flu. I think, it is in *Macedon* where *Alexander* is porn: I tell you, captain, if you look in the maps of the orld, I warrant, that you sall find, in the compa-

---

Entring (and therefore I have said, *Alarms continued*); for we find by *Gower's* first Speech, that the Soldiers had already cut their Prisoners throats, which required some Time to do. The Matter is this. The Baggage, during the Battle (as K. *Henry* had no Men to spare) was guarded only by boys and Lacqueys; which some *French* Runaways getting notice of, they came down upon the *English* Camp-boys, whom they kill'd, and plunder'd and burn'd the Baggage: in Resentment of which Villany it was, that the King, contrary to his wonted Lenity, order'd all Prisoners Throats to be cut. And to this Villany of the *French* Run-aways *Fluellen* is alluding, when he says, *Kill the Poyes and the Luggage*. The Fact is set out (as Mr. *Pope* might have observ'd) both by *Hall* and *Holingshead*   THEOBALD.

Unhappily the King gives one reason for his order to kill the prisoners, and *Gower* another. The King killed his prisoners because he expected another battle, and he had not men sufficient to guard one army and fight another. *Gower* declares that the *gallant king* has *worthily* ordered the prisoners to be destroyed, because the luggage was plundered, and the boys were slain.

risons

460   KING HENRY V.

risons between *Macedon* and *Monmouth*, that the situations, look you, is both alike. There is a river in *Macedon*, there is also moreover a river at *Monmouth*; it is call'd *Wye* at *Monmouth*, but it is out of my prains, what is the name of the other river; but it is all one, 'tis as like as my fingers to my fingers, and there is Salmons in both. If you mark *Alexander's* life well, *Harry* of *Monmouth's* life is come after it indifferent well; for there is figures in all things. *Alexander*, God knows and you know, in his rages, and his furies, and his wraths, and his cholers, and his moods, and his displeasures, and his indignations, and also being a little intoxicates in his prains, did in his ales and his angers, look you, kill his best friend *Clytus*.

Gow. Our King is not like him in that, he never kill'd any of his friends.

Flu. It is not well done, mark you now, to take the tales out of my mouth, ere it is made and finish'd. I speak but in figures, and comparisons of it. As *Alexander* kill'd his friend *Clytus*, being in his ales and his cups; so also *Harry Monmouth*, being in his right wits and his good judgments, turn'd away * the fat Knight with the great belly-doublet. He was full of jests and gypes, and knaveries, and mocks; I have forgot his name.

Gow. Sir *John Falstaff*.

Flu. That is he. I tell you, there is good men porn at *Monmouth*.

Gow. Here comes his Majesty.

SCENE XIV.

Alarm. Enter King Henry, *with* Bourbon *and other prisoners; Lords and Attendants. Flourish.*

K. Henry. I was not angry since I came to *France*, Until this instant. Take a trumpet, herald,

---

* *The fat knight*] This is the last time that *Falstaff* can make sport. The poet was loath to party with him, and has continued his memory as long as he could.

Ride

KING HENRY V. 461

Ride thou unto the horsemen on yon hill.
If they will fight with us, bid them come down,
Or void the field, they do offend our sight;
If they'll do neither, we will come to them;
And make them sker away, as swift as stones
Enforced from the old *Assyrian* slings:
* Besides, we'll cut the throats of those we have;
And not a man of them, that we shall take,
Shall taste our mercy. Go, and tell them so.

Enter Mountjoy.

Exe. Here comes the herald of the *French*, my Liege.

Glou. His eyes are humbler than they us'd to be.

K. Henry. How now, what means their herald?
Know'st thou not,
That I have fin'd these bones of mine for ransom?
Com'st thou again for ransom?

Mount. No, great King:
I come to thee for charitable licence
That we may wander o'er this bloody field,
To book our dead, and then to bury them;
To sort our nobles from our common men;
For many of our Princes, woe the while!
Lie drown'd, and soak'd in mercenary blood;
So do our vulgar drench their peasant limbs
In blood of Princes, while their wounded steeds
Fret fet-lock deep in gore, and with wild rage
Yerk out their armed heels at their dead masters,

---

* *Besides, we'll cut the throats,* &c.] The king is in a very bloody disposition. He has already cut the throats of his prisoners, and threatens now to cut them again. No haste of composition could produce such negligence; neither was this play, which is the second draught of the same design, written in haste. There must be some dislocation of the scenes. If we place these lines at the beginning of the twelfth scene, the absurdity will be removed, and the action will proceed in a regular series. This transposition might easily happen in copies written for the players. Yet it must not be concealed, that in the imperfect play of 1608 the order of the scenes is the same as here.

Killing

Killing them twice. O, give us leave, great King,
To view the field in safety, and difpofe
Of their dead bodies.

K. Henry. I tell thee truly, herald,
I know not, if the day be ours or no;
For yet a many of your horfemen peer,
And gallop o'er the field.

Mount. The day is yours.

K. Henry. Praifed be God, and not our ftrength,
for it!
What is this caftle call'd, that ftands hard by?

Mount. They call it *Agincourt*.

K. Henry. Then call we this the field of *Agincourt*,
Fought on the day of *Crifpin Crifpianus*.

Flu. Your grandfather of famous memory, an't
pleafe your Majefty, and your great uncle *Edward* the
plack Prince of *Wales*, as I have read in the chronicles,
fought a moft prave pattle here in *France*.

K. Henry. They did, *Fluellen*.

Flu. Your Majefty fays very true. If your Majefties
is remember'd of it, the *Welfhmen* did good fervice in
a garden where Leeks did grow, wearing Leeks in their
Monmouth caps, which your Majefty knows to this
hour is an honourable padge of the fervice; and I do
believe your Majefty takes no fcorn to wear the Leek
upon St. *Tavee's* day.

K. Henry. I wear it for a memorable honour:
For I am *Welfh*, you know, good countryman.

Flu. All the water in *Wye* cannot wafh your Majefty's
Welfh plood out of your pody, I can tell you that; God
plefs and preferve it, as long as it pleafes his grace
and his majefty too.

K. Henry Thanks, good my countryman.

Flu. By Jefhu, I am your Majefty's countryman, I
care not who know it; I will confefs it to all the orld;
I need not be afhamed of your Majefty, praifed be
God, fo long as your Majefty is an honeft man.

K. Henry. God keep me fo!

Enter

KING HENRY V.   463
Enter Williams.
Our hearlds go with him.
[*Exeunt Heralds, with* Mountjoy.
Bring me juft notice of the numbers dead
On both our parts——Call yonder fellow hither.

SCENE XV.

Exe. Soldier, you muft come to the King.

K. Henry. Soldier, why wear'ft thou that glove in thy cap?

Will. A'nt pleafe your Majefty, 'tis the gage of one that I fhould fight withàl, if he be alive.

K. Henry. An *Englifhman?*

Will. An't pleafe your Majefty, a rafcal that fwagger'd with me laft night; who, if alive, and if ever he dare to challenge this glove, I have fworn to take him a box o'th' ear; or if I can fee my glove in his cap, which he fwore as he was a foldier he would wear, if alive, I will ftrike it out foundly.

K. Henry. What think you, captain *Fluellen*, is it fit this foldier keep his oath?

Flu. He is a craven and a villain elfe, an't pleafe your Majefty, in my confcience.

K. Henry. It may be, his enemy is a gentleman of
* great fort, † quite from the anfwer of his degree.

Flu. Though he be as good a gentleman as the devil is, as *Lucifer* and *Belzebub* himfelf, it is neceffary, look your Grace, that he keep his vow and his oath. If he be perjur'd, fee you now, his reputation is as arrant a villain and a jackfawce, as eyer his black fhoe trod upon God's ground and his earth, in my confcience law.

K. Henry. Then keep thy vow, firrah, when thou meet'ft the fellow.

Will. So I will, my Liege, as I live.

* *Great fort.*] High rank. So in the ballad of *Jane Shore*, *Lords and ladies of* great fort.
† *Quite from the anfwer of his degree.*] A man of fuch ftation as is not bound to hazard his perfon in *anfwer* to a challenge from one of the foldier's *low degree.*

K. Henry.

K. Henry. Who ſerv'ſt thou under?

Will. Under captain *Gower*, my Liege.

Flu. Gower is a good captain, and is good knowledge and literature in the wars.

K. Henry. Call him hither to me, ſoldier.

Will. I will, my Liege. [*Exit.*

K. Henry. Here, *Fluellen*, wear thou this favour for me, and ſtick it in thy cap. When *Alanſon* and myſelf were down together, I pluck'd this glove from his helm; if any man challenge this, he is a friend to *Alanſon* and an enemy to our perſon; if thou encounter any ſuch, apprehend him if thou doſt love me.

Flu. Your Grace does me as great honours as can be deſir'd in the hearts of his ſubjects. I would fain ſee the man, that has but two legs, that ſhall find himſelf agriev'd at this glove; that is all; but I would fain ſee it once, an pleaſe God of his grace that I might ſee.

K. Henry. Know'ſt thou *Gower?*

Flu. He is my dear friend, and pleaſe you.

K. Henry. Pray thee, go ſeek him, and bring him to my tent.

Flu. I will fetch him. [*Exit.*

K. Henry. My Lord of *Warwick* and my brother *Glo'ſter,*

Follow *Fluellen* cloſely at the heels:
The glove, which I have given him for a favour,
May, haply, purchaſe him a box o'th' ear.
It is the ſoldier's; I by bargain ſhould
Wear it myſelf. Follow, good couſin *Warwick:*
If that the ſoldier ſtrike him, as, I judge
By his blunt bearing, he will keep his word;
Some ſudden miſchief may ariſe of it:
For I do know *Fluellen* valiant,
And, touch'd with choler, hot as gun-powder;
And quickly he'll return an injury.
Follow; and ſee, there be no harm between them.
Come you with us, uncle of *Exeter.* [*Exeunt.*

SCENE

KING HENRY V.

SCENE XVI.

Before King HENRY's *Pavilion.*

Enter Gower *and* Williams.

Will. I Warrant, it is to knight you, captain.

Enter Fluellen.

Flu. God's will and his pleasure.—Captain, I beseech you now come apace to the King; there is more good toward you, peradventure, than is in your knowledge to dream of.
Will. Sir, Know you this glove?
Flu. Know the glove? I know, the glove is a glove.
Will. I know this, and thus I challenge it.
                                [*Strikes him.*
Flu. 'Sblud, an arrant traitor as any's in the universal orld, in *France* or in *England.*
Gower. How now, Sir? you villain!
Will. Do you think I'll be forsworn?
Flu. Stand away, captain *Gower*, I will give treason his payment into plows, I warrant you.
Will. I am no traitor.
Flu. That's a lye in thy throat. I charge you in his Majesty's name apprehend him, he's a friend of the Duke of *Alanson's.*

Enter Warwick *and* Gloucester.

War. How now, how now, what's the matter?
Flu. My Lord of *Warwick*, here is, praised be God for it, a most contagious treason come to light, look you, as you shall desire in a summer's day. Here is his Majesty.

Enter King Henry, *and* Exeter.

K. Henry. How now, what's the matter?

Flu. My Liege, here is a villain and a traitor, that, look your Grace, has struck the glove, which your Majesty is take out of the helmet of *Alanson*.

Will. My Liege, this was my glove, here is the fellow of it, and he, that I gave it to in change, promis'd to wear it in his cap; I promis'd to strike him, if he did; I met this man with my glove in his cap, and I have been as good as my word.

Flu. Your Majesty hear now, saving your Majesty's manhood, what an arrant, rascally, beggarly, lowsy, knave it is. I hope, your Majesty is pear me testimonies, and witnesses, and avouchments, that this is the glove of *Alanson* that your Majesty is give me, in your conscience now.

K. Henry. * Give me thy glove, soldier; look, here is the fellow of it. 'Twas me, indeed, thou promised'st to strike, and thou hast given me most bitter terms.

Flu. An please your Majesty, let his neck answer for it, if there is any martial law in the orld.

K. Henry. How canst thou make me satisfaction?

Will. All Offences, my Lord, come from the heart; never came any from mine, that might offend your Majesty.

K. Henry. It was ourself thou didst abuse.

Will. Your Majesty came not like yourself; you appear'd to me, but as a common man; witness the night, your garments, your lowliness; and what your Highness suffer'd under that shape, I beseech you, take it for your fault and not mine; for had you been as I took you for, I made no offence; therefore, I beseech your Highness, pardon me.

---

* *Give me thy glove, —— look, here is the fellow of it*] It must be, *give me my glove,* for of the soldier's glove the king had not the fellow.

K. Henry.

K. Henry. Here, uncle *Exeter*, fill this glove with crowns,
And give it to this fellow. Keep it, fellow;
And wear it for an honour in thy cap,
Till I do challenge it. Give him the Crowns.
And, captain, you muſt needs be friends with him.

Flu. By this day and this light, the fellow has mettle enough in his pelly. Hold there is twelve pence for you; and I pray you to ſerve God, and keep you out of prawls and prabbles, and quarrels and diſſentions, and, I warrant you, it is the better for you.

Will. I will none of your money.

Flu. It is with a good will; I can tell you, it will ſerve you to mend your ſhoes. Come, wherefore ſhould you be ſo paſhful; your ſhoes are not ſo good. 'Tis a good filling, I warrant you, or I will change it.

SCENE XVII.
Enter Herald.

K. Henry. Now, *Herald*, are the dead number'd?

Her. Here is the number of the ſlaughter'd *French*.

K. Henry. What priſoners of good ſort are taken, uncle?

Exe. [3] *Charles* Duke of *Orleans*, nephew to the King;
John Duke of *Bourbon*, and Lord *Bouchiqualt*:
Of other Lords, and Barons, Knights, and 'Squires,
Full fifteen hundred, beſides common men.

K. Henry. This note doth tell me of ten thouſand *French*
Slain in the field; of Princes in this number,
And nobles bearing banners, there lie dead
One hundred twenty-ſix; added to theſe,
Of Knights, Eſquire, and gallant Gentlemen,
Eight thouſand and four hundred; of the which,
Five hundred were but yeſterday dubb'd Knights;

---
[3] *Charles Duke of Orleans, &c.*] This liſt is copied from *Hali.* POPE.

So that in these ten thousand they have lost,
There are but sixteen hundred * mercenaries:
The rest are Princes, Barons, Lords, Knights, 'Squires,
And gentlemen of blood and quality.
The names of those their nobles, that lie dead,
Charles Delabreth, high constable of *France:*
Jaques Chatilion, admiral of *France*;
The master of the cross-bows, Lord *Rambures*;
Great master of *France*, the brave Sir *Guichard*
    Dauphin;
John Duke of *Alanson*, *Anthony* Duke of *Brabant*
The brother to the Duke of *Burgundy*,
And *Edward* Duke of *Bar:* Of lusty Earls,
Grandpree and *Roussie*, *Faulconbridge* and *Foyes*,
Beaumont and *Marle*, *Vaudemont* and *Lastrale*.
Here was a royal fellowship of death!
Where is the number of our *English* dead?

  Exe. *Edward* the Duke of *York*, the Earl of *Suf-*
    folk,
Sir *Richard Ketley*, *Davy Gam*, Esquire;
None else of name; and of all other men,
But five and twenty.

  K. Henry. O God, thy arm was here!
And not to us, but to thy arm alone,
Ascribe we all. When, without stratagem,
But in plain shock and even play of battle,
Was ever known so great, and little loss,
On one part, and on th' other?—Take it, God,
For it is only thine.

  Ex. 'Tis wonderful!

  K. Henry. Come, go we in procession to the village:
And be it death proclaimed through our host,
To boast of this, or take that praise from God,
Which is his only.

    * *Mercenaries* are in this place own charge, in consequence of
common soldiers, or *hired soldiers*. their tenures.
The gentlemen served at their

Flu.

Flu. Is it not lawful, an pleafe your Majefty to tell how many is kill'd?

K. Henry. Yes, captain; but with this acknowledgement,
That God fought for us.

Flu. Yes, my confcience, he did us great good.

K. Henry. Do we all holy rites [5];
Let there be fung *Non nobis*, and *Te Deum:*
The dead with charity enclos'd in clay;
And then to *Calais*; and to *England* then;
Where ne'er from *France* arriv'd more happy men.
[*Exeunt.*

ACT V. SCENE I.

Enter CHORUS.

Chorus. VOUCHSAFE, to thofe that have not
    read the ftory,
That I may prompt them; and to fuch as have,
I humbly pray them to admit th' excufe
Of time, of numbers, and due courfe of things,
Which cannot in their huge and proper life
Be here prefented. Now we bear the King
Tow'rd *Calais*: grant him there; and there being feen,
Heave him away upon your winged thoughts
Athwart the fea. Behold, the *Englifh* beach
Pales in the flood with men, with wives and boys,
Whofe fhouts and claps out-voice the deep-mouth'd
  fea;

---

[5] *Do we all holy rites;* &c.] The king (fay the chroniclers) caufed the Pfalm, *In exitu Ifrael de Ægypto* (in which, according to the vulgate, is included the Pfalm, *Non nobis, Domine,* &c.) to be fung after the victory.
      Pope.
Which,

KING HENRY V.

Which, like a mighty [6] whiffler 'fore the King,
Seems to prepare his way. So let him land,
And solemnly see him set on to *London*.
So swift a pace hath thought, that even now
You may imagine him upon *Black-heath*,
Where that his Lords desire him to have borne
His bruised helmet, and his bended sword,
Before him through the city; he forbids it;
Being free from vainness and self-glorious pride,
[7] Giving full trophy, signal, and ostent,
Quite from himself to God. But now behold,
In the quick forge and working house of thought,
How *London* doth pour out her citizens;
The Mayor and all his brethren in best sort,
[8] Like to the senators of antique *Rome*,
With the *Plebeians* swarming at their heels,
Go forth and fetch their conqu'ring *Cæsar* in.
As by a lower but by loving [9] likelihood,

Were

[6] *Whiffler.*] An officer who walks first in processions, or before persons in high stations, on occasions of ceremony. The name is still retained in *London*, and there is an officer so called that walks before their companies at times of publick solemnity. It seems a corruption from the *French* Word *Huissier*.
HANMER.

[7] *Giving full trophy.*] Transferring all the honours of conquest, all trophies, tokens, and shews, from himself to God.

[8] *Like to the senators of antique Rome.*] This is a very extraordinary compliment to the *City*. But he ever declines all general satire on them; and in the epilogue to *Henry* VIII. he hints with disapprobation on his contemporary poets who were accustomed to abuse them. Indeed his satire is very rarely partial or licentious. WARBURTON.

[9] *Likelihood,*] *Likelihood*, for similitude. WARBURTON.

The latter editors, in hope of mending the measure of this line, have injured the sense. The folio reads as I have printed; but all the books, since revisal became fashionable, and editors have been more diligent to display themselves than to illustrate their authour, have given the line thus;

As by a low, but loving likelihood.

Thus they have destroyed the praise which the poet designed for *Essex*; for who would think himself honoured by the epithet *low?* The poet, desirous to celebrate that great man, whose popularity was then his boast, and afterwards his destruction,

KING HENRY V.

Were now the General of our gracious Empress
(As in good time he may) from *Ireland* coming,
Bringing rebellion broached on his sword;
How many would the peaceful city quit,
To welcome him? much more, and much more cause,
Did they this *Harry*. Now in *London* place him;
As yet the lamentation of the *French*
Invites the King of *England's* Stay at home:
The Emperor's coming in behalf of *France*,
To order peace between them) and omit
All the occurrences, whatever chanc'd,
Till *Harry's* back return again to *France*;
There must we bring him; and myself have play'd
The int'rim, by remembring you, 'tis past.
Then brook abridgment, and your eyes advance
After your thoughts, straight back again to *France*.

SCENE II.

The English *Camp in* France.

† *Enter* Fluellen *and* Gower.

Gower. NAY, that's right.—But why wear you
your Leek to day? St. *David's* day is past.
Flu. There is occasions and causes why and wherefore in all things. I will tell you as a friend, captain *Gower*; the rascally, scauld, beggarly, lowsy, praging knave, *Pistol*, which you and yourself and all the world know to be no petter than a fellow, look you now, of no merits; he is come to me and prings

ruction, compares him to king *Harry*; but being afraid to offend the rival courtiers, or perhaps the queen herself, he confesses that he is *lower* than a king, but would never have represented him absolutely as *low*.

¹ *We're now the General*, &c.] The Earl of *Essex* in the reign of Queen *Elizabeth*.   POPE.

* *Broached.*] Spitted; transfixed.

† *Enter* Fluellen *and* Gower.] This scene ought, in my opinion, to be concluded the fourth act, and be placed before the last chorus. There is no *English* camp in this act; the quarrel apparently happens before the return of the army to *England*, and not after so long an interval as the chorus has supplied.

me pread and falt yefterday, look you, and bid me eat my Leek. It was in a place where I could breed no contentions with him; but I will be fo pold as to wear it in my cap, 'till I fee him once again; and then I will tell him a little piece of my defires.

Enter Piftol.

Gow. Why, here he comes fwelling like a Turkycock.

Flu. 'Tis no matter for his fwelling, nor his Turkycocks. God pleffe you, aunchient *Piftol:* you fcurvy lowfy knave, God pleffe you.

Pift. Ha! art thou beldam? doft thou thirft, bafe
  Trojan,
² To have me fold up *Parca's* fatal web?
Hence!—I am qualmifh at the fmell of leek.

Flu. I pefeech you heartily, fcurvy lowfy knave, at my defires, and my requefts and my petitions, to eat, look you, this leek; becaufe, look you, you do not love it, and your affections, and your appetites, and your digeftions, does not agree with it, I would defire you to eat it.

Pift. Not for *Cadwallader* and all his Goats.

Flu. There is one Goat for you.   [*Strikes him.* Will you be fo good, fcauld knave, as eat it?

Pift. Bafe *Trojan,* thou fhalt die.

Flu. You fay very true, fcauld knave, when God's will is. I defire you to live in the mean time and eat your victuals; come, there is fauce for it—[*Strikes him.*] You call'd me yefterday Mountain-Squire, but I will make you to day a * Squire of low degree. I pray you, fall to; if you can mock a leek, you can eat a leek.

Gow. Enough, captain; you have † aftonifh'd him.

Flu. I fay, I will make him eat fome part of my leek, or I will peat his pate four days. Pite, I pray

---

² *To have me fold up,* &c.] Doft thou defire to have me put thee to death.

* *Squire of low degree.*] That is, *I will bring you to the ground.*

† *Aftonifh'd him*] That is, you have ftunned him with the blow.

you;

KING HENRY V.

you; it is good for your green wound and your ploody coxcomb.

Pift. Muft I bite?

Flu. Yes, out of doubt, and out of queftions too, and ambiguities.

Pift. By this leek, I will moft horribly revenge; I [3] eat and eat I fwear——

Flu. Eat, I pray you. Will you have fome more fauce to your leek? there is not enough leek to fwear by.

Pift. Quiet thy cudgel; thou doft fee, I eat.

Flu. Much good do you, fcauld knave, heartily. Nay, pray you throw none away, the fkin is good for your proken coxcomb. When you take occafions to fee leeks hereafter, I pray you, mock at 'em. That's all.

Pift. Good.

Flu. Ay, leeks is good. Hold you, there is a groat to heal your pate.

Pift. Me a groat!

Flu. Yes, verily, and in truth, you fhall take it, or I have another leek in my pocket, which you fhall eat.

Pift. I take thy groat in earneft of revenge.

Flu. If I owe you any thing, I will pay you in cudgels; you fhall be a woodmonger, and buy nothing of me but cudgels; God pe wi' you, and keep you, and heal your pate. [*Exit.*

Pift. All hell fhall ftir for this.

Gow. Go, go, you are a counterfeit cowardly knave. Will you mock at an ancient tradition, began upon an honourable refpect, and worn as a memorable trophy of predeceas'd valour, and dare not avouch in your

---

[3] *I eat and eat I fwear*] Thus the firft folio, for which the later editors have put, *I eat and fwear*. We fhould read, I fuppofe, in the frigid tumour of *Piftol's* dialect,

I eat and eke I fwear.

deeds

474 KING HENRY V.

deeds any of your words? I have seen you gleeking and galling at this gentleman twice or thrice. You thought, becauſe he could not ſpeak *Engliſh* in the native garb, he could not therefore handle an *Engliſh* cudgel; you find 'tis otherwiſe; and henceforth let a *Welſh*-correction teach you a good *Engliſh* condition. Fare you well. [*Exit.*

Piſt. Doth [4] fortune play the hufwife with me now?
[*] News have I, that my *Dol* is dead i' th' ſpittle
Of malady of *France*,
And there my rendezvous is quite cut off;
Old I do wax, and from my weary limbs
Honour is cudgell'd. Well, bawd will I turn,
And ſomething lean to cut-purſe of quick hand,
To *England* will I ſteal, and there I'll ſteal;
And patches will I get unto theſe cudgell'd ſcars,
And ſwear, I got them in the *Gallia* Wars [5]. [*Exit* [6].

---

[4] *Fortune doth play the buſwife.*] That is, the *jilt. Huſwife* is here in an ill ſenſe.

[*] *News have I, that my* Dol *is dead,*] We muſt read, *my* Nell *is dead. Dol Tearſheet* was ſo little the favourite of *Piſtol* that he offered her in contempt to *Nym.* Nor would her death have cut off his rendezvous; that is, deprived him of a home. Perhaps the poet forgot his plan.

[5] In the quarto of 1608 theſe lines are read thus,
Doth fortune play the buſwife with me now?
Is honour cudgel'd from my warlike loins?
Well France farewell. News have I certainly,
That Doll is ſick of malady of France.
The wars affordeth nought, but will I trudge,
Bawd will I turn, and uſe the ſlight of hand.
To England *will I ſteal, and there I'll ſteal;*
And patches will I get unto theſe ſcars,
And ſwear I got them in the Gallia *wars.*

[6] The comick ſcenes of the hiſtory of *Henry* the fourth and fifth are now at an end, and all the comick perſonages are now diſmiſſed. *Falſtaff* and Mrs. *Quickly* are dead; *Nym* and *Bardolph* are hanged; *Gadſhill* was loſt immediately after the robbery; *Poins* and *Peto* have vaniſhed ſince, one knows not how; and *Piſtol* is now beaten into obſcurity. I believe every reader regrets their departure.

SCENE

KING HENRY V.   475

SCENE III.

The French *Court, at* Trois *in* Champaigne.

ter at one door King Henry, Exeter, Bedford, War- wick, *and other Lords;* at another, the French King, Queen *Ifabel, Princess* Catharine, *the Duke of* Bur- gundy, *and other* French.

Henry. Peace to this meeting, wherefore we are met [7].
nto our brother *France*, and to our fifter,
ealth and fair time of day; joy and good wifhes,
o our moft fairly and princely coufin *Catharine*;
nd as a branch and member of this royalty,
′ whom this great affembly is contriv'd,
′e do falute you, Duke of *Burgundy*.
nd, Princes *French*, and Peers, health to you all.
Fr. King. Right joyous are we to behold your face;
oft worthy brother *England*, fairly met!
) are you, Princes *Englifh*, every one.
Q. Ifa. So happy be the iffue, brother *England*,
f this good day, and of this gracious meeting,
s we are now glad to behold your eyes,
our eyes, which hitherto have borne in them
gainft the *French*, that met them in their bent,
he fatal balls of murdering bafilifks;
he venom of fuch looks we fairly hope
ave loft their quality, and that this day
ıall change all griefs, and quarrels into love.
K. Henry. To cry *Amen* to that, thus we appear.
Q. Ifa. You *Englifh* Princes all, I do falute you.
Burg. My duty to you both on equal love.
·reat Kings of *France* and *England*. That I've la- bour'd

[7] *Peace to this meeting, where- fore we are met.*] Peace, ·r which we are here met, be to this meeting.
Here, after the chorus, the fifth act feems naturally to begin.
With

With all my wits, my pains, and strong endeavours,
To bring your most imperial Majesties
* Unto this bar and royal interview,
Your Mightnesses on both parts can witness.
Since then my office hath so far prevail'd,
That, face to face and royal eye to eye,
You have congreeted, let it not disgrace me,
If I demand, before this royal view,
What rub or what impediment there is,
Why that the naked, poor, and mangled peace,
Dear nurse of arts, plenties and joyful births,
Should not in this best garden of the world,
Our fertile *France*, put up her lovely visage?
Alas! she hath from *France* too long been chas'd;
And all her husbandry doth lie on heaps,
Corrupting in its own fertility.
⁹ Her vine, the merry chearer of the heart,
Unpruned dies; her hedges even pleach'd,
Like * prisoners, wildly over-grown with hair,
Put forth disorder'd twigs: her fallow leas
The darnel, hemlock, and rank fumitory
Doth root upon; while that the coulter rusts,
That should deracinate such savag'ry:
The even mead, that erst brought sweetly forth
The freckled cowslip, burnet, and green clover,
Wanting the scythe, all uncorrected, rank,
Conceives by idleness; and nothing teems,
But hateful docks, rough thistles, keckfies, burs,
Losing both beauty and utility;

* *Unto this bar.*] To this *barrier*; to this place of congress.

⁹ *Her vine,* ———
Unpruned dyes:] We must read. *lyes*: For neglect of pruning does not kill the vine, but causes it to ramify immoderately, and grows wild; by which the requisite nourishment is withdrawn from its fruit. WARB.
This emendation is physically right, but poetically the vine may be well enough said to die which ceases to bear fruit.

* This image of prisoners is oddly introduced. A *prisoner* may be *overgrown with hair*, but *wildness* is contrary to the state of a prisoner. A *hedge even-pleach'd* is more properly imprisoned.

And

KING HENRY V.

And all our vineyards, fallows, meads, and hedges,
Defective in their nurtures, grow to wildness.
Even so our houses, and ourselves and children
Have lost, or do not learn for want of time,
The sciences, that should become our country;
But grow like savages, as soldiers will,
That nothing do but meditate on blood,
To swearing and stern looks, [1] diffus'd attire,
And every thing that seems unnatural.
Which to reduce into our [2] former favour,
You are assembled; and my speech intreats,
That I may know the Let, why gentle peace
Should not expel these inconveniencies;
And bless us with her former qualities.

K. Henry. If, Duke of *Burgundy*, you would the peace,
Whose want gives growth to th' imperfections
Which you have cited, you must buy that peace
With full accord to all our just demands,
Whose tenours and particular effects
You have, enschedul'd briefly, in your hands.

Burg. The King hath heard them; to the which as yet
There is no answer made.

K. Henry. Well, then the peace
Which you before so urg'd, lies in his answer.

Fr. King. I have but with a cursorary eye
O'er-glanc'd the articles; pleaseth your Grace
T'appoint some of your council presently
To sit with us, once more with better heed

---

[1] —— diffus'd *attire,*] Diffus'd, for extravagant. The military habit of those times was extremely so. Act 3. Scene 7. *Gower* says, *And what a beard of the General's cut, and a* horrid *suit of the camp, will do amongst &c. is wonderful to be thought on.* WARBURTON.

Diffus'd is so much used by our authour for *wild, irregular,* and *strange,* that in the *Merry Wives of* Windsor, he applies it to a song supposed to be sung by fairies.

[2] *Former faveur.*] Former *appearance.*

To

To re-survey them; we will suddenly
³ Pass, or accept, and peremptory answer.

K. Henry. Brother, we shall. Go, uncle *Exeter*,
And brother *Clarence*, and you, brother *Glo'ster*,
Warwick and *Huntingdon*, go with the King;
And take with you free pow'r to ratify,
Augment, or alter, as your wisdoms best
Shall see advantageable for our dignity,
Any thing in, or out of, our Demands;
And we'll consign thereto. Will you, fair sister,
Go with the Princes, or stay here with us?

Q. Isa. Our gracious brother, I will go with them;
Haply, a woman's voice may do some good,
When Articles too nicely urg'd be stood on.

K. Henry. Yet leave our cousin *Catharine* here with us.
She is our capital demand, compris'd
Within the fore-rank of our articles.

Q. Isa. She hath good leave. [*Exeunt.*

SCENE IV.

Manent King Henry, Catharine, *and a Lady.*

K. Henry. Fair *Catharine*, most fair,
Will you vouchsafe to teach a soldier terms,
Such as will enter at a lady's ear,
And plead his love-suit to her gentle heart?

Cath. Your Majesty shall mock at me, I cannot
speak your *England*.

K. Henry. O fair *Catharine*, if you will love me
soundly with your *French* heart, I will be glad to hear
you confess it brokenly with your *English* tongue. Do
you like me, *Kate*?

---

³ ——— *we will suddenly
Pass our accept, and peremptory answer.*] As the *French*
King desires more time to consider deliberately of the articles, 'tis odd and absurd for him to say absolutely, that he would accept them all. He certainly must mean, that he would at once *wave* and *decline* what he dislik'd, and consign to such as he approv'd of. Our author uses *pass* in this manner in other places: As in *King* John.

But if you fondly pass our proffer'd love. WARB.

Cath.

KING HENRY V.

Cath. *Pardonnez moy*, I cannot tell vhat is *like me*.

K. Henry An angel is like you, *Kate*, and you are like an angel.

Cath. *Que dit-il, que je suis semblable à les Anges?*

Lady. *Ouy, vrayment, (sauf voſtre grace) ainſi dit il.*

K. Henry. I said so, dear *Catharine*, and I must not blush to affirm it.

Cath. *O bon Dieu! les langues des hommes ſont pleines de tromperies.*

K. Henry What says she, fair one? that tongues of men are full of deceits?

Lady. *Ouy*, dat de tongues of de mans is be full of deceits. Dat is de Princeſs.

K. Henry. The Princeſs is the better *Engliſh* Woman. I'faith, *Kate*, my wooing is fit for thy underſtanding; I am glad thou canſt ſpeak no better *Engliſh*, for if thou couldſt, thou wouldſt find me ſuch a plain King, [4] that thou wouldſt think I had ſold my farm to buy my Crown. I know no ways to mince it in love, but directly to ſay, *I love you*; then if you urge me further than to ſay, *do you in faith?* I wear out my ſuit. Give me your anſwer; i'faith, do; and ſo clap hands and a bargain. How ſay you, lady?

Cath. *Sauf votre honneur*, me underſtand well.

K. Henry. Marry, if you would put me to verſes, or to dance for your ſake, *Kate*, why, you undid me;

---

[4] —*ſuch a plain king.*] I know not why *Shakeſpeare* now gives the king nearly ſuch a character as he made him formerly ridicule in *Percy*. This military groſsneſs and unſkilfulneſs in all the ſofter arts, does not ſuit very well with the gaieties of his youth, with the general knowledge aſcribed to him at his acceſſion, or with the contemptuous meſſage ſent him by the *Dauphin*, who repreſents him as fitter for the ball room than the field, and tells him that he is not *to revel into dutchies*, or win provinces *with a nimble galliard*. The truth is, that the poet's matter failed him in the fifth act, and he was glad to fill it up with whatever he could get; and not even *Shakeſpeare* can write well without a proper ſubject. It is a vain endeavour for the moſt ſkilful hand to cultivate barrenneſs, or to paint upon vacuity.

for

for the one I have neither words nor meafure; and for the other I have no ftrength in meafure, yet a reafonable meafure in ftrength. If I could win a lady at leap-frog, or by vaulting into my faddle with my armour on my back; under the correction of bragging be it fpoken, I fhould quickly leap into a wife. Or if I might buffet for my love, or bound my horfe for her favours, I could lay on like a butcher, and fit like a jack-a-napes, never off. But, before God, *Kate*, I cannot look greenly, nor gafp out my eloquence, nor have I cunning in proteftation; only downright oaths, which I never ufe 'till urg'd, and never break for urging. If thou canft love a fellow of this temper, *Kate*, whofe face is not worth fun-burning; that never looks in his glafs for love of any thing he fees there; let thine eye be thy cook. I fpeak plain foldier; if thou canft love me for this, take me; if not, to fay to thee that I fhall die, 'tis true; but for thy love, by the Lord, no; yet I love thee too. And while thou liv'ft, *Kate*, take a fellow of plain and uncoined conftancy,[5] for he perforce muft do thee right, becaufe he hath not the gift to woo in other places; for thefe fellows of infinite tongue, that can rhyme themfelves into ladies' favours, they do always reafon themfelves out again. What? a fpeaker is but a prater; a rhyme is but a ballad; a good leg will fall, a ftraight back will ftoop, a black beard will turn white, a curl'd pate will grow bald, a fair face will wither, a full eye will wax hollow; but a good heart, *Kate*, is the fun and the moon; or rather the fun, and not the moon; for it fhines bright and never changes, but keeps his courfe truly. If thou wouldft have fuch a one, take me;

---

[5] — *a fellow of plain and uncoined conftancy*,] i. e. a conftancy in the ingot, that hath fuffered no alloy, as all coined metal has. WARBURTON.

I believe this explanation is more ingenious than true; to *coin* is to *ftamp* and to *counterfeit*. He ufes it in both fenfes; *uncoined* conftancy fignifies *real* and *true* conftancy, *unrefined* and *unadorned*.

ke a foldier; take a King. And what fay'ſt thou then
my love? fpeak, my fair, and fairly, I pray thee.
Cath. Is it poſſible dat I ſhould love de enemy of
rance?

K. Henry. No, it is not poſſible that you ſhould love
e enemy of *France*, *Kate*; but in loving me you
ould love the friend of *France*; for I love *France* ſo
ell, that I will not part with a village of it; I will
ve it all mine; and, *Kate*, when *France* is mine and
am yours, then yours is *France*, and you are mine.
Cath. I cannot tell vhat is dat.

K. Henry. No, *Kate?* I will tell thee in *French*, *
hich, I am fure, will hang upon my tongue like a
married wife about her huſband's neck, hardly to be
ook off, *quand j' ay le poſſeſſion de France, & quand
us aves le poſſeſſion de moi* (let me fee, what then?
. *Dennis* be my ſpeed)! *donc voſtre eſt France, &
us eſtes mienne*. It is as eaſy for me, *Kate*, to conquer
e kingdom, as to fpeak fo much more *French*. I ſhall
ver move thee in *French*, unleſs it be to laugh at me.

Cath. *Sauf voſtre honneur, le François que vous par-
e, eſt meilleur que l' Anglois lequel je parle.*

K. Henry. No, faith, is't not, *Kate*; but thy ſpeak-
g of my tongue and I thine, moſt truly falſly, muſt
eds be granted to be much at one. But, *Kate*, doſt
ou underſtand fo much *Engliſh?* canſt thou love me?
Cath. I cannot tell.

K. Henry. Can any of your neighbours tell, *Kate?*
I aſk them. Come, I know thou loveſt me; and
night when you come into your cloſet, you'll queſ-
n this gentlewoman about me; and I know, *Kate*,
u will to her diſpraiſe thoſe parts in me, that you
ve with your heart; but, good *Kate*, mock me mer-
fully, the rather gentle Princeſs, becauſe I love thee
uelly. If ever thou beeſt mine, *Kate*, (as I have
ving faith within me, tells me, thou ſhalt) I get thee

* *married wife*] Every *wife* ſhould read *new marr.ed*; an epi-
a *married wife*. I ſuppoſe we thet more expreſſive of fondneſs.

with scambling, and thou must therefore needs prove a good soldier-breeder: shall not thou and I, between St. *Dennis* and St. *George*, compound a boy half *French*, half *English*, that shall go to *Constantinople* [6] and take the *Turk* by the beard? shall we not? what say'st thou, my fair Flower-de luce?

Cath. I do not know dat.

K. Henry. No, 'tis hereafter to know, but now to promise. Do but now promise, *Kate*, you will endeavour for your *French* part of such a boy; and for my *English* moiety, take the word of a King and a bachelor. How answer you, *Le plus belle Catharine du monde, mon tres chere & divine deeffe?*

Cath. Your Majestee ave faule French enough to deceive de most sage damoisel dat is *en France*.

K. Henry. Now, fy upon my false *French*; by mine honour, in true *English* I love thee, *Kate*; by which honour I dare not swear thou lov'st me, yet my blood begins to flatter me that thou dost, notwithstanding the poor and untempering effect of my visage [7]. Now beshrew my father's ambition, he was thinking of civil wars when he 'got me; therefore was I created with a stubborn outside, with an aspect of iron, that when I come to woo ladies I fright them; but in faith, *Kate*, the elder I wax, the better I shall appear. My comfort is, that old age, that ill layer up of beauty, can do no more spoil upon my face. Thou hast me, if thou hast me, at the worst; and thou shalt wear me, if thou wear me, better and better; and therefore tell me, most fair *Catharine*, will you have me? Put off your maiden blushes, avouch the thoughts of your heart with the looks of an Empress, take me by the hand and say, *Harry* of *England*, I am thine; which

---

[6] —— *Constantinople*] *Shakespeare* has here committed an anachronism. The *Turks* were not possessed of *Constantinople* before the year 1453, when *Henry* V. had been dead thirty-one years. THEOBALD.

[7] *and* UNTEMPERING *effect*] Certainly, UNTEMPTING. WARBURTON.

word

word thou shalt no sooner bless mine ear withal, but I will tell thee aloud, *England* is thine, *Ireland* is thine, *France* is thine, and *Henry Plantagenet* is thine; who, tho' I speak it before his face, if he be not fellow with the best King, thou shalt find the best King of good fellows. Come, your answer in broken musick; for thy voice is musick, and thy *English* broken: therefore Queen of all, *Catharine*, break thy mind to me in broken *English*, wilt thou have me?

Cath. Dat is, as it shall please *le roy mon pere.*

K. Henry. Nay, it will please him well, *Kate*; it shall please him, *Kate*.

Cath. Den it shall also content me.

K. Henry. Upon that I kiss your hand, and I call you my Queen.

Cath. Laissez, mon seigneur, laissez, laissez: ma foy, je ne veux point que vous abbaissiez vostre grandeur, en baisant la main d'une vostre indigne serviteure; excusez moy, je vous supplie, mon tres puissant Seigneur.

K. Henry. Then I will kiss your lips, *Kate*.

Cath. Les dames & damoiselles pour estre baisées devant leur nopces, il n'est pas le coûtume de France.

K. Henry. Madam my interpreter, what says she?

Lady. Dat it is not be de fashion *pour les* ladies of *France*; I cannot tell, what is *baiser* en *English*.

K. Henry. To kiss.

Lady. Your Majesty *entendre* better *que moy.*

K. Henry. Is it not a fashion for the maids in *France* to kiss before they are married, would she say?

Lady. Ouy, vrayement.

K. Henry. O *Kate*, nice customs curt'sy to great Kings. Dear *Kate*, you and I cannot be confin'd within the weak list of a country's fashion; we are the makers of manners, *Kate*; and the Liberty that follows our places, stops the mouth of all find-faults, as I will do yours, for the upholding the nice fashion of your country in denying me a kiss. Therefore—patiently and yielding—[*Kissing her*] You have witchcraft in your

lips,

lips, *Kate*; there is more eloquence in a touch of them, than in the tongues of the *French* Council; and they should sooner persuade *Harry* of *England*, than a general petition of monarchs. Here comes your father.

SCENE V.

Enter the French *King and Queen, with* French *and* English *Lords.*

Burg. God save your Majesty! My royal cousin, teach you our Princess *English?*

K. Henry. I would have her learn, my fair cousin, how perfectly I love her, and that is good *English.*

Burg. Is she apt?

K. Henry. Our tongue is rough, and my condition is not smooth; so that having neither the voice nor the heart of flattery about me, I cannot so conjure up the spirit of love in her, that he will appear in his true likeness.

Burg. Pardon the frankness of my mirth, [a] if I answer you for that. If you would conjure in her, you must make a circle; if conjure up love in her in his true likeness, he must appear naked and blind. Can you blame her then, being a maid yet ros'd over with the virgin crimson of modesty, if she deny the appearance of a naked blind boy, in her naked seeing self? it were my Lord, a hard condition for a maid to consign to.

K. Henry. Yet they do wink and yield, as love is blind and enforces.

Burg. They are then excus'd, my Lord, when they see not what they do.

[a] *Frankness of my mirth,*] We have here but a mean dialogue for princes; the merriment is very gross, and the sentiments are very worthless.

K. Henry.

K. Henry. Then, good my Lord, teach your cousin to consent to winking.

Burg. I will wink on her to consent, my Lord, if you will teach her to know my meaning. Maids, well summer'd and warm kept, are like flies at *Bartholomew-tide*, blind, though they have their eyes: and then they will endure handling, which before would not abide looking on.

K. Henry * This moral ties me over to time, and a hot summer; and so I shall catch the fly your cousin in the latter end, and she must be blind too.

Burg. As love is, my Lord, before it loves.

K. Henry. It is so; and you may some of you thank love for my blindness, who cannot see many a fair *French* city, for one fair *French* maid that stands in my way.

Fr. King. Yes, my Lord, you see them perspectively; the cities turn'd into a maid; for they are all girdled with maiden walls, that war hath never enter'd.

K. Henry. Shall *Kate* be my wife?

Fr. King. So please you.

K. Henry. I am content, so the maiden cities you talk of may wait on her; so the maid, that stood in the way for my wish, shall shew me the way to my will.

Fr. King. We have consented to all terms of reason.

K. Henry. Is't so, my Lords of *England*?

West. The King hath granted every article:
His daughter first; and then in sequel all,
According to their firm proposed nature.

Exe. Only he hath not yet subscribed this:
Where your Majesty demands, That the King of *France*, having occasion to write for matter of grant, shall name your Highness in this form, and with this addition in *French*: ⁹ *nostre tres cher filz Henry Roy d'Angleterre*,

---

* *This moral*] That is, the application of this fable: the *moral* being the application of a fable, our authour calls any application a *moral*.

thus in *Latin*; PRÆCLARISSI-MUS *filius*] What, is *tres cher*, in *French*, *Præclarissimus* in *Latin*! We should read, PRÆCARISSIMUS. WARBURTON.

⁹ *nostre tres cher filz*——And

heretier de France: and thus in *Latin; Præclarissimus filius noster Henricus Rex Angliæ & hæres Franciæ.*

Fr. King. Yet this I have not (brother) so deny'd,
But your request shall make me let it pass.

K. Henry. I pray you then, in love and dear alliance,
Let that one article rank with the rest,
And thereupon give me your daughter.

Fr. King. Take her, fair son, and from her blood raise up
Issue to me; that these contending Kingdoms,
England and *France,* whose very shores look pale
With envy of each other's happiness,
May cease their hatred; and this dear conjunction
Plant neighbourhood and christian-like accord
In their sweet breasts, that never war advance
His bleeding sword 'twixt *England* and fair *France.*

Lords. Amen!

K. Henry. Now welcome, *Kate*; and bear me witness all,
That here I kiss her as my Sovereign Queen. [*Flourish.*

Q. Isa. God, the best maker of all marriages,
Combine your hearts in one, your realms in one:
As man and wife, being two, are one in love,
So be there 'twixt your kingdoms such a spousal,
That never may ill office, or fell jealousy,
Which troubles oft the bed of blessed marriage,
Thrust in between the paction of these kingdoms,
To make divorce of their incorporate league;
That *English* may as *French, French, Englishmen,*
Receive each other. God speak this Amen!

All. Amen!

---

[1] *Thrust in between the paction of these Kingdoms.*] The old Folio's have it, *the pation*; which makes me believe, the author's Word was *paction*; a Word, more proper on the occasion of a Peace struck up. A Passion of two Kingdoms for one another, is an odd Expression. An Amity and political Harmony may be fixed betwixt two Countries, and yet either People be far from having a Passion for the other. THEOBALD.

K. Henry.

KING HENRY V.

K. Henry. Prepare we for our marriage; on which day,
My Lord of *Burgundy*, we'll take your oath
And all the Peers, for surety of our leagues.
Then shall I swear to *Kate*, and you to me,
And may our oaths well kept, and prosp'rous be!
                                                    [*Exeunt.*

                Enter CHORUS.

Thus far with rough, and all unable, pen
  Our blending author [2] hath pursu'd the story;
In little room confining mighty men,
  Mangling by starts [3] the full course of their glory.
Small time, but, in that small, most greatly liv'd
  This Star of *England*; fortune made his sword,
By which the world's best garden he atchiev'd,
  And of it left his son imperial Lord.
Henry the Sixth, in infant bands crown'd King
  Of *France* and *England*, did this King succeed,
Whose state so many had i'th' managing,
  That they lost *France*, and made his *England* bleed:
Which oft our stage hath shown; and, for their sake,
In your fair minds let this acceptance take. [4]

---

[2] *Our* BENDING *author* ———] We should read,
  BLENDING *author* ———
So he says of him just afterwards, *mangling by starts.*
                    WARBURTON.
[3] — *by starts.*] By touching only on select parts.
[4] This play has many scenes of high dignity, and many of easy merriment. The character of the King is well supported, except in his courtship, where he has neither the vivacity of *Hal*, nor the grandeur of *Henry*. The humour of *Pistol* is very happily continued; his character has perhaps been the model of all the bullies that have yet appeared on the *English* stage.
  The lines given to the chorus have many admirers; but the truth is, that in them a little may be praised, and much must be forgiven; nor can it be easily discovered why the intelligence given by the chorus is more necessary in this play than in many others where it is omitted. The great defect of this play is the emptiness and narrowness of the last act, which a very little diligence might have easily avoided.

THE

FIRST PART

OF

HENRY VI.

Dramatis Personæ.

KING Henry *the Sixth.*
Duke of Gloucester, *Uncle to the King, and Protector.*
Duke of Bedford, *Uncle to the King, and Regent of* France.
Cardinal Beauford, *Bishop of* Winchester, *and great Uncle to the King.*
Duke of Exeter.
Duke of Somerset.
Earl of Warwick.
Earl of Salisbury.
Earl of Suffolk.
Lord Talbot.
Young Talbot, *his Son.*
Richard Plantagenet, *afterwards Duke of* York.
Mortimer, *Earl of* March.
Sir John Fastolfe. Woodvile, *Lieutenant of the* Tower. *Lord Mayor of* London. *Sir* Thomas Gargrave. *Sir* William Glansdale. *Sir* William Lucy.
Vernon, *of the* White Rose, *or* York *Faction.*
Basset, *of the* Red Rose, *or* Lancaster *Faction.*
Charles, *Dauphin, and afterwards King of* France.
Reignier, *Duke of* Anjou, *and Titular King of* Naples.
Duke of Burgundy.
Duke of Alanson.
Bastard of Orleans.
Governor of Paris.
Master Gunner of Orleans. *Boy, his Son.*
An old Shepherd, Father to Joan la Pucelle.

Margaret, *Daughter to* Reignier, *and afterwards Queen to King* Henry.
Countess of Auvergne.
Joan la Pucelle, *a Maid pretending to be inspir'd from Heav'n, and setting up for the Championess of* France.
Fiends, attending her.
Lords, Captains, Soldiers, Messengers, and several Attendants both on the English *and* French.

The SCENE *is partly in* England, *and partly in* France.

[1] The FIRST PART of

King *HENRY* VI.

ACT I. SCENE I.

WESTMINSTER-*Abbey*.

Dead March. Enter the Funeral of King Henry *the Fifth, attended on by the Duke of* Bedford, *Regent of* France ; *the Duke of* Gloucester, *Protector* ; *the Duke of* Exeter, *and the Earl of* Warwick, *the Bishop of* Winchester, *and the Duke of* Somerset.

BEDFORD.

HUNG be the heavens with black, yield day to night!
Comets, importing change of times and states,

Brandish

---

[1] *The* first *Part of K.* HENRY VI.] The Historical Transactions contained in this Play, take in the Compass of above 30 Years. I must observe, however, that our Author, in the three Parts of *Henry* VI. has not been very precise to the Date and Disposition of his Facts; but shuffled them, backwards and forwards, out of Time. For Instance; The Lord *Talbot* is kill'd at the End of the 4th Act of this Play, who in reality did not fall till the 13th of *July* 1453: and the 2d Part of *Henry* VI. opens with the Marriage of the King, which was solemniz'd 8 Years before *Talbot's* Death, in the Year 1445. Again, in

the

² Brandish your cryſtal treſſes in the ſky,
And with them ſcourge the bad revolting ſtars,
That have conſented unto *Harry's* death!
Henry the Fifth, too famous to live long!
England ne'er loſt a King of ſo much worth.

Glou. *England* ne'er had a King until his time:
Virtue he had, deſerving to command.
His brandiſh'd ſword did blind men with its beams,
His arms ſpread wider than a Dragon's wings,
His ſparkling eyes, repleat with awful fire,
More dazzled and drove back his enemies,
Than mid day ſun fierce bent againſt their faces.
What ſhould I ſay? his deeds exceed all ſpeech:
He never lifted up his hand but conquer'd.

Exe. We mourn in black; why mourn we not in blood?
Henry is dead, and never ſhall revive:
Upon a wooden coffin we attend:
And death's diſhonourable victory
We with our ſtately preſence glorify,
Like captives bound to a triumphant car.
What? ſhall we curſe the planets of miſhap,

the 2d Part, Dame *Eleanor Cobham* is introduced to inſult Q. *Margaret*; though her Penance and Baniſhment for Sorcery happened three Years before that Princeſs came over to *England*. I could point out many other Tranſgreſſions againſt Hiſtory, as far as the Order of Time is concerned. Indeed, tho' there are ſeveral Maſter-Strokes in theſe three Plays, which inconteſtably betray the Workmanſhip of *Shakeſpeare*; yet I am almoſt doubtful, whether they were entirely of his Writing. And unleſs they were wrote by him very early, I ſhould rather imagine them to have been brought to him as a Director of the *Stage*; and ſo to have received ſome finiſhing Beauties at his Hand. An accurate Obſerver will eaſily ſee, the *Diction* of them is more *obſolete*, and the *Numbers* more *mean* and *proſaical*, than in the Generality of his genuine Compoſitions. THEOBALD.

² *Brandiſh your* CRYSTAL *treſſes*—] We have heard of a cryſtal heaven, but never of cryſtal comets before. We ſhould read, CRISTED or *creſted*, i. e. treſſes ſtanding an end, or mounted like a creſt. WARBURTON.

I believe *cryſtal* is right.

That

That plotted thus our glory's overthrow?
Or shall we think ³ the subtle-witted *French*
Conj'rers and forc'rers, that, afraid of him,
By magick verse have thus contriv'd his end?

Win. He was a King, bleft of the King of Kings.
Unto the *French*, the dreadful judgment-day
So dreadful will not be as was his fight.
The battles of the Lord of hofts he fought;
The church's pray'rs made him fo profperous.

Glou. The church? where is it? had not church-
  men pray'd,
His thread of life had not-fo foon decay'd.
None do you like but an effeminate Prince,
Whom, like a School-boy, you may over-awe.

Win. Glo'fter, whate'er we like, thou art Protector.
And lookeft to command the Prince and realm;
Thy wife is proud; fhe holdeth thee in awe,
More than God, or religious church-men may.

Glou. Name not religion, for thou lov'ft the flefh;
And ne'er throughout the year to church thou go'ft,
Except it be to pray againft thy foes.

Bed. Ceafe, ceafe thefe jars, and reft your minds in
  peace.
Let's to the altar. Heralds, wait on us.
Inftead of gold we'll offer up our arms,
Since arms avail not now that *Henry's* dead.
Pofterity await for wretched years,
When at their mothers' moift eyes babes fhall fuck;
⁴ Our ifle be made a nourifh of falt tears,

           And

---

³ *The fubtle-witted* French, &c.] There was a notion prevalent a long time, that life might be taken away by metrical charms. As fuperftition grew weaker, thefe charms were imagined only to have power on irrational animals. In our author's time it was fuppofed that the *Irifh* could kill rats by a fong.

⁴ *Our Ifle be made a* Marifh *of falt Tears.*] Thus it is in both the Impreffions by Mr. *Pope:* upon what Authority, I cannot fay. All the old Copies read, a *Nourifh:* and confidering it is
           faid

THE FIRST PART OF

And none but women left to 'wail the dead.
Henry the Fifth! thy ghoſt I invocate;
Proſper this realm, keep it from civil broils,
Combat with adverſe planets in the heavens;
A far more glorious ſtar thy ſoul will make,
Than *Julius Cæſar*, or bright———⁵.

SCENE II.

Enter Meſſenger.

Meſſ. My honourable Lords, health to you all.
Sad tidings bring I to you out of *France*,
Of loſs, of ſlaughter, and diſcomfiture;
Guienne, *Champaign*, and *Rheims*, and *Orleans*,
Paris, *Guyſors*, *Poictiers*, are all quite loſt.

Bed. What ſay'ſt thou, man?—Before dead *Henry's*
    coarſe?———
Speak ſoftly, or the loſs of thoſe great towns
Will make him burſt his lead, and riſe from death.

ſaid in the Line immediately preceding, that Babes ſhall ſuck at their Mothers moiſt Eyes, it ſeems very probable that our Author wrote, a *Nourice*: i. e. that the whole Iſle ſhould be one common *Nurſe*, or *Nouriſher*, of Tears: and thoſe be the Nouriſhment of its miſerable Iſſue.
    THEOBALD.
    Was there ever ſuch nonſenſe! But he did not know that *Mariſh* is an old word for marſh or fen; and therefore very judiciouſly thus corrected by Mr. *Pope*.
    WARBURTON.
  ⁵ *Than* Julius Cæſar, *or bright*———] I can't gueſs the occaſion of the Hemiſtic and imperfect ſenſe in this place; 'tis not impoſſible it might have been filled up with—*Francis Drake*,—tho' that were a terrible anachroniſm; (as bad as *Hector's* quoting *Ariſtotle* in *Troilus and Creſſida*); yet perhaps at the time that brave *Engliſhman* was in his glory, to an *Engliſh*-hearted audience, and pronounced by ſome favourite actor, the thing might be popular, tho' not judicious; and therefore by ſome critick in favour of the author afterwards ſtruck out. But this is a mere ſlight conjecture.   POPE.
    To confute the *ſlight* conjecture of *Pope* a whole page of vehement oppoſition is annexed to this paſſage by *Theobald*. Sir *T. Hanmer* has ſtopped at *Cæſar*—perhaps more judiciouſly.

Glou.

Glou. Is *Paris* loſt, and *Roan* yielded up?
If *Henry* were recall'd to life again,
Theſe news would cauſe him once more yield the ghoſt.

Exe. How were they loſt? what treachery was us'd?

Meſſ. No treachery, but want of men and mony.
Among the ſoldiers this is muttered,
That here you maintain ſev'ral factions,
And, whilſt a field ſhould be diſpatch'd and fought,
You are diſputing of your Generals.
One would have lingring wars with little coſt;
Another would fly ſwift, but wanteth wings;
A third man thinks, without expence at all,
By guileful fair words, peace may be obtain'd.
Awake, awake, *Engliſh* nobility!
Let not ſloth dim your honours, new-begot;
Crop'd are the Flower-de-luces in your Arms,
Of *England's* Coat one half is cut away.

Exe. Were our tears wanting to this funeral,
Theſe tidings would call forth their flowing tides.

Bed. Me they concern. Regent I am of *France*
Give me my ſteeled coat, I'll fight for *France.*
Away with theſe diſgraceful, wailing robes;
Wounds I will lend the *French*, inſtead of eyes,
[6] To weep their intermiſſive miſeries.

SCENE III.

Enter to them another Meſſenger.

2 *Meſſ.* Lords, view theſe letters, full of bad miſchance.
France is revolted from the *Engliſh* quite,
Except ſome petty towns of no import.
The Dauphin *Charles* is crowned King in *Rheims*,

---

[6] *To weep their intermiſſive miſeries.*] i. e. their miſeries, which have had only a ſhort intermiſſion from *Henry* the Fifth's death to my coming amongſt them. WARBURTON.

The bastard *Orleans* with him is join'd,
Reignier, Duke of *Anjou*, doth take his part,
The Duke of *Alanson* flies to his side. [*Exit.*

Exe. The Dauphin crowned King? all fly to him?
O, whither shall we fly from this reproach?

Glou. We will not fly but to our enemies' throats.
Bedford, if thou be slack, I'll fight it out.

Bed. Glo'ster, why doubt'st thou of my forwardness?
An army have I muster'd in my thoughts,
Wherewith already *France* is over-run.

SCENE IV.

Enter a third Messenger.

3 Mess. My gracious Lords, to add to your laments
Wherewith you now bedew King *Henry's* hearse,
I must inform you of a dismal fight
Betwixt the stout Lord *Talbot* and the *French*.

Win. What! wherein *Talbot* overcame? is't so?

3 Mess. O, no; wherein Lord *Talbot* was o'er-
thrown.
The circumstance I'll tell you more at large.
The tenth of *August* last, this dreadful Lord
Retiring from the siege of *Orleans*,
Having scarce full six thousand in his troop,
By three and twenty thousand of the *French*
Was round encompassed and set upon.
No leisure had he to enrank his men,
He wanted pikes to set before his archers,
Instead whereof sharp stakes pluckt out of hedges
They pitched in the ground confusedly
To keep the horsemen off from breaking in.
More than three hours the fight continued;
Where valiant *Talbot* above human thought
Enacted wonders with his sword and lance.
Hundreds he sent to hell, and none durst stand him,
Here, there, and every where, enrag'd he flew,

The

KING HENRY VI.

The *French* exclaim'd, "The devil was in arms!"
All the whole army stood agaz'd on him.
His soldiers, spying his undaunted spirit,
A *Talbot! Talbot!* cried out amain,
And rush'd into the bowels of the battle:
Here had the Conquest fully been seal'd up,
If Sir *John Fastolfe* had not play'd the coward [7];
He being in the vaward, (plac'd behind,
With purpose to relieve and follow them)
Cowardly fled, not having struck one stroke.
Hence grew the gen'ral wreck and massacre;
Enclosed were they with their enemies;
A base *Walloon*, to win the Dauphin's grace,
Thrust *Talbot* with a spear into the back;
Whom all *France* with her chief assembled strength
Durst not presume to look once in the face.

Bed. Is *Talbot* slain? then I will slay myself,
For living idly here in pomp and ease;
Whilst such a worthy leader, wanting aid,
Unto his dastard foe-men is betray'd.

3 *Mess.* O no, he lives, but is took prisoner,
And lord *Scales* with him, and lord *Hungerford*:
Most of the rest slaughter'd, or took likewise.

Bed. His ransom there is none but I shall pay;
I'll hale the Dauphin headlong from his throne,
His Crown shall be the ransom of my friend.
Four of their Lords I'll change for one of ours.
Farewel, my masters, to my task will I;
Bonfires in *France* forthwith I am to make.
To keep our great St. *George's* feast withal.

---

[7] *If Sir John Fastolfe*] Mr. *Pope* has taken Notice, "That *Falstaff* is here introduced again, who was dead in *Henry* V. the occasion whereof is that this Play was written before *Henry* IV. or *Henry* V." But Sir *John Fastolf*, (for so he is called) was a Lieutenant-General, Deputy Regent to the Duke of *Bedford* in *Normandy*, and a *Knight* of the *Garter*: and not the *Comick* Character afterwards introduced by our Author.
THEOBALD.

VOL. IV.   K k   Ten

THE FIRST PART OF

Ten thousand soldiers with me I will take,
Whose bloody deeds shall make all *Europe* quake.

3 Mess. So you had need, for *Orleans* is besieg'd,
The *English* army is grown weak and faint,
The Earl of *Salisbury* craveth supply,
And hardly keeps his men from mutiny,
Since they so few watch such a multitude.

Exe. Remember, Lords, your oaths to *Henry* sworn,
Either to quell the Dauphin utterly,
Or bring him in obedience to your yoke.

Bed. I do remember it, and here take leave,
To go about my preparation. [*Exit* Bedford.

Glou. I'll to the *Tower* with all the haste I can,
To view th' artillery and ammunition;
And then I will proclaim young *Henry* King.

Exe. To *Eltam* will I, where the young King is,
Being ordain'd his special governor;
And for his safety there I'll best devise. [*Exit.*

Win. Each hath his place and function to attend,
I am left out, for me nothing remains
But long I will not be thus out of office;
The King from *Eltam* I intend to send,
And sit at chiefest stern of publick weal. [*Exit.*

SCENE V.

Before Orleans *in* FRANCE.

Enter Charles, Alanson, *and* Reignier, *marching with a Drum and Soldiers.*

Char. MARS his true moving, ev'n as in the heav'ns,
So in the earth to this day is not known;
Late, did he shine upon the *English* side,
Now we are victors, upon us he smiles;
What towns of any moment, but we have?
At pleasure here we lie near *Orleans*,

Tho'

KING HENRY VI.

Tho' still the famish'd *English*, like pale ghosts,
Faintly besiege us one hour in a month.

Alan. They want their porridge, and their fat bull-
  beeves;
Either they must be dieted, like mules,
And have their provender ty'd to their mouths.
Or piteous they will look like drowned mice.

Reig. Let's raise the siege, why live we idly here?
Talbot is taken, whom we wont to fear,
Remaineth none but mad-brained *Salisbury*,
And he may well in fretting spend his gall,
Nor men, nor mony, hath he to make war.

Char. Sound, sound alarum: we will rush on them.
Now for the honour of the forlorn *French*,
Him I forgive my death, that killeth me,
When he sees me go back one foot, or fly. [*Exeunt.*

[*Here Alarm, they are beaten back by the* English
  with great loss.

Re-enter Charles, Alanson, *and* Reignier.

Char. Who ever saw the like? what men have I?
Dogs, cowards, dastards! I wou'd ne'er have fled,
But that they left me midst my enemies.

Reig. Salisbury is a desp'rate homicide,
He fighteth as one weary of his life,
The other lords, like lions wanting food,
Do rush upon us as their hungry prey [8].

Alan. Froysard, a countryman of ours, records,
[9] *England* all *Olivers* and *Rowlands* bred,

---

[8] *As their hungry pr.y.*] I believe it should be read,
  As their hungred pr.y.

[9] *England all* Olivers *and*
  Rowlands *bred,*] These
were two of the most famous in
the list of *Charlemagne's* twelve
Peers; and their exploits are
render'd so ridiculously and equally extravagant by the old ro-
mancers, that from thence arose
that saying amongst our plain
and sensible ancestors, of *giving
one a Rowland for his Oliver,* to
signify the matching one incre-
dible lye with another.
  WARBURTON.

During the time *Edward* the Third did reign;
More truely now may this be verified,
For none but *Sampsons* and *Goliasses*
It sendeth forth to skirmish, one to ten.
Lean raw-bon'd rascals! who would e'er suppose,
They had such courage and audacity!

 Char. Let's leave this town, for they are hair-brain'd slaves,
And hunger will enforce them be more eager;
Of old I know them; rather with their teeth
The walls they'll tear down, than forsake the siege.

 Reig. I think, by some odd [1] gimmals or device
Their arms are set like clocks, still to strike on;
Else they could ne'er hold out so, as they do.
By my consent, we'll e'en let them alone.

 Alan. Be it so.

Enter the Bastard of Orleans.

 Bast. Where's the Prince Dauphin? I have news for him.

 Dau. Bastard of *Orleans*, thrice welcome to us.

 Bast. Methinks, your looks are sad, [2] your chear appall'd;
Hath the late overthrow wrought this offence?
Be not dismay'd, for succour is at hand.
A holy maid hither with me I bring,
Which by a vision, sent to her from heav'n,
Ordained is to raise this tedious siege;
And drive the *English* forth the bounds of *France*.
The spirit of deep prophecy she hath,
Exceeding the [3] nine *Sibyls* of old *Rome*,

---

[1] *Gimmals.*] A *gimmal* is a piece of jointed work, where one piece moves within another, whence it is taken at large for an *engine*. It is now by the vulgar called a *gimcrack*.

[2] *Your chear appall'd.*] *Chear* is countenance, appearance.

[3] ——— *nine* Sibyls *of old* Rome:] There were no nine *Sibyls of Rome*: but he confounds things, and mistakes this for the nine books of Sibylline oracles, brought to one of the *Tarquins*. WARBURTON.

What's paft, and what's to come, fhe can defcry.
Speak, fhall I call her in? * Believe my words,
For they are cerain and infallible.

Dau. Go, call her in. But firft, to try her fkill,
Reignier, ftand thou as Dauphin in my place,
Queftion her proudly, let thy looks be ftern;
By this means fhall we found what fkill fhe hath.

SCENE VI.

Enter Joan la Pucelle.

Reig. Fair maid, is't thou wilt do thefe wond'rous feats?
Pucel. *Reignier*, is't thou that thinkeft to beguile me?
Where is the Dauphin? Come, come from behind,
I know thee well, tho' never feen before.
Be not amaz'd, there's nothing hid from me;
In private will I talk with thee apart.
Stand back, you Lords, and give us leave a while.
Reig. She takes upon her bravely at firft dafh.
Pucel. Dauphin, I am by birth a fhepherd's daughter,
My wit untrain'd in any kind of art.
Heav'n, and our Lady gracious hath it pleas'd
To fhine on my contemptible eftate.
Lo, whilft I waited on my tender lambs,
And to fun's parching heat difplay'd my cheeks,
God's mother deigned to appear to me;
And, in a vifion full of majefty,
Will'd me to leave my bafe vocation,
And free my country from calamity.
Her aid fhe promis'd, and affur'd fuccefs.
In compleat glory fhe reveal'd herfelf;

* *Believe my words.*] It fhould rather be read,
—— *believe her words.*

And, whereas I was black and swart before,
With those clear rays which she infus'd on me,
That beauty am I blest with, which you see.
Ask me what question thou canst possible,
And I will answer unpremeditated.
My courage try by combat, if thou dar'st,
And thou shalt find that I exceed my sex.
Resolve on this, thou shalt be fortunate,
If thou receive me for thy warlike mate.

Dau. Thou hast astonish'd me with thy high terms.
Only this proof I'll of thy valour make,
In single combat thou shalt buckle with me;
And, if thou vanquishest, thy words are true;
Otherwise, I renounce all confidence.

Pucel. I am prepar'd; here is my keen-edg'd sword,
Deck'd with fine Flow'r de-luces on each side;
The which, at *Tourain* in St. *Catherine*'s church,
Out of a deal of old iron I chose forth.

Dau. Then come o'God's name, for I fear no woman.

Pucel. And while I live, I'll ne'er fly from a man.
[*Here they fight*, and Joan la Pucelle *overcomes.*]

Dau. Stay, stay thy hands, thou art an *Amazon*;
And fightest with the sword of *Debora.*

Pucel. Christ's mother helps me, else I were too weak.

Dau. Who-e'er helps thee, 'tis thou that must help me.
Impatiently I burn with thy desire.
My heart and hands thou hast at once subdu'd;
Excellent *Pucelle,* if thy name be so,
Let me thy servant and not Sovereign be,
'Tis the *French* Dauphin sueth to thee thus.

Pucel. I must not yield to any rites of love,
For my profession's sacred from above;
When I have chased all thy foes from hence,
Then will I think upon a recompence.

Dau.

Dau. Mean time, look gracious on thy proſtrate thrall.
Reig. My Lord, methinks, is very long in talk.
Alan. Doubtleſs, he ſhrives this woman to her ſmock;
Elſe ne'er could he ſo long protract his ſpeech.
Reig. Shall we diſturb him, ſince he keeps no mean?
Alan. He may mean more than we poor men do know;
Theſe women are ſhrewd tempters with their tongues.
Reig. My Lord, where are you? what deviſe you on?
Shall we give over *Orleans* or no?
Pucel. Why, no, I ſay; diſtruſtful recreants!
Fight till the laſt gaſp, for I'll be your guard.
Dau. What ſhe ſays, I'll confirm; we'll fight it out.
Pucel. Aſſign'd I am to be the *Engliſh* ſcourge.
This night the ſiege aſſuredly I'll raiſe,
* Expect Saint *Martin's* ſummer, *Halcyon* days,
Since I have enter'd thus into theſe wars.
Glory is like a circle in the water;
Which never ceaſeth to enlarge itſelf,
Till by broad ſpreading it diſperſe to nought.
With *Henry's* death the *Engliſh* circle ends;
Diſpers'd are the glories it included.
Now am I like that proud inſulting ſhip,
Which *Cæſar* and his fortune bore at once.
Dau. Was *Mahomet* inſpired with a Dove?
Thou with an Eagle art inſpired then.
Helen the mother of great *Conſtantine*,
⁵ Nor yet St. *Philip's* daughters, were like thee.
Bright ſtar of *Venus*, fall'n down on the earth,
How may I reverently worſhip thee?
Alan. Leave off delays, and let us raiſe the ſiege.
Reig. Woman, do what thou canſt to ſave our honours;
Drive them from *Orleans*, and be immortaliz'd.

---

* *Expect St.* Martin's *ſummer.*] That is, expect *proſperity* after *misfortune*, like fair weather at *Martlemas*, after winter has begun.

⁵ Meaning the four daughters of *Philip* mentioned in the *Acts*.

THE FIRST PART OF

Dau. Presently try. Come, let's away about it.
No prophet will I trust, if she proves false. [*Exeunt.*

SCENE VII.

Tower-*Gates, in* LONDON.

Enter Gloucester, *with his Serving-men.*

Glou. I AM this day come to survey the *Tower*;
Since *Henry's* death, I fear, there is [6] conveyance.
Where be these warders, that they wait not here?
Open the gates. 'Tis *Gloucester* that calls.
  1 *Ward.* Who's there, that knocketh so imperiously?
  1 *Man.* It is the noble Duke of *Gloucester.*
  2 *Ward.* Whoe'er he be, you may not be let in.
  1 *Man.* Villains, answer you so the Lord Protector?
  1 *Ward.* The Lord protect him! so we answer him;
We do no otherwise than we are will'd.
  Glou. Who willed you? or whose will stands but
    mine?
There's none Protector of the realm but I.
Break up the gates, I'll be your warranty.
Shall I be flouted thus by dunghill grooms?

Gloucester's *men rush at the* Tower-gates, *and* Woodvile *the Lieutenant speaks within.*

Wood. What noise is this? what traitors have we
    here?
  Glou. Lieutenant, is it you, whose voice I hear?
Open the gates; here's *Glo'ster,* that would enter.
  Wood. Have patience, noble Duke; I may not open;
The Cardinal of *Winchester* forbids;
From him I have express commandement,
That thou, nor none of thine, shall be let in.

[6] *Conveyance* means *theft.*   HANMER.
                 Glou.

Glou. Faint-hearted *Woodvile*, prizeft him o'fore me?
Arrogant *Winchefter*, that haughty prelate,
Whom *Henry*, our late Sovereign, ne'er could brook!
Thou art no friend to God, or to the King;
Open the gate, or I'll fhut thee out fhortly.

Serv. Open the gates there to the Lord Protector;
We'll burft them open, if you come not quickly.

Enter to the Protector at the Tower-gates, *Winchefter and his men in tawny coats.*

Win. How now, ambitious *Humphrey*, what means this [7]?

Glou. Piel'd Prieft [8], doft thou command me be fhut out?

Win. I do, thou moft ufurping proditor,
And not protector, of the King or realm.

Glou. Stand back, thou manifeft confpirator;
Thou, that contriv'd'ft to muder our dead Lord;
Thou, that giv'ft whores indulgences to fin [9];
I'll canvafs thee in thy broad Cardinal's hat,
If thou proceed in this thy infolence.

Win. Nay, ftand thou back, I will not budge a foot.
This be *Damafcus*, be thou curfed *Cain* [1],
To flay thy brother *Abel*, if thou wilt.

---

[7] *How now ambitious* umpire, *what means this?*] This Reading has obtained in all the Editions fince the 2d *Folio*. The firft *Folio* has it *Umpheir*. In both the Word is diftinguifh'd in *Italicks*. But why, *Umpire?* Or of what? The Traces of the Letters, and the Word being printed in *Italicks*, convince me, that the Duke's Chriftian Name lurk'd under this Corruption.
THEOBALD.

[8] Piel'd *Prieft*,———] Allud-ing to his fhaven crown.
POPE.

[9] ———*giv'ft whores indulgence to fin*;] The public ftews were formerly under the diftrict of the Bifhop of *Winchefter*.
POPE.

[1] *This be* Damafcus, *be thou curfed* Cain,] N. B. About four miles from *Damafcus* is a high hill, reported to be the fame on which *Cain* flew his brother *Abel*. *Maundrell's* Travels. *page* 131.
POPE.

Glou.

THE FIRST PART OF

Glou. I will not slay thee, but I'll drive thee back.
Thy scarlet robes, as a child's bearing cloth,
I'll use to carry thee out of this place.

Win. Do, what thou dar'st; I beard thee to thy face.

Glou. What? am I dar'd, and bearded to my face?
Draw, men, for all this privileged place.
Blue coats to tawny. Priest, beware thy beard;
I mean to tug it, and to cuff you soundly.
Under my feet I'll stamp thy Cardinal's hat;
In spight of Pope or dignities of Church,
Here by the cheeks I'll drag thee up and down.

Win. Glo'ster, thou'lt answer this before the Pope.

Glou. Winchester Goose [2]! I cry, a rope, a rope.
Now beat them hence, why do you let them stay?
Thee I'll chase hence, thou Wolf in Sheep's array.
Out, tawny coats; out, scarlet hypocrite!

Here Gloucester's *men beat out the Cardinal's; and enter in the burly-burly the Mayor of* London, *and his Officers.*

Mayor. Fy, Lords; that you, being supreme magistrates,
Thus contumeliously should break the peace!

Glou. Peace, Mayor, for thou know'st little of my wrongs;
Here's *Beauford,* that regards not God nor King,
Hath here distrain'd the *Tower* to his use.

Win. Here's *Glo'ster* too, a foe to citizens,
One that still motions war, and never peace,
O'er-charging your free purses with large fines,
That seeks to overthrow religion,
Because he is Protector of the realm,
And would have armour here out of the *Tower,*
To crown himself King, and suppress the Prince.

Glou. I will not answer thee with words, but blows.
[*Here they skirmish again.*

---

[2] *Winchester Goose!* ———] A clap, or rather a strumpet was called a *Winchester* Goose.

KING HENRY VI. 507

Mayor. Nought rests for me in this tumultuous strife,
But to make open proclamation.
Come, officer, as loud as e'er thou canst.

All manner of men assembled here in arms this day, against God's peace and the King's, we charge and command you in his Highness's name, to repair to your several dwelling places, and not wear, handle, or use any sword, weapon, or dagger henceforward upon pain of Death.

Glou. Cardinal, I'll be no breaker of the law,
But we shall meet, and tell our minds at large.
Win. Glo'ster, we'll meet to thy dear cost, be sure;
Thy heart-blood I will have for this day's work.
Mayor. I'll call for clubs, if you will not away.
This Cardinal is more haughty than the devil.
Glou. Mayor, farewel : thou dost but what thou may'st.
Win. Abominable *Glo'ster*, guard thy head,
For I intend to have it, ere be long. [*Exeunt.*
Mayor. See the coast clear'd, and then we will depart.
Good God! that nobles should such stomachs bear!
I myself fight not once in forty year [3]. [*Exeunt.*

---

[3] —— *that nobles should such stomachs bear!*
I myself fight not once in forty year.] The Mayor of *London* was not brought in to be laugh'd at, as is plain by his manner of interfering in the quarrel, where he all along preserves a sufficient dignity. In the line preceding these, he directs his officer, to whom without doubt these two lines should be given. They suit his character, and are very expressive of the pacific temper of the City Guards.
WARBURTON.
I see no reason for this change. The Mayor speaks first as a magistrate, and afterwards as a citizen.

SCENE VIII.

Changes to Orleans *in* France.

Enter the Master-gunner of Orleans, *and his Boy.*

M. Gun. SIRRAH, thou know'st how *Orleans* is
besieg'd,
And how the *English* have the suburbs won.
　Boy. Father, I know, and oft have shot at them,
Howe'er, unfortunate, I miss'd my aim.
　M. Gun. But now thou shalt not. Be thou rul'd
by me.
Chief Master-gunner am I of this town,
Something I must do to procure me grace.
The Prince's 'spials have informed me,
The *English*, in the suburbs close intrench'd,
Went thro' a secret grate of iron bars,
In yonder tow'r, to over-peer the city;
And thence discover how, with most advantage,
They may vex us, with shot or with assault.
To intercept this inconvenience,
A piece of ordnance 'gainst it I have plac'd;
And fully ev'n these three days have I watch'd,
If I could see them. Now, Boy, do thou watch.
For I can stay no longer,———
If thou spy'st any, run and bring me word,
And thou shalt find me at the Governor's. [*Exit.*
　Boy. Father, I warrant you; take you no care;
I'll never trouble you, if I may spy them.

SCENE IX.

Enter Salisbury and Talbot *on the Turrets, with others.*

　Sal. Talbot, my life, my joy, again return'd!
How wert thou handled, being prisoner?

Or

KING HENRY VI.

Or by what means got'st thou to be releas'd?
Discourse, I pr'ythee, on this turret's top.

Tal. The Duke of *Bedford* had a prisoner,
Called the brave Lord *Ponton de Santraile*.
For him was I exchang'd, and ransomed.
But with a baser man of arms by far,
Once, in contempt, they would have barter'd me,
Which I disdaining scorn'd, and craved death
Rather than I would be so vile esteem'd.
In fine, redeem'd I was, as I desir'd.
But, oh! the treach'rous *Fastolfe* wounds my heart;
Whom with my bare fists I would execute,
If I now had him brought into my pow'r.

Sal. Yet tell'st thou not, how thou wert entertain'd.

Tal. With scoffs and scorns, and contumelious taunts.
In open market-place produc'd they me,
To be a publick spectacle to all.
Here, said they, is the terror of the *French*;
The scare-crow, that affrights our children so.
Then broke I from the officers that led me,
And with my nails digg'd stones out of the ground
To hurl at the beholders of my shame.
My grisly countenance made others fly;
None durst come near, for fear of sudden death.
In iron walls they deem'd me not secure:
So great a fear my name amongst them spread,
That they suppos'd, I could rend bars of steel;
And spurn in pieces posts of adamant.
Wherefore a guard of chosen shot I had;
They walk'd about me ev'ry minute-while;
And if I did but stir out of my bed,
Ready they were to shoot me to the heart.

Enter the Boy, *on the other side, with a Linstock.*

Sal. I grieve to hear what torments you endur'd.
But we will be reveng'd sufficiently.
Now it is supper-time in *Orleans:*

Here

Here thro' this grate I can count every one,
And view the *Frenchmen* how they fortify;
Let us look in, the fight will much delight thee.
Sir *Thomas Gargrave*, and Sir *William Glansdale*,
Let me have your express opinions,
Where is best place to make our batt'ry next?

   Gar. I think, at the north gate; for there stand Lords.

   Glan. And I here, at the bulwark of the bridge.

   Tal. For aught I see, this city must be famish'd,
Or with light skirmishes enfeebled.

               [*Here they shoot, and* Salisbury *falls down.*

   Sal. O Lord, have mercy on us, wretched sinners.

   Gar. O Lord, have mercy on me, woful man.

   Tal. What chance is this, that suddenly hath crost us?
Speak, *Salisbury*, at least if thou canst speak;
How far'st thou, mirror of all martial men?
One of thy eyes and thy cheek's side struck off!
Accursed tow'r, accursed fatal hand,
That hath contriv'd this woful tragedy!
In thirteen battles *Salisbury* o'ercame:
Henry the Fifth he first train'd to the wars.
Whilst any trump did sound, or drum struck up,
His sword did ne'er leave striking in the field.
—Yet liv'st thou, *Salisbury?* tho' thy speech doth fail,
One eye thou hast to look to heav'n for grace.
The sun with one eye vieweth all the world.
—Heaven be thou gracious to none alive,
If *Salisbury* wants mercy at thy hands!
—Bear hence his body, I will help to bury it.
Sir *Thomas Gargrave*, hast thou any life?
Speak unto *Talbot*; nay, look up to him.
—O *Salisb'ry*, chear thy spirit with this comfort,
Thou shalt not die, while——
——He beckons with his hand, and smiles on me,
As who should say, *When I am dead and gone,*
Remember to avenge me on the French.

KING HENRY VI.

Plantagenet, I will; and, *Nero*-like,
Play on the lute, beholding the towns burn;
Wretched shall *France* be only in my name.
   [*Here an alarm, and it thunders and lightens.*
What stir is this? what tumults in the heav'ns?
Whence cometh this alarum and this noise?

   Enter a Messenger.

 Mess. My Lord, my Lord, the *French* have ga-
  ther'd head.
The *Dauphin*, with one *Joan la Pucelle* join'd,
A holy Prophetess new risen up.
Is come with a great courage to raise the siege.
   [*Here* Salisbury *lifteth himself up, and groans.*
 Tal. Hear, hear, how dying *Salisbury* doth groan!
It irks his heart, he cannot be reveng'd.
Frenchmen, I'll be a *Salisbury* to you.
* *Pucelle* or *Pussel*, *Dauphin* or *Dog fish*,
Your hearts I'll stamp out with my Horse's heels,
And make a quagmire of your mingled brains.
Convey brave *Salisbury* into his tent,
And then we'll try what dastard *Frenchmen* dare.
   [*Alarm. Exeunt, bearing* Salisbury *and*
    Sir Thomas Gargrave *out.*

SCENE X.

Here an alarm again; and Talbot *pursueth the Dauphin,
 and driveth him: then enter* Joan la Pucelle, *driving*
 Englishmen *before her. Then enter* Talbot.

 Tal. Where is my strength, my valour, and my
  force?
Our *English* troops retire, I cannot stay them.
A woman, clad in armour, chaseth them.

---

 * Pucelle *or* Pussel.] I know not what *pussel* is: perhaps it should be *Pucelle* or *puzzle*. Something with a meaning it should be, but a very poor meaning will serve.

Enter

Enter Pucelle.

Here, here, she comes. I'll have a bout with thee;
Devil or devil's dam, I'll conjure thee.
* Blood will I draw on thee, thou art a witch;
And straitway give thy soul to him thou serv'st.

    Pucel. Come, come, 'tis only I, that must disgrace
        thee.   [*They fight.*

    Tal. Heav'ns, can you suffer hell so to prevail?
My breast I'll burst with straining of my courage,
And from my shoulders crack my arms asunder,
But I will chastise this high-minded strumpet.

    Pucel. Talbot, farewel, thy hour is not yet come;
I must go victual *Orleans* forthwith.

    [*A short alarm. Then enters the town with soldiers.*
O'ertake me if thou canst, I scorn thy strength.
Go, go, chear up thy hunger-starved men.
Help *Salisbury* to make his testament.
This day is ours, as many more shall be. [*Exit* Pucelle.

    Tal. My thoughts are whirled like a potter's wheel,
I know not where I am, nor what I do,
A witch, by fear, not force, like *Hannibal*,
Drives back our troops, and conquers as she lists.
So Bees with smoke, and Doves with noisom stench,
Are from their hives, and houses, driv'n away.
They call'd us for our fierceness *English* dogs,
Now, like their whelps, we crying run away.
                                        [*A short alarm.*
Hark, countrymen! either renew the fight,
Or tear the Lions out of *England's* Coat;
Renounce your soil, give Sheep in Lion's stead.
Sheep run not half so tim'rous from the Wolf,
Or Horse or Oxen from the Leopard,
As you fly from your oft-subdued slaves.
                       [*Alarm. Here another Skirmish.*

---

    * The superstition of those times taught that he that could draw the woman's blood, was free from her power.

KING HENRY VI. 513

not be. Retire into your trenches;
ll consented unto *Salisbury*'s death,
one would strike a stroke in his revenge.
is enter'd into *Orleans*,
ght of us, or aught that we could do.
uld I were to die with *Salisbury*!
ame hereof will make me hide my head.
[*Exit* Talbot.
Alarm, Retreat, Flourish.

SCENE XI.

r on the Wall, Pucelle, Dauphin, Reignier,
Alanson, *and Soldiers.*

lle. Advance our waving colours on the walls,
d is *Orleans* from the *English* Wolves;
Joan la Pucelle hath perform'd her word.
. Divinest creature, bright *Astrea*'s daughter,
hall I honour thee for this success!
romises are like *Adonis*' Garden [7],
That

— *like* Adonis' *Garden,*] them *for* Adonis' *worship; because*
ot be impertinent to take Venus *had once laid him in a let-*
f a dispute between four *tice bed. The next day they were*
of very different orders, *thrown away, &c.* To this Dr.
is very *important* point of *Pierce* replies, *That this account*
dens of Adonis. *Milton* *of the* Gardens *of* Adonis *is right,*
, *and yet* Milton *may be defended*
ore *delicious than those* *for what he says of them: For*
Gardens *feign'd,* *why* (says he) *did the* Grecians
reviv'd Adonis, or —— *on* Adonis' *festival carry these*
Dr. Bentley pronounces *small earthen* Gardens *about in*
; For *hat the* Κῆποι Ἀδώ- *honour of him? It was because*
Gardens *of* Adonis, *so* *they had a* tradition, *that, when*
ly mentioned by Greek *he was alive, he delighted in Gar-*
Plato, Plutarch, &c *were* *dens, and had a magnificent one:*
ut portable earthen Pots, *For proof of this we have* Pliny's
e Lettice or Fennel grow- words, xix. 4. *Antiquitas nihil*
em. On his yearly festi- prius mirata est quàm Hesperi-
ry woman carried one of dum Hortos, ac regum Ado-
IV. L l NIDIS

THE FIRST PART OF

That one day bloom'd, and fruitful were the next,
France, triumph in thy glorious prophetess;
Recover'd is the town of *Orleans*;
More blessed hap did ne'er befal our state.

  Reig. Why ring not out the bells throughout the town?
Dauphin, command the citizens make bonfires,
And feast and banquet in the open streets,
To celebrate the joy, that God hath giv'n us.

  Alan. All *France* will be replete with mirth and joy,
When they shall hear how we have play'd the men.

  Dau. 'Tis *Joan*, not we, by whom the day is won.

ʀɪᴅɪꜱ & Alcinoi. One would now think the question well decided: But Mr. *Theobald* comes, and will needs be Dr. *Bentley's* second. *A learned and reverend gentleman* (says he) *having attempted to impeach Dr.* Bentley *of error, for maintaining that there* ɴᴇᴠᴇʀ ᴡᴀꜱ ᴇxɪꜱᴛᴇɴᴛ *any magnificent or spacious Gardens of* Adonis, *an opinion in which it has been my fortune to second the Doctor, I thought my self concerned, in some part, to weigh those authorities alledged by the objector,* &c. The reader sees that Mr. *Theobald* mistakes the very question in dispute between these two truly learned men, which was not whether *Adonis'* Gardens *were ever existent*, but whether there was *a tradition of any celebrated Gardens cultivated by* Adonis. For this would sufficiently justify *Milton's* mention of them, together with the Gardens of *Alcinous*, confessed by the poet himself to be fabulous. But hear their own words. *There was no such Garden* (says Dr. *Bentley*) *ever existent, or* ᴇᴠᴇɴ ꜰᴇɪɢɴ'ᴅ.

He adds the latter part, as knowing that that would justify the poet; and it is on that assertion only that his adversary Dr. *Pierce* joins issue with him. *Why* (says he) *did they carry the small earthen Gardens? It was because they had a* ᴛʀᴀᴅɪᴛɪᴏɴ, *that when he was alive he delighted in Gardens*. Mr. *Theobald*, therefore, mistaking the question, it is no wonder that all he says, in his long note at the end of the fourth volume, is nothing to the purpose; it being to shew that Dr. *Pierce's* quotations from *Pliny* and others, do not prove the real *existence* of the Gardens. After these, comes the *Oxford Editor*; and he pronounces in favour of Dr. *Bentley* against Dr. *Pierce*, in these words, *The Gardens of* Adonis *were never represented under any local description*. But whether this was said at hazard, or to contradict Dr. *Pierce*, or to rectify Mr. *Theobald's* mistake of the question, it is so obscurely expressed, that one can hardly determine.

                ᴡᴀʀʙᴜʀᴛᴏɴ.

or which I will divide my Crown with her,
nd all the priests and friars in my realm
all in procession sing her endless praise.
statelier pyramid to her I'll rear,
han *Rhodope's* or *Memphis*' ever was!
memory of her, when she is dead,
er ashes, in an urn more precious
han the rich-jewel'd coffer of *Darius*,
ransported shall be at high festivals,
fore the Kings and Queens of *France*.
o longer on St. *Dennis* will we cry,
it *Joan la Pucelle* shall be *France's* Saint.
me in, and let us banquet royally,
ter this golden day of victory. [*Flourish. Exeunt.*

ACT II. SCENE I.

Before ORLEANS.

Enter a Serjeant of a Band, with two Centinels.

SERJEANT.

IRS, take your places, and be vigilant,
If any noise or soldier you perceive
ar to the wall, by some apparent sign
t us have knowledge at the court of guard.
Cent. Serjeant, you shall. [*Exit Serjeant*] Thus are
poor servitors,
hen others sleep upon their quiet beds,
nstrain'd to watch in darkness, rain, and cold.

ter Talbot, Bedford, *and* Burgundy, *with scaling ladders. Their drums beating a dead march.*

Tal. Lord Regent, and redoubted *Burgundy*,
whose approach the regions of *Artois*,
Walloon,

Walloon, and *Picardy* are friends to us;
This happy night the *Frenchmen* are secure,
Having all day carous'd and banquetted,
Embrace we then this opportunity,
As fitting best to quittance their deceit,
Contriv'd by art and baleful sorcery.

Bed. Coward of *France!* how much he wrongs his fame,
Despairing of his own arm's fortitude,
To join with witches and the help of hell!

Bur. Traitors have never other company.
But what's that *Pucelle*, whom they term so pure?

Tal. A maid, they say.

Bed. A maid? and be so martial?

Bur. Pray God, she prove not masculine ere long!
If underneath the standard of the *French*
She carry armour, as she hath begun.

Tal. Well, let them practise and converse with spirits;
God is our fortress, in whose conqu'ring name
Let us resolve to scale their flinty bulwarks.

Bed. Ascend, brave *Talbot*, we will follow thee.

Tal. Not all together; better far I guess,
That we do make our entrance several ways,
That if it chance the one of us do fail,
The other yet may rise against their force.

Bed. Agreed; I'll to yon corner.

Bur. I to this.

Tal. And here will *Talbot* mount, or make his grave.
Now, *Salisbury!* for thee, and for the right
Of *English Henry*, shall this night appear
How much in duty I am bound to both.

Cent. [*within.*] Arm, arm; the enemy doth make assault.

[*The* English, *scaling the Walls, cry,* St. George!
A Talbot!

SCENE

SCENE II.

The French *leap o'er the Walls in their shirts. Enter, several ways,* Bastard, Alanson, Regnier, *half ready and half unready.*

   Alan. How now, my Lords? what all * unready so?
   Bast. Unready? ay, and glad we 'scap'd so well.
   Reig. 'Twas time, I trow, to wake and leave our
       beds;
Hearing alarums at our chamber-doors.
   Alan. Of all exploits, since first I follow'd arms,
Ne'er heard I of a warlike enterprize
More venturous, or desperate than this.
   Bast. I think, this *Talbot* is a fiend of hell.
   Reig. If not of hell, the heav'ns, sure, favour him.
   Alan. Here cometh *Charles*; I marvel how he sped.

Enter Charles *and* Joan.

   Bast. Tut! holy *Joan* was his defensive guard.
   Char. Is this thy cunning, thou deceitful dame?
Didst thou at first, to flatter us withal,
Make us partakers of a little gain;
That now our loss might be ten times as much?
   Pucel. Wherefore is *Charles* impatient with his friend?
At all times will you have my power alike?
Sleeping or waking, must I still prevail?
Or will you blame and lay the fault on me!
Improvident soldiers, had your watch been good,
This sudden mischief never could have fall'n.
   Char. Duke of *Alanson*, this was your default,
That, being captain of the watch to night,
Did look no better to that weighty charge.
   Alan. Had all your quarters been as safely kept,
As that whereof I had the government,
We had not been thus shamefully surpriz'd.

* *Unready* was the current word in those times for *undressed.*

Bast. Mine was secure.

Reig. And so was mine, my Lord.

Char. And for myself, most part of all this night,
Within her quarter, and mine own precinct,
I was employ'd in passing to and fro,
About relieving of the centinels.
Then how, or which way, should they first break in?

Pucel. Question, my Lords, no further of the case,
How, or which way; 'tis sure, they found some part
But weakly guarded, where the breach was made.
And now there rests no other shift but this,
To gather our soldiers, scatter'd and disperst,
And lay new platforms to endamage them. [*Exeunt.*

SCENE III.

Within the Walls of Orleans.

Alarm. Enter a Soldier crying, a Talbot! *a* Talbot! *they fly, leaving their cloaths behind.*

Sol. I'LL be so bold to take what they have left.
The cry of *Talbot* serves me for a sword,
For I have loaden me with many spoils,
Using no other weapon but his name. [*Exit.*

Enter Talbot, Bedford, *and* Burgundy.

Bed. The day begins to break, and night is fled,
Whose pitchy mantle over-veil'd the earth.
Here sound retreat, and cease our hot pursuit. [*Retreat.*

Tal. Bring forth the body of old *Salisbury*,
And here advance it in the market place,
The middle centre of this cursed town.
Now have I pay'd my vow unto his soul,
For ev'ry drop of blood was drawn from him,
There have at least five *Frenchmen* dy'd to-night.
And that hereafter ages may behold
What ruin happen'd in revenge of him,

Within

KING HENRY V.

Within their chiefest temple I'll erect
A tomb, wherein his corps shall be interr'd,
Upon the which, that every one may read,
Shall be engrav'd the Sack of *Orleans,*
The treach'rous manner of his mournful death,
And what a terror he had been to *France.*
But, Lords, in all our bloody massacre,
I muse, we met not with the Dauphin's Grace,
His new-come champion, virtuous *Joan* of *Arc,*
Nor any of his false confederates.

Bed. 'Tis thought, Lord *Talbot,* when the fight began,
Rous'd on the sudden from their drowsy beds,
They did amongst the troops of armed men
Leap o'er the walls, for refuge in the field.

Bur. Myself, as far as I could well discern
For smoke and dusky vapours of the night,
Am sure, I scar'd the Dauphin and his trull,
When, arm in arm, they both came swiftly running,
Like to a pair of loving Turtle Doves,
That could not live asunder day or night.
After that things are set in order here,
We'll follow them with all the pow'r we have.

Enter a Messenger.

Mess. All hail, my Lords. Which of this princely train
Call ye the warlike *Talbot,* for his acts
So much applauded through the realm of *France?*

Tal. Here is the *Talbot,* who would speak with him?

Mess. The virtuous lady, Countess of *Auvergne,*
With modesty, admiring thy renown,
By me intreats, great Lord, thou wouldst vouchsafe
To visit her poor Castle where she lies;
That she may boast she hath beheld the man,
Whose glory fills the world with loud report.

Bur. Is it ev'n so? nay, then, I see, our wars

Will turn into a peaceful comick sport,
When ladies crave to be encounter'd with.
You can't, my Lord, despise her gentle suit.

Tal. Ne'er trust me then; for when a world of men
Could not prevail with all their oratory,
Yet hath a woman's kindness over-rul'd:
And therefore tell her, I return great thanks;
And in submission will attend on her.
Will not your honours bear me company?

Bed. No, truly, that is more than manners will;
And I have heard it said, unbidden guests
Are often welcomest when they are gone.

Tal. Well then, alone, since there's no remedy,
I mean to prove this lady's courtesy.
Come hither, captain. [*Whispers.*]—You perceive my mind.

Capt. I do my Lord, and mean accordingly. [*Exeunt.*

SCENE IV.

The Countess of Auvergne's *Castle.*

Enter the Countess, and her Porter.

Count. POrter, remember what I gave in charge;
And, when you've done so, bring the keys to me.

Port. Madam, I will. [*Exit.*

Count The plot is laid. If all things fall out right
I shall as famous be by this exploit
As *Scythian Tomyris* by *Cyrus*' death.
Great is the rumour of this dreadful Knight,
And his atchievements of no less account.
Fain would mine eyes be witness with mine ears,
To give their censure of these rare reports.

Enter Messenger and Talbot.

Mess. Madam, according as your ladyship

By

KING HENRY VI.

essage crav'd, so is Lord *Talbot* come.
nt. And he is welcome. What! is this the man?
ss. Madam, it is.
nt. [*as musing*] Is this the scourge of *France*?
s the *Talbot* so much fear'd abroad
with his name the mothers still their babes?
 report is fabulous and false;
ight, I should have seen some *Hercules*;
ond *Hector*, for his grim aspect,
large proportion of his strong-knit limbs.
 this is a child, a silly dwarf.
not be, this weak and writhled Shrimp
d strike such terror in his enemies.
'. Madam, I have been bold to trouble you,
nce your ladyship is not at leisure,
rt some other time to visit you.
nt. What means he now? Go ask him, whither
 he goes.
ss. Stay, my Lord *Talbot*; for my lady craves,
now the cause of your abrupt departure.
'. Marry, for that she's in a wrong belief,
o certify her, *Talbot*'s here.

Enter Porter with keys.

int. If thou be he, then art thou prisoner.
'. Pris'ner? to whom?
nt. To me, blood-thirsty Lord,
for that cause I train'd thee to my house.
; time thy shadow hath been thrall to me,
n my gallery thy picture hangs,
ow the substance shall endure the like,
I will chain these legs and arms of thine,
 hast by tyranny these many years
ed our country, slain our citizens,
sent our sons and husbands captivate.
'. Ha, ha, ha.
int. Laughest thou, wretch? thy mirth shall turn
 to moan.
                                        Tal.

Tal. I laugh to see your ladyship so fond,
To think, that you have aught but *Talbot's* shadow
Whereon to practise your severity.

Count. Why? art not thou the man?

Tal. I am, indeed.

Count. Then have I substance too.

Tal. No, no, I am but a shadow of myself,
You are deceiv'd, my substance is not here;
For what you see, is but the smallest part
And least proportion of humanity.
I tell you, Madam, were the whole frame here,
It is of such a spacious lofty pitch,
Your roof were not sufficient to contain it.

Count. This is a riddling merchant for the nonce,
He will be here, and yet he is not here;
How can these contrarieties agree?

Tal. That will I shew you presently.

*Winds his horn; drums strike up; a peal of Ordnance.
Enter Soldiers.*

How say you, Madam? are you now persuaded,
That *Talbot* is but shadow of himself?
These are his substance, sinews, arms and strength,
With which he yoaketh your rebellious necks,
Razeth your cities, and subverts your towns,
And in a moment makes them desolate.

Count. Victorious *Talbot*, pardon my abuse;
I find, thou art no less than fame hath bruited,
And more than may be gather'd by thy shape.
Let my presumption not provoke thy wrath,
For, I am sorry, that with reverence
I did not entertain thee as thou art.

Tal. Be not dismay'd, fair lady; nor misconstrue
The mind of *Talbot*, as you did mistake
The outward composition of his body.
What you have done, hath not offended me,
Nor other satisfaction do I crave,

But

KING HENRY VI.

But only with your patience that we may
Taste of your wine, and see what cates you have;
For soldiers' stomachs always serve them well.

Count. With all my heart, and think me honoured
To feast so great a warrior in my house. [*Exeunt.*

SCENE V.

Changes to London, *in the* Temple *garden.*

Enter Richard Plantagenet, Warwick, Somerset,
Suffolk, *and others.*

Plan. GReat Lords and Gentlemen, what means
this silence?
Dare no man answer in a case of truth?

Suf. Within the Temple-hall we were too loud,
The garden here is more convenient.

Plan. Then say at once, if I maintain'd the truth;
And was not wrangling *Somerset* in th' error [6]?

Suf. 'Faith, I have been a truant in the law;
I never yet could frame my will to it,
And therefore frame the law unto my will.

Som. Judge you, my Lord of *Warwick,* then between us.

War. Between two hawks, which flies the higher
pitch,
Between two dogs, which hath the deeper mouth,
Between two blades, which bears the better temper,
Between two horses, which doth bear him best,
Between two girls, which hath the merriest eye,
I have, perhaps, some shallow spirit of judgment;
But in these nice sharp quillets of the law,
Good faith, I am no wiser than a daw.

[6] All the editions read, *Or else was wrangling* Somerset *i'th' errour?*] Here is apparently a want of opposition between the two questions. I once read, *Or else was wrangling* Somerset *i'th' right?* But I have inserted Sir *T. Hanmer's* emendation.

Plan.

Plan. Tut, tut, here is a mannerly forbearance.
The truth appears so naked on my side,
That any pur-blind eye may find it out.

Som. And on my side, it is so well apparell'd,
So clear, so shining, and so evident,
That it will glimmer thro' a blind man's eye.

Plan. Since you are tongue-ty'd, and so loth to speak,
In dumb significants proclaim your thoughts.
Let him, that is a true-born gentleman,
And stands upon the honour of his birth,
If he suppose that I have pleaded truth,
[7] From off this briar pluck a white rose with me:

Som. Let him that is no coward, and no flatterer,
But dare maintain the party of the truth,
Pluck a red rose from off this thorn with me.

War. I love no [8] colours; and without all colour
Of base insinuating flattery,
I pluck this white rose with *Plantagenet.*

Suf. I pluck this red rose with young *Somerset,*
And say, withal, I think, he held the right.

Ver. Stay, Lords and Gentlemen, and pluck no more,
'Till you conclude, that he, upon whose side
The fewest roses are cropt from the tree,

---

[7] *From off this briar pluck a white rose with me,* &c.] This is given as the original of the two badges of the house of *York* and *Lancaster,* whether truly or not, is no great matter. But the proverbial expression of *saying a thing under the Rose,* I am persuaded, came from thence. When the nation had ranged itself into two great factions, under the *white* and *red* Rose, and were perpetually plotting and counterplotting against one another, then when a matter of faction was communicated by either party to his friend in the same quarrel, it was natural for him to add, that he *said it under the Rose;* meaning that, as it concern'd the faction, it was religiously to be kept secret.

WARBURTON.

Of this proverb other authors give other originals, but the question is not of great importance.

[8] *Colours* is here used ambiguously for *tints* and *deceits.*

Shall

Shall yield the other in the right opinion.

Som. Good master *Vernon*, it is [9] well objected;
If I have fewest, I subscribe in silence.

Plan. And I.

Ver. Then for the truth and plainness of the case,
I pluck this pale and maiden blossom here,
Giving my verdict on the white rose side.

Som. Prick not your finger as you pluck it off,
Left, bleeding, you do paint the white rose red;
And fall on my side so against your will.

Ver. If I, my Lord, for my opinion bleed,
Opinion shall be surgeon to my hurt;
And keep me on the side, where still I am.

Som. Well, well, come on; who else?

Lawyer. Unless my study and my books be false,
The argument, you held, was wrong in you;
[*To* Somerset.
In sign whereof I pluck a white rose too.

Plan. Now, *Somerset*, where is your argument?

Som. Here in my scabbard, meditating that
Shall dye your white rose to a bloody red.

Plan. Mean time, your cheeks do counterfeit our
 Roses;
For pale they look with fear, as witnessing
The truth on our side.

Som. No, *Plantagenet*,
'Tis not for fear, but anger, that thy cheeks
Blush for pure shame to counterfeit our Roses;
And yet thy tongue will not confess thy error.

Plan. Hath not thy Rose a canker, *Somerset*?

Som. Hath not thy Rose a thorn, *Plantagenet*?

Plan. Ay, sharp and piercing to maintain his truth;
Whiles thy consuming canker eats his falshood.

Som. Well, I'll find friends to wear my bleeding
 Roses,

[9] *Well objected.*] Properly thrown in our way, justly proposed.

That

THE FIRST PART OF

That shall maintain what I have said is true,
Where false *Plantagenet* dare not be seen.

Plan. Now by this maiden blossom in my hand,
¹ I scorn thee and thy fashion, peevish boy.

Suf. Turn not thy scorns this way, *Plantagenet*.

Plan. Proud *Pool*, I will; and scorn both him and thee.

Suf. I'll turn my part thereof into thy throat.

Som. Away, away, good *William de la Pool!*
We grace the Yeoman by conversing with him.

War. Now, by God's will, thou wrong'st him, *Somerset*,
His grandfather was *Lyonel* Duke of *Clarence*,
Third son to the third *Edward* King of *England*;
Spring ² crestless Yeomen from so deep a root?

Plan. ³ He bears him on the place's privilege,
Or durst not for his craven heart, say thus.

Som. By him that made me, I'll maintain my words
On any plot of ground in Christendom.
Was not thy father, *Richard*, Earl of *Cambridge*,
For treason headed in our late King's days?
And by his treason stand'st not thou attainted,
⁴ Corrupted and exempt from ancient gentry?
His trespass yet lives guilty in thy blood;
And, till thou be restor'd, thou art a yeoman.

---

¹ *I scorn thee and thy* Fashion,--] So the old copies read, and rightly. Mr. *Theobald* altered it to *Faction*, not considering that by *fashion* is meant the badge of the *red-rose*, which *Somerset* said he and his friends should be distinguish'd by. But Mr. *Theobald* asks, *if* Faction *was not the true reading, why should* Suffolk *immediately reply,*
Turn not thy scorns this way, Plantagenet?
Why? because *Plantagenet* had called *Somerset*, with whom *Suf-*folk sided, *peevish boy*. WARB.

Mr. *Pope* had altered *fashion* to *passion*.

² *Spring* crestless *Yeomen*—] i. e. those who have no right to arms. WARBURTON.

² *He bears him on the place's privilege*.] The *Temple*, being a religious house, was an asylum, a place of exemption, from violence, revenge, and bloodshed.

⁴ *Corrupted and* exempt——] *Exempt*, for excluded.
WARBURTON.
Plan.

KING HENRY VI.

Plan. My father was attached, not attainted;
Condemn'd to die for treason, but no traitor;
And that I'll prove on better men than *Somerset*,
Were growing time once ripen'd to my will.
For your partaker *Pool*, and you yourself,
I'll note you in my book of memory,
[5] To scourge you [6] for this apprehension;
Look to it well and say, you are well warn'd.

Som. Ah, thou shalt find us ready for thee still,
And know us by these colours for thy foes;
For these my friends, in spite of thee shall wear.

Plan. And by my soul, this pale and angry rose,
As cognizance of my blood-drinking hate,
Will I for ever and my faction wear;
Until it wither with me to my grave,
Or flourish to the height of my degree.

Suf. Go forward, and be choak'd with thy ambition:
And so farewell, until I meet thee next. [*Exit.*

Som. Have with thee, *Pool*: farewell, ambitious
Richard. [*Exit.*

Plan. How am I brav'd, and must perforce endure it!

War. This blot, that they object against your house,
Shall be wip'd out in the next Parliament,
Call'd for the truce of *Winchester* and *Glo'ster*,
And if thou be not then created *York*,
I will not live to be accounted *Warwick*.
Mean time, in signal of my love to thee,
Against proud *Somerset* and *William Pool*,
Will I upon thy party wear this rose.
And here I prophesy; this brawl to day,
Grown to this faction, in the Temple-garden,

---

[5] *To scourge you for this Apprehension.*] Tho' this Word possesses all the Copies, I am persuaded, it did not come from the Author. I have ventur'd to read, *Reprehension*: and *Plantagenet* means, that *Somerset* had reprehended or reproach'd him with his Father, the Earl of *Cambridge's* Treason.   THEOBALD.

[6] —— *for this* apprehension;] Apprehension, *i. e.* opinion.
WARBURTON.

Shall

THE FIRST PART OF

Shall send, between the red rose and the white,
A thousand souls to death and deadly night.

Plan. Good master *Vernon*, I am bound to you;
That you on my behalf would pluck a flow'r.

Ver. In your behalf still will I wear the same.

Lawyer. And so will I.

Plan. Thanks, gentle Sir.
Come let us four to dinner; I dare say,
This quarrel will drink blood another day. [*Exeunt.*

SCENE VI.

A PRISON.

Enter Mortimer, *brought in a chair, and Jailors.*

Mor. KIND keepers of my weak decaying age,
⁷ Let dying *Mortimer* here rest himself.
Ev'n like a man new haled from the rack,
So fare my limbs with long imprisonment:
And these grey locks, the pursuivants of death,
Nestor-like aged in an age of care,
Argue the end of ⁸ *Edmund Mortimer.*
These eyes, like lamps whose wasting oil is spent,
Wax dim, as drawing to their * exigent.
Weak shoulders over-born with burd'ning grief,
And pithless arms, like to a wither'd vine
That droops his sapless branches to the ground.
Yet are these feet, whose strengthless stay is numb,
Unable to support this lump of clay,
Swift-winged with desire to get a grave;
As witting, I no other comfort have.

---

⁷ *Let dying* Mortimer *here rest himself.*] I know not whether *Milton* did not take from this hint the lines with which he opens his tragedy.

⁸ This *Edmund Mortimer,* when K. *Richard* II. set out upon his fatal *Irish* expedition, was declared by that Prince heir Apparent to the Crown: for which Reason K. *Henry* IV. and V. took Care to keep him in Prison during their whole Reigns. THEO.

* *Exigent,* end.

But

KING HENRY VI.

But tell me, keeper, will my nephew come?

Keep. *Richard Plantagenet*, my Lord, will come;
We sent unto the Temple, to his chamber,
And answer was return'd that he will come.

Mor. Enough; my soul then shall be satisfy'd.
Poor gentleman, his wrong doth equal mine.
Since *Henry Monmouth* first began to reign,
Before whose glory I was great in arms,
This loathsom sequestration have I had;
And ev'n since then hath *Richard* been obscur'd,
Depriv'd of honour and inheritance;
But now the arbitrator of despairs,
Just death, kind * umpire of men's miseries,
With sweet enlargement doth dismiss me hence.
I would, his troubles likewise were expir'd,
That so he might recover what was lost.

Enter Richard Plantagenet.

Keep. My Lord, your loving nephew now is come.
Mor. *Richard Plantagenet*, my friend? Is he come?
Plan. Ay, noble uncle, thus ignobly us'd,
Your nephew, late despised *Richard*, comes.

Mor. Direct mine arms, I may embrace his neck,
And in his bosom spend my latest gasp.
Oh, tell me, when my lips do touch his cheeks,
That I may kindly give one fainting kiss.
And now declare, sweet stem from *York's* great stock,
Why didst thou say, of late thou wert despis'd?

Plan. First, lean thine aged back against mine arm,
And in that ease I'll tell thee my † Disease.
This day, in argument upon a case,
Some words there grew 'twixt *Somerset* and me,
Amongst which terms he us'd his lavish tongue,
And did upbraid me with my father's death,
Which obloquy set bars before my tongue,

---

* *Umpire of misery.*] That
is, he that terminates or concludes misery. The expression

is harsh and forced.
† *Disease* seems to be here
uneasiness or *discontent*.

Vol. IV.　　　　　M m　　　　　Else

Else with the like I had requited him.
Therefore, good uncle, for my father's sake,
In honour of a true *Plantagenet*,
And for alliance' sake, declare the cause
My father Earl of *Cambridge* lost his head.

   Mor. This cause, fair nephew, that imprison'd me,
And hath detain'd me all my flow'ring youth
Within a loathsome dungeon there to pine,
Was cursed instrument of his decease.

   Plan. Discover more at large what cause that was,
For I am ignorant and cannot guess.

   Mor. I will, if that my fading breath permit,
And death approach not, ere my tale be done.
Henry the Fourth, grandfather to this King,
Depos'd his cousin *Richard*, *Edward's* son
The first-begotten, and the lawful heir
Of *Edward* King, the third of that descent.
During whose reign the *Percies* of the north,
Finding his usurpation most unjust,
Endeavour'd my advancement to the throne.
The reason mov'd these warlike Lords to this,
Was, for that young King *Richard* thus remov'd,
Leaving no heir begotten of his body,
I was the next by birth and parentage,
For by my mother I derived am
From *Lyonel* Duke of *Clarence*, the third son
To the third *Edward*; whereas *Bolingbroke*
From *John* of *Gaunt* doth bring his pedigree,
Being but the Fourth of that heroick Line.
But mark; as in this * haughty great attempt
They laboured to plant the rightful heir;
I lost my liberty, and they their lives.
Long after this, when *Henry* the Fifth
After his father *Bolingbroke* did reign,
Thy father, earl of *Cambridge*, then deriv'd
From famous *Edmund Langley*, Duke of *York*,
Marrying my sister, that thy mother was;
Again in pity of my hard distress,

   * Haughty for high

Levied

KING HENRY VI.

an army, weening to redeem
-inſtal me in the Diadem:
he reſt ſo fell that noble Earl,
as beheaded. Thus the *Mortimers*,
n the title reſted, were ſuppreſt.
. Of which, my Lord, your honour is the laſt.
. True; and thou ſeeſt, that I no iſſue have;
\at my fainting words do warrant death.
\rt my heir. The reſt I wiſh thee gather;
: be wary in thy ſtudious care.
. Thy grave admoniſhments prevail with me;
:, methinks, my father's execution
othing leſs than bloody tyranny.
. With ſilence, nephew, be thou politick;
-fixed is the Houſe of *Lancaſter*,
ike a mountain, not to be remov'd.
w thy uncle is removing hence,
nces do their Courts when they are cloy'd
ong continuance in a ſettled place.
\. O uncle, would ſome part of my young years
 but redeem the paſſage of your age!
. Thou doſt then wrong me, as that ſlaugh-
 t'rer doth,
 giveth many wounds when one will kill.
 not, except thou ſorrow for my good;
\;ive order for my funeral.
\) farewel; [9] and fair be all thy hopes,
roſp'rous be thy life, in peace and war! [*Dies.*
\. And peace, no war, befal thy parting ſoul!
on haſt thou ſpent a pilgrimage,
ike a hermit, over-paſt thy days.

and fair be all *thy Hopes*,]
· knew *Plantagenet's*
were fair, but that the
\iment of the *Lancaſtrian*
ſappointed them: ſure,
\ild wiſh, that his Ne-
fair Hopes might have a
e. I am perſuaded the
ote;

—— *and fair* befal *thy Hopes!*
THEOBALD.
This emendation is received
by Sir *T. Hanmer* and Dr. *Warburton.* I do not ſee how the
readings differ in ſenſe. *Fair* is
lucky, or *proſperous.* So we ſay,
a *fair* wind, and *fair* fortune.

—Well

— Well; I will lock his counsel in my breast;
And what I do imagine, let that rest.
Keepers, convey him hence; and I myself
Will see his burial better than his life.
¹ Here dies the dusky torch of *Mortimer*,
² Choak'd with ambition of the meaner sort.
And for those wrongs, those bitter injuries,
Which *Somerset* hath offer'd to my House,
I doubt not but with honour to redress,
And therefore haste I to the Parliament;
Either to be restored to my blood,
³ Or make my Ill th' advantage of my Good. [*Exit.*

¹ *Here* DIES *the dusky torch*—] The image is of a torch just extinguished, and yet smoaking. But we should read LIES instead of DIES. For when a dead man is represented by an extinguished torch, we must say the *torch lies*: when an extinguished torch is compared to a dead man, we must say the *torch dies*. The reason is plain, because integrity of metaphor requires that the terms proper to the thing *illustrating*, not the thing *illustrated*, be employed. WARBURTON.

² *Choak'd with ambition of the meaner sort.*] We are to understand the speaker as reflecting on the ill fortune of *Mortimer*, in being always made a tool of by the *Percies* of the north in their rebellious intrigues; rather than in asserting his claim to the crown, in support of his own princely ambition. WARBURTON.

³ In the former Editions:
Or make my Will th' Advantage of my Good.] So all the printed Copies: but with very little regard to the Poet's Meaning. I read,
Or make my Ill th' Advantage of my Good.
Thus we recover the *Antithesis* of the Expression. THEOBALD.

ACT

ACT III. SCENE I.

The PARLIAMENT.

...urish. Enter King Henry, Exeter, Gloucester, Win-
...cester, Warwick, Somerset, Suffolk, *and* Richard
Plantagenet. Gloucester *offers to put up a Bill:*
Winchester *snatches it, and tears it.*

WINCHESTER.

COM'ST thou with deep premeditated lines,
With written pamphlets studiously devis'd,
...umphrey of *Glo'ster?* If thou can'st accuse,
*...*aught intend'st to lay unto my charge,
*...*it without invention suddenly;
*...*I with sudden and extemporal speech
*...*urpose to answer what thou canst object.
Glou. Presumptuous Priest, this place commands my patience,
... thou shouldst find, thou hast dishonour'd me.
*...*hink not, altho' in writing I prefer'd
*...*he manner of thy vile outragious crimes,
*...*hat therefore I have forg'd, or am not able
*...*rbatim to rehearse the method of my pen.
*...*o, Prelate, such is thy audacious wickedness,
*...*hy lewd, pestif'rous, and dissentious pranks,
*...*he very Infants prattle of thy pride.
*...*hou art a most pernicious usurer,
*...*roward by nature, enemy to peace,
*...*ascivious, wanton, more than well beseems
... man of thy profession and degree.
*...*nd for thy treach'ry, what's more manifest?
... that thou laid'st a trap to take my life,
*...*s well at *London-bridge,* as at the *Tower.*
*...*eside, I fear me, if thy thoughts were sifted,

The

The King thy Sovereign is not quite exempt
From envious malice of thy swelling heart.

Win. *Glo'ster*, I do defy thee. Lords, vouchsafe
To give me hearing what I shall reply.
If I were covetous, perverse, ambitious,
As he will have me, how am I so poor?
How haps it then, I seek not to advance
Or raise myself, but keep my wonted Calling?
And for dissention, who preferreth peace
More than I do except I be provok'd?
No, my good Lords, it is not that offends;
It is not that, which hath incens'd the Duke;
It is, because no one should sway but he,
No one, but he, should be about the King;
And that engenders thunder in his breast,
And makes him roar these accusations forth.
But he shall know, I am as good———

Glou. As good?
Thou bastard of my grandfather!

Win. Ay, lordly Sir; for what are you, I pray,
But one imperious in another's throne?

Glou. Am not I then Protector, saucy priest?

Win. And am not I a prelate of the Church?

Glou. Yes, as an out-law in a castle keeps,
And uses it to patronage his theft.

Win. Unrev'rend *Glo'ster!*

Glou. Thou art reverend
Touching thy spiritual function, not thy life.

Win. This *Rome* shall remedy.

War. Roam thither then.

Som. My Lord, it were your duty to forbear.

War. Ay, see, the Bishop be not over-borne.

Som. Methinks, my Lord should be religious;
And know the office that belongs to such.

War. Methinks, his Lordship should be humbler then;
It fitteth not a prelate so to plead.

Som. Yes, when his holy state is touch'd so near.

War.

War. State, holy or unhallowed, what of that?
Is not his Grace Protector to the King?
 Rich. *Plantagenet*, I see, must hold his tongue;
Left it be said, ' Speak, sirrah, when you should,
' Must your bold verdict enter talk with Lords?'
Else would I have a fling at *Winchester*.
 K. Henry. Uncles of *Glo'ster*, and of *Winchester*,
The special watchmen of our *English* weal,
I would prevail, if prayers might prevail,
To join your hearts in love and amity.
Oh, what a scandal is it to our Crown,
That two such noble peers as ye should jar!
Believe me, Lords, my tender years can tell
Civil dissention is a vip'rous worm,
That gnaws the bowels of the Common-wealth.
   [*A noise within*; Down with the tawny coats.
 K. Henry. What tumult's this?
 War. An uproar, I dare warrant,
Begun thro' malice of the Bishop's men.
   [*A noise again*, Stones, Stones.

SCENE II.

Enter Mayor.

 Mayor. Oh, my good Lords, and virtuous *Henry*,
Pity the city of *London*, pity us,
The Bishop and the Duke of *Glo'ster's* men,
Forbidden late to carry any weapon,
Have fill'd their pockets full of pebble stones,
And, banding themselves in contrary parts,
Do pelt so fast at one another's pates,
That many have their giddy brains knock'd out;
Our windows are broke down in ev'ry street,
And we for fear compell'd to shut our shops.

    M m 4   *Enter*

THE FIRST PART OF

Enter men in Skirmish with bloody pates.

K. *Henry.* We charge you on allegiance to ourselves,
To hold your slaught'ring hands, and keep the peace,
—Pray, uncle *Glo'ster*, mitigate this strife.

1 *Serv.* Nay, if we be forbidden stones, we'll fall
to it with our teeth.

2 *Serv.* Do what ye dare, we are as resolute.
[*Skirmish again.*

Glou. You of my houshold, leave this peevish broil;
And set this * unaccustom'd fight aside.

3 *Serv.* My Lord, we know your Grace to be a man
Just and upright, and for your royal birth
Inferior to none but to his Majesty;
And ere that we will suffer such a Prince,
So kind a father of the Common-weal,
To be disgraced by an Inkhorn mate,
We, and our wives, and children, all will fight:
And have our bodies slaughter'd by thy foes.

1 *Serv.* Ay, and the very parings of our nails
Shall pitch a field, when we are dead. [*Begin again.*

Glou. Stay, stay, I say;
And if you love me, as you say you do,
Let me persuade you to forbear awhile.

K. *Henry.* O how this discord doth afflict my soul!
Can you, my Lord of *Winchester*, behold
My sighs and tears, and will not once relent?
Who should be pitiful, if you be not?
Or who should study to prefer a peace,
If holy churchmen take delight in broils?

War. My Lord Protector, yield; yield, *Winchester*,
Except you mean with obstinate repulse
To slay your Sovereign, and destroy the Realm.
You see, what mischief, and what murder too,

---

* *Unaccustomed is unseemly, indecent.*
† *An Inkhorn mate.*] A Bookman.

Hath

Hath been enacted thro' your enmity,
Then be at peace, except ye thirst for blood.

Win. He shall submit, or I will never yield.

Glou. Compassion on the King commands me stoop,
Or I would see his heart out, ere the priest
Should ever get that privilege of me.

War. Behold, my Lord of *Winchester*, the Duke
Hath banish'd moody discontented fury,
As by his smoothed brows it doth appear.
Why look you still so stern and tragical?

Glou. Here, *Winchester*, I offer thee my hand.

K. Henry. Fy, uncle *Beaufort*; I have heard you preach,
That malice was a great and grievous sin,
And will not you maintain the thing you teach,
But prove a chief offender in the same?

War. Sweet King! the Bishop hath a kindly gird!
—For shame, my Lord of *Winchester*, relent;
What, shall a child instruct you what to do?

Win. Well, Duke of *Glo'ster*, I will yield to thee;
Love for thy love, and hand for hand, I give.

Glou. Ay, but I fear me, with a hollow heart.
See here, my friends and loving countrymen,
This token serveth for a flag of truce
Betwixt ourselves and all our followers.
So help me God, as I dissemble not!

Win. [*Aside*] So help me God, as I intend it not!

K. Henry. O loving uncle, gentle Duke of *Glo'ster*
How joyful am I made by this contract!
—Away, my masters, trouble us no more;
But join in friendship as your Lords have done.

1 *Serv.* Content. I'll to the Surgeon's.

2 *Serv.* So will I.

3 *Serv.* And I'll see what physick the tavern affords.
[*Exeunt.*

SCENE

THE FIRST PART OF

SCENE III.

War. Accept this scrowl, most gracious Sovereign,
Which in the right of *Richard Plantagenet*
We do exhibit to your Majesty.
   Glou. Well urg'd, my Lord of *Warwick*; for, sweet
        Prince,
An if your Grace mark ev'ry circumstance,
You have great reason to do *Richard* right:
Especially, for those occasions
At *Eltham*-place I told your Majesty.
   K. Henry. And those occasions, uncle, were of force:
Therefore, my loving Lords, our pleasure is,
That *Richard* be restored to his blood.
   War. Let *Richard* be restored to his blood,
So shall his father's wrongs be recompens'd.
   Win. As will the rest, so willeth *Winchester*.
   K. Henry. If *Richard* will be true, not that alone,
But all the whole inheritance I give,
That doth belong unto the house of *York*;
From whence you spring by lineal Descent.
   Rich. Thy humble servant vows obedience,
And faithful service, till the point of death.
   K. Henry. Stoop, then, and set your knee against
        my foot.
And in [5] reguerdon of that duty done,
I gird thee with the valiant sword of *York*.
Rise, *Richard*, like a true *Plantagenet*,
And rise created Princely Duke of *York*.
   Rich. And so thrive *Richard*, as thy foes may fall!
And as my duty springs, so perish they,
That grudge one thought against your Majesty!
   All. Welcome, high Prince, the mighty Duke of
        York!

[5] *Reguerdon.*] Recompence, return.

Som.

Som. Perish, base Prince, ignoble Duke of *York!*
[*Aside.*

Glou. Now will it best avail your Majesty
To cross the seas, and to be crown'd in *France:*
The presence of a King engenders love
Amongst his subjects and his loyal friends,
As it disanimates his enemies.

K. Henry. When *Glo'ster* says the word, King *Henry*
goes;
For friendly counsel cuts off many foes.

Glou. Your ships already are in readiness. [*Exeunt.*

Manet Exeter.

Exe. Ay, we may march in *England* or in *France*,
Not seeing what is likely to ensue;
This late dissention, grown betwixt the peers,
Burns under feigned ashes of forg'd love;
And will at last break out into a flame.
As fester'd members rot but by degrees,
Till bones and flesh, and sinews, fall away;
So will this base and envious discord breed [6].
And now I fear that fatal Prophecy,
Which in the time of *Henry*, nam'd the Fifth,
Was in the mouth of every sucking babe;
That *Henry*, born at *Monmouth*, should win all:
And *Henry* born at *Windsor* should lose all;
Which is so plain, that *Exeter* doth wish,
His days may finish ere that hapless time. [*Exit.*

[6] *So will — discord breed.*] That is, so will the malignity of this discord *propagate itself* and *advance.*

SCENE

THE FIRST PART OF

SCENE IV.

Changes to Roan *in* France.

Enter Joan la Pucelle *disguis'd, and four Soldiers with Sacks upon their backs.*

Pucel. THese are the city gates, the gates of *Roan*,
Thro' which our policy must make a breach,
Take heed, be wary, how you place your words,
Talk like the vulgar sort of market-men,
That come to gather money for their corn.
If we have entrance (as I hope we shall)
And that we find the slothful Watch but weak,
I'll by a sign give notice to our friends,
That *Charles* the Dauphin may encounter them.

Sol. Our sacks shall be a mean to sack the city,
And we be Lords and rulers over *Roan*;
Therefore we'll knock.   [*Knocks.*

Watch. Qui va là?

Pucel. Paisans, pauvres gens de France.
Poor market-folks, that come to sell their corn.

Watch. Enter, go in, the market-bell is rung.

Pucel. Now, *Roan*, I'll shake thy bulwarks to the ground.

Enter Dauphin, Bastard, and Alanson.

Dau. St. *Dennis* bless this happy stratagem!
And once again we'll sleep secure in *Roan*.

Bast. Here enter'd *Pucelle*, and her practisants [7].
Now she is there, how will she specify
Where is the best and safest passage in?

Reig. By thrusting out a torch from yonder tow'r,

---

[7] —— *practisants.*] *Practice,* in the language of that time, was *treachery*, and perhaps in the softer sense *stratagem. Practisants* are therefore *confederates in the stratagem.*

Which,

KING HENRY VI.

Which, once discern'd, shews that her meaning is,
⁸ No way to that for weakness which she enter'd.

Enter Joan la Pucelle *on the top, thrusting out a torch burning.*

Pucel. Behold, this is the happy wedding torch,
That joineth *Roan* unto her countrymen;
But burning fatal to the *Talbotites.*
Bast. See, noble *Charles,* the beacon of our friend,
The burning torch, in yonder turret stands.
Dau. Now shines it like a comet of revenge,
A prophet to the fall of all our foes.
Reig. Defer no time, delays have dangerous ends;
Enter and cry, the *Dauphin!* presently,
And then do execution on the Watch.
[*An Alarm;* Talbot *in an Excursion.*
Tal. France, thou shalt rue this treason with thy tears,
If *Talbot* but survive thy treachery.
Pucelle, that witch, that damned sorceress,
Hath wrought this hellish mischief unawares,
That hardly we escap'd the pride of *France* ⁹. [*Exit.*

⁸ *No way to that—*] That is, *no way equal to that,* no way so fit as that.

⁹ *That hardly we escap'd the pride of* France.] *Pride* signifies the *haughty power.* The same speaker says afterwards, Act 4. Scene 6.

And from the pride *of* Gallia *rescu'd thee.*

One would think this plain enough. But what won't a puzzling critic obscure! Mr. Theobald says, Pride of France *is an absurd and unmeaning expression,* and therefore alters it to *Prize of France;* and in this is followed by the *Oxford Editor.*
WARBURTON.

SCENE

SCENE V.

An alarm: Excursions. Bedford *brought in, sick, in a chair.* Enter Talbot *and* Burgundy, *without;* within, Joan la Pucelle, Dauphin, Bastard, *and* Alanson [1], *on the walls.*

Pucel. Good morrow, gallants, want ye corn for bread?
I think, the Duke of *Burgundy* will fast,
Before he'll buy again at such a rate.
'Twas full of darnel; do you like the taste?
    Burg. Scoff on, vile fiend, and shameless courtizan!
I trust, ere long, to choak thee with thine own,
And make thee curse the harvest of that corn.
    Dau. Your Grace may starve, perhaps, before that time.
    Bed. Oh let not words, but deeds, revenge this treason!
    Pucel. What will you do, good grey-beard? break a lance,
And run a tilt at death within a chair?
    Tal. Foul fiend of *France*, and hag of all despight,
Incompass'd with thy lusty paramours,
Becomes it thee to taunt his valiant age,
And twit with cowardise a man half dead?
Damsel, I'll have a bout with you again,
Or else let *Talbot* perish with his shame.
    Pucel. Are you so hot? yet, *Pucelle*, hold thy Peace;
If *Talbot* do but thunder, rain will follow.
        [Talbot *and the rest whisper together in council.*
God speed the parliament! who shall be the speaker?
    Tal. Dare ye come forth, and meet us in the field!
    Pucel. Belike, your Lordship takes us then for fools,

---

[1] *Alanson* Sir T. Hanmer has replaced here, instead of *Reig-nier*, because *Alanson*, not *Reig-nier*, appears in the ensuing scene.

To try if that our own be ours, or no.

Tal. I speak to not that railing *Hecate*,
But unto thee, *Alanson*, and the rest.
Will ye, like soldiers, come and fight it out?

Alan. Seignior, no.

Tal. Seignior, hang.——Base muleteers of *France!*
Like peasant foot-boys do they keep the walls,
And dare not take up arms like gentlemen.

Pucel. Captains, away; let's get us from the walls,
For *Talbot* means no goodness by his looks.
God be wi' you, my Lord: we came, Sir, but to tell you
That we are here. [*Exeunt from the walls.*

Tal. And there will we be too, ere it be long,
Or else reproach be *Talbot's* greatest fame!
Vow, *Burgundy*, by honour of thy House,
Prick'd on by publick wrongs sustain'd in *France*,
Either to get the town again, or die.
And I, as sure as *English Henry* lives,
And as his father here was Conqueror,
As sure as in this late-betrayed town
Great *Cœurdelion's* heart was buried,
So sure I swear, to get the town, or die.

Burg. My vows are equal patners with thy vows.

Tal. But ere we go, regard this dying Prince,
The valiant Duke of *Bedford*. Come, my Lord,
We will bestow you in some better place:
Fitter for sickness, and for crazy age.

Bed. Lord *Talbot*, do not so dishonour me:
Here I will sit before the walls of *Roan*,
And will be partner of your weal and woe.

Burg. Couragious *Bedford*, let us now persuade you.

Bed. Not to be gone from hence; for once I read,
That stout *Pendragon*, in his litter sick,
Came to the field, and vanquished his foes.
Methinks, I should revive the soldiers' hearts;
Because I ever found them as myself.

Tal. Undaunted spirit in a dying breast!
Then be it so. Heav'ns keep old *Bedford* safe!

And

And now no more ado, brave *Burgundy*,
But gather we our forces out of hand,
And fet upon our boafting enemy. [*Exit.*

An Alarm : excurfions. Enter Sir John Faftolfe, *and a Captain.*

Cap. Whither away, Sir *John Faftolfe*, in fuch hafte?
Faft. Whither away? to fave myfelf by flight.
We are like to have the overthrow again.
Cap. What! will you fly, and leave Lord *Talbot*?
Faft. Ay, all the *Talbots* in the world to fave my life. [*Exit.*
Cap. Cowardly Knight, ill-fortune follow thee! [*Exit.*

Retreat: excurfions. Pucelle, Alanfon, *and Dauphin fly.*

Bed. Now, quiet foul, depart, when heav'n fhall pleafe,
For I have feen our enemies' overthrow.
What is the truft or ftrength of foolifh man?
They, that of late were daring with their fcoffs,
Are glad and fain by flight to fave themfelves.
[*Dies, and is carried off in his chair.*

SCENE VI.

Within the walls of Roan.

An Alarm: Enter Talbot, Burgundy, *and the reft.*

Tal. LOST and recover'd in a day again?
This is a double honour, *Burgundy*;
Yet, heav'ns have glory for this victory!
Burg. Warlike and martial *Talbot, Burgundy*
Infhrines thee in his heart; and there erects
Thy noble deeds, as Valour's monuments.
Tal. Thanks, gentle Duke. But where is *Pucelle* now?
I think,

I think, her old Familiar is asleep.
Now where's the bastard's braves, and *Charles* his glikes?
What, all a mort? *Roan* hangs her head for grief;
That such a valiant company are fled.
Now we will take some order in the town,
Placing therein some expert officers,
And then depart to *Paris* to the King;
For there young *Henry* with his Nobles lies.

Burg. What wills Lord *Talbot*, pleaseth *Burgundy*.

Tal. But yet before we go, let's not forget
The noble Duke of *Bedford*, late deceas'd;
But see his exequies fulfill'd in *Roan*.
A braver soldier never couched lance,
A gentler heart did never sway in Court.
But Kings and mightiest Potentates must die,
For that's the end of human misery. [*Exeunt.*

SCENE VII.

Enter Dauphin, Bastard, Alanson, *and* Joan la Pucelle.

Pucel. Dismay not, Princes, at this accident,
Nor grieve that *Roan* is so recovered.
Care is no cure, but rather corrosive,
For things that are not to be remedy'd.
Let frantick *Talbot* triumph for a while;
And, like a Peacock, sweep along his tail,
We'll pull his plumes and take away his train,
If Dauphin and the rest will be but rul'd.

Dau. We have been guided by thee hitherto,
And of thy cunning had no diffidence.
One sudden foil shall never breed distrust.

Bast. Search out thy wit for secret policies,
And we will make thee famous through the world.

Alan. We'll set thy statue in some holy place,
And have thee reverenc'd like a blessed Saint.
Employ thee then, sweet virgin, for our good.

Pucel. Then thus it muſt be, this doth *Joan* deviſe
By fair perſuaſions mixt with ſugar'd words,
We will entice the Duke of *Burgundy*
To leave the *Talbot*, and to follow us.

Dau. Ay, marry, ſweeting, if we could do that,
France were no place for *Henry's* warriors;
Nor ſhall that Nation boaſt it ſo with us,
But be extirped from our provinces.

Alan. For ever ſhould they be expuls'd from *France*,
And not have title of an Earldom here.

Pucel. Your honours ſhall perceive how I will work,
To bring this matter to the wiſhed end.
[*Drum beats afar off.*
Hark, by the ſound of drum, you may perceive
Their powers are marching unto *Paris*-ward.
[*Here beat an* Engliſh *March.*
There goes the *Talbot* with his Colours ſpread,
And all the troops of *Engliſh* after him. [French *March.*
Now, in the rereward, comes the Duke and his,
Fortune, in favour, makes him lag behind.
Summon a parley, we will talk with him.
[*Trumpets ſound a parley.*

SCENE VIII.

Enter the Duke of Burgundy *marching.*

Dau. A parley with the Duke of *Burgundy.*——
Burg. Who craves a parley with the *Burgundy?*
Pucel. The princely *Charles* of *France*, thy country-man.
Burg. What ſayſt thou, *Charles?* for I am march-ing hence.
Dau. Speak, *Pucelle*, and enchant him with thy words.
Pucel. Brave *Burgundy*, undoubted hope of *France!*
Stay, let thy humble hand-maid ſpeak to thee.
Burg. Speak on, but be not over-tedious.
Pucel.

KING HENRY VI.

Pucel. Look on thy country, look on fertile *France*;
And see the cities, and the towns defac'd,
By wasting ruin of the cruel foe.
As looks the mother on her lowly babe [2],
When death doth close his tender dying eyes;
See, see the pining malady of *France*.
Behold the wounds, the most unnat'ral wounds,
Which thou thyself hast giv'n her woful breast.
Oh, turn thy edged sword another way;
Strike those that hurt; and hurt not those that help:
One drop of blood, drawn from thy country's bosom,
Should grieve thee more than streams of common gore;
Return thee, therefore, with a flood of tears,
And wash away thy country's stained spots.

Burg. Either she hath bewitch'd me with her words,
Or nature makes me suddenly relent.

Pucel. Besides, all *French* and *France* exclaim on thee;
Doubting thy birth, and lawful progeny.
Whom join'st thou with, but with a lordly nation
That will not trust thee but for profit's sake?
When *Talbot* hath set footing once in *France*,
And fashion'd thee that instrument of Ill;
Who then but *English Henry* will be Lord,
And thou be thrust out like a fugitive?
Call we to mind, and mark but this for proof?
Was not the Duke of *Orleans* thy foe?
And was not he in *England* prisoner?
But when they heard he was thine enemy,
They set him free without his ransom paid;
In spight of *Burgundy*, and all his friends.
See then, thou fight'st against thy countrymen;
And join'st with them, will be thy slaughter-men.

[2] —— *on her* LOWLY *babe,*] It is plain *Shakespeare* wrote, LOVELY *babe,* it answering to *fertile France* above, which this domestic image is brought to illustrate. WARBURTON. The alteration is easy and probable, but perhaps the poet by *lowly babe* meant the *babe* lying *low* in death. *Lowly* answers as well to *towns defaced* and *wasting ruin,* as *lovely* to *fertile.*

548 THE FIRST PART OF

Come, come, return; return, thou wand'ring Lord.
Charles, and the rest will take thee in their arms.

Burg. I'm vanquished. These haughty words of hers
Have battered me like roaring cannon-shot [3],
And made me almost yield upon my knees.
Forgive me, country, and sweet countrymen;
And, Lords, accept this hearty kind embrace.
My forces and my pow'r of men are yours.
So farewel, *Talbot*, I'll no longer trust thee.

Pucel. Done like a *Frenchman:* turn, and turn again [4]!

Dau. Welcome, brave Duke! thy friendship makes
us fresh.

Bast. And doth beget new courage in our breasts.

Alan. *Pucelle* hath bravely play'd her part in this,
And doth deserve a Coronet of gold.

Dau. Now let us on, my Lords, and join our powers,
And seek how we may prejudice the foe. [*Exeunt.*

SCENE IX.

Changes to PARIS.

Enter King Henry, Gloucester, Winchester, York, Suffolk, Somerset, Warwick, Exeter, *&c. To them* Talbot, *with his Soldiers.*

Tal. MY gracious Prince and honourable Peers,
Hearing of your arrival in this realm,

[3] —— *These haughty words of hers Have batter'd me like roaring cannon shot,*] How these lines came hither I know not; there was nothing in the speech of *Joan* haughty or violent, it was all soft entreaty and mild expostulation.

[4] *Done like a* Frenchman: *turn, and turn again!*] This seems to be an offering of the poet to his royal mistress's resentment, for *Henry* the Fourth's last great turn in religion, in the year 1593. WARBURTON.

The inconstancy of the *French* was always the subject of satire. I have read a dissertation written to prove that the index of the wind upon our steeples was made in form of a cock, to ridicule the *French* for their frequent changes.

I have

I have a while giv'n truce unto my wars,
To do my duty to my Sovereign.
In sign whereof, this arm, that hath reclaim'd
To your obedience fifty fortresses,
Twelve cities, and sev'n walled towns of strength,
Beside five hundred prisoners of esteem;
Lets fall the sword before your Highness' feet:
And with submissive loyalty of heart
Ascribes the glory of his Conquest got,
First to my God, and next unto your Grace.

 K. Henry. Is this the fam'd Lord *Talbot*, uncle *Glo'ster*,
That hath so long been resident in *France?*

 Glou. Yes, if it please your Majesty, my Liege.

 K. Henry. Welcome, brave Captain, and victorious Lord.
When I was young, as yet I am not old,
I do remember how my father said,
A stouter champion never handled sword.
Long since we were resolved of your truth,
Your faithful service and your toil in war;
Yet never have you tasted your reward,
Or been reguerdon'd with so much as thanks,
Because 'till now we never saw your face;
Therefore stand up, and, for these good deserts,
We here create you *Earl* of *Shrewsbury*,
And in our Coronation take your place. [*Exeunt.*

Manent Vernon *and* Basset.

 Ver. Now, Sir, to you that were so hot at sea,
Disgracing of these colours that I wear
In honour of my noble Lord of *York*;
Dar'st thou maintain the former words thou spak'st?

 Bas. Yes, Sir, as well as you dare patronage
The envious barking of your saucy tongue
Against my Lord, the Duke of *Somerset*.

 Ver. Sirrah, thy Lord I honour as he is.

 Bas. Why, what is he? as good a man as *York*.

550   THE FIRST PART OF

Ver. Hark ye; not so: in witness, take you that.
                              [*Strikes him.*

Bas. Villain, thou know'st, the law of arms is such,
That, whoso draws a sword, 'tis present death [5];
Or else this blow should broach thy dearest blood.
But I'll unto his Majesty, and crave
I may have liberty to venge this wrong;
When thou shalt see, I'll meet thee to thy cost.

Ver. Well, miscreant, I'll be there as soon as you;
And, after, meet you sooner than you would. [*Exeunt.*

ACT IV. SCENE I.

PARIS.

Enter King Henry, Gloucester, Winchester, York, Suffolk, Somerset, Warwick, Talbot, Exeter, *and Governor of* Paris.

GLOUCESTER.

LORD Bishop, set the Crown upon his head.
Win. God save King *Henry*, of that name the Sixth!
Glou. Now, Governor of *Paris*, take your oath,
That you elect no other King but him;
Esteem none friends, but such as are his friends;
And none your foes, but such as shall pretend [6]
Malicious practices against his state.
This shall ye do, so help you righteous God!

---

[5] *That, whoso draws a sword, 'tis present death;*] *Shakespeare* wrote,
—— *draws a sword i'th' presence 't's death;*
i.e. in the Court, or in the presence Chamber. WARBURTON.
   This reading cannot be right, because, as Mr. *Edwards* observed, it cannot be pronounced.

" —— *such as shall pretend.*] To *pretend* is to *design*, to intend

                                                      Enter

Enter Faſtolfe.

Faſt. My gracious Sovereign, as I rode from *Calais*,
To haſte unto your Coronation;
A letter was deliver'd to my hands,
Writ to your Grace from th' Duke of *Burgundy*.
  Tal. Shame to the Duke of *Burgundy*, and thee!
I vow'd, baſe Knight, when I did meet thee next,
To tear the Garter from thy craven leg,
Which I have done; becauſe unworthily
Thou waſt inſtalled in that high degree.
Pardon, my Princely *Henry*, and the reſt;
This daſtard, at the battle of *Poictiers*,
When but in all I was ſix thouſand ſtrong,
And that the *French* were almoſt ten to one,
Before we met, or that a ſtroke was given,
Like to a truſty 'ſquire, did run away.
In which aſſault we loſt twelve hundred men;
Myſelf and divers gentlemen beſide
Were there ſurpriz'd, and taken priſoners.
Then judge, great Lords, if I have done amiſs;
Or whether that ſuch cowards ought to wear
This ornament of knighthood, yea or no?
  Glou. To ſay the truth, this fact was infamous,
And ill beſeeming any common man;
Much more a knight, a captain, and a leader.
  Tal. When firſt this Order was ordain'd, my Lords,
Knights of the Garter were of noble birth;
Valiant and virtuous, full of haughty courage [7];
Such as were grown to Credit by the wars;
Not fearing death, nor ſhrinking for diſtreſs,
But always reſolute in moſt extremes.
He then, that is not furniſh'd in this ſort,
Doth but uſurp the ſacred name of Knight,
Profaning this moſt honourable Order;

---

[7] ———— *haughty courage*;] *Haughty* is here in its original ſenſe for *high*.

And should, if I were worthy to be judge,
Be quite degraded, like a hedge-born swain
That doth presume to boast of gentle blood.

K. Henry. Stain to thy countrymen! thou hear'st thy doom;
Be packing therefore, thou that wast a Knight;
Henceforth we banish thee on pain of death. [*Exit* Fast.
And now, my Lord Protector, view the letter
Sent from our uncle Duke of *Burgundy*.

Glou. What means his Grace, that he hath chang'd his stile?
No more but plain and bluntly, *To the King*. [*Reading.*
Hath he forgot, he is his Sovereign?
Or doth this churlish superscription
Portend some alteration in good will?
What's here? *I have upon especial cause,* [*Reads.*
Mov'd with compassion of my country's wreck,
Together with the pitiful complaints
Of such as your oppression feeds upon,
Forsaken your pernicious faction,
And join'd with Charles, *the rightful King of* France.
O monstrous treachery! can this be so?
That in alliance, amity, and oaths,
There should be found such false dissembling guile?

K. Henry. What! doth my uncle *Burgundy* revolt?
Glou. He doth, my Lord, and is become your foe.
K. Henry. Is that the worst this letter doth contain?
Glou. It is the worst, and all, my Lord, he writes.
K. Henry. Why then, Lord *Talbot* there shall talk with him,
And give him chastisement for this abuse.
My Lord, how say you, are you not content?

Tal. Content, my Liege? yes: but that I'm prevented,
I should have begg'd I might have been employ'd.

K. Henry. Then gather strength, and march unto him strait:
Let him perceive how ill we brook his treason,

And

And what offence it is to flout his friends.

Tal. I go, my Lord, in heart defiring ftill
You may behold confufion of your foes. [*Exit* Talbot.

SCENE II.

Enter Vernon *and* Baffet.

Ver. Grant me the combat, gracious Sovereign.
Baf. And me, my Lord; grant me the combat too.
York. This is my fervant; hear him, noble Prince.
Som. And this is mine; fweet *Henry*, favour him.
K. Henry. Be patient, Lords, and give them leave
 to fpeak.
—Say, gentlemen, what makes you thus exclaim?
And wherefore crave you combat? or with whom?
Ver. With him, my Lord, for he hath done me
 wrong.
Baf. And I with him, for he hath done me wrong.
K. Henry. What is the wrong whereon you both
 complain?
Firft let me know, and then I'll anfwer you.
Baf. Croffing the fea from *England* into *France*,
This fellow here, with envious, carping tongue,
Upbraided me about the rofe I wear;
Saying, the fanguine colour of the leaves
Did reprefent my mafter's blufhing cheeks;
When ftubbornly he did repugn the truth
About a certain queftion in the law,
Argu'd betwixt the Duke of *York* and him;
With other vile and ignominious terms.
In confutation of which rude reproach,
And in defence of my Lord's worthinefs,
I crave the benefit of law of arms.
Ver. And that is my petition, noble Lord;
For though he feem with forged quaint conceit
To fet a glofs upon his bold intent,
Yet, know, my Lord, I was provok'd by him;

And he first took exceptions at this badge,
Pronouncing, that the paleness of this flow'r
Bewray'd the faintness of my master's heart.
  York. Will not this malice, *Somerset*, be left?
  Som Your private grudge, my Lord of *York*, will out,
Though ne'er so cunningly you smother it.
  K. Henry. Good Lord! what madness rules in brain-
    sick men!
When, for so slight and frivolous a cause,
Such factious emulations shall arise!
Good cousins both of *York* and *Somerset*,
Quiet yourselves, I pray, and be at peace.
  York. Let this dissention first be try'd by fight,
And then your Highness shall command a peace.
  Som. The quarrel toucheth none but us alone;
Betwixt ourselves let us decide it then.
  York. There is my pledge; accept it, *Somerset*.
  Ver. Nay, let it rest, where it began at first.
  Bas. Confirm it so, mine honourable Lord.
  Glou. Confirm it so?—Confounded be your strife,
And perish ye with your audacious prate;
Presumptuous vassals! are you not asham'd
With this immodest clamorous outrage
To trouble and disturb the King, and us?
And you, my Lords, methinks, you do not well
To bear with their perverse objections:
Much less to take occasion from their mouths
To raise a mutiny betwixt yourselves:
Let me persuade you, take a better course.
  Exe. It grieves his Highness. Good my Lords, be
    friends.
  K. Henry. Come hither you, that would be com-
    batants.
Henceforth I charge you, as you love our favour,
Quite to forget this quarrel and the cause.
—And you, my Lords, remember where we are,
In *France*, amongst a fickle wavering nation;
If they perceive dissention in our looks,

And that within ourselves we disagree,
How will their grudging stomachs be provok'd
To wilful Disobedience, and Rebel?
Beside, what infamy will there arise,
When foreign Princes shall be certify'd,
That for a toy, a thing of no regard,
King *Henry*'s Peers and chief Nobility
Destroy'd themselves, and lost the realm of *France*?
O, think upon the Conquest of my father,
My tender years, and let us not forego
That for a trifle, which was bought with blood.
Let me be Umpire in this doubtful strife.
I see no reason, if I wear this rose,
[*Putting on a red rose.*
That any one should therefore be suspicious
I more incline to *Somerset*, than *York*.
Both are my kinsmen, and I love them both.
As well they may upbraid me with my Crown,
Because, forsooth, the King of *Scots* is crown'd.
But your discretions better can persuade
Than I am able to instruct or teach,
And therefore, as we hither came in peace,
So let us still continue peace and love.
Cousin of *York*, we institute your Grace
To be our Regent in these parts of *France*:
And, good my Lord of *Somerset*, unite
Your troops of horsemen with his bands of foot;
And, like true subjects, sons of your progenitors,
Go chearfully together, and digest
Your angry choler on your enemies.
Ourself, my Lord Protector, and the rest,
After some respite, will return to *Calais*;
From thence to *England*; where I hope ere long
To be presented by your victories,
With *Charles*, *Alanson*, and that trait'rous rout.
[*Flourish. Exeunt.*

Manent

THE FIRST PART OF

Manent York, Warwick, Exeter, *and* Vernon.

War. My Lord of *York*, I promise you, the King
Prettily, methought, did play the orator.
 York. And so he did; but yet I like it not,
In that he wears the badge of *Somerset*.
 War. Tush, that was but his fancy, blame him not;
I dare presume, sweet Prince, he thought no harm.
 York. ⁸And, if I wis, he did.—But let it rest;
Other affairs must now be managed. [*Exeunt.*

Manet Exeter.

Exe. Well didst thou, *Richard*, to suppress thy voice:
For had the passion of thy heart burst out,
I fear, we should have seen decypher'd there
More ranc'rous spight, more furious raging broils,
Than yet can be imagin'd or suppos'd.
But howsoe'er, no simple man that sees
This jarring discord of Nobility,
This should'ring of each other in the Court,
This factious bandying of their favourites;
But that he doth presage some ill event.
'Tis much, when scepters are in childrens' hands;
But more, when envy breeds unkind division:
There comes the ruin, there begins confusion. [*Exit.*

---

⁸ In former editions,
 And if I wish he did.] By the Pointing reform'd, and a single Letter expung'd. I have restor'd the Text to its Purity. *And, if I wis, he did.*——*Warwick* had said, the King meant no harm in wearing *Somerset's* Rose: *York* testily replies, "Nay, if I know any thing, he did think harm." THEOBALD.
 This is followed by the succeeding editors, and is indeed plausible enough; but perhaps this speech may become intelligible enough without any change, only supposing it broken.
 And if — I wis—he did.
or perhaps,
 And if he did, I wish——

SCENE

KING HENRY VI.

SCENE III.

Before the Walls of Bourdeaux.

Enter Talbot *with trumpets and drum.*

Tal. GO to the gates of *Bourdeaux*, trumpeter,
Summon their General unto the Wall. [*Sounds.*

Enter General, aloft.

English John Talbot, Captains, calls you forth,
Servant in arms to *Harry* King of *England* ;
And thus he would.———Open your city-gates,
Be humbled to us, call my Sovereign yours,
And do him homage as obedient subjects,
And I'll withdraw me and my bloody pow'r.
But if you frown upon this proffer'd peace,
You tempt the fury of my three attendants,
Lean famine, quartering steel, and climbing fire ;
Who in a moment even with the earth
Shall lay your stately and air-braving tow'rs,
If you forsake the offer of our love [9].

Gen. Thou ominous and fearful owl of death,
Our nation's terror, and their bloody scourge !
The period of thy tyranny approacheth.
On us thou canst not enter, but by death :
For, I protest, we are well fortify'd ;
And strong enough to issue out and fight.
If thou retire, the Dauphin, well appointed,
Stands with the snares of war to tangle thee.
On either hand thee, there are squadrons pitch'd
To wall thee from the liberty of flight,
And no way canst thou turn thee for redress,
But death doth front thee with apparent spoil,

---

[9] The common editions read,———*the offer of their love.* Sir *T. Hanmer* altered it to *our*.

And

And pale destruction meets thee in the face.
Ten thousand *French* have ta'en the sacrament,
To rive their dangerous artillery [1]
Upon no christian soul but *English Talbot*.
Lo! there thou stand'st, a breathing valiant man,
Of an invincible, unconquer'd spirit:
This is the latest glory of thy praise,
That I thy enemy [2] due thee withal;
For ere the glass, that now begins to run,
Finish the process of his sandy hour,
These eyes, that see thee now well coloured,
Shall see thee wither'd, bloody, pale and dead.
                              [*Drum afar off.*
Hark! hark! the Dauphin's drum, a warning bell,
Sings heavy musick to thy tim'rous soul;
And mine shall ring thy dire departure out.
                              [*Exit from the walls.*
Tal. He fables not, I hear the enemy.
Out, some light horsemen, and peruse their wings.
O, negligent and heedless discipline!
How are we park'd, and bounded in a pale?
A little herd of *England's* tim'rous Deer,
Maz'd with a yelping kennel of *French* curs.
If we be *English* Deer, be then in blood; [3]
Not rascal like to fall down with a pinch,
But rather moody, mad, and desp'rate Stags,
Turn on the bloody hounds with heads of steel, [4]
And make the cowards stand aloof at bay.
Sell every man his life as dear as mine,
And they shall find dear Deer of us, my friends.

---

[1] *To rive their dangerous artillery*] I do not understand the phrase *to rive artillery*, perhaps it might be to *drive*; we say *to drive a blow*, and to *drive at a man*, when we mean to express furious assault.

[2] —— *due thee*] To *due* is to *endue*, to *deck*, to *grace*.

[3] —— *be then in blood;*] Be high in spirits; be of true mettle.

[4] —— *with heads of steel,*] Continuing the image of the *deer*, he supposes the lances to be their horns.

God

God and St. *George*, *Talbot*, and *England*'s right,
Prosper our Colours in this dangerous fight! [*Exeunt.*

SCENE IV.

Another Part of France.

Enter a Messenger, that meets York. *Enter* York,
with trumpet, and many soldiers.

York. ARE not the speedy scouts return'd again,
That dogg'd the mighty army of the Dauphin?
Mess. They are return'd, my Lord, and give it out
That he is march'd to *Bourdeaux* with his pow'r,
To fight with *Talbot*; as he march'd along,
By your espyals were discovered
Two mightier troops than that the Dauphin led,
Which join'd with him, and made their march for
Bourdeaux.
York. A plague upon that villain *Somerset*,
That thus delays my promised supply
Of horsemen, that were levied for this siege!
Renowned *Talbot* doth expect my aid,
⁵ And I am lowted by a traitor villain,
And cannot help the noble chevalier:
God comfort him in this necessity!
If he miscarry, farewel wars in *France*.

Enter Sir William Lucy.

Lucy. Thou princely leader of our *English* strength,
Never so needful on the earth of *France*,
Spur to the rescue of the noble *Talbot*;

---

⁵ *And I am lowted*——] To *lowt* may signify to *depress*, to *lower*, to *dishonour*; but I do not remember it so used. We may read, *And I am* flouted. *I am mocked,* and treated with contempt.

Who

Who now is girdled with a waste of iron,
And hem'd about with grim destruction.
To *Bourdeaux*, warlike Duke; to *Bourdeaux*, *York*!
Else farewel *Talbot*, *France*, and *England*'s honour.

  York. O God! that *Somerset*, who in proud heart
Doth stop my cornets, were in *Talbot*'s place!
So should we save a valiant gentleman,
By forfeiting a traitor and a coward.
Mad ire, and wrathful fury, makes me weep,
That thus we die, while remiss traitors sleep.

  Lucy. O, send some succour to the distress'd Lord!

  York. He dies, we lose; I break my warlike word;
We mourn, *France* smiles; we lose, they daily get;
All 'long of this vile traitor *Somerset*.

  Lucy. Then God take mercy on brave *Talbot*'s soul,
And on his son young *John*! whom, two hours since,
I met in travel towards his warlike father;
This sev'n years did not *Talbot* see his son,
And now they meet, where both their lives are done.

  York. Alas! what joy shall noble *Talbot* have,
To bid his young son welcome to his grave!
Away! vexation almost stops my breath,
That sundred friends greet in the hour of death.
Lucy, farewel; no more my fortune can,
But curse the cause; I cannot aid the man.
Maine, *Bloys*, *Poictiers*, and *Tours* are won away,
'Long all of *Somerset*, and his delay.   [*Exit.*

  Lucy. Thus while ' the vulture of sedit'on
Feeds in the bosom of such great commanders.
Sleeping neglection doth betray to loss:
The Conquests of our scarce cold Conqueror,
That ever living man of memory,
Henry the Fifth!—While they each other cross,
Lives, honours, lands, and all, hurry to loss. [*Exit.*

---

⁶ —— *the vulture*] Alluding to the tale of *Prometheus*.

KING HENRY VI.

SCENE V.

Another Part of France.

Enter Somerset, *with his army.*

Som. IT is too late; I cannot send them now.
This expedition was by *York* and *Talbot*
Too rashly plotted; all our gen'ral force
Might with a sally of the very town
Be buckled with. The over-daring *Talbot*
Hath sullied all his gloss of former honour
By this unheedful, desp'rate, wild adventure:
York set him on to fight and die in shame,
That, *Talbot* dead, great *York* might bear the name.

Capt. Here is Sir *William Lucy,* who with me
From our o'er-match'd forces forth for aid.

Enter Sir William Lucy.

Som. How now, Sir *William*, whither were you sent?
Lucy. Whither, my Lord? from bought and sold
Lord *Talbot*,
Who, ring'd about [7] with bold adversity,
Cries out for noble *York* and *Somerset*,
To beat assailing death from his weak legions.
And while the honourable Captain there
Drops bloody sweat from his war-wearied limbs,
And, [*] in advantage ling'ring, looks for rescue;
You, his false hopes, the trust of *England's* honour,
Keep off aloof with worthless emulation [8].
Let not your private discord keep away
The levied succours that should lend him aid;
While he, renowned noble gentleman,

---

[7] *— ring'd about*] Environed, encircled.

[*] *In advantage ling'ring.*] Protracting his resistance by the advantage of a strong post.

[8] *— worthless emulation.*] In this line *emulation* signifies merely *rivalry*, not struggle for superior excellence.

VOL. IV.   O o   Yields

Yields up his life unto a world of odds.
Orleans the *Baſtard, Charles,* and *Burgundy,*
Alanſon, Reignier, compaſs him about;
And *Talbot* periſheth by your default.

Som. *York* ſet him on, *York* ſhould have ſent him aid.

Lucy. And *York* as faſt upon your Grace exclaims;
Swearing, that you with-hold his levied hoſt,
Collected for this expedition.

Som. *York* lies; he might have ſent, and had the horſe;
I owe him little duty and leſs love,
And take foul ſcorn to fawn on him by ſending.

Lucy. The fraud of *England,* not the force of *France,*
Hath now entrapt the noble-minded *Talbot*;
Never to *England* ſhall he bear his life,
But dies, betray'd to fortune by your ſtrife.

Som. Come, go; I will diſpatch the horſemen ſtrait;
Within ſix hours they will be at his aid.

Lucy. Too late comes reſcue; he is ta'en, or ſlain;
For fly he could not, if he would have fled,
And fly would *Talbot* never, though he might.

Som. If he be dead, brave *Talbot,* then adieu!

Lucy. His fame lives in the world, his ſhame in you.
[*Exeunt.*

SCENE VI.

A field of Battle near Bourdeaux.

Enter Talbot *and his ſon.*

Tal. O Young *John Talbot,* I did ſend for thee
To tutor thee in ſtratagems of war,
That *Talbot's* name might be in thee reviv'd,
When ſapleſs age, and weak unable limbs,
Should bring thy father to his drooping chair.
But, O malignant and ill-boding ſtars!
Now art thou come unto * a feaſt of death,

---

* *A feaſt of death.*] To a field where *death* will be *feaſted* with ſlaughter.

A ter-

KING HENRY VI.

A terrible and unavoided danger.
Therefore, dear boy, mount on my swiftest horse;
And I'll direct thee how thou shalt escape
By sudden flight. Come, dally not; begone.

John. Is my name *Talbot?* and am I your son?
And shall I fly? O! if you love my mother,
Dishonour not her honourable name,
To make a bastard and a slave of me.
The world will say, he is not *Talbot's* blood
That basely fled, when noble *Talbot* stood [9].

Tal. Fly, to revenge my death, if I be slain.
John. He that flies so, will ne'er return again.
Tal. If we both stay, we both are sure to die.
John. Then let me stay, and, father, do you fly;
Your loss is great, so * your regard should be,
My worth unknown, no loss is known in me.
Upon my death the *French* can little boast,
In yours they will, in you all hopes are lost.
Flight cannot stain the honour you have won,
But mine it will, that no exploit have done;
You fled for vantage, ev'ry one will swear,
But if I bow, they'll say, it was for fear.
There is no hope that ever I will stay,
If the first hour I shrink, and run away.
Here, on my knee, I beg mortality,
Rather than life preserv'd with infamy.

Tal. Shall all thy mother's hopes lie in one tomb?
John. Ay, rather than I'll shame my mother's womb.
Tal. Upon my blessing, I command thee go.
John. To fight I will, but not to fly the foe.
Tal. Part of thy father may be sav'd in thee.
John. No part of him, but will be shame in me.

[9] For what reason this scene is written in rhyme I cannot guess. If *Shakespeare* had not in other plays mingled his rhymes and blank verses in the same manner, I should have suspected that this dialogue had been a part of some other poem which was never finished, and that being loath to throw his labour away, he inserted it here.

* *Your regard.*] Your care of your own safety.

Tal. Thou never hadſt renown, nor canſt not loſe it.
John. Yes, your renowned name; ſhall flight abuſe it?
Tal. Thy father's charge ſhall clear thee from that ſtain.
John. You cannot witneſs for me, being ſlain,
If death be ſo apparent, then both fly.
Tal. And leave my followers here to fight and die?
My age was never tainted with ſuch ſhame.
John. And ſhall my youth be guilty of ſuch blame?
No more can I be ſever'd from your ſide,
Than can yourſelf yourſelf in twain divide;
Stay, go, do what you will, the like do I,
For live I will not, if my father die.
Tal. Then here I take my leave of thee, fair ſon,
Born to eclipſe thy life this afternoon.
Come, ſide by ſide, together live and die;
And ſoul with ſoul from *France* to heaven fly. [*Exeunt.*

Alarm; excurſions, wherein Talbot's *ſon is hemm'd about, and* Talbot *reſcues him.*

Tal. St. *George*, and victory! fight, ſoldiers, fight:
The Regent hath with *Talbot* broke his word,
And left us to the rage of *France's* ſword.
Where is *John Talbot?* pauſe, and take thy breath;
I gave thee life, and reſcu'd thee from death.
John. O, twice my father! twice am I thy ſon;
The life thou gav'ſt me firſt was loſt and done,
Till with thy warlike ſword, deſpight of fate,
To my determin'd time thou gav'ſt new date.
Tal. When from the Dauphin's creſt thy ſword ſtruck fire,
It warm'd thy father's heart with proud deſire
Of bold-fac'd victory. Then leaden age,
Quicken'd with youthful ſpleen and warlike rage,
Beat down *Alanſon, Orleans, Burgundy,*
And from the pride of *Gallia* reſcu'd thee.

KING HENRY VI.

The ireful baſtard *Orleans*, that drew blood
From thee, my boy, and had the maidenhood
Of thy firſt Fight, I ſoon encountered,
And, interchanging blows, I quickly ſhed
Some of his baſtard blood; and in diſgrace
Beſpoke him thus; Contaminated, baſe,
And miſ-begotten blood I ſpill of thine,
Mean and right poor, for that pure blood of mine,
Which thou didſt force from *Talbot*, my brave boy —
Here, purpoſing the Baſtard to deſtroy,
Came in ſtrong reſcue. Speak, thy father's care,
Art not thou weary, *John?* how doſt thou fare?
Wilt thou yet leave the battle, boy, and fly,
Now thou art ſeal'd the ſon of Chivalry?
Fly, to revenge my death, when I am dead;
The help of one ſtands me in little ſtead.
Oh, too much folly is it, well I wot,
To hazard all our lives in one ſmall boat.
If I to-day die not with *Frenchmens*' rage,
To-morrow I ſhall die with mickle age;
By me they nothing gain; and, if I ſtay,
'Tis but the ſhortning of my life one day;
In thee thy mother dies, our houſhold's name,
My death's revenge, thy youth, and *England's* fame,
All theſe, and more, we hazard by thy ſtay,
All theſe are ſav'd, if thou wilt fly away.

John. The ſword of *Orleans* hath not made me ſmart,
Theſe words of yours draw life-blood from my heart.
Oh what advantage bought with ſuch a ſhame, [1]
To ſave a paultry life, and ſlay bright fame!

[1] *On that advantage, bought with ſuch a Shame, To ſave a paltry life, and ſlay bright Fame!*] This paſſage ſeems to lie obſcure and disjointed. Neither the Grammar is to be juſtified; nor is the Sentiment better. I have ventur'd at a ſlight Alteration, which departs ſo little from the Reading which has obtain'd, but ſo much raiſes the Senſe, as well as takes away the Obſcurity, that I am willing to think it reſtores the Author's

THE FIRST PART OF

Before young *Talbot* from old *Talbot* fly,
The coward horse, that bears me, fall and die!
And like me to the peasant boys of *France*,
To be shame's scorn, and subject of mischance.
Surely, by all the glory you have won,
An if I fly, I am not *Talbot's* son.
Then talk no more of flight, it is no boot;
If son to *Talbot*, die at *Talbot's* foot.

Tal. Then follow thou thy desp'rate Sire of *Crete*,
Thou *Icarus*! thy life to me is sweet:
If thou wilt fight, fight by thy father's side;
And, commendable prov'd, let's die in pride. [*Exeunt.*

SCENE VII.

Alarm. Excursions. Enter old Talbot, *led by the* French.

Tal. Where is my other life? mine own is gone.
O! where's young *Talbot*? where is valiant *John*?
Triumphant Death, * smear'd with captivity!
Young *Talbot's* valour makes me smile at thee.
When he perceiv'd me shrink, and on my knee,
His bloody sword he brandish'd over me,
And, like a hungry Lion, did commence
Rough deeds of rage, and stern impatience;

Author's Meaning;
   Out on that vantage.
              THEOBALD.
Sir *T. Hanmer* reads, *Oh what advantage*, which I have followed, though Mr. *Theobald's* conjecture may be well enough admitted.

   And like me to the peasant boys of France,] *To like one to the peasants* is, to *compare*, to *level by comparison*; the line is therefore intelligible enough by itself, but in this sense it wants connection. Sir *T. Hanmer* reads, *And leave me*, which makes a clear sense and just consequence. But as change is not to be allowed without necessity, I have suffered *like* to stand, because I suppose the author meant the same as *make like*, or *reduce to a level with*.

   * *Death smear'd with captivity.*] That is, death stained and dishonoured with captivity.

But

KING HENRY VI. 567

when my angry Guardant stood alone,
 dring my ruin, and assail'd of none,
y-ey'd fury and great rage of heart
 enly made him from my side to start,
the clustring battle of the *French*,
, in that sea of blood, my boy did drench
 over-mounting spirit; and there dy'd
Icarus! my blossom in his pride!

Enter John Talbot, *borne.*

v. O my dear Lord! lo! where your son is borne.
l. " Thou antick death, which laught'st us here
 to scorn,
, from thy insulting tyranny,
 led in bonds of perpetuity,
Talbots winged ⁵ through the lither sky,
y despight, shall 'scape mortality.
 ou, whose wounds become hard-favour'd death,
k to thy father, ere thou yield thy breath.
 e death by speaking, whether he will or no,
 ine him a *Frenchman*, and thy foe.
 boy! he smiles, methinks, as who should say,
 ad death been *French*, then death had died to day."
e, come, and lay him in his father's arms;
spirit can no longer bear these harms.
 iers, adieu. I have what I would have,
 my old arms are young *John Talbot's* Grave.
 [*Dies.*

endring my ruin, ————]   ⁵ *Through the* lither *sky*] *Li-*
 ing me with tenderness in   *ther* is *flexible* or *yielding*. In
ll.   much the same sense *Milton* says,
Thou antick death.] The   ——— *He with broad sails*
 r antick of the play, made   *Winnow'd the* buxom *air.*
by mocking the graver per-   That is, the obsequious air.
 es.

O o 4   A C T

ACT V. SCENE I.

Continues near Bourdeaux.

Enter Charles, Alanson, Burgundy, *Bastard and* Pucelle.

CHARLES.

HAD *York* and *Somerset* brought rescue in,
We should have found a bloody day of this.
Bast. How the young whelp of *Talbot's* raging brood
Did flesh his puny sword in *Frenchmens'* blood! °
Pucel. Once I encounter'd him, and thus I said:
" Thou maiden youth, be vanquish'd by a maid."
But with a proud, majestical, high scorn
He answer'd thus: " Young *Talbot* was not born
" To be the pillage of a * giglot wench."
So, rushing in the Bowels of the *French*,
He left me proudly, as unworthy fight.
Bur. Doubtless, he would have made a noble Knight:
See, where he lies inhersed in the arms
Of the most bloody nurser of his harms.
Bast. Hew them to pieces, hack their bones asunder;
Whose life was *England's* glory, *Gallia's* wonder.
Char. Oh, no. Forbear. For that which we have fled
During the life, let us not wrong it dead.

° The return of rhyme where young *Talbot* is again mentioned, and in no other place, strengthens the suspicion, that these verses were originally part of some other work, and were copied here only to save the trouble of composing new.

* *Giglet* is a wanton, or a strumpet.

Enter

Enter Sir William Lucy.

Lucy. [7] Conduct me to the Dauphin's tent, to know
Who hath obtain'd the glory of the day.
 Char. On what submissive message art thou sent?
 Lucy. Submission, Dauphin? 'tis a meer *French*
  word,
We *English* warriors wot not what it means.
I come to know what prisoners thou hast ta'en,
And to survey the bodies of the dead.
 Char. For prisoners ask'st thou? hell our prison is.
But tell me whom thou seek'st?
 Lucy. Where is the great *Alcides* of the field,
Valiant Lord *Talbot*, Earl of *Shrewsbury?*
Created, for his rare success in arms,
Great Earl of *Washford, Waterford,* and *Valence,*
Lord *Talbot* of *Goodrig* and *Urchingfield,*
Lord *Strange* of *Blackmere*, Lord *Verdon* of *Alton,*
Lord *Cromwell* of *Wingfield,* Lord *Furnival* of *Shef-*
  field,
The thrice victorious Lord of *Falconbridge,*
Knight of the noble Order of St. *George,*
Worthy St. *Michael,* and the *Golden Fleece,*
Great Marshal to our King *Henry* the Sixth
Of all his wars within the realm of *France.*
 Pucel. Here is a silly, stately, stile, indeed.
The *Turk,* that two and fifty Kingdoms hath,
Writes not so tedious a stile as this.
Him that thou magnify'st with all these titles,
Stinking, and fly-blown, lies here at our feet.
 Lucy. Is *Talbot* slain, the *Frenchmens*' only scourge,

---

[7] *Conduct me to the Dauphin's tent, to know Who hath obtain'd* ——] *Lucy*'s Message implied that he knew who had obtained the victory; therefore Sir *T. Hanmer* reads,

Herald, conduct me to the Dauphin's tent.

Your

Your kingdom's terror and black *Nemesis*?
Oh, were mine eye-balls into bullets turn'd,
That I in rage might shoot them at your faces!
Oh that I could but call these dead to life,
It were enough to fright the realm of *France*!
Were but his picture left among you here,
It would amaze the proudest of you all.
Give me their bodies, that I may bear them hence,
And give them burial as beseems their worth.

  Pucel. I think, this Upstart is old *Talbot's* ghost;
He speaks with such a proud commanding spirit.
For God's sake, let him have 'em; to keep them here,
They would but stink and putrify the air.

  Char. Go, take the bodies hence;
  Lucy. I'll bear them hence;
But from their ashes, Dauphin, shall be rear'd
A Phœnix, that shall make all *France* afear'd.

  Char. So we be rid of them, do what thou wilt.
—And now to *Paris*, in this conqu'ring vein;
All will be ours, now bloody *Talbot's* slain. [*Exeunt.*

SCENE II.

Changes to England.

Enter King Henry, Gloucester, *and* Exeter.

  K. *Henry.* HAVE you perus'd the letters from the Pope,
The Emperor, and the Earl of *Armagnac*?

  Glou. I have, my Lord; and their intent is this;
They humbly sue unto your Excellence,
To have a godly Peace concluded of,
Between the realms of *England* and of *France*.

  K. *Henry.* How doth your Grace affect this motion?

  Glou. Well, my good Lord; and as the only means
To stop effusion of our Christian blood,
And stablish quietness on ev'ry side.

  K. *Henry.*

K. Henry. Ay, marry, uncle; for I always thought
It was both impious and unnatural,
That such immanity and bloody strife
Should reign among professors of one Faith.

Glou. Beside, my Lord, the sooner to effect
And surer bind this knot of amity,
The Earl of *Armagnac,* near kin to *Charles,*
A man of great Authority in *France,*
Proffers his only daughter to your Grace
In marriage with a large and sumptuous dowry,

K. Henry. Marriage? alas! my years are yet too
    young,
And fitter is my study and my books,
Than wanton dalliance with a paramour.
Yet call th' Ambassadors; and, as you please,
So let them have their answers ev'ry one.
I shall be well content with any choice,
Tends to God's glory, and my Country's weal.

Enter Winchester, *and three Ambassadors.*

Exe. What is my Lord of *Winchester* install'd,
And call'd unto a Cardinal's degree?
Then I perceive, that will be verify'd,
Henry the Fifth did sometime prophesy;
" If once he come to be a Cardinal,
" He'll make his Cap coequal with the Crown."

K. Henry. My Lords Ambassadors, your sev'ral suits
Have been considered and debated on;
Your purpose is both good and reasonable;
And therefore are we certainly resolv'd
To draw conditions of a friendly Peace,
Which by my Lord of *Winchester* we mean
Shall be transported presently to *France.*

Glou. And for the proffer of my Lord your master,
I have inform'd his Highness so at large;
As, liking of the lady's virtuous gifts,
Her beauty and the value of her dower,

He

He doth intend she shall be *England's* Queen.

K. Henry. In argument and proof of which Contract,
Bear her this jewel, pledge of my affection.
And, so, my Lord Protector, see them guarded,
And safely brought to *Dover*; where, inshipp'd,
Commit them to the fortune of the sea.
[*Exeunt King and Train.*

Win. Stay, my Lord *Legate*, you shall first receive
The Sum of money which I promised
Should be delivered to his Holiness.
For cloathing me in these grave ornaments.

Legate. I will attend upon your Lordship's leisure.

Win. Now *Winchester* will not submit, I trow,
Or be inferior to the proudest Peer.
Humphry of *Glo'ster*, thou shalt well perceive,
That * nor in birth, or for authority,
The Bishop will be over-borne by thee:
I'll either make thee stoop, and bend thy knee,
Or sack this country with a mutiny. [*Exeunt.*

SCENE III.

Changes to France.

Enter Dauphin, Burgundy, Alanson, *Bastard,*
Reignier, *and* Joan la Pucelle.

Dau. THESE news, my Lords, may chear our
drooping spirits:
'Tis said, the stout *Parisians* do revolt,
And turn again unto the warlike *French.*

Alan. Then march to *Paris,* royal *Charles* of *France,*
And keep not back your Pow'rs in dalliance.

Pucel. Peace be amongst them, if they turn to us,
Else Ruin combat with their Palaces.

---

* *Nor in birth.*] I would read *for* birth, That is, thou shalt not rule me though thy birth is legitimate and thy authority supreme.

Enter

Enter Scout.

Scout. Succefs unto our valiant General,
And happinefs to his accomplices!
Dau. What tidings fend our fcouts? I pr'ythee, fpeak.
Scout. The *Englifh* army, that divided was
Into two parts, is now conjoin'd in one;
And means to give you battle prefently.
Dau. Somewhat too fudden, Sirs, the warning is;
But we will prefently provide for them.
Burg. I truft, the ghoft of *Talbot* is not there;
Now he is gone, my Lord, you need not fear.
Pucel. Of all bafe paffions fear is moft accurft.
Command the Conqueft, *Charles*, it fhall be thine:
Let *Henry* fret and all the world repine.
Dau. Then on, my Lords; and *France* be fortunate. [*Exeunt.*

Alarm: excurfions. Enter Joan la Pucelle.

Pucel. The Regent conquers, and the *Frenchmen* fly.
Now help, [8] ye charming Spells and Periapts;
And ye choice Spirits, that admonifh me,
And give me figns of future accidents; [*Thunder.*
You fpeedy helpers, that are fubftitutes
Under the lordly [9] monarch of the North,
Appear, and aid me in this enterprize.

Enter Fiends.

This fpeedy quick appearance argues proof
Of your accuftom'd diligence to me.

---

[8] —— *ye charming Spells and Periapts;*] Charms fow'd up. Ezek. xiii. 18. *Wo to them that fow pillows to all arm-holes, to hunt fouls.* POPE.

[9] *Monarch of the North.*] The North was always fuppofed to be the particular habitation of bad fpirits. *Milton* therefore affembles the rebel angels in the North.

Now,

574 THE FIRST PART OF

Now, ye familiar spirits, that are cull'd
[1] Out of the pow'rful regions under earth,
Help me this once, that *France* may get the field.
      [*They walk, and speak not.*
Oh, hold me not with silence over long,
Where I was wont to feed you with my blood,
I'll lop a member off, and give it you
In earnest of a further benefit,
So you do condescend to help me now.
      [*They hang their heads.*
No hope to have redress? my body shall
Pay recompence, if you will grant my suit.
      [*They shake their heads.*
Cannot my body, nor blood-sacrifice,
Intreat you to your wonted furtherance?
Then, take my soul; my body, soul and all;
Before that *England* give the *French* the foil.
      [*They depart.*
See, they forsake me. Now the time is come,
That *France* must vail her lofty-plumed crest,
And let her head fall into *England's* lap.
My ancient incantations are too weak,
And Hell too strong for me to buckle with.
Now, *France*, thy glory droopeth to the dust. [*Exit.*

 Excursions. Pucelle *and* York *fight hand to hand.*
  Pucelle *is taken. The* French *fly.*

 York. Damsel of *France*, I think, I have you fast.
Uunchain your spirits now with spelling Charms,
And try if they can gain your liberty.
A goodly prize, fit for the devil's Grace!
See, how the ugly witch doth bend her brows,
As if, with *Circe*, she would change my shape.
 Pucel. Chang'd to a worser shape thou canst not be.
 York. Oh, *Charles* the Dauphin is a proper man;

---

[1] *Out of the pow'rful regions under earth.*] I believe *Shakspeare* wrote *legions*.   WARBURTON.

No shape, but his, can please your dainty eye.

Pucel. A plaguing mischief light on *Charles* and thee!
And may ye both be suddenly surpris'd
By bloody hands, in sleeping on your beds.

York. Fell, banning hag! inchantress, hold thy tongue.

Pucel. I pr'ythee, give me leave to curse a-while.

York. Curse, miscreant, when thou comest to the stake. [*Exeunt.*

SCENE IV.

Alarm. Enter Suffolk, *with Lady* Margaret *in his hand.*

Suf. Be what thou wilt, thou art my prisoner.
[*Gazes on her.*
Oh, fairest beauty, do not fear, nor fly;
For I will touch thee but with reverend hands.
I kiss these fingers for eternal peace,
And lay them gently on thy tender side.
Who art thou? say; that I may honour thee.

Mar. Margaret, my name; and daughter to a King;
The King of *Naples*; whosoe'er thou art.

Suf. An Earl I am, and *Suffolk* am I call'd.
Be not offended, Nature's miracle,
Thou art allotted to be ta'en by me;
So doth the Swan her downy cignets save,
Keeping them pris'ners underneath her wings.
Yet if this servile usage once offend,
Go and be free again, as *Suffolk's* friend. [*She is going.*
Oh, stay!—I have no pow'r to let her pass;
My hand would free her, but my heart says, no.
* As plays the sun upon the glassy streams,

Twink-

---

* *As plays the sun upon the glassy streams,* &c.] This comparison, made between things which seem sufficiently unlike,

Twinkling another counterfeited beam,
So seems this gorgeous beauty to mine eyes.
Fain would I woo her, yet I dare not speak;
I'll call for pen and ink, and write my mind.
Fy, *De la Pole*, [3] disable not thyself;
Hast not a tongue? is she not here thy pris'ner?
Wilt thou be daunted at a woman's sight?
Ay; beauty's princely Majesty is such,
Confounds the tongue, and make the senses rough.

Mar. Say, Earl of *Suffolk*, if thy name be so;
What ransom must I pay before I pass?
For, I peceive, I am thy prisoner.

Suf. How can'st thou tell she will deny thy suit,
Before thou make a trial of her love? [*Aside.*

Mar. Why speak'st thou not? what ransome must
    I pay?

Suf. She's beautiful; and therefore to be woo'd;
She is a woman, therefore to be won. [*Aside.*

Mar. Wilt thou accept of ransom, yea, or no?

Suf. Fond man! remember that thou hast a wife;
Then how can *Margaret* be thy paramour? [*Aside.*

Mar. 'Twere best to leave him, for he will not hear.

Suf. There all is marr'd; there lies a cooling card.

Mar. He talks at random; sure, the man is mad.

Suf. And yet a dispensation may be had.

Mar. And yet I would, that you would answer me.

Suf. I'll win this lady *Margaret*. For whom?
Why, for my King. Tush, that's a wooden thing.

Mar. He talks of wood: it is some carpenter.

Suf. Yet so my fancy may be satisfy'd,
And Peace established between these realms.
But there remains a scruple in that too,

---

is intended to express the softness and delicacy of Lady *Margaret's* beauty, which delighted, but did not dazzle; which was bright, but gave no pain by its lustre.

[3] *Disable not thyself.*] Do not represent thyself so weak. To *disable* the judgment of another was, in that age, the same as to destroy its credit or authority.

For

For though her father be the King of *Naples*,
Duke of *Anjou* and *Maine*, yet he is poor;
And our Nobility will scorn the match. [*Aside.*

Mar. Hear ye me, Captain? Are ye not at leisure?

Suf. It shall be so, disdain they ne'er so much.
Henry is youthful, and will quickly yield.
Madam, I have a secret to reveal.

Mar. What tho' I be inthrall'd, he seems a Knight,
And will not any way dishonour me. [*Aside.*

Suf. Lady, vouchsafe to listen what I say.

Mar. Perhaps, I shall be rescu'd by the *French*;
And then I need not crave his courtesy. [*Aside.*

Suf. Sweet Madam, give me hearing in a cause.

Mar. Tush, women have been captivate ere now.
[*Aside.*

Suf. Lady, wherefore talk you so?

Mar. I cry you mercy, 'tis but *Quid* for *Quo*.

Suf. Say, gentle Princess, would you not suppose
Your bondage happy, to be made a Queen?

Mar. To be a Queen in Bondage, is more vile
Than is a slave in base servility;
For Princes should be free.

Suf. And so shall you,
If happy *England's* royal King be free.

Mar. Why, what concerns his freedom unto me?

Suf. I'll undertake to make thee *Henry's* Queen,
To put a golden Scepter in thy hand,
And set a precious Crown upon thy head,
If thou wilt condescend to be my ——

Mar. What?

Suf. His love.

Mar. I am unworthy to be *Henry's* wife.

Suf. No, gentle Madam; I unworthy am
To woo so fair a dame to be his wife;
And have no portion in the choice myself.
How say you, Madam, are you so content?

Mar. An if my father please, I am content.

Suf. Then call our Captains and our colours forth.

And, Madam, at your father's castle-walls,
We'll crave a parly to confer with him.

Sound. Enter Reignier *on the walls.*

Suf. See, *Reignier,* see thy daughter prisoner.
Reig. To whom?
Suf. To me.
Reig. Suffolk, what remedy?
I am a soldier, and unapt to weep,
Or to exclaim on fortune's fickleness.
Suf. Yes, there is remedy enough, my Lord.
Consent, and for thy honour give consent,
Thy daughter shall be wedded to my King;
Whom I with pain have woo'd and won thereto;
And this her easy-held imprisonment
Hath gain'd thy daughter princely liberty.
Reig. Speaks *Suffolk* as he thinks?
Suf. Fair *Margaret* knows,
That *Suffolk* doth not flatter, face, or feign.
Reig. Upon thy princely warrant I descend;
To give the answer of thy just demand.
Suf. And here I will expect thy coming.

Trumpets sound. Enter Reignier.

Reig. Welcome, brave Earl, into our territories;
Command in *Anjou,* what your Honour pleases.
Suf. Thanks, *Reignier,* happy in so sweet a child,
Fit to be made companion of a King.
What answer makes your Grace unto my suit?
Reig. Since thou dost deign to woo her little worth,
To be the Princely bride of such a Lord;
Upon condition I may quietly
Enjoy mine own, the country *Maine* and *Anjou,*
Free from oppression or the stroke of war,
My daughter shall be *Henry's,* if he please.
Suf. That is her ransom, I deliver her;
And those two counties, I will undertake,
Your Grace shall well and quietly enjoy.

Reig.

KING HENRY VI.

Reig. And I again in *Henry's* Royal name,
As Deputy unto that gracious King,
Give thee her hand for sign of plighted faith.

Suf. *Reignier* of *France*, I give thee kingly thanks,
Because this is in traffick of a King.
And yet, methinks, I could be well content
To be mine own Attorney in this case.   [*Aside.*
I'll over then to *England* with this News,
And make this marriage to be solemniz'd.
So farewell, *Reignier*; set this diamond safe
In golden Palaces, as it becomes.

Reig. I do embrace thee, as I would embrace
The Christian Prince King *Henry*, were he here.

Mar. Farewel, my Lord. Good wishes, praise and pray'rs
Shall *Suffolk* ever have of *Margaret*.   [*She is going.*

Suf. Farewel, sweet Madam; hark you, *Margaret*;
No princely commendations to my King?

Mar. Such commendations as become a maid,
A virgin, and his servant, say to him.

Suf. Words sweetly plac'd, and modestly directed.
But, Madam, I must trouble you again,
No loving token to his Majesty?

Mar. Yes, my good Lord, a pure unspotted heart,
Never yet taint with love, I send the King.

Suf. And this withal.   [*Kisses her.*

Mar. That for thyself.——I will not so presume
* To send such peevish tokens to a King.

Suf. O, wert thou for myself!——but, *Suffolk*, stay;
Thou may'st not wander in that labyrinth;
There Minotaurs, and ugly treasons, lurk.
Sollicit *Henry* with her wond'rous praise,
Bethink thee on her virtues that surmount,
Her nat'ral graces that extinguish art;
Repeat their semblance often on the seas;

---

* *To send such* peevish *tokens*—] *Peevish,* for childish.   WARB.

P p 2   That,

THE FIRST PART OF

That, when thou com'ft to kneel at *Henry's* feet,
Thou may'ft bereave him of his wits with wonder.
[*Exeunt.*

SCENE VI.

Enter York, Warwick, *a Shepherd, and* Pucelle.

York. Bring forth that forcerefs, condemn'd to burn.
Shep. Ah, *Joan!* This kills thy father's heart out-
 right.
Have I fought ev'ry country far and near,
And now it is my chance to find thee out,
Muft I behold thy timelefs, cruel, death?
Ah, *Joan,* fweet daughter, I will die with thee.
 Pucel. Decrepit mifer! bafe ignoble wretch!
I am defcended of a gentler blood.
Thou art no father, nor no friend of mine.
 Shep. Out, out! — my Lords, an pleafe you, 'tis
 not fo;
I did beget her, all the parifh knows,
Her mother, living yet, can teftify,
She was the firft-fruit of my batch'lorfhip.
 War. Gracelefs, wilt thou deny thy parentage?]
 York. This argues, what her kind of life hath been.
Wicked and vile; and fo her death concludes.
 Shep. Fy, *Joan,* that thou wilt be fo obftacle[5]:
God knows, thou art a collop of my flefh,
And for thy fake have I fhed many a tear.
Deny me not, I pray thee, gentle *Joan.*
 Pucel. Peafant, avaunt! You have fuborn'd this
 man
Of purpofe to obfcure [9] my noble birth.

---

[5] *Why wilt thou be fo obftacle?*] A vulgar corruption of *obftinate,* which I think has odly lafted fince our author's time till now.

[6] —— *my noble birth.*
 'Tis true, I gave a noble—&c.] This paffage feems to corroborate an explanation, fomewhat far fetched, which I have given in *Henry* IV. of the *nobleman* and *Royal man.*

Shep.

Shep. 'Tis true, I gave a noble to the prieſt,
The morn that I was wedded to her mother.
Kneel down and take my bleſſing, good my girl.
Wilt thou not ſtoop? now curſed be the time
Of thy nativity! I would, the milk,
Thy mother gave thee when thou ſuck'dſt her breaſt,
Had been a little ratſbane for thy ſake;
Or elſe, when thou didſt keep my lambs a-field,
I wiſh ſome rav'nous wolf had eaten thee.
Doſt thou deny thy father, curſed drab?
O, burn her, burn her; hanging is too good. [*Exit*

York. Take her away, for ſhe hath liv'd too long,
To fill the world with vicious qualities.

Pucel. Firſt, let me tell you, whom you have con-
demn'd.
Not me begotten of a ſhepherd ſwain,
But iſſu'd from the progeny of Kings;
Virtuous and holy, choſen from above,
By inſpiration of celeſtial grace,
To work exceeding miracles on earth:
I never had to do with wicked ſpirits.
But you, that are polluted with your luſts,
Stain'd with the guiltleſs blood of innocents,
Corrupt and tainted with a thouſand vices,
Becauſe you want the grace, that others have,
You judge it ſtreight a thing impoſſible
To compaſs wonders, but by help of devils.
No, miſconceived *Joan of Ark* hath been
A virgin from her tender infancy,
Chaſte and immaculate in very thought;
Whoſe maiden blood thus rig'rouſly effus'd,
Will cry for vengeance at the gates of heav'n.

York. Ay, ay; away with her to execution.

War. And hark ye, Sirs; becauſe ſhe is a maid,
Spare for no faggots, let there be enow;
Place pitchy barrels on the fatal ſtake,
That ſo her torture may be ſhortened.

P p 3 *Pucel.*

Pucel. Will nothing turn your unrelenting hearts?
Then, *Joan*, discover thine infirmity;
That warranteth by law to be thy privilege.
I am with child, ye bloody homicides,
Murder not then the fruit within my womb,
Although you hale me to a violent death.

York. Now heav'n forefend! the holy maid with child!

War. The greatest miracle that ere you wrought.
Is all your strict precisenes come to this?

York. She and the Dauphin have been juggling;
I did imagine, what would be her refuge.

War. Well, go to; we will have no bastards live;
Especially, since *Charles* must father it.

Pucel. You are deceiv'd, my child is none of his;
It was *Alanson* that enjoy'd my love.

York. [7] *Alanson!* that notorious *Machiavel!*
It dies, an if it had a thousand lives.

Pucel. O, give me leave; I have deluded you;
'Twas neither *Charles*, nor yet the Duke I nam'd,
But *Reignier*, King of *Naples*, that prevail'd.

War. A married man! that's most intolerable.

York. Why, here's a girl.—I think, she knows not well.
There were so many, whom she may accuse.

War. It's a sign, she hath been liberal and free.

York. And yet, forsooth, she is a virgin pure.
Strumpet, thy words condemn thy brat and thee;
Use no intreaty, for it is in vain.

Pucel. Then lead me hence; with whom I leave my curse.
May never glorious sun reflect his beams
Upon the country where you make aboad!
But darknes and the gloomy shade of death

---

[7] *Alanson? that notorious Machiavel.*] *Machiavel* being mentioned somewhat before his time, this line is by some of the editors given to the players, and ejected from the text.

Inviron you, 'till mischief and despair
Drive you to break your necks, or hang yourselves!
[*Exit guarded.*

York. Break thou in pieces, and consume to ashes,
Thou foul accursed minister of hell!

SCENE VII.

Enter Cardinal of Winchester.

Car. Lord Regent, I do greet your Excellence
With letters of Commission from the King.
For know, my Lords, the states of Christendom,
Mov'd with remorse of these outragious broils,
Have earnestly implor'd a gen'ral Peace
Betwixt our nation and th' aspiring *French*;
And see at hand the Dauphin, and his train,
Approaching to confer about some matters.

York. Is all our travel turn'd to this effect?
After the slaughter of so many Peers,
So many Captains, gentlemen and soldiers,
That in this quarrel have been overthrown,
And sold their bodies for their country's benefit,
Shall we at last conclude effeminate Peace?
Have we not lost most part of all the towns,
By treason, falshood, and by treachery,
Our great progenitors had conquered?
Oh, *Warwick, Warwick!* I foresee with grief

---

[8] *— 'till mischief and despair Drive you to break your necks,—*] Perhaps *Shakespeare* intended to remark in this execration, the frequency of suicide among the *English*, which has been commonly imputed to the gloominess of their air.

[9] *Betwixt our nation and th' ASPIRING French;*] But would an Ambassador, who came to persuade peace with *France*, use it as an argument, that *France* was *aspiring. Shakespeare* without doubt wrote,

—— th' RESPIRING French. i. e. who had but just got into breath again, after having been almost hunted down by the *English.*   WARBURTON.

The ambassador yet uses no argument; but if he did, *respiring* would not much help the cause. *Shakespeare* wrote what might be pronounced, and therefore did not write *th' respiring.*

THE FIRST PART OF

The utter loss of all the realm of *France*.

War. Be patient, *York*; if we conclude a Peace,
It shall be with such strict and severe covenants,
As little shall the *Frenchmen* gain thereby.

Enter Charles, Alanson, *Bastard, and* Reignier.

Char. Since, Lords of *England*, it is thus agreed,
That peaceful Truce shall be proclaim'd in *France*;
We come to be informed by yourselves,
What the conditions of that league must be.

York. Speak, *Winchester*; for boiling choler chokes
The hollow passage of my prison'd voice,
By sight of these our baleful enemies [1].

Win. *Charles* and the rest, it is enacted thus:
That in regard King *Henry* gives consent,
Of meer compassion and of lenity,
To ease your Country of distressful war,
And suffer you to breathe in fruitful Peace;
You shall become true liegemen to his Crown.
And, *Charles*, upon condition thou wilt swear
To pay him tribute and submit thyself,
Thou shalt be plac'd as Viceroy under him;
And still enjoy thy regal dignity.

Alan. Must he be then a shadow of himself?
Adorn his temples with a Coronet [2],
And yet in substance and authority
Retain but privilege of a private man?
This proffer is absurd and reasonless.

Char. 'Tis known, already that I am possest
Of more than half the *Gallian* Territories,
And therein rev'renc'd for their lawful King.
Shall I, for lucre of the rest un-vanquish'd,
Detract so much from that prerogative,
As to be call'd but Viceroy of the whole?
No, Lord Ambassador, I'll rather keep

---

[1] —— *baleful enemies.*] *Baleful is sorrowful;* I therefore rather imagine that we should read *baneful,* hurtful, or mischievous.

[2] —— *with a Coronet.*] *Coronet* is here used for a *crown.*

That

That which I have, than, coveting for more,
Be caft from poffibility of all.

York. Infulting *Charles*, haft thou by fecret means
Us'd interceffion to obtain a League;
And now the matter grows to compromife,
Standft thou aloof upon comparifon [3]?
Either accept the title thou ufurp'ft,
Of benefit [4] proceeding from our King,
And not of any challenge of defert,
Or we will plague thee with inceffant wars.

Reig. My Lord, you do not well in obftinacy
To cavil in the courfe of this Contract:
If once it be neglected, ten to one,
We fhall not find like opportunity.

Alan. To fay the truth, it is your policy,
To fave your Subjects from fuch maffacre,
Ard ruthlefs flaughters, as are daily feen
By our proceeding in hoftility.
And therefore take this compact of a Truce,
Although you break it, when your pleafure ferves.
[*Afide, to the Dauphin.*

War. How fay'ft thou, *Charles?* fhall our Condition ftand?

Char. It fhall:
Only referv'd, you claim no intereft
In any of our towns of garrifon.

York. Then fwear allegiance to his Majefty.
As thou art Knight, never to difobey,
Nor be rebellious to the Crown of *England*,
Thou, nor thy Nobles, to the Crown of *England*.
[Charles *and the reft give tokens of fealty.*
—So now difmifs your army, when you pleafe;
Hang up your enfigns, let your drums be ftill,
For here we entertain a folemn Peace. [*Exeunt.*

[3] —— *upon comparifon?*] Do you ftand to compare your prefent ftate, a ftate which you have neither right or power to maintain, with the terms which we offer?

[4] — *accept the title thou ufurp'ft, Of benefit* ———] *Benefit* is here a term of law. Be content to live as the *beneficiary* of our king.

SCENE

SCENE VIII.

Changes to England.

Enter Suffolk, *in Conference with King* Henry; Gloucester, *and* Exeter.

K. *Henry.* YOUR wondrous rare description, Noble Earl,
Of beauteous *Marg'ret* hath astonish'd me;
Her virtues, graced with external gifts,
Do breed love's settled passions in my heart.
And, like as rigour of tempestuous gusts
Provokes the mightiest hulk against the tide,
⁵ So am I driv'n by breath of her renown,
Either to suffer shipwreck, or arrive
Where I may have fruition of her love.

Suf. Tush, my good Lord, this superficial tale
Is but a preface to her worthy praise.
The chief perfections of that lovely dame,
Had I suffient skill to utter them,
Would make a volume of inticing lines,
Able to ravish any dull conceit.
And, which is more, she is not so divine,
So full replete with choice of all delights,
But with as humble lowliness of mind
She is content to be at your command,
Command, I mean, of virtuous chaste intent,
To love and honour *Henry* as her Lord.

K. *Henry.* And otherwise will *Henry* ne'er presume.
Therefore, my lord Protector, give consent,
That *Marg'ret* may be *England*'s Royal Queen.

Glou. So should I give consent to flatter sin.
You know, my Lord, your Highness is betroth'd

---

⁵ *So am I driv'n*———] This simile is somewhat obscure; he seems to mean, that as a ship is driven against the tide by the wind, so he is driven by love against the current of his interest.

Unto

Unto another Lady of esteem.
How shall we then dispense with that Contract,
And not deface your honour with reproach?

Suf. As doth a Ruler with unlawful oaths;
Or one, that⁶ at a triumph having vow'd
To try his strength, forsaketh yet the Lists
By reason of his adversary's odds;
A poor Earl's daughter is unequal odds;
And therefore may be broke without offence.

Glou. Why, what, I pray, is *Marg'ret* more than that?
Her father is no better than an Earl,
Although in glorious titles he excel.

Suf. Yes, my good Lord, her father is a King,
The King of *Naples* and *Jerusalem*;
And of such great Authority in *France*,
That his Alliance will confirm our Peace;
And keep the *Frenchmen* in allegiance.

Glou. And so the Earl of *Armagnac* may do,
Because he is near kinsman unto *Charles*.

Exe. Beside, his wealth doth warrant lib'ral Dow'r,
While *Reignier* sooner will receive, than give.

Suf. A Dow'r, my Lords! Disgrace not so your King,
That he should be so abject, base and poor,
To chuse for wealth, and not for perfect love.
Henry is able to enrich his Queen;
And not to seek a Queen to make him rich.
So worthless peasants bargain for their wives,
As market-men for Oxen, Sheep, or Horse.
But marriage is a matter of more worth,
Than to be dealt in * by Attorneyship,
Not whom we will, but whom his Grace affects,
Must be companion of his nuptial bed.
And therefore, Lords, since he affects her most,
It most of all these reasons bindeth us,

---

⁹ —— *at a triumph*] That is, at the sports by which a triumph is celebrated.

* *By attorneyship.*] By the intervention of another man's choice; or the discretional agency of another.

In our opinions she should be preferr'd,
For what is wedlock forced, but a hell,
An age of discord and continual strife?
Whereas the contrary bringeth forth Bliss,
And is a pattern of celestial Peace.
Whom should we match with *Henry*, being a King,
But *Marg'ret*, that is daughter to a King?
Her peerless feature, joined with her birth,
Approves her fit for none, but for a King;
Her valiant courage, and undaunted spirit,
More than in woman commonly is seen,
Answer our hope in Issue of a King;
For *Henry*, son unto a Conqueror,
Is likely to beget more Conquerors;
If with a Lady of so high resolve,
As is fair *Marg'ret*, he be link'd in love.
Then yield, my Lords, and here conclude with me,
That *Marg'ret* shall be Queen, and none but she.

 K. *Henry*. Whether it be through force of your report,
My noble Lord of *Suffolk*; or for that
My tender youth was never yet attaint
With any passion of inflaming love,
I cannot tell; but this I am assur'd,
I feel such sharp dissention in my breast,
Such fierce alarums both of hope and fear,
As I am sick with working of my thoughts.
Take therefore shipping; post, my Lord, to *France*;
Agree to any Covenants; and procure,
That lady *Marg'ret* do vouchsafe to come
To cross the seas to *England*; and be crown'd
King *Henry's* faithful and anointed Queen.
For your expences and sufficient charge,
Among the people gather up a tenth.
Be gone, I say; for 'till you do return,
I am perplexed with a thousand cares.
And you, good Uncle, banish all offence:

If

KING HENRY VI. 589

If you do censure me [7], by what you were,
Not what you are, I know, it will excuse
This sudden execution of my will.
And so conduct me, where, from company,
I may revolve and ruminate my grief.[8] *[Exit.*

Glou. Ay; grief, I fear me, both at first and last.
[Exit Gloucester.

Suf. Thus *Suffolk* hath prevail'd, and thus he goes,
As did the youthful *Paris* once to *Greece*,
We hope to find the like event in love;
But prosper better than the *Trojan* did:
Marg'ret shall now be Queen, and rule the King:
But I will rule both her, the King, and realm. *[Exit.*

[7] *If you do censure me*, &c.]
To *censure* is here simply to *judge*.
If in judging me you consider the
past frailties of your own youth.

[8] —— *ruminate my grief.*]
Grief in the first line is taken
generally for *pain* or *uneasiness*;
in the second specially for *sorrow*.

Of this play there is no copy
earlier than that of the folio in
1623, though the two succeeding parts are extant in two editions in quarto. That the second
and third parts were published
without the first may be admitted
as no weak proof that the copies were surreptitiously obtained, and that the printers of that
time gave the publick those plays
not such as the authour designed,
but such as they could get them.
That this play was written before the two others is indubitably collected from the series of
events; that it was written and
played before *Henry* the fifth is
apparent, because in the epilogue there is mention made of
this play, and not of the other
parts

Henry *the sixth in swaddling
bards crown'd king,*
*Whose state so many had i'th'
managing*
That they lost France, *and made
all* England *rue,*
Which oft our stage hath shewn.
France *is lost* in this play. The
two following contain, as the old
title imports, the contention of
the houses of *York* and *Lancaster*.
The two first parts of *Henry*
VI. were printed in 1600. When
Henry V. was written we know
not, but it was printed likewise
in 1600, and therefore before
the publication of the first and
second parts, the first part of
Henry VI. had been often *shown
on the stage,* and would certainly have appeared in its
place had the authour been the
publisher.

The END of the FOURTH VOLUME.

Lightning Source UK Ltd.
Milton Keynes UK
UKHW02n1118120218
317657UK00005B/818/P